# The Handbook of
# Communication Science

## Second Edition

*To the memory of Steve Chaffee and Gerry Miller,*
*two extraordinary communication scientists*

# The Handbook of
# Communication Science

## Second Edition

Edited by

## Charles R. Berger
*University of California, Davis*

## Michael E. Roloff
*Northwestern University*

## David R. Roskos-Ewoldsen
*Ohio State University*

Los Angeles | London | New Delhi
Singapore | Washington DC

*For information:*

SAGE Publications, Inc.
2455 Teller Road
Thousand Oaks, California 91320
E-mail: order@sagepub.com

SAGE Publications India Pvt. Ltd.
B 1/I 1 Mohan Cooperative Industrial Area
Mathura Road, New Delhi 110 044
India

SAGE Publications Ltd.
1 Oliver's Yard
55 City Road
London EC1Y 1SP
United Kingdom

SAGE Publications Asia-Pacific Pte. Ltd.
33 Pekin Street #02-01
Far East Square
Singapore 048763

Printed in the United States of America.

*Library of Congress Cataloging-in-Publication Data*

The handbook of communication science / editors, Charles R. Berger, Michael E. Roloff, David R. Roskos-Ewoldsen. — 2nd ed.
    p. cm.
Includes bibliographical references and index.
ISBN 978-1-4129-1813-8 (cloth)
    1. Communication. I. Berger, Charles R. II. Roloff, Michael E. III. Roskos-Ewoldsen, David R.

P90.H294 2009
302.2—dc22                          2008044859

This book is printed on acid-free paper.

09   10   11   12   13      10   9   8   7   6   5   4   3   2   1

| | |
|---|---|
| *Acquisitions Editor:* | Todd R. Armstrong |
| *Editorial Assistant:* | Aja Baker |
| *Production Editor:* | Astrid Virding |
| *Copy Editor:* | Gillian Dickens |
| *Typesetter:* | C&M Digitals (P) Ltd. |
| *Proofreader:* | Scott Oney |
| *Indexer:* | Kathy Paparchontis |
| *Cover Designer:* | Gail Buschman |
| *Marketing Manager:* | Carmel Schrire |

# CONTENTS

# PREFACE TO THE SECOND EDITION

More than two decades have passed since publication of the *Handbook of Communication Science*'s first edition. During this time, several handbooks addressing a variety of specific communication contexts and topical areas of communication inquiry have appeared on the communication research landscape. Given these developments, this seems to be an especially propitious time to produce a handbook that serves to integrate these ostensibly diverse areas. As the present volume's chapters aptly demonstrate, there are a number of vectors along which these seemingly diverse areas of inquiry show distinct tendencies for convergence. Some might wonder why a second edition has taken so long. Conversations about a second edition of this handbook took place a few years after its publication; however, at that time the editors were engaged in other long-term research and writing projects. They simply did not have the time to undertake a project of this magnitude. Then, at about the time the editors might have been able to direct their energies toward a second edition, one of them passed away. After this sad and unexpected event, it took additional time to assemble the current editorial ensemble.

At the time the first edition of this handbook was published, the editors noted that the earlier *Handbook of Communication* (Pool, Schramm, Frey, Maccoby, & Parker, 1973) included many authors based in a variety of social science disciplines. The editors further observed that for the first time, a communication handbook included authors whose training and intellectual homes were primarily in communication-related departments. Almost all of the chapters included in this second edition of the *Handbook of Communication Science* are similarly authored by researchers trained and housed in communication departments both in the United States and abroad. Although this tradition has been carried forward from the handbook's first edition, there have been substantial changes in the substantive and methodological contours of the communication science terrain since publication of the first edition.

Given the dynamic nature of communication science, not surprisingly, new domains of inquiry not only have appeared on the scene but also have quickly developed into burgeoning research enterprises. Such areas as computer-mediated communication and human-computer interaction are two obvious cases in point; each of them is represented by a chapter in the present volume. Neither domain received chapter-length treatment in the first edition. In addition to these two chapters, several others in this edition devote considerable space to discussing the ways in which the Internet has altered the conduct of communicative commerce in such contexts as health and politics and how those who seek to understand mass media effects and communication campaigns must take seriously these new communication modalities. New communication technologies are having equally significant impacts on the ways in which interactions that were formerly conducted face-to-face can now be accomplished through technological mediation. Mediated social interaction has begun to play a pivotal role in the development and maintenance of personal relationships, especially those conducted over long distances. Given the increasing costs of transportation and concomitant reductions in physical mobility, mediated social interaction will very likely become an even more pervasive feature of everyday communicative life and an expanding venue for research activity.

Beyond these responses to the dramatic innovations in communication technology, some areas represented in the handbook's first edition have expanded to the point that they now require two chapters to provide adequate coverage of them. The communication and conflict literature was reviewed in just one chapter in the handbook's first edition. The present volume includes separate chapters on interpersonal conflict and intergroup conflict. Similarly, the present volume contains a chapter on persuasion and another on compliance gaining. The first edition included a single chapter focused only on the former. Interpersonal aspects of health communication and issues related to health communication campaigns are considered in two different chapters of this edition, whereas only one chapter was devoted to health communication in the first edition. Although the role of emotion-related processes in communication was mentioned in passing by only a few authors in the first edition, the present edition has an entire chapter devoted to communication and emotion.

First-edition authors were asked to write their chapters using a template featuring the individual, interpersonal, organizational, and macro-social levels of analysis. Each of these levels of analysis was explicated in separate chapters in that edition, and the authors of the remaining chapters were encouraged to consider their particular chapter's substantive focus from the perspective of each of the four levels. With few notable exceptions, most authors found it difficult, if not impossible, to implement this four-level schema in their chapters. The difficulty authors found in using the levels approach does not deny the "levels" nature of the communication science domain. Perhaps the time was not ripe for such a venture. Although we did not attempt to have the present volume's authors employ such a template in writing their chapters, one of this edition's chapters is devoted to issues surrounding levels of analysis. Methodological developments that have come to the fore since the handbook's first edition have fostered increased attention to the importance of different levels of analysis in understanding a variety of communication phenomena. Multilevel modeling and hierarchical linear modeling, methodological tools that enable researchers to tease out intra- and interlevel effects, are among these developments. We suspect that the continuing and increasing use of these methodologies across substantive domains of communication science may enable authors to pen chapters appearing in future editions of this handbook that seriously consider a variety of communication phenomena from a multilevels perspective.

Longitudinal changes in the substantive foci of communication science since the handbook's first edition have been substantial and impressive. Against this highly optimistic backdrop, with both great fondness and sadness, we wish to remember Steve Chaffee, a coeditor of the handbook's first edition, and Gerry Miller, who was an adviser to two of this edition's editors and an author of a chapter in the first edition. Both of these communication scientists were outstanding theoreticians, researchers, and writers, but what is more, today they are both remembered as extremely generous and kind human beings who were fun to work with and to be around. They were both wonderful storytellers. Unfortunately, they both left us too soon. Now, the Gerry and Steve stories that are part of today's communication science folklore do not centrally concern theoretical or research matters; rather, they focus on the humanity of these two fine people. Theories may come and go, but Steve and Gerry will not soon be forgotten. We have thus dedicated this volume to their memory.

This edition of the handbook would not exist were it not for the encouragement of the two people who founded Sage Publications, Sara Miller McCune, the "SA" in SAGE, and George McCune, the "GE" in SAGE. Sara was a driving force who devoted much time and effort to ensuring the publication of the handbook's first edition. Although George has passed away, Sara continues to be active on many other projects and recently has launched the magazine *Miller-McCune*, a publication dedicated to using social science theory and research to ameliorate social problems. This recent development is consistent with what has now become an impressive history of SAGE's continuing support for publishing social scientific communication theory and research.

Finally, we would be remiss if we did not thank our respective families for the forbearance and understanding they accorded us during the inevitable emotional turbulence associated with completing a project like this one. We solemnly promise them and ourselves that considerable time will pass before we contemplate undertaking a project of this scope.

Charles R. Berger
*Davis, California*

Michael E. Roloff
*Evanston, Illinois*

David R. Roskos-Ewoldsen
*Columbus, Ohio*

## ◆ Reference

Pool, I. S., Schramm, W., Frey, F. W., Maccoby, N., & Parker, E. B. (Eds.). (1973). *Handbook of communication.* Chicago: Rand McNally.

## ◆ Reviewer List

Deborah A. Cai (University of Maryland)

Laura K. Guerrero (Arizona State University)

David R. Seibold (University of California, Santa Barbara)

Sandi Smith (Michigan State University)

# PART 1

## OVERVIEW

# 1

# WHAT IS COMMUNICATION SCIENCE?

♦ Charles R. Berger, Michael E. Roloff,
and David R. Roskos-Ewoldsen

W e provide both simple and complex answers to the question posed in this chapter's title. Before attempting to answer the question, however, it is necessary to consider briefly the historical context within which communication emerged as a social scientific discipline. Detailed treatments of the development of communication research are provided in the present volume (Bryant & Pribanic-Smith, Chapter 2, this volume) and elsewhere (Delia, 1987). Our extremely abbreviated excursion into this history is meant to provide a framework that offers a partial explanation for the shape of contemporary communication science as well as some tentative answers to the "What is communication science?" question.

## ♦ Historical Perspective

The social scientific study of human communication is a relatively recent development, one that emerged in the years following World War II (Bryant & Pribanic-Smith, Chapter 2, this volume; Delia, 1987). At that time, there was a great deal of optimism about the future of the social sciences in general, especially with regard to their relevance for improving the conditions of society (Lewin, 1945). Many social sciences already had been established early in the 20th century; however, although studies of communication were conducted during this pre–World War II period, they were carried out by researchers who called psychology, sociology, and political science their disciplinary homes (Schramm, 1964). It was not until the late 1950s and early 1960s that cadres of communication researchers, educated in such communication-related departments as speech and journalism, began to appear on the scene. Thus, in relation to other social science disciplines, communication as a social science was a relatively late arrival to the social science family (McLeod, Chapter 11, Kosicki, & McLeod, this volume).

Because the social scientific study of communication took hold in speech and journalism departments that were then, and still are, dedicated to the inculcation of various communication skills—for example, oratorical and argumentation skills in the case of speech departments and writing and editing skills in the case of journalism departments—from the beginning there was a strong impetus to undertake research addressing practical aims. By using the rapidly developing arsenal of quantitative methods to attack important practical research questions, not only could communication skills be better taught to students, but pressing social problems also could be solved by improving communication effectiveness.

A case in point is the work done on communication and national development. During the 1950s and 1960s, considerable faith was vested in the proposition that the development of mass media systems in Third World countries would create a climate in which individuals would become better educated, less fatalistic, and more civically engaged, thus creating conditions favorable to political and economic development (Lerner, 1958, 1967; Rogers, 1962). Moreover, in these early decades of

the cold war, when there was great fear of a nuclear exchange between the United States and the Soviet Union, communication was seen by some as a key element in the amelioration of conflict (Bowers, 1974; see Ellis, Chapter 17, this volume; Sillars, Chapter 16, this volume) and the prevention of such a conflagration.

At the same time, there were increasing concerns about the potential deleterious effects of the then-new medium of television on members of its mass audiences, especially children (Himmelweit, Oppenheim, & Vince, 1958; Schramm, Lyle, & Parker, 1961). The role of violent television content in promoting aggressive and antisocial behavior, the degree to which soap opera viewing encourages negative views of married life, and the extent to which television consumption promotes escapism were presented as potential toxic effects of media exposure. These concerns about television's effects echoed those voiced almost three decades earlier in the Payne Fund studies of the effects of movies (Charters, 1933). The primary motivation of these inquires was to demonstrate that such undesirable effects occurred among those exposed to particular media content. By using the tools of quantitative social science to document these negative effects, steps could be taken to modify or eliminate such noxious content.

These applied research foci were further buttressed by Paul Lazarsfeld's extensive research program conducted during the 1940s and 1950s that was dedicated to demonstrating a variety of mass media effects within such domains as politics and marketing (Benoit & Holbert, Chapter 25, this volume; Bryant & Pribanic-Smith, Chapter 2, this volume; Delia, 1987; McLeod et al., Chapter 11, this volume). Rather than being aimed at providing ammunition for public policy arguments concerning harmful media content, a substantial amount of this research was motivated by commercial interests, although such notions as the two-step flow hypothesis and opinion leadership that emerged from this research corpus (Benoit & Holbert, Chapter 25, this volume; Katz & Lazarsfeld, 1955) assumed center stage in other lines of applied communication research (Rogers, 1962).

In view of past alarmist responses to the introduction of new communication technologies, quite predictably, the potential negative effects of "new media" such as the Internet on their users have recently become a focus of concern. These effects include Internet addiction (Young, 1998) and the possibility that excessive Internet use potentiates social loneliness (Kraut et al., 1998), although evidence suggests that social loneliness may not necessarily be associated with extensive Internet use (Kraut et al., 2002). Still others have noted that the cloak of anonymity surrounding Internet use may embolden individuals to insult others or to "flame" them—behaviors they would not normally display in most face-to-face encounters (Siegel, Dubrovsky, Kiesler, & McGuire, 1983). Thus, the tradition of revealing potential noxious effects of extensive media use continues to preoccupy researchers to the present.

As these developments unfolded within the mass communication domain, during the late 1950s and early 1960s, the first generation of communication researchers concerned with the study of face-to-face interaction emerged from graduate programs. Among this vanguard were Robert N. Bostrom, John Waite Bowers, and Gerald R. Miller from the University of Iowa and David K. Berlo, Erwin Bettinghaus, and Hideya Kumata from the University of Illinois. During the late 1950s and early 1960s, four of these early figures—Berlo, Bettinghaus, Kumata, and Miller—found their way to the newly formed Department of Communication at Michigan State University. Partially because of the rhetorical background from which some of the researchers emerged, they were interested in communication and persuasion and language behavior. Important touchstone works for them were the monographs that emerged from psychologist Carl Hovland's research program concerning the role communication plays in promoting attitude and behavior change (Hovland, Janis, & Kelley, 1953), social psychologist Leon Festinger's cognitive dissonance theory (Festinger, 1957, 1964), and psychologist Charles Osgood's research in the emerging area of psycholinguistics (Osgood, Suci, & Tannenbaum, 1957). In addition, Kumata had abiding research interests in the then-fledgling area of intercultural communication.

This highly abbreviated overview of communication science's roots suggests at least three important antecedent conditions that continue to influence the ways in which social scientifically oriented communication research has evolved over the ensuing years. First, within the mass communication domain, the research formula *identify a potential toxic media effect* → *document the effect with research findings* → *ameliorate the noxious effect* through media literacy programs, legal intervention, or suasive discourse aimed at media industry decision makers continues to enjoy considerable cachet and financial support. Within this paradigm, theory may be invoked as a way of rationalizing the inquiry and provides it with the appearance of theoretical motivation, with social learning theory frequently being the theory of choice (Bandura, 1977, 1986), but the primary research purpose is to demonstrate that increasing exposure to the undesirable content potentiates socially undesirable attitudes or behaviors and to use the successful demonstration as evidence in advocacy efforts aimed at eliminating the offending content. Rarely does research with this primary motivation directly test theory in general or, even when it is invoked, social learning theory in particular (see Nabi & Oliver, Chapter 15, this volume). Demonstrating the robustness of the bivariate relationship between exposure to toxic content and its noxious effects, while controlling for possible "third variables," is key. The formulation outlined here is not confined solely to mass communication research; however, several researchers have noted the need for increased theoretical elaboration within this domain (Nabi & Oliver, Chapter 15, this volume; McLeod et al., Chapter 11, this volume; Pfau, 2008).

Second, the confluence of interests in communication and social influence processes, increased methodological sophistication, and external funding opportunities have encouraged communication researchers to attack applied communication problems in such contexts as disease prevention and health maintenance. Much of this applied work within the health communication domain has not been motivated by explicit theoretical concerns (see Atkin & Salmon, Chapter 24, this volume; Cegala & Street, Chapter 23, this volume), although again, "theory"—for example, psychological reactance theory (Brehm, 1966)—may sometimes be invoked in a speculative, post hoc fashion to account for communication campaign failures (see Dillard, Chapter 12, this volume). In addition, although establishing that certain "message features" may potentiate desired persuasive outcomes may have important implications for communication praxis, merely demonstrating such effects does not explain why they occur (Dillard, Chapter 12, this volume). Of course, producing successful practical outcomes can motivate theory development efforts; several persuasion theories that appeared during the 1950s and 1960s grew out of the applied persuasion research undertaken during World War II.

Third, because the frames of reference of early mass communication and interpersonal communication researchers emerged from such cognate areas as sociology, social psychology, and political science, when their research was informed by theory, the theory was frequently imported from the cognate discipline. For example, communication research concerning counterattitudinal advocacy (Miller & Burgoon, 1973) was driven primarily by dissonance theory (Brehm & Cohen, 1962; Festinger, 1957, 1964) and incentive theory (Janis & Gilmore, 1965), both of which were imported from social psychology. These borrowing proclivities persist today. For example, the elaboration likelihood model (ELM) of persuasion (Petty & Cacioppo, 1986; Petty & Wegener, 1999), a model that is frequently invoked by communication researchers, originated in social psychology (see Dillard, Chapter 12, this volume). In general, then, these three antecedent conditions and others created a climate that attenuated theory development within the communication science domain and precipitated a theoretical trade deficit in which communication became the debtor discipline (Berger, 1991), although broader purviews of the communication discipline that include humanistic approaches may provide more evidence of original theory development efforts (Craig, 1993). In addition, we recognize that in a few instances, theories imported from other disciplines have been extensively elaborated and extended by communication scientists (Lang, 2000).

The first two of these three antecedent conditions propelled communication researchers in the direction of increased methodological sophistication. From the great expectations surrounding the introduction in the 1960s of high-speed, mainframe computing that enabled re-searchers to analyze ever-increasing numbers of variables, to contemporary fascinations with structural equation modeling and hierarchical linear modeling that are now the stuff of laptop computers, there has been an abiding faith in the notion that sophisticated methodological tools will yield large increments in our understanding of communication processes. Although we certainly agree that such tools are critical in plying the communication research trade, absent theory, they are, after all, merely tools. It is only when theory animates their use that these tools become truly powerful. In short,

"Data without theory are like babies without parents: Their life expectancy is low" (Gigerenzer, 2000, p. 296). Communication science, then, is all about explanation, and explanation is all about theory development (see Pavitt, Chapter 3, this volume).

In providing this short answer to the question of what communication science is, we do not mean to imply that applied communication research should be relegated to second-class status. To the contrary, for those who persist in bifurcating theory and application, we would remind them that the understanding theory provides is more likely to yield successful interventions in practical affairs than are intuitively driven interventions and campaigns based on trial and error (see Atkin & Salmon, Chapter 24, this volume; Dillard, Chapter 12, this volume; Lewin, 1945), even when the trial-and-error-based programs are evaluated with highly sophisticated research methods. Engineering advances based on applications of basic physical science principles provide ample evidence of the synergistic relationship between theory and application. Of course, theory-based interventions presuppose theory on which to predicate desired interventions. We remain somewhat skeptical that contemporary communication theories yet provide stable enough launching pads for such applied efforts (see Cegala & Street, Chapter 23, this volume; Dillard, Chapter 12, this volume). However, we are optimistic about prospects for remedying this lack through increased attention to theory construction within the communication science community (Pfau, 2008). Ultimately, we are reminded of Kurt Lewin, a "founding father" of both social psychology and communication research (Schramm, 1964), who once observed, "Nothing is as practical as a good theory" (Lewin, 1945, p. 129). Now that we have provided some tentative answers to the query, "What is communication science?" we now consider more complex issues.

## ◆ Regularities in Communicative Conduct

As we have already observed, communication science involves something more than using sophisticated and powerful research methods and statistical techniques to assay hypotheses and something more than trying to solve various practical communication problems, for example, devising persuasive messages to encourage people older than 40 years of age to have yearly physical examinations. Communication science practitioners not only wish to identify regularities with respect to communication and its effects but also fundamentally seek to explain why such regularities occur (see Pavitt, Chapter 3, this volume). For communication scientists, the problem to be solved is one of identifying and then explaining regularities by constructing and testing theories.

In the physical world, observing that the sun rises in the east and sets in the west and that its path through the sky changes in a highly predictable way with the changes of the seasons permits generalizations about the sun's behavior; however, by themselves, these generalizations do not explain why the sun behaves in this fashion. Indeed, alternative explanations for these observed regularities precipitated heated conflict between Galileo, an advocate of Copernican explanation, and the Roman Catholic Church concerning the center of the universe. Does the earth rotate around the sun or is the earth at the center of the universe, with all other celestial bodies rotating around it? These theoretical debates almost cost Galileo his life. In this case, the observed regularities were not in doubt—indeed, the sun rises in the east and sets in the west—but their explanation most certainly was.

Although examples of regularities in the physical world readily come to mind, some might argue that in the domain of social action and communication, such regularities are rare, thus raising the issue of whether explanation is a useful pursuit in which to engage. After all, if there are but few regularities to be found in social and communicative commerce, why be concerned with their explanation? There are at least three critical responses to this question. First, the view that physical phenomena are necessarily highly predictable is somewhat naive. There are many physical phenomena that demonstrate stochastic behavior that makes their prediction and explanation difficult. That is, as is the case with the social world, probabilistic relationships abound in the physical world; nonetheless, physical scientists seek to provide explanations for them. Moreover, nonlinear, dynamic systems that may appear to be highly unpredictable and chaotic may, in fact, be predictable, thus calling into question the usefulness of the "predictable-unpredictable" bipolarity in the first place (Kelso & Engstrom, 2006). Rather than being a matter of "either predictable or unpredictable," it may be more a matter of both "either-or" and "both-and."

Second, some have suggested that conversational behavior and language use are considerably more routinized than might be supposed. Because goals recur in everyday social life, conversational routines have evolved so that social actors can satisfy their goals efficiently (Coulmas, 1981). Linguists have estimated that up to 70% of the utterances made in daily social intercourse are formulaic (Sinclair, 1991; Wray & Perkins, 2000). This formulaticity is postulated to be necessary because of both recurrence of goals and the considerable cognitive load requirements associated with message production (see Berger, Chapter 7, this volume). Because of the cognitive demands involved in performing social interaction, individuals typically do not have the time to formulate highly unique utterances. Furthermore, the instrumental use of communication to achieve mundane, recurring goals efficiently simply does not require such

uniqueness (Clark, 1994; Wittgenstein, 1953). Although these observations concern language use in social interaction contexts, given the recurring nature of audience members' goals, we assume that much media content also exhibits considerable formulaticity.

Finally, if regularities in communicative commerce are indeed rare, efforts to devise effective communication "strategies" for achieving practical outcomes such as persuasion would seem to be doomed to failure from their beginnings. Attempting to be "strategic" in the face of abjectly capricious systems, whether the systems are individual or social, would seem like embarking on a fool's errand. Thus, those who design messages to induce some desired change in audience behavior, attitudes, beliefs, or some combination of the three must at least behave "as if" there are "message features" that will be instrumental in bringing about the desired changes (see Dillard, Chapter 12, this volume). The supposed linkages between "message features" and desired changes may be intuitively derived, but nevertheless, even these intuitions represent naive generalizations about what "message features" will prove to be "effective" with specific types of audience members or audiences (see Benoit & Holbert, Chapter 25, this volume). If social actors behave in highly capricious ways, practical attempts to influence audiences would seem to be not worth undertaking.

Such methodological concerns as reliability and validity of measures and the internal and external validity of experiments, as well as the degree to which stimulus sampling permits generalization across message types (see Boster & Sherry, Chapter 4, this volume), are issues that must be addressed in the process of identifying to-be-explained regularities. However, even when the canons of "best methodological practice" have been observed and the regularity duly identified, its explanation remains problematic. One can demonstrate repeatedly that varying a set of antecedent conditions reliably produces a certain set of outcomes, even when potential mediators and moderators are taken into account, but still have to clear the hurdle of explaining why the reliable covariation between the antecedents and consequences occurs, as well as their mediation and moderation. While a useful step in the right direction, becoming swept up in mediation-moderation mania by itself does not necessarily yield theoretical explanations. As observed earlier, theoretical disputes arise even when all parties to them agree on the nature of the observed covariation, including its mediation and moderation.

Although certifying the reliability of covariation, causal or otherwise, between variables through replication studies is critical to the scientific enterprise, the value of replication studies typically has been diminished in current communication science praxis. While this lack of attention to replication is sometimes bemoaned (see Benoit & Holbert, Chapter 25, this volume; Nabi & Oliver, Chapter 15, this volume) and most agree that more replication studies would be better, replication is less valued than the presentation of new findings. Sometimes individual studies purported to demonstrate a relationship between variables are followed by later-published studies that fail to replicate the original findings. However, given the tendency to devalue replication research, frequently on the grounds that it is not "innovative" or "cutting edge," we wonder how many unchallenged published findings would survive the test of studies specifically aimed at their replication. We further wonder how many failures to replicate findings remain unpublished and forever sealed in the files of researchers whose work was rejected by publication outlets. One way to obviate this problem would entail requiring researchers to report a series of studies that adduce replication evidence, rather than just a single demonstration of the key relationship or relationships. Meta-analysis is beginning to play a key

role in determining the robustness of specific relationships across studies and potential moderators of these relationships (Allen & Preiss, 1998; Allen, Burrell, Gayle, & Preiss, 2002; Preiss, Gayle, Burrell, Allen, & Bryant, 2007). Having established that a phenomenon displays regularity, we turn to the issue of theory and its role in communication science.

## ◆ Where Do Communication Theories Come From?

In dealing with issues related to theory and its role in explanation, we do not wish to cover the territory that is aptly presented in Chapter 3 (see Pavitt, Chapter 3, this volume). Instead, we will identify some strategies for generating theoretical explanations for communication phenomena. Before doing so, however, we will enumerate some misuses of the term *theory* that can be found in the current communication science literature. We hope that by identifying at least some of these faux theories, researchers will avoid the pitfalls associated with promoting the illusion of theory without its substance.

### PHENOMENON + "THEORY" ≠ THEORY

Unfortunately, the term *theory* is sometimes misused to characterize a body of research that merely demonstrates that a particular phenomenon occurs or can be produced under a set of conditions. Merely appending the term *theory* to the phenomenon does not constitute a theory. Examples of this kind of error are currently evident in the mass communication effects literature (see Nabi & Oliver, Chapter 15, this volume). Thus, a series of studies designed to demonstrate that priming or framing effects can be induced under a certain set of conditions or within a specific context may be portrayed as evidence for "priming theory" or "framing theory" when in fact, the studies themselves have only demonstrated that the priming or framing effects have occurred. Although observing that news stories "framed" in a particular way reliably give rise to particular types of attributions and interpretations may have important implications for understanding the formation of individual and public opinion, demonstrating these relationships by itself does not explain how the content of the news stories so framed is transmuted into the interpretations, attributions, and opinions. It is one thing to identify the effects of various news story frames, but it is quite another to explain why the observed framing effects occur.

We assume that priming and framing effects arise out of interactions among a variety of cognitive structures and processes. Until the structures and processes are identified and their interactions understood, there can be no "priming theory" or "framing theory" that provides an explanation for why such effects occur. As noted previously, identified regularities need to be explained by recourse to mechanisms that account for the regularity in question. Moreover, while demonstrating that the regularity can be replicated across contexts speaks to the generality of the regularity, generalization studies by themselves do not explain. It is only when research is predicated on the desire to answer the "why" question that one can lay claim to engaging in "theoretically driven" research.

## THEORY ≠ MODEL

Another unfortunate error, one that has become increasingly more frequent with the advent of more sophisticated causal modeling techniques that can be executed with point-and-click ease, is that of equating models and theories. It is not uncommon to find the terms *theory* and *model* used interchangeably. There are obvious examples of

models that offer little in the way of theoretical explanation. A working, radio-controlled model of an airplane that a child successfully flies does not by itself provide a theoretical explanation of the aerodynamics of flight. Similarly, regression models that identify independent variables that account for variability in a dependent variable, by themselves, provide no theoretical account for the shared variance. In this regard, the term *explained variance* in this regression context is misleading. No matter how high the coefficient of determination $(r^2)$ values may be, they do not provide theoretical explanations for the relationships they characterize.

We do not mean to imply that such statistical modeling techniques as hierarchical linear modeling and structural equation modeling are not useful; indeed, when properly used, they are (see Boster & Sherry, Chapter 4, this volume). However, even when models are found to produce much-coveted high $R^2$ values or highly encouraging goodness-of-fit statistics indicating strong concordance between models and data, the task of theoretical explanation may have only just begun, especially if the evaluated model is itself not anchored in theory. Moreover, if the encouraging goodness-of-fit statistics have been achieved by post hoc "model trimming," there should be even less cause for celebration. The manifold and complex relationships between theories and models are explicated in detail elsewhere in this handbook (see Pavitt, Chapter 3, this volume). Here, we simply caution that the two should not be conflated.

## THEORY-LADENNESS OF OBSERVATIONS

Since the 1950s, there has been a continuing debate concerning the degree to which scientific observations are influenced by theoretical (Hanson, 1958) or paradigmatic (Kuhn, 1970) commitments. In contradistinction to the positivist claim that observations consist of raw sensory experience, free from the influence of observers' theoretical affinities, these philosophers suggest that theories and broader paradigmatic perspectives that researchers embrace are likely to influence their judgments of what observations count as relevant data and the degree to which data comport with theories or paradigms to which they subscribe, although Hanson (1958) recognized that language can be used to describe sensory experience in a way that is not theory laden, and Kuhn (1970) suggested that observed anomalies may undermine expectations based on theoretical or paradigmatic commitments (Heidelberger, 2003). In any case, philosophical positions like these have been invoked to raise fundamental questions about the ability of researchers to evaluate theories and hypotheses in ways that avoid potential biases.

In contrast to these views of theory-ladenness, Duhem (1906/1974) recognized that experiments might be predicated on two different motivations. First, experiments might be designed simply to determine whether a causal relationship obtains between two sets of events. A naive laboratory assistant with no knowledge of the theories relevant to the events being observed could carry out such experiments. A second and very different motivation for experimentation is to test theory. In this case, the naive laboratory assistant might be able to produce the predicted results but would be unable to interpret them absent a formal theoretical framework; that is, the assistant could report the results but not understand their significance. Thus, in Duhem's view, it is possible to make observations that are minimally influenced by theory. Duhem further argued that experiments not motivated by theory are more likely to be performed in less developed sciences, perhaps a reasonable characterization of present-day communication science.

Although we find Duhem's distinction between the two different motivations for experimental inquiry plausible, it may be useful to distinguish between intuitive or implicit theories, on one hand, and formally explicated theories, on the other. This distinction is consistent with dual-process approaches to information processing (Stanovich, 2002). Intuitive theories are theories formed through interactions with the physical and social world. They consist of preconsciously processed associations represented in memory that are based on informal observations (Gigerenzer, 2000, 2007; Hogarth, 2001, 2005; Stanovich, 2002). Such intuitively derived theories are the product of System 1 (Kahneman & Frederick, 2002) or experiential processing (Epstein, 1994, 2003)—processing that is affect laden, preconscious, and relatively effortless. By contrast, formal theories are the products of formal reasoning that is governed by logical inference rules. Such theories are the product of System 2 or the rational processing system, which is affect free, conscious, and effortful.

Given the distinction between formal and informal theories and Duhem's differentiation between causality-establishing and theory-testing experiments, it is reasonable to contend that even when experiments are performed merely to establish causal connections between variables in the absence of a formal theory, intuitively based, informal theories guide the selection of plausible causal antecedents for experimental assay. This kind of intuitive, preconscious winnowing process is likely to give rise to the much-vaunted "aha" experience sometimes romantically associated with scientific discovery. Indeed, we suspect that in many communication laboratories, researchers frequently come to work in the morning with "new ideas" that have mysteriously "bubbled up" from their associative-oriented intuitive systems during the night. Because much intuitive knowledge is derived from observations of covariation between variables (Hogarth, 2001; Reber, 1993), it seems plausible that dramatic scientific breakthroughs attributed to creative processes that involve the sudden and unexpected experience of "seeing connections" between phenomena that have not been heretofore perceived as related are at least partially the product of System 1 processing.

In our view, then, all observations are in a sense "theory laden," but the nature of the theory informing them may vary. The appearance of "theory-free" inquiry is merely that; however, theoretical predilections, emanating from either formal or informal theories, may exert varying levels of influence on observations. More important, although informal, intuitive System 1 theories may provide researchers with potentially valuable hunches for productive research avenues and creative insights, they are no substitute for formally articulated System 2 theories. The preconscious nature of System 1 makes it difficult if not impossible to encapsulate its theories in natural language. System 2 theories can be assessed for their internal consistency, and because they are expressed in propositional form and are thus less subject to ambiguity, they are more amenable to falsification, if they are indeed false. In addition, because System 2 theories can be expressed in natural language or mathematics, they can be communicated more easily and shared among research community members. Thus, because System 2 theories are explicit, they reinforce the public nature of science and also facilitate replication attempts by geographically distributed researchers.

## CONFIRMATORY BIASES AND FALSIFICATIONISM

Closely related to the theory-ladenness of observations issue are the confirmatory biases they may promote and attempts to identify and counter these biases. When individuals are given a hypothesis to test concerning another person's personality— for example, whether the person is an introvert—those testing the hypothesis will tend to ask questions in a way that will confirm their hypothesis (Snyder, 1981). Social actors' information-gathering proclivities are biased in the direction of confirming their naive hypotheses about others. This bias may arise from paying inordinate attention to cases that comport with the predicted co-occurrences between variables and ignoring co-occurrences that deviate from those hypothesized or developing hypotheses after the results are known, thus promoting illusory theory conformation (Kerr, 1998). It is doubtful that researchers are immune from these biases, although adequate training in research methods should include careful consideration of such issues. Table 1.1 illustrates a common bivariate situation that might encourage confirmatory bias.

Researchers vested in supporting the hypothesis that those who expose themselves to media violence will be more likely to display aggressive behavior are probably more predisposed to focus on cases that fall in the hypothesis-confirming Absent-Absent and Present-Present cells

**Table 1.1** Bivariate Confirmatory Bias Scenario

| | *Aggressive Behavior* | |
| --- | --- | --- |
| | *Absent* | *Present* |
| Exposure to media violence | | |
| Present | Disconfirming | *Confirming* |
| Absent | *Confirming* | Disconfirming |

of the table than the cases that fall in the disconfirming cells. From the point of view of answering the question of why individuals vary in their propensities to manifest aggressive behavior, this confirmatory orientation is problematic for at least two reasons. First, relatively low correlations ($r$ = .20 to .30) between exposure to media violence and aggressive behavior have been obtained in nonexperimental studies (Huesmann & Taylor, 2006). Although statistically significant and of potential practical significance (Rosenthal, Rosnow, & Rubin, 2000), this relatively low correlation indicates that numerous cases fall into the disconfirming cells of Table 1.1. A second danger is that an intense focus on exposure to violent media content as a cause of aggressive behavior may blind researchers to other, potentially more important causal antecedents of aggressive behavior, such as being raised in a family with a history of family violence. Again, the relatively low correlation suggests that factors other than exposure to media violence act to potentiate aggressive behavior, and these factors may account for more variance in aggression.

Media reform-minded researchers and perhaps those receiving funding from some advocacy groups might be especially prone to fall victim to the confirmatory bias in the above example because their agenda entails demonstrating a positive relationship between exposure to media violence and aggressive behavior. By contrast, researchers operating from a theoretical perspective that is more catholic might be more prone to take seriously the task of trying to explain the "disconfirming" cases. For advocates with vested interests in confirming the relationship between exposure to media violence and aggressive behavior, the disconfirming cells represent a pesky nuisance; by contrast, theoretically motivated researchers would seek to identify the mechanisms that explain both confirming and disconfirming cases. Indeed,

explanations frequently proffered for the relationship between exposure to media violence and violent behavior—for example, social learning and priming—do not necessarily offer coherent explanations for the disconfirming cells. Of course, individuals with theoretical commitments can fall victim to the confirmatory bias (Kerr, 1998); however, researchers whose inquiries are motivated by strong ideological or policy positions that entail specific predictions are probably more likely to do so (McIntyre, 2006).

One potential antidote for this confirmatory bias is for researchers to actively seek disconfirming evidence for their theories. Karl Popper (1963) suggested that researchers should purposely attempt to disconfirm their hypotheses rather than confirm them. He argued that repeated failures to disconfirm hypotheses derived from a theory allow researchers to place greater credence in the theory. In addition, theories themselves may be structured in ways that make their falsification difficult if not impossible. In particular, theories that postulate processes for which there are no independent measures allow those promulgating them the "escape clause" of explaining failures to confirm hypotheses by recourse to the claim that the critical, unmeasured processes were not at work in the disconfirming study. Obviously, in such cases, theories cannot be shown to be false when in fact they may be. Although the plausibility of the notions of theory confirmation and theory disconfirmation can be questioned on logical grounds (Cappella, 1997), confirmatory biases are problematic enough to warrant substantial concern (Kerr, 1998).

## THEORY DEVELOPMENT STRATEGIES

To this point, our explication of communication science has focused on a series of cautions, including faux theories, model-theory confusion, theory-ladenness of observations, and the confirmatory bias and falsification. We now assume a more affirmative stance and outline strategies for devising communication theories. Theory construction is a creative enterprise that is at the same time both intellectually risky and highly entertaining (Berger, 1991). Well-articulated theories that give rise to unambiguous predictions may prove to be false, thus representing a potential threat to the theory developer's self-esteem. Put another way, at least for some, it is much less risky and ego threatening to test someone else's theory or theories than to make public one's own, clearly articulated theory and risk the possibility of its disconfirmation.

We cannot possibly present here a course of therapy designed to assuage the disconfirmation fears of potential theory builders. We only observe that empirical confrontations between theories are one sign of a vital and dynamic scientific enterprise. These confrontations and the debates they precipitate are crucial for the advancement of disciplines. However, even in an earlier era, some expressed the view that communication science practitioners have shown too little evidence of such theoretical controversy (Phillips, 1981), although others disagreed with this indictment (Miller, 1981). Surely, over the past two decades, the level of theory development activity within some sectors of the communication science community has increased, but levels of theoretical confrontation remain relatively low. This state of affairs may be a by-product of the relative youth of the discipline, its theory-borrowing proclivities, and a situation in which the critical mass of researchers is simply too small to coalesce into opposing theoretical camps. Whatever the reason, we look forward to the day when conferences and journals feature more papers in which competing theoretical explanations are at stake. In the interest of hastening that day's arrival, we turn to strategies for developing theory.

*Finding Useful Metaphors and Analogies.* Metaphors and analogies have frequently been used as a basis for developing theories—indeed, for rationalizing entire realms of inquiry. In the latter case, since the 1960s, the digital computer with its input, working memory, memory buffers, scripts, long-term store, and output has been employed as a metaphor for various information-processing theories and models. It is probably no accident that advances in computer technology have paralleled the so-called cognitive revolution, although with increased understanding of the neurophysiology and neurochemistry of the human brain, the computer metaphor may cease to be the guiding analogy for information-processing theory. Another well-known example is McGuire's (1964) use of an analogy taken from immunology to formulate his inoculation theory of resistance to persuasion.

We caution would-be theory builders that merely likening communication processes to some other process—for example, neurochemical "communication" that takes place within the human brain's neural networks—does not by itself explain anything about the communication process so analogized. The proposed metaphor, no matter how intuitively compelling and persuasive, does not alleviate the theorists' obligation to propose a theoretical framework that provides an explanation for the communication process of interest. Metaphors and analogies are potentially highly useful starting points for theory development, but they are not the endpoints.

*Conflicting Findings.* We have already emphasized the need to establish the reliability of regularities before undertaking their explanation; however, a theory development strategy that relies on explaining empirical inconsistencies may motivate theory construction efforts. In this case, contradictory findings gleaned from a body of research are scrutinized for differences among studies that may have been responsible for producing the seeming inconsistency. If artifactual explanations for inconsistencies between or among studies can be set aside, and if the conflicting findings stem from studies performed in the service of testing theories, it may be possible to propose theoretical explanations that account for the apparent discrepancies. Moreover, even if the conflicting empirical studies were not necessarily theoretically motivated, researchers can search for variables that may account for the observed discrepancies. Having identified plausible candidates, researchers can propose further studies designed to assess the source of the discrepancies that include the presumed critical variables, but they can also advance and evaluate theoretical accounts for their predictions.

Unfortunately, sometimes overly large and active egos get in the way of such reconciliation efforts. That is, when predictions derived from theory are not supported by data, and especially when those adducing the data are not among the theorist's "camp followers," some theorists may respond by vociferously impugning the disconfirming studies rather than by entertaining the possibility that at least some aspect of their theory may be in error. Of course, studies and the data they produce may be flawed; however, if theoretically derived predictions are unsupported by a series of studies featuring replication attempts with variations designed to mitigate potential methodological flaws, there comes a time when confronted theorists must capitulate to such evidence. Indeed, in our experience, it is cause for considerable celebration if over 60% of the hypotheses tested in a given study are supported; consequently, if researchers cannot adopt a reasonably appropriate level of humility in the process of advancing a theory, their data ultimately will very likely humble them.

*Anticipating Alternative Explanations.* Attempts to devise theoretical explanations for regularities ideally should both

acknowledge and try to take into account alternative explanations. In some cases, the problem is that in proposing a theory, the potential for alternative explanations is not recognized or is recognized but not explicitly acknowledged. However, it is one thing to acknowledge explicitly explanatory competitors, but it is quite another to demonstrate how the proposed theory takes into account the competitors. One alternative to a priori specification of alternative explanations is to let other members of the research community identify and propose them. Of course, this process will play out over time, no matter how many alternatives are considered within the context of a given theory; however, there are efficiencies to be realized if theorists explicitly recognize the existence of alternative explanations and deal with them in their theorizing. Furthermore, by taking such alternatives explicitly into account, theories may become more comprehensive and potentially more powerful. Explicitly entertaining alternative explanations is a manifestation of the falsificationist perspective discussed previously (Popper, 1963).

*Surrounding One's Self With Skeptics.* Proclivities to fall prey to the confirmatory bias suggest the wisdom of consciously seeking the counsel of those who are likely to be uncongenial or even hostile to one's theoretical arguments. While some scientific theorists and most politicians may derive considerable psychological comfort from the validation they receive from like-minded colleagues, the "cold fusion" and Bay of Pigs fiascos in the realms of physics and public policy, respectively, demonstrate the degraded judgments and decisions that can eventuate from the psychological comfort afforded by congenial supporters (Janis, 1972). It is not hyperbolic to represent groupthink as anathema to scientific theorizing; nevertheless, even though the deleterious effects of groupthink have been clearly demonstrated, many researchers seem to prefer to affiliate with like-minded colleagues and to minimize their interactions with those who do not share their theoretical orientations. The social organization of professional associations and the research areas reflected in journals speak to the proclivities of researchers to adhere to the "birds of a feather flock together" aphorism.

Although we have emphasized the valuable role critics can play in the theory generation process, we would also suggest that research motivated primarily by public policy and other practical concerns might benefit even more from the responses of skeptics. Individuals whose political and ideological predilections lure them in the direction of confirming hypotheses compatible with their ideological and political leanings surely would benefit from interactions with those who do not share or may intensely oppose their ideological predispositions. Thus, for example, research conducted to assess the relationship between the toys that children play with, for example, toy guns, and their proclivities toward aggressive behavior that is initiated by those who favor gun control might well be designed in such a way that the probability of supporting the hypothesized relationship is increased. What is counted as "aggressive behavior" or "toy guns" might be decided in such a way that the study is biased toward confirming a positive relationship. For example, do such behaviors as verbal or nonverbal insults count as aggressive acts? By involving those opposed to gun control in the study's design, confirmatory bias pitfalls might be avoided. Again, we recognize that the ideal of including skeptics in theory construction and research design is one that, for the most part, remains a faint outline on a distant horizon.

*Letting Intuition Work.* Over the past two decades, it has become apparent that a great deal of social perception, judgment, and action result from mental activity that is preconscious and automatic rather than

conscious and calculating (Dijksterhuis, Chartrand, & Aarts, 2007; Moors & De Houwer, 2007). We have already observed that System 1 or the intuitive system is postulated to operate in this way and that even when individuals perform experiments or collect data that are not designed to test an explicit theory, naive, tacit theories may surreptitiously guide their inquiry. However, this distinction between automatic and controlled processing may not be quite as stark as it is sometimes portrayed. People may be conscious of the products of automatic processes but not of the processes themselves. That is, the outputs of these automatic processes are consciously experienced as perceptions, judgments, and actions, as well as "ideas."

It is hardly far-fetched to suppose that repeated exposure to a wide variety of research literatures tends to automate the knowledge contained in them such that System 1 might establish automatically connections between literatures—relationships that were not consciously perceived by the theorist when exposed to the literatures in question. Some have argued that good science results, in part, from exposure to a wide variety of ideas, some of which may be far afield from one's own interests (Thagard, 2006). This kind of catholic purview might well encourage the kind of analogic thinking that has proven so valuable in theory generation. At times, such analogic thinking might be practiced at the System 2 or analytic level, as it was by McGuire (1964) in formulating his inoculation theory. However, at other times, automatically drawn analogies may remain preconscious and give rise to the conscious experience of only vague, gut-level feelings or intuitions concerning explanations for phenomena.

We believe it is important to heed these gut-level feelings, for such feelings and intuitions are probably the product of the same system that enables people to have the experience of falling asleep, having unsuccessfully solved a difficult problem, only to wake up the next morning with the problem's solution. Indeed, temporal separation of an individual's guesses significantly improves the accuracy of their average (Vul & Pashler, 2008). Of course, these intuitions must be subjected to close scrutiny and ultimately be made part of an explicit theory; however, they may prove to be a useful departure point for theory development. Anyone who has done science for a reasonable period of time knows that the full panorama of emotions is operative in scientific endeavors (Thagard, 2006). Thus, dismissing the role that System 1 plays in theory development would be an egregious error.

*Be Not Intimidated by Ideologues.* Those who theorize about communication and social action should be aware of the possibility that their theoretical explanations may sometimes be at variance with the beliefs of those who subscribe to a variety of political and religious ideologies. In commenting on the chilling effect of political ideology on social scientific inquiry, McIntyre (2006) observed,

> At times entire areas of research have been ruled out of bounds simply because their investigation may uncover facts that cause us to question favored ideological assumptions (or violate the basic human prejudice that humans are somehow special). In some instances, this had led to the suggestion that social scientists cannot settle an empirical dispute, simply because it raises political issues that are "controversial." In other instances, well-confirmed facts about human behavior have been rejected altogether simply because they contradict popular political ideology. In this way, the corrosive effect of political ideology reveals its similarity to age-old attempts to resist knowledge, seen throughout the history of scientific inquiry. (p. 62)

We cannot possibly address here the vast panorama of ethical issues associated with the conduct of social scientific inquiry. However, unfettered inquiries, conducted in accordance with the highest ethical standards, which allow researchers to go where their theories and data take them, are very likely to be most productive. The self-correcting nature of scientific inquiry will winnow those theories that are in error and those data that are flawed. The alternative of dogmatic adherence to "ideologically correct" explanations, regardless of their accuracy, is akin to the situation that existed during the Dark Ages (McIntyre, 2006). We submit that social reform attempts based on sound theoretical principles and reliable data are preferable to attempts predicated on dogma of any stripe.

## ◆ Conclusion

The discerning reader may have noted that we have not presented arguments concerning the relative desirability of qualitative and quantitative research methods. Debates concerning these methodologies are legion in the communication discipline. In our view, the significance of these debates pales in comparison to the problem of erecting a body of theory that explains communicative action. As we hope we have demonstrated here, sophisticated research methods of any type in the hands of atheoretically inclined researchers are very likely to yield relatively little insight into the nature of communication processes. Asking fundamental "why" questions and constructing and evaluating theories that answer them are activities that are at the very heart of studying communication as a social science.

## ◆ References

Allen, M., Burrell, N., Gayle, B. M., & Preiss, R. W. (Eds.). (2002). *Interpersonal communication research: Advances thorough meta-analysis.* Mahwah, NJ: Lawrence Erlbaum.

Allen, M., & Preiss, R. W. (1998). *Persuasion: Advances through meta-analysis.* Cresskill, NJ: Hampton Press.

Bandura, A. (1977). *Social learning theory.* Englewood Cliffs, NJ: Prentice Hall.

Bandura, A. (1986). *Social foundations of thought and action: A social cognitive theory.* Englewood Cliffs, NJ: Prentice Hall.

Berger, C. R. (1991). Communication theories and other curios. *Communication Monographs, 58,* 101–113.

Bowers, J. W. (1974). Guest editor's introduction: Beyond threats and promises. *Speech Monographs, 41,* n.p.

Brehm, J. W. (1966). *A theory of psychological reactance.* New York: Academic Press.

Brehm, J. W., & Cohen, A. R. (1962). *Explorations in cognitive dissonance.* New York: John Wiley.

Cappella, J. N. (1997). The development of theory about automated patterns of face-to-face human interaction. In G. Phillipsen & T. L. Albrecht (Eds.), *Developing communication theories* (pp. 57–83). Albany: State University of New York Press.

Charters, W. W. (1933). *Motion pictures and youth: A summary.* New York: Macmillan.

Clark, H. H. (1994). Discourse in production. In M. A. Gernsbacher (Ed.), *Handbook of psycholinguistics* (pp. 985–1021). San Diego: Academic Press.

Coulmas, F. (1981). Introduction: Conversational routine. In P. Coulmas (Ed.), *Conversational routines: Explorations in standardized communication situations and prepatterned speech* (pp. 1–17). The Hague, The Netherlands: Mouton.

Craig, R. T. (1993). Why are there so many communication theories? *Journal of Communication, 43,* 26–33.

Delia, J. G. (1987). Communication research: A history. In C. R. Berger & S. H. Chaffee (Eds.), *Handbook of communication science* (pp. 20–98). Newbury Park, CA: Sage.

Dijksterhuis, A., Chartrand, T. L., & Aarts, H. (2007). Effects of priming and perception on social behavior and goal pursuit. In J. A. Bargh (Ed.), *Social psychology and the unconscious: The automaticity of higher mental processes* (pp. 51–131). New York: Psychology Press.

Duhem, P. (1974). *The aim and structure of physical theory.* New York: Atheneum. (Original work published 1906)

Epstein, S. (1994). Integration of the cognitive and the psychodynamic unconscious. *American Psychologist, 49,* 709–724.

Epstein, S. (2003). Cognitive-experiential self-theory of personality. In T. Millon & M. J. Lerner (Eds.), *Handbook of psychology: Vol. 5. Personality and social psychology* (pp. 159–184). New York: John Wiley.

Festinger, L. (1957). *A theory of cognitive dissonance.* Stanford, CA: Stanford University Press.

Festinger, L. (1964). *Conflict, decision, and dissonance.* Stanford, CA: Stanford University Press.

Gigerenzer, G. (2000). *Adaptive thinking: Rationality in the real world.* New York: Oxford University Press.

Gigerenzer, G. (2007). *Gut feelings: The intelligence of the unconscious.* New York: Viking.

Hanson, N. R. (1958). *Patterns of discovery.* Cambridge, UK: Cambridge University Press.

Heidelberger, M. (2003). Theory-ladenness and scientific instruments in experimentation. In H. Radder (Ed.), *The philosophy of scientific experimentation* (pp. 138–151). Pittsburgh: University of Pittsburgh Press.

Himmelweit, H. T., Oppenheim, A. N., & Vince, P. (1958). *Television and the child.* Oxford, UK: Oxford University Press.

Hogarth, R. M. (2001). *Educating intuition.* Chicago: University of Chicago Press.

Hogarth, R. M. (2005). Deciding analytically or trusting your intuition: The advantages and disadvantages of analytic and intuitive thought. In T. Betsch & S. Haberstroh (Eds.), *The routines of decision making* (pp. 67–82). Mahwah, NJ: Lawrence Erlbaum.

Hovland, C. I., Janis, I. L., & Kelley, H. H. (1953). *Communication and persuasion: Psychological studies of opinion change.* New Haven, CT: Yale University Press.

Huesmann, R., & Taylor, L. D. (2006). The role of media violence in violent behavior. *Annual Review of Public Health, 27,* 393–415.

Janis, I. L. (1972). *Victims of groupthink: A psychological study of foreign-policy decisions and fiascoes.* Boston: Houghton Mifflin.

Janis, I. L., & Gilmore, J. B. (1965). The influence of incentive conditions on the success of role playing in modifying attitudes. *Journal of Personality and Social Psychology, 1*, 17–27.

Kahneman, D., & Frederick, S. (2002). Representativeness revisited: Attribution substitution in intuitive judgment. In T. Gilovich, D. Griffin, & D. Kahneman (Eds.), *Heuristics and biases: The psychology of intuitive judgment* (pp. 49–81). Cambridge, UK: Cambridge University Press.

Katz, E., & Lazarsfeld, P. F. (1955). *Personal influence: The part played by people in the flow of mass communications.* New York: Free Press.

Kelso, J. A. S., & Engstrom, D. A. (2006). *The complementary nature.* Cambridge, MA: Bradford/MIT Press.

Kerr, N. L. (1998). HARKing: Hypothesizing after the results are known. *Personality and Social Psychology Review, 2*, 167–219.

Kraut, R., Kiesler, S., Boneva, B., Cummings, J., Helgeson, V., & Crawford, A. (2002). Internet paradox revisited. *Journal of Social Issues, 58*, 49–74.

Kraut, R., Lundmark, V., Patterson, M., Kiesler, S., Mukopadhyay, T., & Scherlis, W. (1998). Internet paradox: A social technology that reduces social involvement and psychological well-being? *American Psychologist, 53*, 1017–1031.

Kuhn, T. S. (1970). *The structure of scientific revolutions* (2nd ed.). Chicago: University of Chicago Press.

Lang, A. (2000). The limited capacity model of mediated message processing. *Journal of Communication, 50*(1), 46–70.

Lerner, D. (1958). *The passing of traditional society: Modernizing the Middle East.* Glencoe, IL: Free Press.

Lerner, D. (1967). *Communication and change in developing countries.* Honolulu, HI: East-West Center Press.

Lewin, K. (1945). The Research Center for Group Dynamics at Massachusetts Institute of Technology. *Sociometry, 8*, 126–136.

McGuire, W. J. (1964). Inducing resistance to persuasion: Some contemporary approaches. In L. Berkowitz (Ed.), *Advances in experimental social psychology* (Vol. 1, pp. 191–229). New York: Academic Press.

McIntyre, L. (2006). *Dark ages: The case for a science of human behavior.* Cambridge, MA: Bradford/MIT Press.

Miller, G. R. (1981). "'Tis the season to be jolly": A yuletide 1980 assessment of communication research. *Human Communication Research, 7*, 371–377.

Miller, G. R., & Burgoon, M. (1973). *New techniques of persuasion.* New York: Harper & Row.

Moors, A., & De Houwer, J. (2007). What is automaticity? An analysis of its component features and their interrelations. In J. A. Bargh (Ed.), *Social psychology and the unconscious: The automaticity of higher mental processes* (pp. 11–50). New York: Psychology Press.

Osgood, C. E., Suci, G. J., & Tannenbaum, P. H. (1957). *The measurement of meaning.* Urbana: University of Illinois Press.

Petty, R. E., & Cacioppo, J. T. (1986). *Communication and persuasion: Central and peripheral routes to persuasion.* New York: Springer-Verlag.

Petty, R. E., & Wegener, D. T. (1999). The elaboration likelihood model: Current status and controversies. In S. Chaiken & Y. Trope (Eds.), *Dual-process theories in social psychology* (pp. 41–72). New York: Guilford.

Pfau, M. (2008). Tension between breadth and depth in mass communication education. *Communication Monographs, 75*, 119–126.

Phillips, G. M. (1981). Science and the study of human communication: An inquiry from the other side of the two cultures. *Human Communication Research, 7*, 361–370.

Popper, K. R. (1963). *Conjectures and refutations: The growth of scientific knowledge.* London: Routledge & Kegan Paul.

Preiss, R. W., Gayle, B. M., Burrell, N., Allen, M., & Bryant, J. (Eds.). (2007). *Media effects research: Advances through meta-analysis.* Mahwah, NJ: Lawrence Erlbaum.

Reber, A. S. (1993). *Implicit learning and tacit knowledge: An essay on the cognitive unconscious.* New York: Oxford University Press.

Rogers, E. M. (1962). *The diffusion of innovations.* New York: Free Press.

Rosenthal, R., Rosnow, R. L., & Rubin, D. B. (2000). *Contrasts and effect sizes in behavioral research.* Cambridge, UK: Cambridge University Press.

Schramm, W. (1964). *The science of human communication.* New York: Basic Books.

Schramm, W., Lyle, J., & Parker, E. B. (1961). *Television in the lives of our children.* Stanford, CA: Stanford University Press.

Siegel, J., Dubrovsky, V., Kiesler, S., & McGuire, T. (1983). Group processes in computer-mediated communication. *Organizational Behavior and Human Decision Processes, 37,* 694–710.

Sinclair, J. (1991). *Corpus, concordance, collocation.* Oxford, UK: Oxford University Press.

Snyder, M. (1981). "Seek and ye shall find . . ." In E. T. Higgins, C. P. Herman, & M. P. Zanna (Eds.), *Social cognition: The Ontario symposium on personality and social psychology* (pp. 277–304). Hillsdale, NJ: Lawrence Erlbaum.

Stanovich, K. E. (2002). Rationality, intelligence, and levels of analysis in cognitive science: Is dysrationalia possible? In R. J. Sternberg (Ed.), *Why smart people can be so stupid* (pp. 124–158). New Haven, CT: Yale University Press.

Thagard, P. (2006). *Hot thought: Mechanisms and applications of emotional cognition.* Cambridge, MA: Bradford/MIT Press.

Vul, E., & Pashler, H. (2008). Measuring the crowd within: Probabilistic representations within individuals. *Psychological Science, 19,* 645–647.

Wittgenstein, L. (1953). *Philosophical investigations.* Oxford, UK: Basil Blackwell.

Wray, A., & Perkins, M. K. (2000). The functions of formulaic language: An integrated model. *Language and Communication, 20,* 1–28.

Young, K. S. (1998). Internet addiction: The emergence of a new clinical disorder. *CyberPsychology, 1,* 237–244.

# 2

# A HISTORICAL OVERVIEW OF RESEARCH IN COMMUNICATION SCIENCE

◆ Jennings Bryant and
Erika J. Pribanic-Smith

I n the original *Handbook of Communication Science* (Berger & Chaffee, 1987), Delia (1987) provided a classic and expansive chapter titled "Communication Research: A History." Our primary goal in this chapter is to summarize and build upon Delia's rich legacy, synthesize the contributions of other historians who have provided insightful descriptions and interpretations of the evolution of communication research, and then provide a more specialized historical overview of various subdisciplines of communication science that have developed in important ways since the original *Handbook* was published.

## ◆ Laying a Foundation

Delia (1987) placed the origins of modern communication studies in the progressive historical era and indicated that during the early decades of communication science, especially from 1900 to 1940, fragmentation reigned because fledgling communication investigations were being conducted in various social science and humanistic disciplines. Practically the only commonality Delia identified across these investigations was "a conception of direct, undifferentiated, and powerful effects" (p. 21).

In attempting a classification of early scholarly developments in communication, Delia (1987) identified five major fields of research, each of which had its own theoretical foundations and methodologies. (1) Research on communication and political institutions drew from a variety of disciplines and encompassed propaganda analysis, most notably the work of Harold Lasswell (Schramm, 1963), analysis of political and social themes in public communications, qualitative and quantitative analyses of messages, and public opinion research. (2) The Chicago school of sociology exerted tremendous influence on research into communication and social life, and its adherents typically studied communication effects via empirical research, especially field investigations. They employed a variety of methodologies that provided "richness of description and sensitivity to the interrelation of persons' experiences and the social context of their lives" (p. 31). (3) Social psychological studies introduced an experimental approach to communication research but maintained a focus on effects, including an "adoption of concepts treating communication reception and effects in complex mediational terms" (p. 39). (4) Research on communication and education focused largely on the impact of new technology and on instructional strategies. (5) Finally, commercially focused communication research stemmed from the desire of advertisers to study the size and composition of broadcast audiences and the effectiveness of marketing strategies. The stigma of applied research meant that many of these investigations were conducted by marketing faculty in business schools, although several of these scholars explored the roles of psychology and sociology in advertising. By 1940, Paul Lazarsfeld had, through his creation of the Bureau of Applied Social Research at Columbia, "cemented the emerging bridge between academic and commercial interests in communication research and established the theoretical relevance of communication research based on applied problems" (p. 51).

The consolidation of interdisciplinary communication study marked the period from 1940 to 1965, according to Delia (1987). World War II sparked new interest in communication research, drawing scholars from myriad fields. However, interpersonal contacts that developed among leading researchers (including Lazarsfeld and Carl Hovland) allowed for a coalescence of viewpoints, and the field consolidated "around a core that took theory development as its principal goal and a linear-effects perspective as its organizing framework" (p. 69). Tensions arose as American survey, experimental, and statistical research took precedence, and European, historical, cultural, and non-statistical research became marginalized or excluded. Furthermore, theoretical research became insulated from practical communication education.

Delia (1987) asserted that the integration of communication research into journalism schools and speech departments was a significant step in the development of the field. The need for graduate faculty to meet the demands of higher education, along with diverse membership of the National Society for the Study of Communication (later the International Communication Association, or ICA) sparked the rapid expansion of the social scientific approach to communication research within journalism schools and speech departments. Meanwhile, the humanistic research methods traditionally used in journalism and speech research, including historical analysis and rhetorical criticism, were integrated into the established process-and-effects framework.

◆ *Other Historical Overviews*

Wartella (1996) listed Delia's (1987) historical tome among a series of communication research histories published during the 1970s and 1980s and identified several commonalities. The "received history," as she called these collected works, began with public concern about the effects of newly developed mass media on audiences, which instigated research that resulted in Lasswell's model of direct, powerful, and undifferentiated media effects. Researchers of the 1940s, particularly Lazarsfeld and his Columbia colleagues, challenged the idea of powerful effects and contributed to the creation of the two-step flow model. The accepted history ended with the institutionalization of communication research beginning in the 1950s and continuing through the 1960s. Wartella concurred with Delia's assessment that this received history featured (a) an identification of communication research with the study of the media of mass communication, (b) a presumption that the methods of communication research were the methods of social scientific research, (c) the treatment of communication research as an exclusively American research tradition, and (d) an identification of the core concern of communication research as the processes by which communication messages influence audience members.

Wartella (1996) described how this accepted history has been criticized and particularly emphasized the contributions of communication scholarship originating outside of the United States and prior to Lasswell's propaganda research. She also pointed out that whereas the accepted history described a shift from beliefs in powerful media effects to limited effects, the true history had been more cyclical. For the public at large, she argued, media effects continuously have been viewed as powerful. In academia, however,

> what would seem to better describe the literature on media-effects theory historically is the following: (a) Each new technologically or socially prompted media problem generates or attracts its own set of media researchers, many of them unversed in previous media research; (b) these researchers tend to believe, much like the public at large, in

relatively powerful media impact and theorize accordingly; and (c) as they or others come to empirically test these theories on media audiences within the individualistic paradigm present in media-effects research, it very quickly becomes obvious that qualifications on the grand theory need to be made, usually in the initial set of studies. (p. 177)

This argument was extended to claims that shifts in beliefs about the power of the media to affect the audience's knowledge, attitudes, and behavior were rooted in the particular historical context of the research and researchers. Wartella (1996) expressed the need to consider classic media effects studies in their historical context and to realize that the motivations of past scholars stemmed from the society in which they lived.

The contributors to Dennis and Wartella's (1996) *American Communication Research: The Remembered History* discussed in great detail many of the individuals, perspectives, and research developments that Delia (1987) had covered, but this later work cast a slightly larger historical and geographical net. For example, Lang (1996) emphasized that research techniques typically considered to be American were developed in Europe. He noted a particular German influence, either by German-born scholars or by Americans who had studied in Germany, dating from mid-19th-century telegraph studies by Knies. Robinson (1996) referred to a continuous "transcontinental borrowing and intellectual transfer" (p. 165) that included the German influence of the late 19th and early 20th centuries, as well as theoretical exchanges with Canadian, French, and British scholars in the 1960s, 1970s, and 1980s. Like Delia, Robinson observed a comfortable plurality in communication studies since the 1970s, stemming in part from the reintroduction of humanistic research approaches.

Glander (2000) provided the historical context that Wartella (1996) suggested was necessary when examining communication studies of the past. He asserted that circumstances early in the 20th century were highly significant to the institutionalization of communication study and in shaping the field's dominant paradigm. Among the forces at work were concerns with the growing use of propaganda during the two world wars and the questioning of the values of higher education stimulated by economic depression, which forced mass communication scholars to justify and define the meaning and purpose of their work. Following World War II, the United States entered a cold war atmosphere "driven by a mass media system that had redirected its efforts from winning support for World War II to now continuously (and in near unison) warning of the threat of an international communist conspiracy" (Glander, 2000, p. 58). The psychological nature of the cold war required even more intense propaganda than the world wars had, increasing the need for and interest in communication research. Glander argued that the resulting body of media effects studies formed the core of communication research at that time and that effects remained the dominant focus of the field today. Like Delia (1987), Glander pointed to the era after World War II as the period when communication research came of age. He identified Berelson, Stanton, Cantril, Hovland, and Dodd as major figures in establishing communication research on university campuses and called Lazarsfeld and Schramm "the two most important early mass communications researchers" (p. xii), thanks in large part to their creation and direction of research bureaus or institutes.

Glander's (2000) assertions regarding Wilbur Schramm's impact on the field echoed those of Rogers (1994), who labeled Schramm as the central figure in the establishment of communication as its own scholarly field. Rogers noted the European roots of communication study, listing Karl Marx, Charles Darwin, and Sigmund Freud among the intellectuals whose revolutionary ideas and influence on later scholars (such as Lasswell and Adorno) shaped the future of communication research. Rogers profiled the Chicago scholars—Lasswell, Lazersfeld, Hovland, Lewin, Shannon, and Weiner—but named them as precursors to communication study and attached their significance to their influence on Schramm. According to Rogers, Schramm was the one true father of communication study because he was the first to institutionalize it and give it a name. Rogers's main interest in communication study since Schramm lay in the expansion of institutional research and graduate education across the country and internationally (cf. Bryant & Thompson, 1999). He credited research on new communication technologies by Canadian scholars Innis and McLuhan with popularizing communication study in the 1970s.

Whereas other examinations of the history of communication research had emphasized mass communication, McCroskey and Richmond (1996) highlighted research in speech and interpersonal communication. The authors divided communication study into relational and rhetorical approaches. They defined rhetoric as the study of public speaking, which they traced to Aristotle, and discussed the expansion of "speech" programs to include not only traditional rhetoric but also other aspects of oral communication, including theater, broadcast, and film. The authors placed the origins of the relational tradition in Asian philosophy, which is focused more on maintaining valued relationships than exerting influence and control.

Like Delia (1987), McCroskey and Richmond (1996) pointed to the development of the National Society for the Study of Communication (i.e., the ICA) as an important turning point in communication study because the association attracted scholars interested in both interpersonal communication and mass communication effects. The authors described the study of communication in the 1990s as more diversified than ever. The relational and rhetorical approaches both were thriving, and various subfields emerged, including individual differences, pedagogy, family communication, gender studies, and developmental approaches.

Bryant and Miron's (2007) examination of communication research history was far more encompassing than any previous account, spanning several continents from antiquity to the present and including a detailed discussion of communication and mass communication studies. Like McCroskey and Richmond (1996), Bryant and Miron established an East-West dichotomy, rooted in the difference between rhetorical studies that originated in Ancient Greece and relational theories modeled on Asian philosophical systems. As they traced the history of communication studies through the Hellenistic, Sophistic, Middle Ages, Renaissance, Enlightenment, and Romantic eras and into modern times, Bryant and Miron noted several instances in which the East-West dichotomy, which they alternately describe as a polarity between goal and style, resurfaced, regardless of geography.

In addition to noting the origins of research philosophies, Bryant and Miron (2007) examined the evolution of concepts that eventually came under the scrutiny of communication researchers, including mass entertainment (originating with Ancient Roman games) and principles of modern advertising and public relations (first appearing in the rhetoric of Christian Sophists at the end of the 2nd century). The authors also discussed the evolution of media technology, beginning with the invention of the printing press during the Renaissance.

Bryant and Miron (2007) asserted that a normative theory of mass-mediated communication emerged with research and theory on political uses and effects of media during the first half of the 20th century and noted that the intellectual climate was influenced early on by logical positivism, functionalism, trends in biology, pragmatism, and progressivism. The authors pointed to the journalism department as the birthplace of formal mass communication education but asserted that communication scholars borrowed freely from other social scientific fields, creating a relatively well-rounded approach to the study of human communication more generally.

Like Robinson (1996), Lang (1996), and Rogers (1996), Bryant and Miron (2007) noted a distinct German influence during the first half of the 20th century, primarily via scholars fleeing Nazism (cf. Rogers, 1994). They echoed the accepted history in positing that the original linear model of communication was modified into the two-step flow model. Bryant and Miron asserted, however, that later theories added complexity by considering communication as a continuous, interactive process, and they argued that these developments occurred much earlier and more often than is typically presented in the received history. They also contended that by the late 1980s, scholars had begun attempting to reconcile the often-questioned divide between interpersonal and mass communication. During the last half of the 20th century, science came to cover aspects of life not previously considered topics of scientific investigation, resulting in methodological refinements, expansions of communication theories, and development of new insights. New multidisciplinary examinations of the roles, functions, and effects of communication encompassed qualitative (critical-cultural) and quantitative (sociological-psychological) studies.

Bryant and Miron (2007) pointed out that as the 21st century dawned, communication scholars encountered new theoretical problems associated with the emergence of new electronic media (Campbell & Ling, 2009), which blurred distinctions between content and functions, interpersonal and mass communication, and sender and receiver. New communication technologies also created new social issues, including a larger generational gap, increased interdependence, enhanced class divisions, and changing communication patterns, all of which were presumed to affect future communication inquiry.

## ◆ Specialized Areas of Communication Inquiry

As communication scholarship matured, new domains of communication inquiry other than mass communication began to assume more independent identities and relatively autonomous characteristics. The roots and development of these various research traditions warrant independent treatments.

*Interpersonal Communication.* The roots of interpersonal communication research lie in the 1920s and 1930s, with studies on social interaction and relationships in the workplace, children's interaction, symbolic interactionism, and semantics (Knapp, Daly, Albada, & Miller, 2002). Research during the 1940s and 1950s on nonverbal communication and the psychology of interpersonal relations also contributed to the field, but it was not until the 1960s that interpersonal communication came into its own as an identifiable academic discipline.

Early research in this area focused primarily on persuasion and social influence, although some scholars examined group dynamics (Berger, 2005). Social influence studies assumed one-way communication, but interpersonal communication research evolved during the late 1960s and early 1970s to include the role of social interaction in the development, maintenance, and deterioration of personal relationships. By the late 1970s, researchers had begun studying the cognitive structures and processes of social interaction.

Consolidation and maturation of the field occurred in the 1970s and 1980s, thanks to a marked increase in the development of theories and models (Berger, 2005). The field also became institutionalized during that time, as evidenced by the explosion of university courses and textbooks covering aspects of interpersonal communication and relationships, as well as the founding of several scholarly and

professional associations centered on interpersonal communication (Knapp et al., 2002).

The theoretical activity of recent decades can be organized into six main areas: interpersonal adaptation, message production, uncertainty, deceptive communication, dialectical issues, and computer-mediated social interaction. The latter area necessarily emerged within the past 15 years, as new communication technologies have become ubiquitous aspects of American life. Berger (2005) predicted that research in computer-mediated social interaction would continue to grow as technology evolves. He identified several other growing research areas that likely would constitute the future of interpersonal communication scholarship, including social interaction routines that individuals employ across a wide variety of social contexts and relationship types, the variety of important functions emotions play in social interaction, skills and processes involved in message reception and interpretation, and social interaction competence. Berger argued that although researchers have studied these areas of social interaction, theoretical development has been lacking.

*Language and Social Interaction.* Language and social interaction (LSI) emerged within the past three decades, spawned primarily by other areas of communication inquiry. LSI has been described as "a multidisciplinary confederation of research communities assembled within the field of Communication" (Fitch & Sanders, 2005, p. 1). The overarching theme of LSI research is the meaningfulness of what individuals say to certain other individuals in certain circumstances, but the field can be divided into the subgroups of language pragmatics, conversation analysis, language and social psychology, discourse analysis, and ethnography of communication.

The first LSI divisions in a professional association evolved during the 1970s and early 1980s from the National Communication Association's (NCA's) Speech and Language Science division, which gradually switched over to social interaction-based research as speech and language pathology scholars migrated to their own specialized organizations (Tracy & Haspel, 2004). After the NCA division officially changed its name to Language and Social Interaction (in 1987), the ICA began a division of the same name. Prior to that time, most ICA members interested in that line of research had been submitting their scholarly papers to the Interpersonal Communication division.

In both organizations, LSI had been considered an intellectual subgroup of interpersonal communication research, but that tie weakened throughout the 1990s (Tracy & Haspel, 2004). During that time, LSI research evolved from studying message processes and intimate relationships to examining social forces in a wide range of contexts. The study of language, conversation, culture, and discourse increased across disciplines, as evidenced by the publication of several discourse-related journals in the late 1990s. Numerous essays and handbooks published during the late 1990s and early 2000s (e.g., Fitch & Sanders, 2005; Glenn, LeBaron, & Mandelbaum, 2003; van Dijk, 1997) confirm that LSI had become a bona fide academic field, although tremendously multidisciplinary in focus. Scholars from areas such as organizational communication and rhetoric increasingly were looking toward LSI research to help enrich the understanding of their respective disciplines and vice versa (Tracy & Haspel, 2004).

*Organizational Communication.* Although the roots of organizational communication can be traced to principles of ancient rhetoric, formal study originated in the first half of the 20th century (Redding & Tompkins, 1988). During the discipline's "era of preparation" (1900–1950), research focused on the need for prescriptive and skills-based training to achieve effective communication within organizational settings. The succeeding "era of identification and consolidation" (1940–1970) was signaled by the development of graduate

programs, the publication of seminal research articles, and the formation of the professional organizations that would become the NCA and ICA. Research entered an "applied-scientific" phase, emphasizing the scientific method as central to the development of knowledge about organizational communication processes.

The 1970s marked the beginning of the "era of maturity and innovation," when organizational communication was recognized as an established communication studies discipline with ties to a variety of other fields (Taylor, Flanagin, Cheney, & Seibold, 2001). The proliferation of graduate programs throughout the world and the publication of several edited books on organizational communication (e.g., Goldhaber & Barnett, 1988; Jablin, 1987; McPhee & Tompkins, 1985) emphasized the field's maturation and consolidation.

Recent decades have seen a number of intellectual shifts and conceptual debates in this area, instigated in part by the continual change of organizations and their communication processes. Six challenges face current organizational communication researchers: to innovate in theory and methodology, to address the role of ethics, to move from microlevel interpersonal issues to more macrolevel ones, to examine new organizational structures and technologies, to understand the communication of organizational change, and to explore diversity and the intergroup aspects of communication (Jones, Watson, Gardner, & Gallois, 2004).

*Intercultural Communication.* Intercultural communication arose out of the United States' post–World War II emergence as a world power and the global village philosophy promoted by the United Nations. The need to promote better understanding of cultures and communication practices in non-Western societies motivated academic inquiry in the 1950s and 1960s (Kim, 2005). Several of the earliest intercultural communication scholars were former Peace

Corps workers, and the term *intercultural communication* was introduced in a handbook for training American diplomats through the U.S. Foreign Service Institute (Steinfatt & Christophel, 1996).

International and intercultural communication became an organized field in the 1970s and 1980s, when the Speech Communication Association (now NCA) and the ICA created Intercultural Communication divisions. As is the case with most areas of communication studies, intercultural communication encompasses numerous facets, resulting in theoretical and methodological development that draws on a variety of disciplines. Cultural inquiry necessarily involves humanistic research such as ethnography and linguistics, but the discipline also encompasses a number of relevant social scientific traditions rooted in sociological and psychological research (Steinfatt & Christophel, 1996).

A significant amount of work among intercultural communication researchers has been directed toward intracultural communication and cross-cultural comparisons (Kim, 2005). Theoretically, current research addresses five major themes: psychological processes, intercultural communication competence, adaptation to an unfamiliar culture, cultural identity in intercultural contexts, and power inequality in intercultural relations. The field is vibrant, with a broad range of ideas and concepts, but Kim (2005) challenged future researchers to develop a common set of foundational notions.

*Political Communication.* Political communication study has its earliest roots in the classical works of Plato and Aristotle, who were interested in the effects of communication on political and legal institutions. Propaganda studies and empirical research on voting behavior from the 1940s and early 1950s also contributed to the communication field (Kaid, 1996). It was not until later in the 1950s, however, that scholars began to label political communication as its own discipline (Nimmo & Sanders, 1981).

Political communication studies evolved slowly through the 1960s (Kaid, 1996). In contrast, the field reached several significant milestones during the 1970s, including the emergence of focused university courses, the publication of dedicated journals, and the founding of the ICA's Political Communication division. The discipline continued to solidify during the 1980s and early 1990s with the publication of several important books, articles, and resource materials (e.g., Kaid & Sanders, 1985; Nimmo & Sanders, 1981; Swanson & Nimmo, 1990).

Political communication encompasses aspects of mass and interpersonal communication and has drawn concepts from myriad disciplines ranging from journalism to psychology. Nonetheless, four basic perspectives have guided most political communication research: rhetorical, critical, and interpretive; effects; agenda setting; and uses and gratifications (Kaid, 1996). Major topics of interest also include political debates, political advertising, political rhetoric, media coverage of political campaigns, and the role of media in civic learning (Graber, 2005; Kaid, 1996).

The proliferation of new media technologies has opened new areas of political communication research. Scholars must determine whether these technologies will serve to increase civic participation or simply serve as a new tool for current elites to maintain their power. Other areas that are ripe for future study include communication policy formation, press freedom issues, the media and political socialization, public information campaigns, user-friendliness factors, and network analyses (Graber, 2005).

*Journalism.* Adams (1993) defined journalism as "a form of expression used to report and comment in the public media on the events and ideas of the here and now" (p. 11). As so defined, the practice of journalism has existed since the 15th century, when printers began using pamphlets and broadsides to inform European publics.

The formal study of journalism, however, is much younger.

Early journalists learned the trade via apprenticeship. Journalism programs began, generally, under the umbrella of English and other college departments during the 1870s (Weaver, 2003). Separate schools and departments of journalism developed beginning in 1908, and universities soon began establishing PhD minors in journalism (Bryant & Thompson, 1999). During the 1940s, graduate education in journalism grew, as did formal journalism research.

Journalistic research prior to 1927 consisted of "descriptive histories of newspapers and periodicals without much interpretation" (Weaver & Gray, 1980, p. 127). Lasswell's (1927) propaganda research marked a turn toward the social scientific studies that dominated journalism scholarship from the 1930s to the 1950s. Three currents during that time were social histories, which examined the role of forces such as industrialization, urbanization, and technology in the development of journalism; studies of the communication process; and studies of the press in society, including press freedom, press responsibility, and the role of the press in shaping public opinion (Schramm, 1957). Revolution marked the period from the 1950s through 1980, thanks to the introduction of television and the social upheaval of the 1960s (Weaver & Gray, 1980). Quantitative research on uses and effects dominated that era.

Five main areas dominate current journalism study: sociological research emphasizing relationships, behavior, and effects; historical inquiry; the study of language and journalism; examinations of journalism's political role in the making of news; and cultural analyses focusing on contextual factors that shape journalistic practice (Zelizer, 2004). Despite this large body of research, Zelizer (2004) lamented, "As the practices, forms, and technologies for news gathering and news presentation increase in variety, demeanor, and number, the existing body of scholarly material shrinks in relevance" (p. 6). She recommended that future journalism scholars rethink their definition of journalism to be more inclusive of new and nontraditional means of spreading information and that researchers from the various subfields reach across their academic boundaries to form a more complete understanding of journalistic processes, products, and effects. The rapid growth and increasing intellectual sophistication of the journalism division of the ICA in the 21st century bode well for the accomplishment of such goals, as non-U.S. journalism scholars have greatly enriched the breadth and depth of contemporary journalism studies.

*Health Communication.* Although the practice of health communication dates to 18th-century pamphlets and speeches promoting small pox inoculation, theory and research played a minimal role in early health communication efforts (Atkin & Marshall, 1996). The founding of an ICA interest group in the mid-1970s marked the formal emergence of health communication as a recognized area of scholarly study.

Rogers (1996) considered the launching of the Stanford Heart Disease Prevention Program (SHDPP) in 1971 to be the moment when health communication research was born and argued that "SHDPP directly and indirectly spawned a family tree of health communication programs concerned with preventing heart disease, substance abuse, cancer, teenage pregnancy, and HIV/AIDS" (p. 17). The AIDS epidemic in particular spurred interest in health promotion and disease prevention.

Between 1971 and 1996, a number of universities launched specialized programs in health communication (Rogers, 1996). Research during that 25-year span drew theoretically and methodologically from a variety of academic fields, including communication, public health, medicine, marketing, social psychology, and anthropology. Popular topics of study, in addition to those listed above, included improved doctor-patient communication, media advocacy for healthy lifestyles, smoking cessation, and the prevention of drunk-driving accidents. Although a majority of health communication research centers on the effectiveness of public health campaigns, health communication via interpersonal channels also has been an important area of inquiry (Atkin & Marshall, 1996).

Since 1996, health communication has seen tremendous growth (Edgar & Freimuth, 2006). Effectiveness research, particularly regarding HIV/AIDS and smoking cessation campaigns, continues to dominate the field. Scholars have examined a number of other health communication facets, including the way health issues are portrayed in news, advertising, and entertainment media. Recent scholarship also has explored the use of new technologies to communicate about health. Disease prevention, emergency preparedness, environmental health, and workplace safety are among the health issues current researchers study. Parrott (2004) averred that scholars have neglected a number of important topics that future researchers should address, including mental health issues, health care economics, and informed consent.

*Visual Communication.* Visual communication research stemmed from centuries-old traditions of artistic criticism and philosophy. During the late 1950s, however, scholars from varied fields began theoretical studies of visual communication. The emergence of visual studies from its traditional home in the arts can be attributed to increasing observation across disciplines of visuality in culture (Barnhurst, Vari, & Rodriguez, 2004). A number of works from the 1960s and 1970s, ranging from the examination of spatial and nonverbal cues in anthropology to the application of art theory in the study of advertising, contributed to VisCom. During the 1970s and 1980s, organizations such as the Association for Education in Journalism and Mass Communication (AEJMC) founded visual communication

divisions, and several disciplines established visual studies journals.

Visual studies scholars often have pointed to the 1990s as a decade of maturation. In 1993, an ICA steering committee started a Visual Communication Interest Group. The previous year, the journals *Communication* and *Journalism Educator* had published special issues dedicated to visual communication scholarship. Griffin (1992) posited that visual communication merited special attention because of its unique focus on the forms and practices of media itself. He argued that the visual communication tradition provided models for areas neglected by conventional mass communication research: "the ontology of the media event; the structure and form of media products; the nature of media reception and interpretation; the processes by which meanings are 'read,' shared, and related to other cultural phenomena in varying social situations" (p. 81). Texts chosen for study in the special issue of *Communication* included documentary film, photojournalism, TV news, social science textbooks, and advertising.

Three key strains of theory emerge from recent visual communication research (Barnhurst et al., 2004). Rhetorical studies, which have dominated visual research on mass media and popular culture, consider images and designs as persuasive tools. The pragmatic approach has focused on the processes of production and reception. Finally, semantic scholars have examined the internal structures within a design or image. Across theoretical foundations, study of new technologies as visual texts has increased.

Although Barnhurst et al. (2004) proclaimed continued growth in visual communication studies, they cautioned that fragmentation among scholars in varied disciplines was hurting the field. The authors also noted an emerging trend toward combining historical and semantic approaches, which they predicted to be the cutting edge of visual studies during the next decade.

*Instructional and Developmental Communication.* As long as academic communication departments have existed, scholars have been studying communication in instructional settings (Nussbaum & Friedrich, 2005). The scholarly journal *Communication Education* was founded in the 1950s and, for nearly six decades, has published scholarship on discourse and instruction. In 1972, instructional communication was recognized as a formal area of scholarship when the ICA established a division dedicated to research in that field. Teacher characteristics, student characteristics, and teaching strategies were among the dominant areas of study during these early decades of instructional communication research (Staton-Spicer & Wulff, 1984).

During the past 20 years, the number and breadth of topics in instructional communication scholarship have increased exponentially. Analyzing research of the 1990s, Waldeck, Kearney, and Plax (2001) identified 12 major theories associated with instructional communication and six categories of research foci (listed here in order of frequency): student communication, teacher communication, mass media effects on children, pedagogical methods, classroom management, and teacher-student interaction. McCroskey and McCroskey (2006) predicted continued growth and recommended several areas for future study, including technologically mediated instructional communication, communication between teachers and students of different cultures, and instructional communication outside the United States.

In the mid-1980s, the ICA's Instructional Communication division expanded to include developmental communication scholarship. Concerned with the communication process across individuals' life spans, developmental communication draws on developmental psychology research of the 1960s and 1970s. It emerged as its own discipline after a caucus on communication and aging met at the 1979 NCA conference (Nussbaum & Friedrich, 2005). During the late 1980s, several seminal books on the subject were published (e.g., Carmichael, Botan, & Hawkins, 1988; Nussbaum, 1989; Nussbaum, Thompson, & Robinson, 1989).

Research in developmental communication primarily explored issues surrounding communication with, by, and between children and the elderly. Although Nussbaum and Friedrich (2005) proclaimed developmental communication studies to be a rich field built on strong theoretical foundations, they suggested that future researchers do more to address adolescents and midlife adults and to develop methodologies that appropriately measure change across time and across the entire life span.

*Communication and Technology.* Scientists began experimenting with means of transmitting sound at a distance in the late 17th century, and society has been using the fruits of their labors to communicate since the early 19th century (Winston, 1998). The telegraph, telephone, radio, and television all are communication technologies that have been in use for anywhere from 60 to 170 years. When computerized communication tools came on the scene, however, scholars became increasingly interested in studying information and communication technology (ICT) as processes and how they relate to other aspects of communication. Investigators began studying the forms, uses, and implications of ICTs in the 1970s, when the first personal computers were introduced and the U.S. Department of Defense built the first packet-switching network, ARPANET (Lievrouw & Livingstone, 2002). At that time, scholars from myriad disciplines began examining issues such as the economics of information, ICTs and social change, the transformation of "old" media in the wake of new media development, and the impact of ICTs on attitudes, behaviors, organizations, and policies. The latter strain, modeled after the mass communication effects tradition, quickly became the dominant area of American ICT research and seems to remain as such today.

Investigations of communication and technology grew and evolved during the 1980s, as an increasing number and variety of new communication technologies became available to a wider audience. New ICTs of that decade were different from the unidirectional technologies of the past and thus warranted special consideration (Rogers, 1986). Microcomputers, videotext and teletext, teleconferencing, cable television, and VCRs were among the media of interest, and the diffusion of innovations and social impacts of communication technologies became the primary areas of research.

ICT research exploded during the 1990s, resulting in part from the growth of the Internet (Lievrouw & Livingstone, 2002; Walther, Gay, & Hancock, 2005). The Internet is a ripe area for ICT scholarship because of elements such as multimedia capabilities, hypertextuality, packet switching, synchronicity, and interactivity. Despite the alleged "newness" of Internet technology, however, research in that area has yielded surprisingly little new theory. Walther and his colleagues (2005) also noted that some research draws on traditional theories that compare medium to medium, "in which Internet characteristics are insufficiently explicated" (p. 650). A third shortcoming of current ICT research is the narrow, nationalistic nature of study and the failure to compare work across cultural boundaries. Lievrouw and Livingstone (2002) suggested that an internationalization of the field would enrich understanding of ICTs and their impact on society.

*Public Relations.* Ideas inherent in the practice of modern public relations (PR) date back to practices of ancient civilization (Heath, 2005), and PR became a serious professional practice throughout the democratic world by the end of the 19th century (Cutlip, 1994). As an academic discipline, however, public relations has a fairly short history. Only within the past 25 years has a body of scholarly public relations research grown

and theoretical development occurred (Botan & Taylor, 2004; Sriramesh & Vercic, 2003).

Prior to 1985, the slim body of knowledge in public relations had remained at the analytical level (L. A. Grunig, 1996). J. E. Grunig (1984) developed the first public relations theory to achieve widespread adoption and use, and his contribution remained the field's primary theoretical basis until the start of the 21st century. Researchers focused their studies on the extent to which organizations practiced J. E. Grunig's four models of public relations: press agentry/publicity, public information, two-way asymmetrical, and two-way symmetrical. Grunig's models fit neatly into research perspectives that Heath (2001) identified, which included information, persuasion, critical, symmetrical, interpersonal, reflective, and relational.

Botan and Taylor (2004) labeled that sort of research as functional and posited that research is evolving from its focus on public relations as a tool to achieve organizational goals. They declared the field to be in a paradigm shift toward a cocreational perspective, viewing PR as the instrument through which relationships and shared meanings are built. They contended that the "future of public relations lies with whichever cocreationist model emerges as the most useful, the most theoretically valuable" (p. 659).

Regardless of the paradigm, public relations quickly was on its way to becoming one of the most researched areas of communication, as evidenced by the large number of papers submitted to PR divisions in the major communication organizations, as well as specialized PR associations and public relations research journals (Botan & Taylor, 2004). Furthermore, public relations research has become a global phenomenon. Although Sriramesh and Vercic (2003) lamented that theory building has been limited to the United States and a few Western European countries, researchers throughout the world have offered descriptive data regarding their public relations practices. Adopting a global public relations research framework is necessary, the authors asserted, because the field has become such a global enterprise that "*every* public relations professional must have a multicultural and global perspective in order to be effective" (p. xxv).

*Other Specializations Within Communication.* A case could be made that topics corresponding to most if not all of the ICA's 22 divisions and interest groups, as well as to a goodly number of the NCA's 51 divisions and sections, merit additional discussion. Obviously, limited space considerations prohibit such, although it is refreshing to realize that genuine progress in communication science is being made in many of these extremely diverse areas of scholarship.

## ◆ Reflections and Conclusions

When Delia (1987) penned his chapter of the history of communication science two decades ago, communication still was a "debtor nation" in the sense that a great deal of our theory and much of the research we cited came from other disciplines. A recent citation analysis of major communication journals revealed that this is no longer the case (Rice, 2007). Although we undoubtedly cannot as yet claim to have a favorable balance of trade in terms of exporting versus importing theories, the vast majority of the citations in peer-reviewed articles published in major communication journals are to articles published in communication journals. Or, to look at a more arcane index of the evolution of centrality of communication sources to our discipline, in Delia's (1987) history of communication science, on the shoulders of which the present historical overview stands, fewer than 20% of the 375 sources in the reference list were to communication journals, handbooks, or yearbooks, whereas

more than 50% of the citations of the present chapter are to such communication-specific periodical or compilation sources.

Moreover, even a casual examination of journals in psychology, sociology, public health, human development, and the like reveals numerous citations to journals in communication. To provide a specific exemplar, according to *Journal Citation Reports,* the communication journal *Media Psychology* had among the top-10 Thomson-ISI (now Thomson Scientific) impact rankings of the 54 *applied psychology* journals covered by that citation service between 2004 and 2006.

Moreover, in some areas at least, "name-brand theories" have migrated from communication to prominent usage in psychology, sociology, and related social science disciplines. One such area is entertainment theory (e.g., Bryant & Vorderer, 2006), and commonly exported exemplar theories within that domain include Zillmann's (2003) excitation-transfer, disposition, and mood management theories.

It is also apparent that our discipline as a whole has become increasingly prolific. The current *Journal Citation Reports* lists 44 communication journals that meet their relatively rigorous inclusion criteria, but only 13 of those journals were published in 1987, the year the original *Handbook of Communication Science* (Berger & Chaffee, 1987) was published. Obviously, mastering the content of 44 journals is impossible, bearing apt testimony to the degree of sub-disciplinary specialization that now typifies communication.

Although numerous other markers of the manifold qualitative and quantitative changes in the nature of the communication discipline over the past two decades are readily available, we will highlight only one other major change. During the late 1980s, a featured session at seemingly every major communication conference was the need for macro-theory—or even a single unifying theory—in communication. Leading communication scholars of the era (e.g., Steve

Chaffee, Ev Rogers) led such discussions in packed rooms. A search of the programs of all the major communication conferences in 2006 and 2007 failed to reveal even one such session. Apparently, we have become more realistic about the ramifications of our epistemological, methodological, and subdisciplinary pluralism.

One thing is clear. Berelson's (1959) famous pronouncement that the communication field is withering away definitely is not happening. In fact, it seems more realistic to claim that communication science truly has come of age in the digital era.

## ◆ References

Adams, G. C. (1993). *Notes toward a definition of journalism: Understanding an old craft as an art form.* St. Petersburg, FL: The Poynter Institute.

Atkin, C., & Marshall, A. (1996). Health communication. In M. B. Salwen & D. W. Stacks (Eds.), *An integrated approach to communication theory and research* (pp. 479–495). Mahwah, NJ: Lawrence Erlbaum.

Barnhurst, K. G., Vari, M., & Rodriguez, I. (2004). Mapping visual studies in communication. *Journal of Communication, 54,* 616–644.

Berelson, B. (1959). The state of communication research. *Public Opinion Quarterly, 23,* 1–6.

Berger, C. R. (2005). Interpersonal communication: Theoretical perspectives, future prospects. *Journal of Communication, 55,* 415–447.

Berger, C. R., & Chaffee, S. H. (Eds.). (1987). *Handbook of communication science.* Newbury Park, CA: Sage.

Botan, C. H., & Taylor, M. (2004). Public relations: State of the field. *Journal of Communication, 54,* 645–661.

Bryant, J., & Miron, D. (2007). Historical contexts and trends in the development of communication theory. In B. B. Whaley & W. Sampter (Eds.), *Explaining communication: Contemporary theories and exemplars* (pp. 403–431). Mahwah, NJ: Lawrence Erlbaum.

Bryant, J., & Thompson, S. (1999). Graduate communication programs. In W. G. Christ (Ed.), *Leadership in times of change: A handbook for communication and media administrators* (pp. 135–161). Mahwah, NJ: Lawrence Erlbaum.

Bryant, J., & Vorderer, P. (Eds.). (2006). *Psychology of entertainment.* Mahwah, NJ: Lawrence Erlbaum.

Campbell, S. W., & Ling, R. (2009). Effects of mobile communication. In J. Bryant & M. B. Oliver (Eds.), *Media effects: Advances in theory and research* (3rd ed., pp. 592–606). New York: Routledge.

Carmichael, C. W., Botan, C. H., & Hawkins, R. (1988). *Human communication and the aging process.* Prospect Heights, IL: Waveland.

Cutlip, S. C. (1994). *The unseen power: Public relations, a history.* Hillsdale, NJ: Lawrence Erlbaum.

Delia, J. G. (1987). Communication research: A history. In C. R. Berger & S. H. Chaffee (Eds.), *Handbook of communication science* (pp. 20–98). Newbury Park, CA: Sage.

Dennis, E. E., & Wartella, E. (Eds.). (1996). *American communication research: The remembered history.* Mahwah, NJ: Lawrence Erlbaum.

Edgar, T., & Freimuth, V. S. (2006). Introduction: 10 years of health communication research. *Journal of Health Communication, 11,* 7–9.

Fitch, K. L., & Sanders, R. E. (Eds.). (2005). *Handbook of language and social interaction.* Mahwah, NJ: Lawrence Erlbaum.

Glander, T. (2000). *Origins of mass communications research during the American cold war: Educational effects and contemporary implications.* Mahwah, NJ: Lawrence Erlbaum.

Glenn, P. J., LeBaron, C. D., & Mandelbaum, J. S. (Eds.). (2003). *Studies in language and social interaction.* Mahwah, NJ: Lawrence Erlbaum.

Goldhaber, G. M., & Barnett, G. A. (Eds.). (1988). *Handbook of organizational communication.* Norwood, NJ: Ablex.

Graber, D. A. (with Smith, J. A.). (2005). Political communication faces the 21st century. *Journal of Communication, 55,* 479–507.

Griffin, M. (1992). Editor's introduction. *Communication, 13,* 79–84.

Grunig, J. E. (1984). Organizations, environments, and models of public relations.

*Public Relations Research and Education, 1,* 6–29.

Grunig, L. A. (1996). Public relations. In M. B. Salwen & D. W. Stacks (Eds.), *An integrated approach to communication theory and research* (pp. 459–477). Mahwah, NJ: Lawrence Erlbaum.

Heath, R. L. (Ed.). (2001). *Handbook of public relations.* Thousand Oaks, CA: Sage.

Heath, R. L. (Ed.). (2005). *Encyclopedia of public relations.* Thousand Oaks, CA: Sage.

Jablin, F. M. (Ed.). (1987). *Handbook of organizational communication: An interdisciplinary perspective.* Newbury Park, CA: Sage.

Jones, E., Watson, B., Gardner, J., & Gallois, C. (2004). Organizational communication: Challenges for the new century. *Journal of Communication, 24,* 722–750.

Kaid, L. L. (1996). Political communication. In M. B. Salwen & D. W. Stacks (Eds.), *An integrated approach to communication theory and research* (pp. 443–458). Mahwah, NJ: Lawrence Erlbaum.

Kaid, L. L., & Sanders, K. R. (1985). Survey of political communication theory and research. In K. R. Sanders, L. L. Kaid, & D. Nimmo (Eds.), *Political communication yearbook 1984* (pp. 283–308). Carbondale: Southern Illinois University Press.

Kim, Y. Y. (2005). Inquiry in intercultural and development communication. *Journal of Communication, 55,* 554–577.

Knapp, M. L., Daly, J. A., Albada, K. F., & Miller, G. R. (2002). Background and current trends in the study of interpersonal communication. In M. L. Knapp & J. A. Daly (Eds.), *Handbook of interpersonal communication* (3rd ed., pp. 3–20). Thousand Oaks, CA: Sage.

Lang, K. (1996). The European roots. In E. E. Dennis & E. Wartella (Eds.), *American communication research: The remembered history* (pp. 1–20). Mahwah, NJ: Lawrence Erlbaum.

Lasswell, H. D. (1927). *Propaganda technique in the world war.* New York: Knopf.

Lievrouw, L. A., & Livingstone, S. (Eds.). (2002). *Handbook of new media: The social shaping and consequences of ICTs.* Thousand Oaks, CA: Sage.

McCroskey, J. C., & McCroskey, L. L. (2006). Instructional communication: The historical perspective. In T. P. Mottet, V. P. Richmond, & J. C. McCroskey (Eds.), *Handbook of instructional communication: Rhetorical and relational perspectives* (pp. 33–47). Boston: Pearson.

McCroskey, J., & Richmond, V. P. (1996). Human communication theory and research: Traditions and models. In M. B. Salwen & D. W. Stacks (Eds.), *An integrated approach to communication theory and research* (pp. 233–242). Mahwah, NJ: Lawrence Erlbaum.

McPhee, R., & Tompkins, P. K. (Eds.). (1985). *Organizational communication: Traditional themes and new directions.* Beverly Hills, CA: Sage.

Nimmo, D., & Sanders, K. R. (Eds.). (1981). *Handbook of political communication.* Beverly Hills, CA: Sage.

Nussbaum, J. F. (1989). *Life-span communication: Normative processes.* Hillsdale, NJ: Lawrence Erlbaum.

Nussbaum, J. F., & Friedrich, G. (2005). Instructional/developmental communication: Current theory, research, and future trends. *Journal of Communication, 55,* 578–593.

Nussbaum, J. F., Thompson, T., & Robinson, J. D. (1989). *Communication and aging.* New York: Harper & Row.

Parrott, R. (2004). Emphasizing "communication" in health communication. *Journal of Communication, 54,* 751–787.

Redding, W. C., & Tompkins, P. K. (1988). Organizational communication: Past and present tenses. In G. Goldhaber & G. Barnett (Eds.), *Handbook of organizational communication* (pp. 5–34). Norwood, NJ: Ablex.

Rice, R. E. (2007, May). *Citation analyses of major communication journals: Impact factors and local citation environments.* Paper presented at the meeting of the Executive Committee of the International Communication Association, San Francisco.

Robinson, G. J. (1996). Constructing a historiography for North American communication studies. In E. E. Dennis & E. Wartella (Eds.), *American communication research: The remembered history* (pp. 157–168). Mahwah, NJ: Lawrence Erlbaum.

Rogers, E. M. (1986). *Communication technology: The new media in society.* New York: Free Press.

Rogers, E. M. (1994). *A history of communication study: A biographical approach.* New York: Free Press.

Rogers, E. M. (1996). Up-to-date report. *Journal of Health Communication, 1,* 15–23.

Schramm, W. (1957). Twenty years of journalism research. *Public Opinion Quarterly, 21,* 91–107.

Schramm, W. (Ed.). (1963). *The science of human communication.* New York: Basic Books.

Sriramesh, K., & Vercic, D. (Eds.). (2003). *The global public relations handbook: Theory, research, and practice.* Mahwah, NJ: Lawrence Erlbaum.

Staton-Spicer, A. Q., & Wulff, D. H. (1984). Research in communication and instruction: Categorization and synthesis. *Communication Education, 33,* 377–391.

Steinfatt, T., & Christophel, D. M. (1996). Intercultural communication. In M. B. Salwen & D. W. Stacks (Eds.), *An integrated approach to communication theory and research* (pp. 317–334). Mahwah, NJ: Lawrence Erlbaum.

Swanson, D. L., & Nimmo, D. (Eds.). (1990). *New directions in political communication.* Newbury Park, CA: Sage.

Taylor, J. R., Flanagin, A. J., Cheney, G., & Seibold, D. R. (2001). Organizational communication research: Key moments, central concerns, and future challenges. In W. Gudykunst (Ed.), *Communication yearbook 24* (pp. 99–137). Thousand Oaks, CA: Sage.

Tracy, K., & Haspel, K. (2004). Language and social interaction: Its institutional identity, intellectual landscape, and discipline-shifting agenda. *Journal of Communication, 54,* 788–816.

van Dijk, T. A. (Ed.). (1997). *Discourse studies: A multidisciplinary introduction.* London: Sage.

Waldeck, J. H., Kearney, P., & Plax, T. (2001). Instructional and developmental communication theory and research in the 90s: Extending the agenda for the 21st century. In W. Gudykunst (Ed.), *Communication yearbook 24* (pp. 207–230). Thousand Oaks, CA: Sage.

Walther, J. B., Gay, G., & Hancock, J. T. (2005). How do communication and technology researchers study the Internet. *Journal of Communication, 55,* 632–657.

Wartella, E. (1996). The history reconsidered. In E. E. Dennis & E. Wartella (Eds.), *American communication research: The remembered history* (pp. 169–180). Mahwah, NJ: Lawrence Erlbaum.

Weaver, D. H. (2003). Journalism education in the United States. In R. Frohlich & C. Holtz-Bacha (Eds.), *Journalism education in Europe and North America: An international comparison* (pp. 49–64). Cresskill, NJ: Hampton.

Weaver, D. H., & Gray, R. G. (1980). Journalism and mass communication research in the United States: Past, present, and future. In G. C. Wilholt & H. de Bock (Eds.), *Mass communication review yearbook 1* (pp. 124–151). Beverly Hills, CA: Sage.

Winston, B. (1998). *Media technology and society, a history: From the telegraph to the Internet.* New York: Routledge.

Zelizer, B. (2004). *Taking journalism seriously: News and the academy.* Thousand Oaks, CA: Sage.

Zillmann, D. (2003). Theory of affective dynamics: Emotions and moods. In J. Bryant, D. Roskos-Ewoldsen, & J. Cantor (Eds.), *Communication and emotion: Essays in honor of Dolf Zillmann* (pp. 533–567). Mahwah, NJ: Lawrence Erlbaum.

# 3

# ALTERNATIVE APPROACHES TO THEORIZING IN COMMUNICATION SCIENCE

◆ Charles Pavitt

This chapter describes various pathways contributing to our arsenal of scientific communication theory. While including only two of Craig's (1999) seven theoretical traditions (the cybernetic and socio-psychological), it will provide greater precision in classifying scientific communication theories. Two dimensions, form (model) and content (fundamental explanatory principle), will be used to accomplish this task. Consistent with relativistic approaches to science (Kuhn, 1970), it has become commonplace to view explanatory and assumptive differences as marks of conflict over the very nature of science. However, Kuhn (1977) later described qualities that all scientists, regardless of theoretical presumptions, value in scientific theory: accuracy, consistency, breadth of scope, parsimony, and potential for inspiring further research advances. Analogously, this chapter will first describe the characteristics that mark scientific communication theories, no matter their presuppositions about form and content.

## ◆ *The Hallmarks of Scientific Communication Theory*

Scientific theory can be defined as "a formal system of concepts and relationships tying these concepts together, with the functions of explaining, predicting, and allowing potential control over real-world phenomena" (Pavitt, 2000b, p. 111), to which could be added the function of describing. More fundamentally, a scientific theory consists of two major parts, a model and a scientific explanation. These two components will be described in turn.

### MODELS

Hawes (1975) proposed that a model is "[a representation of] salient structural and/or functional features, properties, or characteristics of another object or process" (p. 111). Hawes's distinction among three types of models has inspired a more developed classification (Pavitt, 2000b, pp. 128–130). *Physical models* are actual instantiations of a structure or process. One subtype of physical model, the *scale model,* represents through the use of physical material. A second subtype, the *physical process model,* represents

through actions and events. For example, a scale model of an airplane may be built and its performance evaluated in a wind tunnel. Physical models are not parts of theories per se but are methods for testing them. *Conceptual models* are symbolic representations of a structure or process. One subtype, the *structural model,* demonstrates the content of a theory, usually through drawings; the structural equation diagram is an example. A second subtype, the *symbolic process model,* "acts out" a process in a symbolic world; the idea that vaccination protects against disease can serve as a representation of a method for "inoculating" people against persuasive arguments (McGuire, 1964). *Formal models* map out the relationships among theoretical concepts abstractly, through mathematical equations or computer programs, and are used for simulating the impact of these relationships on the state of the concepts over time. One could, for example, examine hypothetical changes over time in the level of liking between two people through formally modeling its mutual causal relationships with communication, similarity, uncertainty, and other related variables.

Table 3.1 summarizes this classification, listing for each member of the set its category, whether it functions to represent structure or process, and the "object" doing the representation.

**Table 3.1**  Model Classification

| Type | Category | Function | Object |
|------|----------|----------|--------|
| Scale | Physical | Structure | Physical substance |
| Physical process | Physical | Process | Physical activity |
| Structural | Symbolic/conceptual | Structure | Diagram |
| Symbolic process | Symbolic/conceptual | Process | Verbal analogy |
| Formal | Symbolic/formal | Process | Equation or diagram |

## EXPLANATION

The essence of a scientific theory is an explanation. To explain something is to make it understandable in terms of what is already understood. Attempts to characterize scientific explanation as a logical derivation (Hempel & Oppenheim, 1948) have been deemed failures, as there is no necessary connection between logical derivation and understanding (Scriven, 1959). To better understand explanation, one must begin with the everyday process of "explaining" as a discursive act. In this process, an "audience" has a "question" about some confusing phenomenon, and a "speaker" utters a "sentence" with two intentions: first, to answer directly that question and, second, for the audience to recognize that intention (Achinstein, 1983). For the discursive act to be successful, the audience must recognize the speaker's relevant intentions. Finally, the speaker believes the content of that sentence to be true; that content is the explanation. The criteria for judging an everyday explanation's adequacy are equivalent to Grice's (1975) four maxims for cooperative interaction: quantity (explanations should be adequately informative), quality (explanations should be accurate), relation (explanations should be relevant to the audience's question), and manner (explanations should be clear) (Pavitt, 2000a).

To qualify as scientific, an explanation must meet additional criteria. First, unlike explanations of single events (e.g., historical), scientific theory is intended to explain patterns of events displaying some form of regularity (Friedman, 1974), allowing its application to a wide array of circumstances. Second, scientific theory explains by describing how patterns of events follow from some fundamental underlying principle, ideally expressed in the form of microstructures and microprocesses (Bhaskar, 1978). Third, a scientific explanation unifies ostensibly disparate phenomena within the same explanatory framework, thus promoting parsimony (Kitcher, 1989). In summary, an audience seeking a scientific explanation is looking for a description of a general underlying principle that accounts for the occurrence of a regular pattern of events. The specific type of explanation is dependent on the audience's question.

## CAUSAL EXPLANATION

*Causal explanation,* the most prevalent type, is relevant when the audience is interested in learning how a pattern of events came to be. Hume's phenomenalist view of causality as only the "constant conjunction" of a series of events dominated metatheoretical commentary for more than 250 years but is fundamentally flawed (Hirst, 1959). The existence of "force" is an undeniable sensory experience, to which anyone ever knocked over by waves at an ocean beach can attest. Causal explanations are founded on the notion that material objects, as a consequence of their attributes, can be "generative mechanisms"—in other words, have causal efficacy (Harre & Madden, 1975). For causes and effects separated by time and space, causal explanations require the description of both generative mechanisms and the "conduits" responsible for transferring causal force from cause to effect (Salmon, 1984). Such "causal processes" conserve some quantity, be it momentum, energy, or information, from generative mechanism to final outcome (Dowe, 1992).

Specific conceptual models for causal explanation can be distinguished. Two are common in theories of message effects and message production; I will call the first of these the stimulus-processing-response model (SPR) and the second of these the orientation-stimulus-processing-response model (OSPR). These descriptors, rather than the traditional stimulus-organism-response (SOR; Woodworth, 1929) and orientation$_1$-stimulus-orientation$_2$-response (OSOR) terminology (Markus & Zajonc, 1985; McLeod, Kosicki, & McLeod,

2002, and Chapter 11, this volume), are used to disambiguate the stages in each. The OSPR model is the more prevalent of the two. In a general OSPR model for communication effects, people with a preexisting cognitive structure of beliefs, goals, and needs (orientation), upon receiving a message (stimulus), process the message in terms of their orientation, potentially resulting in a changed cognitive structure and/or some relevant behavior (response). In a general OSPR account of message production, those parts of cognitive structures (orientation) made relevant by the situation (stimulus) are chosen through cognitive processes as blueprints for the subsequent message (response).

The second type of causal model prevalent in communication science, the input-process-output (IPO) form, was introduced through the study of small group discussion (Gouran, 1975; Hackman & Morris, 1975) but is common throughout work in interpersonal interaction across contexts (dyadic, group, organizational) and channels (face-to-face vs. mediated). An IPO model represents a causal process by which factors conceptually prior to communication, usually including individual characteristics of the interacting communicators and relevant situational constraints (input), affect communication content (process), which in turn affects factors conceptually subsequent to communication, such as task performance or personal satisfaction (output). Several theories take an "interactive" extension of the IPO model, in which feedback loops among interactants (for exam-ple, "Ann" and "Bob") allow for mutual causal processes. In short, whatever impact Ann's communication has on Bob (output) becomes input for Bob's subsequent messages. Although IPO theories can be reinterpreted in OSPR terms, to do so would obscure a fundamental distinction between them; the P stands for cognitive process in OSPR theories but communicative process in IPO theories, thus highlighting the differing concerns at the heart of their explanations.

## FUNCTIONAL EXPLANATION

Audiences may have questions other than "how," such as "what's the point of it." This question calls for *functional explanation,* which is accomplished through what Achinstein (1983) called either a "good-consequences doctrine" (the function of X as part of system S is to do y if and only if this doing confers some good to S; for example, "the heart functions to pump blood") or a "goal doctrine" (the function of X in system S is to do y if and only if it contributes to a goal related to S; for example, "the thermostat functions to turn heat on and off").

## SCIENTIFIC THEORY IN COMMUNICATION SCIENCE

Most theories in the social and behavioral sciences can be classified as either causal or functional. A scientific *communication* theory requires communication or, at least, interaction to be integral to the theory's explanation, either as a conduit in a causal process or as that which brings about goal achievement in a functional relationship. The large majority of social and behavioral scientific theory is not communicative. For example, in Byrne's (1971) reinforcement-affect theory of interpersonal attraction, degree of liking toward a given person is a function of how rewarding experiences with that person have been. Whether these experiences have been communicative is not inherent to the theory's explanation. In contrast, Thibaut and Kelley's (1959) version of social exchange theory is not truly "communicative" but fundamentally interactive. In addition, proposing scientific communication theory presupposes at least three commitments. First, as scientific theory consists of both model and explanation, the presentation of a model alone provides only a description of the relationship among variables and is incomplete without an explication of a fundamental explanatory principle, couched in terms of microstructure and microprocess, underlying that description. Second, that underlying principle is psychological, sociological, or, on occasion, biological. Communication cannot explain itself, and any attempt to do so limits one to a description. Third, communication does not have material existence and so cannot serve as a generative mechanism in a causal explanation; rather, it functions as a necessary conduit in causal processes. The relevant generative mechanism in a causal explanation in scientific communication theory is always some characteristic of the human being. Noting that communication is not a generative mechanism does not contradict its centrality in causal or functional process; in either explanatory form, communication is "consequential" (Bonito & Hollingshead, 1997).

## ◆ Prevalent Generative Mechanisms in Causal Explanations

Again, the relevant generative mechanism in a causal explanation in scientific communication theory is always some characteristic of the human; moreover, most causal communication theories rely on one of a relatively small number of generative mechanisms. With some notable exceptions, message effects (OSPR and SPR) and interactional (IPO) theories are based on one of three basic psychological needs: hedonistic, understanding, and consistency. Again, with exceptions, message production theories (OSPR) along with a few interactional theories presume that communicators are primarily goal oriented. Although the terms *need* and *goal* have different connotations, for present purposes, a "need" can be viewed as a motivator for acting toward a goal and a "goal" as a

cognitive representation of a desired end state that could be the consequence of a need. A few message effects theories concentrate wholly on cognitive processing, and for these, neither goals nor needs are critical components.

In the following sections, most existing scientific communication theories will be classified according to their model (OSPR/SPR or IPO) within categories defined by a fundamental explanatory principle, in so doing distinguishing theories driven by one of the three basic psychological needs (hedonistic, understanding, and consistency), by communicator goals, or by notions of cognitive processing.

## ◆ Hedonistic Theories

The idea that people act primarily to gain pleasure and escape from pain has intellectual roots going back at least 2,400 years. Further impetus for this notion came from the British Empiricist philosophical tradition; in particular, Bentham (1789) incorporated hedonistic principles into a social psychological framework (Allport, 1969). Thorndike's law of effect ("pleasure stamps in; pain stamps out") became the concept of reinforcement (Thorndike, 1898). Among subsequent directions taken by "learning theorists," the most relevant is drive theory (Miller & Dollard, 1941), in which the degree of reinforcement for a given response to either an internal drive or an external cue determines the likelihood that the response will be reenacted the next time the drive or cue reappears. Learning theorists have tended to accept two basic tenets besides hedonism: *associationism,* that the experience of pleasure and pain becomes associated with that which brings them, and *behaviorism,* that characteristics of the human mind are irrelevant for explaining behavior (Deutsch & Krauss, 1965). A plurality of scientific communication theories is hedonistic, including all of the causal models (SPR, OSPR, standard and interactive IPO) common in communication science. Although often directly influenced by drive theory, all have rejected behaviorism while accepting hedonism and associationism.

## SPR/OSPR

The Yale Communication Research Program (Hovland, Janis, & Kelley, 1953) and Katz's (1960) "functional" approach are based on drive-theoretical principles. Preexisting attitudes (orientation) result from past or expected future reinforcements; when a relevant drive ("I'm thirsty") or cue (a tavern) is present, the mentalistic representation of the most highly reinforced possible response (the attitude) is likely to be enacted ("Coorsweiser is my beer"). Messages implying that a different option would be more rewarding (stimulus), if attended to, comprehended, and accepted (process), can lead to attitude change ("Old Madison is now my beer"), interpreted as a shift in the "implicit response" likely called forth when the drive or cue reappears.

Allport (1969) considered the need for homeostasis as a variant of the hedonistic principle, as it implies a desire to escape from pain. Zillmann and Bryant's (1985) theory of affect-dependent stimulus arrangement is an example. First encounters with media are considered in SPR form. For example, a randomly chosen television program (stimulus) is found either pleasurable or not (process) depending on whether its content matches the viewer's present drive for stimulation (i.e., a bored person wants excitement, whereas a stressed person wants something calming). Degree of match leads the viewer to decide whether to continue with that program or try another (response). The viewer remembers which programs were pleasurable, and, as the memory affects future program choice, the theory switches to OSPR form for later media encounters. The activation theory of information exposure (Donohew, Lorch, &

Palmgreen, 1988) works similarly, with a media consumer's attention to a media stimulus based on his or her drive for stimulation as determined by the characteristic level of sensation seeking.

Social learning theory (Bandura, 1977) also uses a SPR model for first encounters with media and an OSPR model for consequences of that encounter. Attention-getting media presentations in which media characters are rewarded for aggressive behavior (stimulus) produce memories of both the relevant behavioral sequence and the association between performing that sequence and reward (response). If facing a later situation in which aggression is a viable option (stimulus), these memories (orientation) come into play (process), which, when motivated by what was viewed, result in aggressive behavior (response).

Theories concerning emotional responses to messages have been cast in SPR form, although they presume an appraisal process requiring consideration of the message receiver's preexisting goals and beliefs. In Witte's (1992) extended parallel process approach, message characteristics (stimulus) lead to estimates of threat, which, when sufficiently substantial, stimulate estimates of personal efficacy and feelings of fear (process). Differing combinations of these factors result in either adaptive or maladaptive responses or no response at all. Nabi's (1999) cognitive-functional theory is general to negative emotions. Emotional message appeals (stimulus) conjure up either approach (e.g., anger) or avoidance (e.g., fear) tendencies, in turn influencing the message receiver's motivation and ability to process the message's recommendations, resulting in either message acceptance or rejection and the subsequent probability of attitude change (response).

McGuire's (1964) inoculation theory of resistance is explicitly in OSPR mold. The reception of a stimulus message providing arguments contrary to a person's beliefs creates a feeling of personal threat that, when linked with example counterarguments, leads the person to think about how to defend the relevant beliefs. The result is greater ability to resist later attempts at persuasion through contradictory arguments. One final OSPR message effects proposal, M. Burgoon's (M. Burgoon, Dillard, & Doran, 1983) persuasion theory of expectancy violations, states that people have expectations (orientation) about normative communication behaviors (e.g., degree of message intensity). Message stimuli are judged against those expectations (processing). Those that negatively violate expectations inhibit persuasion, while those that positively violate them facilitate persuasion (response).

## STANDARD IPO

Two hedonistic-based communication theories in standard IPO model form are relevant to the impact of stress on the communicative process. Bradac, Bowers, and Courtright's (1980) explanation for degree of lexical variation in messages begins with a speaker's degree of cognitive stress (input), which affects the intensity, diversity, and immediacy of the speaker's word choice (process), in turn affecting a receiver's judgments of the speaker's competence, beliefs concerning similarity between the speaker and receiver, and attitude reinforcement or change. In Karau and Kelly's (1992) work on the impact of time on group performance, time pressure and task demands determine member arousal level and amount of attentional focus directed to task completion rather than nontask activity (input), with time restriction leading the group discussion pro-cess toward task orientation. Task performance follows the classic arousal curve, with intermediate levels of arousal leading to task focus without panic and optimum results (output).

In communication accommodation theory (Giles & Ogay, 2007), communicators' knowledge about their own and their interaction partner's relevant social categories and their desire for approval or disapproval lead to attempts at either convergence or divergence in speech and nonverbal style with the partner. In general, if approval from the other is desired, convergence is likely; if self-approval or, assuming one identifies with one's own social group, approval from that group is paramount, divergence is expected.

## INTERACTIVE IPO

As mentioned previously, social exchange theories (Homans, 1958; Thibaut & Kelley, 1959) do not include "communication" as a central theoretical concept within them; nonetheless, they are fundamentally interactive. Ann and Bob (our imaginary co-interlocutors in interactive IPO theories) each desire valued resources, including affection, goods, information, money, services, and status (Foa & Foa, 1976). They more highly value their relationship as they find exchanges of resources more pleasurable than painful. Intangible resources (i.e., affection, information, and status) are most effectively exchanged through communication. To increase their relationship's value, Ann uses her knowledge of the situation and of Bob (input) to plan a message (process) providing some resource she believes Bob will find pleasurable. If Bob perceives the resource that way (output), he uses his relevant knowledge analogously as input into his verbal response. Later social exchange theories focused on the specific roles of equity in exchange (Adams, 1965), self-disclosure (Altman & Taylor, 1973), and resources invested in relationships (Rusbult, 1980).

Although not originally proposed in interactive form, theories regarding communicators' responses to one another's intimacy behaviors were probably intended to be interpreted that way. All presume that one party's response to another's intimacy behaviors follows from the extent to which the person finds those behaviors pleasurable or painful.

In Argyle and Dean's (1965) equilibrium theory, a balance of approach and avoidance forces determines one person's desired degree of behavioral intimacy with another. Thus, as Bob's behaviors imply increased intimacy (e.g., Bob moves closer), Ann feels anxiety and compensates to decrease her intimacy (she gazes less often at Bob). Bob could then respond in turn, continuing the "negotiation" of intimacy. Subsequent theories also allowed for reciprocity; an increase in Bob's intimacy could lead to an increase in Ann's, implying greater liking between them. According to J. K. Burgoon and Hale's (1988) nonverbal expectancy violations theory, Ann has expectations of the intimacy level implied by Bob's behaviors based on their relational history and the situation. Discrepancies above a threshold level between Bob's behavior and Ann's expectation result in a violation of Ann's expectations and increased arousal on her part. If Ann finds interaction with Bob rewarding, she responds to the arousal by reciprocating; if Bob is considered punishing, Ann compensates. Comparable approaches include arousal-labeling theory (Patterson, 1976), discrepancy arousal theory (Cappella & Greene, 1982), cognitive valence theory (Andersen, 1998), and interaction adaptation theory (J. K. Burgoon & White, 1997), which differ from nonverbal expectancy violations theory in terms of the proposed psychological process by which Ann's arousal affects her subsequent actions. Each theory either explicitly states or implies interactivity; Ann's behavioral output becomes input to Bob, who will respond both psychologically and behaviorally in analogous ways.

## ◆ Understanding-Driven Theories

Gestalt psychology (Kohler, 1959) was influenced by Kantian arguments that our experience is an active attempt to understand the world and that perception is fundamentally holistic. Gestalt psychologists attended to the manner in which perceptions organize the world in order to make sense of it, as instantiated in tendencies to see broken circles as complete and similar or symmetrical figures as related. These tendencies were believed to apply beyond perception to cognitive processes in general.

Theories founded on the motivation to understand followed from the work of Gestaltists Kurt Lewin and Fritz Heider. Lewin's influence is most explicit in his student Festinger's theories of social communication (1950) and social comparison (1954), specifically as a need to evaluate the level of our abilities and the correctness of our cognitions. However, these understanding needs are only tangentially related with Festinger's major concern: pressure toward uniformity in group members' opinions. In both theories, Festinger claimed that the need to evaluate one's cognitions implies a desire to agree with one's group, but this implication does not follow; a person can be aware of but unconcerned with disagreement with their groupmates. Both are input-process theories relating various factors to the desire to discuss relevant topics (social communication theory) or change the discrepant opinions of others (social comparison theory).

### SPR/OSPR

Heider's impact is most apparent in his attribution theory (1958) and in the theories of impression formation his work inspired (Jones & Davis, 1965; Kelley, 1967). These view people as "naive scientists" who, when observing one another's behavior, are motivated to form a theory about the other allowing for that behavior's explanation (through trait attribution) and prediction of future behavior (through implication from the attributed trait). These theories were presented in SPR form; behavioral observation (stimulus) leads to a psychological inference process resulting in an explanatory trait (response). More recent work has articulated the cognitive processes by which attribution occurs

(Reed & Miller, 1998). Full-blown impression formation theories are OSPR, beginning with a belief structure delineating the relationships among behaviors and traits at the foundation of the attribution process (Pavitt, 1989).

Both the elaboration likelihood (Petty & Cacioppo, 1986) and heuristic/systematic (Chaiken, Liberman, & Eagly, 1989) theories of persuasion begin with the explicit Festinger-inspired postulates that people are motivated to hold correct attitudes. Central concerns are how people act on that motivation when faced with a message inconsistent with their attitude. They stand as exemplar OSPR effects theories; one's motivation and ability to process messages and one's preexisting attitude (orientation), upon receiving the message (stimulus), influence the extent to which one analyzes message content (process), resulting in influence toward the message, a boomerang away from it, or no change at all (response). Sharing the basic assumption of understanding needs, Shrum (2002) adopted the heuristic-systematic model for a discussion of cultivation effects (i.e., how people come to believe that television content reflects the conditions of real life).

Agenda-setting theory (Shaw & McCombs, 1977) is a model case of the desire to understand as a motivator. Depending on interest in and knowledge about politics, a media audience member's degree of "need for orientation" motivates politically relevant media use (orientation). Although the theory includes the process by which news media organizations choose what political issues to include and emphasize, what is relevant here is that the degree to which given issues are emphasized (stimulus), in interaction with their need for orientation, influences the extent to which audience members attend to those issues (processing), determining their relevant knowledge and behavior (response). Eveland's (2001) cognitive mediation model of learning from the news is comparable. Greater levels of "surveillance gratifications," the desire to gain information about one's environment

(orientation), lead to greater attention and deeper message processing with exposure to media news (stimulus), resulting in more learning about public affairs (response). Also analogous is Kim's (1977) explanation for acculturation of foreign immigrants, which hinges on "acculturation motivation," consisting in part of the immigrant's desire to learn about the host culture. Acculturation motivation and knowledge of the host culture's language (orientation), when paired with sufficient opportunity to engage in interpersonal interaction and consume mass media (stimulus), result in greater knowledge about the host culture (response).

For Weick (1979), organizing is a process of reducing environmental uncertainty, or "equivocality." When facing a novel circumstance (stimulus), groups of people attempt to work together to bring certainty to it. Organizing proceeds through coordinated behavioral sequences ("interlocking cycles"), some communicative. Those interlocking cycles that have proven successful in reducing equivocality are retained in memory as "assembly rules" (orientation) and are selected again as responses when a similar circumstance occurs. Similarly, the mediational approach to group leadership asserts that the major function of group leadership is clarifying an uncertain environment for the group (Barge & Hirokawa, 1989). Task complexity, group climate, and role relationship clarity are situational factors that call on the leader's communication skills (orientation), influencing the successful leader's choice and enactment of varying types of task- and relationally oriented communication.

## INTERACTIVE IPO

Uncertainty reduction theory (Berger & Calabrese, 1975) can be interpreted as an account of interactional processes running in parallel to the psychological processes described in attribution and impression formation theories. In this case, Ann and Bob are strangers whose initial high uncertainty about one another (input) motivates each to seek information and reciprocate one another's comments (process), lowering uncertainty (output), which leads (as input) to increased verbalizations and nonverbal affiliative behavior (process), resulting in even lower uncertainty and increases in liking (output). In contrast, Sunnafrank (1986) proposed that the beginning motivation to understand the other becomes superseded by a hedonistic-fueled estimate of whether continued interaction would lead to positive outcomes. Knowledge gained from uncertainty-inspired talk (output) receives a positive/negative evaluation, which serves as input for a subsequent process. Other related theories cite both hedonistic (anxiety) and understanding (uncertainty) needs as motivators. Gudykunst's (1993) OSPR anxiety/uncertainty management theory, relevant to strangers attempting to communicate in intergroup or intercultural settings, includes a host of personal (orientation) and situational (stimulus) factors affecting the stranger's anxiety and uncertainty about the upcoming interaction (process). Anxiety and uncertainty levels, in turn, determine "mindfulness" (further process) and subsequent message effectiveness (response). The OSPR theory of motivated information management (Afifi & Weiner, 2004) sees anxiety as a consequence of discrepancies between the uncertainty level desired (orientation) and that engendered by the situation (stimulus). Anxiety motivates an estimation of the outcome value of a search for uncertainty-reducing information and the likelihood of lowering anxiety as a result of this search (process). A decision of whether to conduct the information search behavior follows (response).

## ◆ Consistency-Driven Theories

The notion of a need for *cognitive consistency*, such that perceived inconsistency motivates restoration of psychological balance, follows from the Gestalt contention that the mind strives to experience the world in orderly and symmetrical patterns. A further impetus may be what Allport (1969, p. 13) considered a "disguised version of hedonism," in which a motivation for tension reduction underlay some versions of drive theory.

The 1950s saw several relevant and influential OSPR theories of cognitive organization and change, one fundamentally communicative (Osgood & Tannenbaum, 1955) and the others easily interpreted as such. In balance theories (Heider, 1945; Newcomb, 1953), people desire consistency between their degree of attraction toward and amount of agreement with another person. If Ann, who likes Bob but dislikes Senator Loudmouth (orientation), hears Bob say he likes the senator (stimulus), Ann enters an imbalanced state resolvable by cognition re-arrangement (process), coming to either like the senator or dislike Bob, depending on which sentiment is held less deeply (response). Congruity theory (Osgood & Tannenbaum, 1955) is relevant when a person is unaware of inconsistency between two related attitudes. A message exposing that inconsistency motivates the person to reduce it (process), resulting in his or her convergence. In cognitive dissonance theory (Festinger, 1957), a person with a set of consonant beliefs (orientation) may experience a message (stimulus) inconsistent with those beliefs, causing dissonance but also demonstrating how to rearrange those beliefs and restore consonance (process), leading to attitude change (response).

The disposition theory of enjoyment for dramatic media presentations (Raney, 2004) seems best served by a cognitive consistency interpretation. Media consumers possess beliefs about the morality of various actions, the type and degree of punishment deserved for immoral actions, and expectations concerning the actions of role types, for example, physician, police officer, or drug dealer (orientation). Media content (stimulus) leads to comparisons among these orientations. Consumer enjoyment of the media presentation depends on cognitive balance (i.e., the good guys get rewarded and the bad guys get punished).

The work summarized thus far reveals the extent to which theorists have envisioned specific needs as central concepts in scientific communication theory. Two further classes of causal theories do not presume any particular need as a primary generative mechanism for message production or reception. One posits that communicative activity is goal driven, without presupposing any specific goal. The other bypasses the concepts of "need" and "goal" while concentrating on message processing alone.

## ◆ Goal-Driven Theories

### OSPR

Several theories relevant to message production include a representation of beliefs about the relationships among goals, situations, and actions, or "procedural knowledge units," instructing what to do to achieve a given goal in a given situation (orientation). The experienced situation (stimulus) triggers cognitive processing, during which procedural knowledge units relevant to the situation and communicator goals (either predating the situation or made salient by it) are singled out and organized into a message (response). Greene's (1984) action assembly theory exemplifies this formula. Berger's (1997) planning theory allows for plans preexisting in memory, simplifying the processing stage. Planning theory also considers the impact of relevant "declarative knowledge" (known facts) and includes a second process for revision of failed original plans. Meyer's (1997) work emphasizes the editing of formulated plans judged either ineffective or socially unsuitable.

Some approaches include both message production and message reception accounts. Current constructivist theory (Burleson, 2007) considers cognitive structures relevant to message production to include, along with procedural knowledge units, constructs or bipolar trait adjectives describing social knowledge. The more complex (i.e., numerous and interconnected) these constructs, the more sophisticated the message planning, and the more person centered the resulting message. On the receiver side, greater construct complexity implies deeper message processing, resulting in a more sophisticated understanding of the intentions and motives behind the communicator's message. Smith's (1982) contingency rules theory of interpersonal compliance-gaining message production begins with procedural knowledge units that, when called up by contextual beliefs about the communicator's relationship with the message receiver, determine message design. For receivers, the persuasive message is successful to the extent that the procedural knowledge units its content calls into mind are associated with the receiver's goals. Buck's (1997) readout theory of spontaneous affect display considers such displays to be biologically based responses to some motivational state (orientation) activated by "challenging" stimuli. As part of our biological inheritance (orientation), observations of spontaneous displays are automatically processed and recognized by receivers.

Politeness theory (Brown & Levinson, 1987), unlike other message production theories, legislates objective situational constraints. Communicators are presumed to have an interactional goal either showing disregard for the receiver (threaten positive face) or impeding the receiver's freedom of action (threaten negative face). The situation, defined by social distance and relative power between communicator and receiver and implied degree of "imposition" for the receiver, serves as stimulus. The communicator then calculates the optimum amount of face threat the situational constraints imply (process) and words his or her message accordingly (response). Face negotiation theory (Ting-Toomey & Kurogi, 1998) extends these ideas to intercultural conflict interactions by including degree of self-construal independence versus interdependence within a person's orientation; these, in turn, are partly a function of his or her native culture's degree of individualism versus collectivism.

Outside of message production theories, Lang's (2000) limited-capacity model of mediated message processing presumes that people approach media consumption with relevant goals and knowledge structures (orientation) that direct attention to specific aspects of media content (stimulus), although content presentation salience can also influence attentional focus. Depending on available processing capacity, part of what is attended to is then encoded into memory (process), resulting in changes in knowledge structures (response).

## INTERACTIVE IPO

Within interpersonal deception theory (Buller & Burgoon, 1996), deceiver Ann's relevant knowledge, skill, and goals (input) determine her behavioral display (process); upon perception of the display, Bob judges its veracity (output). This judgment, along with Bob's knowledge and skills, affects his behavioral response (process), which Ann then uses to evaluate Bob's degree of suspicion (output), affecting Ann's next behavioral display (process) and so on, with the final output of Ann's success at deception juxtaposed with Bob's success at detection.

The original version of the coordinated management of meaning theory (Pearce & Cronen, 1980) also takes the interactive IPO form. On the basis of her understanding of contextually relevant regulative rules (input), Ann constructs a message for Bob (process), which Bob interprets based on his conception of contextually relevant constitutive rules (output), following which he uses his beliefs about regulative rules (input) to design a response (process) and so on throughout the interchange. The degree of coordination depends on the extent to which Ann and Bob's understandings match.

## ◆ *Process-Driven Theories*

Social judgment-involvement theory (Sherif, Sherif, & Nebergall, 1965) treats an individual's attitude on a specific issue (orientation) as a bipolar dimension anchored by extreme positions toward that issue, divided into regions defining positions the individual finds acceptable, objectionable, or neither (neutrality). If a message stimulus is perceived, people judge that message's position relative to these regions; one within their "latitude of acceptance" is assimilated toward their view, one within their "latitude of rejection" is contrasted from it, and one within their "latitude of noncommitment" is judged accurately (process). Only the last of these can lead to attitude change consistent with the message (response).

In Fishbein and Ajzen's (1975) theory of reasoned action, an attitude toward either an object or action (orientation) is determined by "salient" beliefs (those most closely associated with the object or action in long-term memory; Roskos-Ewoldsen & Fazio, 1997) about object attributes or action consequences along with affective evaluations of these beliefs. Message stimuli can lead to attitude change (response) through changing either the content or evaluation of a preexisting belief or adding a new belief. An attitude toward an action and beliefs about how valued others evaluate that action influence in turn behavioral intentions and behaviors as possible further responses. Each intervening step from beliefs through behaviors implies some cognitive processing. Palmgreen and Rayburn's (1982) expectancy value approach to media choice is based on this conception. One's attitude toward a specific media source is a function of beliefs about that source and evaluation of those beliefs. These attitudes predict one's tendency to use that media source (orientation). A person will compare his or her experience with a given media source with the beliefs and evaluations making up the attitude (process), possibly leading to change in attitude and tendency to return to that media source (response).

## ♦ Functional Theories

Communication serves many functions in human life, leading scholars to propose lists of functions performed by communication in various contexts. A list, however, does not a scientific theory make. Functional theories are as responsible for meeting the criteria for adequate scientific theory as are causal theories—in particular, the requirement to account for patterns of events through some fundamental underlying principle analogous to the generative mechanism. Very few relevant proposals have been made, and even fewer meet that requirement; those that have succeeded have done so through the goal doctrine variant of functional explanation.

One example is Bales's (1953) equilibrium theory of group decision-making discussion, an example of structural-functional theorizing, in which social systems are proposed as having goals (in this case, successful task completion and group maintenance) that people's actions function to achieve. As progress toward the first goal leads to tension among members that threatens the achievement of the second, group process consists of alternating sequences of tension-producing task-relevant communication (proposal generation/discussion/evaluation) and tension-reducing positive relational communication. Furthermore, leadership structures responsible for task- and relationally oriented discussion must evolve. In addition, task talk must

proceed in a sequential three-phase pattern of problem analysis, criteria generation, and proposal evaluation because logic requires that later phases cannot occur before the earlier ones.

A second example is Ball-Rokeach's media dependency theory of media effects (DeFleur & Ball-Rokeach, 1982). Media, the generalized media audience, and various social systems (most notably the economic and political) each have goals requiring interaction with one another. For example, to achieve its goal of surviving, media attempts to satisfy the economic and political systems through types of programming. Audiences have goals that media can meet, such as gaining information and entertainment, and media content can perform various cognitive and emotional functions for that audience.

Other proposals could easily meet the criteria of functional theory. Gouran and Hirokawa's (Gouran, Hirokawa, Julian, & Leatham, 1993) approach to group task work features a list of functions associated with positively evaluated decisions, meeting the good consequences variant of functional explanation but lacking any fundamental underlying principle (VanderVoort, 2002). However, critics (Billingsley, 1993; Stohl & Holmes, 1993) have found that principle in Gouran et al.'s presumptions that group members are sufficiently rational and motivated to make a good decision. The "pragmatic" tradition of relational power beginning with Watzlawick, Beavin, and Jackson (1967) could be formulated analogously to Bales (1953) under the assumptions of a personal need for power and sufficient rationality (Pavitt, 2000a). Marriages have the goals of task performance and maintenance, with the former requiring the more competent spouse to take the dominant role and the latter requiring both spouses to have opportunities to be dominant. Fights for dominance occur when these goals collide, requiring both people to exchange periods of domination for a healthy marriage.

## ◆ Conclusion

This chapter's goals have been to describe the attributes of scientific communication theory and to classify existing scientific communication theories within a system defined by form, or type of model (SPR, OSPR, standard and interactive IPO, functional) and content, or fundamental explanatory principle (presuming hedonistic, understanding, or consistency needs as motivators; presuming goals as motivators; or making no such presumption and concentrating on the details of cognitive processing). The result is a thumbnail sketch of the current state of scientific communication theory. The remainder of this chapter will outline three areas in which further developments would be beneficial. First, as often as researchers write about the functions performed by communication, they have barely begun to theorize about them. Lists of the functions performed by communication, both in general (McQuail, 1987) and in specific areas (e.g., persuasion; Stewart, Smith, & Denton, 1989), abound. Developing these lists into theories would add valuable examples of this form.

Second, seriously considering the processual (i.e., over-time) nature of communication can improve already existing theories. Many SPR and OSPR theories featuring cognitive change in response to message stimuli and cognitive processing fail to consider how this change feeds back into the orientation with which the communicator processes subsequent messages. Examining two theories that do (Bandura, 1977; Zillmann & Bryant, 1985) reveals how the results of earlier encounters with media might influence, through explicit feedback loops, later thought processes and actions. The existence of interactive IPO theories, which consider how both co-interlocutors' perspectives unfold over time, raises the question of whether most or all of standard, noninteractional IPO theory can be explicated in interactive form.

Third, although approaches such as adaptive structuration theory (Poole & DeSanctis, 1990) and dialectical theory (Baxter & Braithwaite, 2007) do not fit the molds of causal or functional explanatory form, it would be foolhardy to ignore the contributions these and analogous theories can provide. Whether they can be explicated in OSPR or IPO terms or whether other forms of scientific communication theory can be generated for these cases remains to be seen.

## ◆ References

Achinstein, P. (1983). *The nature of explanation*. New York: Oxford University Press.

Adams, J. (1965). Inequity in social exchange. In L. Berkowitz (Ed.), *Advances in experimental social psychology* (Vol. 2, pp. 267–300). New York: Academic Press.

Afifi, W. A., & Weiner, J. L. (2004). Toward a theory of motivated information management. *Communication Theory, 14*, 167–190.

Allport, G. W. (1969). The historical background of modern social psychology. In G. Lindzey & E. Aronson (Eds.), *Handbook of social psychology* (2nd ed., Vol. 1, pp. 10–68). Reading, MA: Addison-Wesley.

Altman, I., & Taylor, D. (1973). *Social penetration*. New York: Holt, Rinehart & Winston.

Andersen, P. A. (1998). The cognitive valence theory of intimate communication. In M. T. Palmer & G. A. Barnett (Eds.), *Progress in communication sciences* (Vol. 14, pp. 39–72). Stamford, CT: Ablex.

Argyle, M., & Dean, J. (1965). Eye-contact, distance and affiliation. *Sociometry, 28*, 289–304.

Bales, R. F. (1953). The equilibrium problem in small groups. In T. Parsons, R. F. Bales, & E. A. Shils (Eds.), *Working papers in the theory of action* (pp. 111–161). Glencoe, IL: Free Press.

Bandura, A. (1977). *Social learning theory*. Englewood Cliffs, NJ: Prentice Hall.

Barge, J. K., & Hirokawa, R. Y. (1989). Toward a communication competency model of group leadership. *Small Group Behavior, 20*, 167–189.

Baxter, L. A., & Braithwaite, D. O. (2007). Social dialectics: The contradictions of relating. In B. B. Whaley & W. Samter (Eds.), *Explaining communication* (pp. 275–292). Mahwah, NJ: Lawrence Erlbaum.

Bentham, J. (1789). *An introduction to the principles of morals and legislation.* London: T. Payne.

Berger, C. R. (1997). *Planning strategic interaction.* Mahwah, NJ: Lawrence Erlbaum.

Berger, C. R., & Calabrese, R. J. (1975). Some explorations in initial interaction and beyond: Toward a developmental theory of interpersonal communication. *Human Communication Research, 1,* 99–112.

Bhaskar, R. (1978). *A realist view of science* (2nd ed.). Atlantic Highlands, NJ: Humanities Press.

Billingsley, J. M. (1993). An evaluation of the functional perspective in small group communication. In S. A. Deetz (Ed.), *Communication yearbook 16* (pp. 615–622). Newbury Park, CA: Sage.

Bonito, J. A., & Hollingshead, A. B. (1997). Participation in small groups. In B. R. Burleson (Ed.), *Communication yearbook 20* (pp. 227–261). Thousand Oaks, CA: Sage.

Bradac, J. J., Bowers, J. W., & Courtright, J. A. (1980). Lexical variations in intensity, immediacy, and diversity: An axiomatic theory and causal model. In R. N. St. Clair & H. Giles (Eds.), *The social and psychological contexts of language* (pp. 193–223). Hillsdale, NJ: Lawrence Erlbaum.

Brown, P., & Levinson, S. C. (1987). *Politeness: Some universals in language usage.* Cambridge, UK: Cambridge University Press.

Buck, R. (1997). From DNA to MTV: The spontaneous communication of emotional messages. In J. O. Greene (Ed.), *Message production: Advances in communication theory* (pp. 313–339). Mahwah, NJ: Lawrence Erlbaum.

Buller, D. R., & Burgoon, J. K. (1996). Interpersonal deception theory. *Communication Theory, 6,* 203–242.

Burgoon, J. K., & Hale, J. L. (1988). Nonverbal expectancy violations: Model elaboration and application to immediacy behavior. *Communication Monographs, 55,* 58–79.

Burgoon, J. K., & White, C. H. (1997). Researching nonverbal message production: A view from interaction adaptation theory. In J. O. Greene (Ed.), *Message production: Advances in communication theory* (pp. 279–312). Mahwah, NJ: Lawrence Erlbaum.

Burgoon, M., Dillard, J. P., & Doran, N. E. (1983). Friendly or unfriendly persuasion: The effects of violations of expectations by males and females. *Human Communication Research, 10,* 283–294.

Burleson, B. R. (2007). Constructivism: A general theory of communication skill. In B. B. Whaley & W. Samter (Eds.), *Explaining communication: Contemporary theories and exemplars* (pp. 105–128). Mahwah, NJ: Lawrence Erlbaum.

Byrne, D. (1971). *The attraction paradigm.* New York: Academic Press.

Cappella, J. N., & Greene, J. O. (1982). A discrepancy-arousal explanation of mutual influence in expressive behavior for adult and infant-adult interaction. *Communication Monographs, 49,* 89–114.

Chaiken, S., Liberman, A., & Eagly, A. (1989). Heuristic and systematic information processing within and beyond the persuasion context. In J. S. Uleman & J. A. Bargh (Eds.), *Unintended thought* (pp. 212–252). New York: Guilford.

Craig, R. T. (1999). Communication theory as a field. *Communication Theory, 9,* 119–161.

DeFleur, M. L., & Ball-Rokeach, S. J. (1982). *Theories of mass communication* (2nd ed.). New York: Longman.

Deutsch, M., & Krauss, R. (1965). *Theories in social psychology.* New York: Basic Books.

Donohew, L., Lorch, E. P., & Palmgreen, P. (1988). Applications of a theoretic model of information exposure to health interventions. *Human Communication Research, 24,* 454–468.

Dowe, P. (1992). Wesley Salmon's process theory of causality and the conserved quantity theory. *Philosophy of Science, 59,* 195–216.

Eveland, W. P., Jr. (2001). The cognitive mediation model of learning from the news: Evidence from non-election, off-year election, and presidential election. *Communication Research, 28,* 571–601.

Festinger, L. (1950). Informal social communication. *Psychological Review, 57,* 271–282.

Festinger, L. (1954). A theory of social comparison processes. *Human Relations, 7,* 117–140.

Festinger, L. (1957). *A theory of cognitive dissonance*. Stanford, CA: Stanford University Press.

Fishbein, M., & Ajzen, I. (1975). *Belief, attitude, intention, and behavior*. Reading, MA: Addison-Wesley.

Foa, E., & Foa, U. (1976). Resource theory of social exchange. In J. Thibaut, J. Spence, & R. Carson (Eds.), *Contemporary topics in social psychology* (pp. 99–131). Morristown, NJ: General Learning Press.

Friedman, M. (1974). Explanation and scientific explanation. *Journal of Philosophy, 71*, 5–19.

Giles, H., & Ogay, T. (2007). Communication accommodation theory. In B. B. Whaley & W. Samter (Eds.), *Explaining communication: Contemporary theories and exemplars* (pp. 293–310). Mahwah, NJ: Lawrence Erlbaum.

Gouran, D. S. (1975). The paradigm of unfulfilled promise: A critical examination of the history of research on small groups in speech communication. In T. W. Benson (Ed.), *Speech communication in the 20th century* (pp. 90–108). Carbondale: Southern Illinois University Press.

Gouran, D. S., Hirokawa, R. Y., Julian, K. M., & Leatham, G. B. (1993). The evolution and current status of the functional perspective on communication in decision-making and problem-solving groups. In S. A. Deetz (Ed.), *Communication yearbook 16* (pp. 573–600). Newbury Park, CA: Sage.

Greene, J. O. (1984). A cognitive approach to human communication: An action assembly theory. *Communication Monographs, 51*, 289–306.

Grice, H. P. (1975). Logic and conversation. In P. Cole & J. L. Morgan (Eds.), *Syntax and semantics 3: Speech acts* (pp. 41–58). New York: Academic Press.

Gudykunst, W. B. (1993). Toward a theory of effective interpersonal and intergroup communication: An anxiety/uncertainty management (AUM) perspective. In R. L. Wiseman & J. Koester (Eds.), *Intercultural communication competence* (pp. 33–71). Newbury Park, CA: Sage.

Hackman, J. R., & Morris, C. G. (1975). Group tasks, group interaction process, and group performance effectiveness: A review and proposed integration. In L. Berkowitz (Ed.), *Advances in experimental social psychology* (Vol. 8, pp. 45–99). New York: Academic Press.

Harre, R., & Madden, E. H. (1975). *Causal powers*. Totowa, NJ: Rowman & Littlefield.

Hawes, L. C. (1975). *Pragmatics of analoguing*. Reading, MA: Addison-Wesley.

Heider, F. (1945). Attitudes and cognitive organization. *Journal of Psychology, 21*, 107–112.

Heider, F. (1958). *The psychology of interpersonal relations*. New York: John Wiley.

Hempel, C. G., & Oppenheim, P. (1948). Studies in the logic of explanation. *Philosophy of Science, 15*, 135–175.

Hirst, R. J. (1959). *The problems of perception*. London: Allen & Unwin.

Homans, G. (1958). Social behavior as exchange. *American Journal of Sociology, 63*, 597–606.

Hovland, C. I., Janis, I. L., & Kelley, H. H. (1953). *Communication and persuasion*. New Haven, CT: Yale University Press.

Jones, E. E., & Davis, K. E. (1965). From acts to dispositions: The attribution process in person perception. In L. Berkowitz (Ed.), *Advances in experimental social psychology* (Vol. 2, pp. 236–305). New York: Academic Press.

Karau, S. J., & Kelly, J. R. (1992). The effects of time scarcity and time abundance on group performance quality and interaction process. *Journal of Experimental Social Psychology, 28*, 542–571.

Katz, D. (1960). The functional approach to the study of attitudes. *Public Opinion Quarterly, 24*, 163–204.

Kelley, H. H. (1967). Attribution theory in social psychology. *Nebraska Symposium on Motivation, 15*, 192–238.

Kim, Y. Y. (1977). Communication patterns of foreign immigrants in the process of acculturation. *Human Communication Research, 4*, 66–77.

Kitcher, P. (1989). Explanatory unification and the causal structure of the world. In P. Kitcher & W. C. Salmon (Eds.), *Minnesota studies in the philosophy of science: Vol. 13. Scientific explanation* (pp. 410–505). Minneapolis: University of Minnesota Press.

Kohler, W. (1959). Gestalt psychology today. *American Psychologist, 14*, 727–734.

Kuhn, T. S. (1970). *The structure of scientific revolutions* (2nd ed.). Chicago: University of Chicago Press.

Kuhn, T. S. (1977). *The essential tension.* Chicago: University of Chicago Press.

Lang, A. (2000). The limited capacity model of mediated message processing. *Journal of Communication, 50,* 46–70.

Markus, H., & Zajonc, R. B. (1985). The cognitive perspective in social psychology. In G. Lindzey & E. Aronson (Eds.), *The handbook of social psychology* (3rd ed., Vol. 1, pp. 137–230). New York: Random House.

McGuire, W. J. (1964). Inducing resistance to persuasion: Some contemporary approaches. In L. Berkowitz (Ed.), *Advances in experimental social psychology* (Vol. 1, pp. 191–229). New York: Academic Press.

McLeod, D. M., Kosicki, G. M., & McLeod, J. M. (2002). Resurveying the boundaries of political communications effects. In J. Bryant & D. Zillmann (Eds.), *Media effects: Advances in theory and research* (2nd ed., pp. 215–267). Mahwah, NJ: Lawrence Erlbaum.

McQuail, D. (1987). Functions of communication: A nonfunctionalist overview. In C. R. Berger & S. H. Chaffee (Eds.), *Handbook of communication science* (pp. 327–349). Newbury Park, CA: Sage.

Meyer, J. R. (1997). Cognitive influences on the ability to address interaction goals. In J. O. Greene (Ed.), *Message production: Advances in communication theory* (pp. 71–90). Mahwah, NJ: Lawrence Erlbaum.

Miller, N. E., & Dollard, J. (1941). *Social learning and imitation.* New Haven, CT: Yale University Press.

Nabi, R. L. (1999). A cognitive-functional model for the effects of discrete negative emotions on information processing, attitude change, and recall. *Communication Theory, 9,* 292–320.

Newcomb, T. M. (1953). An approach to the study of communicative acts. *Psychological Review, 60,* 393–404.

Osgood, C. E., & Tannenbaum, P. H. (1955). The principle of congruity in the prediction of attitude change. *Psychological Bulletin, 62,* 42–55.

Palmgreen, P., & Rayburn, J. D., II. (1982). Gratifications sought and media exposure: An expectancy value model. *Communication Research, 9,* 561–580.

Patterson, M. L. (1976). An arousal model of interpersonal intimacy. *Psychological Review, 83,* 235–245.

Pavitt, C. (1989). Accounting for the process of communicative competence evaluation: A comparison of predictive models. *Communication Research, 16,* 405–433.

Pavitt, C. (2000a). Answering questions requesting scientific explanations for communication. *Communication Theory, 10,* 379–404.

Pavitt, C. (2000b). *Philosophy of science and communication theory.* Huntington, NY: Nova Science.

Pearce, W. B., & Cronen, V. E. (1980). *Communication, action, and meaning.* New York: Praeger.

Petty, R. E., & Cacioppo, J. T. (1986). *Communication and persuasion.* New York: Springer-Verlag.

Poole, M. S., & DeSanctis, G. (1990). Understanding the use of group decision support systems: The theory of adaptive structuration. In J. Fulk & C. Steinfield (Eds.), *Organizations and communication technology* (pp. 175–195). Newbury Park, CA: Sage.

Raney, A. A. (2004). Expanding disposition theory: Reconsidering character liking, moral evaluations, and enjoyment. *Communication Theory, 14,* 348–369.

Reed, S. J., & Miller, L. C. (1998). On the dynamic construction of meaning: An interactive activation and competition model of social perception. In S. J. Reed & L. C. Miller (Eds.), *Connectionist models of social meaning and social behavior* (pp. 27–68). Mahwah, NJ: Lawrence Erlbaum.

Roskos-Ewoldsen, D. R., & Fazio, R. H. (1997). The role of belief accessibility in attitude formation. *Southern Communication Journal, 62,* 107–116.

Rusbult, C. E. (1980). Commitment and satisfaction in romantic associations: A test of the investment model. *Journal of Experimental Social Psychology, 16,* 172–186.

Salmon, W. C. (1984). *Scientific explanation and the causal structure of the world.* Princeton, NJ: Princeton University Press.

Scriven, M. (1959). The covering law position: A critique and an alternative analysis. In P. Gardiner (Ed.), *Theories of history* (pp. 443–471). New York: Free Press.

Shaw, D. L., & McCombs, M. E. (1977). *The emergence of American political issues: The agenda setting function of the press.* St. Paul, MN: West.

Sherif, C., Sherif, M., & Nebergall, R. (1965). *Attitude and attitude change: The social judgment-involvement approach.* Philadelphia: W. B. Saunders.

Shrum, L. J. (2002). Media consumption and perceptions of social reality: Effects and underlying processes. In J. Bryant & D. Zillmann (Eds.), *Media effects: Advances in theory and research* (2nd ed., pp. 69–95). Mahwah, NJ: Lawrence Erlbaum.

Smith, M. J. (1982). Cognitive schemata and persuasive communication: Toward a contingency rules theory. In M. Burgoon (Ed.), *Communication yearbook 6* (pp. 330–362). Beverly Hills, CA: Sage.

Stewart, C. J., Smith, C. A., & Denton, R. E., Jr. (1989). *Persuasion and social movement* (2nd ed.). Prospect Heights, IL: Waveland.

Stohl, C., & Holmes, M. E. (1993). A functional perspective for bona fide groups. In S. A. Deetz (Ed.), *Communication yearbook 16* (pp. 601–614). Newbury Park, CA: Sage.

Sunnafrank, M. (1986). Predicted outcome value during initial interactions: A reformulation of uncertainty reduction theory. *Human Communication Research, 13,* 3–33.

Thibaut, J. W., & Kelley, H. H. (1959). *The social psychology of groups.* New York: John Wiley.

Thorndike, E. L. (1898). Animal intelligence: An experimental study of the associative processes in animals. *Psychological Review Monograph Supplement, 2*(4), 1–109.

Ting-Toomey, S., & Kurogi, A. (1998). Facework competence in intercultural conflict: An updated face-negotiation theory. *International Journal of Intercultural Relations, 22,* 187–225.

VanderVoort, L. (2002). Functional and causal explanations in group communication research. *Communication Theory, 12,* 469–486.

Watzlawick, P., Beavin, J. H., & Jackson, D. D. (1967). *Pragmatics of human communication.* New York: W. W. Norton.

Weick, K. E. (1979). *The social psychology of organizing* (2nd ed.). Reading, MA: Addison-Wesley.

Witte, K. (1992). Putting the fear back into fear appeals: The extended parallel process model. *Communication Monographs, 59,* 329–349.

Woodworth, R. S. (1929). *Psychology: A study of mental life* (2nd ed.). New York: Holt.

Zillmann, D., & Bryant, J. (1985). Affect, mood, and emotion as determinants of selective exposure. In D. Zillmann & J. Bryant (Eds.), *Selective exposure to communication* (pp. 157–190). Hillsdale, NJ: Lawrence Erlbaum.

# 4

# ALTERNATIVE METHODOLOGICAL APPROACHES TO COMMUNICATION SCIENCE

◆ Franklin J. Boster and John L. Sherry

As musical instruments extend the human voice, so too technology extends the observational capacity of scientists. The last decade of the 20th century was termed the "Decade of the Brain" and was marked by substantial advances in our understanding of human cognition and affect. These advances came largely from other disciplines and subdisciplines but had a substantial impact on the conduct of communication science. Cognitive and affective processes are believed to mediate or moderate the relationship between numerous attributes of messages and important outcome variables, as well as between situational and individual differences and message generation. Consequently, measuring cognitive and affective processes is pivotal to conducting the research that parses explanations of known empirical generalizations and for generating additional research questions and opportunities.

Universities in general, and communication departments in particular, are under increased pressure to seek extramural funding, and the increased competition for these limited funds drives many research agenda. Grantors demand methodological, analytic, and theoretical innovativeness, and the coveted but scarce funds come with concomitant demands for improved sampling, instrumentation, and analysis techniques. The demands of university internal review boards (IRBs) constitute another challenge to the usual manner in which communication scholars pursue their research agenda.

This chapter addresses these issues and discusses advances made in these areas. Initially, the topic of sampling is examined, followed by comments about advances in measurement and finally data analysis.

## ◆ Sampling

The ongoing project of communication science demands valid data upon which theory can be built. Using humans as subjects raises problems that are not inherent in sciences such as physics and chemistry. Unlike physics and chemistry, human cognition and culture interact with the process of research, making claims of external validity particularly difficult. As defined by Cook and Campbell (1979), external validity refers to the extent to which a causal relationship holds over variations in persons, settings, and times. In the communication context, we may add sampling across messages to the list (Reeves & Geiger, 1994). The difficulty of making claims of external validity has led to lively discussion in the field.

### CONVENIENCE SAMPLING AND EXTERNAL VALIDITY

Potter, Cooper, and Dupagne (1993) asserted that the vast majority of communication research was "prescientific," due largely to the widespread use of convenience samples. Sparks (1995a, 1995b) challenged their conclusions in a series of replies, arguing that externally valid research can be conducted without national random samples. The exchange stimulated a series of articles addressing issues of using nonprobability samples in communication research (Courtright, 1996), the use of inferential statistics in experiments that do not use probability samples (Lang, 1996), the use of student samples (Basil, 1996), and the validity of comparing communication research results across generational cohorts (Abelman, 1996).

The issue of external validity has not been settled, as there is no evidence of a comprehensive agreement of externally valid methodology in the field. Nevertheless, researchers are engaging in research that broadens the scope of validity claims beyond the apocryphal "college sophomore." An examination of articles from four of the top general communication journals—*Human Communication Research, Journal of Communication, Communication Monographs,* and *Communication Research*—between 2000 and 2006 shows that communication scientists have moved toward addressing the Potter et al. (1993) critique. Across 87 studies, only one third ($n = 29$) used convenience samples consisting of college students, and 74% of those studies employed experimental designs, a generally accepted practice. Interestingly, the sample reveals a broad array of sample types, including national random samples, local random samples, online samples, and child/teen samples.

There are more reasoned ways to address issues of external validity. Shadish, Cook, and Campbell (2002) provide five principles for evaluating external validity claims. First, the principle of *surface similarity* addresses the extent to which a causal relationship observed with one type of person, setting, time, or message will generalize to other persons, settings, times, or messages. Second is the principle of *ruling out irrelevancies*. This principle is used to identify attributes of persons, settings, times, or messages that are irrelevant because they are unlikely to change a generalization. The third principle is that of *making discriminations* to identify features of persons, settings, times, or messages that limit the ability to generalize from an observed causal relationship. Fourth is the principle of *interpolation and extrapolation,* which pertains to the extent that observed causal relationships within a population can be estimated both between known values and extending from known values. Finally, the principle of *causal explanation* involves theorizing the conditions under which the causal relationship is likely.

Mook (1983, 1989) observes that the Shadish et al. (2002) approach to external validity is unnecessarily narrow because it only speaks to the extent to which research generalizes to other persons, settings, times, and messages. Drawing a distinction between research that seeks prediction and research that seeks understanding, Mook (1983, 1989) points out that generalization to the "real world" is not necessary for understanding. Instead, research that seeks understanding need only generalize to the theory tested. For example, if we want to predict whether juvenile delinquents imitate video game violence, we need a valid sample of juvenile delinquents. However, if we are interested in understanding the mechanism by which a person could come to imitate media violence, any sample will do.

## NATIONAL DATABASES

One of the best options for improving external validity in some types of communication research is to employ national survey samples. Two options for this type of work have emerged: dedicated national communication research and piggybacking on national surveys such as those conducted by the Institute for Survey Research or the National Opinion Research Center. Excellent examples of dedicated communication research include national health communication studies such as the Kaiser Family Foundation–funded evaluation of the CDC VERB national fitness campaign (Huhman et al., 2005) and the Westat/ Annenberg School for Communication evaluation of the National Youth Anti-Drug

Media Campaign (Hornik et al., 2003). Kaiser Family Foundation has sponsored a number of national media surveys such as *Parents, Children & Media: A Kaiser Family Foundation Survey* (Rideout, 2007); *The Media Family: Electronic Media in the Lives of Infants, Toddlers, Preschoolers, and Their Parents* (Rideout & Hamel, 2006); and *Generation M: Media in the Lives of 8–18 Year-Olds* (D. F. Roberts, Foehr, & Rideout, 2005).

A less expensive option is to buy questionnaire space on national studies. Alternatively, some communication researchers have used publicly available databases from national studies to conduct secondary analyses of survey data. The problem with this approach is that the researcher does not choose which variables are on the survey or how the questions are phrased. Furthermore, few interpersonal, group, or organizational communication research projects would benefit from this approach.

## WORLD WIDE WEB SAMPLING

The Internet holds promise for drawing national samples inexpensively (cf. Dochartaigh, 2001; Fraley, 2004; Hewson, Yule, Laurent, & Vogel, 2002; Malhotra & Krosnick, 2007). Moreover, it provides access to groups engaging in specific communication behavior such as online video game playing, using health information sites, and taking part in social networking or chat Web sites. These groups are often the target sample for computer-mediated communication (CMC) research and are easy to locate because they select themselves into Web sites based on content. Although random sampling methodology on the World Wide Web has proven elusive, many other sampling methods can still be effective. Furthermore, the Web can erase distances to particular populations. For example, a comparative study of soccer fans in the

United States, England, Germany, and Korea can be conducted without need for travel.

Sampling the Web also has disadvantages. The same distance that the Web defeats keeps the subject out of direct observation and control of the researcher. Although the Web may solve some external validity problems, it introduces others. We cannot be sure that respondents are who they say they are. We may not be able to control the number of times someone responds to a survey or how long it takes to respond.

## ◆ Data Collection

### OBSERVATION

The advent of low-cost, high-power personal computers has affected communication science research in many ways. In addition to expanding the potential pool of subjects, computer technology has put high-end physiological measurement tools within the reach of communication scientists. Recently, communication researchers have expanded use of physiological measurement equipment from fairly simple technologies, such as heart rate and skin conductance (see Lang, 1994), to functional magnetic resonance imaging (fMRI; Weber, Ritterfeld, & Mathiak, 2006) and saliva samples (Floyd & Roberts, in press). Concurrently, communication scientists have advanced compelling arguments advocating better understanding of the biological processes involved in human communication (Beatty & McCroskey, 2001; Sherry, 2004). We present some physiological measures being used in communication research in descending order from the most powerful and recent to older, more established technologies.

### EXPERIENTIAL SAMPLING

Experiential sampling is an observational methodology used to track responses to media during daily life. Respondents are asked to carry an electronic paging device and a media diary at all times. The paging device is set to ring randomly during the day, at which time respondents fill out a diary stating their current activity and emotional state. Estimates of media use and affective disposition in daily life are reconstructed from the data. This method has been used to estimate a number of communication-related behaviors, including media use (Kubey, 1986; Kubey & Larson, 1990), work life (Snir & Dov Zohar, 2007), affect (Kashdan & Steger, 2006), music use (R. Larson & Kubey, 1983), and relational communication (Feeney & Hill, 2006).

### FINE OBSERVATION

A number of methodologies allow researchers to track interpersonal behavior. Many researchers videotape interpersonal interactions, which are subsequently coded for verbal and nonverbal behavior. For example, the Family Interaction Coding System is used to classify 29 nonverbal behavior categories at 6-second intervals, resulting in three general categories: aversive behavior, neutral behavior, and positive behavior (Milner, 1994). In addition, verbal exchanges may be videotaped and conversational turn taking coded. For example, J. Larson, Christensen, Abbott, and Franz (1996) coded physician conversations about case evaluations noting when new and shared information was exchanged and who shared the most information (medical student, intern, or resident).

Linguists and conversation analysts code at an even finer level. Naturally occurring conversations are recorded and transcribed with careful attention to language features such as words, sounds, silences, in breaths, out breaths, cutoffs, pitch change, and many other language features (F. Roberts & Robinson, 2004). The goal of much of this research is to understand the complex systems by which human speech is constructed and interpreted.

## PHYSIOLOGICAL MEASUREMENT

*Functional Neuroimaging.* The phrase *functional neuroimaging* refers to technologies that measure and graphically present online brain activity during mental function. These technologies use a variety of scanning techniques, connected to a powerful computational system, to track secondary indicators of brain activity (e.g., fMRI, positron emission tomography [PET], near-infrared spectroscopic imaging [NIRSI], magneto-encephalography [MEG], and electro-encephalography [EEG]) or focus primarily on brain structure (e.g., computer tomography [CT]). PET and fMRI use powerful magnetic systems to detect and localize changes in blood oxygen levels, NIRSI uses infrared light to detect change in blood oxygen, CT employs slices of X-ray images to create three-dimensional images of the brain, and both MEG and EEG are technologies that detect electrical activity in the brain at different frequencies.

Functional neuroimaging technologies are distinguished by the varying accuracy and speed of their spatial and temporal resolution. Spatial resolution refers to the degree to which the imaging technology provides a clear and detailed picture. PET, fMRI, and NIRSI capture multiple slices of brain data from a variety of angles, which are then reassembled into a three-dimensional image. Hence, these technologies tend to provide the greatest spatial resolution. An earlier technology that also provides good spatial resolution is CT scans, which are a series of X-ray slices, also converted into a high-resolution, three-dimensional image by a computer. Because the multiple scans taken to produce enough data for a reconstructed image take longer to collect, these systems sacrifice temporal resolution, the number of complete scans taken of the target area per second, for spatial resolution. Technologies that are high in temporal resolution, such as MEG and EEG, allow researchers to track more closely rapid online changes in neural activity.

Alternatively, EEG and MEG, which monitor electrical activity in the cortex, provide low spatial resolution. Medical researchers are working with systems that mix high spatial resolution technology with high temporal resolution technology to mitigate the weakness of a single system.

The high-end imaging techniques most frequently used by communication researchers are fMRI and EEG. Researchers have used fMRI to observe neural activity during media use, such as during violent video game play (Weber et al., 2006; for another application, see D. R. Anderson, Fite, Petrovich, & Hirsch, 2006). However, the high cost of using fMRI often places the technology out of reach for communication researchers. Often, grant support and collaboration with university radiology departments are necessary.

*Electromyography.* Electromyography (EMG) is the direct measure of electrical potential resulting from muscle contraction. Although EMG typically involves inserting needles through skin and into muscle tissue, communication researchers use the less invasive facial EMG technique. Facial EMG involves placing electrical sensors on the skin near muscle groups that are implicated in emotional processing of messages. For example, a humor response can be measured by placing electrodes near the zygomatic major group of muscles, which are used when smiling. Thus, EMG is able to track more subtle muscle movement than is typically perceivable by eye. Raw data from facial EMG are typically spiked and not readily interpretable, so a conversion algorithm is necessary to facilitate interpretation.

Several communication researchers have used facial EMG to study responses to television and radio advertising, fear stimuli, and leadership displays. For example, Bucy and Bradley (2003) measured participants' smile and frown reactions to nonverbal displays of the president during a variety of presidential news stories. Their EMG data showed that viewers displayed negative reactions when the president displayed positive reactions to intense news stories. Thunberg and Dimberg (2000) found that women displayed more intense and exaggerated reactions to scary stimuli than did men. Bolls, Lang, and Potter (2001) demonstrated the validity of using facial EMG for measuring emotional responses to radio messages.

*Peripheral Nervous System Physiology Measures: EKG, Heart Rate, EDA (GSR), and Blood Pressure.* The most common measures of the peripheral nervous system are heart rate (HR) and skin conductance levels/responses (SCL/SCR, also known as electrodermal activity [EDA] and galvanic skin response [GSR]). HR and blood volume are frequently measured using a photo-plethysmograph, which employs laser light to monitor pressure changes on the skin that result from pulse activity. Skin conductance is measured in one of two major ways: endosomatic measures and exosomatic measures. Endosomatic measurement is used to detect changes in the potential of the electrical signal naturally given off by skin tissue. Exosomatic measurement employs a small DC current sent across the skin from one electrode to another, recording changes in electronic resistance to the current. These measures are considered highly valid and reliable indicators for arousal and attention but provide few insights into neurophysiology and neural activity. Relatively simple and inexpensive peripheral nervous system measures are important to monitor research participants and provide control variables in neurophysiological research designs, or they may be used to explore basic assumptions before investing money in expensive brain imaging studies. These measures have a history of use in communication research. Both Lang (1994) and Ravaja (2004) provide useful summaries of these and other physiological measures in communication research.

*Hormone Measures.* Recently, Floyd (Floyd & Roberts, in press) has been most closely associated with communication research involving hormone levels. Hormones are chemicals secreted by glands that affect the activity of targeted cells. They are released in response to contextual cues but also influence responses to those cues. For example, frustration from video game play is likely to increase testosterone levels. When testosterone increases, one is more likely to respond aggressively during interpersonal conflicts (e.g., Cohan, Booth, & Granger, 2003). Anticipation of giving a speech, as well as actually giving a speech, has been shown to increase levels of the stress hormone cortisol (J. B. Roberts, Sawyer, & Behnke, 2004).

Hormone activity is studied in one of two ways: tonic or phasic. Tonic studies look for individual differences in hormone level among people who do or do not exhibit a target behavior (e.g., comparing the testosterone levels of those who like and those who do not like violent video games). Phasic research involves monitoring the magnitude or valence of hormone-level change relative to a varied stimulus. Using the phasic approach, a researcher may look at fluctuations in hormone levels induced by fear- or anger-arousing media.

Hormones are measured by drawing a sample of bodily fluid, most commonly saliva, blood, or urine. Recently, saliva has become a noninvasive source for a variety of hormones, including the stress hormone cortisol and the reproductive hormones testosterone, progesterone, and estrogen. Saliva is a preferred medium for testing hormone levels as it is easier to obtain and has been shown to be a more precise measure of the level of certain hormones such as progesterone (Dollbaum & Duwe, 1997). Slightly more invasive is urine sampling, which measures hormonal traces of neurotransmitters that are not readily available in saliva, such as epinephrine, norepinephrine, serotonin, follicle-stimulating hormone, oxytocin, and glucose. Finally, the most invasive method is blood sample draws to test for hormones such as vasopressin, oxytocin, endogenous opioids, epinephrine, and norepinephrine.

At this point, communication research involving hormones is largely descriptive, seeking to ascertain if people with a higher average level of a particular hormone act differently from those with a lower average level of that hormone or if hormone levels vary in response to communication situations (see Floyd & Roberts, in press), such as comforting, verbal aggressiveness, or media portrayals. Hormone testing provides a window into individual differences as well as reactivity in several areas such as stress, aggression, sexual attraction, metabolism, and fear responses.

*Technological Promise.* The power these technologies have for promoting the understanding of human communication must be tempered by a realistic understanding of the data they create. Often, reading the data from these advanced technologies is as much art as science. For example, fMRI and PET scans detect changes in blood oxygenation levels, which are assumed to be an indication of neural activity. Although it is expected that cells using energy will require more oxygen, this assumption remains untested. Data sets produced by these technologies are large and complex, often introducing additional untested assumptions. Furthermore, neurophysiological research is far from understanding the highly networked processes involved in human thought. Neuroscientists can generally say "something changes in this region when people perform X activity," but why change occurs and what those changes mean transcend current scientific understanding. Finally, use of these technologies requires an in-depth understanding of cellular and magnetic physics, as well as advanced mathematics such as neural networks and complex contingent time-series analysis. For this reason and due to the high cost of using neurophysiological equipment, communication scientists often must team with researchers from other areas, although they still need to understand the measurement process.

## SELF-REPORT

Participants' reports of their own behavior, cognitive states, emotional states, demographic characteristics, and other attributes are a rich source of data for communication scholars. Although it is well understood, it is rarely stated explicitly that self-report data are useful to the extent that the participants are both willing and able to respond accurately. Consequently, practices that promote participants' willingness and ability to report on features of their communication behavior provide substantial benefits to the research community.

*Willingness to Report Accurately.* Evidence indicates that participants will be more willing to report as the sensitivity of the item decreases (Tourangeau & Yan, 2007). On the other hand, sensitive information is the focus in some research applications, such as when investigators ask participants if they have used illegal substances. Even in more mundane inquiry, it is not unusual to question participants regarding their income, and some may be reluctant to report this information or to report it accurately.

Warner (1965) presented the random response technique as a means of reducing participants' reluctance to report sensitive information. There are a number of variations of this technique. In one variation, participants are asked to flip a coin to determine whether they respond to a sensitive question or a nonsensitive question with which they will agree with a known probability. The investigator is unaware of the question to which any given participant is responding but can infer the prevalence of agreement with the sensitive item from the number of affirmative responses, the probability of responding to the sensitive question (.5 with a fair coin), and the probability of responding affirmatively to the nonsensitive question.

An alternative to the random response technique is Droitcour et al.'s (1991) item count technique. With this technique, half of the participants are asked to respond to a list of nonsensitive items, and the other half of the participants are asked to respond to this list and one additional sensitive item. The difference in the mean number of items endorsed by these two groups of participants serves as the estimate of the prevalence of those responding affirmatively to the sensitive item.

Although such methods may be effective at producing more accurate prevalence estimates (e.g., Lensvelt-Mulders, Hox, van der Heijden, & Maas, 2005; Tourangeau & Yan, 2007), they are relatively inefficient and limited. They require relatively large sample sizes, and they do not allow complex sets of associations among variables to be examined. Computer technology, however, may provide solutions that circumvent these challenges. One example is Anthony, Heeter, and Reed's (2007) Longitudinal Study Engine (LSE). It is an Internet-based data collection tool that offers participants anonymity and thus may promote greater disclosure on sensitive issues. Participants log in to the system anonymously, create their own user ID and passwords, and then are exposed to survey items. They may be invited to return for follow-up surveys. Experiments that compare response rate and prevalence data collected via tools such as the LSE with other techniques thought or known to be relatively effective at eliciting accurate self-reports of sensitive information (e.g., Roese & Jamieson, 1993) will ultimately judge the extent to which Internet technology can reduce underreporting on sensitive items.

*The Ability to Report Accurately.* It has long been known that people have limitations in their ability to report accurately on their cognitive processes, reasons for their preferences, frequencies with which they perform activities, and other features of their experience about which communication scientists would like to know (e.g., see Nisbett & Wilson, 1977; Smith & Miller, 1978; Wilson, 2002; also see Kashy & Kenny, 1990; Killworth & Bernard, 1976).

Despite being willing to report accurately and being confident in the self-reports they provide, participants may be inaccurate. Studies performed in the legal environment provide dramatic examples of confident eye-witnesses producing mistaken self-reports (Cutler & Penrod, 1995; Sporer, Penrod, Read, & Cutler, 1995). They show that innocent suspects may come to believe that they are guilty and confess (Kassin, 2005; Kassin & Kiechel, 1996).

Ericsson and Simon's (1980) argument emphasizing the importance of modeling the processes that produce self-reports is sound and has produced a number of important insights. For instance, Ericsson and Simon (1993) have shown that there is a close relationship between thought and verbal report when the thinking-aloud technique is employed, but asking participants to generate explanations has reactive effects. Moreover, it is an argument to which cognitive scientists have responded rapidly (e.g., Bradburn, Rips, & Shevell, 1987) and often (e.g., Schwarz, 1999; Sirken et al., 1999), attending carefully to matters such as question wording, response scale format, and the context in which items are embedded.

For instance, to provide an accurate answer to an item, participants must first understand it in a manner that matches what the investigator has in mind (Schwarz, 1999). Although the literal meaning of the words that comprise the item may be clear and unambiguous, the pragmatic meaning of the item, taken as a whole, may not. Thus, Schwarz (1999) suggests Grice's (1975) cooperativeness principle (be clear, informative, relevant, and truthful) as a guide to item writing to facilitate the ability of the participants to make sense of the items to which they respond (for an interesting application, see Holbrook, Krosnick, Carson, & Mitchell, 2000).

Deceptively simple item response scale choices, such as ratings made on a scale ranging from 0 to 10 versus one ranging from −5 to +5, have been shown to affect participants' interpretation of items and their responses to them. More dramatic choices, such as whether to employ an open-ended or closed-ended format, have produced even more striking effects. For example, Schuman and Presser (1981) found that in response to an item asking participants to report the most important thing to prepare children for life presented on a list, 61.5% checked the option, "To think for themselves"; only 4.6% provided an answer that could be coded in this manner when responding in an open-ended format. Finally, the context in which items are presented may have a substantial impact on the manner in which items are interpreted and how participants respond to them. Subtle features, such as the letterhead on the questionnaire and the immediately adjacent items to which participants are asked to respond, have been shown to have a substantial impact on the ensuing answer.

This large and burgeoning literature continues to inform the design of surveys and interviews. Although best practices emerge, results obtained from such studies defy the development of a set of simple rules that, if followed, will allow the investigator to develop a set of items for which participants can provide accurate answers. They do underscore, however, the importance of taking Ericsson and Simon's (1980) advice seriously. Self-report data involve a complex conversation between investigator and participant that must be modeled carefully if responses are to be understood.

## EXPERIMENTATION

Although not viewed commonly in this manner, experimentation can be conceived as an alternative means of measuring an independent variable(s)—the dependent variable(s) being measured by observation or self-report. When relatively successful, assignment of participants to conditions serves to vary the induced attribute(s), which fulfills a function similar to assessing natural variation by observation or self-report.

Thus, it is reasonable to include a discussion of experimentation within a section on data collection.

Much about experimentation is common knowledge. The logic of experimentation is well known. Threats to the validity of experiments have been enumerated and examined thoroughly. Social, environmental, and instructional inductions continue to be the strategies employed to vary independent variables. Most often experimentation is equated with laboratories or classrooms in university buildings, and indeed, many communication experiments employ instructional inductions and take place in university laboratories or classrooms. There are field experiments that serve as notable exceptions (e.g., Hocking, Margreiter, & Hylton, 1977), but despite the fact that such inquiry has the potential to increase the external and ecological validity of communication experiments without serious sacrifice to internal validity, they are rare. The well-known arguments concerning drawing substantive conclusions from a body of inquiry predicated upon the responses of college sophomores must be taken seriously when studying some important communication problems (Sears, 1986).

In addition to being subject to ecological validity critiques, experiments that are conducted in university laboratories or classrooms present certain practical challenges. For example, temporal and spatial constraints involved in scheduling participants, confederates, or experimenters may delay or postpone experimental projects. They may also limit the number of participants and, pertinent to the problem of ecological validity, the range of individual differences of the sample. Multisite trials may reduce these limitations, but perhaps not as much as desired. By contacting participants on the Internet and allowing them to respond via computer, technology provides an avenue by which these limitations can be reduced. For many types of experiments, sessions may be conducted at any time and any place where the investigator has the necessary software and the participant has access to a computer and the Internet.

MediaLab is the software most familiar to those who conduct experiments. Alternatively, the LSE (Anthony et al., 2007) allows the presentation of sophisticated stimuli (e.g., video, audio, graphics, games), insertion of instructional inductions such as messages, randomization of participants to conditions, reinforcement for participation (e.g., Amazon gift certificates), response tracking over time for repeated-measures experiments, and complete anonymity to research participants, a particularly useful feature for experiments in which responses are highly sensitive (following an electronic mail invitation with attached URL, participants log in anonymously, creating their own user identification number and password).

It would be wrong to conceive of the LSE as a replacement for a laboratory, rather than a supplement. It might not be possible to vary features of the environment (e.g., room temperature) or to employ social inductions (e.g., vary responses of confederates) with the LSE. Not knowing the conditions under which participants are exposed to stimuli could serve as a limitation (or advantage) in some cases. Nevertheless, it is a tool that promises high utility under a wide range of conditions. Imagine, for example, a participant watching and listening to a health prevention message in her home in Milan while the investigator sleeps in Palo Alto, or a participant watching and listening to the same message at a cyber café in Lima while the investigator teaches a persuasion class in Madison. Both scenarios are possible with technology such as the LSE.

## ◆ Data Analysis

Although counterexamples can be provided, the linear model provides the analytic framework employed most often by those who collect quantitative data. Specifically,

the analysis of variance and linear regression remain the most commonly used statistical tools. Six characteristics of these techniques, as commonly employed, merit particular scrutiny. First, they posit linear relationships between and among variables. Moreover, regression models typically posit additive relationships (i.e., they exclude interaction terms), an attribute not shared by analysis of variance (ANOVA) models. Second, they examine direct effects. Third, they include no measurement model. Fourth, they are generally used to examine cross-sectional data. Fifth, they are used to examine quantitative dependent variables. Sixth, they are used in studies in which observations are independent of one another. When relationships between and among variables are nonlinear, when effects are indirect, when there is substantial error of measurement, when longitudinal data are collected, when a dependent variable is dichotomous or polychotomous, or when there is substantial nonindependence in the data, they may require extension, modification, or substitution in order for accurate conclusions to be drawn. To varying extents, recent quantitative communication research has extended these features of the linear model, and these issues are considered below.

## NONLINEARITY AND NONADDITIVITY

Prior to fitting nonlinear models, data may compel the researcher to consider the possibility that a particular relationship is nonlinear. Techniques for examining the hypothesis of linearity are well known. Scatterplots may be perused, various error plots may be observed, and certain statistics may be calculated (e.g., the deviation from linearity). Such results are reported infrequently.

Specification errors may be sufficiently subtle as to defy clear identification; consider the challenge of distinguishing between a linear bivariate relationship and an exponential bivariate relationship (i.e., $Y = ae^{bX}$) when $N$ is small, the range of the independent variable is limited, and $b$ is small. Theories that generate hypotheses that involve nonlinear relations provide motivation to examine nonlinearities as well, but such hypotheses are rarely found in communication journals. When nonlinear relationships are expected or detected, there are classic textbooks that provide useful discussions of nonlinear regression techniques and contrast coefficients (e.g., Darlington, 1990; Keppel, 1991). Moreover, commonly used statistical software includes nonlinear regression and contrast coding options.

Nonadditivity is more likely to receive attention from communication scholars because interaction effects are predicted commonly. Nevertheless, statistical tests for nonadditivity may lack power. Rosenthal and Rosnow (1985) made this point in the context of analyzing experimental data by pointing out that ANOVA is often substantially underpowered, which can be corrected by applying pertinent contrast coefficients. Recently, Hayes (2005) made this point in the regression context, pointing out the problems with the common procedure of dichotomizing or polychotomizing continuous variables so as to enable the use of ANOVA and explaining the moderated multiple regression model.

*Causal Analysis.* Relaxing the restriction of direct effects has become more common. Methods of assessing indirect and spurious effects, such as path analysis and structural equation modeling, are now used with considerably greater frequency. This change has produced benefits. Theories may predict indirect effects. The mathematics of causal analysis indicate clearly that in some causal structures, these mediated effects are expected to be substantially smaller (if the theory is correct) than direct effects. Therefore, using direct effect models, such as ANOVA and regression, to evaluate mediated effects can produce errors in evaluating indirect effects. Those who rely on

the null hypothesis statistical significance tests (NHSSTs) to evaluate mediated relationships may employ radically underpowered tests.

Although causal relationships cannot be established with certainty, causal inference is improved when analyses allow matters of causal order to be clarified. Because causal models make different predictions about the structure of correlation matrices, they may allow competing models to be distinguished. Scholars' ability to test for the possibility of spurious relationships is also facilitated by causal analysis. Causal analysis allows sophisticated types of spuriousness to be examined, as well as permitting the assessment of multiple spurious relationships within the same model.

A final benefit of causal analysis has been to improve measurement. Confirmatory factor analysis may be viewed as a causal model with unmeasured variables. This family of algorithms provides a welcome alternative to the exploratory model because the evaluation of proposed factor structures accounts for differential item reliability and sampling error more rigorously than does the exploratory model.

Statistical software has made the practice of causal modeling easier. Many programs are available (e.g., AMOS, EQS, PATH, LISREL). In the main, these programs allow the investigator to enter variables, either observed or latent, and draw paths indicating direct causal effects between them. The software does the rest, and the investigator may have little idea of what "the rest" is. The result has not been altogether salutary; too many causal models are absurd substantively. They include a surfeit of marginally relevant variables, little compelling argument for model specification, failure to remove paths when the data indicate a trivial link, and, in general, a disconnect between ordinary language theorizing, the resulting causal diagram, and the equations that the diagram implies.

Moreover, some questionable practices have become standard operating procedure. Structural equation modeling combines measurement models and a theoretical model so as to produce an overall test of fit. As J. C. Anderson and Gerbing (1988) point out, benefits accrue from separating these two procedures. In addition, most statistical software allows the investigator to incorporate correlated errors into causal models. This option allows the possibility of specious model fitting. For example, consider the following simple causal string, $X \rightarrow Y \rightarrow Z$. It is well known that this predicts that the XZ correlation is the product of the XY and YZ correlations. What is less well known is that, when the path coefficients are nonzero, this outcome holds only when the correlation between the error terms for Y and Z are uncorrelated. By specifying a particular correlation among the error terms, multiple sets of correlations could be claimed to fit this model.

Given these practices, investigators would be well advised to use these techniques cautiously. They might also be advised that if cross-sectional relationships arise from the impact of past causal forces, then investigators would benefit from generating cross-section causal models from the differential equations that produce them. If a substantively sensible set of change equations cannot be constructed that yield the posited cross-sectional causal model, then that cross-sectional model lacks plausibility. Second, it might be best to avoid using computer programs when one does not yet have a reasonable understanding of the mathematics that they employ.

*Error of Measurement.* ANOVA and regression have no model of measurement error. It has long been known that bivariate, linear, cross-sectional coefficients are attenuated by error of measurement when the variables in question are measured with high validity. The correction for attenuation due to error of measurement is also well known and provides an estimate of the association between

two variables that would exist had they been measured without error. Nevertheless, this figure is reported rarely. It is less well known that corrected coefficients can be used to correct multivariate statistics, such as standardized regression coefficients or ANOVA parameters.

*Longitudinal Research.* Generally, communication has been defined as a process, and communication scholars have recognized the methodological implication that longitudinal data are crucial for answering many substantive questions. Paradoxically, data collection is most frequently cross-sectional, with occasional pretest and posttest experiments.

There is no dearth of longitudinal statistical models. Repeated-measures experimental designs (in which time serves as at least one of the repeated factors), Markov models, autoregressive integrated moving average (ARIMA) models, lag sequential models, and others are available but infrequently employed. Most often, structural equation models are used to examine growth and decay in latent variables. Notably, only the latter technique models the effect of measurement error and factors it into estimates of pivotal parameters. The classical theory of error, with its emphasis on random response error of measurement, will generally be adequate to model cross-lag and cross-sectional relationships, but this model may be inadequate to account for errors of measurement that affect test-retest coefficients.

*Dependence of Observations.* Recently, communication scholars have begun addressing issues that demand multilevel designs. Data collected from such designs may exhibit nonindependence. Consequently, results obtained using the individual as the unit of analysis may be misleading unless the effects of larger units in which they are nested are controlled. Perhaps the most familiar analytic strategy is the hierarchical linear model introduced by Bryk and

Raudenbush (1992). Interpersonal scholars might be more familiar with the Kenny, Kashy, and Cook (2006) models. Less well known but very readable is Gonzalez and Griffin's (2001) approach. Presently, the relatively recent applications of this class of techniques render judgment of their utility moot. In particular, it will be interesting to ascertain if, or how, common effect size metrics from these techniques will be able to be cumulated across studies so that sense may be made of large bodies of literature that employ them.

*Noncontinuous Dependent Measures.* Some of the criterion variables of substantive interest to communication scholars are dichotomies or polychotomies (e.g., health communication scholars might want to predict whether middle school students will smoke tobacco). Traditionally, the chi-square test for independence has been employed to examine relationships between one dichotomous variable or polychotomous variable and a second dichotomous or polychotomous variable. This test has served well for decades. But when two or more dichotomous or polychotomous variables are used to predict a dichotomous or polychotomous criterion, this standard technique must be extended. One option is the log-linear model and its variants (e.g., Goodman, 1970). This approach to analysis compares saturated and various unsaturated models to reach conclusions and thus is different from the traditional linear model. Nevertheless, this class of models has introduced interesting statistics for assessing the magnitude of effects, relative risk, and the odds ratio.

*Another Consideration.* In addition to expanding the linear model, one other data-analytic trend is worthy of brief mention. It involves a major shift in the manner in which literature is reviewed. From early work (e.g., Boster & Mongeau, 1984; Dillard, Hunter, & Burgoon, 1984) to contemporary articles (e.g., O'Keefe & Jensen, 2006) to a compilation volume (Allen & Preiss, 1998), meta-analyses have ceased being a novelty in communication journals. Although particular meta-analyses have clarified what was known at the time and set future research agenda, perhaps the greatest impact is on the manner in which thoughtful scholars think about the nature and importance of the single study. Compared with a thorough meta-analytic review, the single study is likely to be less informative, and it can be viewed as both more and less important than it has been in the past. It can be seen as more important because, if it meets certain criteria, it contributes to the cumulative base of knowledge. It can be seen as less important because it is only one of many studies that does so.

To contribute to the knowledge base, the single study must report results in such a way that those performing meta-analytic reviews can record effect sizes. This emphasis, although not yet producing less use of the NHSST, represents an important advance. It shifts the conversation of results from "is there an effect" to "how large is the effect" and may eventually lead to an increase in reported confidence intervals and the use of the probability of replication statistic, $p_{rep}$ (Killeen, 2005), as well as effect sizes.

## ◆ Conclusion

This chapter may be construed as an update on how human communication research is conducted. The research environment that surrounds the communication scholar has become more complex. Sampling exigencies are more pressing, IRBs are increasingly involved in shaping research agenda, data collection procedures have expanded while challenging past practice, and data analysis has expanded. To say that one is sophisticated methodologically in 2009 requires much more than it did 20 years ago, a point that requires careful consideration when designing graduate curricula for the next generation of communication scientists.

# ◆ References

Abelman, R. (1996). Can we generalize from Generation X? Not! *Journal of Broadcasting & Electronic Media, 40,* 441–447.

Allen, M., & Preiss, R. W. (1998). *Advances through meta-analysis.* Cresskill, NJ: Hampton.

Anderson, D. R., Fite, K. V., Petrovich, N., & Hirsch, J. (2006). Cortical activation while watching video montage: An fMRI study. *Media Psychology, 8,* 7–24.

Anderson, J. C., & Gerbing, D. W. (1988). Structural equation modeling in practice: A review and recommended two-step approach. *Psychological Bulletin, 103,* 411–423.

Anthony, J. C., Heeter, C., & Reed, P. J. (2007). *The Longitudinal Study Engine (LSE) software: An overview of background, history, concepts, and research protocols* (Technical Report Series). East Lansing: Department of Epidemiology, College of Human Medicine, Michigan State University. www.epi.msu.edu/lse/trs1.html

Basil, M. D. (1996). The use of student samples in communication research. *Journal of Broadcasting & Electronic Media, 40,* 431–441.

Beatty, M. J., & McCroskey, J. C. (with Valencic, K. M.). (2001). *The biology of communication: A communibiological perspective.* Cresskill, NJ: Hampton.

Bolls, P. D., Lang, A., & Potter, R. F. (2001). The effects of message valance and listener arousal on attention, memory, and facial muscular responses to radio advertisements. *Communication Research, 28,* 627–652.

Boster, F. J., & Mongeau, P. (1984). Fear-arousing persuasive messages. In R. N. Bostrom & B. H. Westley (Eds.), *Communication yearbook 8* (pp. 330–375). Beverly Hills, CA: Sage.

Bradburn, N. M., Rips, L. J., & Shevell, S. K. (1987). Answering autobiographical questions: The impact of memory and inference on surveys. *Science, 236,* 157–161.

Bryk, A. S., & Raudenbush, S. W. (1992). *Hierarchical linear models: Applications and data analysis methods.* Newbury Park, CA: Sage.

Bucy, E., & Bradley, S. (2003, May). *Engaging the surveillance system: Cognitive, emotional, and physiological responses to inappropriate leader displays.* Paper presented at the annual meeting of the International Communication Association, San Diego.

Cohan, C. L., Booth, A., & Granger, D. A. (2003). Gender moderates the relationship between testosterone and marital interaction. *Journal of Family Psychology, 17,* 29–40.

Cook, T. D., & Campbell, D. T. (1979). *Quasi-experimentation: Design and analysis issues for field settings.* Boston: Houghton Mifflin.

Courtright, J. A. (1996). Rationally thinking about nonprobability. *Journal of Broadcasting & Electronic Media, 40,* 414–422.

Cutler, B. L., & Penrod, S. D. (1995). *Mistaken identification: The eyewitness, psychology, and the law.* New York: Cambridge University Press.

Darlington, R. B. (1990). *Regression and linear models.* New York: McGraw-Hill.

Dillard, J. P., Hunter, J. E., & Burgoon, M. (1984). Sequential-request persuasive strategies: Meta-analysis of foot-in-the-door and door-in-the-face. *Human Communication Research, 10,* 461–488.

Dochartaigh, N. O. (2001). *The Internet research handbook: An introductory guide for the social sciences.* London: Sage.

Dollbaum, C. M., & Duwe, G. F. (1997, September). *Direct comparison of plasma and saliva levels after topical progesterone application absorption of progesterone after topical application: Plasma and saliva levels.* Paper presented at the 7th Annual Meeting of the North American Menopause Society, Boston.

Droitcour, J., Caspar, R. A., Hubbard, M. L., Parsley, T. L., Visscher, W., & Ezzati, T. M. (1991). The item count technique as a method of indirect questioning: A review of its development and a case study application. In P. P. Biemer, R. M. Groves, L. E. Lyberg, N. A. Mathiowetz, & S. Sudman (Eds.), *Measurement errors in surveys* (pp. 185–210). New York: John Wiley.

Ericsson, K. A., & Simon, H. A. (1980). Verbal reports as data. *Psychological Review, 87,* 215–251.

Ericsson, K. A., & Simon, H. A. (1993). *Protocol analysis: Verbal reports as data.* Cambridge, MA: Bradford Books/MIT Press.

Feeney, J. A., & Hill, A. (2006). Victim-perpetrator differences in reports of hurtful events. *Journal of Social and Personal Relationships, 23,* 587–608.

Floyd, K., & Roberts, J. B. (in press). Principles of endocrine system measurement in communication research. In M. J. Beatty & J. C. McCroskey (Eds.), *Biology and communication*. Boston: Allyn & Bacon.

Fraley, R. C. (2004). *How to conduct behavioral research over the Internet: A beginner's guide to HTML and CGI/Perl*. New York: Guilford.

Gonzalez, R., & Griffin, D. W. (2001). A statistical framework for modeling homogeneity and interdependence in groups. In G. J. O. Fletcher & M. S. Clark (Eds.), *Blackwell handbook of social psychology: Interpersonal processes* (pp. 505–534). Malden, MA: Blackwell.

Goodman, L. A. (1970). The multivariate analysis of qualitative data: Interactions among multiple classifications. *Journal of the American Statistical Association, 65*, 226–256.

Grice, H. P. (1975). Logic and conversation. In P. Cole & J. L. Morgan (Eds.), *Syntax and semantics: Vol. 3. Speech act* (pp. 41–58). New York: Academic Press.

Hayes, A. F. (2005). *Statistical methods for communication science*. Mahwah, NJ: Lawrence Erlbaum.

Hewson, C., Yule, P., Laurent, D., & Vogel, C. (2002). *Internet research methods: A practical guide for the social and behavioural sciences*. Thousand Oaks, CA: Sage.

Hocking, J. E., Margreiter, D. G., & Hylton, C. (1977). Intra-audience effects: A field test. *Human Communication Research, 3*, 240–249.

Holbrook, A. L., Krosnick, J. A., Carson, R. T., & Mitchell, R. C. (2000). Violating conversational conventions disrupts cognitive processing of attitude questions. *Journal of Experimental Psychology, 36*, 465–494.

Hornik, R., Maklan, D., Cadell, D., Barmada, C. H., Jacobsohn, L., Prado, A., et al. (2003). *Evaluation of the National Youth Anti-Drug Media Campaign: Fifth semi-annual report of findings*. http://www.mediacampaign.org/publications/westat5/credits.html

Huhman, M., Potter, L. D., Wong, F. L., Banspach, S. W., Duke, J. C., & Heitzler, C. D. (2005). Effects of a mass media campaign to increase physical activity among children: Year-1 results of the VERB campaign. *Pediatrics, 116*, 277–288.

Kashdan, T. B., & Steger, M. F. (2006). Expanding the topography of social anxiety: An experience-sampling assessment of positive emotions, positive events, and emotion suppression. *Psychological Science, 17*, 120–128.

Kashy, D. A., & Kenny, D. A. (1990). Do you know whom you were with a week ago Friday? A re-analysis of the Bernard, Killworth, and Sailer studies. *Social Psychology Quarterly, 53*, 55–61.

Kassin, S. M. (2005). On the psychology of confessions: Does innocence put innocents at risk? *American Psychologist, 60*, 215–228.

Kassin, S. M., & Kiechel, K. L. (1996). The social psychology of false confessions: Compliance, internalization, and confabulation. *Psychological Science, 7*, 125–128.

Kenny, D. A., Kashy, D. A., & Cook, W. L. (2006). *Dyadic data analysis*. New York: Guilford.

Keppel, G. (1991). *Design and analysis: A researcher's handbook*. Upper Saddle River, NJ: Prentice Hall.

Killeen, P. R. (2005). An alternative to null-hypothesis significance tests. *Psychological Science, 16*, 345–353.

Killworth, P. D., & Bernard, H. R. (1976). Informant accuracy in social network data. *Human Organization, 35*, 269–286.

Kubey, R., & Larson, R. (1990). The use and experience of the new video media among children and young adolescents. *Communication Research, 17*, 107–130.

Kubey, R. W. (1986). Television use in everyday life: Coping with unstructured time. *Journal of Communication, 36*, 108–123.

Lang, A. (1994). *Measuring psychological responses to media messages*. Hillsdale, NJ: Lawrence Erlbaum.

Lang, A. (1996). The logic of using inferential statistics with experimental data from non-probability samples: Inspired by Cooper, Dupagne, Potter, and Sparks. *Journal of Broadcasting & Electronic Media, 40*, 422–431.

Larson, J., Jr., Christensen, C., Abbott, A., & Franz, T. (1996). Diagnosing groups: Charting the flow of information in medical decision-making teams. *Journal of Personality & Social Psychology, 71*, 315–330.

Larson, R., & Kubey, R. (1983). Television and music: Contrasting media in adolescent life. *Youth and Society, 15*, 13–31.

Lensvelt-Mulders, G. J. L. M., Hox, J., van der Heijden, P. G. M., & Maas, C. J. M. (2005). Meta-analysis of randomized response research. *Sociological Methods & Research, 33,* 319–348.

Malhotra, N., & Krosnick, J. A. (2007). The effect of survey mode and sampling on inferences about political attitudes and behavior: Comparing the 2000 and 2004 ANES to Internet surveys with nonprobability samples. *Political Analysis, 15,* 286–323.

Milner, I. S. (1994). Assessing physical child abuse risk: The Child Abuse Potential Inventory. *Clinical Psychology Review, 14,* 547–583.

Mook, D. G. (1983). In defense of external validity. *American Psychologist, 38,* 379–387.

Mook, D. G. (1989). The myth of external validity. In L. W. Poon, D. C. Rubin, & B. A. Wilson (Eds.), *Everyday cognition in adulthood and late life* (pp. 25–43). New York: Cambridge University Press.

Nisbett, R. E., & Wilson, T. D. (1977). Telling more than we can know: Verbal reports on mental processes. *Psychological Review, 84,* 231–259.

O'Keefe, D. J., & Jensen, J. D. (2006). The advantages of compliance or the disadvantages of noncompliance? A meta-analytic review of the relative persuasive effectiveness of gain-framed and loss-framed messages. *Communication Yearbook, 30,* 1–43.

Potter, W. J., Cooper, R., & Dupagne, M. (1993). The three paradigms of mass media research in mainstream communication journals. *Communication Theory, 3,* 317–335.

Ravaja, N. (2004). Contributions of psychophysiology to media research: Review and recommendations. *Media Psychology, 6,* 193–235.

Reeves, B., & Geiger, S. (1994). Designing experiments that assess psychological responses to media messages. In A. Lang (Ed.), *Measuring psychological responses to media* (pp. 165–180). Hillsdale, NJ: Lawrence Erlbaum.

Rideout, V. (2007). *Parents, children & media: A Kaiser Family Foundation survey.* http://www.kff.org/entmedia/entmedia061907pkg.cfm

Rideout, V., & Hamel, E. (2006). *The media family: Electronic media in the lives of infants, toddlers, preschoolers, and their parents.* http://www.kff.org/entmedia/7500.cfm

Roberts, D. F., Foehr, U. G., & Rideout, V. (2005). *Generation M: Media in the lives of 8–18 year-olds.* http://www.kff.org/entmedia/entmedia030905pkg.cfm

Roberts, F., & Robinson, J. (2004). Interobserver agreement on first-stage conversation analytic transcription. *Human Communication Research, 30,* 376–410.

Roberts, J. B., Sawyer, C. R., & Behnke, R. R. (2004). A neurological representation of speech state anxiety: Mapping salivary cortisol levels of public speakers. *Western Journal of Communication, 68,* 219–231.

Roese, N. J., & Jamieson, D. W. (1993). Twenty years of bogus pipeline research: A critical review and meta-analysis. *Psychological Bulletin, 114,* 363–375.

Rosenthal, R., & Rosnow, R. L. (1985). *Contrast analysis: Focused comparisons in the analysis of variance.* Cambridge, UK: Cambridge University Press.

Schuman, H., & Presser, S. (1981). *Questions and answers in attitude surveys.* New York: Academic Press.

Schwarz, N. (1999). Self-reports: How the questions shape the answers. *American Psychologist, 54,* 93–105.

Sears, D. O. (1986). College sophomores in the laboratory: Influences of a narrow data base on social psychology's view of human nature. *Journal of Personality and Social Psychology, 51,* 515–530.

Shadish, W. R., Cook, T. D., & Campbell, D. T. (2002). *Experimental and quasi-experimental designs for generalized causal inference.* Boston: Houghton-Mifflin.

Sherry, J. L. (2004). Media effects theory and the nature/nurture debate: A historical overview and directions for future research. *Media Psychology, 6,* 63–109.

Sirken, M. G., Herrmann, D. J., Schechter, S., Schwarz, N., Tanur, J. M., & Tourangeau, J. M. (1999). *Cognition and survey research.* New York: John Wiley.

Smith, E. R., & Miller, F. D. (1978). Limits on perception of cognitive processes: A reply to Nisbett and Wilson. *Psychological Review, 85,* 355–362.

Snir, R., & Dov Zohar, D. (2007). Workaholism as discretionary time investment at work: An experience-sampling study. *Applied Psychology (OnlineEarly Articles).* Retrieved September 1, 2007, from http://www.blackwell-synergy.com/doi/abs/10.1111/j.1464-0597.2006.00270.x

Sparks, G. G. (1995a). Comments concerning the claim that mass media research is "prescientific": A response to Potter, Cooper & Dupagne. *Communication Theory, 5,* 273–280.

Sparks, G. G. (1995b). A final reply to Potter, Cooper & Dupagne. *Communication Theory, 5,* 286–289.

Sporer, S., Penrod, S., Read, D., & Cutler, B. L. (1995). Choosing, confidence, and accuracy: A meta-analysis of the confidence-accuracy relation in eyewitness identification studies. *Psychological Bulletin, 118,* 315–327.

Thunberg, M., & Dimberg, U. (2000). Gender differences in facial reactions to fear-relevant stimuli. *Journal of Nonverbal Behavior, 24,* 45–51.

Tourangeau, R., & Yan, T. (2007). Sensitive questions in surveys. *Psychological Bulletin, 133,* 859–883.

Warner, S. L. (1965). Random response: A survey technique for eliminating evasive answer bias. *Journal of the American Statistical Association, 60,* 63–69.

Weber, R., Ritterfeld, U., & Mathiak, K. (2006). Does playing violent video games induce aggression? Empirical evidence of a functional magnetic resonance imaging study. *Media Psychology, 8,* 39–60.

Wilson, T. D. (2002). *Strangers to ourselves: Discovering the adaptive unconscious.* Cambridge, MA: Harvard University Press.

# PART 2

# COMMUNICATION CODES

# 5

# LANGUAGE AND COMMUNICATION

◆ Jordan Soliz and Howard Giles

Communication is often considered synonymous with language and, acknowledging that nonverbal cues are a fundamental aspect of communication (Manusov & Patterson, 2006), we agree with Jacobs's (2002) contention that "communication scholars will recognize that the use of language to formulate messages and to perform social actions is the paradigm case of communication" (p. 213). In the chapter "Language, Social Comparison, and Power" (Giles & Weimann, 1987) for the earlier edition of this handbook, as well as in other works later (e.g., Bull, 2002; Holtgraves, 2002; Weatherall, Gallois, & Watson, 2007), historical approaches to studying language have been discussed, and we provide a very brief overview here (Fitch & Sanders, 2004).

With his contention of humans' natural and inherent knowledge of appropriate grammar and syntactic structure, Chomsky's (1965) seminal work on transformational grammar propelled the area of psycholinguistics into an exciting area of inquiry. Although a catalyst for research on language use and development, this approach inspired many to embrace what could be caricatured as an *a*social view on language. However, over the next 20 or so years, research on language and social context was informed by three approaches: language is *determined by, builds upon,* and *determines* context. The earliest of this research was guided by the assumption that language was driven by the

◆ 75

situation. For example, a social context (e.g., football game, church service) may influence, consciously or nonconsciously, the language choices of individuals (e.g., Fishman, 1972). However, with theoretical advancements in communication science, the latter two approaches provided an enhanced understanding of language use and communication by highlighting the significance of intersubjectivity and shared assumptions of individuals and, more important, recognizing the constitutive nature of communication (Rommetveit & Blakar, 1979).

In summarizing these approaches, Giles and Weimann (1987) argued that theorizing and, hence, future inquiries needed to focus on the "functions of language in individual, relational, and multiple group identities . . . focus upon the creative role of majority and minority collectivities in society . . . and feature the interface between the ways language reflects, builds upon, and determines social reality as well as highlight the dynamic, skeptical, crafty communicative qualities we all share" (p. 368). Now, two decades later, we can see the considerable advancements in the study of and theorizing on language as these relate to social context (see Fiedler, 2007; Robinson, 2003; Robinson & Giles, 2001).

## ◆ Perspectives on the Study of Language

The study of language and communication is a cross-disciplinary effort, and there are as many questions, methods, and orientations guiding research as there are languages and dialects. Perhaps one of the most fundamental areas of language inquiry is language development (Hoff & Shatz, 2006). Whereas this approach centers on phonological acquisition and production, other perspectives focus on language as a social behavior. Noels, Giles, and Le Poire (2003) summarize some of the central theoretical approaches to studying

language and social behavior. The *pragmatic* perspective emphasizes the function of speech acts. One of the more utilized theories emerging from this perspective is P. Brown and Levinson's (1987) politeness theory, which frames language as a strategy for managing face concerns of self and others. The *dialogic* perspective centers on the coordinated negotiation of meaning during interactions (e.g., Baxter & Montgomery, 1996). In contrast to the previous perspective, meaning emerges from the dialogue between individuals rather than individual speech acts. Theories emerging from the *interpersonal adaptation* perspective highlight language modifications and their role in engendering a sense of relational affiliation or distinctiveness (Burgoon, Floyd, & Guerrero, Chapter 6, this volume; Burgoon, Stern, & Dillman, 1995). Finally, a *discursive psychology* perspective assumes that communication is constitutive in that reality is a product of language and interactions (e.g., Edwards & Potter, 1992; Potter & Edwards, 2001). Moreover, rather than aiming for lawlike generalizations about cognition and communication, the focus is on the subjective understanding of individuals (J. Jaworski & Coupland, 1999).

Although studied from the perspective of multiple disciplines and corresponding methodologies, our orientation toward the study of language draws attention to the cognitive processes associated with communicative behaviors and evaluations, demonstrating how communication both affects and is affected by social identities and personal relationships (Giles & Coupland, 1991). Individual programs of research have necessarily focused on specific aspects of language, such as its role in relational development and maintenance (Stafford, Dainton, & Haas, 2000), coping and emotional support (Burleson & Goldsmith, 1998), intergroup communication and attitudes (Harwood & Giles, 2005), and institutionalized language policies (Bourhis, 2001). Although seemingly unrelated, when examined as a whole, the overall picture is that language has the power to both sustain and erode relationships and create and ameliorate intergroup discrimination. Thus, this chapter's objective is to explicate what Robinson (2001) labels the five "ints" that compose the function of language: "intentions and interpretations in interpersonal and intergroup interactions" (p. xvi).

## LANGUAGE OF INTERPERSONAL AND INTERGROUP INTERACTIONS

Some early work on language and social relations concerned the realm of ethnic identity (Giles, 1977). Much of this work has its roots in the tenets of social identity theory (Tajfel & Turner, 1986), which proposes that an individual's self-concept is, in part, influenced by his or her identification with social groups (e.g., ethnic, religious, age). Specifically, the evaluative and affective aspects of group memberships are an inherent part of self-concepts and the desire to maintain positive distinctiveness for social groups; hence, self-images induce individuals to make intergroup comparisons. These comparisons are at the core of prejudice and discrimination in society (see Ellis, Chapter 17, this volume). Moving from a cognitive to a more communicative approach, initial studies investigated evaluations of language behaviors. Giles, Taylor, and Bourhis (1977) investigated linguistic, geographic, and cultural aspects of Welsh identity for Welsh bilinguals and English-only Welsh speakers. Results demonstrated that language and, to a lesser extent, cultural background are important indicators of ethnic identity. For example, Welsh bilinguals perceived more similarity with other Welsh bilinguals, especially those living in close geographic proximity. One of the major implications of this research was the salience of Welsh language use and proficiency as a determinant of "Welsh" identity regardless of being born Welsh. In Bourhis and Giles's (1976) study, Welsh-speaking respondents reacted more favorably to requests in Welsh-accented English compared with those same requests using the higher status variety of English (Received Pronunciation). The findings were predictably the mirror image for the English-speaking informants in that they responded more positively to the higher status English. That said, other work has shown that certain nonstandard speech forms can have covert prestige to such an extent that those who do not use them—even in public settings—can be denigrated as cultural traitors (see Marlow & Giles, 2007, for the case of Hawaiian Pidgin).

A fundamental question guiding this work was the following: What were the motivating factors that determined these linguistic shifts and attitudes? Giles, Bourhis, and Taylor (1977) proposed that the social and linguistic status of an ethnic group, the overall number and dispersion of the ethnic group population, and institutional policies and practices (e.g., bilingual representation in education and media) are all factors in determining the overall so-called group vitality of an ethnic group (Harwood, Giles, & Bourhis, 1994). In turn, the vitality of an ethnolinguistic group is influential in language use, maintenance, and acquisition. Extending this, ethnolinguistic identity theory (ELIT; Giles & Johnson, 1987) was formulated to articulate how a desire for a positive self-image was a motivating factor in identifying with an ethnolinguistic group. For example, if a group member's language is that of a high-status group, then a positive self-image is associated with use of that language. Conversely, if one's language is indicative of a low-status group, then one's social identity is threatened. Sachdev and Bourhis (2005) outlined strategies for confronting these threats. If plausible, individuals may choose to embrace the higher status language in the public domain and, if desired, limit native language to more private contexts in order to assimilate into the majority culture. Although this may benefit the individual in terms of a positive sense of self, the cumulative effect of individuals opting for another language may have detrimental long-term effects on the group's ethno-linguistic vitality. Thus, other strategies include social movements or language norms to contest the social status and public policy of the majority linguistic group.

ELIT was actually an extension of communication accommodation theory (CAT; Gallois, Ogay, & Giles, 2005), which augments the social identity perspective to include communicative features of contact (Burgoon et al., Chapter 6, this volume). The theory has grown from a relatively straightforward focus on linguistic shifts to a more complex delineation of the personal, contextual, social identity, and sociohistorical factors associated with a wide array of communicative behaviors (Giles, Coupland, & Coupland, 1991).

*Approximation* strategies incorporate the focus of the theory's early development, and thus the preceding discussion on language and ethnicity represents this core aspect of the theory. Approximation is typically discussed in terms of convergence, divergence, and maintenance to highlight the manner in which communication is adapted (or not adapted) to styles, preferences, or needs of conversation partners. Motivation for adapting one's communication may be interpersonal similarity (i.e., seeking affiliation) or a desire to emphasize differences and display distinctiveness. *Discourse management* strategies refer to modifications based on partners' conversation needs (e.g., topics of conversation, face management). Speakers may also employ *interpretability* strategies to improve communication clarity in an attempt to facilitate a partner's ability to understand (Clark, 1996). Finally, through *interpersonal control* strategies, speakers attend to power, control, and dominance in relational roles.

Communication involves adjustment of multiple sociolinguistic strategies in a specific interaction. For example, a speaker may not only converge toward a partner's speech style but also introduce topics of shared interest in order to show similarity or transcend differences. Thus, broadly applied, communication adaptation is typically referred to as *appropriate accommodation, underaccommodation,* or *overaccommodation.* Overaccommodation occurs when communication exceeds what is needed or desired by a conversation partner, oftentimes resulting in a perceived patronizing style of communication (Hummert & Ryan, 2001). Conversely, speakers may be perceived as *under*accommodating when their partner feels adjustments are lacking, as in young people's beliefs that their elders typically do not listen to them but follow their own conversational agenda (Williams & Nussbaum, 2002). As demonstrated in Harwood's (2000) research on relational solidarity, grandchildren's perceptions of grandparents' accommodative involvement and appropriate accommodation were positively associated with communication satisfaction and emotional closeness, whereas overaccommodation was negatively associated with liking of the grandparent and communication satisfaction.

CAT has been applied to various contexts of communication to demonstrate how psychological distinctiveness or affiliation is achieved through communication and thus is one of the theories of interpersonal adaptation (Noels et al., 2003) that attends to *both* interpersonal and intergroup dynamics of language and communication. Of course, this is not to suggest that CAT serves as the *only* theoretical framework for research on language (e.g., Guerrero, Alberts, & Heisterkamp, 2001; see also Lakin, Jefferis, Cheng, & Chartrand, 2003, on the highly related "chameleon effect"). However, the theory underscores the significance of both idiosyncratic features of conversational partners and social context (e.g., influence of social group identity) in understanding motivational processes of language use and evaluation. Thus, we now turn our attention to the interpersonal and intergroup contexts to demonstrate how personal, relational, and identity goals are manifested in language and communication.

## INTERPERSONAL COMMUNICATION: CONTROL AND RELATIONAL SOLIDARITY

Interpersonal research has received considerable attention from communication scholars and spawned more specific and, some argue, separate contexts of inquiry (e.g., relational communication, family communication). In general, the language of interpersonal communication varies based on the goals and context of the relationship (Knapp & Daly, 2002). We focus here on two fundamental aspects of language and interpersonal dynamics: control and relational solidarity.

Interpersonal control is a central function of language in relationships as our communication reflects, sustains, and creates social power. The issue of power dominated much of the early work on interpersonal communication (Berger, 1994). Initial studies on relational development and maintenance investigated control moves and strategies in an attempt to understand the function of messages (Millar & Rogers, 1988). Specifically, relational partners will engage in a series of communicative "movements" that either announce or concede relational control. For example, a partner who, by asserting a topic change, signals a "one-up" move with his or her partner relenting to such a shift of focus (i.e., a one-down move) is an occasion when both relational partners are exerting control, yet the transaction is, nonetheless, complementary. Conversely, if that assertion had been matched by another power move, then the relational partners would again be exerting control but in a more competitive manner. Thus, by examining the patterns of these control moves in interactions, we gain insight into the nature of relationships.

Issues of power also have been investigated in various nonromantic contexts, for example, patient-physician interactions (Walker, Arnold, Miller-Day, & Webb, 2002), where life span changes in relational control have been highlighted. More specifically, traditional family roles support parental power and the unidirectional enactment of control (parent → child). Yet, Morgan and Hummert's (2000) research on control strategies in later life, mother-daughter interactions demonstrates that children acquire power as they age, but that it is enacted differently for younger and older generations. Specifically, middle-aged daughters deemed direct control strategies—messages with little concern for protecting a partner's face needs—more appropriate for 70-year-old mothers than did 20-year-old daughters. Because direct control messages are perceived as less satisfying, less respectful, and less nurturing, the findings suggest that older parent-child dyads may experience more contentious interactions with the changes in and varying expectations of family roles and enacted control as parents and children age.

Moreover, as Noels et al. (2003) suggest, "Language serves control functions in at least three manners, including reflecting and creating control, depoliticizing control, and routinizing control" (p. 241). The first indicates that language may be a function of social status. For example, the language styles in parent-child interactions are dependent on the role relations between the two. Thus, in early and middle childhood, attention has been afforded the socializing role of parents (Kunkel, Hummert, & Dennis, 2006). But, as discussed above, role relations change throughout the life span, creating different communicative goals and patterns of communication. Perhaps this is no more evident than in adolescence, during which the goals of independence and negotiation of identity can lead to more conflict-ridden communication with parents (Laursen & Collins, 2004).

The second manner suggests that control may be indirectly exploited by using linguistic strategies that conceal social power, oftentimes by various strategies of silencing others (see A. Jaworski, 1993). Finally, patterns of interaction may reflect power differentials that seem normative and expected (e.g., gendered communication in cross-sex friendships or romantic relationships). Language can also challenge or, perhaps, change the power structure of interpersonal relations. For example, McDevitt and Chaffee (2002) point out that child-initiated conversations about civic responsibility have the potential to reverse traditional views on political socialization in that children can influence parents' political involvement through their initiation of political discussion. In general, this research demonstrates that social power is enacted through communicating control, which is a function of an individual's communication competence, self-presentation, and the context and development of the relationship (Giles & Weimann, 1987).

Another function of language in interpersonal interactions is to develop a sense of relational solidarity. Early work on relationships focused on the communicative acts associated with stages of development, as evidenced in Knapp's (1984) model of relationship development. Likewise, in their social penetration theory, Altman and Taylor (1973) proposed that relational progression coincides with more frequent and personal disclosures in interactions. The role of disclosure in personal relationships has received considerable scholarly attention (Derlega, Metts, Petronio, & Margulis, 1993), resulting in a more nuanced conceptualization that distinguishes between emotional and informational disclosure and posits that expectations of disclosure may vary. For instance, Mathews, Derlega, and Morrow (2006) identified topics of disclosure that were deemed highly personal by young adults (e.g., sex, psychological problems, family relationships). More important, they found that the disclosure of personal information also depends on the type of relationship (e.g., mother, friend). In fact, to account for the importance and complexity of disclosure in our relationships, communication privacy management theory (Petronio, 2002) was developed to understand the motivation and process for disclosing as well as concealing private information.

Extending this emphasis on self-disclosure and relational development, research has also focused on additional relational maintenance strategies embedded in messages. Stafford and Canary (1991) demonstrated that messages that convey positivity, openness, and assurances are important in maintaining satisfying relationships. Furthermore, theorizing has moved from a linear view of relational development to a focus on the dialogic and constitutive nature of communication in relationships (Baxter & Montgomery, 1996). An additional communicative act that has been linked to relational solidarity as well as overall physical and mental well-being is supportive communication (Burleson & MacGeorge, 2002). Goldsmith (1992) stated that supportive communication is "a category of speech acts and events that are culturally recognized as intending to convey various kinds of assistance" (p. 276). This communication can include informational support, providing advice, eliciting support, and, especially prudent to our relational outcomes, comforting communication. Moreover, successful comforting messages are those that convey active involvement, demonstrate attentiveness to thoughts and feelings of the conversational partner, and are nonjudgmental (Burleson, 1990).

Whereas self-disclosure and supportive communication have received considerable scholarly attention, the more routine acts of our everyday talk have also emerged as important factors in quality relationships (Duck, Rutt, Hurst, & Strejc, 1991). In fact, most of the everyday communication in our relationships is nonintimate and informal, as in recapping the day's events and gossip (Jaeger, Skelder, & Rosnow, 1998). As scholars delve more deeply into the interpersonal interaction domain, the types of communicative behaviors analyzed are becoming more diverse. For example, stories and storytelling have been examined to understand their role in shaping and reflecting our personal and relational identities (Bochner, 2002; Koenig Kellas, 2005).

Given the breadth and scope of interpersonal communication research, there is still a relative absence of consideration of social identity influences on personal interactions. Attempting to understand language and communication *without* attention to these dynamics is failing to take into consideration the wider social context of the interactions, including the ways in which they are enacted within complex community networks (Giles, Katz, & Myers, 2006). In fact, only very rarely can it be said that interpersonal communication is not influenced, to some extent, by larger macro-level factors (see McLeod, Kosicki, & McLeod, Chapter 11, this volume).

## INTERGROUP COMMUNICATION: SOCIAL COMPARISON

The social identity tradition stipulates that social categorization and identification can lead to intergroup comparison and thus in-group favoritism (Capozza & Brown, 2000). Building on this perspective, intergroup communication refers to an interactional context in which communicative behaviors—as well as the interpretation of these behaviors—are influenced by individuals' social group identifications (e.g., age, ethnicity, religion, gender, social class, political affiliation) and the corresponding evaluative nature of group categorization (Harwood, Giles, & Palomares, 2005). The notion that in-group favoritism and social stereotyping can be observed in language variations is now given much more empirical attention (see Ellis, Chapter 17, this volume; Wigboldus & Douglas, 2007).

Maass, Salvi, Arcuri, and Semin (1989) formulated the linguistic intergroup bias model to demonstrate that the level of abstractness in our language choices depends on the behavior of in-group and out-group members. Specifically, the model stipulates that individuals use abstract language when describing positive actions of in-group members or negative actions of out-group members. Conversely, more concrete language is used to describe negative actions of in-group members and positive actions of out-group members. The rationale for this prediction is based on the idea that abstract language reflects a more general and stable disposition of a person or group of persons. Hence, the notion of in-group favoritism suggests that this type of language would be used to explain expected and self-promoting behavior, such as the positive actions of in-group members. Concrete language, on the other hand, is situational and reflects the specific context or circumstances surrounding a specific action. Thus, this type of language would be used to explain unexpected or identity-threatening behavior, such as negative actions of in-group members. In Gorham's (2006) experiment on reactions to media reports, White participants reacted much more favorably to abstract language describing African American suspects and were more likely to embrace concrete language in descriptions of White suspects. In a similar vein, studies have also shown that this linguistic bias can be an implicit indicator of racial and gender prejudice (von Hippel, Sekaquaptewa, & Vargas, 1997).

Our initial discussion of language and ethnic identity represents some of the earlier work on intergroup communication—and this focus on language and identity continues today. For instance, in regions with multiethnic and multilingual populations, linguistic behaviors are associated with regional or ethnic identity as well as social acceptance. Ros, Huici, and Gómez (2000) discuss the notion of comparative identity to explain identification with different categories such that, in Spain, one can simultaneously identify with regional or national groups at various levels of inclusion (Clément & Noels, 1992). Thus, the extent to which individuals embrace a regional or national identity is reflected in their use of regional (e.g., Catalan) or national (i.e., Castilian) languages.

Much of the personal relations research assumes monolingualism, although multilingualism is the norm in many societies around the world. As evidenced above, language proficiency and use have significant relational and identity implications. For example, language use in multilingual immigrant families is associated with language maintenance among younger generations, ethnic identity of family members, and overall familial solidarity (Ng, 2007). The family context is just one example of the significance of multilingual communication and how the process of linguistic code switching relates to identity and relational goals (Auer, 1998).

In taking more interest in the applied consequences of attitudes concerning language and sociolinguistic groups, scholars have begun to critically assess public policy related to language (e.g., English-only laws: Barker et al., 2001). In their interactive acculturation model (IAM), Bourhis, Moise, Perreault, and Senécal (1997) demonstrate how state policies regarding immigration affect acculturation of minority group members as well as the nature of the relationship between minority and majority groups (see Kim, Chapter 26, this volume). The IAM delineates four ideologies that majority groups can embrace that dictate official policy. All the ideologies expect minority groups to adhere to values of the dominant culture, yet they vary on the respect and freedom given to minority (i.e., immigrant) cultural practices. At one end of the ideological spectrum is the *pluralism* ideology that dictates sovereignty of cultural practices and no restrictions on minority social involvement. Moreover, the state may financially or politically support the vitality of minority groups. At the opposite end of the spectrum is the *ethnist* ideology; minority groups are expected, or legally forced, to forsake cultural practices, but there is no intention of accepting these groups into the mainstream society. Although cultural

practices include various aspects of a social group (e.g., religious practice, celebrations), these ideologies have significant implications for language maintenance or loss of minority groups (Sachdev & Bourhis, 2005).

An intergroup approach has also informed research on various contexts of interaction, such as communication and disability (Ryan, Bajorek, Beaman, & Anas, 2005), interactions between homosexuals and heterosexuals (Hajek & Giles, 2002), gender differences and communication (Boggs & Giles, 1999), police-civilian contact (Giles et al., 2007), and organizational identity (Scott, 2007), to name a few. In these contexts, the findings further demonstrate the link between language behaviors and social identities (see also Cameron & Kulik, 2006; Noels & Giles, in press).

One area of inquiry that has received considerable attention from an intergroup perspective is intergenerational relations (Harwood, 2007). Although age is a progressive interval, we make sense of our age as members of cohorts (e.g., baby boomers, Generation X), and age is a salient identity for many, especially younger adults (Harwood, Giles, & Ryan, 1995). Like all social groups, age-groups are distinguished by linguistic and communicative markers. For example, adolescents enact a variety of communicative behaviors with peers and adults (Williams & Thurlow, 2005), which can either facilitate a sense of affiliation or demonstrate social distinctiveness. Thus, in the intergenerational context, communication behaviors and evaluations of others' communication are influenced by our attitudes toward age-groups (Williams & Giles, 1996). Considering relatively negative views toward older age-groups and aging in general (Kite & Johnson, 1988), it is not surprising that young adults' attitudes toward intergenerational interactions are somewhat negative.

Harwood et al. (1995) summarize some of these perceptions, which suggest that younger adults view older adults as less competent as well as less skilled and effective in communicating. In fact, Ryan, Giles, Bartolucci, and Henwood's (1986) communication predicament model of aging demonstrates how negative stereotypes of older adults lead to modified—and often patronizing—communication toward older adults that constrains the interactions. This, in turn, reinforces the negative stereotypes of older adults, resulting in harmful implications for the older adults' self-concept and overall well-being. However, not all intergenerational interactions are destined for this fate (Williams & Coupland, 1998). Researchers have identified positive and negative stereotypes of older adults and developed the age stereotypes in interaction model to demonstrate the role of context (e.g., hospital vs. family dinner), characteristics of the individuals, and positive/negative stereotypes in the quality of communication (Hummert, Garstka, Ryan, & Bonnesen, 2004).

Although research has focused on attitudes toward older adults, younger adults are not immune from age-related perceptions. Hummert et al.'s (2004) work also identified positive and negative stereotypes of *younger* adults. Young adults have indicated that older generations perceive them as irresponsible and unskilled communicators, incompetent, reckless, and so on (Garrett & Williams, 2005). As such, young adults view patronizing language and unsolicited advice from older adults as a result of these negative attitudes. Moreover, with the emergence of the younger generation's cyberculture and proclivity for newer techno-mediated communication (McKay, Thurlow, & Zimmerman, 2005), techno- and computer-mediated communication will not only serve as a characteristic of this age cohort but may also act as an additional barrier to successful intergenerational interactions (Lee & Sundar, Chapter 29, this volume; Thurlow, 2007; Walther, Chapter 28, this volume). Thus, intergenerational communication brings together

multiple individual and social dynamics of communication. Whereas some research has pointed out that productive capabilities vary based on age and impair intergenerational interactions (Kemper, Kynette, & Norman, 1992), it is the contextual, relational (e.g., grandparent vs. stranger), social (e.g., attitudes toward age-groups), and communicative factors that play a major role in differentiating positive and negative intergenerational interactions.

Whether considering group vitality (i.e., the social power of a language group) or status of social groups in general, the intergroup perspective demonstrates how language can reflect social identification, categorization, and comparison. In other words, power and social status evident in society are reflected in personal interactions. Even some of the communicative behaviors of interpersonal interactions (e.g., gendered communication norms) reflect aspects of more macrosocial influences. Thus, to understand the underlying process of language and, just as important, evaluations and consequences of speech styles, we must attend to both intergroup and interpersonal influences on interactions.

## CONCEPTUALIZING INTERGROUP-INTERPERSONAL INFLUENCES ON LANGUAGE AND COMMUNICATION

More traditional theorizing positioned interpersonal and intergroup as competing ends of a spectrum. On the basis of this perspective, we can still witness today the academic partitions in our research on language and communication in that many scholars seem to focus on either micro-level (i.e., interpersonal) or macro-level (i.e., group) influences. However, alternative perspectives suggest that communication can be influenced by the *simultaneous* salience or lack thereof of interpersonal and intergroup factors (Gallois, 2003; Harwood et al., 2005). As Harwood (2006) states, "We need to understand collective identities as a key aspect of human behavior, and we need to think about incorporating this higher-level sense of self into our communication research as a more routine practice" (p. 89).

At first, this may seem counterintuitive since many people consider *inter*group contact to refer to interactions between strangers. Yet, there are various contexts in which intergroup factors are present in what is typically considered an interpersonal interaction, such as persons in interracial/interethnic friendships and romantic relationships (Gaines et al., 1999), cross-faith friendships (Paolini, Hewstone, Cairns, & Voci, 2004), and heterosexual-homosexual relationships (Vonofakou, Hewstone, & Voci, 2007). Thus, each of these represents situations in which individuals must communicatively manage social group influences while aiming for interpersonal affiliation and relational satisfaction.

In fact, even families—typically considered as quite personal—are not immune from intergroup influences (Harwood, Soliz, & Lin, 2006). As such, gender roles (Tannen, 2003) as well as age (Harwood, 2000) and racial/ethnic differences (Killian, 2001) may influence social functioning, communication, and relational solidarity in families. Interracial/interethnic couples, for instance, may opt for "codes of silence" or directly address situations or topics (i.e., racism) in which intergroup distinctions are heightened. Family disapproval or lack of support for the relationship can also be a relational stressor as familial and racial/ethnic allegiances are challenged. Furthermore, multiracial/multiethnic families, including those formed through transracial and international adoption, must communicatively negotiate individual, cultural, and family identities (Galvin, 2003; Root, 2003) through open discussion of similarities and differences, affirmation of identities, recognition of language differences, and development of family and cultural rituals.

## LANGUAGE AND MEDIATED COMMUNICATION

With advancements in communication technologies, the changing landscape of information and entertainment options, and the subsequent changes in daily communication practices (e.g., text messaging), we would be remiss to ignore the interplay of language and mediated communication. Although much recent attention has been devoted to computer-mediated communication (CMC), investigating the role of technology in everyday interactions is not a new area of inquiry for communication scholars. For example, Buzzanell, Burrell, Stafford, and Berkowitz (1996) researched asynchronous communication in callers' interactions with answering machines. Answering machines are not typically conceptualized as "mediated communication," but this study demonstrates the interest scholars have in the potential differences evident in non-face-to-face interactions.

In fact, shifting from this focus on "wired" communication, researchers have turned their attention to norms, perceptions, and uses of mobile communications. Campbell (2006a) completed a cross-cultural study of wireless phone use and perceptions. The most significant trend in the findings is that there seems to be a cultural conformity in cell phone practices, with younger people being more tolerant of them (Campbell, 2006b). Likewise, research has shown that the goals and uses of mediated communication with cell phones mirror face-to-face communication goals (e.g., social support, identity management; Campbell & Kelley, 2006). Although the rise in cell phones has been dramatic over the past decade, the technological advancements in and prevalence of text-based CMC (e.g., e-mail, texting, instant messaging) have created an important area of inquiry for language and mediated communication (see Walther, Chapter 28, this volume).

Addressing this, Walther (2004) outlined three reasons for studying language and CMC. First, we need to understand how technology influences or changes our language use, perceptions, and outcomes, with Ling and Baron (2007) documenting language differences between text messaging and instant messaging. As demonstrated in Lee's (2007) study on instant messaging, technical constraints of the hardware (e.g., inability to produce certain symbols) influenced individuals' preference for English over Cantonese or, at least, code switching between the two when technical issues warranted this linguistic shift. Moreover, participants indicated this would not be the case in face-to-face interactions. Second, we should investigate how our language is adapted to transcend any barriers in CMC. For instance, in purely online romantic relationships, textual messages are the fundamental aspect of the relationship as nonverbal cues, physical contact, and public interactions are absent (Anderson & Emmers-Sommer, 2006). Thus, relational partners are more actively engaged in the production of written messages and are more aware of the potential interpretations and effects of their online language.

Finally, as social scholars, we should be interested in developing technologies that facilitate the attainment of conversational and social goals. For example, Postmes and Baym (2005) discuss the benefits of online intergroup contact in which positive outcomes may emerge without the negative consequences of face-to-face interaction and conflict. Of course, these examples cannot do justice to the burgeoning area of language and CMC that has recently spawned new specialized journals and scholarly books (e.g., Howard & Jones, 2003). As we attempt to delve more deeply into our understanding of motivations and outcomes of language use, it will be necessary to consider

the impact of technology and the role of CMC on our everyday interactions (see Walther, Chapter 28, this volume).

Mediated communication also refers to language use and practices in the mass media. Our discussion of accommodation, for instance, has centered on dyadic interactions, whereas Bell (1991) contends that accommodative strategies are also important in effectively communicating to mass audiences. For example, Koslow, Shamdasani, and Touchstone (1994) suggest that mixed-language advertisements—those employing both Spanish and English—may be more effective in reaching Hispanic populations in the United States compared with monolingual advertisements—as this communicatively affirms the dimensions of identity for Hispanic Americans. Furthermore, interpretations of mass media messages are contingent on our social identification, such that we may be more critical of, reinterpret, or even reject messages from out-group sources (Harwood & Roy, 2005). In other words, factors associated with language use and outcomes in mass media as well as strategies for effective communication may mirror those in dyadic or small group interactions.

Although the term *mass media* typically refers to messages sent to a large public audience, there is a growing interest in the development of mediated relationships between audience members and characters in films, television, and the like. Horton and Wohl (1956) argued that the cognitive processes associated with mediated relationships, which were originally conceptualized as parasocial interaction, are similar to those in face-to-face relationships. Support for this is evident in Cohen's (2004) research on emotional attachment to parasocial relationships. Extending this notion and incorporating intergroup theorizing, Schiappa, Gregg, and Hewes (2005) put forth the parasocial contact hypothesis to determine if mediated contact with out-group members would reduce levels of prejudice. Specifically, after viewing shows with gay or transvestite characters, viewers generally reported lower levels of prejudice toward these groups. The notion of parasocial relationships is an intriguing area for language scholars because the research to date has focused on the association between media exposure and cognition but given little attention to the language of these relationships. If, as the evidence suggests, we develop relationships with mediated others that operate in a fashion similar to actual relationships, then we can expect that language use and outcomes would also be similar.

## ◆ Conclusion

What does the foregoing add to our understanding of language? In a general sense, it accentuates the mutual influence of self, interpersonal, relational, and social identities. Because personal interactions are situated in a larger social context, it is possible that, through our language choices, perceptions of individuals and specific interactions as well as social groups, in general, can be improved (R. Brown & Hewstone, 2005). Traditional research in this realm has focused on basic conceptualizations of intergroup contact (i.e., focusing on positive-negative valence of contact). However, recent work has concentrated on identifying specific language behaviors that are associated with the intergroup salience of the interaction (Harwood, Raman, & Hewstone, 2006) as well as those behaviors that can improve perceptions of the out-group as a whole. For example, Soliz and Harwood (2006) linked (non)accommodative behaviors in grandparent-grandchild relationships with perceptions of older adults and aging.

In a similar vein, the link between language and ideology, as reflected in our public discourse, provides insight into the presence or absence of political, economic, and social injustice (Schaffner & Wenden, 1995). Thus, it is through language that our identities, goals, status, and power are manifested. Thus, language can function as both  a control and a mechanism for relational closeness. Likewise, it can both create and reflect intergroup conflict. But, more important, by transforming our styles and goals of language to reflect—in face-to-face as well as in old and new media settings in a globalizing world (see, e.g., Lamb, 2004)—a more inclusive and other-oriented perspective, interethnic, interfaith, and other even allegedly intractable intergroup conflicts may be resolved (see Ellis, 2006, and Chapter 17, this volume).

## ◆ References

Altman, I., & Taylor, D. (1973). *Social penetration: The development of interpersonal relationships.* New York: Holt, Rinehart and Winston.

Anderson, T., & Emmers-Sommer, T. (2006). Predictors of relationship satisfaction in online romantic relationships. *Communication Studies, 57,* 153–172.

Auer, P. (1998). *Code-switching in conversation.* New York: Routledge.

Barker, V., Giles, H., Noels, K., Duck, J., Hecht, M., & Clément, R. (2001). The English-only movement: A communication analysis of changing perceptions of language vitality. *Journal of Communication, 51,* 3–37.

Baxter, L. A., & Montgomery, B. M. (1996). *Relating: Dialogues and dialectics.* New York: Guilford.

Bell, A. (1991). Audience accommodation and the mass media. In H. Giles, J. Coupland, & N. Coupland (Eds.), *Contexts of accommodation* (pp. 69–102). Cambridge, UK: Cambridge University Press.

Berger, C. R. (1994). Power, dominance, and social interaction. In M. L. Knapp & G. R. Miller (Eds.), *Handbook of interpersonal communication* (pp. 450–507). Thousand Oaks, CA: Sage.

Bochner, A. P. (2002). Perspectives on inquiry III: The morals of stories. In M. L. Knapp & J. A. Daly (Eds.), *Handbook of interpersonal communication* (pp. 73–101). Thousand Oaks, CA: Sage.

Boggs, C., & Giles, H. (1999). The canary in the coalmine: The nonaccommodation cycle in the gendered workplace. *International Journal of Applied Linguistics, 9,* 223–245.

Bourhis, R. Y. (2001). Acculturation, language maintenance, and language loss. In J. Klatter-Falmer & P. Van Avermaet (Eds.), *Theories on language maintenance and loss of minority languages* (pp. 5–37). New York: Waxmann Verlag.

Bourhis, R. Y., & Giles, H. (1976). The language of co-operation in Wales: A field study. *Language Sciences, 42,* 13–16.

Bourhis, R. Y., Moise, L. C., Perreault, S., & Senécal, S. (1997). Towards an interactive acculturation model: A social psychological approach. *International Journal of Psychology, 32,* 369–386.

Brown, P., & Levinson, S. C. (1987). *Politeness: Some universals in language usage.* Cambridge, UK: Cambridge University Press.

Brown, R., & Hewstone, M. (2005). An integrative theory of intergroup contact. *Advances in Experimental Social Psychology, 37,* 255–343.

Bull, P. (2002). *Communication under the microscope.* London: Routledge.

Burgoon, J. K., Stern, L. A., & Dillman, L. (1995). *Interpersonal adaptation: Dyadic interaction patterns.* Cambridge, UK: Cambridge University Press.

Burleson, B. R. (1990). Comforting as social support: Relational consequences of supportive behaviors. In S. Duck (with R. C. Silver) (Eds.), *Personal relationships and social support* (pp. 66–82). London: Sage.

Burleson, B. R., & Goldsmith, D. J. (1998). How the comforting process works: Alleviating emotional distress through conversationally induced reappraisals. In P. A. Anderson & L. K. Guerrero (Eds.), *Communication and emotion: Theory, research, and applications* (pp. 245–280). Orlando, FL: Academic Press.

Burleson, B. R., & MacGeorge, E. L. (2002). Supportive communication. In M. L. Knapp & J. A. Daly (Eds.), *Handbook of interpersonal communication* (pp. 374–422). Thousand Oaks, CA: Sage.

Buzzanell, P. M., Burrell, N. A., Stafford, R. S., & Berkowitz, S. B. (1996). When I call you up and you're not there: Application of communication accommodation theory to telephone answering machines. *Western Journal of Communication, 60,* 310–336.

Cameron, D., & Kulick, D. (Eds.). (2006). *The language and sexuality reader.* London: Routledge.

Campbell, S. W. (2006a). A cross-cultural comparison of perceptions and uses of mobile telephony. *New Media and Society, 9,* 343–363.

Campbell, S. W. (2006b). Perceptions of mobile phones in college classrooms: Ringing, cheating, and classroom policies. *Communication Education, 55,* 280–294.

Campbell, S. W., & Kelley, M. J. (2006). Mobile phone use in AA networks: An exploratory study. *Journal of Applied Communication Research, 34,* 191–208.

Capozza, D., & Brown, R. (Eds.). (2000). *Social identity processes.* London: Sage.

Chomsky, N. (1965). *Aspects of the theory of syntax.* Cambridge: MIT Press.

Clark, H. H. (1996). *Using language.* Cambridge, UK: Cambridge University Press.

Clément, R., & Noels, K. A. (1992). Towards a situated approach to ethnolinguistic identity: The effects of status on individuals and groups. *Journal of Language and Social Psychology, 11,* 203–232.

Cohen, J. (2004). Parasocial break-up from favorite television characters: The role of attachment styles and relationship intensity. *Journal of Social and Personal Relationships, 21,* 187–202.

Derlega, V. J., Metts, S., Petronio, S., & Margulis, S. T. (1993). *Self disclosure.* London: Sage.

Duck, S., Rutt, D. J., Hurst, M. H., & Strejc, H. (1991). Some evident truths about conversations in everyday relationships: All communications are not created equal. *Human Communication Research, 18,* 228–267.

Edwards, D., & Potter, J. (1992). *Discursive psychology.* London: Sage.

Ellis, D. G. (2006). *Transforming conflict: Communication and ethnopolitical conflict.* Lanham, MD: Rowman & Littlefield.

Fiedler, K. (Ed.). (2007). *Social communication.* New York: Psychology Press.

Fishman, J. A. (1972). The relationship between micro- and macro-sociolinguistics in the study of who speaks what language to whom and when. In J. B. Pride & J. Holms (Eds.), *Sociolinguistics* (pp. 15–32). Harmondsworth, UK: Penguin.

Fitch, K. L., & Sanders, R. E. (Eds.). (2004). *Handbook of language and social interaction.* Mahwah, NJ. Lawrence Erlbaum.

Gaines, S. O., Jr., Granrose, C. S., Rios, D. I., Garcia, B. F., Youn, M. S., Farris, K. R., et al. (1999). Patterns of attachment and response to accommodative dilemmas among interethnic/interracial couples. *Journal of Social and Personal Relationships, 16,* 275–285.

Gallois, C. (2003). Reconciliation through communication in intercultural encounters: Potential or peril. *Journal of Communication, 53,* 5–15.

Gallois, C., Ogay, T., & Giles, H. (2005). Communication accommodation theory: A look back and a look ahead. In W. Gudykunst (Ed.), *Theorizing about intercultural communication* (pp. 121–148). Thousand Oaks, CA: Sage.

Galvin, K. (2003). International and transracial adoption: A communication research agenda. *Journal of Family Communication, 3,* 237–253.

Garrett, P., & Williams, A. (2005). Adults' perceptions of communication with young people. In A. Williams & C. Thurlow (Eds.), *Talking adolescence* (pp. 35–52). New York: Peter Lang.

Giles, H. (Ed.). (1977). *Language, ethnicity, and intergroup relations.* London: Academic Press.

Giles, H., Bourhis, R. Y., & Taylor, D. M. (1977). Towards a theory of language in ethnic group relations. In H. Giles (Ed.), *Language, ethnicity, and intergroup relations* (pp. 307–348). London: Academic Press.

Giles, H., & Coupland, N. (1991). *Language: Contexts and consequences.* Milton Keynes, UK: Open University Press.

Giles, H., Coupland, N., & Coupland, J. (1991). Accommodation theory: Communication, context, and consequence. In H. Giles, N. Coupland, & J. Coupland (Eds.), *Contexts of accommodation* (pp. 1–68). Cambridge, UK: Cambridge University Press.

Giles, H., Hajek, C., Barker, V., Chen, M.-L., Zhang, B. Y., Hummert, M. L., et al. (2007). Accommodation and institutional talk: Communicative dimensions of police-civilian interactions. In A. Weatherall, B. Watson, & G. Gallois (Eds.), *Language, discourse and social psychology* (pp. 131–159). New York: Palgrave Macmillan.

Giles, H., & Johnson, P. (1987). Ethnolinguistic identity theory: A social psychological approach to language maintenance. *International Journal of the Sociology of Language, 68,* 69–99.

Giles, H., Katz, V., & Myers, P. (2006). Language attitudes and the role of communication infrastructures. *Moderna Språk, 100,* 38–54.

Giles, H., Taylor, D. M., & Bourhis, R. Y. (1977). Dimensions of Welsh identity. *European Journal of Social Psychology, 7,* 165–174.

Giles, H., & Weimann, J. M. (1987). Language, social comparison, and power. In C. R. Berger & S. H. Chaffee (Eds.), *Handbook of communication science* (pp. 350–384). Newbury Park, CA: Sage.

Goldsmith, D. (1992). Managing conflicting goals in supportive interaction: An integrative theoretical framework. *Communication Research, 19,* 264–286.

Gorham, B. W. (2006). News media's relationship with stereotyping: The linguistic intergroup bias in response to crime news. *Journal of Communication, 56,* 289–308.

Guerrero, L. K., Alberts, J. K., & Heisterkamp, B. (2001). Discrepancy arousal and cognitive valence theory. In W. P. Robinson & H. Giles (Eds.), *The new handbook of language and social psychology* (pp. 57–78). Chichester, UK: Wiley.

Hajek, C., & Giles, H. (2002). The old man out: An intergroup analysis of intergenerational communication among gay men. *Journal of Communication, 52,* 698–714.

Harwood, J. (2000). Communicative predictors of solidarity in the grandparent-grandchild relationship. *Journal of Social and Personal Relationships, 17,* 743–766.

Harwood, J. (2006). Social identity. In G. Shepherd, J. St. John, & T. Striphas (Eds.), *Communication as . . . : Perspectives on theory* (pp. 84–90). Thousand Oaks, CA: Sage.

Harwood, J. (2007). *Understanding communication and aging.* Thousand Oaks, CA: Sage.

Harwood, J., & Giles, H. (2005). *Intergroup communication.* New York: Peter Lang.

Harwood, J., Giles, H., & Bourhis, R. Y. (1994). The genesis of vitality theory: Historical patterns and discoursal dimensions. *International Journal of the Sociology of Language, 108,* 167–206.

Harwood, J., Giles, H., & Palomares, N. A. (2005). Intergroup theory and communication processes. In J. Harwood & H. Giles (Eds.), *Intergroup communication* (pp. 1–20). New York: Peter Lang.

Harwood, J., Giles, H., & Ryan, E. B. (1995). Aging, communication and intergroup theory: Social identity and intergenerational communication. In J. F. Nussbaum & J. Coupland (Eds.), *Handbook of communication and aging research* (pp. 133–160). Mahwah, NJ: Lawrence Erlbaum.

Harwood, J., Raman, P., & Hewstone, M. (2006). The family and communication dynamics of group salience. *Journal of Family Communication, 6,* 181–200.

Harwood, J., & Roy, A. (2005). Social identity theory and mass communication research. In J. Harwood & H. Giles (Eds.), *Intergroup communication* (pp. 189–211). New York: Peter Lang.

Harwood, J., Soliz, J., & Lin, M.-C. (2006). Communication accommodation theory: An intergroup approach to family relationships. In D. O. Braithwaite & L. Baxter (Eds.), *Engaging theories in family communication* (pp. 19–34). Thousand Oaks, CA: Sage.

Hoff, E., & Shatz, M. (2006). *Blackwell handbook of language development.* Malden, MA: Blackwell.

Holtgraves, T. M. (2002). *Language as social action.* Mahwah, NJ: Lawrence Erlbaum.

Horton, D., & Wohl, R. R. (1956). Mass communication and para-social interaction. *Psychiatry, 19,* 215–229.

Howard, P. E. N., & Jones, S. (2003). *Society online: The internet in context.* Thousand Oaks, CA: Sage.

Hummert, M. L., Garstka, T. L., Ryan, E. B., & Bonnesen, J. (2004). The role of age stereotypes in interpersonal communication. In J. F. Nussbaum & J. Coupland (Eds.), *Handbook of communication and aging research* (2nd ed., pp. 91–115). Mahwah, NJ: Lawrence Erlbaum.

Hummert, M. L., & Ryan, E. B. (2001). Patronizing. In W. P. Robinson & H. Giles (Eds.), *The new handbook of language and social psychology* (pp. 253–270). New York: John Wiley.

Jacobs, S. (2002). Language and interpersonal communication. In M. L. Knapp & J. A. Daly (Eds.), *Handbook of interpersonal communication* (pp. 213–239). Thousand Oaks, CA: Sage.

Jaeger, M. E., Skelder, A. A., & Rosnow, R. L. (1998). Who's up on the low down: Gossip in interpersonal relationships. In B. H. Spitzberg & W. R. Cupach (Eds.), *The dark side of close relationships* (pp. 103–188). Mahwah, NJ: Lawrence Erlbaum.

Jaworski, A. (1993). *The power of silence: Social and pragmatic perspectives.* Newbury Park, CA: Sage.

Jaworski, J., & Coupland, N. (Eds.). (1999). *The discourse reader* (2nd ed.). London: Routledge.

Kemper, S., Kynette, D., & Norman, S. (1992). Age difference in spoken language. In R. West & J. Sinnot (Eds.), *Everyday memory and aging* (pp. 138–154). New York: Springer-Verlag.

Killian, K. D. (2001). Reconstituting racial histories and identities: The narratives of interracial couples. *Journal of Marital and Family Therapy, 27,* 27–42.

Kite, M. E., & Johnson, B. T. (1988). Attitudes toward older and younger adults: A meta-analysis. *Psychology and Aging, 3,* 233–244.

Knapp, M. L. (1984). *Interpersonal communication and human relationships.* Boston: Allyn & Bacon.

Knapp, M. L., & Daly, J. A. (2002). *Handbook of interpersonal communication.* Thousand Oaks, CA: Sage.

Koenig Kellas, J. (2005). Family ties: Communicating identity through jointly told family stories. *Communication Monographs, 72,* 365–389.

Koslow, S., Shamdasani, P. N., & Touchstone, E. E. (1994). Exploring language effects in ethnic advertising: A sociolinguistic perspective. *Journal of Consumer Research, 20,* 575–585.

Kunkel, A., Hummert, M. L., & Dennis, M. R. (2006). Social learning theory: Modeling and communication in the family context. In D. O. Braithwaite & L. Baxter (Eds.), *Engaging theories in family communication* (pp. 260–275). Thousand Oaks, CA: Sage.

Lakin, J. L., Jefferis, V. E., Cheng, C. M., & Chartrand, T. L. (2003). The chameleon effect as social glue: Evidence for the evolutionary significance of nonconscious mimicry. *Journal of Nonverbal Behavior, 27,* 145–162.

Lamb, M. (2004). Integrative motivation in a globalizing world. *System, 32,* 3–19.

Laursen, B., & Collins, W. A. (2004). Parent-child communication during adolescence. In A. L. Vangelisti (Ed.), *Handbook of family communication* (pp. 333–348). Mahwah, NJ: Lawrence Erlbaum.

Lee, C. K.-M. (2007). Affordance and text-making practices in online instant messaging. *Written Communication, 24,* 223–249.

Ling, R., & Baron, N. S. (2007). Text messaging and IM: Linguistic comparison of American college data. *Journal of Language and Social Psychology, 26,* 291–298.

Maass, A., Salvi, D., Arcuri, L., & Semin, G. R. (1989). Language use in intergroup context. *Journal of Personality and Social Psychology, 57,* 981–993.

Manusov, V., & Patterson, M. L. (2006). *The Sage handbook of nonverbal communication.* Thousand Oaks, CA: Sage.

Marlow, M., & Giles, H. (2007). "Who you tink You, talkin propah?" Language choices and discursive perceptions among locals in Hawai'i. *Journal of Multicultural Discourses, 3,* 53–69.

Mathews, A., Derlega, V. J., & Morrow, J. (2006). What is highly personal information and how is it related to self-disclosure decision-making? The perspective of college students. *Communication Research Reports, 23,* 85–92.

McDevitt, M., & Chaffee, S. (2002). From top-down to trickle-up influence: Revisiting assumptions about the family in political socialization. *Political Communication, 19,* 281–301.

McKay, S., Thurlow, C., & Zimmerman, H. T. (2005). Wired whizzes or techno-slaves? Young people and their emergent communication technologies. In A. Williams & C. Thurlow (Eds.), *Talking adolescence* (pp. 185–206). New York: Peter Lang.

Millar, F. E., & Rogers, L. E. (1988). Power dynamics in marital relationships. In P. Noller & M. A. Fitzpatrick (Eds.), *Perspectives on marital interaction* (pp. 78–97). Philadelphia: Multilingual Matters.

Morgan, M., & Hummert, M. L. (2000). Perceptions of communicative control strategies in mother-daughter dyads across the life-span. *Journal of Communication, 50,* 48–64.

Ng, S. H. (2007). From language acculturation to communication acculturation: Addressee orientations and communication brokering in conversations. *Journal of Language and Social Psychology, 26,* 75–90.

Noels, K. A., & Giles, H. (in press). Social identity and language learning. In T. K. Bhatia & W. C. Ritchie (Eds.), *Elsevier new handbook of second language acquisition.* Oxford, UK: Elsevier.

Noels, K. A., Giles, H., & Le Poire, B. (2003). Language and communication processes. In M. A. Hogg & J. Cooper (Eds.), *The Sage handbook of social psychology* (pp. 232–257). London: Sage.

Paolini, S., Hewstone, M., Cairns, E., & Voci, A. (2004). Effects of direct and indirect cross-group friendships on judgments of Catholics and Protestants in Northern Ireland: The mediating role of an anxiety-reduction mechanism. *Personality and Social Psychology Bulletin, 30,* 770–786.

Petronio, S. (2002). *Boundaries of privacy: Dialectics of disclosure.* Albany: State University of New York Press.

Postmes, T., & Baym, N. (2005). Intergroup dimensions of the internet. In J. Harwood & H. Giles (Eds.), *Intergroup communication* (pp. 214–238). New York: Peter Lang.

Potter, J., & Edwards, D. (2001). Discursive social psychology. In W. P. Robinson & H. Giles (Eds.), *The new handbook of language and social psychology* (pp. 103–118). Chichester, UK: Wiley.

Robinson, W. P. (2001). Prologue. In W. P. Robinson & H. Giles (Eds.), *The new handbook of language and social psychology* (pp. xv–xx). New York: John Wiley.

Robinson, W. P. (2003). *Language in social worlds.* Oxford, UK: Blackwell.

Robinson, W. P., & Giles, H. (Eds.). (2001). *The new handbook of language and social psychology.* New York: John Wiley.

Rommetveit, R., & Blakar, R. M. (Eds.). (1979). *Studies of language, thought and verbal communication.* London: Academic Press.

Root, M. P. P. (2003). Multiracial families and children: Implications for educational research and practice. In J. A. Banks & C. A. McGee Banks (Eds.), *Handbook of research on multicultural education* (pp. 110–124). San Francisco: Jossey-Bass.

Ros, M., Huici, C., & Gómez, A. (2000). Comparative identity, category salience, and intergroup relations. In D. Capozza & R. Brown (Eds.), *Social identity processes* (pp. 81–95). London: Sage.

Ryan, E. B., Bajorek, S., Beaman, A., & Anas, A. P. (2005). "I just want you to know that 'them' is me": Intergroup perspectives on communication and disability. In J. Harwood & H. Giles (Eds.), *Intergroup communication* (pp. 117–140). New York: Peter Lang.

Ryan, E. B., Giles, H., Bartolucci, G., & Henwood, K. (1986). Psycholinguistic and social psychological components of communication by and with the elderly. *Language and Communication, 6,* 1–24.

Sachdev, I., & Bourhis, R. Y. (2005). Multilingual communication and social identification. In J. Harwood & H. Giles (Eds.), *Intergroup communication* (pp. 65–92). New York: Peter Lang.

Schaffner, C., & Wenden, A. L. (1995). *Language and peace.* Amsterdam: Harwood.

Schiappa, E., Gregg, P. B., & Hewes, D. E. (2005). The parasocial contact hypothesis. *Communication Monographs, 72,* 95–118.

Scott, C. R. (2007). Communication and social identity theory: Existing and potential connections in organizational identification research. *Communication Studies, 58,* 123–138.

Soliz, J., & Harwood, J. (2006). Shared family identity, age salience, and intergroup contact: Investigation of the grandparent-grandchild relationship. *Communication Monographs, 73,* 87–107.

Stafford, L., & Canary, D. J. (1991). Maintenance strategies and romantic relationship type, gender, and relational characteristics. *Journal of Social and Personal Relationships, 8,* 217–242.

Stafford, L., Dainton, M., & Haas, S. (2000). Measuring routine and strategic relational maintenance: Scale revision, sex versus gender roles, and the prediction of relational characteristics. *Communication Monographs, 37,* 306–323.

Tajfel, H., & Turner, J. C. (1986). The social identity theory of intergroup behavior. In S. Worchel & W. Austin (Eds.), *Psychology of intergroup relations* (pp. 7–24). Chicago: Nelson-Hall.

Tannen, D. (2003). Gender and family interaction. In J. Holmes & M. Meyerhoff (Eds.), *The handbook of language and gender* (pp. 179–201). Malden, MA: Blackwell.

Thurlow, C. (2007). Fabricating youth: New-media discourse and the technologization of

young people. In S. Johnson & A. Erisslin (Eds.), *Language in the media* (pp. 213–233). London: Continuum.

von Hippel, W., Sekaquaptewa, D., & Vargas, P. (1997). The linguistic intergroup bias as an implicit indicator of prejudice. *Journal of Experimental Social Psychology, 33,* 490–509.

Vonofakou, C., Hewstone, M., & Voci, A. (2007). Contact with out-group friends as a predictor of meta-attitudinal strength and accessibility of attitudes towards gay men. *Journal of Personality and Social Psychology, 92,* 804–820.

Walker, K. L., Arnold, C., Miller-Day, M., & Webb, L. (2002). Investigating the physician-patient relationship: Examining emerging themes. *Health Communication, 14,* 45–68.

Walther, J. B. (2004). Language and communication technology: Introduction to the special issue. *Journal of Language and Social Psychology, 23,* 384–396.

Weatherall, A., Gallois, C., & Watson, B. (2007). Introduction: Theoretical and methodological approaches to language and discourse in social psychology. In A. Weatherall, B. Watson, & C. Gallois (Eds.), *Language, discourse and social psychology* (pp. 1–12). New York: Palgrave Macmillan.

Wigboldus, D., & Douglas, K. (2007). Language, stereotypes, and intergroup relations. In K. Fiedler (Ed.), *Social communication* (pp. 79–106). New York: Psychology Press.

Williams, A., & Coupland, N. (1998). Epilogue: The socio-political framing of communication and aging research. *Journal of Applied Communication Research, 26,* 139–154.

Williams, A., & Giles, H. (1996). Intergeneration conversations: Young adults' retrospective accounts. *Human Communication Research, 23,* 220–250.

Williams, A., & Nussbaum, J. F. (2002). *Intergenerational communication across the lifespan.* Mahwah, NJ: Lawrence Erlbaum.

Williams, A., & Thurlow, C. (2005). *Talking adolescence.* New York: Peter Lang.

# 6

# NONVERBAL COMMUNICATION THEORIES OF INTERACTION ADAPTATION

◆ Judee K. Burgoon, Kory Floyd, and Laura K. Guerrero

Among the quintessential features that characterize intelligent life forms is the ability of species' mates to coordinate and adapt communication to one another. The question of how humans accomplish this, and under what conditions, has attracted theoretical and empirical attention from scholars in many fields. In the latter half of the 20th century, social scientists advanced a number of theories and principles to account for adaptation and coordination, including the principle of reciprocity (Gouldner, 1960), equilibrium theory (Argyle & Dean, 1965), arousal-labeling theory (Patterson, 1973), motor mimicry (Bavelas, Black, Chovil, Lemery, & Mullett, 1988), and the sequential-functional model (Patterson, 1983). These various sociological and psychological models—which emphasized, respectively, the role of social norms, physiological arousal, affective perceptions related to arousal, communicative mimicking of projections of another's state, and a combination of psychological, physiological, and social factors—were foundational to the communication theories elaborated in this chapter.

## ◆ Communication Theories of Nonverbal Adaptation

Although many areas of communication research are theoretically bereft, theories that attempt to explain responses to nonverbal communication have been a rich source of inquiry for decades (Andersen, Guerrero, Buller, & Jorgensen, 1998). These theories focus on *nonverbal adaptation,* which is the process by which people alter nonverbal behavior when interacting with others (Burgoon, Stern, & Dillman, 1995). Within the communication field, five theories are at the forefront when it comes to explaining patterns of nonverbal adaptation: communication accommodation theory (CAT), expectancy violations theory (EVT), discrepancy-arousal theory (DAT), cognitive valence theory (CVT), and interaction adaptation theory (IAT). These five theories are, in many respects, complementary rather than competitive in that they each make sensible predictions within specific domains, channels, or communication functions.

All five theories rest on the principle that people use nonverbal communication to coordinate and approach or avoid interaction with others. CAT focuses on patterns of accommodation—behavioral patterns that are similar or dissimilar to one another. The other four theories focus more on patterns of reciprocity and compensation (although some also address other forms of adaptation). Reciprocity and compensation occur when an individual alters her or his nonverbal behavior in response to a partner's change in behavior, whereas accommodation can involve gradual or rapid movement toward or away from a partner's communication style, regardless of whether the partner's style is changing or static.

Theories of reciprocity and compensation often examine nonverbal immediacy or involvement behaviors. Immediacy behaviors, such as smiling, gaze, and close distances, communicate physical and psychological closeness, approachability, sensory stimulation, interest, and interpersonal warmth (Andersen, 1985). Involvement behaviors, such as vocal and kinesic expressiveness, communicate engagement and interest in the interaction at hand (Coker & Burgoon, 1987). When combined with affective cues such as smiling and vocal warmth, involvement behaviors communicate intimacy and closeness (Prager & Roberts, 2004). The five communication theories of nonverbal adaptation are described next, along with research supporting or refuting them. The reader is directed to other handbook chapters and volumes (e.g., Burgoon & Bacue, 2003; Burgoon & Hoobler, 2002; Manusov & Patterson, 2006) for a more generic review of nonverbal communication principles and the theories that undergird them.

### COMMUNICATION ACCOMMODATION THEORY

CAT, which was initially called speech accommodation theory, was one of the first communication theories that explained patterns of nonverbal adaptation. The theory originally focused on vocalic behaviors such as accent and speaking rate but now includes a wide variety of nonverbal cues (see Giles, Mulac, Bradac, & Johnson, 1987; Shepard, Giles, & Le Poire, 2001; Soliz & Giles, Chapter 5, this volume). A major premise of CAT is that people use accommodation strategies to help negotiate social distance and promote various types of social relationships, such as in-groups and out-groups. In-groups are related to people's affiliations, such as the social, cultural, and co-cultural groups to which they belong.

CAT revolves primarily around two forms of accommodation: convergence and divergence. *Convergence* is the process of adapting one's communication style so that it becomes more similar to another person's or group's style, whereas *divergence* is the process of adapting one's communication style so that it becomes more different than another person's or group's style. Both types of accommodation vary based on the degree to which they are upward versus downward, partial versus full, symmetrical versus asymmetrical, and unimodal versus multimodal (Shepard et al., 2001). Accommodation is upward or downward depending on whether the person is moving toward a more or less socially prestigious communication style, respectively. An example of upward accommodation is trying to speak "the Queen's English" or using Received Pronunciation. Downward accommodation would occur if the Queen tried to relate to subjects from a rural area by altering her accent to match theirs. The distinction between partial and full accommodation rests on the degree to which people end up converging with or diverging from one another. Full convergence would result in partners or group members looking or sounding identical, while full divergence would result in partners or group members looking or sounding very different. Partial accommodation, which happens more frequently, occurs when people move toward or away from another person's style but still retain some of their own. Symmetrical accommodation involves both people converging or diverging so that both become either similar to or different from one another. Asymmetrical accommodation, by contrast, occurs when one person converges and the other diverges. Finally, accommodation is unimodal when only one behavior (perhaps smiling or body positioning) shows a pattern of convergence or divergence. When accommodation is multimodal, convergence or divergence occurs for multiple behaviors (perhaps smiling, body positioning, gesturing, and vocal tone).

According to CAT, accommodation is influenced by intrapersonal, intergroup, individual, and situational factors. *Intrapersonal factors* revolve around social and personal identity issues, *intergroup factors* encompass perceptions of in-groups and out-groups, and an *individual's initial orientation* includes behavioral predispositions and tendencies. *Situational factors* are

"norms and roles that prescribe behavior in any given context" (Shepard et al., 2001, p. 48), including sociopsychological states involving motivation, emotion, stereotypes, expectations, and goals. Goals, such as wanting to be seen as approachable, likable, or competent, help guide people in deciding whether to converge or diverge to another person's communication style (although such adjustments often occur outside of one's conscious awareness). People then evaluate (also often unconsciously) whether their accommodation helped them achieve their goals, and they store this information to help them cope with future accommodative situations. Overall, research suggests that convergence is especially likely among in-group members, close relational partners, and people who like or respect one another. Divergence is more likely when people communicate with out-group members or people they dislike, when they want to convey superior status, and when they want to assert their personal identity, such as adolescents diverging from parents (Giles & Wadleigh, 2008; Shepard et al., 2001).

A considerable amount of research spanning several disciplines, contexts, and populations has examined patterns of accommodative behavior, showing that people enact convergence and divergence by using nonverbal behaviors such as accent (Giles, 1973), gaze (Mulac, Studley, Wiemann, & Bradac, 1987), response latency (Street, 1984), smiling (Gallois, Giles, Jones, Cargile, & Ota, 1995), speaking rate (Street, 1984), talk time (Willemyns, Gallois, Callan, & Pittam, 1997), and vocal pitch (Gregory, Dagan, & Webster, 1997). Empirical research has also verified that CAT is applicable to a wide variety of contexts, including business interactions (Baker, 1991; Bourhis, 1991), the courtroom, intercultural interaction (e.g., Gallois et al., 1995), intergenerational communication (Giles, Fox, & Smith, 1993), interviews (Street, 1984; Willemyns et al., 1997), law enforcement (Giles, Willemyns, Gallois, & Anderson, 2007), and persuasion situations

(Buller & Aune, 1988, 1992). For example, Buller and Aune (1988) demonstrated that people were more likely to comply with phone requests if the caller's voice sounded similar to the receiver's voice. CAT has also been used to explain differences in communication between men and women (Boggs & Giles, 1999; Mulac et al., 1987), between people of unequal status (e.g., Thakerar, Giles, & Cheshire, 1982), and between minority groups and the larger culture (e.g., Bourhis & Giles, 1977). Although considerable empirical evidence supports CAT, Shepard et al. (2001) suggested that further research remains to be done to validate the specific details and propositions of CAT. In particular, more work is necessary to learn how intrapersonal, intergroup, and situational factors interact to predict patterns of nonverbal accommodation.

## EXPECTANCY VIOLATIONS THEORY

Like CAT, EVT was one of the first theories to examine patterns of nonverbal adaptation. Originally, this theory focused on how people respond to personal space violations (Burgoon, 1978). Since its inception, however, EVT has been expanded to include various forms of nonverbal communication, such as facial expression, touch, eye contact, and vocal behavior (Burgoon & Hale, 1988). EVT postulates that people hold expectations about their own and others' behaviors; deviations from these expectations have predictable effects on the reactions of others. Expectations can be *predictive* (i.e., based on what a person believes will occur in a given situation) or *prescriptive* (i.e., based on what a person believes *should* occur in a given situation). For example, you may know that a friend gets uptight during job interviews, so you would have the predictive expectation that he will sound nervous when meeting with a prospective employer. However, you might also have the prescriptive expectation that

he should look composed during the interview. According to EVT, expectations are primarily derived from three sources: personal characteristics (e.g., gender, knowledge of someone's personality), relational characteristics (e.g., type and state of relationship), and contextual factors (e.g., situation, culture).

Nonverbal communication can either confirm or violate expectancies. Most of the time, people's behavior conforms to expectations and goes largely unnoticed. When expectancies are violated, however, people pay attention to the unexpected behavior. Specifically, expectancy violations heighten receivers' arousal and lead to a series of cognitive appraisals that help the receivers interpret and respond to the unexpected behavior. Two primary variables influence how receivers react to the unexpected behavior: violation valence and communicator reward level.

Violation valence refers to whether the unexpected behavior is judged to be positive or negative. In general, unexpected behaviors are regarded as positive when they are evaluated as better than what was expected and as negative when they are evaluated as worse than what was expected. Thus, receiving a quick hug from someone could be considered a positive expectancy violation if a person only expected a comforting glance, but the same quick hug could be considered a negative expectancy violation if the individual expected a longer embrace. Some behaviors tend to have fairly unambiguous meanings and therefore are likely to be evaluated as negative or positive across a number of situations. For instance, being yelled at is usually valenced negatively, whereas being smiled at is usually valenced positively. However, even these behaviors can be interpreted differently depending on the situation. Sometimes yelling can be valenced positively (e.g., yelling to warn someone of danger), and smiling can be valenced negatively (e.g., smiling in a condescending manner). Other nonverbal behaviors, such as moving close to someone or speaking in a nervous voice, are inherently more ambiguous.

When the valence of a behavior is ambiguous, the reward value of the communicator who enacted the unexpected behavior becomes significant as a means of assigning a valence to the behavior. Reward value refers to the degree to which the person who engaged in the unexpected behavior is regarded favorably or unfavorably. People who are socially skillful, physically attractive, popular, or famous or who have high status are likely to be high in reward value. Rewarding individuals have more leeway to engage in unexpected behaviors and still be evaluated positively. For example, a hug or personal space violation is likely to be evaluated positively if enacted by a rewarding individual but negatively if enacted by an unrewarding individual.

According to EVT, reward value and violation valence predict how people respond to unexpected nonverbal behavior. Specifically, when a rewarding person engages in higher than expected immediacy (a positive violation), the receiver is theorized to reciprocate by increasing immediacy (e.g., Kari smiles and moves closer to Sarah; Sarah smiles and touches Kari's arm). By contrast, when a rewarding partner engages in lower than expected immediacy (a negative violation), the receiver is theorized to compensate in an effort to return the interaction to a more comfortable level of intimacy (e.g., Kari moves away from Sarah; Sarah moves closer and asks, "What's wrong?"). In either of these situations, people respond to the unexpected behavior of rewarding communicators by, at least initially, increasing immediacy. Over time, however, if the overtures of increased immediacy fail to elicit a reciprocal response, the theory predicts that a person will eventually reciprocate rewarding communicators' decreased levels of immediacy (Guerrero, Jones, & Burgoon, 2000; Le Poire & Burgoon, 1994).

The opposite pattern is predicted for unrewarding communicators. According to EVT, if unrewarding communicators use unexpectedly high levels of immediacy (a negative violation), receivers are theorized to compensate by engaging in low levels of immediacy (i.e., Jake moves into Tyler's personal space; Tyler frowns and moves away). If unrewarding communicators use unexpectedly low levels of immediacy, receivers are theorized to reciprocate by acting less immediate (e.g., Jake looks away from Tyler; Tyler moves away from Jake). Either way, receivers are more likely to engage in low levels of nonverbal immediacy when interacting with unrewarding communicators. Thus, EVT suggests that unrewarding communicators should confirm rather than violate expectations if they want to be evaluated positively (Floyd, Ramirez, & Burgoon, 2008).

EVT has garnered considerable empirical support since its inception in the late 1970s (see Burgoon, Stern, & Dillman, 1995, for a review), but much of that work has focused on interaction *outcomes* such as credibility or persuasion rather than on interaction *processes* that relate to reciprocity and compensation. Of the investigations that have examined reactions to changes in immediacy and involvement (e.g., Burgoon, Olney, & Coker, 1987; Burgoon, Le Poire, & Rosenthal, 1995; Burgoon, Stern, & Dillman, 1995; Hale & Burgoon, 1984), the general findings have been that people (a) reciprocate positively valued communication styles such as increased involvement, (b) compensate for specific discomfiting interaction behaviors such as excessive proximity or eye contact, (c) show more variable responses but generally a reciprocal suppression of involvement or pleasantness in response to persistent low involvement or unpleasantness by a partner, and (d) compensate initially for undesirable behaviors such as unpleasantness, reductions in involvement, or shows of skepticism but abandon those behavior patterns over time if they fail to elicit a reciprocal response. Thus, reciprocity and compensation can occur in parallel, the former in terms of more global communication patterns and the latter in terms of specific behaviors related to physical and psychological comfort. Consistent with EVT predictions, positive violations elicit mostly reciprocity and matching. However, negative violations provoke more variable responses, including some initial compensatory or nonaccommodative responses but reciprocity of decreased involvement and pleasantness over time. Thus, a mix of patterns may be evident simultaneously and, depending on which measure is examined, can support any of the theories. This can be problematic when it comes to validating any given prediction, and it points to the possible need to invoke a parallel processing mechanism.

## DISCREPANCY AROUSAL THEORY

Cappella and Greene's (1982) DAT also focuses on explaining patterns of reciprocity and compensation in response to changes in nonverbal behavior. Using Stern's (1974) work on parent-child interaction, Cappella and Greene argued that patterns of nonverbal adaptation occur rapidly, with little time for cognitive evaluation. Thus, they theorized that automatic changes in and responses to arousal are primarily responsible for determining how people react to unexpected nonverbal behaviors by senders. The theory focuses on causal links between (a) discrepancy levels and arousal change, (b) degree of arousal change and affective response, and (c) affective responses and behavioral responses.

*Discrepancy* refers to the difference between expected and actual behavior. Expectations about behavior are theorized to be based on personal preferences, past experiences, cultural and social norms, and situational variables (Cappella & Greene, 1982). Expected behavior falls within an *acceptance region;* in other words, expected behaviors conform to what is typically accepted from a particular person in a certain situation. When behaviors clearly fall within the acceptance

region, there is no discrepancy and no arousal change. However, when a behavior falls outside of the acceptance region, it is highly discrepant and leads to high levels of arousal change. When actual behavior is somewhat discrepant from expected behavior but still falls within the acceptance range, it leads to moderate levels of arousal change. Overall, then, DAT predicts that degree of discrepancy is positively associated with level of arousal change.

The degree of arousal change is then theorized to associate with a receiver's affective response. Because expected behaviors are not arousing, DAT specifies that they do not lead to affective reactions. Moderate increases in arousal, however, are theorized to lead to positive affective reactions such as happiness, relief, or pleasant surprise, whereas very high increases in arousal are theorized to lead to negative affective reactions, such as disappointment, anger, or discomfort. Thus, according to DAT, unexpected behaviors that fall within the acceptance region lead to moderate arousal change and positive affect; unexpected behaviors that fall outside the acceptance region lead to high arousal change and negative affect.

The last link in the DAT chain of predictions is between affect and behavior. Positive affective reactions are predicted to increase approach and reciprocity, whereas negative affective reactions are predicted to result in avoidant or compensatory behavior. Therefore, if a sender is unexpectedly warm and expressive (perhaps by smiling and moving close), the receiver's response will depend on how discrepant, and therefore arousing, the unexpected behavior is. If the unexpectedly warm behavior falls within the acceptance region, DAT predicts that the receiver will experience moderate arousal change and positive affect, leading to approach behavior (e.g., the receiver will smile back). However, if the unexpectedly warm behavior falls outside the acceptance region, DAT predicts that the receiver will experience high levels of arousal and negative affect, leading to avoidant behavior (e.g., backing away). Unclear from the original statement of the theory is whether unexpectedly unpleasant behavior, such as being contemptuous and aloof, that falls outside the acceptance region and elicits high levels of arousal should prompt reciprocal avoidant behavior or compensatory approach behavior.

Empirical support for DAT has been mixed. In an initial test, Cappella and Greene (1984) argued that high-sensation seekers would have wider acceptance regions related to spatial invasions than low-sensation seekers. Therefore, compared with high-sensation seekers, they expected low-sensation seekers to react with more arousal change, negative affect, and compensation when their space was invaded. When two groups that differed in terms of trait sensation seeking (high vs. low) were compared, no significant differences emerged. However, a supplementary analysis that involved participants' actual evaluations of the violation (rather than just the trait measure) did lend some support to DAT. Specifically, people who evaluated the space violation more negatively displayed more compensation in the form of less gaze, less lean, and more indirect body orientation.

Two other studies pitted DAT against other theories of nonverbal adaptation. Le Poire and Burgoon (1994) had confederates pose as medical students and manipulate their level of nonverbal involvement when they interacted with student participants. Their data did not support the proposed DAT link between the level of involvement behavior displayed by the confederates and the level of arousal change experienced by the participants. Their data did, however, support the link between size of involvement change by confederates and the affective responses of participants. Specifically, the smaller the involvement change by the confederates, the more participants were likely to report experiencing positive affect. In another study, Andersen et al. (1998) examined physiological and behavioral

responses to changes in the nonverbal immediacy of a cross-sex friend (who, unbeknownst to the participant, was acting as a confederate). Consistent with principles from DAT, participants experienced more arousal change in response to large increases in immediacy compared with moderate increases in immediacy. Also consistent with DAT, they found that moderate increases in a confederate's level of nonverbal immediacy led to reciprocity, whereas large increases in nonverbal immediacy led to a mix of reciprocity and compensation.

## COGNITIVE VALENCE THEORY

EVT and DAT examine reactions to both increases and decreases in nonverbal behaviors such as immediacy and expressiveness, whereas Andersen's (1985, 1998) CVT was developed to predict how people react to increased immediacy only. When developing CVT, Andersen focused on combining elements from past theories to create an explanation for nonverbal adaptation that includes both physiological and cognitive variables. Arousal plays a key role in the theory, with high or low levels of arousal change theorized to lead to automatic responses. Moderate levels of arousal change are theorized to produce more complicated responses, with people quickly assessing the situation to determine whether they regard the increase in immediacy favorably or unfavorably. Six cognitive valencers are posited as the mechanisms by which this determination occurs: cultural appropriateness, personal predispositions, interpersonal valence, relational appropriateness, situational appropriateness, and psychological or physical states.

Before any of these cognitive valencers are activated, however, Andersen (1995, 1998) specifies that the increase in nonverbal immediacy must be perceived by the receiver, and the arousal change must be moderate. If the increase in immediacy goes unnoticed, if there is no arousal change, or if the arousal change is low, Andersen predicts that there will be no behavioral reaction to the increase in immediacy; rather, receivers will continue interacting in their typical fashion. If arousal change is high, CVT (like DAT) specifies that negative emotion and compensation will follow. In essence, Andersen predicts that people engage in a flight-or-fight response to situations that elicit high levels of arousal and accompanying negative emotions such as fear, discomfort, or panic. It is only under situations of moderate arousal change, which Andersen believes to be most common, that receivers evaluate the increase in immediacy on the basis of the six aforementioned cognitive valencers.

According to CVT, all six of the cognitive valencers must be evaluated positively for reciprocity and positive relational outcomes (such as increased closeness) to occur (Andersen, 1992, 1998). Culture is a major determinant of how people interpret and react to increased immediacy. For example, in some cultures, it is appropriate and even expected for strangers to kiss one another's faces when they meet; in other cultures, these actions are inappropriate. Personal predispositions of the receiver refer to traits such as gender, age, and socioeconomic status, as well as personality variables such as extraversion, shyness, and level of social skill. Interpersonal valence refers to the personal aspects of the sender, such as how attractive, powerful, and friendly a sender is perceived to be. Interpersonal valence is similar to the concept of reward value in EVT. The relationship also plays a critical role. The stage, type, and characteristics of relationships determine how appropriate and desired increased levels of nonverbal immediacy are. Situational variables include where (e.g., public vs. private; work vs. home) and when (e.g., at the beginning vs. end of a date) the interaction occurs. Finally, psychological and physical states include temporary conditions such as being in a good mood, having a headache, or feeling nervous. Andersen (1998) believes that

these six cognitive valencers are constantly in place, helping receivers quickly make sense of increases in immediacy without having to exert much cognitive effort. In other words, people do not have to think about the valencers; instead, they are used so routinely that they become automatic.

So far, few studies have formally tested CVT. Andersen et al. (1998) examined CVT within the context of cross-sex friendships. As both CVT and DAT predict, participants experienced higher levels of negative arousal and displayed more defensiveness in response to greater changes in immediacy. Like the EVT experiments, results also showed a mix of reciprocity and compensation. As CVT predicts, friends compensated for especially high levels of nonverbal immediacy by engaging in blocking and distancing behaviors, patterns suggestive of a flight response. However, they also reciprocated by engaging in behaviors showing positive affect, such that the moderate-immediacy condition did not differ from the high-immediacy condition on positivity. Similarly, degree of arousal experienced (as measured by physiological indices, such as heart rate) was not related to variability in behavioral responses to immediacy. Instead, participants tended to respond to moderate changes in nonverbal immediacy with reciprocity, as would be predicted by DAT.

Other studies focusing on how specific cognitive valencers are associated with responses to changes in immediacy have found relational appropriateness to be an important cognitive valencer for determining whether increases in immediacy are wanted or unwanted (Andersen, 1992), as well as if such increases are perceived as sexually harassing (Wertin & Andersen, 1996). Guerrero and Johnson (2009) also found that people believe that they would respond more positively if they regarded the sender as highly attractive and if the situation was informal (a party) rather than formal (a job interview fair). Contrary to CVT, there were times when one or two of the cognitive valencers were evaluated negatively, but participants still thought they would generally react positively both emotionally and behaviorally (Guerrero & Johnson, 2008). This was especially true if the sender was evaluated as highly attractive, which comports with EVT's prediction that the reward value of a communicator is an important determinant of how people ultimately respond to unexpected nonverbal behavior.

## INTERACTION ADAPTATION THEORY

IAT (Burgoon, Dillman, & Stern, 1993) is the most recent communication theory of nonverbal adaptation. Intended to provide a broader explanation of nonverbal adaptation than EVT while still retaining parsimony, IAT examines how three elements influence patterns of reciprocity and compensation: requirements (R), expectations (E), and desires (D). The R element refers primarily to biological and emotional factors, such as hunger, mood, or anxiety, which can constrain communicators and interfere with the interaction (Miczo, Miczo, & Burgoon, 2008). The E element refers "to what is anticipated, based on social norms, social prescriptions, or individuated knowledge of the other's behavior, and includes the general communication functions or goals operative in the situation" (Burgoon, Stern, et al., 1995, p. 265). Finally, the D element includes personal preferences and goals that represent what we want in a given interaction.

According to IAT, the RED elements combine to form an *interaction position,* which is then compared with the actual behavior enacted by one's conversational partner (Burgoon, Allspach, & Miczo, 1997; Burgoon et al., 1993; Burgoon, Stern, et al., 1995). Nonverbal adaptation is then determined by the match between a person's interactional position and the partner's actual behavior. When the partner's

actual behavior matches or exceeds what a receiver initially required, expected, or desired, the receiver is theorized to reciprocate. In contrast, when the partner's behavior falls below the interactional position, the receiver is theorized to compensate.

Although IAT is comparatively new, several studies have already tested some of its predictions. Burgoon, Stern, et al. (1995) reported results from four dyadic interaction experiments. An interview experiment in which confederate interviewees greatly increased or decreased involvement after a baseline period showed weak reciprocity and matching effects when correlational analyses were used but stronger evidence of adaptation when time-series analyses (which are most appropriate for identifying temporal adjustments) were used. Adaptation was more prevalent when the confederate decreased involvement and when kinesic and proxemic behaviors were measured. When vocal adaptation occurred, it more often took the form of matching than of complementarity, consistent with both CAT and IAT predictions. An interesting nonlinear pattern occurred in which interviewer changes in involvement closely mirrored those of confederate interviewees, suggesting that interviewers figuratively "put on the brakes" to prevent the interaction from escalating too rapidly.

A second study, originally designed to test EVT and reported in Burgoon, Le Poire, and Rosenthal (1995), conducted a similar multimodal, multimethod analysis of partner responses to a confederate's actual and expected increases or decreases in pleasantness and involvement. Correlational analyses again showed partners largely reciprocating confederate behavior in both the "increase" and "decrease" conditions except for a complementary response on general involvement in the "decrease" condition. Temporal analyses likewise showed primarily reciprocity and matching, especially when the confederate increased pleasantness/involvement, but a mix of patterns when the confederate decreased pleasantness/involvement. Across the two investigations, virtually all measures were implicated in adaptation processes in one or more analyses.

Two additional deception experiments found strong evidence of reciprocity but also instances of compensation across a variety of behaviors and channels. Burgoon, Stern, et al. (1995) concluded,

> Compensation may be more common when interactions depart from "normalcy"—that is, when factors such as suspicion, deception, and differential knowledge and experience with the task are introduced. One reason these elements may evoke compensation is that they create interaction patterns that are outside the desired or expected range, causing interactants to engage in behaviors designed to model desired responses or to "pull" the interaction back to a more typical pattern. (pp. 246–247)

Guerrero and Burgoon (1996) used IAT to predict patterns of nonverbal adaptation based on a receiver's attachment style. Of particular interest to IAT were the preoccupied and dismissive attachment styles. Preoccupied individuals desire excessive amounts of intimacy and have unrealistic expectations regarding how much intimacy their partner will display. Dismissive individuals, on the other hand, desire relatively low amounts of intimacy. Thus, according to IAT, preoccupied individuals should reciprocate increased nonverbal immediacy and compensate for decreased nonverbal immediacy. Dismissive individuals should follow the opposite pattern (i.e., compensate increases in immediacy and reciprocate decreased immediacy). To test this conjecture, undergraduate students with varying attachment styles were asked to bring their romantic partner with them to participate in an experiment. Their partners were then told to either surreptitiously increase or decrease their level of nonverbal immediacy during the second of two interactions. Consistent with IAT's predictions, individuals with a preoccupied attachment style tended to compensate for decreased nonverbal

immediacy, but dismissive individuals tended to reciprocate decreased nonverbal immediacy. Both preoccupied and dismissive individuals reciprocated increased nonverbal immediacy, although preoccupieds did so to a greater extent than dismissives.

Another experiment (Burgoon et al., 1998) examined how interactants in same- versus mixed-culture conversations adapted to changes in one another's level of responsiveness and engagement. During a baseline period, interactants showed weak but increasingly reciprocal interaction patterns in both same- and mixed-culture dyads. Subsequently, when one partner was enlisted to change his or her level of responsivity, partner reciprocity became even more pronounced, with those in the high-responsivity condition increasing involvement and those in the low-responsivity condition decreasing it. Mixed-culture participants were slower to converge toward unresponsiveness than were same-culture participants; that is, they did more to offset an undesirable communication pattern. The IAT-predicted role of interaction desires was also investigated. Those who placed more importance on creating a supportive relational climate showed more approach behaviors; those with more concerns for managing arousal showed more avoidance. Thus, this investigation supported several IAT predictions.

Yet another study examined what happens when the D and E elements of the theory are consistent versus inconsistent (Floyd & Burgoon, 1999). Naive participants were paired with trained confederates for a "get acquainted" task. Prior to the task, participants were primed to expect that their confederate partners either would or would not like them. They were also induced to want to make the confederate either like or dislike them during the task. These conditions (expect to be liked or disliked and desire to be liked or disliked) were crossed with the confederates' behavior during the task. Half of the time, confederates behaved as though they liked the participants (by engaging in high-immediacy behaviors); the other half of the time, they behaved as though they disliked the participants (by engaging in low-immediacy behaviors). The principal outcome variable was the extent to which participants matched or compensated for the confederates' nonverbal behaviors. On the basis of IAT, Floyd and Burgoon (1999) predicted that participants would behaviorally match confederates when they expected, wanted, and received liking behavior and also when they expected, wanted, and received disliking behavior. These behavioral patterns were obtained in the study. When participants had incongruent desires and expectations, however, Floyd and Burgoon found that desires were more potent. That is, participants matched the behaviors they desired and compensated for the behaviors they did not desire, irrespective of their expectations. At least in this case, therefore, it appears that the D element was a stronger predictor of behavioral adaptation than the E element.

More recent experiments in progress are examining the adaptation patterns when interactants are truthful or deceptive. Based on findings from White and Burgoon (2001), among others, predictions are that accommodation will be more difficult when senders are preoccupied with producing deceptive messages but that they will attempt to compensate for signs of skepticism from receivers by becoming more involved and pleasant so as to boost their credibility.

## ◆ Controversies, Unresolved Issues, and Future Directions

### THE ROLE OF AROUSAL CHANGE

There are several unresolved issues regarding the role that arousal change plays in determining nonverbal adaptation. This issue is especially prominent in DAT, CVT, and EVT. First, according to DAT and CVT, especially high levels of arousal change are automatically connected to negative emotion and flight-or-fight responses, leading people to compensate when increased immediacy results in high levels of arousal change. Conversely, rather than predicting an automatic association between high arousal change and aversive affective reactions, EVT specifies that high levels of arousal change can be evaluated positively or negatively based on the valence of the violation and the reward value of the communicator, both of which depend on characteristics of the communicator, context, and interpersonal relationship. Further research is needed to clarify the association between arousal change and patterns of nonverbal adaptation so that scholars better understand if and when arousal change becomes so great that it is automatically associated with negative reactions. One reason that this question remains controversial is that it is difficult to falsify the claim that extremely high levels of arousal are associated with flight-or-fight responses because scholars can always say that they did not induce enough arousal change to produce this result. Thus, scholars studying CVT and DAT need to set a priori thresholds for what constitutes high levels of arousal change, perhaps based on clinical literature or physiological measures of changes from a baseline.

A second arousal-related issue deals with whether both arousal change and affective responses are needed in an explanatory calculus for predicting patterns of nonverbal adaptation. As reported earlier, Le Poire and Burgoon (1994) found that level of involvement change was related to affective responses but not arousal per se. Thus, theories of nonverbal adaptation might be just as predictive, but more parsimonious, if they examined emotional reactions rather than both arousal and affect. Emotion may also play a more central role in CAT, CVT, and IAT than is currently thought. Indeed, in IAT, the emotional responses that occur when the interpersonal position and the actual behavior are discrepant may be the driving force in determining whether a person reciprocates or compensates.

A third issue related to arousal and affect is one of operationalizations. The more prominently arousal and emotion figure into these models, the more the issue of how best to measure them becomes salient as well. Ideally, arousal and emotional states should be measured rather than inferred. But the wide array of possible measures raises the question of which ones and how many should be used. Clear specification of which types of arousal are implicated is essential to addressing this issue. The deployment of multiple measures relates in turn to the next issue.

## MIXED MULTIMODAL RESPONSES

Empirical findings suggest that people sometimes engage in a mix of reciprocal and compensatory responses when they encounter a change in their partner's nonverbal communication. The several investigations reported in Burgoon, Stern, et al. (1995) revealed mixed rather than consistent results across the multiple cues and codes measured. Other investigations have likewise found a mix of reciprocity and compensation simultaneously or serially within the same condition, with concomitant challenges to interpretation. For example, in response to very high increases in nonverbal immediacy by a cross-sex friend, Andersen et al. (1998) found that people reciprocated with positive affect cues but compensated by using some distancing and blocking behaviors. Similarly, Guerrero et al. (2000) found that people responded to decreased nonverbal immediacy by a romantic partner by compensating verbally (e.g., asking questions such "What is wrong?" and "Is everything okay?") while reciprocating nonverbally (e.g., showing

less positive affect and expressiveness). None of the theories discussed in this chapter, however, does a good job of explaining when and why such a mixed reaction might occur.

There are, however, possibilities for explaining mixed responses within each of the theories. In CAT, a mixed pattern of convergence and divergence might occur when some of the factors predicting accommodation are contradictory. For instance, it is possible to dislike a person who has high status. In EVT, situations that involve contradictions between violation valence and communicator reward value may lead to such mixed responses, as seems to be the case for rewarding communicators who engage in negative behaviors. When evaluating DAT, Guerrero, Alberts, and Heisterkamp (2001) argued that behaviors falling well within the acceptance region may be most likely to elicit approach responses, whereas behaviors falling outside the acceptance region appear most likely to elicit avoidant responses. However, responses on the fringe—near but not outside the edge of the acceptance region— "may produce more ambivalent, mixed responses" (p. 70). The same logic can be applied to both CVT and IAT. When the cognitive valencers in CVT or the RED factors in IAT are mixed, the behavioral response might also be mixed.

## WITHIN-DYADS VERSUS BETWEEN-DYADS APPROACHES

Mixed patterns may also result depending on whether one takes a between-dyads or within-dyads approach. Most interaction adaptation models are based on the tacit assumption that one and only one pattern characterizes an interaction at a given point in time. Complementarity, compensation, and divergence are viewed as opposites of matching, reciprocity, and convergence. This makes it logically impossible for similar and dissimilar interaction patterns to occur simultaneously. However, this unitary perspective is overly simplistic and invalid. It results from failing to take into account both how different dyads behave at a given point in time and how the same dyads behave over time and from viewing adaptation as an on/off binary state rather than a matter of degree.

As Burgoon et al. (1998) noted,

> Theoretically, complementarity, compensation, and divergence may be coextensive with matching, reciprocity, and convergence. First, mean levels of a given behavior may show one pattern, while changes over time may show a different one. For example, a person interacting with a highly disinterested other may complement that pattern by showing a fairly high degree of engagement on average and yet over time, drift toward lower involvement in accord with the other person's pattern. . . . Second, interaction patterns in reality may not be "present" or "absent" but rather may be manifest to different degrees in each interaction. That is, rather than reflecting dichotomies, the various patterns can be conceptualized as continua so that manifestations of them appear in varying degrees of two "opposing" forms. On this view, it is possible to show an abbreviated pattern that only partially resembles that of the interaction partner, a pattern that could be described, say, as either partial matching or partial complementarity. (p. 200)

Emerging theorizing about coordination dynamics takes the argument further in proposing that coordination between organisms is a dynamic and nonlinear process that does not fit neat oppositional dichotomies. Instead, mind and body are viewed as nonstatic and self-organizing such that they follow increasingly complex—or simple—but ever-shifting and complementary patterns that can range from the extremes of reciprocal or compensatory behavior to all states in between (Kelso, 1995; Kelso & Engstrom, 2006). These newer perspectives on dynamical systems challenge not only some of the premises and principles of interaction adaptation patterns but also

theories of psychology and interpersonal communication more generally, while at the same time perhaps supplying some of the missing links that increase the viability of the theories discussed herein.

## ◆ Conclusion

The processes whereby people adapt their communication to one another are among the most fundamental for understanding how humans develop and maintain social relationships. Theories of how this adaptation is accomplished provide insight into broader issues of what it means to communicate and what factors govern the communication processes and outcomes. The five theories reviewed here offer complementary perspectives on the relative importance of physiological, cognitive, and social variables in the advertent and inadvertent achievement of coordinated interaction. If there is one common conclusion to be drawn, it is that there appears to be an overriding predisposition toward interactional reciprocity and similarity that often swamps other "local" forms of adjustment. That is, the empirical default "main effect" pattern for most interactions is one of matching, reciprocity, and coordination. Why this is so depends on the theory upon which one draws and may have evolutionary as well as social organizational significance. Compensatory or maintenance patterns tend to be more transitory and related either to alleviating undesirable conditions such as negative arousal and emotional states or to asserting social distance. That is, consistent with the principle found in many of the models, communicators may unconsciously adjust their interaction style to restore a more comfortable level of involvement, may alter their style deliberately to create a more desirable dyadic interaction pattern, or both. Ultimately, the theory or theories that will persist are those that best account for how deviations from these default patterns are managed.

## ◆ References

Andersen, P. A. (1985). Nonverbal immediacy in interpersonal communication. In A. W. Siegman & S. Feldstein (Eds.), *Mulitchannel integrations of nonverbal behavior* (pp. 1–36). Hillsdale, NJ: Lawrence Erlbaum.

Andersen, P. A. (1992, July). *Excessive intimacy: An account analysis of behaviors, cognitive schemata, affect, and relational outcomes.* Paper presented at the International Conference on Personal Relationships, Orono, ME.

Andersen, P. A. (1998). The cognitive valence theory of intimate communication. In M. Palmer & G. A. Barnett (Eds.), *Progress in communication sciences: Vol. 14. Mutual influence in interpersonal communication theory and research in cognition, affect, and behavior* (pp. 39–72). Norwood, NJ: Ablex.

Andersen, P. A., Guerrero, L. K., Buller, D. B., & Jorgensen, P. F. (1998). An empirical comparison of three theories of nonverbal immediacy exchange. *Human Communication Research, 24,* 501–535.

Argyle, M., & Dean, J. (1965). Eye-contact, distance and affiliation. *Sociometry, 28,* 289–304.

Baker, M. A. (1991). Reciprocal accommodation: A model for reducing gender bias in managerial communication. *Journal of Business Communication, 28,* 113–130.

Bavelas, J. B., Black, A., Chovil, N., Lemery, C. R., & Mullett, J. (1988). Form and function in motor mimicry: Topographic evidence that the primary function is communicative. *Human Communication Research, 14,* 275–300.

Boggs, C., & Giles, H. (1999). "The canary in the cage": The nonaccommodation cycle in the gendered workplace. *International Journal of Applied Linguistics, 22,* 223–245.

Bourhis, R. Y. (1991). Organization communication and accommodation: Toward some conceptual and empirical links. In H. Giles, J. Coupland, & N. Coupland (Eds.), *Contexts of accommodation: Developments in applied sociolinguistics* (pp. 270–304). Cambridge, UK: Cambridge University Press.

Bourhis, R. Y., & Giles, H. (1977). The language of intergroup distinctiveness. In H. Giles (Ed.), *Language, ethnicity and intergroup relations* (pp. 119–135). London: Academic Press.

Buller, D. B., & Aune, R. K. (1988). The effects of vocalics and nonverbal sensitivity on compliance: A speech accommodation theory explanation. *Human Communication Research, 14,* 301–332.

Buller, D. B., & Aune, R. K. (1992). The effects of speech rate similarity on compliance: Application of communication accommodation theory. *Western Journal of Communication, 56,* 37–53.

Burgoon, J. K. (1978). A communication model of personal space violations: Explication and an initial test. *Human Communication Research, 4,* 129–142.

Burgoon, J. K., Allspach, L. E., & Miczo, N. (1997, February). *Needs, expectancies, goals and initial interaction: A view from interaction adaptation theory.* Paper presented to the Western States Communication Association, Monterey, CA.

Burgoon, J. K., & Bacue, A. (2003). Nonverbal communication skills. In B. R. Burleson & J. O. Greene (Eds.), *Handbook of communication and social interaction skills* (pp. 179–219). Mahwah, NJ: Lawrence Erlbaum.

Burgoon, J. K., Dillman, L., & Stern, L. A. (1993). Adaptation in dyadic interaction: Defining and operationalizing patterns of reciprocity and compensation. *Communication Theory, 4,* 293–316.

Burgoon, J. K., Ebesu, A., White, C., Koch, P., Alvaro, E., & Kikuchi, T. (1998). The many faces of interaction adaptation. In M. T. Palmer & G. A. Barnett (Eds.), *Progress in communication sciences* (Vol. 14, pp. 191–220). Stamford, CT: Ablex.

Burgoon, J. K., & Hale, J. L. (1988). Nonverbal expectancy violations: Model elaboration and application to immediacy behaviors. *Communication Monographs, 55,* 58–79.

Burgoon, J. K., & Hoobler, G. (2002). Nonverbal signals. In M. L. Knapp & J. Daly (Eds.), *Handbook of interpersonal communication* (pp. 240–299). Thousand Oaks, CA: Sage.

Burgoon, J. K., Le Poire, B. A., & Rosenthal, R. (1995). Effects of preinteraction expectancies and target communication on perceiver reciprocity and compensation in dyadic interaction. *Journal of Experimental Social Psychology, 31*, 287–321.

Burgoon, J. K., Olney, C. A., & Coker, R. A. (1987). The effects of communicator characteristics on patterns of reciprocity and compensation. *Journal of Nonverbal Behavior, 11*, 146–165.

Burgoon, J. K., Stern, L. A., & Dillman, L. (1995). *Interpersonal adaptation: Dyadic interaction patterns.* New York: Cambridge University Press.

Cappella, J. N., & Greene, J. O. (1982). A discrepancy-arousal explanation of mutual influence in expressive behavior for adult and infant-adult interaction. *Communication Monographs, 49*, 89–114.

Cappella, J. N., & Greene, J. O. (1984). The effects of distance and individual differences in arousability on nonverbal involvement: A test of discrepancy-arousal theory. *Journal of Nonverbal Behavior, 8*, 259–286.

Coker, D. A., & Burgoon, J. K. (1987). The nature of conversational involvement and nonverbal encoding patterns. *Human Communication Research, 13*, 463–494.

Floyd, K., & Burgoon, J. K. (1999). Reacting to nonverbal expressions of liking: A test of interaction adaptation theory. *Communication Monographs, 66*, 219–239.

Floyd, K., Ramirez, A., & Burgoon, J. K. (2008). Expectancy violations theory. In L. K. Guerrero & M. L. Hecht (Eds.), *The nonverbal communication reader* (3rd ed., pp. 503–510). Prospect Heights, IL: Waveland.

Gallois, C., Giles, H., Jones, E., Cargile, A. C., & Ota, H. (1995). Accommodating intercultural encounters: Elaborations and extensions. In R. Wiseman (Ed.), *Intercultural communication theory* (pp. 115–147). Thousand Oaks, CA: Sage.

Giles, H. (1973). Accent mobility: A model and some data. *Anthropological Linguistics, 15*, 87–109.

Giles, H., Fox, S., & Smith, E. (1993). Patronizing the elderly: Intergenerational evaluations. *Research in Language and Social Interaction, 26*, 129–149.

Giles, H., Mulac, A., Bradac, J. J., & Johnson, P. (1987). Speech communication theory: The next decade and beyond. In M. McLaughlin (Ed.), *Communication yearbook 10* (pp. 13–48). Newbury Park, CA: Sage.

Giles, H., & Wadleigh, P. M. (2008). Accommodating nonverbally. In L. K. Guerrero, J. A. De Vito, & M. L. Hecht (Eds.), *The nonverbal communication reader* (3rd ed., pp. 491–502). Prospect Heights, IL: Waveland.

Giles, H., Willemyns, M., Gallois, C., & Anderson, M. C. (2007). Accommodating a new frontier: The context of law enforcement. In K. Fiedler (Ed.), *Social communication* (pp. 129–162). New York: Psychology Press.

Gouldner, A. W. (1960). The norm of reciprocity: A preliminary statement. *American Sociological Review, 25*, 161–178.

Gregory, S. W., Dagan, K., & Webster, S. (1997). Evaluating the relation of vocal accommodation in conversation partners' fundamental frequencies to perceptions of communication quality. *Journal of Nonverbal Behavior, 21*, 23–43.

Guerrero, L. K., Alberts, J. K., & Heisterkamp, B. (2001). Discrepancy arousal theory and cognitive valence theory. In W. P. Robinson & H. Giles (Eds.), *The new handbook of language and social psychology* (pp. 57–77). Chichester, UK: Wiley.

Guerrero, L. K., & Burgoon, J. K. (1996). Attachment styles and reactions to nonverbal involvement change in romantic dyads: Patterns of reciprocity and compensation. *Human Communication Research, 22*, 335–370.

Guerrero, L. K., & Johnson, S. L. (2009). *A test of cognitive valence theory.* Manuscript in preparation.

Guerrero, L. K., Jones, S. M., & Burgoon, J. K. (2000). Responses to nonverbal intimacy change in romantic dyads: Effects of behavioral valence and degree of behavioral change on nonverbal and verbal reactions. *Communication Monographs, 67*, 325–346.

Hale, J. L., & Burgoon, J. K. (1984). Models of reactions to changes in nonverbal immediacy. *Journal of Nonverbal Behavior, 8*, 287–314.

Kelso, J. A. S. (1995). *Dynamic patterns: The self-organization of brain and behavior.* Cambridge: MIT Press.

Kelso, J. A. S., & Engstrom, D. (2006). *The complementary nature.* Cambridge, MA: MIT/Bradford Press.

Le Poire, B. A., & Burgoon, J. K. (1994). Two contrasting explanations of involvement violations: Expectancy violations theory versus discrepancy arousal theory. *Human Communication Research, 20*, 560–591.

Manusov, V., & Patterson, M. L. (Eds.). (2006). *Handbook of nonverbal communication.* Thousand Oaks, CA: Sage.

Miczo, N., Miczo, L. E., & Burgoon, J. K. (2008). Converging on the phenomenon of interpersonal adaptation: Interaction adaptation theory. In L. K. Guerrero & M. L. Hecht (Eds.), *The nonverbal communication reader* (3rd ed., pp. 521–530). Prospect Heights, IL: Waveland.

Mulac, A., Studley, L. B., Wiemann, J. W., & Bradac, J. J. (1987). Male-female gaze in same-sex and mixed-sex dyads: Gender-linked differences and mutual influence. *Human Communication Research, 13,* 323–344.

Patterson, M. L. (1973). Compensation in nonverbal immediacy behaviors: A review. *Sociometry, 36,* 237–252.

Patterson, M. L. (1983). *Nonverbal behavior: A functional perspective.* New York: Springer-Verlag.

Prager, K. J., & Roberts, L. J. (2004). Deep intimate connection: Self and intimacy in couple relationships. In D. J. Mashek & A. P. Aron (Eds.), *Handbook of closeness and intimacy* (pp. 43–60). Mahwah, NJ: Lawrence Erlbaum.

Shepard, C. A., Giles, H., & Le Poire, B. A. (2001). Communication accommodation theory. In W. P. Robinson & H. Giles (Eds.), *The new handbook of language and social psychology* (pp. 33–56). Chichester, UK: Wiley.

Stern, D. N. (1974). Mother and infant at play: The dyadic interaction involving facial, vocal, and gaze behavior. In M. Lewis & L. A. Rosenblum (Eds.), *The effect of the infant on its caregiver* (pp. 187–213). New York: John Wiley.

Street, R. L., Jr. (1984). Speech convergence and speech evaluation in fact-finding interviews. *Human Communication Research, 11,* 139–169.

Thakerar, J., Giles, H., & Cheshire, J. (1982). Psychological and linguistic parameters of speech accommodation theory. In C. Fraser & K. R. Scherer (Eds.), *Advances in the social psychology of language* (pp. 205–255). Cambridge, UK: Cambridge University Press.

Wertin, L., & Andersen, P. A. (1996, February). *Cognitive schemata and perceptions of sexual harassment.* Paper presented at the annual meeting of the Western States Communication Association, Pasadena, CA.

White, C. H., & Burgoon, J. K. (2001). Adaptation and communicative design: Patterns of interaction in truthful and deceptive conversations. *Human Communication Research, 27,* 9–37.

Willemyns, M., Gallois, C., Callan, V. J., & Pittam, J. (1997). Accent accommodation in the job interview: Impact of interviewer accent and gender. *Journal of Language and Social Psychology, 16,* 3–22.

# PART 3

# FUNDAMENTAL
# PROCESSES

# 7

# MESSAGE PRODUCTION PROCESSES

◆ Charles R. Berger

Message production is fundamental to communication whether the message being produced is verbal, nonverbal, or both and regardless of the particular context within which communication takes place. Communicators must transmute their thinking into speech, writing, or some nonverbal medium of expression. This is the case whether the communication situation is mediated or unmediated, whether the audiences for messages are physically present or available only through mediation, or whether audiences are imagined, as when individuals create messages for mass audiences or imagine social interactions with others. As this chapter will demonstrate, the processes that enable the encoding of conceptual representations of messages into such expressive media as speech, writing, and action can be studied and understood at several different levels of analysis; moreover, as will become apparent, some researchers opt to focus primarily on understanding the fundamental processes that enable message producers to achieve efficient and almost error-free performances when they speak or write, with little regard for the effectiveness of those performances with respect to audiences. By contrast, others concern themselves with the pragmatic effects of these performances rather than the fundamental mechanisms that enable the performances themselves.

The chapter will begin by providing an overview of language production models, most of which attempt to describe the processes by

◆ 111

which communicators transmute thought into speech. In the next section, these individually oriented speech production models will be augmented by accounts of how individuals are able to achieve communication efficiencies by establishing common ground and shared knowledge in their social commerce with others. Finally, the goal-directed nature of message production and the "effects" perspective it implies will be examined. This latter perspective has animated most of the communication research conducted since the appearance of the discipline, but at the same time, it has remained relatively isolated from the literatures considered in the chapter's first two sections. The potential advantages of merging some aspects of these research domains will be adumbrated at the chapter's close.

## ◆ Language Production Models

Although the great bulk of theory and research seeking to illuminate how individuals process language has been concerned with the structures and processes that subserve the comprehension and interpretation of text and discourse (see Roskos-Ewoldsen & Roskos-Ewoldsen, Chapter 8, this volume), psycholinguists and cognitive psychologists have shown increased interest in the language production domain, with most of this effort focused on speech production (Bock & Griffin, 2000). The commonplace assumption that speaking is simply the reverse of listening is belied by the fact that it may take up to five times longer for speakers to generate words in their native languages than to recognize the same words when presented with them (Griffin & Ferreira, 2006). Intention is a prerequisite for speaking and writing, while word recognition is frequently automatic when listening or reading. Although this differential in retrieval time between word recognition and word production may be due to different lexical retrieval processes, it is also possible that message production entails choosing among more alternatives than does message comprehension. This differential is observed in the early stages of language acquisition; children can comprehend and conceptualize quantitatively more than they can say.

Typically, normal adults produce speech at the rate of 120 to 180 words per minute (Maclay & Osgood, 1959), and speech is accomplished with minimal error. Even though adult speakers know tens of thousands of words (Oldfield, 1963), lexical selection errors are extremely rare in normal speech. Error estimates range from 0.25 (Deese, 1984) through 0.41 (Garnham, Shillcock, Brown, Mill, & Cutler, 1982) to 2.3 (Shallice & Butterworth, 1977) per 1,000 words uttered. Even when speakers accelerate their speech rate to 420 words per minute, their speech remains relatively error free (Deese, 1984). Slips of the tongue are so rare in everyday discourse that methods have been developed to elicit them in the laboratory (Motley, Baars, & Camden, 1983). Thus, despite the fact that lexical retrieval in the service of speech production characteristically takes longer than word recognition, speech production is a highly developed skill among adults.

A number of speech production models have been proposed that differ with respect to details (e.g., Bock & Levelt, 1994; Levelt, 1989; Levelt, Roelofs, & Meyer, 1999; MacKay, 1987); however, in general terms, most models posit similar steps through which speech producers must pass in order to realize their intentions in articulation (Ferreira & Englehardt, 2006; Griffin & Ferreira, 2006). Much of the evidence for these production steps or stages has been adduced from analyses of speech production errors such as slips of the tongue, tip of the tongue phenomena, speech onset latencies and pauses, studies of speech-related pathologies, and, more recently, brain imaging studies.

Language production models typically begin with conceptualization, a process during which messages are composed of abstract semantic propositions and pragmatic features or lexical concepts. This initial stage is generally postulated to be prelinguistic and is conceived of as the interface between thought and language. In the next step, or formulation stage, which involves lexical selection and grammatical encoding, the abstract propositions and concepts of the conceptualization stage are represented as lemmas or lexical entries selected to represent the abstract message. At this stage, lemmas are assigned a functional role in the projected utterance, but they must subsequently be processed and assigned a positional order. Once this positional order is determined, phonological encoding occurs, which, in turn, leads to articulation. Among a number of controversies with respect to these models are such issues as the number of steps involved in grammatical encoding (one vs. two) and the degree to which the outputs of these stages feed back and constrain one another (Ferreira & Englehardt, 2006). However, all of these models begin with a conceptual message, which is ultimately realized in phonological encoding, which, in turn, leads to articulation.

Some have observed that the nature of the initial conceptualization stage has generally been underspecified in these language production models (Horton & Gerrig, 2005). However, some attempts have been made to explicate the nature of the conceptualization stage and its relationships to subsequent lexical and grammatical encodings of the conceptual inputs during formulation processes (Smith, 2000). Two general approaches have been used to characterize the relationship between the conceptualization and formulation stages. The rationalist approach postulates a one-to-one relationship between grammatical encoding of language and the structure of the conceptual system; that is, grammatical encoding represents the structure of the conceptual system. By contrast, on the empiricist view, there is no such isomorphism between the

two systems, and the conceptual system is not linguistic. Consistent with this latter perspective, rather than viewing the conceptual message as consisting of abstract semantic propositions, Smith (2000) suggests that "clausal-like" units that include information about time, space, and viewpoint represent analogically based world knowledge and that lexical and grammatical encoding digitizes this conceptual output in the formulation stage. Thus, the same concept may be rendered similarly by multiple lexical and grammatical formulations, and a given lexical item may represent a multiplicity of concepts. This latter possibility is illustrated by the Korean word *bae* (배), which can refer to a (a) surname, (b) boat, (c) pear, or (d) stomach but be perfectly understandable in the following sentence: "While Mr. Bae was riding in a boat he ate a pear and his stomach began to ache" "배씨는 배를타면서 배를 먹어 배가 아프게 됐다."

Given the differing natures of the conceptualization and formulation stages, conceptual messages are almost never fully realized in the output of the formulation processes. That is, there is almost always some slippage of meaning between the conceptual message, on one hand, and the way it is lexicalized and grammatically formulated, on the other hand. Indeed, in order to avoid the aforementioned processing costs associated with lexical retrieval and grammatical formulation, language producers do not fully specify conceptual messages at the formulation stage; rather, they specify them only to a level sufficient to ensure comprehensibility, thus shifting some of the processing burden to those who receive their messages. Thus, in requesting the salt at the dinner table, uttering only the noun *salt* may be sufficient to achieve the desired result. In addition to underspecifying conceptual messages, another way to minimize language production costs is to employ preformulated utterances. Estimates are that up to 70% of utterances are formulaic (Altenberg, 1990), suggesting that language producers routinely reduce formulation costs by using preformulated utterances (Smith, 2000; Wray & Perkins, 2000).

Although, for the sake of reducing production costs, speakers generally do not completely specify conceptual representations of messages in the formulation stage, there may be occasions when speakers provide too much specification, as when they continue to add details to an explanation even when addressees have already fully apprehended their intended meaning. Such aphorisms as "beating a dead horse" reflect this kind of addressee-based frustration and may lead to reductions in the addressee's attention to the speaker. Moreover, speakers' overspecification may induce addressees to judge speakers to be patronizing. Conversely, speakers may underspecify conceptual representations to the point that addressees have difficulty understanding what it is they are talking about, again creating frustration and the possibility of reduced attention to the speaker. These possibilities imply that the fundamental cognitive processes enabling the transmutation of thought into language have potentially important pragmatic consequences in everyday communication contexts.

◆  *Common Ground: Language Production in Social Contexts*

Although the production of speech and writing that are comprehensible is generally a prerequisite for communicative effectiveness under many conditions, as suggested previously, it is far from the entire story. It is possible to envision circumstances in which individuals might generate, either intentionally or unintentionally, incomprehensible or nonfluent speech, writing, and action for the sake of achieving certain goals. Or, on the other side of the coin, individuals might produce highly fluent and comprehensible speech but do so in a relatively socially inappropriate way. For example, those afflicted with Williams syndrome, a rare genetic disorder that occurs in approximately 1 out of 20,000 births and involves a range of physical problems and some form of mental retardation, may be highly loquacious, friendly, and social; however, their conduct in social situations may seem somewhat out of place and awkward (Bellugi, Lichtenberger, Mills, Galaburda, & Korenberg, 1999). Thus, the capacity to generate fluent and comprehensible speech by itself does not, ipso facto, guarantee communicative success in social transactions.

When individuals generate messages in social interaction contexts, whether the contexts are face-to-face or technologically mediated, their ability to coordinate their discourse and actions and to communicate efficiently critically depends on the degree to which they share common ground (Schober & Brennan, 2003). Common ground consists of the totality of the presupposition individuals have concerning shared beliefs, assumptions, and knowledge (H. H. Clark, 1994; H. H. Clark & Carlson, 1982; H. H. Clark & Marshall, 1981; Lewis, 1969; Schiffer, 1972; Stalnaker, 1978). Common ground can arise from at least two sources. Communal common ground pertains to the beliefs, assumptions, and knowledge typical of the communities to which the interacting parties belong. Personal common ground is generated by inferences based on interacting parties' shared experience (H. H. Clark, 1994, 1996).

This difference between communal and personal common ground resembles G. R. Miller and Steinberg's (1975) distinction between social interactions predicated mostly on cultural- and sociological-level knowledge, on one hand, and those driven primarily by psychological-level or individual-specific knowledge, on the other hand. In their view, as individuals acquire more psychological-level knowledge about each other, their communication becomes more interpersonal and less impersonal because co-interlocutors are able to base their predictions about each other on individuating information. Lack of communal common ground in particular may make communication between members of different cultures less efficient and more effortful (see Kim, Chapter 26, this volume). As social actors interact through time, common ground accretes and current discourse and actions are interpreted within the updated common ground (H. H. Clark, 1994).

Initial interaction rituals are designed to facilitate the development of common ground. The first few minutes of conversations between American strangers are usually dominated by questions aimed at revealing each other's biographical and demographic attributes such as birthplace, where one grew up, current residence, education, occupation, and marital status (Berger, Gardner, Clatterbuck, & Schulman, 1976; Berger & Kellermann, 1983). This demographic information may be used as attributional grist for making proactive inferences about attitudes and opinions and other more personal information not yet revealed; moreover, the same demographic information may be employed retroactively, as causal inferences, to explain differences in preferences, attitudes, and behavior that become evident later in conversations (Berger, 1975). The degree to which co-interlocutors share mutual knowledge is readily apparent to those who observe their conversations. Not only does the content of conversations between friends show more evidence of mutual knowledge than does the content of strangers' conversations (Planalp, 1993), but observers of conversations can accurately differentiate between those of acquaintances and friends (Planalp & Benson, 1992). In the latter study, when observers were queried about how they were able to differentiate between acquaintances' and friends' conversations, they cited the amount of mutual knowledge shared by the co-interlocutors as the most important parameter.

During social interaction, common ground is essential for communication efficiency. When given a referential communication task in which the goal of a "director" is

to describe an array of abstract figures to a "matcher" such that the "matcher" arranges the figure array to duplicate the director's, over successive trials, directors use fewer words, and dyads take less time and fewer speaking turns to achieve correct solutions. These parameters are taken to be indicators of communication efficiency. During early trials, directors tend to make indirect references to the figures in the array, whereas on later trials, direct references to figures become more frequent (H. H. Clark & Wilkes-Gibbs, 1986; Isaacs & Clark, 1987; Krauss & Weinheimer, 1964, 1966; Schober & Clark, 1989; Wilkes-Gibbs & Clark, 1992). When individuals (side participants) were allowed to sit next to directors as they communicated with matchers and then assume the role of director, the observed decrement in their communication efficiency on their first trial as a director was significantly less than that of simple bystanders who merely listened to directors and matchers in the same room, omniscient bystanders who watched directors and matchers on a remote video hookup, or naive partners who worked on a completely different task in another room while the director and matcher interacted (Wilkes-Gibbs & Clark, 1992). Apparently, because of their observational viewpoint, the side participants were able to establish more common ground with matchers when they assumed the director role than were simple bystanders, omniscient bystanders, or naive partners.

Critical to establishing common ground and efficient communication is the ability to make at least somewhat accurate estimates of conversational partners' knowledge. Initiating a conversation topic about which a co-interlocutor has little knowledge may result in awkward silences and face loss, perhaps creating the need to divert conversational resources to face repair efforts. Although research suggests that individuals are fairly adept at estimating conversational partners' knowledge, these estimates tend to be biased toward the knowledge of those making the estimates (Fussell & Krauss,

1992; Krauss & Fussell, 1992). In addition to reasoning from their own memory, individuals generate inferences based on a small group of people's or others' likely behaviors to make estimates of their partners' knowledge. Moreover, even when additional information about partners is made available to them, individuals tend to rely on their prior beliefs about their partners' knowledge to fashion their messages.

Although the common-ground construct has prompted considerable research, as evidenced in the foregoing review, some have argued that its usefulness as an explanatory construct is somewhat limited in the language production domain (Horton & Gerrig, 2005). Viewing common ground as a fund of shared beliefs and knowledge provides little purchase for explicating the processes that enable language producers to move from conceptual representations of messages to formulation processes and then on to phonological encoding and articulation. In reformulating the common-ground construct within the language production context, Horton and Gerrig (2005) argue that when speakers design utterances for addressees, they must address two distinct issues: (a) the degree to which the addressee shares knowledge with the speaker and (b) how to construct utterances that take into account this shared knowledge. They refer to these processes as commonality assessment and message formulation, respectively, and argue that both processes involve ordinary memory processes acting on ordinary memory representations. Thus, they argue that the effects that have been heretofore attributed to the accretion of common ground can be explained by recourse to memory processes. Reconceptualizing common ground in this way holds the promise of integrating the phenomena it encompasses into language production models. Of course, commonality assessments may be faulty and thus give rise to incomprehensible utterances. For example, when a speaker refers to the first name of a person but the addressee either knows no

one by that first name or knows several different people with the same first name, the name reference is ambiguous. It is possible, of course, that the addressee could know the referred-to person only by a formal name.

As much as speakers may believe they know what addressees know, during the course of conversations, unexpected revelations and actions may confound co-interlocutors. One study revealed that unexpected negative revelations made when conversational partners shared similar impressions resulted in attempts to revise their impression through further interaction; however, during these impression revision attempts, participants manifested a tendency to seek information in such a way that it confirmed rather than disconfirmed the negative revelation (Ruscher & Hammer, 1994). Thus, attempts to update a knowledge base about another person in response to contradictory information may result in the acquisition of faulty information. Moreover, other studies have found that when addressees indicate that they have failed to understand speakers for reasons that have nothing to do with acoustical failure, speakers will frequently respond by repeating what they have just uttered but do so at a higher level of vocal intensity (Berger, 1997b; Berger & diBattista, 1993). This kind of speaker response to understanding failure suggests that when utterances fail to bring about desired results, speakers do not necessarily "redesign" utterances in ways that will overcome encountered difficulties. Default responses to communication failure, such as increasing vocal intensity or speaking more slowly, may substitute for more nuanced and functional message adjustments.

Although a fund of mutual knowledge may be available to co-interlocutors, thus increasing common ground and the efficiency with which they communicate, an overlooked issue with respect to knowledge, shared or otherwise, is the degree to which it is accessible to social actors. During conversations, individuals may experience memory failures such that they are aware that they know a particular item but are unable to recall it when needed. Memory failures such as these can occur both at the individual level and at the group level, when all conversational participants are unable to recall a specific word or referent. When people think back over just-completed conversations, it is not uncommon for them to remember things that they could have said but that they did not remember to say during the conversation. Thus, even when individuals have large amounts of knowledge germane to co-interlocutors and topics being discussed, the inability to retrieve this knowledge during conversations should act to reduce communication efficiency, as social actors struggle to access it.

◆ *Message Production for Goal Pursuit*

Some have argued that because humans are genetically programmed to preserve and replicate themselves, the necessity of developing guidance toward specific goals that will enable these preservation goals has led to the development of the human cognitive system (Bogdan, 1994). People gather, process, and store data from their environments in order to locate and guide themselves toward goals. A well-developed cognitive system makes goal attainment surer and more efficient. Similar observations have been made regarding the functional significance of language (Austin, 1962; H. H. Clark, 1994; Wittgenstein, 1953). H. H. Clark (1994) observed, "People engage in discourse not simply to use language, but to accomplish things. They want to buy shoes or get a lost address or arrange a dinner party or trade gossip or teach a child improper fractions. Language is simply a tool for achieving these aims" (p. 1018). Wittgenstein (1953) put it even more concisely when he averred, "Language in an instrument" (para. 569). Some have argued that the design features

of communication systems result from complex interactions between system constraints and the demands of the job required of the system, the latter being germane to goal pursuit (Hauser, 1996).

Language and discourse are not the only tools humans use to attain goals; humans' ability to interpret others' goals is postulated to have evolved out of the necessity for knowing whether others' current goals facilitate or interfere with the pursuit of one's own goals (Bogdan, 1997). Within the language use domain, some have argued that inferences about others' goals and plans are fundamental to understanding discourse and texts. In making this point, Green (1996) opined, "Understanding a speaker's intention in saying what she said and the way she said it amounts to inferring the speaker's plan, in all of its hierarchical glory, although there is considerable latitude regarding the details" (p. 13). Achieving an understanding of co-interlocutors' goals and plans is vital to the language production process in general; furthermore, it plays a key role in the initial conceptualization stage of language production. Messages conceptualized at this stage must take into account co-interlocutors' goals and plans; not to do so would be to risk formulating potentially incomprehensible utterances, failure to achieve desired goals, or both.

*GOAL-PLAN DETECTION*

Efficient and effective message production partially hinges on the ability of message producers to make relatively accurate inferences about the goals message addressees are pursuing and the plans they are employing to reach them (Berger, 2000). This postulate is not only germane to face-to-face and mediated social interaction but also relevant to communication contexts in which messages are conceived and formulated for mass audiences. Although the processes involved in goal and plan detection resemble the previously discussed notion of commonality assessment, they are different. Commonality assessments of addressees' knowledge and beliefs are conducted in the service of designing and formulating utterances that addressees will comprehend (Horton & Gerrig, 2005). The commonality assessment concept is rationalized within the context of Grice's (1975) notions of the cooperative principle and the conversational maxims. This Gricean purview postulates that social actors are bound to make clear, truthful, relevant, and parsimonious utterances in their commerce with others, although Grice recognized that these four maxims might be flouted in everyday conversations for a variety of reasons. Consistent with this perspective, most common-ground studies have employed referential communication tasks that explicitly require participants to act cooperatively and match arrangements of abstract figures without being able to see each other's arrangements.

In contrast to the commonality assessment construct, detection of addressees' goals and plans enables message producers to conceptualize messages such that they increase the likelihood that they will reach their instrumental and communication goals. These goals might include persuasion, deception, or threatening a co-interlocutor's face. Perpetrating deception may require that certain Gricean maxims—for example, the quality maxim—be violated by making untruthful utterances that appear to be truthful (McCornack, 1992, 1997), and speakers might try to belittle addressees by using a lexicon that exceeds the addressees' ability to comprehend it, thus violating the injunction to be clear (manner maxim) and belying the notion that common ground tends to accrete over time. Although establishing some level of common knowledge is a necessary condition for referential understanding and communication, it is hardly sufficient to guarantee success in reaching goals that everyday message producers typically seek to achieve. To put it another way,

addressees may understand completely a speaker's well-formulated utterances but, much to the speaker's chagrin, be utterly uninfluenced by them.

Although relatively little work has been done to illuminate the processes by which goals and plans are detected, some theorists have suggested that cognitive representations of commonly encountered social contexts are associated with specific goals; hence, once social actors encounter such a context—for example, shopping in a grocery store or eating in a restaurant—the goals of the social actors in the context are automatically activated (Palomares, 2008; Wilson, 1990, 1995). In such transparent communication contexts, under ordinary conditions, most observers would find it absurd for an adult language user to ask why particular individuals, such as check-out counter personnel, waiters, waitresses, and customers, are doing what they are doing because adults know what goals are being met by the actions deployed by those in the situation (Berger, 2007). In these transparent contexts, the degree to which observers are certain about their goal inferences is high (Palomares, 2008), and communication routines for interacting in such recurring situations are readily available (Coulmas, 1981; Leidner, 1993; Wray & Perkins, 2000). Other social contexts, however, may be considerably more opaque, thus making goal inferences less certain (Palomares, 2008). In addition to social contexts, goals may be associated with various tactics in long-term memory such that goals are automatically activated when a given tactic is deployed; for example, the tactical assertion of making a promise activates the goal of enforcing an obligation (Wilson, 1990, 1995). Of course, like goals, tactics may be opaque or transparent but incompatible with social contexts, thus making goal detection more difficult. With respect to social contexts and tactics, the fewer the number of goals linked with the social context or tactic, the greater the confidence with which goal inferences are made (Palomares, 2008).

## FORGING MESSAGE PLANS

Making rapid and relatively accurate inferences about co-interlocutors' goals does not by itself ensure communicative success. Once these goals are ascertained, social actors must formulate discourse and action plans that foster the achievement of their own goals in relation to those of the other parties. The plan construct not only played a prominent role during the early stages of the cognitive revolution (G. A. Miller, Galanter, & Pribram, 1960) but also has been widely invoked as a knowledge structure that enables the comprehension of discourse and text (Carberry, 1990; Green, 1996; Schank & Abelson, 1977; Wilensky, 1983), as well as guides goal-directed actions (Berger, 1995, 1997b; Bratman, 1987, 1990; Sacerdoti, 1977). Generally, plans are conceived of as cognitive structures that organize knowledge about the actions necessary to achieve goals. It is assumed that cognitive representations of these actions are arranged hierarchically with abstract representations of action types at the tops of the hierarchies and progressively more concrete actions nested below them. Thus, a plan to reach the goal of attaining compliance from another person might have an abstract representation of an "Offer Reward" action type at the top of its hierarchy that is successively specified such that representations of the verbal and nonverbal actions necessary to realize the abstract type are delineated at the hierarchy's lowest level. Action production theories have postulated constructs—for example, procedural records—that resemble plans. Procedural records are thought to be cognitive structures that contain links between representations of actions and outcomes, but these records are more elemental than are plans; however, they can become associatively linked to form unitized assemblies that resemble plans (Greene, 1984, 1997). Although individuals may be forced by circumstance, usually when encountering relatively novel situations or novel discourse and actions in otherwise familiar situations, to formulate plans from incoming data in a bottom-up fashion, plans that are repeatedly used to achieve goals in transparent communication contexts can be stored in long-term memory, retrieved, and used top-down, sometimes with minor adjustments, when recurring goals arise (Berger, 1997b; Hammond, 1989).

Plans vary in their complexity. As plans are specified in greater detail, their complexity increases. In addition, the degree to which plans anticipate the possibility that specific actions contained in them may not bring about desired goals and provide alternative actions in response to such failures, the more complex the plans become (Berger, 1997b). Although anticipating goal failures by including contingencies in message plans affords message producers the advantage of recovering more quickly in the event that such failures are actually encountered while pursuing their goals, having too many available alternatives may slow down the speed with which messages are delivered when failure occurs. Consistent with this reasoning, individuals who prepared one or six maps or one or six arguments in advance of direction giving or persuasion tasks, respectively, showed significantly longer speech onset latencies when their first plan failed than did individuals who prepared three maps or three arguments, respectively (Knowlton & Berger, 1997). Having too many alternatives in the event of failure was as debilitating to performance subsequent to failure as was having too few.

Other studies in this research program demonstrated the viability of the hierarchy principle. This principle asserts that alterations to message plans at more abstract levels entail higher levels of cognitive load than do alterations at lower levels (Berger, 1997b), thus encouraging individuals to give priority to lower level alterations in the event of goal failure. Consistent with the principle, direction givers who were informed by confederates that their directions could not be understood because they gave them too quickly, included too few landmarks in them, or provided a route that was unfamiliar to the confederate took the least amount of time to render the second rendition of their directions in the first speech rate condition and the greatest amount of time in the route reformulation condition (Berger, Knowlton, & Abrahams, 1996). Reformulating the entire walk route in the second rendition of the directions was clearly more demanding of cognitive resources than was repeating the same walk route at a reduced speech rate.

In experiments such as those just described, message plans were formulated "off line" in advance of the communication episode. There is evidence that individuals devise message plans "on line" as they attempt to achieve goals in their interactions. In a series of studies, individuals who participated in interactions in which they tried to achieve specific goals were given the opportunity to review a videotape of the just-completed interaction and indicate, whenever possible, what they were thinking (Waldron, 1990, 1997). Analyses of thought lists generated by this procedure revealed that close to 50% of the recalled items concerned the goals being pursued in the interaction and the plans being used to achieve them (Waldron, 1990). Other studies in this series demonstrated that individuals who were judged to be more effective in achieving their goals during their conversations tended to (a) take into account their co-interlocutor's goals in their message plans, (b) plan at more concrete levels, (c) look further ahead in the conversation, and (d) devise more complex plans than did those judged to be less effective at reaching their goals during the interaction (Waldron, 1990, 1997; Waldron & Applegate, 1994; Waldron, Caughlin, & Jackson, 1995; Waldron & Lavitt, 2000).

## AUDIENCE ADAPTED COMMUNICATION

Like the goal-plan-action approach to message production, the constructivist approach to communication (Delia, O'Keefe, & O'Keefe, 1982), which is based on Kelly's (1955) theory of personal constructs, focuses on the ways in which communication is employed to reach goals. This functional perspective argues that the degree to which individuals have highly differentiated systems of constructs for construing other people (i.e., the more they are cognitively complex), the more effective they are likely to be in achieving their instrumental and communication goals. High cognitive complexity is assumed to promote social perspective taking, that is, the ability to understand others' construals of the same situation in which one finds oneself (Applegate, 1990). Increases in social perspective-taking skill enable message producers to adapt and tailor their messages to addressees, which, in turn, increases the likelihood of goal achievement. Consistent with this line of reasoning, early studies found positive correlations between measures of cognitive complexity and judges' ratings of the potential persuasive effectiveness of messages (R. A. Clark & Delia, 1977; Delia & Clark, 1977). This research revealed that the persuasive messages generated by cognitively complex individuals evidenced greater acknowledgment of co-interlocutors' goals and perspectives than did the persuasive messages of cognitively simple individuals. These studies also revealed positive correlations between age and cognitive complexity. Later work reported under the aegis of message design logics found that cognitively complex individuals are more likely to employ rhetorical logics than are their less complex counterparts, especially in complex communication situations in which message producers are trying to satisfy multiple goals simultaneously (O'Keefe, 1988; O'Keefe & Shepherd, 1987). However, later work that examined the relationships among cognitive complexity, the complexity of plans generated during interaction, and the degree to which individuals successfully achieved their interaction goals demonstrated that while cognitive complexity and plan complexity were significantly and positively related, only plan complexity was significantly and positively related to communication effectiveness during the interaction (Waldron & Applegate, 1994). Thus, while cognitively complex individuals tend to generate more complex message plans than do their cognitively simple counterparts, it is the complexity of message plans that seems to determine communication effectiveness rather than cognitive complexity with respect to the construal of others. Because message plans serve to organize goal-directed actions and discourse, while cognitive complexity measures provide general assessments of proclivities to construe other people by using more or fewer personal constructs, these results are not surprising.

*REMOTE MASS AUDIENCES*

Much of the theory and research considered under the rubric of communication as an instrument for attaining goals has focused on communication occurring in face-to-face interaction contexts. Planning messages for producing effects among members of mass audiences presents particularly unique and difficult problems. Commonality assessments, message formulation, and goal and plan detection are substantially more difficult to carry out with any degree of precision in this communicative arena (see Atkin & Salmon, Chapter 24, this volume). Unlike data gathered during ongoing, goal-directed social interactions, data acquired through public opinion polling and focus groups are more hypothetical and potentially more time bound and generally do not allow for the kind of fine-grained resolution of audience

members' goals and plans that data derived from ongoing social interaction can provide. The difference in both the quantity and quality of data obtained in these two contexts may explain why meta-analyses of professionally designed and implemented public information campaigns that seek to alter various behaviors in mass audiences typically produce no direct behavioral changes among 90% to 95% of those exposed to them (Atkin & Salmon, Chapter 24, this volume; Atkin & Shiller, 2002). Although larger proportions of audience members may show increases in awareness and knowledge as a result of exposure to media campaigns and such increases may eventually lead to behavioral change, these disappointing outcomes are not difficult to understand. While message producers in face-to-face interaction contexts may have to deal with a number of sources of uncertainty involving co-interlocutors' communication skills, goals, plans, affective states, and beliefs (Berger, 1997a), such uncertainties are magnified significantly in the relatively impersonal, mass audience context. The inability of mass audience message producers to obtain detailed information about addressees and to modulate their message plans over a wide range, or at least a range that is wide enough to take into account the degree of variability among audience members' goals and plans, is a sure formula for limited success. Moreover, the fact that segments of mass audiences may be exposed inadvertently to messages designed for other audience segments may produce boomerang effects that further undermine the induction of desired behavioral change.

## ◆ Intersecting Production Levels

As indicated at this chapter's beginning, and as this review has demonstrated, one way to construe the state of affairs in message production theory and research is simply to observe that message production phenomena are studied at different levels of analysis and leave well enough alone. However democratic and celebratory of diversity this "different levels" characterization may appear, it suffers from the myopia that ignores two important facts. First, the same cognitive system writ large is responsible for producing both fluent and comprehensible speech and understandable writing, on one hand, and messages that are more or less functional in achieving goals, on the other. Moreover, under certain conditions, these two seemingly independent processes may become intertwined. Numerous studies have demonstrated, for example, that speech disfluencies may produce deleterious effects on audience members' judgments of speaker credibility (Burgoon, Birk, & Pfau, 1991; G. R. Miller & Hewgill, 1964). Reductions in audiences' credibility perceptions might undermine a speaker's ability to realize his or her instrumental goals. Second, surely it would be difficult to sustain the contention that speakers' and writers' goals, plans, and inferences about co-interlocutors' goals and plans are not somehow implicated in conceptual representations of messages, their lexicalization, and even their syntactical and phonological encoding. The effective pursuit of goals may require choosing the "right" words for the occasion and perhaps sometimes ordering these words in unique and ungrammatical strings to achieve desired effects. Moreover, phonological encoding may also be influenced by goals and plans and inferences about co-interlocutors' mental states. Skill in being able to lay differential stress on strings of syntactically encoded lemmas during phonological encoding may be vital to achieving certain communication goals.

Moving beyond the referential communication realm of matching abstract figure arrays in the laboratory to the more expansive domain of goal pursuit in everyday communication situations requires that functional demands be acknowledged and rationalized within language production models. After all, if the conjecture that cognitive and communication systems have developed in response to fundamental survival and procreation demands is plausible, it is difficult to see why such functional considerations are not center stage in such models. While these production systems feature speed and accuracy that can be enhanced with practice (Greene, 2003), obviously the speed and accuracy with which phonological and orthographic coding of languages is generated are not the only attributes that determine communicative success in the social world. A line of research that moves in the direction of going beyond this relatively narrow production speed and accuracy purview is Burleson's (2003) work in the area of emotional comforting and support. An explicitly stated aim of this research program is to identify message features of comforting messages that are associated with demonstrable reductions in emotional distress. One important implication of this perspective is that the content of comforting messages, as well as the way in which they are delivered, is important to communicative success in this realm.

In addition to identifying message features that are associated with successful goal attainment, another potentially useful direction communication researchers might take in the message production realm concerns the ways in which message producers conceive of audiences and the kinds of messages that will "work" with audiences possessing particular attributes. Such naive theories of audiences might share some similarities with naive theories of persuasion (Roskos-Ewoldsen, 1997), although the range of goals subsumed by naive theories of audiences would go well beyond persuasion and include such goals as informing and entertaining. Doubtlessly, mass media message producers, including both advertising and program creators, harbor naive theories of audiences. Such theories would likely link discernible audience attributes with message features deemed to be potentially effective in reaching desired goals. The extensive use of demographic attributes to characterize and segment mass media audiences suggests the plausibility of the notion that media message producers employ such implicit theories. Moreover, in the social interaction domain, individuals may predicate message production choices on audience attribute-message feature linkages. As previously discussed, strangers may employ funds of cultural-level knowledge in guiding communicative choices during initial encounters; their naive theories may serve to link cultural-level attributes with message features.

From the point of view of communicative effectiveness, implicit theories of audiences have the potential to reveal multiple sources of goal failure. A message producer may identify what are thought to be relevant audience attributes and predicate message feature choices on the attributes only to find that the attributes are irrelevant to achieving a particular goal. Thus, a message producer might deem a message target's age to be an important attribute on which to predicate message feature choices when, in fact, age is an irrelevant attribute with respect to the message's ultimate success. Or an audience attribute that is relevant to success may be identified, but the message features linked to it may not be functional for achieving the desired goal. In the present context, the notion of message features includes not only message content options but also stylistic choices with respect to how the message is rendered. These would include various schemes that might be used to organize messages and nonverbal accompaniments to verbally delivered messages, as well as stylistic variations in written communications.

Some theorists have argued that speakers can bring almost any speech parameter—for example, speech rate, vocal intensity, vocal intonation, and pausing—under conscious control if they so desire (Levelt, 1989). In addition to such speech parameters,

individuals can consciously choose to vary the correctness of their grammar or the difficulty of their lexicon, depending on audience members' attributes and the goals the message producer is attempting to achieve. Writers can also make such conscious choices. Of course, it almost goes without saying that repeated encounters with the same or similar audiences that eventuate in successful goal achievement may serve to automate these previously conscious choices to the point that they are made preconsciously (Aarts & Dijksterhuis, 2000; Bargh, 1997; Gollwitzer & Bargh, 2005). The range of yet-to-be-addressed questions in the message production domain is vast. How message sources design and deploy messages in the service of achieving their goals is a domain of communication inquiry that has important theoretical and practical implications. We have only begun to explore these implications.

## ◆ References

Aarts, H., & Dijksterhuis, A. (2000). Habits as knowledge structures: Automaticity in goal-directed behavior. *Journal of Personality and Social Psychology, 78,* 53–63.

Altenberg, B. (1990). Speech as linear composition. In G. Caie, K. Haastrup, A. L. Jakobsen, J. E. Nielsen, J. Sevaldsen, H. Specht, et al. (Eds.), *Proceedings from the Fourth Nordic Conference for English Studies* (Vol. 1, pp. 133–143). Copenhagen: University of Copenhagen, Department of English.

Applegate, J. L. (1990). Constructs and communication: A pragmatic integration. In G. Neimeyer & R. Neimeyer (Eds.), *Advances in personal construct psychology* (Vol. 1, pp. 203–230). Greenwich, CT: JAI.

Atkin, C., & Shiller, L. (2002). The impact of public service advertising. In L. Shiller & T. Hoff (Eds.), *Public service advertising in a new media age* (pp. 21–30). Menlo Park, CA: Kaiser Family Foundation.

Austin, J. (1962). *How to do things with words.* Oxford, UK: Oxford University Press.

Bargh, J. A. (1997). The automaticity of everyday life. In R. S. Wyer (Ed.), *Advances in social cognition* (Vol. 10, pp. 1–62). Mahwah, NJ: Lawrence Erlbaum.

Bellugi, U., Lichtenberger, L., Mills, D., Galaburda, A., & Korenberg, J. R. (1999). Bridging cognition and the brain: Evidence from Williams syndrome. *Trends in Neuroscience, 22,* 197–207.

Berger, C. R. (1975). Proactive and retroactive attribution processes in interpersonal communication. *Human Communication Research, 2,* 33–50.

Berger, C. R. (1995). A plan-based approach to strategic communication. In D. E. Hewes (Ed.), *Cognitive bases of interpersonal communication* (pp. 141–179). Hillsdale, NJ: Lawrence Erlbaum.

Berger, C. R. (1997a). Message production under uncertainty. In J. O. Greene (Ed.), *Message production: Advances in communication theory* (pp. 221–244). Mahwah, NJ: Lawrence Erlbaum.

Berger, C. R. (1997b). *Planning strategic interaction: Attaining goals through communicative action.* Mahwah, NJ: Lawrence Erlbaum.

Berger, C. R. (2000). Goal detection and efficiency: Neglected aspects of message production. *Communication Theory, 10,* 156–166.

Berger, C. R. (2007). Transparent and opaque communication: Coping with uncertainty in message production and processing. In M. B. Hinner (Ed.), *The role of communication in business transactions and relationships* (pp. 57–73). Frankfurt am Main, Germany: Peter Lang.

Berger, C. R., & diBattista, P. (1993). Communication failure and plan adaptation: If at first you don't succeed, say it louder and slower. *Communication Monographs, 60,* 220–238.

Berger, C. R., Gardner, R. R., Clatterbuck, G. W., & Schulman, L. S. (1976). Perceptions of information sequencing in relationship development. *Human Communication Research, 3,* 29–46.

Berger, C. R., & Kellermann, K. A. (1983). To ask or not to ask: Is that a question? In R. N. Bostrom (Ed.), *Communication yearbook 7* (pp. 342–368). Newbury Park, CA: Sage.

Berger, C. R., Knowlton, S. W., & Abrahams, M. F. (1996). The hierarchy principle in strategic communication. *Communication Theory, 6,* 111–142.

Bock, K., & Griffin, Z. M. (2000). Producing words: How mind meets mouth. In L. Wheeldon (Ed.), *Aspects of language production* (pp. 7–47). Hove, UK: Psychology Press.

Bock, K., & Levelt, W. J. M. (1994). Language production: Grammatical encoding. In M. A. Gernsbacher (Ed.), *Handbook of psycholinguistics* (pp. 945–984). San Diego: Academic Press.

Bogdan, R. J. (1994). *Grounds for cognition: How goal-guided behavior shapes the mind.* Hillsdale, NJ: Lawrence Erlbaum.

Bogdan, R. J. (1997). *Interpreting minds: The evolution of a practice.* Cambridge: MIT Press.

Bratman, M. E. (1987). *Intention, plans and practical reason.* Cambridge, MA: Harvard University Press.

Bratman, M. E. (1990). What is intention? In P. R. Cohen, J. Morgan, & M. E. Pollack (Eds.), *Intentions in communication* (pp. 15–31). Cambridge: MIT Press.

Burgoon, J. K., Birk, T., & Pfau, M. (1990). Nonverbal behaviors, persuasion and credibility. *Human Communication Research, 17,* 140–169.

Burleson, B. R. (2003). Emotional support skill. In J. O. Greene & B. R. Burleson (Eds.), *Handbook of communication and social skills* (pp. 551–594). Mahwah, NJ: Lawrence Erlbaum.

Carberry, S. (1990). *Plan recognition in dialogue and discourse.* Cambridge: MIT Press.

Clark, H. H. (1994). Discourse in production. In M. A. Gernsbacker (Ed.), *Handbook of psycholinguistics* (pp. 985–1021). San Diego: Academic Press.

Clark, H. H. (1996). Communities, commonalities, and communication. In J. Gumperz & S. Levinson (Eds.), *Rethinking linguistic relativity* (pp. 324–355). Cambridge, UK: Cambridge University Press.

Clark, H. H., & Carlson, T. B. (1982). Hearers and speech acts. *Language, 58,* 332–373.

Clark, H. H., & Marshall, C. R. (1981). Definite reference and mutual knowledge. In A. K. Joshi, B. Weber, & I. A. Sag (Eds.), *Elements of discourse understanding* (pp. 10–63). Cambridge, UK: Cambridge University Press.

Clark, H. H., & Wilkes-Gibbs, D. (1986). Referring as a collaborative process. *Cognition, 22,* 1–89.

Clark, R. A., & Delia, J. G. (1977). Cognitive complexity, social perspective taking, and functional persuasion skills in second- to ninth-grade children. *Human Communication Research, 3,* 128–134.

Coulmas, F. (1981). Introduction: Conversational routine. In F. Coulmas (Ed.), *Conversational routine: Explorations in standardized communication situations and prepatterned speech* (pp. 1–17). The Hague, The Netherlands: Mouton.

Deese, J. (1984). *Thought into speech: The psychology of language.* Englewood Cliffs, NJ: Prentice Hall.

Delia, J. G., & Clark, R. A. (1977). Cognitive complexity, social perception, and the development of listener-adapted communication in six-, eight-, ten-, and twelve-year-old boys. *Communication Monographs, 44,* 326–345.

Delia, J. G., O'Keefe, B. J., & O'Keefe, D. J. (1982). The constructivist approach to communication. In F. E. X. Dance (Ed.), *Human communication theory* (pp. 147–191). New York: Harper & Row.

Ferreira, F., & Englehardt, P. E. (2006). Syntax and production. In M. J. Traxler & M. A. Gernsbacher (Eds.), *Handbook of psycholinguistics* (2nd ed., pp. 61–91). Amsterdam: Elsevier.

Fussell, S. R., & Krauss, R. M. (1992). Coordination of knowledge in communication: Effects of speakers' assumptions about what others know. *Journal of Personality and Social Psychology, 62,* 378–391.

Garnham, A., Shillcock, R. C., Brown, G. D., Mill, A. I. D., & Cutler, A. (1982). Slips of the tongue in the London-Lund corpus of spontaneous conversation. In A. Cutler (Ed.), *Slips of the tongue and language production* (pp. 251–263). Berlin: Mouton.

Gollwitzer, P. M., & Bargh, J. A. (2005). Automaticity in goal pursuit. In A. Elloit & C. Dweck (Eds.), *Handbook of competence and motivation* (pp. 624–646). New York: Guilford.

Green, G. M. (1996). *Pragmatics and natural language understanding* (2nd ed.). Hillsdale, NJ: Lawrence Erlbaum.

Greene, J. O. (1984). A cognitive approach to human communication: An action assembly theory. *Communication Monographs, 51,* 289–306.

Greene, J. O. (1997). A second generation action assembly theory. In J. O. Greene (Ed.), *Message production: Advances in communication theory* (pp. 151–170). Mahwah, NJ: Lawrence Erlbaum.

Greene, J. O. (2003). Models of adult communication skill acquisition: Practice and the course of performance improvement. In J. O. Greene & B. R. Burleson (Eds.), *Handbook of communication and social skills* (pp. 51–91). Mahwah, NJ: Lawrence Erlbaum.

Grice, H. P. (1975). Logic and conversation. In P. Cole & J. L. Morgan (Eds.), *Syntax and semantics: Vol. 3. Speech acts* (pp. 41–58). New York: Academic Press.

Griffin, Z. M., & Ferreira, V. S. (2006). Properties of spoken language production. In M. J. Traxler & M. A. Gernsbacher (Eds.), *Handbook of psycholinguistics* (2nd ed., pp. 21–60). Amsterdam: Elsevier.

Hammond, K. J. (1989). *Case-based planning: Viewing planning as a memory task.* New York: Academic Press.

Hauser, M. D. (1996). *The evolution of communication.* Cambridge: MIT Press.

Horton, W. S., & Gerrig, R. J. (2005). Conversational common ground and memory processes in language production. *Discourse Processes, 40,* 1–35.

Isaacs, E., & Clark, H. H. (1987). References in conversation between experts and novices. *Journal of Experimental Psychology: General, 116,* 26–37.

Kelly, G. A. (1955). *The psychology of personal constructs.* New York: Norton.

Knowlton, S. W., & Berger, C. R. (1997). Message planning, communication failure, and cognitive load: Further explorations of the hierarchy principle. *Human Communication Research, 24,* 4–30.

Krauss, R. M., & Fussell, S. R. (1992). Implementing architectural designs: On the carpentry of intersubjectivity. In A. H. Wold (Ed.), *The dialogical alternative: Towards a theory of language and mind* (pp. 195–217). Oslo, Norway: Scandinavian Press.

Krauss, R. M., & Weinheimer, S. (1964). Changes in reference phrases as a function of usage in social interaction: A preliminary study. *Psychonomic Science, 1,* 113–114.

Krauss, R. M., & Weinheimer, S. (1966). Concurrent feedback, confirmation, and the encoding of referents in verbal communication. *Journal of Personality and Social Psychology, 4,* 343–346.

Leidner, R. (1993). *Fast food, fast talk: Service work and the routinization of everyday life.* Berkeley: University of California Press.

Levelt, W. J. M. (1989). *Speaking: From intention to articulation.* Cambridge: MIT Press.

Levelt, W. J. M., Roelofs, A., & Meyer, A. S. (1999). A theory of lexical access in speech production. *Behavioral and Brain Science, 22,* 1–45.

Lewis, D. (1969). *Convention.* Cambridge, MA: Harvard University Press.

MacKay, D. G. (1987). *The organization of perception and action: A theory for language and other cognitive skills.* New York: Springer-Verlag.

Maclay, H., & Osgood, C. E. (1959). Hesitation phenomena in spontaneous English speech. *Word, 15,* 19–44.

McCornack, S. A. (1992). Information manipulation theory. *Communication Monographs, 59,* 1–16.

McCornack, S. A. (1997). The generation of deceptive messages: Laying the groundwork for a viable theory of interpersonal deception. In J. O. Greene (Ed.), *Message production: Advances in communication theory* (pp. 91–126). Mahwah, NJ: Lawrence Erlbaum.

Miller, G. A., Galanter, E., & Pribram, K. H. (1960). *Plans and the structure of behavior.* New York: Holt, Rinehart & Winston.

Miller, G. R., & Hewgill, M. A. (1964). The effect of variations in nonfluency on audience ratings of source credibility. *Quarterly Journal of Speech, 50,* 36–44.

Miller, G. R., & Steinberg, M. (1975). *Between people: A new analysis of interpersonal communication.* Chicago: Science Research Associates.

Motley, M. T., Baars, B. J., & Camden, C. T. (1983). Experimental verbal slip studies: A review and editing model of language encoding. *Communication Monographs, 50,* 79–101.

O'Keefe, B. J. (1988). The logic of message design: Individual differences in reasoning about messages. *Communication Monographs, 55,* 80–103.

O'Keefe, B. J., & Shepherd, G. J. (1987). The pursuit of multiple objectives in face-to-face persuasive interactions: Effects of construct differentiation on message organization. *Communication Monographs, 54,* 396–419.

Oldfield, R. C. (1963). Individual vocabulary and semantic currency: A preliminary study. *British Journal of Social and Clinical Psychology, 2,* 122–130.

Palomares, N. A. (2008). Toward a theory of goal detection in social interaction: Effects of contextual ambiguity and tactical functionality on goal inferences and inference certainty. *Communication Research, 35,* 109–138.

Planalp, S. (1993). Friends' and acquaintances' conversations II: Coded differences. *Journal of Social and Personal Relationships, 10,* 339–354.

Planalp, S., & Benson, A. (1992). Friends' and acquaintances' conversations I: Perceived differences. *Journal of Social and Personal Relationships, 9,* 483–506.

Roskos-Ewoldsen, D. R. (1997). Implicit theories of persuasion. *Human Communication Research, 24,* 31–63.

Ruscher, J. B., & Hammer, E. D. (1994). Revising disrupted impressions through conversation. *Journal of Personality and Social Psychology, 66,* 530–541.

Sacerdoti, E. (1977). *A structure for plans and behavior.* Amsterdam: Elsevier.

Schank, R. C., & Abelson, R. P. (1977). *Scripts, plans, goals and understanding: An inquiry into human knowledge structures.* Hillsdale, NJ: Lawrence Erlbaum.

Schiffer, S. R. (1972). *Meaning.* Oxford, UK: Blackwell.

Schober, M. F., & Brennan, S. E. (2003). Processes of interactive spoken discourse: The role of the partner. In A. C. Graesser, M. A. Gernsbacher, & S. R. Goldman (Eds.), *Handbook of discourse processes* (pp. 123–164). Mahwah, NJ: Lawrence Erlbaum.

Schober, M. F., & Clark, H. H. (1989). Understanding by addressees and overhearers. *Cognitive Psychology, 21,* 211–232.

Shallice, T., & Butterworth, B. (1977). Short-term impairment in spontaneous speech. *Neuropsychologia, 15,* 729–735.

Smith, M. (2000). Conceptual structures in language production. In L. Wheeldon

(Ed.), *Aspects of language production* (pp. 331–374). Hove, UK: Psychology Press.

Stalnaker, R. C. (1978). Assertion. In P. Cole (Ed.), *Syntax and semantics 9: Pragmatics* (pp. 315–332). New York: Academic Press.

Waldron, V. R. (1990). Constrained rationality: Situational influences on information acquisition plans and tactics. *Communication Monographs, 57,* 184–201.

Waldron, V. R. (1997). Toward a theory of interactive conversational planning. In J. O. Greene (Ed.), *Message production: Advances in communication theory* (pp. 195–220). Mahwah, NJ: Lawrence Erlbaum.

Waldron, V. R., & Applegate, J. L. (1994). Interpersonal construct differentiation and conversational planning: An examination of two cognitive accounts for the production of competent verbal disagreement tactics. *Human Communication Research, 21,* 3–35.

Waldron, V. R., Caughlin, J., & Jackson, D. (1995). Talking specifics: Facilitating effects of planning on AIDS talk in peer dyads. *Health Communication, 7,* 249–266.

Waldron, V. R., & Lavitt, M. (2000). Welfare to work: Assessing communication competencies and client outcomes in a job-training program. *Southern Communication Journal, 66,* 1–15.

Wilensky, R. (1983). *Planning and understanding: A computational approach to human reasoning.* Reading, MA: Addison-Wesley.

Wilkes-Gibbs, D., & Clark, H. H. (1992). Coordinating beliefs in conversation. *Journal of Memory and Language, 31,* 183–194.

Wilson, S. R. (1990). Development and text of a cognitive rules model of interaction goals. *Communication Monographs, 57,* 81–103.

Wilson, S. R. (1995). Elaborating a cognitive rules model of interaction goals: The problem of individual differences in goal formation. In B. R. Burleson (Ed.), *Communication yearbook 18* (pp. 3–25). Thousand Oaks, CA: Sage.

Wittgenstein, L. (1953). *Philosophical investigations.* Oxford, UK: Basil Blackwell.

Wray, A., & Perkins, M. K. (2000). The functions of formulaic language: An integrated model. *Language and Communication, 20,* 1–28.

# 8

# MESSAGE PROCESSING

◆ David R. Roskos-Ewoldsen
and Beverly Roskos-Ewoldsen

M uch research has been conducted on the effects of communication.
Clearly, the study of social influence has a long-standing history with communication scholars (see Dillard, Chapter 12, this volume; Wilson, Chapter 13, this volume). Likewise, a major area of
research on the media explores the consequences of exposure to media
messages (see Nabi & Oliver, Chapter 15, this volume). Similarly,
whom we choose to communication with is another major research
focus. The study of interpersonal networks, including families
(Koerner, Chapter 27, this volume) and organizations (Krone, Kramer,
& Sias, Chapter 10, this volume), illustrates this linc of research, but
research on entertainment theory (Klimmt & Vorderer, Chapter 20,
this volume) also involves people's choice of messages to be exposed
to. There is also a growing body of research on message production
(Berger, Chapter 7, this volume). However, as will become evident, not
much research has focused on what people are doing while they are
actually processing communicative exchanges or messages. Rather,
researchers have generally left alone questions surrounding attention
to or comprehension of mediated communicative messages. While
there is little research on media in this domain, there is even less
research on attention and comprehension in other communicative
domains such as interpersonal communication, organizational communication, or social influence. This chapter will focus on the limited
research on attention and comprehension in the media.

Attention is one of those difficult concepts to define. People know what it means to "pay attention" but find it hard to explain what it means. Formally, attention involves the processes whereby information is made accessible for analysis by the cognitive system (Anderson & Kirkorian, 2006). In other words, attention involves selecting some information in the environment to process while other information is excluded. This is referred to as selective attention (Lang, 2000). However, the selection process may not be under individuals' conscious control. Research on attention differentiates automatic processes from controlled processes. Within this context, automatic processing refers to those processes that are outside of an individual's conscious control. For example, people automatically comprehend words that are spoken in a language they understand. Likewise, people automatically orient their attention to a loud banging noise. Controlled processes, on the other hand, are under an individual's control. For example, when a person is first learning to read, determining what word a string of letters stands for requires deliberation and takes cognitive effort. Likewise, if a person puts a DVD in the DVD player to watch, he or she has formed the intention to engage in this activity. Typically, controlled processes require substantially more cognitive resources than automatic processes.

There are two major lines of research involving attention to the media and another involving media comprehension. One line focuses on whether children's attention to TV is passive, whereby their attention is "captured" by TV, or active, whereby they select what to attend to in their environment. The second line of research focuses more on people's attentional processing of media messages and the impact of limited attentional cognitive resources. The third line focuses on understanding how we comprehend the media. This chapter will present each line of research, focusing on the theoretical contributions to understanding how we process media messages.

## ◆ Children's Attention to Television

Historically, the introduction of any new media technology—whether it is radio or the new video game technologies—has been accompanied by fears about the effects of that medium on children (Rogers, 1994). One of the early fears about TV involved it turning children into mindless zombies who were captured by the vivid images offered by TV (Anderson & Field, 1983). In response to these fears, media scholars and developmental psychologists began studying which factors influenced children's allocation of attention to TV. Is TV a monster that can shrivel children's minds while controlling what they watch? Or do children exhibit intentional processing while watching TV, strategically allocating attention to maximize their comprehension while minimizing the energy required for attending to the TV?

The question of passive versus active processing has formed the basis for much of the research in this tradition. However, before we describe the research, we will offer several observations about it. First, this research relies primarily on eyes-on-screen measures of attention. Eyes-on-screen measures record whether a viewer is looking at the TV or not. There is no attempt to measure how much effort is involved in the look or where on the screen children are looking. Second, while this research relies on an eyes-on-screen methodology, which suggests the focus is primarily on the visual, the auditory channel of TV is also important. The soundtrack provides much of the information that is presented on TV and in movies. A person can often understand much of what is occurring on a TV program simply by listening to that program. Indeed, one of the criticisms of contemporary cinema is that there are now few directors such as Alfred Hitchcock, who successfully used the medium's visual component (Bordwell, 2005).

Third, part of this research focuses on the formal features of TV. Formal features are the features or codes of TV that are independent of content and result from the editing and production process, but formal features do inform the content of a program (Anderson & Kirkorian, 2006; Huston & Wright, 1983). Formal features of TV include such things as edits, pacing, special effects, zooms, dissolves, fades, music, pans, voice-overs, and sound effects. Formal features often operate as a syntax for TV and movies by offering a structure for the programming (Huston & Wright, 1983). For example, fades indicate a change in location and time.

Generally, the research in this area has been atheoretical, which is surprising given its 30-plus years of research history (Anderson & Kirkorian, 2006). Nevertheless, a wealth of descriptive details of children's attention to TV has been identified. We will summarize the major findings of the research, first, descriptively as principles of children's TV watching behaviors; second, as they relate to the passive versus active models of attention to TV; and third, as they have evolved into new models of attention.

## PRINCIPLES OF CHILDREN'S TV-WATCHING BEHAVIORS

Anderson and Field (1983) provided a list of 16 principles of how children attend to TV. While it is unclear whether these have achieved the status of principles, we believe that this list is constructive because it provides a useful summary of what has been learned about children's attention to TV over the past 40 years of research and because any theory of children's attention to TV will need to be able to account for these findings. Below is a summary of the 10 principles most relevant to this chapter.

*1. Attention to TV begins during infancy.* Children begin attending to TV by 6 months of age (Hollenbeck & Slaby, 1979) and exhibit clear preferences for different types of programs by 18 months (Anderson & Kirkorian, 2006).

*2. Attention length increases during childhood.* How long children look at a TV increases from infancy through about age 12, where it generally peaks (Anderson, Lorch, Field, Collins, & Nathan, 1986). For example, Alwitt, Anderson, Lorch, and Levin (1980) observed children in three 1-hour sessions. The percentage of eyes-on-screen time increased from 38.5% for 3-year-olds to 48% for 5-year-olds. Not surprisingly, children look at TV more with programs that are aimed at children than with programs not aimed at children. This increase in attention probably reflects higher levels of comprehension of the programming.

*3. Attentional looks are brief.* Typically, children engage in a large number of looks at a TV program, and no single look is particularly long. Preschool children will look at and away from TV more than 2 times a minute, averaging over 150 times an hour (Anderson, Lorch, Smith, Bradford, & Levin, 1981). More than 60% of the time, a child looks at the TV less than 5 seconds before looking away again. The same pattern of looking at TV is found in adults (Hawkins et al., 2005). More than 45% of the looks at the screen for undergraduates watching TV were less than 1.5 seconds.

*4. Attention has inertia.* Although children tend to have many short looks at TV, the longer they look at TV, the less likely they are to stop looking at it. This phenomenon is known as attentional inertia (Anderson & Field, 1983; Krull & Husson, 1979). In other words, as attention to TV is sustained, it becomes more impervious to distractions (Anderson, Choi, & Lorch, 1987). Attentional inertia may play an important role in children's learning of the syntax of formal features. Attentional inertia probably results in the child paying attention to TV when he or she normally would not because it has become incomprehensible, which means the child may be exposed to new formal features he or she will slowly become familiar with (Anderson & Lorch, 1983). Attentional inertia is also found in adults (Burns & Anderson, 1993). Attentional inertia may reflect, at least in part, viewers' greater involvement with a program because attentional inertia appears to be stronger when viewers are engaged in the program (Hawkins, Tapper, Bruce, & Pingree, 1995).

5. *Attention and comprehension are dynamic.* There is a dynamic relationship between attention and comprehension in children (Lorch & Castle, 1997). Anderson et al. (1981, Experiment 2) manipulated the comprehensibility of a *Sesame Street* episode by either substituting an unknown foreign language (Greek) onto the soundtrack or maintaining the original dialogue but splicing it in backward so that the sounds were synced to mouth movements. In this manner, the formal features of the program were identical, but comprehension was degraded. The participants in this study were 2-, 3½-, or 5-year-old English-only-speaking children. As the comprehensibility of the program decreased, children's attention to the program likewise decreased. Collapsing across the age-groups, children had their eyes on the screen 46.9% of the time in the normal condition, compared with 32% for the foreign language clips and 29.4% for the backward dialogue.

6. *Not all formal features attract attention.* Some formal features of TV are more likely to automatically attract children's attention than are other formal features (Anderson & Field, 1983; Anderson & Kirkorian, 2006). These features are likely to attract children's attention even when the content of the show is not comprehensible or the child has not been paying attention to (i.e., looking at) the show. Alwitt et al. (1980) found that the following formal features tend to elicit children's attention: movement, major transitions (e.g., from the show to a commercial), applause, laughter, other sound effects, animation, women's voices, children's voices, and the presence of puppets.

7. *Some formal features decrease attention to TV.* Alwitt et al. (1980) hypothesized

that children have learned that these formal features typically signal content that is less appropriate for or less comprehensible to children. Indeed, formal features found to decrease children's attention to TV include the use of still pictures, male voices, the presence of animals, long zooms and pans (particularly for younger children), and slow music.

8. *Cues are used strategically to watch TV.* Children learn how to use the formal features of TV to guide their attention to and comprehension of TV programs, and they begin to learn how to use these codes by the time they are 4 years old (Calvert, Huston, Watkins, & Wright, 1982; Krull & Husson, 1979; Rice, Huston, & Wright, 1983). Children begin paying greater attention to structured rather than random programming as early as 18 months (Anderson & Kirkorian, 2006). Research also suggests that children transfer what they learn about formal features of a particular program to other programs that are similar (Crawley et al., 2002). Furthermore, children as young as 3 years old use the behavior of other people who are viewing the TV to guide their attention to TV (Anderson et al., 1981).

9. *Multitasking is common.* Children usually engage in multiple tasks while watching TV (Anderson & Field, 1983). While viewing TV, children often talk with other people who are present, play with toys, or engage in other activities (Anderson & Lorch, 1983). The advent of new communication technologies means that children are engaging in more multitasking with different media (Foehr, 2006). Children are developing the skills and strategies for dual tasking by the age of 5. As children gain experience with a program, they are more likely to engage in more secondary tasks (Crawley et al., 2002).

10. *Auditory information provides cues for attention.* Children monitor the auditory track of a TV program to determine when they need to pay more attention to the program (Anderson & Kirkorian, 2006). Clearly, if children are using the formal

features of TV to guide when they need to look to the screen to comprehend the program, then auditory features must play an important role in signaling to the child that important things are about to occur in the story (Bickham, Wright, & Huston, 2001).

## MODELS OF CHILDREN'S ATTENTION TO TV

As the descriptive principles of children's TV viewing developed, three models focusing on different aspects of children's attention also emerged. One model contends that children's viewing is active rather than passive. Another model, the traveling lens model, states that the attentional lens through which children view TV changes (i.e., travels) with increasing familiarity with the programming. The third model, the sampling model, purports that children sample TV shows for cues and then use those cues to guide attention and behavior.

*Passive Versus Active Processing Models.* In many ways, the passive model was a straw caricature of a model, but it was a foundation against which a great deal of this research was conducted. With no real adherents, no program of research vigorously defended the passive model. Rather, the passive model reflected cultural truisms that were quickly debunked by research.

According to the passive model, TV captures our attention and then controls what we attend to in our environment. The model assumes, first, that TV is a highly salient visual stimulus that easily captures people's (especially children's) attention through various tricks that are particular to the medium—the formal features of television—and that TV maintains people's attention by offering programming that is novel or in some way reinforces the viewer (Anderson & Field, 1983; Bickham et al., 2001). The role of viewer's intentions and goals is minimal (Anderson & Lorch, 1983). Second, it assumes

that attention to TV leads to comprehension. Consequently, according to the passive model, educational TV can be made more effective by simply making it more attention grabbing. As Bickham et al. (2001) note, this model is captured by the phrases we use to describe children's viewing such as, "They vegged out in front of the TV."

The alternative model is the *active model.* The active model assumes that children work dynamically to comprehend what is going on when watching television. The model assumes that when children look at TV, the look has a functional reason such as aiding comprehension (Anderson & Field, 1983; Bickham et al., 2001). The formal features of TV are used to guide the allocation of attention. For example, animation is a formal feature that cues the viewer that the content is likely to be aimed at children. Indeed, children tend to pay more attention to animated programming. Conversely, a male voice often signals that the content is aimed at adults, and research finds that children are more likely to stop looking at TV when there is a male voice as compared with a female or child voice (Alwitt et al., 1980).

Evidence of the strategic nature of children's TV viewing comes from studies where children watched the same program with toys either present or absent in their environment. When toys were absent, children looked at the TV two times as often (87% of the time) than when toys were present (44% of the time). Despite the lower rates of attention to the TV when toys were present, the children in the toy condition comprehended the program as well as the children in the no-toy condition (Lorch, Anderson, & Levin, 1979). Clearly, children in the toy condition must have been attending to the critical elements of the program for comprehension to have been comparable to comprehension in the no-toy condition. According to the model, ease of comprehension drives the allocation of attention (Anderson & Field, 1983). If a show is easy to understand, the child does not need to pay much attention to the program and will look away and engage in other activities. Similarly, if a program is too complex for the child to understand, the child will stop looking at the TV and will engage in other activities, unless TV is the only option. Children pay the most attention to programs that they can comprehend but that are not too easy to comprehend (Anderson & Field, 1983; Bickham et al., 2001).

Although the available data strongly support the active view of children's TV attention, it is difficult to argue that this framework is actually a theory. In addition, it is clear that very young children are perhaps better characterized by the passive model (Valkenberg & Vroone, 2004), even though as they age and learn how to watch television, they develop fairly quickly into active users of TV (Rice et al., 1983).

*Traveling Lens Model.* One model that is predictive of children's TV viewing behavior is the traveling lens model (Rice et al., 1983). According to the model, attention to television is a function of familiarization and habituation. At high levels of familiarization, children are less likely to pay attention to TV because they have learned how to use the formal cues of TV to guide their processing of the content efficiently or else they are so habituated to the programming that is it no longer of interest. At the other extreme are programs that use techniques that are unfamiliar to children or programs where the topic is so novel it is beyond the children's ability to understand. In either case, attention to the program is very low. Between these two extremes, attention to the TV follows a curvilinear function such that, as familiarity increases to an optimal level, attention to the program will increase to the point where there is too much novelty or lack of understanding of the formal features, and children will pay less attention to the programming. In other words, programming that is moderately comprehensible to the

child will result in the highest levels of attention (Valkenburg & Vroone, 2004).

As children develop and gain more experience with TV, the entire distribution of the television content that children will attend to shifts to the right. What were once programs that were attended to with great detail are now programs that have become habitualized, and what were once novel and complex programs are now moderately comprehensible. Research on the program *Blue's Clues* found that children who had experience watching the program looked at the screen less during periods when typical as opposed to unique content appeared. Children who were inexperienced with the program watched the show equally during typical and unique content (Crawley et al., 2002).

*Attentional Sampling Model.* Another predictive model is the sampling model of attention (Huston & Wright, 1983). It is designed to explain how children strategically use formal features and random samples of looks at TV to guide their viewing of TV. This model argues that children take small samples of TV programming to determine if it is interesting and comprehensible. When a sampling gaze captures programming that is important to the show, children become more engaged in their viewing. This pattern may explain, at least in part, why viewing times become progressively longer and attentional inertia sets in (Hawkins et al., 2005). This sampling is almost certainly not systematic or random. Rather, children's sampling may be driven, at least partly, by the formal features of the program, as well as what is occurring in the auditory track of the program. How systematically children sample is predicted by the overall comprehensibility of the TV program (Hawkins, Yong-Ho, & Pingree, 1991). Recent research suggests that attentional inertia is tied to children's and adults' strategic viewing of TV (Hawkins et al., 2005).

◆ *Attentional Processing of Media Messages and Limited Cognitive Resources*

The second approach to attention focuses more on the dynamics of attention within information-processing models of cognition. The dominant model in this area is the limited-capacity model of motivated mediated message processing (LC4MP; Lang, 2000, 2006; Lang, Bradley, Park, Shin, & Chung, 2006). Lang (2000) notes two basic assumptions of this approach. First, people actively process information within the cognitive system and, second, their ability to process information is limited by that same cognitive system.

## LIMITED COGNITIVE RESOURCES

The information-processing framework underlying the first assumption maintains that there are three basic cognitive processes: encoding, storage, and retrieval (Basil, 1994; Lang, 2000). Each of these three stages is composed of further subprocesses (Lang, 2000), but a discussion of these is beyond the scope of this chapter. Encoding encompasses those processes involved with bringing information into the cognitive system, including attention and perception. Storage involves incorporating the attended-to information in a mental representation and storing it in memory. Although the LC4MP is not tied to a particular model of memory (Lang, 2000, 2006), it is typically discussed using network models of memory in which information is stored in memory as concept nodes that are connected to related concept nodes through pathways along which energy spreads. The final process is retrieval, which involves activating information that has been stored in memory. Activation from memory allows the information to aid the comprehension of incoming information. The representation of the activated information may be elaborated through the creation of linkages in memory to the new information while the new information is

stored in memory or through modifications of the already stored information. Although it is easy to think of these three stages as discrete and following a linear progression, the three processes interact dynamically, and all three operate simultaneously.

Concerning the second assumption, numerous limitations exist in the cognitive system. People can attend to only a limited amount of information in the environment at any particular moment. Furthermore, the amount of information that can be held for processing is limited by the capacity of short-term memory. Finally, additional cognitive processing requires resources that are also in limited supply. For example, the task may require a lot of resources if a person is trying to understand a complex lecture in a required class. Conversely, the task may require few resources if a person is watching a highly familiar TV show. How limited the supply is varies according to the specific resource pool model one adopts. Some models assume that each process has its own resource pool (Kahneman, 1973). However, the work on media, including the LC4MP, has generally assumed and found evidence consistent with a single resource pool, so that attention, encoding, and retrieval all vie for the same pool (Basil, 1994; Lang, 2000).

There are several key concepts in the LC4MP: total resources, resources allocated, resources required, resources remaining, and resources available. *Total resources* are the total resources in the resource pool. *Resources allocated* are the resources that are actually available for a processing task. The resource allocated to a task may be equivalent to the total resources but probably is not. *Resources required* are the amount of resources necessary to complete a task. *Resources remaining* constitute the difference between total resources and resources required. Again, resources remaining and resources allocated may be the same if total resources are equivalent to allocated resources, but this is unlikely the case. *Resources available* are the difference between the resources allocated and the resources required.

The reasons for these fine-tuned distinctions are several. First, people may not allocate all of the available resources to a task at hand because they are cognitive misers. Unless highly motivated, people tend to use as few resources as necessary. Thus, a distinction is made between total resources and allocated resources. Second, people will allocate resources only as required by the task. If people are watching a program they have seen before, fewer resources may be required because of the familiarity of the program. Conversely, if the production is such that the visual elements of the programming are important (e.g., many of Hitchcock's movies; Bordwell, 2005), then more resources may be required. In both cases, the same amount of resources may have been allocated to the TV program, but different amounts were actually used, leaving some allocated resources available in one case but not in another. Third, some elements in the environment will automatically draw resources. For example, formal features automatically attract attention (e.g., unrelated cuts), drawing required resources from the total pool of resources without conscious allocation of resources. In this case, the difference between the automatic attraction (i.e., required) of resources and the total resources leaves some remaining resources for allocation to other tasks.

Within this model, media messages may receive insufficient or limited processing for two basic reasons. First, there may not be enough resources available to process the message fully (i.e., the required resources exceed the total resources). For example, a message on a topic that a person does not understand may require so many resources— perhaps trying to retrieve information from long-term memory—that, even though all resources may have been allocated to the task, the required resources for retrieval leave neither remaining nor available resources for attending to and encoding the message. Second, there may be enough resources available to process the message, but those resources are not allocated to the

task for reasons such as insufficient motivation or because the person is multitasking (e.g., resources required exceed resources allocated). For example, when a person is cooking and watching TV at the same time, there may not be enough resources available to process the TV program entirely.

## PROCESSING MEDIA MESSAGES

Watching TV involves a number of simultaneous cognitive processes. TV viewing often requires people to engage in processing auditory and visual information and integrating these two channels of information (Lang, Potter, & Bolls, 1999). At the same time, both the auditory and visual information include the content of the program as well as the formal features of TV, which, as we saw in the last section, can act as syntax for the programming. The viewer must integrate all of this information to understand the program. In addition, viewers are storing new information in memory and activating existing knowledge to aid in comprehending the program. Research under the rubric of the LC4MP model focuses on how resources are allocated to the various processes that are occurring and the effects of differential resource allocation on attention, encoding, and retrieval.

Methodologically, the LC4MP uses three primary sets of measures to study how people allocate resources and process information. Secondary task reaction time (STRT) is a measure of the amount of resources allocated to attention. STRT involves people engaging in a primary task such as watching TV while also monitoring a second task such as pressing a button whenever a cue such as a tone sounds or a light comes on (Lang & Basil, 1998; Reeves & Thorson, 1986). The amount of resources that are available (e.g., resources allocated – resources required) has been demonstrated to influence how long it takes people to respond in the STRT (Lang & Basil, 1998). When there are a lot of resources available, people quickly notice the light or tone and are quick to press a button. But when resources are low or taxed, people take longer to notice the light or tone and are slower to respond. For example, a cut to an unrelated scene tends to tax resources because of the new information that needs to be processed, and STRT is slower. Critically, STRT is a function of both the resources allocated to the task and the resources required by the task (Lang et al., 2006).

A second set of methodological tools involves physiological measures such as heart rate, galvanic skin responses (sweating), or muscle activity. Heart rate is used as a measure of whether an orienting response has occurred (Lang, 2000; Lang, Geiger, Strickwerda, & Sumner, 1993). When people show a startle response, their heart rate drops (i.e., decelerates) for a few seconds before returning toward their baseline. Likewise, an increase in skin conductance is evidence of a startle response. Thus, the combined evidence of heart rate deceleration and an increase in skin conductance provides convergent evidence that an orienting response has occurred.

A final set of methodological tools involves measures of memory, including recall and recognition measures (Fox, Park, & Lang, 2007; Lang, 2000). The measures of memory are used to make inferences about encoding and retrieval processes. For example, if messages are simple, increasing people's attention to a message through the inclusion of formal features that orient attention, such as edits, results in improvements in memory for the message. This finding suggests that there were available resources (i.e., more resources allocated than required) that could be diverted to encoding processes. Conversely, with a complex message, the addition of features that increase orienting responses tends to lead to decrements in memory, which suggests that orienting responses automatically drew resources away from encoding processes and resulted in worse memory. The decreased performance on memory tests is one indication that the resources required have exceeded the resources allocated to the task.

Although the LC4MP is a theoretically oriented model of message processing, it provides important practical insights for message production. For example, if a message is primarily intended to convey information, then the message should be constructed to maximize the resources that are available for encoding information. In this instance, the number of structural features of the message that will result in orienting responses should be tied to the informational complexity of the message. As information complexity increases, the message should minimize the number of orienting responses because they may interfere with encoding processes by requiring more resources than allocated or even more resources than in the total pool (Fox et al., 2007; Lang, 2006). Anyone interested in using the LC4MP for message production or in other practical situations should read Lang (2006) for a guide on how to use the theory in applied settings. A final point concerns the applicability of the model. While the name of the model suggests it is limited to attention to mediated messages, the model should apply across contexts. Obviously, in interpersonal settings, the focus would not be on cuts and edits, but the same underlying dynamics would be in operation.

## ◆ Message Comprehension

A third tradition of research on message processing focuses on people's comprehension of a media message. Comprehension involves understanding the story as it is written or seen. It is based in part on a person's own experiences. As a result, two people with different experiences may understand a message differently. On the flip side, the more shared experiences and cultural knowledge, the more similar the understanding.

There are three major approaches to understanding how we comprehend media stories, each with its own methodology. One approach focuses on relationships among characters within a story. A second focuses on the role of situation models in the comprehension of visual and text stories, and a third focuses on the ease with which events within a story are identified and its impact on story comprehension. We present these approaches, focusing on their theoretical and methodological contributions to understanding how we understand the media. It is important to understand that while these models have been studied using mediated messages, they clearly apply in interpersonal and other contexts as well. The focus on the media simply reflects the area that has received the most research attention.

## RELATIONSHIPS AMONG CHARACTERS AND STORY COMPREHENSION

One of the first lines of research on comprehension of the media began in the late 1980s. This research explored whether people form a unified mental representation of a movie or TV series (Livingstone, 1989, 1990a, 1990b). As Livingstone (1987) cogently argued, previous research had focused on the consequences of viewing the media without understanding how people comprehended the messages and, perhaps more important, represented the messages in memory. If these memory representations could be tapped, they would reflect how people understand the message.

This research has focused on people's perceptions of the characters within a story to identify the memory representation of the story. Although perceptions of characters may not seem to be directly related to one's understanding of a story, we believe that they are. First, stories are often understood as a dynamic between the various characters involved in the story, making perceptions of the characters directly relevant to the story. Second, people's interpretation of a story is

tied to how they perceive and identify with the main characters within a story. Again, perceptions of the characters are directly tied to comprehension of the story.

The earliest study within this tradition focused on whether representations that resulted from reading a book versus watching a fairly faithful film adaptation of the book differed (Rowell & Moss, 1986). Importantly, although the adaptation of the book is very close, one of the characters— the donkey—is treated more simplistically in the movie than in the book. Participants either read Orwell's (1945) *Animal Farm* or watched Halas and Bachelor's (1955/2004) animated adaptation of the book. To understand whether and how theses stories were represented differently, people rated how similar the characters were. These similarities were transformed into a multidimensional scaling (MDS) solution. A MDS solution presents an $n$-dimensional space (typically, two-dimensional). The characters are represented as locations within this space, with smaller distances representing greater similarity. Two solutions were created, one for the book condition and one for the movie condition. Overall, the MDS representations for the book and the movie were meaningfully related to the major themes of the story. In addition, however, the spatial representation that resulted from watching the movie was simpler than the representation that resulted from reading the book. Finally, the specific differences in the two representations appeared to be tied to the complexity of the donkey character in the two different formats.

A newer set of studies explored whether people's representations of a story reflected the polysemic nature of the story (Crawford, Roskos-Ewoldsen, & Roskos-Ewoldsen, 2004; Roskos-Ewoldsen, Roskos-Ewoldsen, Yang, & Crawford, 2003). These studies used the movie *Falling Down*, which is a story of an unemployed defense worker (D-Fens) who reacts with progressively higher levels of violence to the frustrations that he faces as he tries to go home. There is clearly something amiss with his intention to go home, as indicated by the panic his intention produces. Around 95% of the viewers in the study perceived D-Fens as being mentally ill. Approximately half of these viewers also perceived him as a hero—a man who fought back against an insane world—whereas the other half did not. Clearly, these two groups comprehended the movie differently. To investigate whether they created different representations of the movie, researchers instructed participants to watch the entire movie and then rate the similarity of 10 main characters in the movie. There were clear differences in the MDS spatial representation of the movie between participants who saw D-Fens as a hero and those who did not, indicating that people with different understandings of the movie developed different mental representations of the movie.

The follow-up study focused on how the mental representations of the movie evolved across time. In this study, participants' mental representations of the movie *Falling Down* were measured at three critical points in the movie or at the end of the movie. That is, four separate groups of people rated the similarities of the characters at the three critical points or at the end. All participants continued watching the entire movie. At the end, all participants indicated their interpretations of the movie, resulting in the same two groups as in the first study. Not only did the representations of the movie change across time, reflecting the dynamics between the characters in the movie, but the changes were distinct for the two groups that had different interpretations of the movie. In the hero interpretation, viewers' representations tended to focus on D-Fens versus everybody else. In the nonhero interpretation of the movie, the representation of the movie focused on the relationships between the various characters who were trying to protect D-Fens's family while bringing him to justice. These findings suggest that what people attended to while watching the movie was tied to their comprehension of the movie, which

again points to the dynamic relationship between attention and comprehension.

## SITUATION MODELS AND COMPREHENSION

A second approach to studying comprehension is the situation model approach. Situation models are constructs in memory that represent what a situation or event described in a text is *about,* rather than a literal representation of the text itself (van Dijk, 1995). More specifically, a situation model is a representation of a specific story or episode that has specific temporal and spatial constraints (Wyer, 2004). Situation models have two properties that make them unique from other models of memory (Wyer & Radvansky, 1999). First, they are malleable such that their components (i.e., characters, setting, relations among each) are interchangeable, much like building blocks that can be used to construct various shapes. For example, the setting for a story could be an urban city, a rural area, or even the Amazon jungle, as long as it is a setting. Situation models are also dynamic. That is, they are subject to user control and may be manipulated to generate inferences, test different scenarios, or draw conclusions about information that may or may not be contained in a text or situation. As an example, movie viewers may use cinematic features (e.g., editing techniques, costumes, music, dialogue) as cues to make predictions about future events or to make inferences about previous events. When anomalous information is foregrounded by filmmakers, viewers attempt to figure out why such information was presented (Magliano, Dijkstra, & Zwaan, 1996).

One situation model that has been used successfully to predict people's comprehension of a story is the landscape model (e.g., van den Broek, Risden, Fletcher, & Thurlow, 1996; see also Roskos-Ewoldsen, Roskos-Ewoldsen, Yang, & Lee, 2007). The landscape model is a computational model of text comprehension that focuses on coherence by looking at the relationship between the on-line processing of a story, the memorial representation of that story, and recall for the story. The model gets its name from the observation that, as one reads a story, information is being activated at various levels across time. If one were to construct a three-dimensional matrix, with the concepts relevant to the movie along the $x$-axis, the different scenes in the movie along the $z$-axis, and the level of activation along the $y$-axis, one would have a landscape of activations with hills and troughs corresponding to activation levels of the concepts across time. Higher elevations in the landscape indicate higher levels of activation of that concept. Troughs in the landscape would represent the absence of activation of that concept.

The model assumes that there are four general sources of activation of concepts while attending to a story (van den Broek, Young, Tzeng, & Linderholm, 1999). First, the immediate environment activates concepts in memory. Specifically, concepts within the current sentence (for a book) or scene (for a movie) will be activated. Second, because activation dissipates across time, concepts from the immediately preceding sentence or scene should still be activated, albeit at a lower level of activation. Furthermore, concepts from previous scenes are hypothesized to have higher levels of activation if they were the focal point of the previous scene, were related to active goals of the protagonists or antagonists in the previous scene, or involved events that were antecedents to some subsequent event. Third, concepts from earlier in the story may be reactivated because they are necessary for maintaining the coherence of the story. Fourth, world knowledge that is necessary for understanding the story will be activated.

The landscape model was used as the theoretical basis for an investigation of how audiences process brand placements within a movie (Yang & Roskos-Ewoldsen, 2007). According to the model, the greater the activation of the brand while viewing the

movie, the greater the likelihood that the brand will be recalled in the future. If a brand is tied to the comprehension of the show by serving as an enabler, it will receive a higher level of activation than brands that are in the background. For example, the Reese's Pieces that Elliot placed on the ground to lure an alien into his house in the movie *E.T.* were enablers because they played an important role in the story (luring the alien inside). Simply presenting the brand as a background in the scene in the movie would lead to a low level of activation because the brand placement is not related to story comprehension, and consequently, later recall of the brand will be unlikely.

In the study, we used three levels of brand placement: (a) in the background, (b) used by the character, and (c) used as an enabler. In the *background* condition, the product was shown with one of the main characters, but the character did not use the product. In the *used by character* condition, the product was used by one of the main characters but was not central to the story. In the *story enabler* condition, the product played a role in the storyline, such as saving the main character or helping to solve a problem in the movie. Participants watched one of these clips, completed an unrelated task for 10 minutes, and then took a recognition test of product brands. The results were consistent with the theoretical predictions from the landscape model. People were more likely to recognize the brands placed in a movie when the brand was an enabler than when it was used by a character or was simply part of the background.

## EVENT INDEXING AND COMPREHENSION

The final approach for investigating story comprehension is based on the event indexing model (Zwaan, Langston, & Graesser, 1995). The event indexing model focuses on events and their interconnectedness within the story. This emphasis is in contrast to the landscape model, which focuses on the activation pattern of the concepts in a story, rather than events. The event indexing model assumes that people monitor and cluster information while creating a situation model of the story; the clusters represent events in the story. According to the model, people use five indices to create these clusters (Magliano, Miller, & Zwaan, 2001): changes in time, changes in space, establishment of a causal relationship between antecedents and consequences, focus on the protagonists' goal, and focus on different agents or objects. These indices capture who has what intention, when and where, and whether the current event is the cause of other events. The event indexing model further assumes that as more of the indices change simultaneously (i.e., a change from night to day concurrently with a change in location), people are more likely to update their situation model of the story, compared with the case where there is continuity along each of the indices (Magliano et al., 2001). As part of the updating process, forward and backward inferences, as well as elaborations of the event, are made.

We investigated the extent to which people make inferences during the normal course of watching a movie (Lee, Roskos-Ewoldsen, & Roskos-Ewoldsen, 2004). We compared these inferences with a situation in which the usual comprehension process is disrupted. That is, we disrupted the ease with which changes in indices were detected, which we argued would lead to fewer updates to a person's situation model. As a result, inferences would be hindered. We used two versions of *Rear Window* (directed by Alfred Hitchcock in 1946); one was the English-language version, and the other was the French-dubbed version with English subtitles. Participants watched the last half of the movie. As they watched the movie, they wrote down any thoughts that came to mind. Any inferences reported by the participants were coded as backward, current, and forward inferences. A backward inference

was one that used information presented earlier in the movie and linked that information with what was currently occurring in the movie. Backward inferences play an important role in creating global coherence for the story. A forward inference was one that predicted future events, and a current inference was one that concerned only the immediate event. By linking events within the current scene together, current inferences aid in maintaining local coherence.

We expected that more inferences would be made in the English-language version than in the French-dubbed/English subtitle version, assuming that the normal updating process would be disrupted by viewers having to split their attention between the visual content of the French film and its subtitles. To our surprise, there was no overall difference in the number of inferences made in the two conditions. However, there were significant differences in the types of inferences made. Participants generated more backward inferences in the English condition than in the French condition, whereas participants generated more current inferences in the French condition than in the English condition. The results of this experiment suggest that when it is difficult to link together events that are temporally separated, the chance of making backward inferences is reduced. In addition, the movie's global coherence and comprehension decline.

## ◆ Conclusion

How messages are processed is a critical part of the communication process. However, communication scholars have largely ignored these processes. Instead, attention to and comprehension of messages is typically taken as a given. Consequently, we have a limited understanding of factors that influence attention to and comprehension of mediated messages or how these processes dynamically interact. We hope that the recent research in both of these domains highlights how communication scholars can study attention and comprehension in mediated messages. Critically, the theories and methodologies that have been outlined in this chapter can also be used to understand attention and comprehension in contexts outside of the media such as interpersonal and group settings.

## ◆ References

Alwitt, L. F., Anderson, D. R., Lorch, E. P., & Levin, S. R. (1980). Preschool children's visual attention to attributes of television. *Human Communication Research, 7,* 52–67.

Anderson, D. R., Choi, H. P., & Lorch, E. P. (1987). Attentional inertia reduces distractability during children's TV viewing. *Child Development, 58,* 798–806.

Anderson, D. R., & Field, D. E. (1983). Children's attention to television: Implications for production. In M. Meyer (Ed.), *Children and the formal features of television: Approaches and findings of experimental and formative research* (pp. 56–96). Munich, Germany: K. G. Saur.

Anderson, D. R., & Kirkorian, H. L. (2006). Attention and television. In J. Bryant & P. Vorderer (Eds.), *Psychology of entertainment* (pp. 35–56). Mahwah, NJ: Lawrence Erlbaum.

Anderson, D. R., & Lorch, E. P. (1983). Looking at television: Action or reaction? In J. Bryant & D. R. Anderson (Eds.), *Children's understanding of television: Research on attention and comprehension* (pp. 1–33). New York: Academic Press.

Anderson, D. R., Lorch, E. P., Field, D. E., Collins, P. A., & Nathan, J. G. (1986). Television viewing at home: Age trends in visual attention and time with TV. *Child Development, 57,* 1024–1033.

Anderson, D. R., Lorch, E. P., Smith, R., Bradford, R., & Levin, S. R. (1981). Effects of peer presence on preschool children's television-viewing behavior. *Developmental Psychology, 17,* 446–453.

Basil, M. D. (1994). Multiple resource theory I: Application to television viewing. *Communication Research, 21,* 177–207.

Bickham, D. S., Wright, J. C., & Huston, A. C. (2001). Attention, comprehension, and the educational influences of television. In D. G. Singer & J. L. Singer (Eds.), *Handbook of children and the media* (pp. 101–119). Thousand Oaks, CA: Sage.

Bordwell, D. (2005). *Figures traced in light: On cinematic staging.* Berkeley: University of California Press.

Burns, J. J., & Anderson, D. R. (1993). Attentional inertia and recognition memory in adult television viewing. *Communication Research, 20,* 777–799.

Calvert, S. L., Huston, A. C., Watkins, B. A., & Wright, J. C. (1982). The relation between selective attention to television forms and children's comprehension of content. *Child Development, 53,* 601–610.

Crawford, Z. A., Roskos-Ewoldsen, B., & Roskos-Ewoldsen, D. R. (2004, April). *Dynamic mental models of a movie.* Paper presented at the annual meeting of the Midwestern Psychological Association, Chicago.

Crawley, A. M., Anderson, D. R., Santomero, A., Wilder, A., Williams, M., Evens, M. K., et al. (2002). Do children learn how to watch television? The impact of extensive experience with *Blue's Clues* on preschool children's television viewing behavior. *Journal of Communication, 52,* 264–280.

Foehr, U. G. (2006). *Media multitasking among American youth: Prevalence, predictors, and pairings.* Menlo Park, CA: Henry J. Kaiser Family Foundation.

Fox, J., Park, B., & Lang, A. (2007). When available resources become negative resources: The effects of cognitive overload on memory sensitivity and criterion bias. *Communication Research, 34,* 277–296.

Halas, J., & Bachelor, J. (Directors). (2004). *Animal farm* [DVD]. Chicago: Home Vision Entertainment. (Original movie released 1955)

Hawkins, R. P., Pingree, S., Hitchon, J., Radler, B., Gorham, B. W., Kahlor, L., et al. (2005). What produces television attention and attention style? Genre, situation, and individual differences as predictors. *Human Communication Research, 31,* 162–187.

Hawkins, R. P., Tapper, J., Bruce, L., & Pingree, S. (1995). Strategic and nonstrategic explanations for attentional inertia. *Communication Research, 22,* 188–206.

Hawkins, R. P., Yong-Ho, K., & Pingree, S. (1991). The ups and downs of attention to television. *Communication Research, 18,* 53–76.

Hollenbeck, A. R., & Slaby, R. G. (1979). Infant visual and vocal responses to television. *Child Development, 50,* 41–45.

Huston, A. C., & Wright, J. C. (1983). Children's processing of television: The informative functions of formal features. In J. Bryant & D. R. Anderson (Eds.), *Children's understanding of television: Research on attention and comprehension* (pp. 39–68). New York: Academic Press.

Kahneman, D. (1973). *Attention and effort.* Englewood Cliffs, NJ: Prentice Hall.

Krull, R., & Husson, W. (1979). Children's attention: The case of TV viewing. In E. Wartella (Ed.), *Children communicating: Media and development of thought, speech, understanding* (pp. 83–114). Beverly Hills, CA: Sage.

Lang, A. (2000). The limited capacity model of mediated message processing. *Journal of Communication, 50*(1), 46–70.

Lang, A. (2006). Using the limited capacity model of motivated mediated message processing to design effective cancer communication messages. *Journal of Communication, 56,* S57–S80.

Lang, A., & Basil, M. (1998). What do secondary task reaction times measure anyway? In M. Roloff (Ed.), *Communication yearbook 21* (pp. 443–470). Thousand Oaks, CA: Sage.

Lang, A., Bradley, S. D., Park, B., Shin, M., & Chung, Y. (2006). Parsing the resource pie: Using STRTs to measure attention to mediated messages. *Media Psychology, 8,* 369–394.

Lang, A., Geiger, S., Strickwerda, M., & Sumner, J. (1993). The effects of related and unrelated cuts on viewers' memory for television: A limited capacity theory of television viewing. *Communication Research, 20,* 4–29.

Lang, A., Potter, R. F., & Bolls, P. D. (1999). Something for nothing: Is visual encoding automatic? *Media Psychology, 1,* 145–163.

Lee, M., Roskos-Ewoldsen, D. R., & Roskos-Ewoldsen, B. (2004, May). *Mental representations of news stories.* Paper presented at the annual meeting of the International Communication Association, New Orleans, LA.

Livingstone, S. M. (1987). The implicit representation of characters in *Dallas:* A multidimensional scaling approach. *Human Communication Research, 13,* 399–420.

Livingstone, S. M. (1989). Interpretive viewers and structured programs: The implicit representations of soap opera characters. *Communication Research, 16,* 25–57.

Livingstone, S. M. (1990a). Interpreting a television narrative: How different viewers see a story. *Journal of Communication, 40*(1), 72–85.

Livingstone, S. M. (1990b). *Making sense of television: The psychology of audience interpretation.* Oxford, UK: Pergamon.

Lorch, E. P., Anderson, D. R., & Levin, S. R. (1979). The relationship of visual attention to children's comprehension of television. *Child Development, 50,* 722–727.

Lorch, E. P., & Castle, V. J. (1997). Preschool children's attention to television: Visual attention and probe response times. *Journal of Experimental Child Psychology, 66,* 111–127.

Magliano, J. P., Dijkstra, K., & Zwaan, R. A. (1996). Generating predictive inferences while viewing a movie. *Discourse Processes, 22,* 199–224.

Magliano, J. P., Miller, J., & Zwaan, R. A. (2001). Indexing space and time in film understanding. *Applied Cognitive Psychology, 15,* 533–545.

Orwell, G. (1945). *Animal farm.* London: Penguin.

Reeves, B., & Thorson, E. (1986). Watching television: Experiments on the viewing process. *Communication Research, 13,* 343–361.

Rice, M. L., Huston, C. A., & Wright, J. C. (1983). The forms of television: Effects on children's attention, comprehension, and social behavior. In M. Meyer (Ed.), *Children and the formal features of television: Approaches and findings of experimental and formative research* (pp. 21–55). Munich, Germany: K. G. Saur.

Rogers, E. M. (1994). *A history of communication study: A biographical approach.* New York: Free Press.

Roskos-Ewoldsen, B., Roskos-Ewoldsen, D. R., Yang, M., & Crawford, Z. (2003, May/June). *Mental models of a movie.* Poster session presented at the annual meeting of the American Psychological Society, Atlanta, GA.

Roskos-Ewoldsen, B., Roskos-Ewoldsen, D. R., Yang, M., & Lee, M. (2007). Comprehension of the media. In D. R. Roskos-Ewoldsen & J. Monahan (Eds.), *Communication and social cognition: Theories and methods* (pp. 319–350). Mahwah, NJ: Lawrence Erlbaum.

Rowell, J. A., & Moss, P. D. (1986). Mental models of text and film: A multidimensional scaling analysis. *Educational Psychology, 6,* 321–333.

Valkenberg, P. M., & Vroone, M. (2004). Developmental changes in infants' and toddlers' attention to television entertainment. *Communication Research, 31,* 288–311.

van den Broek, P., Risden, K., Fletcher, C., & Thurlow, R. (1996). A "landscape" view of reading: Fluctuating patterns of activation and the construction of a stable memory representation. In B. Britton & A. Graesser (Eds.), *Models of understanding text* (pp. 165–188). Mahwah, NJ: Lawrence Erlbaum.

van den Broek, P., Young, M., Tzeng, Y., & Linderholm, T. (1999). The landscape model of reading: Inferences and the online construction of a memory representation. In H. van Oostendorp & S. R. Goldman (Eds.), *The construction of mental representations during reading* (pp. 71–98). Mahwah, NJ: Lawrence Erlbaum.

van Dijk, T. A. (1995). On macrostructures, mental models, and other inventions: A brief personal history of the van Dijk-Kintsch theory. In C. A. Weaver, S. Mannes, & C. R. Fletcher (Eds.), *Discourse comprehension: Essays in honor of Walter Kintsch* (pp. 383–410). Hillsdale, NJ: Lawrence Erlbaum.

Wyer, R. S. (2004). *Social comprehension and judgment: The role of situation models, narratives, and implicit theories.* Mahwah, NJ: Lawrence Erlbaum.

Wyer, R. S., & Radvansky, G. A. (1999). The comprehension and validation of social information. *Psychological Review, 106,* 89–118.

Yang, M., & Roskos-Ewoldsen, D. R. (2007). The effectiveness of brand placements in the movies: Levels of placements, explicit and implicit memory, and brand choice behavior. *Journal of Communication, 57,* 469–489.

Zwaan, R. A., Langston, M. C., & Graesser, A. C. (1995). The construction of situation models in narrative comprehension: An event-indexing model. *Psychological Science, 6,* 292–297.

# THE NATURE OF INTERPERSONAL COMMUNICATION

## A Message-Centered Approach

◆ Brant R. Burleson

T he first edition of the *Handbook of Communication Science* included a chapter that focused on definitions and fundamental questions about interpersonal communication (Cappella, 1987). In this handbook's second edition, I continue this tradition. In the sciences, definitions of central concepts (and the models these imply) are core theoretical equipment. Differences in opinion about definitions crop up even in mature sciences, and these disagreements may be healthy, serving as the harbinger of significant conceptual advances. However, a radical lack of consensus about fundamental conceptual matters undermines coherence in research areas, creating confusion and discord. At present, little consensus exists about the meaning of *interpersonal communication*. This is not a good situation—scientifically, pedagogically, or politically.

To address this situation, I propose a new definition grounded in the idea that interpersonal communication fundamentally involves an exchange of messages. Although this notion hardly seems novel, some of the most influential definitions of interpersonal communication downplay or even exclude this necessary feature. To make the case for the new definition, I begin by describing the current state of dissensus about the fundamental nature of interpersonal communication and detail the undesirable consequences that follow from this. Next, I review and critique three popular definitions of interpersonal communication. I then present my message-centered definition and explicate its key terms. A subsequent section demonstrates how the conceptual model implied by this definition can serve as an organizing framework for theory and research on communication processes, structures, functions, and contexts. Finally, I comment on several potential objections to the proposed definition and consider directions for further conceptual development.

◆ *Dissensus in*
   *Conceptualizations of*
   *Interpersonal Communication*

Since "interpersonal communication" emerged as a recognizable area of theory, research, and teaching in the early 1970s, its scholarship has been reviewed in three editions of the *Handbook of Interpersonal Communication* (most recently, Knapp & Daly, 2002). Other edited volumes in the 1970s (e.g., Miller, 1976a), 1980s (e.g., Roloff & Miller, 1987), 1990s (e.g., Daly & Wiemann, 1994), and the current decade (e.g., Smith & Wilson, 2009) provide important research reviews. In addition, numerous articles have (a) described the historical development of interpersonal communication as a distinguishable area of teaching and research (e.g., Delia, 1987; Knapp, Daly, Fudge, & Miller, 2002; Rawlins, 1985), (b) explored the concept of interpersonal communication (e.g., Burleson, Metts, & Kirch, 2000; Cappella, 1987; Miller, 1978; Motley, 1990; Sillars & Vangelisti, 2006), and

(c) reviewed prominent theories and research findings in this area of study (e.g., Berger, 1977, 2005; Hallsten, 2004; Roloff & Anastasiou, 2001).

Although there is some overlap among scholars in how interpersonal communication is conceptualized, there are also substantial differences. For example, consider some of the definitions of interpersonal communication that appear in recent textbooks:

• "Interpersonal communication [refers] to dyadic communication in which two individuals, sharing the roles of sender and receiver, become connected through the mutual activity of creating meaning" (Trenholm & Jensen, 2008, p. 29).

• "Interpersonal communication is a distinctive form of human communication that . . . is defined not just by the number of people who communicate, but also by the quality of the communication. Interpersonal communication occurs not when you simply interact with someone, but when you treat the other as a unique human being" (Beebe, Beebe, & Redmond, 2002, p. 6).

• "Interpersonal communication refers to the exchange of messages, verbal and nonverbal, between people, regardless of the relationship they share. . . . Thus, interpersonal communication includes the exchange of messages in all sorts of relationships, ranging from functional to casual to intimate" (Guerrero, Andersen, & Afifi, 2007, p. 11).

These definitions all represent interpersonal communication as involving some form of mutual activity, interaction, or exchange, but they also differ significantly. For Beebe et al. (2002), interpersonal communication occurs in close relationships; for Trenholm and Jensen (2008), it transpires within dyads—any two-person system. Guerrero et al. (2007) are even less restrictive; for them, interpersonal communication is any exchange of messages between people, where a "message" can be any feature or behavior of another, intended or not, interpreted by a receiver (p. 12), with no restriction on the number of persons involved in the exchange.

The lack of consistency and consensus in definitions of interpersonal communication has been noted regularly by reviewers of this area over the past 30 years. For example, Berger (1977) observed, "While no attempt will be made here to define interpersonal communication, it should be stressed that this definitional problem remains unresolved" (p. 217). In subsequent years, other reviewers made similar observations (Cappella, 1987; Roloff & Anastasiou, 2001).

Does this lack of definitional consensus really matter? After all, as analytic propositions, definitions can never be "right or wrong" or "true or false"; definitions are, in some sense, arbitrary. But all definitions are NOT equally good. Definitions differ in their clarity, coherence, degree to which they explicate and illuminate, and especially their utility for given ends. Thus, to evaluate the worth of particular definitions, we need to know about the tasks for which these definitions are formulated. Roloff and Anastasiou (2001) suggest that definitions "set the central focus and boundaries" for research areas. So, definitions detail the logical elements of an entity and thus suggest the objects of study within a domain, as well as questions to be pursued with respect to those objects.

Moreover, science is a social enterprise and, as such, is maximally effective at producing knowledge when its practitioners form a community around shared understandings of the objects of study, relevant questions about these objects, and research exemplars focused on those objects. Thus, theorists and researchers need not only *good* definitions of central concepts (i.e., those that are clear, coherent, and enlightening), but also *shared* definitions of those concepts—definitions that have earned consensus among the practitioners in that scholarly community. The history of science indicates that rapid progress in an area is most likely to be achieved when there is community harmony about core concepts and research practices, not cacophony.

There have been three broad responses to this definitional dissensus. Some scholars simply seem to accept the lack of consensus, seeing definitional dissensus as inevitable. Others respond to the definitional dissensus by offering broad, inclusive definitions that attempt to synthesize different conceptualizations and models (e.g., defining communication as a "process of acting upon information"); unfortunately, such definitions are so abstract that they are all but useless in directing theory and research. A third group has forwarded specific definitions of interpersonal communication, arguing for their merits and demonstrating their implications for theory and research. This is the most productive response to definitional dissensus, as it presents a concrete conceptualization of interpersonal communication that can be evaluated. Of course, the definition, as well as the theory and research that follow from it, may ultimately be replaced by an alternative. But offering bold conjectures that invite focused refutations is the path of progress in the sciences (Popper, 1963); I next examine several such bold conjectures about the nature of interpersonal communication.

## ◆ Three Popular Definitions of Interpersonal Communication

Although little consensus about the definition of interpersonal communication currently exists, three broad definitional perspectives are often identified: the situational, the developmental, and the interactional.

## THE SITUATIONAL PERSPECTIVE

Miller (1990) contends that the situational perspective was the first substantive perspective on the nature of interpersonal communication to emerge (probably in the late 1960s) and was the most influential viewpoint on interpersonal communication until at least the mid-1970s. Although quite influential, the origins of the situational approach are unclear.

The situational perspective distinguishes types of communication on the basis of features of the communicative context, the most important of which include the number of communicators, the physical proximity of those communicators, the availability of sensory or communication channels (especially nonverbal ones), and the immediacy of feedback received by communicators (see Miller, 1978; Trenholm, 1986). Thus, interpersonal communication typically transpires between two people engaged in face-to-face interactions who use both verbal and nonverbal channels and have access to immediate feedback. Group, organizational, public, and mass communication involve increasing numbers of persons and decreasing levels of physical proximity, channel availability, and feedback immediacy. *Dyadic communication* often serves as a synonym for interpersonal communication in this perspective. The definition by Trenholm and Jensen (2008) presented at the outset of this chapter embodies the situational perspective on interpersonal communication.

The situational perspective leads to research on ways that contextual factors, especially features of the physical setting, influence processes and outcomes of interaction. Research questions consistent with the situational perspective include the following: Do dyads or groups make better decisions? Does the greater availability of nonverbal cues in dyadic interaction enhance communication fidelity? Does the use of emoticons in the "impoverished" environment of computer-mediated communication increase communicator satisfaction?

The situational perspective has been criticized extensively for highlighting less central interaction features (numbers of actors and qualities of the physical setting) while ignoring more substantive features, such as the relationship between the interactants and the content of their exchange. Miller (1978) maintains that "situational views of interpersonal communication imply a static, nondevelopmental perspective rather than a dynamic, developmental viewpoint of the process" (p. 166). Thus, for example, the situational view equates a face-to-face conversation between a postal clerk and a customer with a conversation between a pair of longtime lovers. Perhaps even more problematic, the situational view maintains that the interaction between the postal clerk and customer is *more* "interpersonal" than a letter from a soldier to his family that details his deepest thoughts and feelings. More generally, Miller contends that the situational perspective invites an ahistorical concern with the number of people in a context, excludes consideration of other features of the context (such as the quality of the relationship among participants) that may more profoundly influence communication processes and outcomes, and leads to pursuing trivial questions such as "how many people can participate in an interaction before it is no longer 'interpersonal.'" Furthermore, the situational perspective provides little guidance for research "save for suggesting that researchers manipulate this or that situational variable to determine its impact on the communication process" (Miller, 1976b, p. 10).

## THE DEVELOPMENTAL PERSPECTIVE

In response to the inadequacies of the situational perspective, Miller (Miller, 1976b, 1978, 1990; Miller & Steinberg, 1975) proposed an alternative: the developmental perspective of interpersonal communication (also see Stewart, 1973). This perspective begins by distinguishing between "impersonal" and "interpersonal" communication. In impersonal communication, interactants relate to one another as social roles rather than as distinct persons and base their predictions about how message options will affect the other on general cultural and sociological knowledge rather than psychological information. In contrast, in interpersonal communication, interactants relate to one another as unique persons and base their predictions about message options on specific psychological information about the other (e.g., the other's distinguishing traits, dispositions, attitudes, or feelings). Impersonal and interpersonal communication form a continuum; when people initially meet, they can only engage in impersonal communication, but if interaction continues and the participants reveal and exchange more personalizing information about each other, their relationship and interactions may become progressively more interpersonal in character. As Roloff and Anastasiou (2001) note, this perspective "makes the study of intimate relationships the central context for studying interpersonal communication" (p. 53; see Solomon & Vangelisti, Chapter 19, this volume). The definition by Beebe et al. (2002) presented at the outset of this chapter embodies the developmental perspective.

The developmental perspective has informed considerable research on processes of relationship development, including research on interpersonal attraction, uncertainty reduction, and self-disclosure, as well as research on other aspects of interaction such as compliance gaining, social exchange, and empathy (see reviews by Hallsten, 2004; Miller, 1990). The developmental perspective continues to enjoy broad acceptance and guides several lines of contemporary theory and research on interpersonal communication.

Despite its popularity, the developmental perspective has been the target of increasing criticism. Several critics argue that intimate relationships are not the only significant associations in life and that "role-specific interactions should be as much a part of the domain of interpersonal inquiry as are more personalized interactions" (Cappella, 1987, p. 186). Even more problematic, although the developmental perspective illuminates the processes that lead to the formation of intimate relationships and the nature of these relationships, it does not provide any analysis of communication per se. Thus, within the developmental perspective, it is unclear what people are doing when they communicate with each other, whatever their degree of knowledge about each other. Indeed, both the developmental perspective and the situational perspective promote the view that there is a qualitatively distinct form of communication that exists in, respectively, interpersonal relationships or interpersonal settings; the focus of these perspectives is thus on clarifying the character of "interpersonal-ness." Contrary to this view, Swanson and Delia (1976) argue, "There is one basic process of communication. . . . *The basic process of communication operates in every context in fundamentally the same way, even though each context requires slightly different skills or special applications of general communication principles*" (p. 36).

The critiques of the developmental perspective and its limited view of interpersonal communication appear to be increasingly influential. Indeed, no less a proponent of the developmental perspective than Charles Berger (2005) recently observed, "Because the domain encompassed by the term *social interaction* is considerably more expansive than the one represented by the interpersonal communication-as-close-relationship-development formulation, it seems wise to adopt the broader and more diverse purview afforded by the social interaction term" (p. 431). We next examine an approach that defines interpersonal communication in terms of social interaction.

## THE INTERACTIONAL PERSPECTIVE

Unlike the situational and developmental perspectives, the interactional perspective treats most, if not all, cases of social interaction as instances of interpersonal communication. Thus, this perspective focuses on unpacking the nature and implications of human interaction rather than attempting to identify a distinguishing essence of interpersonal communication. The origins of the interactional perspective can be traced to the analysis of communication provided by Watzlawick, Beavin, and Jackson (1967). Cappella (1987) provides the most systematic articulation of the interactional perspective, defining interpersonal communication as *mutual adjustment or influence* (see Roloff & Li, Chapter 18, this volume). Cappella explains that the essential commitment of this perspective "is to the interactional character of interpersonal communication, emphasizing that for interpersonal communication to occur, each person must affect the other's observable behavior patterns relative to their typical or baseline patterns" (p. 189). Cappella further underscores that "all encounters that are interactions are interpersonal" (p. 189). The definition by Guerrero et al. (2007) presented at the outset of this chapter embodies this interactional perspective.

Clearly, interpersonal communication involves interaction, but there is disagreement about whether interaction is a sufficient condition for interpersonal communication or simply a necessary one. For example, Delia, O'Keefe, and O'Keefe (1982) maintain that "interaction is not communication, although all communication is a form of interaction and thus shares the characteristics of interaction in general" (p. 159). There are obvious instances of interaction that appear to have little to do with interpersonal communication. For example, people routinely engage in mutual adjustments to the presence and movements of others on a crowded sidewalk, as well as on a crowded freeway. Most would not refer to such interaction as "interpersonal communication."

Missing from the interactional perspective is the idea of a *message*—behavioral expressions typically consisting of symbols that are intended convey internal states, create shared meanings, and accomplish goals (see Motley, 1990). Cappella (1987) anticipates this objection and counterargues that even if features such as the intentional use of symbols in messages "are required, it is premature for us to make our definitions so narrow and it is unproductive for us to debate issues [about the nature, existence, and assessment of intentions and similar internal states] that are unresolvable on empirical grounds" (p. 191). But a major purpose of definitions is to narrow the domain of concepts such as "interpersonal communication" by excluding phenomena that fall outside a desired range (such as interactions that lack any exchange of messages). Moreover, overly broad definitions may be even more unproductive than overly narrow definitions; their inclusion of extraneous phenomena creates confusion and obscures essential distinctions. Furthermore, unless one is willing to treat human communication only as a series of emitted noises, twitches, and squiggles, one must allow meanings, goals, symbols, and intentions as *necessary* features of communicative interactions and develop a conceptual apparatus that accommodates these (see Fay & Moon, 1977).

In sum, although the situational, developmental, and interactional perspectives each contribute important insights about the nature of interpersonal communication, they all have significant limitations, and none provides an optimal foundation for theory, research, and teaching. Missing from all three of these perspectives is a focus on what seems central to the idea of communication: the production and interpretation of messages.

## ◆ A Message-Centered Approach to Defining Interpersonal Communication

The message-centered perspective developed here maintains that interpersonal communication is productively conceptualized as a particular type of social interaction centered on the processes of producing and interpreting messages. I show that a definition focused on this species of interaction provides a framework for coordinating theory and research on the fundamental processes, structures, functions, and contexts associated with interpersonal communication. The current analysis refines some of my previous efforts to characterize essential characteristics of interpersonal communication (Burleson, 1992; Burleson et al., 2000) and is indebted to early conceptual work on the nature of the communication process by Delia and his associates (Delia et al., 1982; Swanson & Delia, 1976).

I offer the following definition: *Interpersonal communication is a complex, situated social process in which people who have established a communicative relationship exchange messages in an effort to generate shared meanings and accomplish social goals.* In what follows, I seek to clarify this definition by explicating its key terms.

A precondition for interpersonal communication is the establishment of a *communicative relationship* between interactants. This relationship is constituted by a peculiar structure of reciprocal expressive and interpretive intentions among interactants. An *expressive intention* is the aim by one party (a source) to convey (make accessible) some internal state (an idea, thought, feeling, etc.) to a second party (the recipient), whereas an *interpretive intention* is the aim by a recipient to comprehend the source's expressions. Thus, a communicative relationship comes into being when (a) a source has the intention to convey some internal state to a recipient, (b) the recipient recognizes the source's expressive intention and signals the complementary intention to attend to the source's expressions, and (c) the source recognizes that his or her expressive intention has been recognized and accepted by the recipient.[1]

With the establishment of a communicative relationship, interactants can engage in an exchange of messages in the effort to create shared meanings and achieve social goals. *Meanings* are the internal states (thoughts, ideas, beliefs, feelings, etc.) that communicators seek to express or convey in a message and interpret a message as expressing or conveying. When communicating, persons strive to align their expressions and interpretations of messages with one another so as to achieve shared meaning—a common understanding of the internal states associated with messages.

*Messages* are sets of behavioral expressions, typically consisting of shared symbols, which are produced in the effort to convey some internal state. Although the connection between symbols and that which they signify is arbitrary, communication is possible, in part, because most symbols used by interactants have a conventional interpretation within a community. However, the conventional (denotative) meaning associated with symbols is rarely sufficiently precise to convey adequately a source's contextually specific (connotative) meanings. So, the symbols composing a message must be interpreted by recipients in a contextually sensitive manner. Communication thus has a fidelity characteristic (Motley, 1990); the interpretations by source and recipient given to the symbols composing a message can differ to a greater or lesser extent, affecting the degree of shared meaning achieved.

A message is more than symbols that compose words and sentences; a message is fundamentally a *speech act*—the performance of an action through the expression of words and gestures (see Tracy, 2002). Indeed, Searle (1969) maintains that in using symbols to produce a message, a source actually performs a whole set of actions, including one or more illocutionary acts (e.g., declaring, asserting, directing, expressing, or committing), as well as multiple propositional acts (e.g., referring and predicating) and utterance acts (e.g., generating words, sentences, and gestures). All of the actions performed by a source through a message must be interpreted by the recipient, and each represents a potential source of misunderstanding; a recipient may not understand what was said (confusion about words or sentences), what was meant (confusion about reference or predication), what was done (confusion about the speaker's illocutionary act), what the speaker wanted to achieve (confusion about the intended outcome), or the speaker's underlying motivation for these interrelated actions.

In interpersonal communication, achieving a shared understanding about the meaning of a message is primarily a means to an end. That is, people do not produce and interpret messages as ends in themselves; rather, they engage in these activities to accomplish particular *social goals*—goals that in some way focus on, include, or require the participation of others. As discussed in detail below, sources may pursue a variety of instrumental objectives through the messages they produce (e.g., entertaining, informing, persuading, supporting), while recipients pursue a variety of objectives with regard to these messages (e.g., understanding what messages mean, do, imply, and request). Moreover, both message sources and recipients typically pursue multiple goals pertaining to the management of identities and relationships throughout the course of an interaction, as well as goals related to managing the interaction itself (e.g., changing topics, moving to close the interaction). Although people sometimes say they are "just talking to pass the time," phrases like these generally refer to communicative activity focused on social goals such as recreating or relationship enhancement.

Of course, people are not always consciously aware of the goals they pursue when communicating and typically have even less awareness of the strategic process through which they pursue goals (Motley, 1990); although communicative behavior is inherently strategic, it is also primarily automatic (Kellermann, 1992). Furthermore, people may pursue goals that are harmful to self and other, as well as pursue those that are beneficial. Of particular importance, messages vary enormously in their effectiveness or success with respect to goal attainment; a given message may be fully successful, partially successful, or wholly unsuccessful in achieving its pragmatic objectives. Thus, a central objective of communication research lies in identifying the features of messages that are reliably associated with greater (and lesser) degrees of goal achievement, and a central task of communication theory lies in developing testable explanations about why certain message features more consistently lead to goal attainment than do others.

To sum to this point: To the extent that the recipient recognizes the source's intention to convey an internal state, and the source recognizes the recipient's intention to interpret, the source and receiver enter into a communicative relationship; to the extent that the recipient interprets the symbols and context of the source's message in a manner similar to the source, communication occurs; and to the extent that the recipient responds to the message in a manner consistent with the source's goal, the message is effective.

There are several other notable properties of interpersonal communication. First, it is a *complex process*. That is, interpersonal communication is not a single process but rather is composed of several interrelated processes that need to be carefully coordinated. These processes include message production, message processing (or reception), interaction coordination, and social perception; each of these processes receives additional consideration later in this chapter. This viewpoint implies that the character of interpersonal communication will be illuminated by distinct theories of particular processes rather than by one general theory.

Second, interpersonal communication is a *situated process;* it never occurs in the abstract but always in a specific, concrete situation. This is highly consequential since particular communicative situations substantially influence roles and identities, goals, selections and interpretations of specific message elements, expectations for self and other, availability of expressive and interpretive resources (e.g., sensory channels, communicative media), and a host of related factors. Moreover, as symbolic interactionists emphasize (e.g., McCall & Simmons, 1978), situations are fluid and the factors that compose them are dynamic; thus the nature of the situation and its underlying components may evolve over the course of an interaction, sometimes substantially. What remains invariant across situations is the fundamental nature of the interpersonal communication process (as described above); of course, many of the factors that influence the manner, substance, and outcomes of interpersonal communication *do* vary as a function of the situation.

Third, interpersonal communication is a *social process*. Its component processes are executed and coordinated by two or more beings that are mutually oriented toward each other in the unfolding situation. As a species of social interaction, communication necessarily involves mutual influence and joint action.

## ◆ Implications of the Message-Centered Definition for the Study of Interpersonal Communication

The terms in the message-centered definition, as well as the underlying conceptual model they imply, point to several key aspects of interpersonal communication that have been the focus of considerable research, including fundamental communication processes, structures, functions, and contexts. Thus, this definition, as well as its underlying model, offers an integrative conceptual framework for organizing theory and research on central aspects of interpersonal communication.

### PROCESSES OF INTERPERSONAL COMMUNICATION

Interpersonal communication is composed of the interrelated processes of message production, message processing, interaction coordination, and social perception. *Message production* is the process of generating verbal and nonverbal behaviors designed to convey an internal state to another to accomplish social goals. *Message processing* (sometimes called "message reception" or "decoding") involves interpreting the communicative behavior of others in the effort to understand the meaning and implications of their behavior. *Interaction coordination* is the process of synchronizing message production and message-processing activities (along with other behaviors) over the course of a social episode so as to achieve smooth and coherent interchanges. Finally, *social perception* is the set of processes through which we make sense of the social world, including experiences of ourselves, other people, social relationships, and social institutions.

Research on these processes has sought to clarify the nature of each of them by (a) specifying the component structures and processes through which each proceeds, (b) describing different modes of operation for each (e.g., automatic vs. controlled) and the factors that invoke particular modes, (c) detailing essential features of their characteristic outputs (i.e., messages for production, interpretations for processing, interactions for coordination, and various perceptions and inferences for social perception) and how these vary as a function of operating mode, and (d) identifying factors (such as emotional arousal) that generally affect their operation and outputs.

Numerous theoretical models of the message production process have been proposed, including Berger's (2007) planning theory, Dillard's (2008) goals-plans-actions theory, Greene's (2007) action assembly theory, and several other variants (for review, see Berger, 2003, and Chapter 7, this volume). Although these theories differ in important ways, they provide similar analyses of the message production process: (a) Interpretation of a situation, in conjunction with enduring values and motivational orientations, gives rise to a set of interaction goals; (b) these goals, in conjunction with representations of the ongoing situation, lead to the retrieval from memory of existing message plans or schemes that might be adaptable to current needs, if such exist; (c) if a suitable plan is not located in memory, a new plan is generated; and (d) the abstract message plan (either retrieved or generated) is concretized and populated with appropriate content and subsequently articulated. The enacted plan is (e) monitored for its impact and may subsequently be (f) modified and rearticulated if that appears desirable. Message production has been a very active research area for more than two decades, with the accumulated findings leading to increasingly more sophisticated understandings of this process (see review by Berger, 2005, and Chapter 7, this volume).

Although message processing is an understudied phenomenon (see Berger, 2005), the broad outlines of the process can be sketched: The message recipient (a) detects physical signals carrying what is interpreted to be a message from a source, and (b) these signals are parsed into words and phrases, which form the basis for inferences about what the source (c) has said (syntactic analysis), (d) means (semantic analysis), (e) is doing (pragmatic analysis), and (f) wants to accomplish (motivational analysis). The recipient may also (g) evaluate various aspects of the message (e.g., its truth, its appropriateness) and the source (e.g., his or her sincerity) and (h) respond internally to this set of inferences and judgments. Certain aspects of message processing have received detailed theoretical attention (e.g., Roskos-Ewoldsen & Roskos-Ewoldsen, Chapter 8, this volume; Wyer & Adaval, 2003), and research has examined phenomena such as how recipients correct for what they view as bias in a message (Hewes, 1995), are taken in by deceptive efforts (McCornack, 2008), and either closely scrutinize message content or process it superficially (Bodie & Burleson, 2008).

Burgoon (1998) compares the coordinated exchange of messages between interactants to a dance, with "each dancer's movement seeming to anticipate that of the partner" (p. 53). Achieving such fine coordination requires, at a minimum, learning and developing facility with the social rules governing particular interchanges (e.g., the rules for turn and topic management in face-to-face conversations, the rules for interaction in classroom discussions, the rules for contributions and comments in instant messenger exchanges; see Tracy, 2002). More generally, interaction adaptation theory (see Burgoon, Floyd, & Guerrero, Chapter 6, this volume; White, 2008) details how individuals achieve highly synchronous interactions through both behavioral reciprocity and matching, while communication accommodation theory (Giles & Ogay, 2007; Soliz & Giles, Chapter 5, this volume) describes how interactants mutually alter their verbal and nonverbal behaviors so that these converge to express solidarity and diverge to express distinctness (for a recent review of these and related theories, see Berger, 2005).

Strictly speaking, social perception is not a communicative process per se since it does not necessarily involve the production, processing, or coordination of messages; rather, it is an aspect of social cognition. However, social perception enters into communication in numerous ways, such as through defining the social situation, including who is in the situation, what their roles are, and what actions they are performing; inferring relevant cognitive, affective, and behavioral qualities of others in the situation on the basis of their dress, movements, expressions, and spontaneous (i.e., symptomatic) nonverbal behavior; ascertaining whether a potential message recipient appears cognizant of one's communicative intentions; evaluating whether a message has been comprehended and accepted and is likely to be acted upon in the desired manner; assessing how the parties to the transaction are feeling about each other; and so forth. In service of these ends, people employ a variety of distinguishable social perception processes, including identifying affect states, making attributions for actions, forming impressions, integrating information, and taking the perspective of the other; all of these processes have been the subject of extensive research (see Fiske & Taylor, 2007).

## STRUCTURES OF INTERPERSONAL COMMUNICATION

The message-centered conception of interpersonal communication focuses on messages—a particular type of behavioral structure that is generated, interpreted, and coordinated through numerous cognitive, linguistic, social, and behavioral structures. Linguists and psychologists study the lexical, syntactic, semantic, and pragmatic message structures that enable people to produce comprehensible, informationally adequate, and pragmatically relevant messages (see Clark & Bly, 1995). Communication scholars (along with a few social and educational psychologists) give particular attention to the strategic plans people use to shape discourse that aims to achieve desired goals. Research has focused on the nature and constituents of these plans, how they are generated or learned initially, how they are stored in and retrieved from memory, how abstract plans get concretized and applied in specific situations, and how people alter or change message plans when their initial plans prove inadequate (see review by Berger, 2003). Researchers and educators have also identified a host of strategic plans that are (or can be) used in the pursuit of numerous communicative objectives (e.g., "advance organizers," the inverted pyramid, and the "5Ws" in informative communication; the motivated sequence and two-sided arguments in persuasive communication; the support-analyze-advise sequence when giving advice).

Structures implicated in social perception processes, interactional coordination, and message production and processing have been examined by scholars from several different disciplines. For example, social psychologists have identified a variety of cognitive structures (e.g., schemas, scripts, constructs, prototypes, exemplars) used in the interpretation of the self, other people, social actions, and social situations (see Fiske & Taylor, 2007).

Conversational analysts detail how various behavioral structures (e.g., the turn-taking system, adjacency pairs, repair structures for managing overlap and gap) generate coherent, smoothly flowing conversational interactions (e.g., Mandelbaum, 2008). A related set of structures governs social uses and forms of talk, such as rules that specify who may say what to whom when and where. These structures are typically studied by sociolinguists, sociologists, anthropologists, and others interested in the ethnography of communication since investigation of these rule systems necessarily involves examining larger systems of social roles, norms, power, and organization (Tracy, 2002). Researchers working within these traditions emphasize that communicative interactions not only are constrained by these structures but also serve to generate or reproduce these structures. That is, communication is a *constitutive activity* that both creates and is constrained by myriad social structures (Seibold & Myers, 2006).

## FUNCTIONS OF INTERPERSONAL COMMUNICATION

The message-centered definition of interpersonal communication emphasizes its fundamentally pragmatic character; people produce and interpret messages to accomplish social goals or functions. Multiple typologies of communication functions have been proposed by theorists (see Robinson, 2001); here, I describe three broad classes of function: interaction management functions, relationship management functions, and instrumental functions (see Burleson et al., 2000).

*Interaction management functions* are those associated with establishing and maintaining coherent conversation. Goals here include (a) initiating and ending conversational interactions, as well as maintaining them by directing their topical focus and turn distribution (Slugoski & Hilton, 2001); (b) producing comprehensible, informationally adequate, and pragmatically relevant messages that fit appropriately into the turn structure of conversation (Clark & Bly, 1995); (c) defining social selves and situations (McCall & Simmons, 1978); (d) managing impressions and maintaining face (Metts & Grohskopf, 2003); and (e) monitoring and managing affect (see Planalp, Metts, & Tracy, Chapter 21, this volume; Saarni, 2000). Accomplishment of these generally tacit and nonproblematic goals forms a "background consensus" within which other goals may be pursued.

*Relationship management functions* are associated with the initiation, maintenance, and repair of a relationship. These goals focus on establishing the relationship, achieving desired levels of privacy and intimacy, managing tensions, dealing with threats to the relationship's integrity and endurance (e.g., geographic separations, jealousy), resolving conflicts, and ending the relationship or altering its basic character. The need for relationship management arises from routine differences between individuals, competition between partners over limited resources, natural "bumps" in the course of relationship development, and strains inherent in balancing "dialectical tensions" (Baxter & Braithwaite, 2007; see Solomon & Vangelisti, Chapter 19, this volume).

*Instrumental functions* are those that typically define the focus of an interaction and serve to distinguish one interactional episode from another (Dillard, 2008). Common instrumental goals include gaining or resisting compliance, requesting or presenting information, soliciting or giving support, and seeking or providing amusement.

The *manner* in which instrumental tasks are communicatively addressed will typically reflect—albeit implicitly—the speaker's feelings about the relationship with the recipient and how the self is viewed in regard to the other. Research suggests that this "relational" level of communication is especially important in expressing feelings regarding control, trust, and intimacy (Courtright, 2007).

Research on communicative functions generally addresses the following groups of questions:

• What is the nature of the particular communicative function? That is, what does it mean to comfort, entertain, inform, persuade, manage conflict, and so on? What are the dimensions or aspects of these? What are the outcomes of interest associated with various functions?

• What message structures are generally more and less effective at pursuing particular functions, what are the key features of these message structures, why are some structures more effective than others, and what factors moderate or qualify the effects of specific message structures for various outcomes?

• What abilities and motivations do individuals need to control if they are to reliably enact message strategies likely to achieve desired outcomes? What do communicators need to know about their topic, audience, and occasion to generate messages that will be appropriate and effective? Furthermore, what motivations underlie the expenditure of effort to produce messages likely to be effective? How do individuals acquire these competencies over the course of development, and what training can enhance these competencies?

Extensive programs of research have addressed these questions for some functions, including emotional support (Burleson,

2003), informing (Rowan, 2003), and persuading (Dillard, 2003, and Chapter 12, this volume), among others. In other areas (e.g., initiating and managing romantic relationships), research has identified some relevant goals and strategies but has yet to detail the effectiveness of different strategies and the factors that affect their use and outcomes (e.g., Dindia & Timmerman, 2003).

## CONTEXTS OF INTERPERSONAL COMMUNICATION

The message-centered definition emphasizes the situatedness of interpersonal communication. Communication context turns out to be a complex construct, and several theorists (e.g., Knapp et al., 2002) have proposed typologies of its dimensions. Applegate and Delia (1980) suggest five dimensions of context for communication situations: the physical setting (the space, environment, and channels employed), the social/relational setting (e.g., friends, spouses, coworkers, neighbors), the institutional setting (e.g., home, work, school, church), the functional setting (the primary goal pursued, e.g., informing, persuading, supporting), and the cultural setting (including ethnicity, nationality, social class, and other relevant groupings). Any specific instance of interpersonal communication occurs in the intersection of these multiple dimensions of context; this intersection is commonly called a situation.

Context matters because it influences the operation and outcomes of the four basic interpersonal communication processes. Aspects of context affect what people do and the form and content of the messages they produce. The roles people play with each other in a particular situation (along with the channels, norms, rituals, rules, codes, etc., associated with particular situations and roles) shape and may even mandate the pursuit of various goals, the strategies used in pursuing particular goals,

the manner or style in which these strategies are instantiated (e.g., language styles, communication channels), the competencies needed to realize particular goals, and criteria for effective performance (see Berger, 2007). Context powerfully influences the interpretation and outcome of messages, affecting which features of the message and situation receive attention, how these features get processed (e.g., superficially vs. systematically), what these features are taken to mean or imply, and how the recipient can allowably respond (Bodie & Burleson, 2008). Context shapes how people coordinate their interactions, influencing (and sometimes determining) the typical turn and topic structure for interactions (e.g., board meetings vs. bull sessions) and the devices that can be used for controlling turns and topics (e.g., raising a hand in the classroom to signal interest in having a turn at talk; see Tracy, 2002), the degree of convergence versus divergence attained (Giles & Ogay, 2007), and the modes and extent of reciprocity and compensation exhibited (White, 2008). Finally, context profoundly influences virtually every aspect and process of social perception, from schema activation to attention, memory, and inference (Fiske & Taylor, 2007).

Context also matters because it and many of the elements composing it are created, maintained, and transformed through the communicative activities of participants (Burleson et al., 2000). Communication is often the critical process in defining the nature of a social situation (McCall & Simmons, 1978). The messages and interactions that people produce sustain, re-create, and reinforce a multitude of social structures, including those that intimately influence communicative conduct (e.g., roles, rules, norms, rituals) and, more fundamentally, those that underlie the very possibility of communication itself (e.g., verbal and nonverbal codes, systems of speech acts, the turn structure of interaction, plans and strategies for messages, schemes for interpreting others and their messages). Moreover, contexts are both mutable and fluid, which means that communicative practices can modify or even transform contexts through a variety of means (e.g., changing the physical or institutional setting, altering the relationship between the participants, shifting the functions pursued, and modifying the relevance of particular cultural rules and understandings). This understanding of the relationship between communication and context has led to research exploring the interactional tensions that motivate redefinitions of situations (Baxter & Braithwaite, 2007), how interactants use talk to redefine the situations in which they find themselves (e.g., Tracy, 2002), and the message structures most likely to accomplish a redefinition of the situation effectively (O'Keefe, 1988).

## ◆ Conclusion

Definitions of a discipline's core concepts matter, and this is particularly true in areas where there is widespread dissensus about these definitions. In an effort to address the inadequacies of extant definitions, deepen our understanding of interpersonal communication, and perhaps decrease the degree of definitional dissensus in this area, I proposed a message-centered definition of interpersonal communication. This definition appears to provide a useful organizing framework for much current theory and research on interpersonal communication by connecting diverse lines of work on communication processes, structures, functions, and contexts. Although the approach taken here has strengths, several criticisms can be directed at it; for some, the definition will be too broad, for others too narrow, for still others it will be too psychological, and for some it will completely miss the essential character of communication. In concluding, I briefly describe and address some of these criticisms.

The message-centered perspective treats "interpersonal communication" as

communication *between people*. Miller (1976b) criticized this idea, observing that such a definition "captures the etymology of the terms 'inter' and 'personal' but does nothing to distinguish interpersonal communication from all other human communicative transactions" (p. 10). To this indictment I must plead guilty as charged. But Miller's criticism appears premised on the false assumption that there really are different kinds of communication that show up in different contexts. Unfortunately, this assumption is given credence by the accepted nomenclature for describing the domains of study in our discipline (i.e., interpersonal communication, group communication, organizational communication)—locutions that certainly suggest that there are different underlying substances examined in each of these areas. This, however, is an unproductive way of conceptualizing communication; I agree with Swanson and Delia (1976) that there is *one* underlying nature of communication, the character of which I seek to capture in my message-centered definition. Thus, rather than using misleading labels such as *interpersonal communication* and *group communication*, perhaps we should refer to communication in dyadic settings, communication in group settings, and so forth. This latter terminology emphasizes that what varies is the context in which communication transpires but not the fundamental nature of communication itself.

While the message-centered definition of interpersonal communication is likely to be viewed as overly broad by proponents of the situational and developmental perspectives, advocates of the interactional perspective are likely to view it as overly narrow in that it excludes phenomena they regard as significant. Although the message-centered perspective certainly is more exclusive than Cappella's (1987) interactional perspective and is vastly more exclusive than the even more encompassing interactional view advocated by Watzlawick et al. (1967), there is considerable merit in focusing on instances of interaction characterized by the exchange of messages. This does not mean that phenomena falling outside the exchange of messages are unimportant and should not be examined by communication scholars; indeed, I have emphasized the vital role in communication played by numerous social perception processes and the phenomena on which these focus. Moreover, I recognize that there are numerous borderline cases of "quasi-communicative" behavior in which neither the interactants nor observers are clear about whether a communicative relationship has been established, shared meaning has been achieved, or goals have been accomplished; these borderline cases are interesting and need to be examined. But these borderline cases are brought into relief and given texture, in part, by the message-centered conception of communication, which provides conceptual tools for exploring problems associated with the establishment of a communication relationship, achieving shared meaning, and accomplishing functional goals. These all represent areas that will benefit from further conceptual development, as well as focused empirical research (e.g., how do potential interactants recognize and respond to difficulties encountered with establishing a communicative relationship?).

For some, the message-centered perspective on interpersonal communication will be problematic because it includes and requires analyses of numerous psychological states, including intentions, goals, plans, meanings, and so forth. This is a concern to some because these entities are notoriously slippery, and it has not always been made clear how these mental entities arise, function, and change in the course of communicative interactions (e.g., Bavelas, 1991). I acknowledge the legitimacy of this concern and further admit that I do not provide precise treatments of these constructs here. But this is not a principled objection against the inclusion of mental or intentional states, and there are sophisticated treatments of these concepts available (e.g., Kellermann,

1992) that can be drawn upon in further refining the framework proposed here.

A more radical critique of the message-centered perspective holds that its concern with psychological states is symptomatic of a fundamentally flawed approach to conceptualizing communication as a process in which individuals transmit information, share meanings, and accomplish goals. In particular, proponents of social constructionist and postmodernist approaches to interpersonal communication (Cronen, 1998; Deetz, 1994) maintain that psychological approaches to communication fail to recognize the fundamentally constitutive character of communication. On this view, communication is not so much a vehicle for sharing meaning and accomplishing goals as it is the medium in which meanings and their attendant social structures (roles, norms, rules, rituals, codes, etc.) are constituted. Communication *is* a constitutive activity; it produces (and reproduces) a host of social and interactional structures while being constrained by these structures. Although this is an extremely important (albeit usually unintentional) effect of communication, it is but one of *many* effects (e.g., achieving instrumental goals, managing relationships, managing interactions). Importantly, approaches that focus on the constitutive properties of communication almost never provide any analysis of the communication process; they do not explain what communication is, how it works, and how it manages to generate its myriad effects. But there is no necessary incompatibility between viewing communication as an intentional activity grounded in psychological processes through which individuals seek to achieve goals and viewing it as a social activity that, among other outcomes, constitutes social structures, including some of the structures that regulate and make possible the very activity of communication itself.

As a 35-year member of the cantankerous group that constitutes the communication discipline, I do not expect (or desire) that the definition of interpersonal communication offered here will end deliberation about the fundamental nature of this subject matter. Indeed, given the history of debates in our discipline about its essential concepts, I would be surprised if the approach advocated here generates more consensus than controversy. Regardless of whether the definition offered here wins widespread acceptance, my hope is that the analysis presented in this chapter helps clarify some core issues in conceptualizing interpersonal communication and aids readers in developing an understanding of this phenomenon that promotes theory, research, and teaching.

## ◆ Note

1. Some modification of this formulation is needed when considering communication between parties separated by time or space (e.g., writing a letter to someone far away; reading an essay written by a long-dead author). In such cases, the source may *assume* that his or her expressive intentions *will be* recognized and accepted by the recipient, and the recipient may recognize the source's expressive intentions and attend to them but *not* signal his or her interpretive intention. Communication between parties separated by time or space is possible because the participants are intimately familiar with the nature of communication in shared time and space and thus can make the necessary accommodations to adjust for temporal or spatial separation.

## ◆ References

Applegate, J. L., & Delia, J. G. (1980). Person-centered speech, psychological development, and the contexts of language usage. In R. S. Clair & H. Giles (Eds.), *The social and psychological contexts of language usage* (pp. 245–282). Hillsdale, NJ: Lawrence Erlbaum.

Bavelas, J. B. (1991). Some problems with linking goals to discourse. In K. Tracy (Ed.), *Understanding face-to-face interaction: Issues linking goals and discourse* (pp. 119–130). Hillsdale, NJ: Lawrence Erlbaum.

Baxter, L. A., & Braithwaite, D. O. (2007). Social dialectics: The contradictions of relating. In B. B. Whaley & W. Samter (Eds.), *Explaining communication: Contemporary theories and exemplars* (pp. 275–292). Mahwah, NJ: Lawrence Erlbaum.

Beebe, S. A., Beebe, S. J., & Redmond, M. V. (2002). *Interpersonal communication: Relating to others*. Boston: Allyn & Bacon.

Berger, C. R. (1977). Interpersonal communication theory and research: An overview. In B. D. Ruben (Ed.), *Communication yearbook 1* (pp. 217–228). New Brunswick, NJ: Transaction.

Berger, C. R. (2003). Message production skill in social interaction. In J. O. Greene & B. R. Burleson (Eds.), *Handbook of communication and social interaction skills* (pp. 257–289). Mahwah, NJ: Lawrence Erlbaum.

Berger, C. R. (2005). Interpersonal communication: Theoretical perspectives, future prospects. *Journal of Communication, 55,* 415–447.

Berger, C. R. (2007). Plans, planning, and communication effectiveness. In B. B. Whaley & W. Samter (Eds.), *Explaining communication: Contemporary theories and exemplars* (pp. 149–164). Mahwah, NJ: Lawrence Erlbaum.

Bodie, G. D., & Burleson, B. R. (2008). Explaining variations in the effects of supportive messages: A dual-process framework. In C. Beck (Ed.), *Communication yearbook 32* (pp. 354–398). New York: Routledge.

Burgoon, J. K. (1998). It takes two to tango: Interpersonal adaptation and implications for relational communication. In J. S. Trent (Ed.), *Communication: Views from the helm for the 21st century* (pp. 53–59). Boston: Allyn & Bacon.

Burleson, B. R. (1992). Taking communication seriously. *Communication Monographs, 59,* 79–86.

Burleson, B. R. (2003). Emotional support skills. In J. O. Greene & B. R. Burleson (Eds.), *Handbook of communication and social interaction skills* (pp. 551–594). Mahwah, NJ: Lawrence Erlbaum.

Burleson, B. R., Metts, S., & Kirch, M. W. (2000). Communication in close relationships. In

C. Hendrick & S. S. Hendrick (Eds.), *Close relationships: A sourcebook* (pp. 244–258). Thousand Oaks, CA: Sage.

Cappella, J. N. (1987). Interpersonal communication: Definition and fundamental questions. In C. R. Berger & S. H. Chaffee (Eds.), *Handbook of communication science* (pp. 184–238). Newbury Park, CA: Sage.

Clark, H. H., & Bly, B. (1995). Pragmatics and discourse. In J. L. Miller & P. D. Eimas (Eds.), *Speech, language, and communication* (pp. 371–410). San Diego: Academic Press.

Courtright, J. A. (2007). Relational communication: As viewed from the pragmatic perspective. In B. B. Whaley & W. Samter (Eds.), *Explaining communication: Contemporary theories and exemplars* (pp. 311–332). Mahwah, NJ: Lawrence Erlbaum.

Cronen, V. E. (1998). Communication theory for the twenty-first century: Cleaning up the wreckage of the psychology project. In J. S. Trent (Ed.), *Communication: Views from the helm for the 21st century* (pp. 18–38). Boston: Allyn & Bacon.

Daly, J. A., & Wiemann, J. M. (Eds.). (1994). *Strategic interpersonal communication.* Hillsdale, NJ: Lawrence Erlbaum.

Deetz, S. A. (1994). Future of the discipline: The challenges, the research, and the social contribution. In S. A. Deetz (Ed.), *Communication yearbook 17* (pp. 565–600). Thousand Oaks, CA: Sage.

Delia, J. G. (1987). Communication research: A history. In C. R. Berger & S. H. Chaffee (Eds.), *Handbook of communication science* (pp. 20–98). Newbury Park, CA: Sage.

Delia, J. G., O'Keefe, B. J., & O'Keefe, D. J. (1982). The constructivist approach to communication. In F. E. X. Dance (Ed.), *Human communication theory: Comparative essays* (pp. 147–191). New York: Harper & Row.

Dillard, J. P. (2003). Persuasion as a social skill. In J. O. Greene & B. R. Burleson (Eds.), *Handbook of communication and social interaction skills* (pp. 479–514). Mahwah, NJ: Lawrence Erlbaum.

Dillard, J. P. (2008). Goals-plan-action theory of message production. In L. A. Baxter & D. O. Braithwaite (Eds.), *Engaging theories in interpersonal communication: Multiple perspectives* (pp. 65–76). Thousand Oaks, CA: Sage.

Dindia, K., & Timmerman, L. (2003). Accomplishing romantic relationships. In

J. O. Greene & B. R. Burleson (Eds.), *Handbook of communication and social interaction skills* (pp. 685–722). Mahwah, NJ: Lawrence Erlbaum.

Fay, B., & Moon, J. D. (1977). What would an adequate philosophy of social science look like? *Philosophy of Social Science, 7,* 209–227.

Fiske, S. T., & Taylor, S. E. (2007). *Social cognition: From brains to culture.* Boston: McGraw-Hill.

Giles, H., & Ogay, T. (2007). Communication accommodation theory. In B. B. Whaley & W. Samter (Eds.), *Explaining communication: Contemporary theories and exemplars* (pp. 293–310). Mahwah, NJ: Lawrence Erlbaum.

Greene, J. O. (2007). Formulating and producing verbal and nonverbal messages: An action assembly theory. In B. B. Whaley & W. Samter (Eds.), *Explaining communication: Contemporary theories and exemplars* (pp. 165–180). Mahwah, NJ: Lawrence Erlbaum.

Guerrero, L. A., Andersen, P. A., & Afifi, W. A. (2007). *Close encounters: Communication in relationships* (2nd ed.). Thousand Oaks, CA: Sage.

Hallsten, J. (2004). Theories of interpersonal communication. In J. R. Baldwin, S. D. Perry, & M. A. Moffitt (Eds.), *Communication theories for everyday life* (pp. 106–121). Boston: Allyn & Bacon.

Hewes, D. E. (1995). Cognitive processing of problematic messages: Reinterpreting to "unbias" texts. In D. E. Hewes (Ed.), *The cognitive bases of interpersonal communication* (pp. 113–138). Hillsdale, NJ: Lawrence Erlbaum.

Kellermann, K. (1992). Communication: Inherently strategic and primarily automatic. *Communication Monographs, 59,* 288–300.

Knapp, M. L., & Daly, J. A. (Eds.). (2002). *Handbook of interpersonal communication* (3rd ed.). Thousand Oaks, CA: Sage.

Knapp, M. L., Daly, J. A., Fudge, K. A., & Miller, G. R. (2002). Background and current trends in the study of interpersonal communication. In M. L. Knapp & J. A. Daly (Eds.), *Handbook of interpersonal communication* (3rd ed., pp. 3–20). Thousand Oaks, CA: Sage.

Mandelbaum, J. (2008). Conversation analysis theory. In L. A. Baxter & D. O. Braithwaite

(Eds.), *Engaging theories in interpersonal communication: Multiple perspectives* (pp. 175–188). Thousand Oaks, CA: Sage.

McCall, G. J., & Simmons, J. L. (1978). *Identities and interactions: An examination of human associations in everyday life* (Rev. ed.). New York: Free Press.

McCornack, S. A. (2008). Information manipulation theory. In L. A. Baxter & D. O. Braithwaite (Eds.), *Engaging theories in interpersonal communication: Multiple perspectives* (pp. 215–226). Thousand Oaks, CA: Sage.

Metts, S., & Grohskopf, E. (2003). Impression management: Goals, strategies, and skills. In J. O. Greene & B. R. Burleson (Eds.), *Handbook of communication and social interaction skills* (pp. 357–399). Mahwah, NJ: Lawrence Erlbaum.

Miller, G. R. (Ed.). (1976a). *Explorations in interpersonal communication*. Beverly Hills, CA: Sage.

Miller, G. R. (1976b). Foreword. In G. R. Miller (Ed.), *Explorations in interpersonal communication* (pp. 9–16). Beverly Hills, CA: Sage.

Miller, G. R. (1978). The current status of theory and research in interpersonal communication. *Human Communication Research, 4,* 164–178.

Miller, G. R. (1990). Interpersonal communication. In G. L. Dahnke & G. W. Clatterbuck (Eds.), *Human communication: Theory and research* (pp. 91–122). Belmont, CA: Wadsworth.

Miller, G. R., & Steinberg, M. (1975). *Between people: A new analysis of interpersonal communication*. Chicago: Science Research Associates.

Motley, M. T. (1990). On whether one can(not) not communicate: An examination via traditional communication postulates. *Western Journal of Speech Communication, 54,* 1–20.

O'Keefe, B. J. (1988). The logic of message design: Individual differences in reasoning about communication. *Communication Monographs, 55,* 80–103.

Popper, K. (1963). *Conjectures and refutations: The growth of scientific knowledge*. New York: Harper & Row.

Rawlins, W. K. (1985). Stalking interpersonal communication effectiveness: Social, individual, or situational integration? In T. W. Benson (Ed.), *Speech communication in the 20th century* (pp. 109–129). Carbondale: Southern Illinois University Press.

Robinson, W. P. (2001). Language in communication: Frames of reference. In W. P. Robinson & H. Giles (Eds.), *The new handbook of language and social psychology* (pp. 3–32). Chichester, England: Wiley.

Roloff, M. E., & Anastasiou, L. (2001). Interpersonal communication research: An overview. In W. B. Gudykunst (Ed.), *Communication yearbook 24* (pp. 51–71). Thousand Oaks, CA: Sage.

Roloff, M. E., & Miller, G. R. (Eds.). (1987). *Interpersonal processes: New directions in communication research*. Newbury Park, CA: Sage.

Rowan, K. E. (2003). Informing and explaining skills: Theory and research on informative communication. In J. O. Greene & B. R. Burleson (Eds.), *Handbook of communication and social interaction skills* (pp. 403–438). Mahwah, NJ: Lawrence Erlbaum.

Saarni, C. (2000). Emotional competence: A developmental perspective. In R. Bar-On & J. D. A. Parker (Eds.), *The handbook of emotional intelligence* (pp. 68–91). San Francisco: Jossey-Bass.

Searle, J. R. (1969). *Speech acts: An essay in the philosophy of language*. Cambridge, UK: Cambridge University Press.

Seibold, D. R., & Myers, K. K. (2006). Communication as structuring. In G. J. Shepherd, J. St. John, & T. Striphas (Eds.), *Communication as . . . : Perspectives on theory* (pp. 143–152). Thousand Oaks, CA: Sage.

Sillars, A. L., & Vangelisti, A. L. (2006). Communication: Basic properties and their relevance to relationship research. In A. L. Vangelisti & D. Perlman (Eds.), *The Cambridge handbook of personal relationships* (pp. 331–352). New York: Cambridge University Press.

Slugoski, B. R., & Hilton, D. J. (2001). Conversation. In W. P. Robinson & H. Giles (Eds.), *The new handbook of language and social psychology* (pp. 193–220). Chichester, England: Wiley.

Smith, S. W., & Wilson, S. R. (Eds.). (2009). *New directions in interpersonal communication*. Thousand Oaks, CA: Sage.

Stewart, J. (1973). Introduction: Bridges not walls. In J. Stewart (Ed.), *Bridges not walls: A book about interpersonal communication* (pp. 2–26). Reading, MA: Addison-Wesley.

Swanson, D. L., & Delia, J. G. (1976). *The nature of human communication.* Chicago: Science Research Associates.

Tracy, K. (2002). *Everyday talk: Building and reflecting identities.* New York: Guilford.

Trenholm, S. (1986). *Human communication theory.* Englewood Cliffs, NJ: Prentice Hall.

Trenholm, S., & Jensen, A. (2008). *Interpersonal communication* (6th ed.). New York: Oxford University Press.

Watzlawick, P., Beavin, J. H., & Jackson, D. D. (1967). *Pragmatics of human communication.* New York: John Wiley.

White, C. H. (2008). Expectancy violations theory and interaction adaptation theory: From expectations to adaptation. In L. A. Baxter & D. O. Braithwaite (Eds.), *Engaging theories in interpersonal communication: Multiple perspectives* (pp. 189–202). Thousand Oaks, CA: Sage.

Wyer, R. S., Jr., & Adaval, R. (2003). Message reception skills in social communication. In J. O. Greene & B. R. Burleson (Eds.), *Handbook of communication and social interaction skills* (pp. 291–355). Mahwah, NJ: Lawrence Erlbaum.

# 10

# THEORETICAL DEVELOPMENTS IN ORGANIZATIONAL COMMUNICATION RESEARCH

◆ Kathleen J. Krone, Michael W. Kramer, and Patricia M. Sias

Organizational communication began to emerge as an identifiable academic field in the United States in the 1940s and 1950s (Redding, 1985), forming around a set of highly practical questions concerning what makes managerial communication in organizations effective. From the 1950s to the 1970s, the field's boundaries expanded to address the effects of small group networks, superior-subordinate communication, and communication climate on employee satisfaction and performance (Putnam & Cheney, 1985). Since that time, the field's identity has grown to include a concern for nonmanagerial voices, the technical rationality that underlies most organizational decision making, understanding the very nature of "organization," and the role of organizations in democratic societies (Mumby & Stohl, 1996). The use of multiple theoretical perspectives has vastly expanded the areas of research conducted to better understand organizational communication and its problems.

In the field's early development, scholars tended to view communication as one of many variables operating in patterned and predictable ways in organizations, which themselves were viewed as objects to be described, predicted, and controlled (Deetz, 2001). Working within this tradition, scholars adopted administrative or social scientific theories of organizations and communication and used these to form questions about causal relationships between organizational and communication variables. Over time, scholars began reconceptualizing preexisting organizational theories in communication-centered terms, while continuing to search in more methodologically sophisticated ways for regularities and causal relationships among communication processes and various organizational outcomes (K. I. Miller, 2000). Such a postpositivist perspective continues to drive many research programs in organizational communication, including those centering on communication during organizational change (e.g., Kramer, Dougherty, & Pierce, 2004; Lewis, 1999), member socialization into workgroups (Myers & McPhee, 2006), and network formation (e.g., Monge & Contractor, 2004).

In the early 1980s, Linda Putnam and her colleagues convincingly argued for a shift toward using an interpretive paradigm in organizational communication research (Putnam & Pacanowsky, 1983). Rooted in beliefs that organizations are socially constructed rather than naturally existing objects and pluralistic systems rather than highly unified, cooperative ones, research began focusing on multiple voices in organizational life and meaning-centered understandings of communication to show how particular realities are socially produced and maintained. The development of descriptive theories grounded in the experiences of research participants in particular social/cultural sites or the use of theoretical concepts as general sensitizing devices was pursued, to complement research grounded in formal predictive theories.

The interpretive paradigm laid the groundwork for critical models of organizational communication research as scholars began arguing that complex social processes of organizing and meaning formation as well as knowledge claims about these processes can never be politically neutral (Deetz & Kersten, 1983). Thus, the field's theoretical boundaries further expanded throughout the 1980s and 1990s as critical scholars began examining how various forms of domination and asymmetrical power relations embedded in larger political and economic systems shape the social construction of reality (Mumby, 2000). Guided by social theorists and philosophers, critical researchers challenge what they take to be the narrow technical and economic interests of corporations and place the study of organizations in a wider social context, often calling for changes that would develop the human capacity to participate in less distorted forms of communication and the organizational capacity to contribute more meaningfully to the development of democratic societies (Cheney, 1995; Deetz, 1992).

In the 1990s, postmodern theoretical developments pushed the boundaries of the field even further. Rather than critiquing organizational experiences in light of macroforces of domination and distorted communication, scholars began examining organizations as discursively produced for the purpose of reclaiming conflicts suppressed in everyday experience (Deetz, 2001). Postmodern scholars seek to illuminate hidden points of resistance and demonstrate how power and resistance operate together through the use of language in organizations. Assuming that meaning is never fixed and final but continually renegotiated, these scholars attempt to de-stabilize dominant meaning structures and to illuminate the fragmented nature of individual and organizational identities (Deetz, 2001).

It is important to acknowledge that this brief characterization of the field's history risks oversimplification and may also gloss over alternative explanations of the field's development (Clair, 1999a). We constructed such an account mainly to illustrate the field's breadth, as each perspective understands and problematizes organizational communication differently. At its best, research conducted within each tradition provides unique theoretical insights for the scientific study of organizational communication. While these insights may sometimes complement, contradict, or even seem irrelevant to each other, within the field they each represent valid ways of trying to understand the ultimately mysterious domain of organizational communication (Krone, 2000). Rather than one perspective crowding out or dominating all others, paradigmatic pluralism has become a hallmark of organizational communication studies and a principle around which the field has developed (Corman & Poole, 2000; Putnam & Krone, 2006). While the contribution of various research traditions can strengthen the field and contribute to its vitality (Cooren, 2006), the use of social scientific approaches to study organizational communication has been critical to the field's development and remains a constant and influential presence.

In that spirit, we discuss several prominent research areas notable for having inspired studies across multiple paradigms. The choice of these four areas is somewhat arbitrary, to be sure. It would be easy to make a case for many different areas given the breadth of topics in organizational communication handbooks. However, we chose these four areas because they represent distinct areas of theoretical development in organizational communication.

## ◆ Supervisor–Subordinate Communication

As noted earlier, the study of management and supervisory communication can be traced back to the very roots of the subfield of organizational communication and continues to this day. The earliest research focused on supervisors and ways in which their communication increased employee productivity, decreased turnover, and increased satisfaction. This body of work concluded that more effective supervisors tend to be communication minded (e.g.,

they enjoy talking and speaking up at meetings and talking with employees, and they are able to explain instructions and policies), are willing and empathic listeners, are more likely to "ask" or "persuade" rather than to "order" or "demand," and are more open in providing reasons underlying policies and information regarding impending change (Redding, 1972). While generally informing, the tendency to focus exclusively on the supervisor's communication positioned employees as passive recipients of supervisory messages and also overlooked the larger organizational context in which the supervisory relationship is embedded (Jablin, 1979).

As research in this area has developed, a variety of theories have been used to pose more sophisticated questions about supervisory and managerial communication, the communication of employees with supervisors, and the communicative nature of the relationship itself, rooted as it is in formal status and power inequality. Excellent summaries of results from this very long research tradition are available elsewhere (for extensive reviews, see Fairhurst, 2001; Jablin, 1979, 2001). The present discussion is designed to highlight what have been influential theories in superior-subordinate communication research.

Testing the importance of the social needs for approval and autonomy, scholars have relied on theories of politeness (e.g., P. Brown & Levinson, 1978) to examine the nature of supervisory feedback and its effects on employee performance. In one set of studies, while managers and administrators advocated the use of greater face support in controlling poor performance (i.e., showing some degree of approval for the employee and providing the employee with autonomy in solving the problem) and believed it might be most effective in controlling poor performance, they tended to maintain more punitive forms of control in actual performance control situations (Fairhurst, Green, & Snavely, 1984). Other research also demonstrates supervisors' preference for the routine use of politeness strategies to protect the "face" of employees when delivering bad news (Wagoner & Waldron, 1999). Specifically, through the use of expressions of solidarity, approbation, and tact, respondents encouraged change in employees' performance while also conveying some degree of approval for them.

More recently, research on effective managerial communication has been guided by theories of reflexivity. The challenges presented by globalization and increased multiculturalism make it more challenging to effectively analyze groups of diverse employees and to strategically adapt messages to their needs. Instead, Barge (2004) explicates the communicative dynamics of reflexive managerial practice in which managers position themselves as being in ongoing conversation with organizational members. Research suggests that managers trained in the practice of reflexivity become more aware of how their contributions to conversations create opportunities and constraints for themselves and for others, rely on employee storytelling to help them understand situations from multiple vantage points, and engage in invitational reflexivity by inviting relational connections that convey appreciation and respect for alternative moral logics (Barge, 2004). Of particular relevance to this section, Barge's study highlights the relational nature of reflexivity, demonstrating how reflexive practice enables managers to be "relationally responsive" by providing a respectful, inclusive, and safe "way of being with others" (p. 78).

Research on employee communication with supervisors initially operated from an information-oriented view of communication. For instance, studies indicated that an employee's willingness to provide accurate information to his or her supervisor, rather than engage in "upward distortion" (i.e., distorting information through lying or omission), depends on a number of factors, including the amount of influence the supervisor has over the employee's career advancement, the extent to which the information reflects favorably on the employee, and the extent to which the employee trusts his or her supervisor (Jablin, 1979). This type of research also addressed the reciprocal nature of information exchange between supervisors and employees demonstrating that supervisors are most likely to receive quality information from employees when they also provide quality information to those employees (e.g., Jablin, 1979).

In addition, studies of downward and upward influence in supervisory relationships drew upon and contributed to the development of theories of strategic message production. According to a recent meta-analysis (Higgins, Judge, & Ferris, 2003), rationality and ingratiation tend to be the most effective tactics employees can use to garner positive performance assessments from supervisors and greater extrinsic success (i.e., salary increases and promotion). Supervisors engaging in downward influence tend to rely on the exchange of benefits and assertiveness (for related reviews, see Fairhurst, 2001; Waldron, 1999).

Influenced by systems theory, organizational communication scholars began reconceptualizing the supervisor-subordinate relationship as influencing and being influenced by the vertical chains of authority in which any single supervisory dyad is embedded (McPhee, 1988). Guided by relational control theory, scholars demonstrated that, consistent with Burns and Stalker's (1961) theory of management systems, mechanistic systems, characterized by hierarchical forms of control, and organic systems, characterized by dispersed forms of control, produced different kinds of superior-subordinate interaction patterns. For example, interaction in the mechanistic system was characterized by competitive exchanges, interruptions, and statements of nonsupport, compared with the organic system in which question-answer exchanges and statements that elaborated upon the previous utterance were more prominent (Courtright, Fairhurst, & Rogers,

1989). The use of systems theory enabled scholars to identify ways in which micro-processes of superior-subordinate communication are influenced by macro-systems of organizational control.

Organizational communication scholars studying supervisor-subordinate communication have been heavily influenced by leader-member exchange (LMX) theory. Originally developed by management scholar George Graen and his colleagues (Graen & Cashman, 1975), LMX theory departs from early management and leadership theories by proposing that leaders form relationships of varying quality across subgroups of subordinates rather than relating to them uniformly. According to the theory, leaders and members form in-group, mid-group, or out-group relationships with each other. In-group relationships are characterized by high levels of mutual support and influence between the two parties, while out-group and mid-group relationships are less mutually supportive. Although LMX theory has been widely used by management and organizational communication scholars (see Graen & Uhl-Bien, 1995, for a thorough review), our summary here focuses on communication-centered studies of LMX theory.

Along these lines, many communication scholars have studied the socially constructed nature of leader-member relationships. Notably, Fairhurst and Chandler (1989) studied routine conversations involving disagreement between a leader and three of his employees, examining them for how their use of language displayed the social structure of each relationship. Consistent with the theory, this leader used language in ways that both neutralized and displayed power and social distance across relational types. For example, in-group interaction consisted of both parties interrupting each other, the subordinate actively trying to influence and also deferring to his supervisor's authority, and the supervisor offering support for whatever choice the employee was about to make. In contrast, out-group interaction consisted of a very brief conflict episode in which the supervisor

made direct suggestions and the employee complied. In the mid-group dyad, power and social distance were more ambiguously displayed as the employee readily disagreed with her supervisor, but his response was to change the subject, and rather than returning to her original point, she followed his lead. Studies such as this began to demonstrate the ways in which day-to-day interaction constructs and sustains variability in leader-member relationships.

More recent studies also identify ways in which communication distinguishes low-quality and high-quality LMX relationships. Yrle, Hartman, and Galle (2003) found two communication patterns that were positively associated with LMX quality—coordination and participation. Coordination refers to the extent to which managers coordinate activities with subordinates in a two-way rather than unidirectional manner, and participation refers to the extent to which supervisors invite employees to participate in decision making. Relatedly, Fix and Sias (2006) found that employees who perceived that their supervisor used a "person-centered" communication style (e.g., messages that encourage employee autonomy and reflection on the complexities of a given situation) reported higher quality LMX relationships than employees whose supervisors tended toward a more "position-centered" communication style (e.g., messages to discourage reflection and that emphasize status differences between the supervisor and employee). In addition, Sias (2005) found that "in-group" employees enjoy a clear advantage over "out-group" employees with respect to the amount and the quality of information they receive from their supervisors. Huang (2002) studied links between LMX and computer-mediated communication and found a positive relationship between the frequency with which subordinate employees communicate with their supervisors via e-mail and their perceptions of LMX. Taken together, these studies reveal a number of important ways LMX relationships are communicatively distinct from one another.

LMX theory also has been used to study variability in relational *maintenance* tactics across in-group and out-group relationships (Lee & Jablin, 1995; Waldron, 1991). These studies suggest that, in general, ingroup employees tend to rely on personal and direct communication tactics to maintain their leader-member relationship, while out-group employees rely more on "regulative" tactics (e.g., talking superficially, avoiding discussion of problems).

LMX theory has been used creatively in tandem with other theories, such as equity theory (Adams, 1965), to examine how employees socially construct perceptions of the relationships of other coworkers with their supervisors (Sias & Jablin, 1995) and how employees socially construct their relationships with one another based on the configuration of leader-member relationships in the workgroup (Sias, 1996). These studies indicate that the types of relationships a supervisor develops with his or her various employees affects the relationships among those employees. Sias and Jablin (1995), for example, found that employees perceived by their coworkers to be the "boss's pet" (i.e., they unfairly receive favorable differential treatment from the supervisor) tend to be isolated from the group's social network because they are disliked and mistrusted by those coworkers. "Boss's victims" (i.e., those perceived by coworkers to be unfairly picked on or victimized by the supervisor), in contrast, tend to be drawn into the group's social network due to sympathy for the victim and anger directed at the supervisor. In sum, communication scholars have expanded the boundaries of LMX theory by building a communication-centered understanding of leader-member relationships.

Organizational communication scholars have also focused on the supervisory relationship as a site of struggle due to the ways in which patterns of domination and asymmetrical power relations embedded in the larger society inevitably intersect with supervisory relationships. One such study illustrated how a patronizing and condescending

interaction between an older White male employee and his younger African American female supervisor undercut her formal authority in the relationship (Fairhurst, 1993). Another project questioned the culturally and racially neutral nature of leadership theories by studying the leadership communication of African American women in leadership positions in White, male-dominated organizations. These leaders effectively challenged traditional (i.e., masculine) leadership practices and instead enacted a unique form of collaboration and control that redefines control as "interactive and personal, rather than competitive and distant" (Parker, 2001, p. 43). This was accomplished through five primary communication practices: interactive communication, challenging others to produce results, communication openness, participative decision making, and effective boundary spanning.

Relatedly, organizational communication scholars have examined the supervisory relationship as a site of domination through the abuse of power. For example, Clair (1993) found that when telling their stories of sexual harassment, victims sometimes trivialize their experience or refer to it as a "simple misunderstanding." Framing their experiences these ways keeps victims from speaking up and operates as a hegemonic device to maintain the interests of the dominant managerial group (Clair, 1993). Building on this line of work, Bingham (1994) and Dougherty (2001) found that communication not only functions to suppress victims of sexual harassment from speaking up, but also can be used to transform abusive workplace environments.

In a study of the dynamics of abusive supervision, Tepper (2000) relied on organizational justice and interactional justice theory (Bies & Moag, 1986) to develop and test a model of subordinates' responses to abusive treatment from their supervisors. He distinguished abusive supervision from other forms of "bad behavior," clarifying it as a sustained display of hostile verbal and nonverbal behavior. The model provides evidence that employees of abusive supervisors were more likely to leave their jobs and report lower job and life satisfaction, lower commitment, and greater work-family conflict and psychological distress. Most of these effects were moderated, though, by organizational justice (i.e., perceptions of procedural and distributive justice) and job mobility.

As the above discussion indicates, organizational communication scholars study supervisor-subordinate communication by focusing on issues of message production and information exchange and by examining how communication constitutes the supervisor-subordinate relationship itself. We consider a strength of this body of work to be researchers' reliance on a wide variety of theories and theoretical perspectives to address the broad and complex topic of supervisor-subordinate research.

## ◆ Organizational Assimilation/Socialization

A long tradition of research based on predictive and descriptive theories has explored questions regarding the communication processes by which newcomers become organizational members. Since this research is voluminous and largely summarized elsewhere (Jablin, 2001; Jablin & Krone, 1987; Waldeck & Myers, 2007), we selected representative examples of this work to illustrate the breadth of theoretical understandings that have resulted from the systematic study of communication and organizational assimilation/socialization processes.

Relying on theories of uncertainty reduction and information management, scholars have addressed questions concerning how individuals come to understand their organizational roles. Using the seminal work by Shannon and Weaver (1949), whose mathematical theory of communication postulates that as information increases, freedom of choice and uncertainty decrease, Berger and Calabrese (1975) proposed uncertainty reduction theory to explore how individuals respond to uncertainty (lack of predictability), especially in initial interactions with strangers. From these interpersonal communication roots, uncertainty theories have been applied especially to the process of newcomers managing uncertainty as they join organizations and interact with others. Factor analysis results identified a range of strategies newcomers use to reduce their uncertainty: (a) overt questions in which the target of uncertainty is queried, (b) indirect questions in which hinting or noninterrogative questions are used, (c) third-party inquiry in which someone other than the source of uncertainty is questioned, (d) testing limits in which perceived norms are violated to see the reactions, (e) disguising conversations in which topics are discussed without direct inquiries, (f) observing for specific information, and (g) surveillance, a more general monitoring for available information (V. D. Miller & Jablin, 1991). Other research has identified the sources individuals use to reduce uncertainty, including coworkers, supervisors, subordinates, friends, partners, and family (Teboul, 1994). Certain sources are preferred for certain types of information. For example, newcomers preferred to receive technical information from their supervisors but preferred peers for information about group norms (Morrison, 1993b). Various combinations of strategies and sources affect newcomers' adjustment, such as their involvement, commitment, and acceptance (Myers & McPhee, 2006). For example, performance feedback improved role clarity (Morrison, 1993a).

Building on these findings for newcomers, assimilation research rooted in uncertainty theory also has examined information seeking in other contexts. For example, in the study of job transfers (geographical movements within the same organization), Kramer (1995) found that quality of supervisor communication immediately after the transfer was a more significant predictor of initial and long-term transferees' uncertainty reduction than supervisor communication after one year. By contrast, peer communication reduced uncertainty throughout the first year (Kramer, 1996). Communication also plays an important role after force reductions or layoffs. After reductions in force, information deprivation led to career uncertainty and propensity to leave; immediate supportive communication from supervisors reduced this negative effect, although supervisor support later on had no effect (Johnson, Bernhagen, Miller, & Allen, 1996). Information deprivation increases job insecurity while reducing the use of direct inquiry and increasing the use of third-party inquiry (Casey, Miller, & Johnson, 1997).

An important theoretical development from this research is the recognition that individuals often manage uncertainty rather than trying to reduce it (Brashers, 2001; Kramer, 2004). By managing information (Afifi & Weiner, 2004), individuals manage uncertainty by increasing, maintaining, or decreasing uncertainty depending on circumstances. For example, an employee may prefer to maintain uncertainty about a potential second round of layoffs rather than knowing for certain that they will occur in an effort to remain hopeful about job prospects.

As an alternative to uncertainty and information theories, other researchers base their examination of the assimilation process on Weick's (1995) sensemaking theory and theories of organizational culture (e.g., Martin, 1992). Along this line, newcomers compare their previous experiences to their current experiences to make sense or create an understanding of the unanticipated surprises they experience in their new situations (Louis, 1980). Organizational stories or memorable messages from peers or supervisors help newcomers make sense of the policies, procedures, and practices of their new organizations by representing the prevailing values and cultural beliefs (M. H. Brown, 1985; Stohl, 1986). For example, the

occupational narratives of iron ore miners socialize them into blue-collar careers and reinforce their work identities (Lucas & Buzzanell, 2004). Some stories or messages become turning points in newcomer socialization, with informal messages typically more important than formal ones (Bullis & Bach, 1989), particularly when newcomers must make sense of contradictory messages (see, e.g., DiSanza, 1995).

Instead of considering newcomers a homogeneous group, some researchers have called for increased examination of the socialization experiences of underrepresented groups (Allen, 1996). Along these lines, Dallimore (2003) found that not only do women experience socialization differently, but their experiences are treated as the "other" compared with the more dominant male experience. Some scholars have reconceptualized organizational socialization as a systematic, exclusionary process for members of marginalized groups (Bullis & Stout, 2000) due to conceptualizations of "organization as container" (Smith & Turner, 1995) and the devaluing of certain types of work (e.g., self-employment, independent artistic work; Clair, 1996).

The confluence of these and other concerns led to a discussion of points of commonality and tension between different perspectives in the December 1999 issue of *Communication Monographs* (Bullis, 1999; Clair, 1999b; Kramer & Miller, 1999; V. D. Miller & Kramer, 1999; Turner, 1999). Collectively, the systematic study of organizational socialization suggests that communication operates as both information exchange to reduce uncertainty and meaning making for making sense, as both inclusionary by allowing some individuals to feel they become part of an organization and exclusionary by making other individuals feel marginalized, and as both rational when individuals seek information to reduce uncertainty and counterrational when individuals experience and make sense of contradictory messages.

## ◆ Emotion Management

Organizational communication research on emotions was inspired by descriptive theories from a number of influential studies emerging from sociology and organizational theory. Chief among these was Arlie Hochschild's (1983) groundbreaking study of flight attendants, in which she coined the term *emotional labor* to refer to ways in which human feeling is increasingly commodified in service work and managed for corporate ends (see Planalp, Metts, & Tracy, Chapter 21, this volume). Also influential was the empirical work of Sutton and Rafaeli (1988), who discovered an unexpected negative relationship between the positive display of emotion among convenience store clerks and rates of sales; instead of positive displays correlating with greater sales, positive emotional displays were more normative in slower paced, low-volume stores. The work of Van Maanen and Kunda (1989) also was influential as they demonstrated how a variety of corporate cultural processes operate to control emotional displays among Disney employees as well as ways in which employees creatively resist these norms.

Inspired by these foundational studies, organizational communication scholars began studying the experience and expression of emotions in organizations. In an early project, Waldron and Krone (1991) examined the relationships between characteristics of employees' self-reports of positive and negative emotional encounters in a corrections organization and a variety of relational and organizational outcomes. Targets of emotional encounters were more likely to be supervisors or someone outside the immediate work group, negative events were experienced more intensely than positive ones, and emotional events resulted in changed perceptions of relationships with the targets. Relational change was especially likely when respondents repressed negative emotional messages such as "protests" and "justifications."

Organizational communication scholars also have extended the study of emotional labor as originally conceptualized by Hochschild (1983). Kruml and Geddes (2000) contributed to the refinement of a model and measure of emotional labor by identifying two distinct dimensions: "emotive effort" and "emotive dissonance," each of which produced different effects. Others have identified instances in which employees actually sought out emotional labor as a rewarding part of their work that helped build a sense of community (Shuler & Sypher, 2000). K. I. Miller's (2002) study of her experiences as a professor during the months following the tragic bonfire accident at Texas A&M University also demonstrated how emotional labor contributed to a larger sense of community. Projects such as these de-emphasize the harmful effects of emotional labor, foregrounding the ways in which employees voluntarily manage emotion.

Continuing to study emotion management more broadly and using expectancy violation theory (Omdahl, 1995), Kramer and Hess (2002) found that employees across a range of occupations expected "professional" behavior, a type of emotion management in which negative emotions were neutralized and positive emotions were not overly exuberant. Similarly, the professional display norms in a health care setting constrained actors to perform along their scripted roles and discouraged the negotiation of display rules (Morgan & Krone, 2001). Taken together, these studies suggest that emotions are managed in accordance with professional and occupational rules and not just in line with corporate norms.

Departing from a U.S. cultural context, emotion management also has been studied among high-level managers in mainland China. In contrast to dominant understandings of rationality and emotionality as separate and distinct processes in the West, this group of Chinese managers talked about processes of emotion management in light of the importance of maintaining continuity between thought and feeling (Krone, Chen, Sloan, & Gallant, 1997). Similarly, an analysis of the metaphorical language used when describing their feelings suggests that these Chinese managers understood emotion management as a homeostatic process of learning rather than as a simple process of containment (Krone & Morgan, 2000).

Challenging the view that rationality and emotion are mutually exclusive, organizational communication scholars have assumed a dialectical purview in which neither process can be well understood without considering the other. In one such study, Mumby and Putnam (1992) critiqued the underpinnings of the classic organizational construct of "bounded rationality" (Simon, 1976) by creating the alternative construct of "bounded emotionality." Rather than being grounded in organizational limitations, bounded emotionality is grounded in the intersubjective limitations between people. Rather than emphasizing the reduction of ambiguity, bounded emotionality emphasizes tolerance of ambiguity. And while bounded rationality unreflectively reinforces the importance of gendered and occupational feeling rules, bounded emotionality emphasizes the importance of relational feeling rules. Bounded emotionality highlights the importance of expressing work feelings to building community in organizations (Putnam & Mumby, 1993).

Organizational communication scholars also have recast the psychological discomfort of emotional labor identified by Hochschild (1983) in more social terms. For example, Tracy (2000) analyzed emotional labor, self-subordination, and the discursive construction of identity in a total institution and concluded that the pain of emotional labor comes not just from the experience of emotive dissonance but also from the inability to discuss such tensions with coworkers or to express a preferred identity. Tracy (2005) further illustrated this point by highlighting how occupational ideologies of emotion and everyday processes such as

organizational identification operate together to contribute to the same dynamic (see Planalp et al., Chapter 21, this volume).

In an effort to integrate these various theoretical perspectives, several projects illustrate connections between various streams of emotion research. One of these incorporates much of the research into a framework representing the process of emotions. The process includes expectations, discrepancies as catalysts, physical and psychological awareness, emotion management decisions, and communication that affects future expectations (Fiebig & Kramer, 1998). Another presents a category system for the various understandings of emotion that have emerged through organizational communication research (e.g., emotional labor, emotional work, emotion at work, and emotion toward work), illustrating ways in which scholars have contributed to, extended, and moved beyond the original construct of emotional labor (K. I. Miller, Considine, & Garner, 2007). Overall, scholars have used a variety of theories to study emotion and in the process have created a large and diverse set of knowledge claims that scholars can draw upon in framing subsequent studies.

## ◆ Power and Control

Many scholars have studied power and control as defining characteristics of organizations. Again, space limitations prevent a full review of the large body of research in this area (see Mumby, 2001, for an extensive review). Instead, we focus on how research has evolved over time to more communication-centered studies of power and control in organizations.

Similar to supervisor-subordinate communication, early research on organizational power and control tended to be unidirectional, centering power in the formal organizational hierarchy, and focused on how managers and supervisors control and influence employees. Such research identified relatively overt forms of power and control such as French and Raven's (1959) typology of power sources, including coercive, reward, legitimate, referent, and expert power. Pfeffer's (1981) research grounded in resource dependency theory revealed how power derives from control over critical resources such as money and budgets, rewards, and sanctions. These theories and studies largely privilege supervisors and others in positions of formal authority (see Seibold, Meyers, & Shoham, Chapter 14, this volume). Conceptualizing subordinates as participants in power and control processes, subsequent research examined "upward influence" and identified several tactics subordinate employees use to influence their supervisors, with rationality and ingratiation tending to be the most effective tactics for garnering positive performance assessments and greater extrinsic success (e.g., salary increases; Higgins et al., 2003).

In the early 1980s, Putnam and Pacanowsky (1983) provided an important turning point for scholars studying power and control by directing scholarly attention to power outside obvious authority holders and toward unobtrusive forms of control and influence that operate in the "deep structure" of the organization. Grounded largely in social construction theory, this move brought attention to informal power and control and, in particular, to the constitutive role of communication in organizational power and control dynamics (Mumby, 2001).

This conceptualization opened the door for communication-centered theorizing that focused on "the relationships among communication, power and meaning" (Mumby, 2001, p. 595). Power from this perspective represents the ability to manage meaning through communication at two levels. The first level focuses on power and politics at a micro level, examining power and control in the context of social relations among individuals and groups (Mumby, 2000). Theory and research at this level examine the discursive construction of meaning, power, and identity in everyday communication. Along these lines, critical studies have identified methods of "concertive" control. In contrast to bureaucratic, authoritarian, and technological forms of control, concertive control emerges from the employees when they reach a consensus on how to shape their behaviors according to core values established by the organization's management through documents such as vision statements (Barker, 1993).

Similarly, Kunda's (1992) study of engineers revealed how employees create and manage meaning in their everyday conversations. These conversations, rather than being simply idle chitchat, are important sites of meaning creation and meaning management; in other words, organizational power. Thus, concertive control is a particularly powerful form of control created and maintained by the workers themselves via socially constructed normative rules and "rationalities."

Along these lines, researchers have also examined how individuals "consent" or participate in the construction of identities that are both enabling and constraining. Howard and Geist's (1995) study of a corporate merger exemplifies this approach. Their study, grounded in structuration theory, and specifically Giddens's (1979) notion of the "dialectic of control," revealed contradictions employees experienced in the merger process (e.g., empowerment and powerlessness). Positioning employees as active agents in the creation and reproduction of organizational power structures, the authors identified several ideological positions employees discursively expressed regarding the merger (e.g., active acceptance, passive rejection) to deal with these contradictions.

At a second, macro level, organizational communication research centers on revealing the hegemonic processes by which "discourses" of meaning, identity, and knowledge are constructed, reproduced, and maintained and how such discourses function to support and reify dominant power and political structures in society (e.g., Deetz, 1992). Grounded in theories such as Habermas's (1979) theory of communicative action, scholars highlight the societal dominance of technical reasoning or technical rationality, which frames knowledge and meaning in reference to efficiency, predictability, rationality, and control (Deetz, 2005; Habermas, 1984; Mumby, 2000). Such knowledge constrains our participation as active agents not only in the context of organizations but also in how we organize everyday life—what Deetz (1992) refers to as the "corporate colonization of the life-world."

Also concerned with power and control, feminist scholars generally conceptualize organizations as communicative constructions of dominance and power, particularly with respect to gender (Mumby, 1993). As Trethewey (2000) noted, feminist scholars grapple with the problem of giving unique voice to women and at the same time deconstructing the binary male/female notion of gender. Standpoint feminist theory addresses the former concern, theorizing women's unique and marginalized organizational positions (e.g., Allen, 1996; Parker, 2001). Discursive feminist approaches address the latter concern, conceptualizing gender as performance and organizations as gendered constructions. This research reveals the discursive "gendering" of organizations that privileges patriarchal and masculine organizational practices such as bureaucracy, technical rationality, and instrumental reasoning and the removal of emotion from the organizing process (e.g., Clair, 1994; Putnam & Mumby, 1993).

Organizational communication scholars have also acknowledged how organizations are situated in a "postmodern condition" that is ambiguous, fragmented, and discontinuous and that questions long-standing assumptions about reality, authority, and knowledge. Research in this tradition examines power and control by "exploring the complex relationships of power, knowledge, and discourse created in the struggle between social groups" (Taylor, 2005, p. 113). Such studies center on discourse and conceptualize organizations as fluid, fragmented, and contested texts (Taylor, 2005). Trethewey (1999), for example, revealed how organizational power and control are exercised through irony, paradox, and ambiguity. Others have focused on control embedded in "language games" that are constituted in forms of organizational discourse such as stories, memos, and meetings (Jeffcutt, 1993; Taylor & Trujillo, 2001).

Using a variety of theories and theoretical perspectives, organizational communication scholars have obtained rich and complex insights into organizational power and control processes. As research has evolved over time toward a communication-centered perspective on organizations and organizing processes, we have developed a dynamic understanding of how organizational power and control are constituted in member, organizational, and societal discourse.

◆ *Discussion and Conclusions*

The task of summarizing the breadth of organizational communication research for a handbook of communication appeared daunting given the breadth of theoretical and empirical research in the field. As a result, after reviewing the history of the field from its roots in problem-driven research to the development of broad theoretical perspectives (May & Mumby, 2005), we chose to provide more in-depth coverage of four representative topics of research rather than attempting to summarize the plethora of micro-theories that populate the field. These areas are by no means a comprehensive list; other topics equally appropriate for inclusion were omitted due to space restrictions.

Our discussion reflects the spirit of "complementary holism" introduced by

Albert et al. (1986). The goal of complementary holism is to develop bodies of knowledge using multiple theoretical or intellectual frameworks that together provide a holistic understanding. Thus, while recognizing that most scholars tend to conduct research using a particular theoretical framework, we encourage scholars to appreciate and develop an understanding of others who study the same phenomenon from various perspectives. Together, such a community of scholars can build rich, complex, and interconnected bodies of scientific knowledge instead of creating and defending islands of disconnected knowledge. We believe the field of organizational communication is ripe for developing complementary holism.

Since the 1987 publication of the first edition of the *Handbook of Communication Science,* organizational communication researchers have drawn upon multiple theoretical perspectives to increasingly position communication as constitutive of selves, supervisory relationships, and organizing. Organizational communication researchers are increasingly working across multiple levels of analysis using multiple methods and theoretical perspectives. In many ways, the set of questions around which the field emerged endures, but both the questions and the answers have grown more complex over time. We believe that organizational communication scholars are well positioned to provide new understandings of such classic problems and to contribute creatively to the formation of new questions and understandings.

## ◆ References

Adams, J. S. (1965). Inequity in social exchange. In L. Berkowitz (Ed.), *Advances in experimental social psychology* (Vol. 2, pp. 267–299). New York: Academic Press.

Afifi, W. A., & Weiner, J. L. (2004). Toward a theory of motivated information management. *Communication Theory, 14,* 167–190.

Albert, M., Cagan, L., Chomsky, N., Hahnel, R., King, M., Sargent, L., et al. (1986). *Liberating theory.* Boston: South End.

Allen, B. J. (1996). Feminist standpoint theory: A Black woman's (re)view of organizational socialization. *Communication Studies, 43,* 257–271.

Barge, J. K. (2004). Reflexivity and managerial practice. *Communication Monographs, 71,* 70–96.

Barker, J. R. (1993). Tightening the iron cage: Concertive control in self-managing teams. *Administrative Science Quarterly, 38,* 408–437.

Berger, C. R., & Calabrese, R. (1975). Some explorations in initial interaction and beyond: Toward a developmental theory of interpersonal communication. *Human Communication Research, 1,* 99–112.

Bies, R. J., & Moag, J. S. (1986). Interactional justice: Communication criteria of fairness. *Research on Negotiation in Organizations, 1,* 43–55.

Bingham, S. G. (1994). Introduction: Framing sexual harassment: Defining a discursive focus of study. In S. G. Bingham (Ed.), *Conceptualizing sexual harassment as discursive practice* (pp. 17–30). Westport, CT: Praeger.

Brashers, D. E. (2001). Communication and uncertainty management. *Journal of Communication, 51,* 477–497.

Brown, M. H. (1985). That reminds me of a story: Speech action in organizational socialization. *Western Journal of Speech Communication, 49,* 27–42.

Brown, P., & Levinson, S. (1978). Universals in language usage: Politeness phenomena. In E. Goody (Ed.), *Questions and politeness: Strategies in social interaction* (pp. 56–289). Cambridge, UK: Cambridge University Press.

Bullis, C. (1999). Mad or bad: A response to Kramer and Miller. *Communication Monographs, 66,* 368–373.

Bullis, C., & Bach, B. W. (1989). Socialization turning points: An examination of change in organizational identification. *Western Journal of Speech Communication, 53,* 273–293.

Bullis, C., & Stout, K. R. (2000). Organizational socialization: A feminist standpoint approach. In P. M. Buzzanell (Ed.), *Rethinking organizational and managerial communication from feminist perspectives* (pp. 47–75). Thousand Oaks, CA: Sage.

Burns, T., & Stalker, G. M. (1961). *The management of innovation*. London: Tavistock.

Casey, M. K., Miller, V. D., & Johnson, J. R. (1997). Survivors' information seeking following a reduction in workforce. *Communication Research, 24,* 755–781.

Cheney, G. (1995). Democracy in the workplace: Theory and practice from the perspective of communication. *Journal of Applied Communication Research, 23,* 167–200.

Clair, R. P. (1993). The use of framing devices to sequester organizational narratives: Hegemony and harassment. *Communication Monographs, 60,* 113–136.

Clair, R. P. (1994). Resistance and oppression as a self-contained opposite: An organizational communication analysis of one man's story of sexual harassment. *Western Journal of Communication, 58,* 235–262.

Clair, R. P. (1996). The political nature of the colloquialism, "a real job": Implications for organizational socialization. *Communication Monographs, 63,* 249–267.

Clair, R. P. (1999a). Standing still in an ancient field: A contemporary look at the organizational communication discipline. *Management Communication Quarterly, 13,* 283–293.

Clair, R. P. (1999b). Ways of seeing: A review of Kramer and Miller's manuscript. *Communication Monographs, 66,* 374–381.

Cooren, F. (2006). The organizational communication/discourse tilt: A refugee's perspective. *Management Communication Quarterly, 19,* 653–660.

Corman, S. R., & Poole, M. S. (2000). *Perspectives on organizational communication: Finding common ground.* New York: Guilford.

Courtright, J. A., Fairhurst, G. T., & Rogers, L. W. (1989). Interaction patterns in organic and mechanistic management systems. *Academy of Management Journal, 32,* 773–802.

Dallimore, E. J. (2003). Memorable messages as discursive formations: The gendered socialization of new university faculty. *Women's Studies in Communication, 26,* 214–265.

Deetz, S. A. (1992). *Democracy in an age of corporate colonization: Developments in communication and the politics of everyday life.* Albany: State University of New York Press.

Deetz, S. A. (2001). Conceptual foundations. In F. M. Jablin & L. L. Putnam (Eds.), *The new handbook of organizational communication: Advances in theory, research, and methods* (pp. 3–46). Thousand Oaks, CA: Sage.

Deetz, S. A. (2005). Critical theory. In S. May & D. K. Mumby (Eds.), *Engaging organizational communication theory and research: Multiple perspectives* (pp. 85–112). Thousand Oaks, CA: Sage.

Deetz, S. A., & Kersten, A. (1983). Critical models of interpretive research. In L. L. Putnam & M. E. Pacanowsky (Eds.), *Communication and organizations: An interpretive approach* (pp. 147–171). Beverly Hills, CA: Sage.

DiSanza, J. R. (1995). Bank teller organizational assimilation in a system of contradictory practices. *Management Communication Quarterly, 9,* 191–218.

Dougherty, D. S. (2001). Sexual harassment as [dys]functional process: A feminist standpoint analysis. *Journal of Applied Communication Research, 29,* 372–402.

Fairhurst, G. T. (1993). The leader-member exchange patterns of women leaders in industry: A discourse analysis. *Communication Monographs, 60,* 321–351.

Fairhurst, G. T. (2001). Dualisms in leadership research. In F. M. Jablin & L. L. Putnam (Eds.), *The new handbook of organizational communication: Advances in theory, research, and methods* (pp. 379–439). Thousand Oaks, CA: Sage.

Fairhurst, G. T., & Chandler, T. A. (1989). Social structure in leader-member interaction. *Communication Monographs, 56,* 215–239.

Fairhurst, G. T., Green, S. G., & Snavely, B. K. (1984). Face support in controlling poor performance. *Human Communication Research, 11,* 272–295.

Fiebig, G. V., & Kramer, M. W. (1998). A framework for the study of emotions in organizational contexts. *Management Communication Quarterly, 11,* 336–372.

Fix, B., & Sias, P. M. (2006). Person-centered communication, leader-member exchange, and job satisfaction. *Communication Research Reports, 23,* 35–44.

French, J. R., & Raven, B. (1959). The bases of social power. In D. Cartwright (Ed.), *Studies in social power* (pp. 150–167). Ann Arbor: University of Michigan Press.

Giddens, A. (1979). *Central problems in social theory.* London: Macmillan.

Graen, G., & Cashman, J. F. (1975). A role-making model of leadership in formal organizations: A developmental approach. In J. G. Hunt & L. L. Hunt (Eds.), *Leadership frontiers* (pp. 143–165). Kent, OH: Kent State University Press.

Graen, G. B., & Uhl-Bien, M. (1995). Relationship-based approach to leadership: Development of a leader-member exchange (LMX) theory of leadership over 25 years— Applying a multi-level multi-domain perspective. *Leadership Quarterly, 6,* 219–247.

Habermas, J. (1979). *Communication and the evolution of society* (T. McCarthy, Trans.). Boston: Beacon.

Habermas, J. (1984). *The theory of communicative action: Vol. 1. Reason and the rationalization of society* (T. McCarthy, Trans.). Boston: Beacon.

Higgins, C., Judge, T. A., & Ferris, G. R. (2003). Influence tactics and work outcomes: A meta-analysis. *Journal of Organization Behavior, 24,* 89–106.

Hochschild, A. R. (1983). *The managed heart.* Berkeley: University of California Press.

Howard, L. A., & Geist, P. M. (1995). Ideological positioning in organizational change: The dialectic of control in a merging organization. *Communication Monographs, 62,* 110–131.

Huang, A. J. (2002). E-mail communication and supervisor-subordinate exchange quality: An empirical study. *Human Systems Management, 21,* 193–204.

Jablin, F. M. (1979). Superior-subordinate communication: The state of the art. *Psychological Bulletin, 86,* 1201–1222.

Jablin, F. M. (2001). Organizational entry, assimilation, and disengagement/exit. In F. M. Jablin & L. L. Putnam (Eds.), *The new handbook of organizational communication: Advances in theory, research, and methods* (pp. 732–818). Thousand Oaks, CA: Sage.

Jablin, F. M., & Krone, K. J. (1987). Organizational assimilation and levels of analysis in organizational communication research. In C. Berger & S. Chaffee (Eds.), *Handbook of communication science* (pp. 711–746). Newbury Park, CA: Sage.

Jeffcutt, P. (1993). From interpretation to representation. In J. Hassard & M. Parker (Eds.), *Postmodernism and organizations* (pp. 25–48). Newbury Park, CA: Sage.

Johnson, J. R., Bernhagen, M. J., Miller, V., & Allen, M. (1996). The role of communication in managing reductions in work force. *Journal of Applied Communication Research, 24,* 139–164.

Kramer, M. W. (1995). A longitudinal study of superior-subordinate communication during job transfers. *Human Communication Research, 22,* 39–64.

Kramer, M. W. (1996). A longitudinal study of peer communication during job transfers: The impact of frequency, quality, and network multiplexity on adjustment. *Human Communication Research, 23,* 59–86.

Kramer, M. W. (2004). *Managing uncertainty in organizational communication.* Mahwah, NJ: Lawrence Erlbaum.

Kramer, M. W., Dougherty, D. S., & Pierce, T. A. (2004). Communication during a corporate merger: A case of managing uncertainty during organizational change. *Human Communication Research, 30,* 71–101.

Kramer, M. W., & Hess, J. A. (2002). Communication rules for the display of emotions in organizational settings. *Management Communication Quarterly, 16,* 66–80.

Kramer, M. W., & Miller, V. D. (1999). A response to criticisms of socialization research: In support of contemporary conceptualizations of assimilation. *Communication Monographs, 66,* 358–367.

Krone, K. J. (2000). Becoming deeply multiperspectival: Commentary on finding common ground in organizational communication research. In S. R. Corman & M. S. Poole (Eds.), *Perspectives on organizational communication* (pp. 144–151). New York: Guilford.

Krone, K. J., Chen, L., Sloan, D. K., & Gallant, L. M. (1997). Managerial emotionality in Chinese factories. *Management Communication Quarterly, 11,* 6–50.

Krone, K. J., & Morgan, J. M. (2000). Emotion metaphors in management: The Chinese experience. In S. Fineman (Ed.), *Emotion in organizations* (pp. 83–100). London: Sage.

Kruml, S. M., & Geddes, D. (2000). Exploring the dimensions of emotional labor: The heart of Hochschild's work. *Management Communication Quarterly, 14,* 8–49.

Kunda, G. (1992). *Engineering culture: Control and commitment in a high-tech corporation.* Philadelphia: Temple University Press.

Lee, J., & Jablin, F. M. (1995). Maintenance communication in superior-subordinate work relationships. *Human Communication Research, 22,* 220–257.

Lewis, L. K. (1999). Disseminating information and soliciting input during planned organizational change: Implementers' targets, sources, and channels of communication. *Management Communication Quarterly, 13,* 43–75.

Louis, M. R. (1980). Surprise and sense-making: What newcomers experience in entering unfamiliar organizational settings. *Administrative Science Quarterly, 25,* 226–251.

Lucas, K., & Buzzanell, P. M. (2004). Blue-collar work, career, and success: Occupational narratives of *Sisu. Journal of Applied Communication Research, 32,* 273–292.

Martin, J. (1992). *Cultures in organizations: Three perspectives.* New York: Oxford University Press.

May, S., & Mumby, D. K. (Eds.). (2005). *Engaging organizational communication theory & research: Multiple perspectives.* Thousand Oaks, CA: Sage.

McPhee, R. D. (1988). Vertical communication chains: Toward an integrated view. *Management Communication Quarterly, 1,* 455–493.

Miller, K. I. (2000). Common ground from the post-positivist perspective: From "straw person" argument to collaborative coexistence. In S. R. Corman & M. S. Poole (Eds.), *Perspectives on organizational communication: Finding common ground* (pp. 46–67). New York: Guilford.

Miller, K. I. (2002). The experience of emotion in the workplace: Professing in the midst of tragedy. *Management Communication Quarterly, 15,* 517–600.

Miller, K. I., Considine, J., & Garner, J. (2007). "Let me tell you about my job": Exploring the terrain of emotion in the workplace. *Management Communication Quarterly, 20,* 231–260.

Miller, V. D., & Jablin, F. M. (1991). Information seeking during organizational entry: Influences, tactics, and a model of the process. *Academy of Management Review, 16,* 92–120.

Miller, V. D., & Kramer, M. W. (1999). A reply to Bullis, Turner, and Clair. *Communication Monographs, 66,* 390–392.

Monge, P. R., & Contractor, N. S. (2004). *Theories of communication networks.* New York: Oxford University Press.

Morgan, J. M., & Krone, K. J. (2001). Bending the rules of "professional" display: Emotional improvisation in caregiver performances. *Journal of Applied Communication Research, 29,* 317–340.

Morrison, E. W. (1993a). Longitudinal study of the effects of information seeking on newcomer socialization. *Journal of Applied Psychology, 78,* 173–183.

Morrison, E. W. (1993b). Newcomer information seeking: Exploring types, modes, sources, and outcomes. *Academy of Management Journal, 36,* 557–589.

Mumby, D. K. (1993). Feminism and the critique of organizational communication: A critical reading. In S. Deetz (Ed.), *Communication yearbook 16* (pp. 155–166). Newbury Park, CA: Sage.

Mumby, D. K. (2000). Common ground from the critical perspective: Overcoming binary oppositions. In S. R. Corman & M. S. Poole (Eds.), *Perspectives in organizational communication: Finding common ground* (pp. 68–86). New York: Guilford.

Mumby, D. K. (2001). Power and politics. In F. M. Jablin & L. L. Putnam (Eds.), *The new handbook of organizational communication: Advances in theory, research and methods* (pp. 585–623). Thousand Oaks, CA: Sage.

Mumby, D. K., & Putnam, L. L. (1992). The politics of emotion: A feminist reading of bounded rationality. *Academy of Management Review, 17,* 465–486.

Mumby, D. K., & Stohl, C. (1996). Disciplining organizational communication studies. *Management Communication Quarterly, 10,* 50–72.

Myers, K. K., & McPhee, R. D. (2006). Influences on member assimilation in workgroups in high-reliability organizations: A multi-level analysis. *Human Communication Research, 32,* 440–468.

Omdahl, B. L. (1995). *Cognitive appraisal, emotion, and empathy.* Mahwah, NJ: Lawrence Erlbaum.

Parker, P. S. (2001). African-American women executives' leadership communication within dominant-culture organizations: (Re)conceptualizing notions of collaboration and instrumentality. *Management Communication Quarterly, 15,* 42–82.

Pfeffer, J. (1981). *Power in organizations.* Marshfield, MA: Pitman.

Putnam, L. L., & Cheney, G. (1985). Organizational communication: Historical development and future directions. In T. W. Benson (Ed.), *Speech communication in the 20th century* (pp. 130–156). Carbondale: Southern Illinois University Press.

Putnam, L. L., & Krone, K. J. (2006). Editors' introduction. In L. L. Putnam & H. J. Krone (Eds.), *Organizational communication* (pp. xxiii–xliii). London: Sage.

Putnam, L. L., & Mumby, D. K. (1993). Organizations, emotion, and the myth of rationality. In S. Fineman (Ed.), *Emotion in organizations* (pp. 36–57). Newbury Park, CA: Sage.

Putnam, L. L., & Pacanowsky, M. E. (Eds.). (1983). *Communication and organizations: An interpretive approach.* Beverly Hills, CA: Sage.

Redding, W. C. (1972). *Communication within the organization: An interpretive review of theory and research.* New York: Industrial Communication Council.

Redding, W. C. (1985). Stumbling toward identity: The emergence of organizational communication as a field of study. In R. D. McPhee & P. K. Tompkins (Eds.), *Organizational communication: Traditional themes and new directions* (pp. 15–54). Beverly Hills, CA: Sage.

Shannon, C. E., & Weaver, W. (1949). *The mathematical theory of communication.* Urbana: University of Illinois Press.

Shuler, S., & Sypher, B. D. (2000). Seeking emotional labor: When managing the heart enhances the work experience. *Management Communication Quarterly, 14,* 50–89.

Sias, P. M. (1996). Constructing perceptions of differential treatment: An analysis of coworker discourse. *Communication Monographs, 63,* 171–187.

Sias, P. M. (2005). Workplace relationship quality and employee information experiences. *Communication Studies, 56,* 375–396.

Sias, P. M., & Jablin, F. M. (1995). Differential superior-subordinate relations, perceptions of fairness, and coworker communication. *Human Communication Research, 22,* 5–38.

Simon, H. (1976). *Administrative behavior* (3rd ed.). New York: Free Press.

Smith, R. C., & Turner, P. K. (1995). A social constructionist reconfiguration of metaphor analysis: An application of "SCMA" to organizational socialization theorizing. *Communication Monographs, 62,* 151–181.

Stohl, C. (1986). The role of memorable messages in the process of organizational socialization. *Communication Quarterly, 34,* 231–249.

Sutton, R. I., & Rafaeli, A. (1988). Untangling the relationship between displayed emotions and organizational sales: The case of convenience stores. *Academy of Management Journal, 31,* 461–487.

Taylor, B. C. (2005). Postmodern theory. In S. R. May & D. K. Mumby (Eds.), *Engaging organizational communication theory and research: Multiple perspectives* (pp. 113–140). Thousand Oaks, CA: Sage.

Taylor, B. C., & Trujillo, N. (2001). Qualitative research methods. In F. M. Jablin & L. L. Putnam (Eds.), *The new handbook of organizational communication: Advances in theory, research, and methods* (pp. 161–194). Thousand Oaks, CA: Sage.

Teboul, J. C. B. (1994). Facing and coping with uncertainty during organizational encounters. *Management Communication Quarterly, 8,* 190–224.

Tepper, B. J. (2000). Consequences of abusive supervision. *Academy of Management Journal, 43,* 178–190.

Tracy, S. J. (2000). Becoming a character for commerce: Emotional expression and organizational culture. *Management Communication Quarterly, 14,* 90–128.

Tracy, S. J. (2005). Locking up emotion: Moving beyond dissonance for understanding emotion labor discomfort. *Communication Monographs, 72,* 261–283.

Trethewey, A. (1999). Isn't it ironic: Using irony to explore the contradiction of organizational life. *Western Journal of Communication, 63,* 140–167.

Trethewey, A. (2000). The shifting common ground: Feminism(s), organizational communication, and productive pragmatic tensions. In S. R. Corman & M. S. Poole (Eds.), *Perspectives on organizational communication: Finding common ground* (pp. 200–210). New York: Guilford.

Turner, P. K. (1999). What if you don't? A response to Kramer and Miller. *Communication Monographs, 66,* 382–389.

Van Maanen, J., & Kunda, G. (1989). "Real feelings": Emotional expression and organizational culture. *Research in Organizational Behavior, 11,* 43–103.

Wagoner, R., & Waldron, V. (1999). How supervisors convey routine bad news:

Face-work at UPS. *Southern Communication Journal, 64,* 193–210.

Waldeck, J., & Myers, K. (2008). Organizational assimilation theory, research, and implications for multiple areas of the discipline: A state of the art review. In C. S. Beck (Ed.), *Communication yearbook 31* (pp. 322–367). New York: Lawrence Erlbaum.

Waldron, V. R. (1991). Achieving communication goals in superior-subordinate relationships: The multi-functionality of upward maintenance tactics. *Communication Monographs, 58,* 289–306.

Waldron, V. R. (1999). Communication practices of followers, members, and protégés: The case of upward influence tactics. In M. E. Roloff (Ed.), *Communication yearbook 22* (pp. 251–299). Thousand Oaks, CA: Sage.

Waldron, V. R., & Krone, K. J. (1991). The experience and expression of emotion in the workplace. *Management Communication Quarterly, 4,* 287–309.

Weick, K. E. (1995). *Sensemaking in organizations.* Thousand Oaks, CA: Sage.

Yrle, A. C., Hartman, S. J., & Galle, W. P. (2003). Examining communication style and leader-member exchange: Considerations and concerns for managers. *International Journal of Management, 20,* 92–101.

# 11

# LEVELS OF ANALYSIS AND COMMUNICATION SCIENCE

◆ Jack M. McLeod, Gerald M. Kosicki, and Douglas M. McLeod

A t the heart of social, political, and cultural processes, communication phenomena are increasingly important in the contemporary world. Communication institutions do not merely relay information from powerful sources neutrally, although sometimes they do exactly that. They frame information of critical importance for understanding political, social, and economic life. As communication researchers seek to understand the influence of mass media on society, they must address the rapidly occurring transformations of both media systems and the global world system. Communication scientists struggle to keep pace with these changes, but there is much progress to report. Despite its status as a multilevel, variable field, communication continues to be dominated by research at the individual level of analysis. Psychological approaches are tightening their grip on the discipline, as cognitive perspectives bring an expanding

AUTHORS' NOTE: We dedicate this chapter to Dr. Jay G. Blumler, Professor Emeritus at the University of Leeds and the University of Maryland, former ICA president, and coauthor of the original 1987 version of this chapter. His inspirational leadership is responsible for much of the progress that has been made in comparative, collaborative, multilevel, multimethod, and all other forms of macro-research in political communication.

set of theories to guide research inquiries. Cognitive theory provides flexible tools that revolutionize research but cannot fully explain macrosocial communication processes. As the discipline commits itself to micro-individual approaches through graduate student training, selection of journal editors, and preferred research methods, important macrosocial phenomena remain understudied. The discipline needs to pay more attention to systematic cross-level accounts of the way institutions and macrosocial processes provide social contexts that affect individual behavior.

The implications of undervaluing macrosocial theory are many. The lack of theoretical and empirical connections between levels has produced explanations of communication phenomena that center on internal mental states rather than on social, economic, and political conditions. The focus on individual agency at the expense of structural factors contributes to the cultural tendency to "blame the victim" for social problems. To produce a more comprehensive understanding of communication processes, the discipline must create theoretically rich and methodologically robust research that is relevant to real-world concerns and public policy debates and responsive to a host of questions. How generalizable are the findings? To what other situations, communities, times, and societies can the findings be applied? Can communication research withstand the withering scrutiny of the toughest critics and survive cross-examination when it is introduced in public hearings and courtrooms?

When the need for macrosocial scholarship was raised in the previous *Handbook of Communication Science* (Berger & Chaffee, 1987), three fundamental arguments for macro-level scholarship were identified (J. M. McLeod & Blumler, 1987). First, it is imperative to formulate and test communication hypotheses at various levels of analysis beyond the individual level to generate a more comprehensive understanding of media processes, extending the external validity and significance of our theoretical explanations. Key studies can be replicated across communities with different characteristics and across societies. Theories should be generally applicable, not situation specific, and help us understand how phenomena differ under various social conditions. Theories must be validated with high-quality empirical evidence, gathered in defensible ways that correspond to the best social science practices.

Second, a major impetus for macrotheories is the desire for relevance to the formulation and maintenance of public policy about communication. Such policy making typically applies at institutional and organizational levels. When considering the level of public knowledge in society, equal opportunity to participate in the information society, or the effects of commercialism embedded in news, the discussion is likely to be about media structure and the relationships of media to other institutions. Scientific inquiry cannot provide definitive answers to normative and policy questions, but careful research can illuminate the likely impact of alternatives and guide reforms that will strengthen cherished values of freedom, equality, and informed participation in public affairs.

Finally, the structure of communication systems and their relationships to political and economic systems are critical subjects for communication research. For example, does it matter that more people are reading news online, often using sources other than newspapers? Will citizens' knowledge about important issues and events happening in their own communities lag behind their awareness of issues of national and international significance? If so, how will this transference of public attention away from local communities affect participatory democracy?

## ◆ The Neglect of Macro-Level Theory and Research

The vast body of micro-individual-level communication research stands in sharp contrast to the modest attention devoted to macro-level and cross-level influences. Most empirical communication research is conducted by U.S. and Western European scholars from *individualistic* rather than *collectivist* cultures. Consequently, researchers may adopt the theoretical perspectives that reflect the cultural tendency to see individual behavior as determined by stable individual dispositions rather than by situational factors. Beyond such cultural influences, the dominance of individual-level theorizing may be best understood through an examination of the historical development of the discipline.

## ORIGINS OF
## THE MODERN FIELD

As detailed in the previous handbook (J. M. McLeod & Blumler, 1987), a vibrant tradition of macrosocial communication research was diminished by World War II and was slow to reemerge in the two decades that followed. That history shapes the field as it is today.

*Limited Legacies of Macro-Research (1950s).* A strong case can be made that Wilbur Schramm's (1954) *The Process and Effects of Mass Communication* marked the beginning of communication as an autonomous academic field. Schramm stitched together more than three dozen selections by social scientists from various disciplines. Roughly half were conceptualized in macro terms. Schramm's selections filled in Paul Lazarsfeld's 16-cell matrix of potential media effects (Lazarsfeld, 1958). Although Lazarsfeld studied only a few of these, he provided suitable examples for the empty cells of potential within-level and cross-level media effects. Thus, both early communication research agenda included the possibilities for macro-level scholarship.

Lazarsfeld's research had a strong impact on the emerging communication field in the late 1950s. His studies of voting (Berelson, Lazarsfeld, & McPhee, 1954; Lazarsfeld, Berelson, & Gaudet, 1948) and personal influence (Katz & Lazarsfeld, 1955) were particularly influential. Evidence from his Erie County (Ohio) panel study of the 1940 presidential election found that the persuasive effects of media on voters' decisions were quite limited *in comparison with* the unsubstantiated claims made two decades earlier that World War I propaganda controlled the masses. The Decatur (Illinois) study of personal influence (Katz & Lazarsfeld, 1955) expanded the concepts of opinion leadership and the two-step flow of communication from the voting studies and redirected research attention to interpersonal processes. Today, interpersonal discussion is seen as a key antecedent to civic engagement, though discussion and media use are now more likely to be conceived as interdependent rather than competing processes.

Lazarsfeld's studies showed that interactions within *social networks* influenced voting and consumer purchase decisions but offered limited insight into more macro-level processes. The macro-*societal* theory in the voting studies was simply a rejection of top-down control articulated by mass society theory (Kornhauser, 1959) rather than a comprehensive macrosocial analysis. Lazarsfeld's implicit societal model was a loose form of functionalism that dominated American sociology in the middle of the 20th century. Society was understood as composed of balanced pluralistic interests, integrated at the bottom by networks of interpersonal relationships (Berelson, 1952). As with most functional analyses, the emphasis on social control and stability ignored internal conflict and social change. Three structural characteristics—socioeconomic status, religious affiliation, and rural-urban residence—were reduced to individual *predispositions* that produced selective effects of mediated and interpersonal influence.

The Columbia view of mass media from an *industry/organizational perspective* stressed concentrated ownership and control, producing *propaganda* for election campaigns, "letting loose upon the land to control or inform, to constrain or tease potential voters into the appropriate decision" (Lazarsfeld et al., 1948, p. 120). Journalists were lumped with party workers, cartoonists, and "local sages" as partisan leaders of opinion. The Columbia researchers equated all forms of campaign content (e.g., news, editorials, candidate speeches, and advertising) with propaganda.

The Columbia research was conducted in Sandusky (Ohio), Elmira (New York), and Decatur (Illinois), but they were not *community*-level studies. Each city was described, but no theoretical or empirical *contextual* connection was made between the community's distinctive political and economic structure and the decisions facing its citizens. Lazarsfeld et al. (1948) noted their failure to relate micro-network influences "to the total flow of influences and decisions within the community" and to "study the total community in greater detail" (p. xxxix).

Collections of earlier research encouraged leaders such as Schramm, Ralph Nafziger, and David Berlo to develop communication curricula, research centers, and doctoral programs in the late 1950s. The research of scholars hired in emerging communication programs reflected their disciplinary origins (i.e., psychology, sociology, social psychology, and political science). Developing new concepts and theories sensitive to the distinctive problems of communication would take another 20 years.

*Searching for Legitimacy and Support (1960s).* Communication scholars arrived a decade late at the table of social science celebration. Scholars from the more established social sciences had already found funding from government agencies and private foundations. Eager to use the new and improved techniques of data gathering and analysis to advance their claims of being "objective and scientific," the postwar social scientists conspicuously avoided "arm-chair theorizing" and the older qualitative techniques that characterized most macro-level research. Optimists believed

technology could be used to attack economic and social problems throughout the world. Communication was seen as an unproblematic vehicle to *transmit* technology and knowledge to the "underdeveloped" peoples of the world. It would be several years before this approach would be challenged by questioning its assumed neutrality and ethnocentrism, as well as assailing the simplicity of its communication process models.

When the new crop of self-designated communication researchers arrived in the 1960s, they found that many of Schramm's scholars had retired or left the field for other pursuits. The communication focus of the voting studies had been lost along with their shift to the University of Michigan. Sociology had drifted away from communication topics, and the emerging behavioral political scientists were largely uninterested in exploring media influences on voting. Funding agencies declined to support investigations of media effects, accepting the common wisdom derived from Klapper (1960) and Berelson (1959) that everything that could be known about communication was already known and that media effects were minor and embedded in a host of necessary conditions.

The new cohort of communication scholars sought guidance from allied disciplines. Social psychology seemed an excellent field to emulate, as it was a successful relative latecomer to social science. Communication processes appeared among the variables social psychologists examined, and their bi-level theorizing had considerable appeal to communication scholars. If emulating social psychology was a good choice generally, it was not a productive one for communication at the macro levels of society, organization, and community. The "social" side of social psychology quickly reduced to the presence of other people, judgments of others, or groups created in laboratory settings.

The search for legitimacy took many paths for the new communication scholars, but few gravitated toward macro-level research. Some tried to articulate highly abstract models that would capture the communication process at all levels, but these proved to be overly general and lacking in testable theoretical propositions. Others found solace in statistical and methodological techniques that were seized upon as keys to the success of the communication discipline: factor analysis, the semantic differential, and Q-methodology. While these contributed to our arsenal of data analysis weapons, none has proven sufficient to replace sound logic and imaginative theory in the building of a research tradition. Most communication researchers sought to develop general theories of communication rather than looking for variation in effects for different societies and social conditions that might have led them to consider macro-influences more fully.

The 1960s brought improvements in basic research practices of the discipline in terms of design, sampling, measurement, and analysis. The ideas of formal comparison, probability sampling, reliability of indices, and the need for control became well known and sometimes practiced. The use of statistical controls, however, may have inadvertently deflected attention away from macro-level concerns. Communication researchers analyzing nonexperimental survey data reflexively control for demographic variables such as education, income, gender, and age. Statistical control is generally a good practice for ensuring internal validity of survey-based analyses, though these are not necessarily the most relevant controls. Moreover, by controlling out these factors, we may be removing structural influences that may interact with and alter the impact of the media effects.

*Expanding Theory and Research (1970s– 1990s).* Communication research expanded and matured starting in the early 1970s with a dramatic rise in the number of communication professors conducting research. With more scholars examining new topics with more rigorous and sensitive tools, it is

not surprising that evidence of stronger and more diverse media effects emerged. Evidence spread slowly to the other social sciences. In political science, television began to replace party affiliation as the major source of influence on voting decisions after the stability of political preferences and their antecedents were challenged (Nie, Verba, & Petrocik, 1976). Political scientists' attention to the role of mass media in politics eventually led to closer connections with communication scholars.

The broadening of media effects beyond attitude change led to the elevation of knowledge gain as a more direct but no less important outcome. Social micro-to-macro effects were considered, if not often investigated. The form of effects was expanded to include delayed effects and the indirect effects that Klapper had dismissed as being of minimal importance. Media use came to be seen as a more complex activity when researchers went beyond mere exposure to examine audience activity such as gratifications sought (Blumler & Katz, 1974), attention (Chaffee & Schleuder, 1986), and information-processing strategies (Kosicki & McLeod, 1990). Multivariate statistical techniques, such as hierarchical regression, reached communication during the 1970s that would two decades later provide better answers to multilevel research questions.

Three of the most prominent and productive communication theoretical perspectives of the past half century were first published during this decade: the knowledge gap hypothesis (Tichenor, Donohue, & Olien, 1970), cultivation (Gerbner, 1973), and agenda setting (McCombs & Shaw, 1972). Each used individual-level data, but notably, they connected individual data with macro-level concepts and theories regarding community-level structure, societal processes, and news media organizations, respectively.

The macro aspects of these theories were poorly recognized. McCombs and Shaw (1972) linked their agenda-setting hypothesis to Cohen's (1963) remark that "the press may not be very successful in telling us what to think, but it is stunningly successful in telling us what to think about" (p. 13). The last half of the slogan, referring to readers judging as most important the issues that have appeared most prominently in news, has been documented by 35 years of research. However, the macro-level assertion that the media are autonomous decision-making agencies has been assumed rather than studied. Few agenda-setting studies even control for real-world conditions.

The decision by President Bush to attack Iraq in 2003 provides a case study of the struggle for control of the media news agenda. An analysis of 393 on-camera news sources used by network and public television before the war indicated over half were either current or former government or military officials (Fairness & Accuracy in Reporting, 2003). The media agenda had been set by these official sources, leading the *New York Times* and a few other prominent dailies to later express regret for being too deferential in the coverage leading up to the invasion.

A study of public comments of President Bush and seven of his administration's top officials found 532 instances of erroneous information being disseminated in the 2 years following the September 11, 2001, terrorist attacks. President Bush made 232 false statements about weapons of mass destruction in Iraq and another 28 about Iraq's links to Al Qaeda (Lewis & Reading-Smith, 2008). Three months after the start of the Iraq war, 73% of Americans thought that the United States had found weapons of mass destruction, and 67% believed that evidence of an Iraq–Al Qaeda link had been discovered (Kull, Ramsay, & Lewis, 2003–2004). Belief in both statements was linked to support for the Iraq war. Simple notions that "the media set the agenda" ignore broader macro-social processes at work. Government-media relations for centuries have been characterized by secrecy, disinformation, and control of messages by framing and priming of issues.

Thus, it is crucial to understand how officials control social issue agenda by using the news media as their docile messengers.

New communication journals born in the 1970s helped scholars around the world increase mutual awareness of their research. This expanded the international base of scholars but had the unfortunate effect of stoking tensions between behavioral, critical, and cultural scholars that culminated in "Ferment in the Field" (Gerbner, 1983). Mistrust of the evidence the opposing camps used to understand macro-level systems had a dampening effect on macro-research. Fortunately, the wars seem to have subsided into an uneasy truce that may now lessen their reticence to understand one another.

## LEVELS OF ANALYSIS

*Levels of analysis* are hierarchical systems of categories arranged according to the degree of abstraction of the concepts used to analyze the units whose variation we are trying to explain. More abstract *units of analysis* are larger and often contain one or more levels of more concrete units. For example, a particular daily newspaper could be analyzed at four levels: as part of an *industry* (most abstract), as an *organization* within the industry, as a *department* within the organization (e.g., city desk, sports, advertising), and as *individual* journalists (least abstract). The more abstract level in any comparison can be labeled *macro* relative to any less abstract *micro* level. In the above example, the department is *macro* relative to the individual employee but *micro* when compared with the larger industry or organization.

The number of levels distinguished by social scientists varies from two (e.g., macro/micro) to many. One common scheme used in sociology is a three-level system: *macro structural* (social institutions and patterns of social behavior), *meso interactional* (relationships among individuals interacting with others), and *micro individual* (psychological processes and properties of human experience). We use a five-category system: *societal/global, industry/organizational,* and *community/neighborhood* as *macro-level* social systems; *network/primary groups* as *microsocial*-level systems; and *individual* as a *micro*-system.

Understanding levels of analysis and micro-macro issues is of critical importance to theory construction and research in communication. Theory building requires concepts that are defined and measured at the same level as the phenomena being explained. The history of communication research, unfortunately, is replete with examples of the mixing of "psychological" and "sociological" variables in a giant stepwise regression analysis to maximize prediction. This results in ambiguous assertions of causality and little understanding. Another problem is "system jumping" by inappropriately using a concept defined at one level of analysis as an explanation of behavior of units at another level.

Levels of analysis are important in shaping theories, though they do not in themselves constitute theories. They belong in the realm of meta-theories: theories about theories. What determines a level of analysis of any theoretical or empirical work is the unit being observed and the degree of abstraction of concepts used to analyze those units. Communication research at the *physiological* level uses variables describing cellular, brain, or nervous system functioning. *Individual* (intrapersonal) level variables describe cognitive, personality, and attitudinal processes. *Interpersonal* communication theory adds variables reflecting relationships and exchanges between individuals. *Macrosocial* systems are analyzed in terms of the structures and processes of organized collections of individuals, including institutions, laws, and norms.

*Communication as a Variable Field.* Development of the social sciences over more than a century has produced disciplines with distinguishable positions regarding levels of analysis. The status of communication as a cross-level *variable* field rather than a *level* field underscores issues of levels of analysis (Paisley, 1984). Level fields such as anthropology (cultures), sociology (social organizations), and psychology (individuals) are organized around a single level of analysis. Economics, political science, geography, and communication are fields that are organized around their respective phenomena of interest. Though level fields have suffered tensions between their specialists, variable fields have been able to achieve much less integration of their knowledge base. Communication scholars from different intellectual traditions tend to use concepts and methods within a particular level, rarely venturing beyond their level of "residence" (Pan & McLeod, 1991, p. 141). The result has been theoretical "islands" mapped by distinctive terminology, each surrounded by mutually noncomparable "seas" of research evidence.

*Controversies Surrounding Levels of Analysis.* All who contemplate constructing unified communication theory connecting levels should be aware they are entering a controversial area of debates that began in 19th-century philosophy and continue in contemporary philosophy of science. In 20th-century social science, micro/macro *ontological* debates continued as part of the claims of legitimacy and the turf wars within and between academic fields. A key concept underlying these debates is that of *emergence,* the claim that less abstract individual component units collaboratively create a given collective entity that is not *reducible* to explanation in terms of individual units. In other words, the whole does not equal the sum of its parts. The relationship of individual and collective properties was a central question for 19th-century founders of sociology and later in the sociological paradigms of structural functionalism, exchange theory, and rational choice theory (Sawyer, 2001). Psychologists rejecting behaviorism in the *cognitive revolution* argued that cognitive processes were emergent and not reducible to less abstract variables of behavior.

Two philosophical questions concern emergence: the *ontological* question of whether the emergent macro-phenomena are *real* rather than nominal analytic constructs and the *empirical* question of whether the macro-phenomena are reducible to explanation by concepts of less abstract individual components. For summaries of micro-macro link issues, see Eulau (1986) and Sawyer (2001). For communication applications, see Blumler, McLeod, and Rosengren (1992); J. M. McLeod and Blumler (1987); J. M. McLeod, Pan, and Rucinski (1995); Ritchie and Price (1991); and Slater, Snyder, and Hayes (2006).

Pan and McLeod (1991) suggest that an *epistemological* view of levels of analysis may be a more fruitful approach in that it does not depend on holding any particular position in the ontological debate. Substantive questions call for the clarification of concepts, the location of variance within and among the concepts, and the specification of theoretical as well as operational linkages of the concepts (Hage, 1972). The locus of the variation and the nature of the mechanisms determine the appropriate level or levels of analysis. Treating levels as falling on a micro- and macro-continuum lessens the burden of lacking "natural units" in communication such as those found in education (e.g., system, school, classroom) or in political science research (e.g., national, state, local).

*Constructing Macro-Level Variables.* The selection, conceptualization, and measurement of variables appropriate for macro-level research are crucial and difficult processes. The pull toward individual-level analyses is made even stronger because it is usually easier to collect data from individuals in sufficient numbers than from macro-units. Aggregation of individual data is the dominant form used to measure macro-level units. For example, nations or other macro-units can be compared on their mean level of income, literacy rates, or per capita time spent watching television. These are examples of what Lazarsfeld (1958) called *analytical* variables. They can be aggregated as means (macro-unit averages) that have an individual counterpart in that each person earns some level of income, may or may not be literate, and watches TV a number of hours per day. The same individual data could have been aggregated in ways that have no direct counterpart. For example, we could calculate the dispersion (variance) of income across the population. Average values and dispersion of the same macro-variable may have very different outcomes.

Lazarsfeld (1958) specified two other variable types more directly relevant to the analysis of macro-level units. *Structural* variables describe relations between individuals (e.g., *reciprocity* in sociometric choices in networks) or between units in more abstract levels (e.g., strength of communication links between community organizations). *Global* variables deal with collective properties of macro-units regardless of their relation to individual members (e.g., *social capital* as the number of voluntary organizations available in communities).

## ◆ Forms of Multilevel Analysis

Most empirical research in communication is conducted with concepts measured at a single level of analysis. If our explanations remain solely at the individual level, we are guilty of disciplinary reductionism and risk missing important social influences, implicitly blaming individuals for problems whose remedies would be better sought through institutions. Cross-level analyses are referred to as *multilevel* because potentially the patterns of influence may cross more than two levels. It may be useful to conceive the processes of some intermediate level as intervening to adapt or direct (i.e., mediate) the effects of a higher on a lower level or the reverse.

We will illustrate four forms of macro-to-micro analysis but only one form in the reverse (micro-to-macro) direction. That imbalance reflects the history of sociological theorizing that emphasized social determinism and neglected the processes of human *agency,* individuals working together to achieve social change. We should avoid the temptation to equate macro-to-micro influence with *social control* and micro-to-macro influence with *social change.* Downward influence of governments may sometimes act to induce change (e.g., the civil rights legislation of the 1960s), and individuals may band together to frustrate change (e.g., the segregationists who blocked the doorway at Little Rock high school in the same era).

## MACRO-TO-MICRO INFLUENCE

*Comparative* is research where "comparisons are made across two or more geographically (spatially) or historically (temporally) defined systems" (Blumler et al., 1992, p. 7). All sound scientific research is comparative in containing at least one formal comparison, but comparative research as used here "creates a need to think structurally, to conceptualize in macro terms, to stretch vertically across levels and horizontally across systems" (p. 8). Multilevel analysis represents a set of comparative analytic strategies distinctive in both theory and methods. Operationalization of concepts in multilevel research is unusual in two ways: (1) It frequently uses a mixture of Lazarsfeld's (1958) analytical, structural, and global macro-measures, and (2) it often analyzes data gathered from various sources (e.g., sample surveys, statistical records, historical data, observation).

Kohn (1989) proposed four roles that the *nation* unit could play in cross-national comparison research: (1) *objects* of analysis where our interest is in the *particular* countries per se or for institutional patterns (e.g., levels of Internet penetration) rather than for testing hypotheses; (2) *contexts* for predicted relationships between variables conceived at a less abstract level (e.g., Internet news use and civic participation); (3) *units* of analysis, described by particular variables of interest measured at the national level; and (4) *components* of larger international or global systems. We review macro-research in communication with variations of the first three of Kohn's analytic forms and then add two additional forms.

*Particularistic Macro-Analysis.* When the researcher's interest is in the particular nation or other macro-unit for its own sake, rather than as a setting for testing some general hypotheses, the unit (e.g., nation, community) is treated as an *object of analysis,* comparing various communication and political variables measured at a single macro level. Variables with continuous measurement can be used to assess variance across units for further multilevel analyses.

*Comparative Macro-Analysis.* Where the interest is in testing relationships between concepts, the macro-units serve as *units of analysis.* This approach seldom strays across levels because macro-theorists are interested in elaborating dynamics at a specific level. They may thereby miss the opportunities to shift their intellectual focus, which can contribute to "forcing a redefinition of existing concepts and fashioning of new ones transportable across space and time, and a framing of new problems and questions" (Gurevitch & Blumler, 1990, p. 319). Macro-comparative theories can be expanded to other levels if a correspondence in hypothesized sets of concepts can be found at each level. For example, if a theory of community-level civic engagement found support for the hypothesis that cities with rich news media systems have a greater number of voluntary associations (macro), then we might predict a positive interaction with local news use in stimulating membership in local voluntary associations.

*Contextual Analysis.* Influence across levels is a more direct concern in contextual analysis. Contexts are broadly defined as properties of macro-units that operate as *constraints,* shaping individual-level (or lower level) phenomena through *incentives* or reducing patterns by *deterrents* or *sanctions.* Considerable thought should be given to the theoretical questions of how various macro-level units and their processes might act to moderate or mediate communication behaviors and their effects at lower levels.

The best-known example of contextual analysis is the research program of Tichenor, Donohue, and Olien (1973), focused on the concept of structural pluralism, a community-level variable that is defined as the degree of differentiation in the community's specialized interests, organizations, power factions, and economic infrastructure. Their theory uses structural pluralism as the key contextual variable that explains significant variance not only in the opinions, attitudes, and behaviors of institutional representatives, citizens, and journalists (Donohue, Olien, & Tichenor, 1985a) but also in the media content produced within a community. For example, highly pluralistic communities devote more attention to covering local community conflicts (Donohue, Olien, & Tichenor, 1985b).

*Temporal Analysis.* Using the arguments of Blumler et al. (1992), we also expand Kohn's (1989) examples of geographically sited *space* variations in nations to suggest contextual influences based on *time* (e.g., year, generational cohort, life cycle, and economic changes over time). For example, downward trends in campaign media attention across elections (the time unit) reduce news consumption and its effect on political knowledge. Long-term trends and campaign-specific influences on both the level of media use (dosage) and media effects (potency) were shown across presidential election campaigns and across the life cycle (Sotirovic & McLeod, 2004). Systematic investigations of macro-variations in time as well as space are essential because levels and effects strengths vary in complex ways.

*Sociotropic Analysis.* Political communication scholars interested in civic engagement face a paradox. They assume that communication processes are essential to producing an informed and active citizenry. Yet these scholars view citizens as unmotivated, uninterested, and uninformed about politics, pursuing their own rather than collective interests and seldom participating in civic affairs. Scholars from Lazarsfeld et al. (1948) onward have located the sources of citizen apathy in low education and other structural factors. Rather than seeking the processes by which structural variables influence participation, however, scholars tend to blame or pity the apathetic citizen and remove the "why" question by statistically controlling out the influence of social factors on civic engagement. The various approaches to multilevel analysis attempt to answer the "why" question by facing the paradox directly. The ideal conditions for testing multilevel macro-influences are often difficult to obtain in the real world of communication research, however. Most often we must accept less than ideal conditions by conducting secondary analyses using large data sets with less than ideal measures of communication and civic engagement. We suggest sociotropic analysis as an approach to understanding macro-influences using individual-level perceptions of the world and social institutions.

The sociotropic approach is based on evidence showing that voting decisions are made less on the basis of pocketbook self-interest than on sociotropic estimates of how well the country is doing economically (Fiorina, 1981; Kinder & Kiewiet, 1981). Average citizens distinguish their own interests from those of their community and nation. Their awareness ("knowledge of") is likely to be greater than their detailed understanding ("knowledge about") of institutions and events that are remote from their immediate world. The citizen has experiential knowledge of the *lifeworld* (Habermas, 1987) but only lay *"theories"* of social systems constructed from fragmentary information emanating from media and personal networks. These lay theories can be seen as attempts of average citizens to reconcile expectations about what they *should* know as citizens with what they really know from their immediate lifeworld. Lay theories, both *normative and empirical,* affect learning from the news (Kosicki & McLeod, 1990).

Citizens who strongly value the normative *pluralistic* roles of the media (as a forum for ideas and activation) pay more attention to the news and are more informed participatory citizens than those advocating *consensual roles* (promoting the local economy and guiding opinions; J. M. McLeod, Sotirovic, & Holbert, 1998). Holding strong *postmaterial* values (e.g., freedom to express ideas, helping each other) strongly stimulates news use, discussion, and reflection on news (Sotirovic & McLeod, 2001). Strong *material* values (e.g., maintain order) dampen citizen action. *Fatalism* (e.g., believing "what will be, will be") is a strong *moderator* in virtually eliminating the media effects on knowledge and participation.

## MICRO-TO-MACRO INFLUENCE

*Aggregation.* This refers to how macro-units emerge as entities that are more than the summation of individual-level phenomena. For example, Cooley (1909) referred to public opinion as "no mere aggregate of separate individual judgments, but an organization, a cooperative product of communication and reciprocal influence" (p. 121). Despite Cooley's promising observation, much research has treated

public opinion as the average of individual opinions. The question becomes how real public opinion emerges, beyond averaging polling data.

This question has been addressed most directly in studies of deliberation, which connect ideas of public opinion and interpersonal discussion. Price and Neijens (1997) studied long-standing questions in public opinion in terms of deliberation and opinion quality. Price (2006) studied deliberation, public opinion, and interactive technology, noting that online environments may be suited to fostering deliberation as they offer relative anonymity and reduced nonverbal, facial, and vocal cues.

Fishkin (1995) pioneered the Deliberative Poll, a set of procedures that provides randomly sampled respondents with oral and written briefing materials and opportunities for discussion in order to assess potential outcomes if the public were exposed to the same information and the same intensive opportunities for discussion as the study participants. The focus on informed public opinion goes beyond the typical formulations of public opinion as the result of simply averaging the views of individuals questioned in sample surveys. Studies of public opinion combining elements of collective rationality are reconnecting the empirical study of public opinion with the oldest and most fundamental normative controversies about public opinion and citizen competence (Althaus, 2003; Page & Shapiro, 1992).

At least three deliberative mechanisms promote positive outcomes on public opinion. The first suggests that group members learn from more knowledgeable and experienced members. A second explanation is that information sharing aggregates group knowledge on a particular topic. Finally, real payoffs are believed to occur when information sharing achieves new breakthroughs through synergistic interactions that lead to unexpected solutions far superior to previous practices (Sunstein, 2006).

Group interactions are prone to difficulties, ranging from groupthink (Janis & Mann, 1977) to hidden profiles, the phenomenon of group members withholding information from discussion (Sunstein, 2006). People are often reluctant to offer their true opinion for fear of social isolation or sanctions. The resulting dysfunctional policies are adopted based on too little information and accompanied by increasing commitments of resources. Online worlds are not immune to such problems, but new communication tools that facilitate interpersonal sharing, discussion, and collaboration across great distances are reshaping social life, business, and government (Benkler, 2006).

## ◆ Prospects for Multilevel Research

The growing interest in multilevel communication research, as evidenced by a number of recent publications (Hayes, Slater, & Snyder, 2008; Park, Eveland, & Cudeck, 2008; Slater et al., 2006), has been driven by an awareness of rapidly changing political arrangements and economic markets and the consolidation and decline of traditional media industries. News forms are changing, audiences require rethinking, and the Internet looms as the elephant, but we are no longer sure where the room is.

Multilevel communication research has been sparse relative to other fields such as public health and education. Slow growth in communication applications may not be a bad idea, however. The frantic search for the magic method (e.g., factor analysis, the semantic differential) in early communication research did little to build theory. Multilevel research requires adequate concepts and theoretical models at each level of analysis along with the daunting auxiliary theories that explain connections between levels (Hannan, 1971; Hauser, 1974). Developing such complex theoretical structures will take

an unusually large amount of thought and empirical validation.

## DEVELOPING STRONG WITHIN-LEVEL MODELS

Connecting two or more levels of analysis through multilevel modeling requires an empirically grounded theoretical model. For the communication and civic engagement topic featured in this chapter, a strong model would provide answers to two interrelated questions: First, why do individual citizens use sources of public affairs information with varying frequency and patterns of use? Second, how does public affairs information influence citizen participation? Unfortunately, these two questions became decoupled more than three decades ago and only recently have been brought closer together in proposals for an O-S-O-R model (D. M. McLeod, Kosicki, & McLeod, 2002).

*Explanations of Media Use.* For more than 60 years, media audiences have been described by their demographic characteristics. However useful these locators were for media planners, they are not explanations of *why,* for example, lower socioeconomic categories use public affairs content less and entertainment content more than more advantaged groups. Uses and gratifications research of the 1970s documented a diverse set of audience motivations (Blumler & Katz, 1974) and content effects (J. M. McLeod & Becker, 1974). The sociotropic approach presented earlier suggests examining orientations as concepts "horizontally" distant from media but closer to their social structural origins. Qualitative approaches could be combined with standard behavioral methods to build orientation measures of how citizens subjectively resolve the contradictions between democratic expectations and the social constraints. The identification of "level-friendly" *mediators* and *moderators* of structural influences on media use is crucial to the development of individual-level models more compatible with macro levels of analysis.

*Effects of Media Use.* The past 30 years of effects research improved measurement of public affairs media use by including exposure and attention measures as well as information-processing strategies (Kosicki & McLeod, 1990). Such measurement has been complicated by the rise of the Internet as a source of public affairs information. The online availability of traditional media content has created ambiguity about how to deal with exposure to a given medium that may at times be accessed through traditional media conduits and other times online. An additional issue concerns measuring differences between online information use, exchange, and creation, which all may predict civic engagement, particularly among younger cohorts (Shah, Cho, Eveland, & Kwak, 2005; Shah, McLeod, & Yoon, 2001).

The O-S-O-R model suggested here for application to multilevel models requires expansion of "level-friendly" ($O^1$) and more complex postexposure cognitive orientations ($O^2$), along with optimal measures of exposure (S) and civic engagement (R). Structural equation modeling (SEM) is the preferred approach to evaluate complex structural models (Jöreskog & Sörbom, 1988). For potential uses and misuses of SEM to communication, see Holbert and Stephenson (2008). Most applications of SEM in communication have tested models with a small number of conceptually close variables. We recommend larger models with greater conceptual distance, as, for example, choosing sociotropic values for preexposure orientations rather than media-centric gratifications and adding more complex mediators to knowledge as postexposure mediators of communication effects.

LISREL provides three major advantages in interpreting complex models: indices of overall model fit, indices revealing poorly fitting paths, and coefficients dividing effects for each predictor variable into its *direct, indirect,* and *total* impact on subsequent variables. Indirect effects, once discounted as unimportant (Klapper, 1960), have become essential to more nuanced theoretical explanations of communication effects processes.

## OPPORTUNITIES AND HAZARDS OF MULTILEVEL MODELING

Multilevel modeling (MLM) provides a remarkably flexible set of interrelated statistical models that have great promise to solve multilevel problems (Bryk & Raudenbush, 1987). It overcomes the statistical problem of nonindependence of variance between levels (common in ordinary least squares [OLS] regression models) by analyzing the variance of two or more levels simultaneously (e.g., between communities and individuals within communities). This alleviates the dangers of committing either the *ecological fallacy,* making inferences about individuals based on macro-level results (Robinson, 1950), or the *individualistic* fallacy, generalizing individual-level results to the macro level (Alker, 1969). Applications of MLM came rather slowly to communication research, first to organizational and interpersonal communication and then to mass communication, as represented by the contextual analysis studies presented earlier. Fortunately, clear introductory materials have recently appeared (Slater et al., 2006), along with an MLM primer (Hayes, 2006) and other MLM background (Park et al., 2008).

Despite the vast opportunities MLM opens to connecting theory and research across levels, there are some necessary decisions and potential hazards of applying it appropriately. Researcher-controlled data are apt to have better measurement but smaller and less representative samples from less dispersed geographical areas, while archived data sets for secondary analysis may be larger but lacking in measurement quality.

*Which Macro Levels to Choose?* Research should begin with research questions and then choose the macro level most likely to impinge on the key concepts and relationships specified in the individual-level model. The necessity of assigning individuals to macro-units brings complications. The availability of data sets and measures may lead to a less than optimal choice. The use of *nations* as the unit is possible when comparable communication and political data are gathered from citizens regarding a common event, as in the seminal study of the first Direct Election to the European Parliament in nine countries (Blumler, 1983). Cho (2008) used *television markets* as the macro-unit in a study of campaign advertising effects on communication behavior. *Communities* are attractive units of aggregation if very large data sets are available (Cho & McLeod, 2007) or if data from repeated cross-sectional surveys from the same communities are combined (Paek, Yoon, & Shah, 2005). *Neighborhoods* are ideal for studying the processes of discussion networks. Kim and Ball-Rokeach (2006) grouped respondents into neighborhoods using GIS software to connect citizens with census tract data regarding ethnic heterogeneity, residential stability, and spatial dependence as neighborhood-level measures. Many archived data sets contain markers for geographic locations that permit widespread analysis of neighborhood units. Total *discussion networks* are potential units, although they have become geographically dispersed by the advent of the Internet.

*What Macro-Variables to Use?* Theoretical considerations are essential to selection of macro-variables. Most multilevel communication research uses measures of community integration: *residential stability, institutional confidence,* and *connectedness* (Shah et al., 2001); *home ownership, social interaction,* and aggregated *local print media use* (Paek et al., 2005); and *cohesion, density,* and *education* (Cho & McLeod, 2007). Community stability provides an environment conducive to civic engagement. Stable communities had higher levels of interpersonal trust and cross-level contextual effects from interacting with Internet use to generate interpersonal trust and participation among younger citizens (Shah et al., 2001). Kim and Ball-Rokeach (2006) found that the individual-level influence of integrated storytelling networks on civic participation was stronger in *residentially unstable* and *ethnically heterogeneous* neighborhoods.

Multilevel political communication research is growing in sophistication and complexity. Cho (2008) measured the *volume of political advertising* exposure by combining ad-tracking data in specific media markets at particular *time intervals* with the respondent's time–part television viewing behavior from the National Annenberg Election Survey daily survey data. *Political ad exposure* stimulated news exposure, Web use for political information, and political talk. Surveillance motivation was offered as an auxiliary theory accounting for the cross-level contextual effect. The use of multiple data sources for macro-level measures rather than only aggregated individual data expands the growing sophistication first evidenced in Kim and Ball-Rokeach (2006) and Cho and McLeod (2007).

## FUTURE DIRECTIONS OF MULTILEVEL RESEARCH AND THEORY

Multilevel research and theory in communication is poised for long-term growth. The early 21st century brought tremendous innovation along with an accompanying mix of instability, fear, and optimism. Unrelenting innovation in communication devices, services, and opportunities is shrinking the world, lowering costs, and increasing communication possibilities. This is unleashing tremendous creativity, collaboration, and optimism about unlocking human potential and creating new wealth, social capital, and improvements in governance. At the same time, many interpret change as weakening many of our long-standing communication institutions that are struggling to adapt to the new environment.

Newspapers are being challenged by Internet-based search engines that empower news aggregators to deliver information that is owned by others, redirecting advertising dollars accordingly. Celebrity news is widely available, but new "content providers" do not stress high-quality local news and investigative and explanatory journalism. This is bad news for many journalists and the local communities they serve.

Journalism's fundamental role in democratic processes has been recognized since the early writings on mass communication and society (e.g., Cooley, 1909). But a new system of news and technology is emerging, along with unfamiliar ownership structures, unclear norms of accuracy and accountability, and new standards of editorial independence. The Internet has enabled more direct and deliberative forms of democracy (Benkler, 2006) but has complicated issues of property rights, security, privacy, and economic viability. This systemic upheaval raises the imperative and visibility of macrosocial inquiry.

Technology is changing communication research as well. New, larger, and less expensive data from populations can be gathered over time in credible, representative ways online through such cost-effective services as the Knowledge Networks panel. New, large, over-time and increasingly international data collections are impressive technical achievements capable of yielding rich troves of publicly shared data that enable new forms of analysis (e.g., Romer, Kenski, Winneg, Adaziewicz, & Jamieson, 2006). Storing, handling, manipulating, and analyzing the complex data required for multilevel modeling are facilitated by various technological advances. Relational databases simplify the process of adding contextual variables to individual-level survey data. Innovations in sampling and geocoding can make survey samples representative of complex spatial arrangements such as sprawling urban communities and gerrymandered political districts. New databases and methods for capturing, storing, and coding video, voice, graphics, and text will enhance and simplify the study of media content. Pushing the boundaries of levels, new tools are popularizing physiological responses.

As we have noted, technology alone will not produce great research without interesting multilevel problems and creative theoretical ideas. Together, these factors offer the potential for tremendous research breakthroughs. J. M. McLeod and Blumler (1987) concluded that "communication science without a macro component would be impoverished and seriously incomplete" (p. 277). A quarter century later, macrosocial research is beginning to thrive, but it is still more rare than it should be.

## ◆ References

Alker, H. R. (1969). A typology of ecological fallacies. In M. Dogan & S. Rokkan (Eds.), *Quantitative ecological analysis in the social sciences* (pp. 69–86). Cambridge: MIT Press.

Althaus, S. L. (2003). *Collective preferences in democratic politics: Opinion surveys and the will of the people.* New York: Cambridge University Press.

Benkler, Y. (2006). *The wealth of networks: How social production transforms markets and freedom.* New Haven, CT: Yale University Press.

Berelson, B. (1952). Democratic theory and public opinion. *Public Opinion Quarterly, 16,* 313–330.

Berelson, B. (1959). The state of communication research. *Public Opinion Quarterly, 23,* 1–16.

Berelson, B. R., Lazarsfeld, P. F., & McPhee, W. N. (1954). *Voting: A study of opinion formation in a presidential campaign.* Chicago: University of Chicago Press.

Berger, C. R., & Chaffee, S. H. (Eds.). (1987). *Handbook of communication science.* Newbury Park, CA: Sage.

Blumler, J. G. (Ed.). (1983). *Communicating to voters: Television in the first European Parliamentary elections.* Beverly Hills, CA: Sage.

Blumler, J. G., & Katz, E. (Eds.). (1974). *Uses of mass communications: Current perspectives on gratifications research.* Beverly Hills, CA: Sage.

Blumler, J. G., McLeod, J. M., & Rosengren, K. E. (1992). An introduction to comparative communication research. In J. G. Blumler, J. M. McLeod, & K. E. Rosengren (Eds.), *Comparatively speaking: Communication and culture across time and space* (pp. 3–18). Newbury Park, CA: Sage.

Bryk, A. S., & Raudenbush, S. W. (1987). Application of hierarchical linear-models to assessing change. *Psychological Bulletin, 101,* 147–158.

Chaffee, S. H., & Schleuder, J. (1986). Measurement and effects of attention to media news. *Human Communication Research, 13,* 76–107.

Cho, J. (2008). Political ad and citizen communication. *Communication Research, 35,* 423–451.

Cho, J., & McLeod, D. M. (2007). Structural antecedents to knowledge and participation: Extending the knowledge gap concept to participation. *Journal of Communication, 57,* 205–228.

Cohen, B. C. (1963). *The press and foreign policy.* Princeton, NJ: Princeton University Press.

Cooley, C. H. (1909). *Social organization: A study of the larger mind.* New Brunswick, NJ: Transaction.

Donohue, G. A., Olien, C. N., & Tichenor, P. J. (1985a). Leader and editor views of role of press in community development. *Journalism Quarterly, 62,* 367–372.

Donohue, G. A., Olien, C. N., & Tichenor, P. J. (1985b). Reporting conflict by pluralism, newspaper type and ownership. *Journalism Quarterly, 62,* 489–499, 507.

Eulau, H. (1986). *Politics, self, and society: A theme and variations.* Cambridge, MA: Harvard University Press.

Fairness & Accuracy in Reporting. (2003, May 18). *In Iraq crisis, networks are megaphones for official views.* Retrieved January 14, 2008, from http://www.fair.org

Fiorina, M. P. (1981). *Retrospective voting in American national elections.* New Haven, CT: Yale University Press.

Fishkin, J. S. (1995). *The voice of the people: Public opinion and democracy.* New Haven, CT: Yale University Press.

Gerbner, G. (1973). Cultural indicators: The third voice. In G. Gerbner, L. Gross, & W. Melody (Eds.), *Communications technology and social policy: Understanding the new "cultural revolution"* (pp. 555–573). New York: John Wiley.

Gerbner, G. (Ed.). (1983). Special issue: Ferment in the field. *Journal of Communication, 33,* 1–368.

Gurevitch, M., & Blumler, J. G. (1990). Comparative research: The expanding frontier. In D. L. Swanson & D. Nimmo (Eds.), *New directions in political communication: A resource book* (pp. 305–325). Newbury Park, CA: Sage.

Habermas, J. (1987). *The theory of communicative action: Lifeworld and system: A critique of functionalist reason* (Vol. 2). Boston: Beacon.

Hage, J. (1972). *Techniques and problems of theory construction in sociology.* New York: John Wiley.

Hannan, M. T. (1971). *Aggregation and disaggregation in sociology.* Lexington, MA: Lexington Books.

Hauser, R. M. (1974). Contextual analysis revisited. *Sociological Methods & Research, 2,* 365–375.

Hayes, A. F. (2006). A primer on multilevel modeling. *Human Communication Research, 32,* 385–410.

Hayes, A. F., Slater, M. D., & Snyder, L. B. (2008). *The Sage handbook of advanced data analysis methods for communication research.* Thousand Oaks, CA: Sage.

Holbert, R. L., & Stephenson, M. T. (2008). Commentary on the uses and misuses of structural equation modeling in communication research. In A. F. Hayes, M. D. Slater, & L. B. Snyder (Eds.), *The Sage handbook of advanced data analysis methods for communication research* (pp. 185–218). Thousand Oaks, CA: Sage.

Janis, I., & Mann, L. (1977). *Decision making: A psychological analysis of conflict, choice and commitment.* New York: Free Press.

Jöreskog, K., & Sörbom, D. (1988). *LISREL 7: A guide to the program and applications.* Chicago: SPSS.

Katz, E., & Lazarsfeld, P. F. (1955). *Personal influence: The part played by people in the flow of mass communications.* Glencoe, IL: Free Press.

Kim, Y. C., & Ball-Rokeach, S. J. (2006). Community storytelling network, neighborhood context, and civic engagement: A multilevel approach. *Human Communication Research, 32,* 411–439.

Kinder, D. R., & Kiewiet, D. R. (1981). Sociotropic politics: The American case. *British Journal of Political Science, 11,* 129–161.

Klapper, J. T. (1960). *Effects of mass communication.* Glencoe, IL: Free Press.

Kohn, M. L. (1989). Introduction. In M. L. Kohn (Ed.), *Cross-national research in sociology* (pp. 17–31). Newbury Park, CA: Sage.

Kornhauser, W. (1959). *The politics of mass society.* Glencoe, IL: Free Press.

Kosicki, G. M., & McLeod, J. M. (1990). Learning from political news: Effects of media images and information-processing strategies. In S. Kraus (Ed.), *Mass communication and political information processing* (pp. 69–83). Hillsdale, NJ: Lawrence Erlbaum.

Kull, S., Ramsay, C., & Lewis, E. (2003–2004). Misperceptions, the media, and the Iraq war. *Political Science Quarterly, 118,* 569–598.

Lazarsfeld, P. F. (1958). Evidence and inference in social research. In D. Lerner (Ed.), *Evidence and inference* (pp. 107–135). New York: Free Press.

Lazarsfeld, P. F., Berelson, B. R., & Gaudet, H. (1948). *The people's choice* (7th ed.). New York: Columbia University Press.

Lewis, C., & Reading-Smith, M. (2008). *False pretenses.* Retrieved January 23, 2008, from http://www.publicintegrity.org/WarCard/

McCombs, M. E., & Shaw, D. L. (1972). The agenda-setting function of the mass media. *Public Opinion Quarterly, 36,* 176–187.

McLeod, D. M., Kosicki, G. M., & McLeod, J. M. (2002). Resurveying the boundaries of political communication effects. In J. Bryant & D. Zillmann (Eds.), *Media effects:*

*Advances in theory and research* (2nd ed., pp. 215–267). Hillsdale, NJ: Lawrence Erlbaum.

McLeod, J. M., & Becker, L. B. (1974). Testing the validity of gratification measures through political effects analysis. In J. G. Blumler & E. Katz (Eds.), *The uses of mass communication: Current perspectives on gratifications research* (pp. 137–164). Beverly Hills, CA: Sage.

McLeod, J. M., & Blumler, J. G. (1987). The macrosocial level of communication science. In C. Berger & S. Chaffee (Eds.), *Handbook of communication science* (pp. 271–322). Newbury Park, CA: Sage.

McLeod, J. M., Pan, Z., & Rucinski, D. (1995). Levels of analysis in public opinion research. In T. L. Glasser & C. T. Salmon (Eds.), *Public opinion and communication of consent* (pp. 55–85). New York: Guilford.

McLeod, J. M., Sotirovic, M., & Holbert, R. L. (1998). Values as sociotropic judgments influencing communication patterns. *Communication Research, 25,* 453–480.

Nie, N. H., Verba, S., & Petrocik, J. R. (1976). *The changing American voter.* Cambridge, MA: Harvard University Press.

Paek, H. J., Yoon, S. H., & Shah, D. V. (2005). Local news, social integration, and community participation: Hierarchical linear modeling of contextual and cross-level effects. *Journalism and Mass Communication Quarterly, 82,* 587–606.

Page, B. I., & Shapiro, R. Y. (1992). *The rational public.* Chicago: University of Chicago Press.

Paisley, W. (1984). Communication in the communication sciences. In B. Dervin & M. J. Voight (Eds.), *Progress in communication sciences* (Vol. 5, pp. 1–43). Norwood, NJ: Ablex.

Pan, Z., & McLeod, J. M. (1991). Multi-level analysis in mass communication research. *Communication Research, 18,* 138–171.

Park, H. S., Eveland, W. P., Jr., & Cudeck, R. (2008). Multilevel modeling: People within groups and contexts. In A. F. Hayes, M. D. Slater, & L. B. Snyder (Eds.), *The Sage handbook of advanced data analysis methods for communication research* (pp. 219–245). Thousand Oaks, CA: Sage.

Price, V. (2006). Citizens deliberating online: Theory and some evidence. In T. Davies & B. S. Noveck (Eds.), *Online deliberation:*

*Design, research and practice.* Stanford, CA: CSLI Publications.

Price, V., & Neijens, P. (1997). Opinion quality in public opinion research. *International Journal of Public Opinion Research, 9,* 336–360.

Ritchie, L. D., & Price, V. (1991). Of matters micro and macro: Special issues for communication research. *Communication Research, 18,* 133–139.

Robinson, W. S. (1950). Ecological correlations and the behavior of individuals. *American Sociological Review, 15,* 351–357.

Romer, D., Kenski, K., Winneg, K., Adaziewicz, C., & Jamieson, K. H. (2006). *Capturing campaign dynamics: The National Annenberg Election Survey.* Philadelphia: University of Pennsylvania Press.

Sawyer, R. K. (2001). Emergence in sociology: Contemporary philosophy of mind and some implications for sociological theory. *American Journal of Sociology, 107,* 351–386.

Schramm, W. L. (1954). *The process and effects of mass communication.* Urbana: University of Illinois Press.

Shah, D. V., Cho, J. C., Eveland, W. P., & Kwak, N. (2005). Information and expression in a digital age: Modeling Internet effects on civic participation. *Communication Research, 32,* 531–565.

Shah, D. V., McLeod, J. M., & Yoon, S. H. (2001). Communication, context, and community: An exploration of print, broadcast, and Internet influences. *Communication Research, 28,* 464–506.

Slater, M. D., Snyder, L., & Hayes, A. F. (2006). Thinking and modeling at multiple levels: The potential contribution of multilevel modeling to communication theory and research. *Human Communication Research, 32,* 375–384.

Sotirovic, M., & McLeod, J. M. (2001). Values, communication behavior, and political participation. *Political Communication, 18,* 273–300.

Sotirovic, M., & McLeod, J. M. (2004). Knowledge as understanding: The information processing approach to political learning. In L. Kaid (Ed.), *Handbook of political communication research* (pp. 357–394). Mahwah, NJ: Lawrence Erlbaum.

Sunstein, C. R. (2006). *Infotopia: How many minds produce knowledge.* New York: Oxford University Press.

Tichenor, P. J., Donohue, G. A., & Olien, C. N. (1970). Mass media flow and differential growth knowledge. *Public Opinion Quarterly, 34,* 159–170.

Tichenor, P. J., Donohue, G. A., & Olien, C. N. (1973). Mass communication research: Evolution of a structural model. *Journalism Quarterly, 50,* 419–426.

# PART 4

## FUNCTIONS

# 12

# PERSUASION

◆ James Price Dillard

**P**ersuasion may be defined as the use of symbols (sometimes accompanied by images) by one social actor for the purpose of changing or maintaining another social actor's opinion or behavior. The foregoing statement implies some degree of agency and fore-thought on the part of the message producer, though not necessarily a great deal of planfulness. In fact, much persuasive discourse can be seen in off-the-cuff responses to a perceived moment of opportunity (Dillard, Anderson, & Knobloch, 2002). Other persuasive efforts, especially those that are the product of marketing departments and political campaigns, are carefully constructed and consciously orches-trated (Zhao, 2002).

The definition also gives a nod to the fundamentally social nature of persuasion. We make efforts to persuade *other people*. When people make reference to self-persuasion, they are really talking about individual decision making. The ability to change the views of others should be viewed as one of the most fundamental of social skills (Dillard & Marshall, 2003).

The phrase *the use of symbols* is important to the definition because it makes clear that persuasion is a form of communication. This point deserves emphasis given that research on persuasion—a communicative phenomenon—has, historically, been tightly intertwined with the study of attitude change—a psychological phenomenon. However, attitude change can result from a variety of nonsymbolic processes. For instance, it is well established that attitudes toward various stimuli—polygons, photographs, drawings, matrices, and people—can be made more favorable simply by repeatedly exposing individuals to those stimuli (Bornstein, 1989). Similarly, when ownership of an object is experimentally manipulated by giving some subjects objects to keep and others objects on loan, those who have ownership of the objects value them more highly (Thaler, 1980). While such processes are interesting and important, they fall outside of the domain of persuasion. With this limited explication of persuasion as a backdrop, I turn next to a sketch of the history of persuasion.

## ◆ A Brief History of Persuasion Research

Any history of persuasion research would be incomplete without some acknowledgment of the contributions of rhetoric. Corax is often credited with having been the first person to equate rhetoric and persuasion (in roughly 467 B.C.) and to advance the notion that the function of rhetoric is to assist in ascertaining not absolute truth but rather that which is likely (B. Smith, 1921). Subsequent students of rhetoric elaborated systems of argument such as Aristotle's well-known distinctions among pathos (affect), logos (logic), and ethos (credibility). Even relatively recent writers offer conceptions of rhetoric that are not markedly different from what has just been described as persuasion. Bitzer (1968) presents a case in point when he writes that "the rhetor alters reality by bringing into existence a discourse of such a character that the audience, in thought and action, is so engaged that it becomes a mediator of change. In this sense rhetoric is always persuasive" (p. 4).[1]

Of course, the study of rhetoric has been and continues to be undertaken using the tools of humanistic inquiry. Writing in 1916, Woolbert argued for the development of a new field—speech science—that broke with humanistic

tradition and embraced the scientific method. Thus were sown the seeds for what would become communication science, a contemporary application of the scientific model to the study of persuasion.

While interest in the scientific view of persuasion grew slowly but steadily in communication, there was an explosion of research activity in social psychology following from the appearance of *Communication and Persuasion* (Hovland, Janis, & Kelley, 1953). The Yale Group, as they were known, was theoretically eclectic but organized their empirical efforts around a single question: Who says what to whom with what effect (Lasswell, 1948, p. 37)? In 1957, Festinger published his theory of cognitive dissonance, which influenced attitude research for decades to come. In 1960, Katz presented his work on attitude functions, which suggested that attitudes serve a variety of psychological purposes (see also M. B. Smith, Bruner, & White, 1956). Just a year later, McGuire (1961) began to develop his thinking on resistance to persuasion. After almost half a century, many of the ideas of these pioneering attitude change researchers continue to have an impact on the kinds of questions that are asked about persuasion today.

In this chapter, I will provide coverage of what are mostly social psychological theories of attitude change. Indeed, not to do so would create a seriously distorted image of the research literature. But there are notable differences between psychologists and communication scientists regarding the utility of these theories, and I will highlight these differences where appropriate. As with any review of this length, it is necessarily selective and inevitably incomplete. Nonetheless, my hope is that readers unfamiliar with the persuasion literature might take away a feel for the breadth of the area and that persons who are already steeped in the research can find a useful summary of contemporary thought.

## ◆ *Theoretical Perspectives on Persuasion*

### FUNCTIONAL THEORIES

Katz (1960) asserted that virtually all attitudes help to structure an understanding of the environment (see also M. B. Smith et al., 1956). This *knowledge function* is performed, at some level, by all attitudes (Fazio, Roskos-Ewoldsen, & Powell, 1994). Some attitudes operate so as to maximize rewards and minimize punishments from objects in the environment (the *utilitarian function*), whereas others foster a connection with social groups (the *social identity function*). Still other attitudes serve a *value expressive function*—that is, they provide a means for the expression of personal values and core aspects of the self-concept.

Although the list of functions varies from author to author, all functional theorists agree on one fundamental principle: Matching message content to attitude function is the means by which persuasion can be achieved. Briñol and Petty (2006) have speculated that there may be multiple mechanisms underlying the matching effect. These include, among others, increased depth of message processing, biased message processing, and processing fluency. In a significant paper, Hullett and Boster (2001) identified and repaired an internal contradiction in existing functional theory. Their contributions were twofold. First, and most important, they noted the ambiguity associated with the value expressive function. To which of the many possible values that one might hold does it refer? And if one wishes to design a persuasive message that matches the values of the target audience, to which value should one appeal? This insight led them to suggest that audiences might be comprehensively studied using existing typologies of values. Their second important contribution was to recognize that the *social adjustive function* (i.e., attitudes that enable affiliation with others) did not deserve

stand-alone status. Rather, this function could be sensibly viewed as the value that individuals place on getting along with others. Subsequent investigations using this framework examined the persuasive effect of emotions provoked by matched and mismatched messages (e.g., Hullett, 2004).

### DISCREPANCY MODELS

Research in this tradition revolves around the assumption that persuasion is the result of some process of comparison. The models differ in terms of what gets compared with what.

*Social Judgment Theory (SJT).* Perhaps the oldest of the discrepancy models, SJT holds that attitude change follows from a comparison of one's preexisting attitude with the position advocated in the message (Sherif & Hovland, 1961). A recipient's attitude may be divided into three regions. The latitude of acceptance includes his or her own position as well as all of the other positions that are acceptable to that individual. The latitude of rejection encompasses all of those positions that are definitely at odds with the individual's own position. The latitude of noncommitment, which lies between acceptable and unacceptable positions, contains positions that the individual neither explicitly embraces nor explicitly disavows. The relative size of the latitudes of acceptance and rejection is thought to be a function of involvement with the issue. Higher levels of involvement produce smaller latitudes of acceptance and larger latitudes of rejection.

When a message proposes a change that falls in the latitude of acceptance, SJT predicts an assimilation effect such that the recipient will see the position as more similar to his or her own than it is in fact. This will produce more change than would be expected from an accurate perception of the position. If a message presents a position that is substantially different from one's own position—in the latitude of rejection—the theory anticipates a contrast effect such that the message is perceived as more different than it really is. It is expected that this misperception will yield less attitude change than a veridical comparison or that it will produce a boomerang effect (i.e., attitude change opposite to that intended).

Although there are few data consistent with the notion that the proposed perceptual processes mediate the effects of message discrepancy on attitude change, the theory is not without value. The core ideas are sufficiently appealing that they remain common currency in the persuasion literature despite the lack of empirical support. And SJT does make the important prediction that change is best accomplished in a series of steps in which each message falls fairly close to the target's initial attitude (i.e., not in the latitude of rejection). This feature of the theory was cleverly exploited by S. W. Smith, Atkin, Martell, Allen, and Hembroff (2006) in a study of drinking among students at Michigan State University. Those researchers conducted an effective social norms campaign by first ascertaining that the normative information they would be providing to students fell relatively close to the target audience's own position (i.e., not in the latitude of rejection), then creating a series of messages that gradually moved that boundary.

*Social Norms Approach (SNA).* More of an idea than a theory, the SNA holds simply that (a) behavior is influenced by the perceived behavior of others, and (b) most individuals live in a state of pluralistic ignorance insofar as they do not perceive the frequency of others' behavior accurately. Typically, individuals believe that others engage in risky health behaviors, such as binge drinking, more often than is actually the case. The implication is that correcting this misperception will cause individuals to bring their own drinking more in line with the true behavioral norm. For example, a message that said "2 out of 3 Penn State students don't drink so much that they forget what they did last night" was intended to reduce alcohol consumption among Penn State students: It did not (L. LaSalle, personal communication, January 9, 2008). Despite some successes, serious questions remain about the validity of the approach. Some investigations show that providing normative data does cause shifts in attitudes and beliefs toward those data but without any corresponding change in behavior (e.g., Steffian, 1999). Other research reports reactance-like effects of social norms messages among those most at risk (e.g., heavy drinkers; Cameron & Campo, 2006; Campo & Cameron, 2006). And even when social normative information does produce change in the desired direction, the specific type of normative information that is effective varies across types of health behavior (Cameron & Campo, 2006). The fact that almost half of the colleges in the United States have used or are using the SNA in an effort to curb student drinking (Wechsler, Seibring, Liu, & Ahl, 2004) suggests an ill-advised rush to implement an unproven persuasive strategy. Greater theoretical specification is needed (e.g., Lapinski & Rimal, 2005) as well as enhanced recognition that SNA must be supplemented with other campaign strategies if they are to have any positive effect at all (e.g., Lederman & Stewart, 2005).

*Language Expectancy Theory (LET).* LET proposes that individuals develop expectations about the linguistic behavior of others as a result of their cultural experiences (Burgoon, Denning, & Roberts, 2002). Persuasive speakers who depart from those expectations may do so in one of two ways. Positive violations exceed expectations in some desirable way and, in so doing, enhance persuasion. Negative violations that depart from linguistic expectations, reflect upon the speaker in an unflattering manner, and yield diminished persuasive effects or boomerangs. In its original conception, LET focused primarily on understanding language intensity in combination with social categories such as males versus females. Subsequently, it was (a) expanded to include a larger variety of message variables, including fear appeals, opinionated language, profanity, and verbal aggression, and (b) taken into new domains such as health communication and interpersonal influence (Burgoon, Denning et al., 2002, provide a review).

## COGNITIVE MODELS

*Cognitive Response Model.* This perspective, originally proposed by Greenwald (1968), asserts that attitude change is a function of thinking. *Cognitive responses* are thoughts that individuals have in reaction to a persuasive message. Although the theory itself is mute regarding the algorithm that computes attitudes from thoughts, the procedures used by researchers are straightforward. After exposure to a message, research participants are asked to list all of the thoughts that came to mind during the message. The resulting cognitive responses have been classified in a variety of ways (Cacioppo, Harkins, & Petty, 1981), but the overwhelming majority of investigations in this tradition have used valence coding. For example, favorable thoughts, that is, those that evaluate the message positively, are coded 1. Unfavorable thoughts, that is, those that are critical of the message, are coded –1. A *dominant cognitive response index* can then be formed by subtracting the sum of the unfavorable thoughts from the sum of the favorable thoughts.

Because the cognitive response model locates dominant cognitive response as the proximal cause of attitude, one important question is whether there is empirical support for that claim. Various different forms of evidence suggest that this is the case. For example, there is a substantial correlation between cognitive responses and attitude (e.g., Petty & Cacioppo, 1979). Other investigations, using some form of statistical mediation analysis,

produced data compatible with the claim of proximal causation (e.g., Hale, Mongeau, & Thomas, 1991). Finally, experimental manipulation of the valence of cognitive responses produced the anticipated effects on attitude (Killeya & Johnson, 1998). Although none of these investigations alone offers ironclad evidence, when considered together, they make a compelling case for the idea that cognitive responses precede attitude change.

The central insight of the cognitive response model is that persuasion will take place only to the extent that a message prompts thinking that is compatible with the major thrust of the appeal. This leads naturally to the question of what might bring about variation in the number and valence of cognitive responses. It was precisely this issue that framed research on the direct descendant of the cognitive response model, that is, the elaboration likelihood model.

*Elaboration Likelihood Model (ELM).* According to Petty and Cacioppo (1986), the general answer to the question of what determines the number and valence of cognitive responses is ability and motivation. Message recipients who are both motivated and able to process a persuasive message are said to engage in *central route processing*. This is an attentive frame of mind in which individuals carefully scrutinize the content and structure of the message. If either motivation or ability is absent, then messages are processed via the *peripheral route*, in which attitude change depends on simple cues, including associative learning, inference from one's own behavior, negative motivation states (e.g., dissonance and reactance), mere exposure, subliminal priming, and memory-based heuristics. While the peripheral route is best viewed as a set of processes, ELM-instigated empirical research is largely limited to the study of heuristics.

Consideration of one of the early studies in this research stream will help to shed light on key features of the model. Petty, Cacioppo, and Goldman (1981) sought to better understand the role of involvement in persuasion. Research participants listened to a message for the supposed purpose of evaluating its broadcast quality. All of the messages argued in favor of the position that college seniors pass a comprehensive examination in their major area of study as a requirement for graduation. One version of the message contained strong arguments, such as the claim that comprehensive exams had been shown to reverse the decline in standardized achievement scores at other universities. Another version was built around weak arguments in which a friend of the author had to take a comprehensive exam and now had a prestigious academic position. The messages were attributed to either a high credibility source—the Carnegie Commission on Higher Education—or a low credibility source—a "report produced by a class at the local high school." The third factor in the design was involvement. It was manipulated by informing participants that the university chancellor was considering implementing the exams either next year (high involvement) or in 10 years (low involvement).

The hypotheses were as follows: When involvement was low, participants would be unwilling to devote much thought to the message and thus would look for a cognitively effortless way to arrive at an attitudinal judgment. The experimenters provided such a means by way of the source credibility cue. In the high-involvement conditions, it was anticipated that participants would be motivated to carefully analyze the message given that it could have a significant impact on their lives. Accordingly, they were expected to pay close attention to argument quality but give little or no weight to source credibility. The results conformed perfectly to these predictions.

There are several noteworthy features of the study, some of which presaged larger movements in the study of attitude change and persuasion. First, the results

for involvement helped to rekindle an interest in the forms and effects of involvement that continues to this day. Second, the argument strength variable proved central to ELM inquiry as a sensitive indicator of depth of message processing. Argument strength in this and later studies was assessed in pretests according to the number of favorable or unfavorable cognitions that the message generated. In other words, under conditions that almost surely reflect central route processing, individuals were asked to list their thoughts about individual arguments within a message. Arguments that produced predominantly *favorable* thoughts (> 65%) were labeled strong, while those that yielded mostly *unfavorable* thoughts (> 65%) were called weak. ELM researchers then proceeded to identify and test for conditions that reduced or eliminated individuals' ability or motivation to discriminate between the two types of messages. From the viewpoint of psychology, this is a perfectly reasonable research strategy: First develop some stimuli that produce the desired psychological effect, and then examine variables that moderate the effect.

From the perspective of communication research, there are at least two problems with this approach. For one, to characterize the arguments as strong or weak is to confuse the effect of the appeals (i.e., variation in cognitive response) with a property of the message (i.e., strength). Whereas Petty and his colleagues (1981) wanted to use the pretested arguments as a methodological tool for understanding message processing, communication researchers take the linkage between message features and message effects as their object of study.

The second problem with argument strength is closely connected to the first. A communication researcher might ask, "How do I design a persuasive message?" but the psychologist's answer appears to be, "Conduct a pretest to determine which messages have strong or weak arguments."

Hence, the ELM seemingly provides no theoretical counsel to individuals whose disciplinary orientation predisposes them to a concern with creating effective persuasive messages. In this regard, the ELM is a viable theory of attitude change but not an especially useful theory of persuasion.

Perhaps the single most important contribution of the ELM is the observation that any given variable can influence attitude change in four ways: (a) by affecting the degree of elaboration, (b) by serving as a cue, (c) by serving as an argument, or (d) by biasing message processing. And there is no requirement that a variable function in only one of these roles. For example, individuals seeking to understand why an expert would endorse a particular position might self-generate arguments (Petty, Wheeler, & Bizer, 1999). Conversely, source expertise might operate as a persuasion cue when involvement is low, as it did in the Petty et al. (1981) study discussed above. Finally, an attorney might point to a witness's expertise in an effort to strengthen him or her argument for the defendant's guilt.

The great value of the ELM's multiple-role postulate is that it makes clear the complexity of the persuasive process. This is not a trivial contribution. The primary shortcoming of the multiple-role postulate is the absence of supporting theoretical architecture that clarifies the conditions under which a given variable will serve one of the four functions. This degree of conceptual flexibility has made it necessary for some researchers to seek the advice of the theory's developer to ascertain what the theory predicts (e.g., Kumkale & Albarracín, 2004, p. 143).

*Heuristic-Systematic Model (HSM).* Chaiken's (Todorov, Chaiken, & Henderson, 2002) heuristic-systematic model (HSM) is often treated as if it were identical to the ELM. It does make many of the same predictions. But it can also be distinguished from the ELM along several lines, perhaps the most

fundamental of which revolves around the notion of dual process. The HSM describes two *types* of message processing: heuristic and systematic. These two modes of message processing are specified to be qualitatively different. In contrast, the ELM posits the existence of two *classes* of mental processes: central (i.e., thinking) and peripheral, which, as discussed above, includes all manner of processes that are low in cognitive effort. This is a key difference between the two theories.

Another important distinction concerns the motivations for message processing. The ELM asserts that the primary (perhaps only) reason for processing is to form an accurate attitude. In contrast, the HSM explicitly recognizes that different forms of involvement underlie different processing motives. Outcome-relevant involvement produces a desire to accurately evaluate the appeal. Impression-relevant involvement prompts the formation of attitudes that align with those of socially desirable others. Value-relevant involvement can stimulate biased processing in an effort to ward off the persuasive attack. Evidence supportive of these distinctions can be found in Johnson and Eagly (1989) and, more recently, in Cho and Boster (2005). However, Slater (2002) has suggested that communication research demands a lengthier list of motivations.

A third point of contrast involves the notion of concurrent processing. Presumably, message processing under the ELM occurs at some specific point on the elaboration likelihood continuum. Thus, if a message processor is engaged in central route processing, he or she is not simultaneously capable of peripheral route processing. But HSM explicitly allows for concurrent processing, a distinctive prediction that has received empirical support (e.g., Bohner, Ruder, & Erb, 2002).

*Unimodel.* The key evidence supporting the dual-process models is the observation that cues and arguments both interact with motivational factors in opposite ways. For example, in the Petty et al. (1981) study described above, source expertise influenced attitude change under conditions of low involvement, but argument quality determined attitude change when involvement was high. The same general pattern was observed for ability factors as well (e.g., Petty, Wells, & Brock, 1976). However, as Kruglanski and his colleagues have pointed out, the cue information in these studies was typically presented prior to the message arguments, and it was much shorter and less complex than the argument information. In other words, the cue versus argument information was confounded with ordinal position and length (Kruglanski et al., 2006).

Is this confound of any consequence? Kruglanski et al. (2006) would certainly answer yes. They base their response on a series of investigations that seem to refute the key evidence supporting the dual-process models. For example, Kruglanski and Thompson (1999) conducted a study that showed that brief arguments had a greater attitudinal impact than lengthy arguments under conditions of low involvement, but the reverse held for high involvement. Other investigations discussed in Kruglanski et al. also run counter to the position that there are two routes to persuasion. Consideration of this evidence *in toto* led Kruglanski et al. to propose that the dual-process models had erroneously posited the existence of two processes when, in fact, only one exists. The single-process account of message processing shows considerable similarity to argumentation theory (e.g., Hample, 2003). It asserts that individuals glean information from persuasive messages (i.e., evidence), which they then proceed to evaluate syllogistically. On this view, an argument or a peripheral cue could serve equally well as the major premise in a syllogism. Accordingly, the logic of the unimodel specifies one and only one process by which suasory messages yield an effect.

Although Kruglanski et al. (2006) make an interesting case for the value of the unimodel, it is not altogether clear that it represents a significant advance in our theoretical understanding of persuasion. One criticism that might be leveled against it is that it covers much of the same ground as the dual-process models. Indeed, two of the three foci of the model—the ability factors and motivational factors that underlie processing—are embodied in the ELM and HSM. It might also be said that the third focus (i.e., the structure of evidence) has also been the target of considerable dual-process research. Even the notion that arguments might serve as cues and cues as arguments has, to some degree, been anticipated by the ELM's multiple-role postulate. In short, it is too soon to know whether the unimodel has the capacity to alter the conceptual terrain of the study of persuasion. But the fact that it has successfully challenged conventional wisdom concerning the underpinnings of the persuasive process and provided the impetus for reexamining what had become taken for granted is all to the good.

*Inoculation Theory.* After observing that two-sided messages were more effective at producing attitude change than one-sided messages, Lumsdaine and Janis (1953) speculated that two-sided messages "inoculated" against persuasive counterattacks. McGuire (1961) subsequently elaborated this germ of an idea into a full-blown theory of resistance to persuasion. Hewing closely to the biological metaphor, he proposed that cultural truisms (i.e., beliefs that had never been challenged) were susceptible to persuasive influence. One means of creating resistance to persuasive attacks might be to provide additional supportive information about the rightness of the beliefs, a strategy much akin to eating right and getting plenty of exercise to maintain one's health. But just as with biological attacks, a more effective strategy might be to present the organism with some weakened but still identifiable form of the disease that would stimulate the body's defenses. In persuasive form, this meant exposing individuals to arguments that were strong enough to demonstrate that their beliefs might be incorrect, then showing those same individuals how to counterargue the attack. This effectiveness of this refutational preemption was thought to depend on motivating the message recipient via threat, then providing argumentative content capable of fending off the attack.

In subsequent years, a great deal was learned about the process of creating resistance. One finding of considerable note was that inoculation is not, as McGuire (1961) originally thought, limited to cultural truisms. Rather, individuals can be inoculated on all manner of controversial topics (e.g., Burgoon & Chase, 1973). Second, much progress has been made, primarily by communication researchers, toward illuminating the psychological processes instigated by refutational preemption. That work shows evidence of counterarguing but also affective change as well as variations in effectiveness due to attitude accessibility (Szabo & Pfau, 2002, provide a comprehensive review). Given the considerable importance of inoculation processes in applied areas such as health and politics, it seems likely that this vigorous research tradition will continue unabated for the foreseeable future.

## COMPUTATIONAL THEORIES

Theories in this section all embrace the idea that the mind bears some resemblance to a computer. They assume that message processing can be modeled using equations similar to the following:

$$A = \Sigma b_i e_i,$$

where $A$ represents an attitude toward some behavior, $b$ represents a belief about the likelihood of some consequence of that behavior, and $e$ represents an evaluation of the outcome. Thus, the process of forming an attitude involves (a) identifying the consequences of an action (of which there may be several, as indicated by the subscripts associated with $b$ and $e$), (b) making judgment of $b$ and $e$, (c) forming the cross-products of $b$ and $e$, and then (d) summing the cross-products. Whether or not the mind actually uses exactly this algorithm is not at issue. Rather, it can be said the mind is doing something similar to Equation 1 because the right side of the equation has proven to predict independent measures of attitude with a high level of precision (Hale, Householder, & Greene, 2002). In this respect, then, attitude formation is a logical and often computationally intense process, though not necessarily one that occurs with conscious awareness.

The equation given above is well known as Fishbein's (1967) theory of attitude. This framework was later expanded into the theory of reasoned action (TRA; Fishbein & Ajzen, 1975), which added the concept of subjective norms, that is, the notion that individuals also take into account the wishes of others. Specifically, subjective norms are aggregated perceptions of the extent to which the target individual believes that particular social entities (i.e., people, groups, institutions) believe that he or she *should* engage in a behavior. Hence, they are conceptually distinct from the descriptive norms that are the focus of the social norms approaches discussed earlier.[2]

In the TRA, attitudes and subjective norms influence behavioral intentions, which, in turn, influence behavior. The theory is one of "reasoned behavior" insofar as individuals compute the most desirable course of action as they see it. In other words, reasoning occurs from a subjective standpoint. It may or may not correspond to objective reality and thus may or may not be rational.

The theory was reformulated again as Ajzen's (n.d.) theory of planned behavior (TPB; see also Fishbein & Yzer, 2003). The major change in this instance was the addition of perceived behavioral control as an antecedent of intention. Broadly speaking, perceived behavioral control is the actor's perception of the relative difficulty of performing the behavior. This move makes plain what was implicit in the TRA—that the computational theories attempt to explain deliberate *volitional* behavior.

In either one of its contemporary forms—Ajzen's TPB or Fishbein and Yzer's integrated model (IM)—this is a mature theory that has successfully withstood many years of testing, stimulated an enormous amount of research, and been applied to a plethora of behavioral phenomena. And, more so than many other theories, it has some fairly straightforward implications for message design. The TPB/IM suggests that, to change intentions, one must change attitudes, subjective norms, or perceived behavioral control. Each of these three constructs is composed of subordinate constructs (e.g., beliefs and evaluations) that help to identify more specific targets of change. Hornik and Woolf (1999) have suggested three criteria for identifying the beliefs that should be targeted in a persuasive intervention: (a) The belief should be significantly associated with intention, (b) there should be a sufficient number of people who do not already subscribe to the belief to justify the intervention, and (c) it should be possible to develop a compelling argument in favor of belief change. For message designers, these guidelines provide added value to a theory that has already contributed a great deal to the study of persuasion.

## HOT PROCESS THEORIES

Whereas cognitive and computational theories accord a privileged role to thought as a precursor to persuasion, other approaches emphasize motivational or "hot processes."

*Message-Irrelevant Affect.* Affective states that exist prior to message exposure and have no logical implications for message evaluation have been termed *message-irrelevant affects* (Dillard & Meijnders, 2002). Research in this area, which has focused on mood, demonstrates that message-irrelevant affect can have a considerable influence on message processing despite the absence of any logical connection. The first study to link mood effects with the dual-process models of persuasion was Mackie and Worth's (1989) investigation. The authors reasoned that because positive mental associations are more tightly interconnected than negative ones, placing people in a positive mood would consume cognitive capacity and thereby render them less capable of discriminating strong from weak arguments. The data were consistent with prediction. In contrast, Bohner, Crow, Erb, and Schwarz (1992) suggested that the findings could be interpreted as a motivational rather than cognitive deficit. Borrowing from emotion theory, these writers advanced the notion that positive moods signal that all is well in the environment. By implication, message recipients can safely concur with any suasory appeal that they might encounter without any need to expend cognitive energy assessing argumentative content.

Contrary to both of these positions, the hedonic contingency model holds that individuals make efforts to manage their moods so as to achieve or maintain favorable affective states (Wegener & Petty, 1994). According to this view, persuasive messages possess content and stylistic features that have hedonic consequences for message processors. For instance, loss-framed or counterattitudinal messages might threaten a positive mood. As a result, the model predicts that individuals in a good mood will be unmotivated to process systematically. In contrast, persons in a negative mood have nowhere to go affectively speaking, except toward the positive end of the scale. Hence, they are expected to be less discriminating in their decisions regarding which messages to process systematically. Hullett's (2005) meta-analysis of the mood and persuasion literature reveals a pattern of data that aligns most closely with the hedonic contingency model. Specifically, positive mood appears to reduce systematic processing when messages possess counterhedonic features but seems to increase systematic processing when messages are proattitudinal.

*Reactance.* Psychological reactance is "the motivational state that is hypothesized to occur when a freedom is eliminated or threatened with elimination" (S. S. Brehm & Brehm, 1981, p. 37). The theory contends that when a perceived freedom is eliminated or threatened with elimination, the individual will be motivated to reestablish that freedom. *Direct restoration* of the freedom involves doing the forbidden act. In addition, freedoms may be restored indirectly by (a) increasing liking for the threatened choice, (b) derogating the source of threat, (c) denying the existence of the threat, or (d) exercising a different freedom to gain feelings of control and choice. Although all of these means for reducing reactance have been the focus of at least some research, reduced or boomerang attitude change has captured the lion's share of attention.

There are four essential elements to reactance theory: freedom, threat to freedom, reactance, and restoration of freedom. The concept of free behaviors is defined broadly so as to include actions, as well as emotions and attitudes (J. W. Brehm, 1966). Individuals possess freedoms only to the extent that they have knowledge of them and perceive that they are capable of enacting the behavior. Given that an individual perceives a specific freedom, any force on the individual that makes it more difficult for him or her to exercise that freedom constitutes a threat (J. W. Brehm, 1966). Even an impersonal event, such as the weather, can be viewed as a threat if it renders more difficult the exercise of a

freedom. However, social influence as a threat to freedom is most pertinent to questions of persuasive communication. It is quite common to see the specter of reactance invoked whenever a persuasive appeal or campaign fails to produce the expected effect (for a review, see Burgoon, Alvaro, Grandpre, & Voulodakis, 2002). Such post hoc explanations may be entirely accurate, but the fact that reactance was never measured directly renders them speculative. A series of recent investigations has shown that reactance can be modeled as an amalgam of anger and negative cognitions (Dillard & Shen, 2005; Quick & Stephenson, 2007; Rains & Turner, 2007). Together, these papers refute the claim that reactance cannot be measured (J. W. Brehm, 1966) and pave the way for research that traces the effects of message features through the entire process delineated by reactance theory. Perhaps most important, this work suggests that reactance theory can be folded into broader perspectives on emotion and persuasion (discussed below). To do so sacrifices none of the theory and research that has accumulated to date. However, it does make clear that reactance can be studied as just one part of a larger conceptual undertaking.

Miller, Lane, Deatrick, Young, and Potts (2007) make a valuable contribution to the message design literature by demonstrating that a postscript that emphasizes choice may be a means of reducing the reactance induced by a persuasive appeal. Finally, there is emerging evidence that loss-framed messages may suffer persuasive deficits relative to gain-framed messages by inducing a state of reactance (Reinhart, Marshall, Feeley, & Tutzauer, 2007). In sum, recent research activity on the nature and antecedents of reactance suggest that the theory is enjoying a resurgence of interest.

*Fear and Persuasion.* Rogers's original version of protection motivation theory (PMT) was a thoroughly cognitive perspective that eschewed emotion entirely (Rogers &

Prentice-Dunn, 1997). The theory predicted a three-way interaction between perceptions of (a) the severity of a threat, (b) one's susceptibility to it, and (c) the likelihood that the recommended action would reduce or eliminate the threat. Over the years, that interaction was almost never supported. Under the weight of accumulating evidence, fear was installed as a variable that could influence cognitive appraisals as well as exert a direct influence on protection motivation (Rogers & Prentice-Dunn, 1997). In the addition, the complex interactions were eliminated in favor of two main effects: one for threat (severity plus susceptibility) and one for recommendation (response efficacy plus self-efficacy). Finally, drawing from the health belief model (Janz & Becker, 1984), concepts such as barriers and benefits were incorporated, thereby rendering what was once a precise but inaccurate theory into something more cumbersome but realistic. In its current formulation, PMT provides a nearly comprehensive summary of the issues that message designers must confront in the implementation of threat appeals.

A second framework that borrows heavily from both PMT and Leventhal's (1971) parallel processing model is Witte's extended parallel processing model (EPPM; Witte & Allen, 2000). The EPPM is attractive for its straightforward condensation of issues into a compact and intuitively attractive framework. However, the theory unequivocally predicts an interaction between threat and recommendation that is not borne out in the literature. The most telling evidence against the interaction prediction can be found in Witte and Allen's (2000) meta-analysis when they write, "Overall, the additive model [i.e., main effects model] receives the greatest support in these analyses" (p. 600). Still, like the PMT, the EPPM offers a summary of the many questions that surround the use of threat appeals, and it remains useful in that regard. The innovative attempt to extend the EPPM into the realm of attitude accessibility offered by Roskos-Ewoldsen, Arpan-Ralstin, and St. Pierre (2002) is beginning to generate

empirical interest (Roskos-Ewoldsen, Yu, & Rhodes, 2004).

*Multiemotion Models.* Recent thinking on the role of emotion in persuasion has embraced the idea that messages have the potential to evoke multiple emotions and that those emotions may exert contradictory influences on the persuasive process (Dillard & Nabi, 2006). For example, one study of messages that were structured as fear appeals found that most individuals actually experienced changes in three or more emotions (Dillard, Plotnick, Godbold, Freimuth, & Edgar, 1996). The same investigation showed that some emotions (e.g., fear and sadness) were positively correlated with persuasion, whereas others showed the opposite influence (e.g., anger and puzzlement). Subsequent research has verified the capacity for messages to arouse multiple emotions and for those emotions to exert a complex pattern of influence on attitude (Dillard & Peck, 2000, 2001).

Nabi's (1999) cognitive-functional model (CFM) emphasizes emotional approach and avoidance tendencies as determinants of attention and depth of message processing. Whereas the theory is designed around five negative emotions, empirical testing to date has focused on just two. That research reveals that anger, relative to fear, is associated with more careful message processing (Nabi, 2002). Other research in this stream indicates that emotions have the potential to frame interpretation of persuasive messages by stimulating a desire for emotion-consistent information (Nabi, 2003).

*Narratives and Exemplars.* One area of inquiry that is attracting increased research attention is that of narrative persuasion (e.g., Green, 2006). Proponents of the approach suggest that the investigation of narrative holds great promise because storytelling is a basic mode of human interaction (Fisher, 1987). When individuals are transported or absorbed by the storyline, they may experience the story as if it were actually taking place, will be less likely to counterargue the story's propositions, and will manifest strong emotional engagement with the characters and the plot (Green, 2006; Slater & Rouner, 2002). Tal-Or, Boninger, Poran, and Gleicher (2004) demonstrated that narratives that prompt counterfactual thinking about one's self (e.g., "If I had only worn a seat belt . . .") produce greater and longer lasting persuasive effects. The study of narrative also offers a broad housing for Zillmann's (2006) exemplification theory, with its emphasis on the number and type of exemplars that are included in news stories. Although it is far too soon to tell with any degree of certainty, this focus on narrative persuasion is sufficiently engaging and distinct from the existing paradigm (i.e., the dual-process models of persuasion) that we may be seeing the cusp of a paradigm shift. Perhaps contributors to the next edition of the *Handbook of Communication Science* will have a better vantage point from which to evaluate the veracity of this forecast.

◆ **Notes**

1. Although Bitzer (1968) contends that all rhetoric is persuasive, it is doubtful that he would agree that all persuasion is rhetoric.

2. My discussion of SNA and TRA aligns these perspectives with descriptive and injunctive norms, respectively. Such a division oversimplifies the messier reality in which some SNA researchers have sought to understand injunctive norms. Moreover, Ajzen (n.d.) now asserts that descriptive norms should sometimes be regarded as instances of subjective (i.e., injunctive) norms.

◆ **References**

Ajzen, I. (n.d.). *The theory of planned behavior.* Retrieved March 28, 2008, from http://people.umass.edu/aizen/tpb.html

Bitzer, L. F. (1968). The rhetorical situation. *Philosophy & Rhetoric, 1,* 1–14.

Bohner, G., Crow, K., Erb, H., & Schwarz, N. (1992). Affect and persuasion: Mood effects on the processing of message content and context cues and on subsequent behavior. *European Journal of Social Psychology, 22,* 511–530.

Bohner, G., Ruder, M., & Erb, H. P. (2002). When expertise backfires: Contrast and assimilation effects in persuasion. *British Journal of Social Psychology, 41,* 495–519.

Bornstein, R. F. (1989). Exposure and affect: Overview and meta-analysis of research 1968–1987. *Psychological Bulletin, 106,* 265–289.

Brehm, J. W. (1966). *A theory of psychological reactance.* New York: Academic Press.

Brehm, S. S., & Brehm, J. W. (1981). *Psychological reactance: A theory of freedom and control.* New York: Academic Press.

Briñol, P., & Petty, R. E. (2006). Fundamental processes leading to attitude change: Implications for cancer prevention communication. *Journal of Communication, 56,* S81–S104.

Burgoon, M., Alvaro, E., Grandpre, J., & Voulodakis, M. (2002). Revisiting the theory of psychological reactance: Communicating threats to attitudinal freedom. In J. P. Dillard & M. Pfau (Eds.), *The persuasion handbook* (pp. 213–232). Thousand Oaks, CA: Sage.

Burgoon, M., & Chase, L. J. (1973). The effects of differential linguistic patterns in messages attempting to induce resistance to persuasion. *Speech Monographs, 40,* 1–7.

Burgoon, M., Denning, V. P., & Roberts, L. (2002). Language expectancy theory. In J. P. Dillard & M. Pfau (Eds.), *The persuasion handbook* (pp. 117–136). Thousand Oaks, CA: Sage.

Cacioppo, J. T., Harkins, S. G., & Petty, R. E. (1981). The nature of attitudes and cognitive responses and their relationships to behavior. In R. E. Petty, T. M. Ostrom, & T. C. Brock (Eds.), *Cognitive responses in persuasion* (pp. 31–54). Hillsdale, NJ: Lawrence Erlbaum.

Cameron, K. A., & Campo, S. (2006). Stepping back from social norms campaigns: Comparing normative influences to other predictors of health behaviors. *Health Communication, 20,* 277–288.

Campo, S., & Cameron, K. A. (2006). Differential effects of social norms campaigns: A cause for concern. *Health Communication, 19,* 209–219.

Cho, H., & Boster, F. J. (2005). Development and validation of value-, outcome-, and impression-relevant involvement scales. *Communication Research, 32,* 235–264.

Dillard, J. P., Anderson, J. W., & Knobloch, L. K. (2002). Interpersonal influence. In M. Knapp & J. Daly (Eds.), *The handbook of interpersonal communication* (pp. 423–474). Thousand Oaks, CA: Sage.

Dillard, J. P., & Marshall, L. (2003). Persuasion as a social skill. In J. O. Greene & B. Burleson (Eds.), *The handbook of interaction and communication skill* (pp. 479–514). Mahwah, NJ: Lawrence Erlbaum.

Dillard, J. P., & Meijnders, A. (2002). Persuasion and the structure of affect. In J. P. Dillard & M. W. Pfau (Eds.), *The persuasion handbook* (pp. 309–328). Thousand Oaks, CA: Sage.

Dillard, J. P., & Nabi, R. (2006). The persuasive influence of emotion in cancer prevention and detection messages. *Journal of Communication, 56,* S123–S139.

Dillard, J. P., & Peck, E. (2000). Affect and persuasion: Emotional responses to public service announcements. *Communication Research, 27,* 461–495.

Dillard, J. P., & Peck, E. (2001). Persuasion and the structure of affect: Dual systems and discrete emotions as complementary models. *Human Communication Research, 27,* 38–68.

Dillard, J. P., Plotnick, C. A., Godbold, L. C., Freimuth, V. S., & Edgar, T. (1996). The multiple affective consequences of AIDS PSAs: Fear appeals do more than scare people. *Communication Research, 23,* 44–72.

Dillard, J. P., & Shen, L. (2005). On the nature of reactance and its role in persuasion. *Communication Monographs, 72,* 144–168.

Fazio, R. H., Roskos-Ewoldsen, D., & Powell, M. C. (1994). Attitudes, perception, and attention. In P. M. Niedenthal & S. Kitayama (Eds.), *The heart's eye: Emotional influences in perception and attention* (pp. 197–216). San Diego: Academic Press.

Festinger, L. (1957). *A theory of cognitive dissonance.* Evanston, IL: Row, Peterson.

Fishbein, M. (1967). A behavior theory approach to the relation between beliefs and an object and the attitude toward the objects. In M. Fishbein (Ed.), *Readings in attitude theory and measurement* (pp. 389–400). New York: John Wiley.

Fishbein, M., & Ajzen, I. (1975). *Beliefs, attitudes, intentions, and behavior: An introduction to theory and research.* Reading, MA: Addison-Wesley.

Fishbein, M., & Yzer, M. C. (2003). Using theory to design effective health behavior interventions. *Communication Theory, 13,* 164–183.

Fisher, W. R. (1987). *Human communication as narration: Toward a philosophy of reason, value, and action.* Columbia: University of South Carolina Press.

Green, M. (2006). Narratives and cancer communication. *Journal of Communication, 56,* S153–S183.

Greenwald, A. G. (1968). Cognitive learning, cognitive response to persuasion and attitude change. In A. G. Greenwald, T. C. Brock, & T. M. Ostrom (Eds.), *Psychological foundations of attitudes* (pp. 147–170). New York: Academic Press.

Hale, J. L., Householder, B. J., & Greene, K. L. (2002). The theory of reasoned action. In J. P. Dillard & M. Pfau (Eds.), *The persuasion handbook* (pp. 259–288). Thousand Oaks, CA: Sage.

Hale, J. L., Mongeau, P. A., & Thomas, R. (1991). Cognitive processing of one- and two-sided messages. *Western Journal of Speech Communication, 55,* 380–389.

Hample, D. (2003). Arguing skill. In J. O. Greene & B. R. Burleson (Eds.), *Handbook of communication and social interaction skills* (pp. 439–478). Mahwah, NJ: Lawrence Erlbaum.

Hornik, R., & Woolf, K. D. (1999). Using cross-sectional surveys to plan message strategies. *Social Marketing Quarterly, 5,* 34–41.

Hovland, C. I., Janis, I. L., & Kelley, H. H. (1953). *Communication and persuasion.* Princeton, NJ: Princeton University Press.

Hullett, C. (2004). Using functional theory to promote sexually transmitted disease (STD) testing: The impact of value-expressive messages and guilt. *Communication Research, 31,* 363–396.

Hullett, C. (2005). The impact of mood on persuasion: A meta-analysis. *Communication Research, 32,* 423–442.

Hullett, C., & Boster, F. J. (2001). Matching messages to the values underlying value-expressive and social-adjustive attitudes: Reconciling an old theory with a contemporary measurement approach. *Communication Monographs, 68,* 133–153.

Janz, N. K., & Becker, M. H. (1984). The health belief model: A decade later. *Health Education Quarterly, 11,* 1–47.

Johnson, B. T., & Eagly, A. H. (1989). Effects of involvement on persuasion: A meta-analysis. *Psychological Bulletin, 106,* 290–314.

Katz, D. (1960). The functional approach to the study of attitudes. *Public Opinion Quarterly, 24,* 468–474.

Killeya, L. A., & Johnson, B. T. (1998). Experimental induction of biased systematic processing: The directed thought technique. *Personality and Social Psychology Bulletin, 24,* 471–484.

Kruglanski, A. W., Chen, X., Pierro, A., Mannetti, L., Erb, H.-P., & Spiegel, S. (2006). Persuasion according to the unimodel: Implications for cancer communication. *Journal of Communication, 56,* S105–S122.

Kruglanski, A. W., & Thompson, E. P. (1999). Persuasion by a single route: A view from the unimodel. *Psychological Inquiry, 10,* 83–109.

Kumkale, T. G., & Albarracín, D. (2004). The sleeper effect in persuasion: A meta-analytic review. *Psychological Bulletin, 130,* 143–172.

Lapinski, M. K., & Rimal, R. N. (2005). An explication of social norms. *Communication Theory, 15,* 127–147.

Lasswell, H. D. (1948). The structure and function of communication in society. In L. Bryson (Ed.), *The communication of ideas: Religion and civilization series* (pp. 37–51). New York: Harper & Row.

Lederman, L. C., & Stewart, L. P. (Eds.). (2005). *Changing the culture of college drinking: A socially situated health communication campaign.* Creskill, NJ: Hampton.

Leventhal, H. (1971). Fear appeals and persuasion: The differentiation of a motivational construct. *American Journal of Public Health, 61,* 1208–1224.

Lumsdaine, A. A., & Janis, I. L. (1953). Resistance to "counterpropaganda" produced by one-sided and two-sided "propaganda" presentations. *Public Opinion Quarterly, 17,* 311–318.

Mackie, D. M., & Worth, L. T. (1989). Processing deficits and the mediation of positive affect in persuasion. *Journal of Personality and Social Psychology, 57,* 27–40.

McGuire, W. A. (1961). The effectiveness of supportive and refutational defenses in immunizing and restoring beliefs against persuasion. *Sociometry, 24,* 184–197.

Miller, C. H., Lane, L. T., Deatrick, L. M., Young, A. M., & Potts, K. A. (2007). Psychological reactance and promotional health messages. *Human Communication Research, 33,* 219–240.

Nabi, R. (1999). A cognitive-functional model for the effects of discrete negative emotions on information processing, attitude change, and recall. *Communication Theory, 9,* 292–320.

Nabi, R. (2002). Anger, fear, uncertainty, and attitudes: A test of the cognitive-functional model. *Communication Monographs, 69,* 204–216.

Nabi, R. (2003). Exploring the framing effects of emotion: Do discrete emotions differentially influence information accessibility, information seeking, and policy preference? *Communication Research, 30,* 224–247.

Petty, R. E., & Cacioppo, J. T. (1979). Effects of message repetition and position on cognitive response, recall, and persuasion. *Journal of Personality and Social Psychology, 37,* 1915–1926.

Petty, R. E., & Cacioppo, J. T. (1986). The elaboration likelihood model of persuasion. In L. Berkowitz (Ed.), *Advances in experimental social psychology* (Vol. 19, pp. 123–205). San Diego: Academic Press.

Petty, R. E., Cacioppo, J. T., & Goldman, R. (1981). Personal involvement as a determinant of argument-based persuasion. *Journal of Personality and Social Psychology, 41,* 847–855.

Petty, R. E., Wells, G. L., & Brock, T. C. (1976). Distraction can enhance or reduce yielding to propaganda: Thought disruption versus effort justification. *Journal of Personality and Social Psychology, 34,* 874–884.

Petty, R. E., Wheeler, S. C., & Bizer, G. Y. (1999). Is there one persuasion process or more? Lumping versus splitting in attitude change theories. *Psychological Inquiry, 10,* 156–163.

Quick, B. L., & Stephenson, M. T. (2007). Further evidence that psychological reactance can be modeled as a combination of anger and negative cognitions. *Communication Research, 34,* 255–276.

Rains, S. A., & Turner, M. M. (2007). Psychological reactance and persuasive health communication. *Human Communication Research, 33,* 241–269.

Reinhart, A. M., Marshall, H. M., Feeley, T. H., & Tutzauer, F. (2007). The persuasive effects of message framing in organ donation: The mediating role of psychological reactance. *Communication Monographs, 74,* 229–255.

Rogers, R. W., & Prentice-Dunn, S. (1997). Protection motivation theory. In D. S. Gochman (Ed.), *Handbook of health behavior research I: Personal and social determinants* (pp. 113–132). New York: Plenum.

Roskos-Ewoldsen, D. R., Arpan-Ralstin, L., & St. Pierre, J. (2002). Attitude accessibility and persuasion: The quick and the strong. In J. P. Dillard & M. Pfau (Eds.), *The persuasion handbook* (pp. 39–61). Thousand Oaks, CA: Sage.

Roskos-Ewoldsen, D. R., Yu, H. J., & Rhodes, N. (2004). Fear appeals messages affect accessibility of attitudes toward threat and adaptive behavior. *Communication Monographs, 71,* 49–69.

Sherif, M., & Hovland, C. I. (1961). *Social judgment: Assimilation and contrast effects in communication and attitude change.* New Haven, CT: Yale University Press.

Slater, M. D. (2002). Involvement as goal-directed strategic processing: Extending the elaboration likelihood model. In J. P. Dillard & M. Pfau (Eds.), *The persuasion handbook* (pp. 175–194). Thousand Oaks, CA: Sage.

Slater, M. D., & Rouner, D. (2002). Entertainment-education and elaboration likelihood: Understanding the processing of narrative persuasion. *Communication Theory, 12,* 173–191.

Smith, B. (1921). Corax and probability. *Quarterly Journal of Speech Education, 6,* 13–42.

Smith, M. B., Bruner, J. S., & White, R. W. (1956). *Opinions and personality.* New York: John Wiley.

Smith, S. W., Atkin, C. K., Martell, D., Allen, R., & Hembroff, L. (2006). A social judgment theory approach to conducting formative research in a social norms campaign. *Communication Theory, 16,* 141–152.

Steffian, G. (1999). Correlation of normative misperceptions: An alcohol abuse prevention program. *Journal of Drug Education, 29,* 115–138.

Szabo, E. A., & Pfau, M. (2002). Nuances in inoculation: Theory and applications. In J. P. Dillard & M. W. Pfau (Eds.), *The persuasion handbook* (pp. 233–258). Thousand Oaks, CA: Sage.

Tal-Or, N., Boninger, D. S., Poran, A., & Gleicher, F. (2004). Counterfactual thinking as a mechanism in narrative persuasion. *Human Communication Research, 30,* 301–328.

Thaler, R. (1980). Toward a positive theory of consumer choice. *Journal of Economic Behavior and Organization, 1,* 39–60.

Todorov, A., Chaiken, S., & Henderson, M. D. (2002). The heuristic-systematic model of information processing. In J. P. Dillard & M. W. Pfau (Eds.), *The persuasion handbook* (pp. 195–212). Thousand Oaks, CA: Sage.

Wechsler, H., Seibring, M., Liu, I. C., & Ahl, M. (2004). Colleges respond to student binge drinking: Reducing student demand or limiting access. *Journal of American College Health, 52,* 159–168.

Wegener, D. T., & Petty, R. E. (1994). Mood management across affective states: The hedonic contingency hypothesis. *Journal of Personality and Social Psychology, 66,* 1034–1048.

Witte, K., & Allen, M. (2000). A meta-analysis of fear appeals: Implications for public health campaigns. *Health Education and Behavior, 27,* 591–615.

Woolbert, C. H. (1916). The organization of departments of speech science in universities. *Quarterly Journal of Public Speaking, 2,* 64–67.

Zhao, X. (2002). A variable-based typology and a review of advertising-related persuasion to research during the 1990s. In J. P. Dillard & M. Pfau (Eds.), *The persuasion handbook* (pp. 495–512). Thousand Oaks, CA: Sage.

Zillmann, D. (2006). Exemplification effects in the promotion of safety and health. *Journal of Communication, 56,* S221–S237.

# SEEKING AND RESISTING COMPLIANCE

◆ Steven R. Wilson

◆ *Compliance Gaining*

*Compliance gaining* refers to interactions in which one individual attempts to induce another person to perform a desired behavior that the target person otherwise might not have performed (Wheeless, Barraclough, & Stewart, 1983). Offering advice, asking favors, and enforcing obligations are among the many reasons people seek compliance from others (Wilson, Aleman, & Leatham, 1998). Others may resist attempts to gain compliance for many reasons too: What is being advised or asked for may not be feasible, or the supposed "obligation" may not be something the other person ever promised to fulfill. Seeking another person's compliance might involve such actions as explaining why the request is being made or why the requested action is beneficial, offering flattery, calling in past favors, or threatening dire consequences (Marwell & Schmitt, 1967; Tracy, Craig, Smith, & Spisak, 1984; Wiseman & Schenk-Hamlin, 1981). Others might resist compliance-gaining attempts by refusing or temporarily withholding agreement, asking questions, explaining why they are not able to comply, claiming the request is unreasonable, or suggesting alternative ways the desired outcome can be achieved (McLaughlin, Cody, & Robey, 1980; Sanders & Fitch, 2001; Wilson, Cruz, Marshall, & Rao, 1993).

Compliance gaining was discussed in a chapter on persuasion in the first edition of the *Handbook of Communication Science* (G. R. Miller, 1987).

Although both compliance gaining and persuasion involve intentional attempts to influence others, they differ in several respects (see Dillard, Chapter 12, this volume). Persuasion scholars typically focus on public or mass communication contexts, whereas compliance-gaining scholars investigate how friends, family members, and coworkers influence one another. Influence in interpersonal contexts has unique qualities; for example, participants constantly adapt to each other's behavior (Sanders & Fitch, 2001), and dyadic patterns (e.g., demand-withdraw sequences; Caughlin & Scott, 2009) can be investigated. Persuasion scholars focus on *message processing or effects,* whereas compliance-gaining research also focuses on *message production or choices.* Compliance-gaining research explores the conditions under which individuals are most likely to comply with requests (Goei & Boster, 2005; Cialdini, 2001). Complementing this effects focus, however, is a large body of research that explores why individuals say what they do when seeking or resisting another person's compliance. For instance, why are college students more likely to explain their decision when turning down rather than agreeing to a date (Folkes, 1982)? Why do mothers with a predisposition toward verbal aggressiveness issue numerous commands and suggestions when playing with their young children (Wilson, Roberts, Rack, & Delaney, 2008)? Questions about message choices and effects are complementary. If particular patterns of compliance gaining are associated with negative relational outcomes (effects), researchers might turn their attention to understanding why participants are producing messages that perpetuate those patterns (choices).

Seeking and resisting compliance are important for such professions as sales, management, and health care. But compliance gaining also offers a glimpse into how relationships are created and sustained. Close relationships are those in which the parties influence one another's thoughts, feelings, and actions frequently and consequentially on a range of topics over time (Kelley et al., 1983; Knobloch & Solomon, 2004; Solomon & Vangelisti, Chapter 19, this volume). Relational power and intimacy shape how participants seek and resist one another's compliance, and reciprocally, such attempts often confirm yet can challenge or renegotiate existing levels of power and intimacy (Brown & Levinson, 1987; Millar & Rogers, 1987). Compliance gaining also offers insight into cultural and individual differences. People from different cultural backgrounds ascribe different meanings to actions such as telling others what to do or saying what they want clearly and directly (Fitch, 1998; Kim, 2002), and members from the same society may hold different implicit theories or beliefs about what is appropriate or relevant to say when seeking or resisting another person's compliance (O'Keefe, 1988). This chapter describes how compliance gaining as an area of research has evolved from an initial flurry of activity motivated by a groundbreaking study, to the development of theoretical frameworks, and then to a period of applying theory and research to problems of social importance.

## ◆ In the Beginning . . .

Within communication, the study of compliance gaining was initiated by Gerald R. Miller and three of his then students in a pioneering investigation of how people select compliance-gaining strategies (G. R. Miller, Boster, Roloff, & Seibold, 1977). The "MBRS" study was couched within a developmental perspective on interpersonal communication. Miller presumed that people want to maintain some control over their social environment and hence acquire strategies for influencing others. When trying to influence individuals whom they do not know well (what Miller termed a *noninterpersonal* relationship), people must rely primarily on sociological and cultural knowledge—that is, information about how the target is similar to others, such as group stereotypes or cultural norms for interaction—to predict the target person's reactions. When trying to influence those who are familiar (what he termed an *interpersonal* relationship), people also can rely on psychological knowledge—that is, information about the target's unique attributes that make him or her different from others—to predict the target's reactions. On the basis of these ideas, G. R. Miller et al. (1977) investigated how compliance-seeking strategies could be grouped and whether people's choice of strategies varied across situations.

To address these questions, G. R. Miller et al. (1977) had participants (a mix of college students and working adults) read four hypothetical scenarios designed to manipulate two situational variables: (a) whether the relationship between the message source and target was interpersonal or noninterpersonal and (b) whether the request had long-term relational consequences or short-term consequences. After reading each scenario, participants rated how likely they would be to use each of 16 compliance-seeking strategies in that situation. A decade earlier, two sociologists (Marwell & Schmitt, 1967) had developed the typology of strategies based on theories of social power, but their typology had received little attention until the MBRS study.[1]

The MBRS study revealed that participants' likelihood-of-use ratings for strategies varied across scenarios. In general, a smaller number of strategies were rated as likely to be used in the interpersonal as opposed to the noninterpersonal scenarios. G. R. Miller et al. (1977) speculated that participants may have rated more strategies as likely to be used in noninterpersonal scenarios because they were less certain what would work with unfamiliar message targets and hence tried anything that seemed plausible. Attempts to reduce the 16 strategies to a smaller number of clusters also revealed a different number of underlying factors in different scenarios.

Despite this variability, participants as a group displayed a strong tendency to rate "prosocial" or "socially appropriate" strategies (e.g., altruism, liking) as likely to be used and "antisocial" or "socially inappropriate" strategies (e.g., aversive stimulation, moral appeal) as unlikely to be used in all four scenarios.

The MBRS study stimulated a large body of subsequent research.[2] Scholars debated the merits of different typologies of compliance-seeking strategies (Boster, Stiff, & Reynolds, 1985; Clark & Delia, 1979; Wiseman & Schenk-Hamlin, 1981) and developed typologies of compliance-resisting strategies (McLaughlin et al., 1980; McQuillen, 1986). Researchers analyzed dimensions along which people distinguished compliance-gaining scenarios (e.g., rights to request, anticipated resistance, intimacy and power, benefits to self and other; Cody & McLaughlin, 1980) and assessed whether likelihood-of-use ratings for strategies differed across these dimensions (e.g., Cody et al., 1986; Dillard & Burgoon, 1985). They also investigated whether personality variables such as communication apprehension, dogmatism, locus of control, Machiavellianism, self-monitoring, and verbal aggressiveness predicted strategy ratings (see Seibold, Cantrill, & Meyers, 1985). All of these studies addressed questions outlined by G. R. Miller and his colleagues; most also were modeled on methods employed in the MBRS study. Despite this collective effort, very few reliable predictors of compliance-seeking strategy use were identified. This first generation of research suffered from conceptual and methodological shortcomings that are summarized here briefly.

Conceptually, research inspired by the MBRS study lacked theoretical grounding. Kellermann and Cole (1994) argued that typologies of compliance-gaining strategies were ad hoc lists that did not distinguish strategies systematically using one or a few message features. Strategies can be distinguished based on their underlying basis of power (Wheeless et al., 1983), the degree to which they are polite or socially appropriate (Burleson et al., 1988), and so forth. Because strategies are not clustered or arrayed systematically along any dimension, it is difficult to interpret differences in strategy ratings.

Researchers also investigated predictors of strategy choice in an ad hoc fashion. Although the MBRS study was grounded in G. R. Miller's developmental view, researchers quickly lost sight of this framework as they investigated a host of personality attributes and situational dimensions that might predict strategy ratings. Researchers often began with hunches rather than a clear rationale for why particular attributes might predict particular qualities of compliance-seeking messages. The few attempts to develop theoretical models (e.g., Hunter & Boster, 1987) made unrealistic assumptions such as that people's choices were based on a single factor rather than on attempts to manage multiple, conflicting goals (Dillard, Segrin, & Harden, 1989).

Methodologically, validity concerns were raised about the "strategy selection" procedure. Debate ensued over whether the procedure made the social appropriateness of strategies salient, leading participants as a group to underselect antisocial strategies (Boster, 1988; Burleson & Wilson, 1988; Burleson et al., 1988; Seibold, 1988). Bolstering such concerns were two studies showing that "message selection data . . . exhibits a degree of correspondence to reported and/or actual compliance-gaining behavior that is less than optimal" (Dillard, 1988, p. 180). G. R. Miller, Boster, Roloff, and Seibold (1987) suggested that participants may be more mindful, face less formidable information-processing demands, and be influenced less by emotion when responding to scenarios than when engaging in interaction. They advocated using a broader range of methods to offset concerns about the external validity of scenario-based research.

Although the MBRS-inspired research program suffered conceptual and methodological limitations, it nevertheless highlighted the importance of influence in relationships and initiated a "source-oriented" perspective on influence. Questions from this research also stimulated theories about why people say what they do when seeking or resisting compliance.

## ◆ The Emergence of Theoretical Frameworks

As the problems just described became apparent, scholars moved toward grounding analyses of compliance gaining in theoretical frameworks. Communication scholars drew on and contributed to theories emerging from cognitive science, social psychology, pragmatics, conversation analysis, and the ethnography of communication. Much of this work can be organized around the concepts of directives, face, goals, and obstacles.

### DIRECTIVES

Research on the social uses of language has been used to understand compliance gaining. Speech act theorists have grappled with how speakers are able to make their intentions apparent through talk and how hearers are able to recognize a speaker's intentions (Austin, 1962; Searle, 1969). Directives refer to the class of speech acts (e.g., recommending, requesting, commanding) in which a speaker attempts to get a hearer to do something that the hearer otherwise might not have done (Searle, 1976). Directives are defined by a set of constitutive rules (also called felicity conditions) that specify necessary and sufficient conditions for performing that act. When requesting, a speaker assumes that the requested action needs to be performed (or there is no need for action), the target person wasn't going to perform the requested action already (or there is no need to request), and the target plausibly might be willing or feel obligated to comply (or there is no point in requesting; Labov & Fanshel, 1977; Searle, 1969).

By seeking another person's compliance, a speaker implicitly assumes that the conditions for issuing a directive exist in the current situation; hence, much of what speakers say should function, in part, to justify these assumptions. A study by Tracy et al. (1984) shows this to be the case. Individuals spoke aloud exactly what they would say after reading each of 24 favor-requesting scenarios. Scenarios varied in terms of the relative status and familiarity of the speaker and hearer as well as the size of the favor being asked. Across scenarios, speakers nearly always explained why they had a legitimate need to make the request (i.e., established a need for action) and inquired about the speaker's willingness to perform the requested action.

Although speakers may say things relevant to the preconditions for requesting when seeking compliance, the degree to which this occurs depends on relational closeness as well as the size of the request. Drawing on the distinction between communal and exchange relationships (Mills & Clark, 1994), Roloff and colleagues argue that intimacy can "substitute" for persuasion (e.g., the need to explain why a request is being made or to induce willingness) because intimates are "obligated to monitor each other's needs and be responsive to them" (Roloff, Janiszewski, McGrath, Burns, & Manrai, 1988, p. 367). To test this reasoning, the authors asked under-graduates to think about another student in the class whom they considered a stranger, acquaintance, or friend. Participants wrote out what they would say if they wanted to borrow that student's class notes for 30 minutes (small request) or for 3 days (large request). Protocols were divided into grammatical clauses, which were coded for the presence of requests plus four other categories: apologies, explanations, induce-ments, and contingencies. As predicted,

request elaboration (i.e., the number of clauses beyond the request itself) was highest when participants asked to borrow notes from a stranger and lowest when the target was a friend; elaboration also was higher when the request was large rather than small.

In sum, speakers, by seeking compliance, implicitly assume that the preconditions for directives are met, and their talk can be understood as responding to a possible need to justify these assumptions. Because the target may not agree with the speaker's assessment, speech act theory also can be used to analyze potential obstacles to compliance (Ifert, 2000). Speech act theory has been criticized for treating context as given rather than as created in part by speech acts, making overly broad assump-tions about the defining conditions for speech acts, and paying too little attention to how actions are recognizable from institutional roles and preceding talk as well as how meanings depend on the goals being pursued via speech acts (Ellis, 1999; Streeck, 1980). These critiques suggest a need to include concepts from speech act theory within larger frameworks that address how speakers strategically use implicit knowledge of the conditions for requesting in pursuit of conversational goals (e.g., Brown & Levinson, 1987; Jacobs & Jackson, 1989; MacGeorge, Feng, Butler, & Budarz, 2004; O'Keefe, 1988; Wilson et al., 1998).

## FACE

Face refers to the importance individuals attach to situated identities they try to project during interaction with others (Goffman, 1967). Brown and Levinson's (1987) politeness theory distinguishes two face wants: the desire to have one's actions and attributes approved of by significant others (positive face) and the desire to maintain one's autonomy and not have one's actions or resources restricted without cause (negative face). People want to maintain their own face, but because face wants are interdependent, they also typically have some motivation to support their conversational partner's face.

Many speech acts run contrary to the speaker's or hearer's face and are intrinsically face threatening (called FTAs). For example, directives presume the message target might be willing or feel obligated to perform an action that was not already planned. Making assumptions about what a message target might be willing to do constrains that person's negative face. Consistent with this logic, requesting or recommending nearly always is perceived as creating some constraint on the message target's autonomy and also can threaten the speaker's own autonomy as well as both parties' desire for approval (Kunkel, Wilson, Olufowote, & Robson, 2003; Lim & Bowers, 1991; Wilson et al., 1998). Message targets in turn constrain the requester's options (negative face) by resisting compliance and also can threaten both parties' positive face (Johnson, Roloff, & Riffee, 2004; Metts, Cupach, & Imahori, 1992).

Although directives constrain the target's negative face, Brown and Levinson (1987) argue that the degree to which this is true (i.e., the "weightiness" of an FTA) depends on three factors: power, distance, and rank. Requests are more face threatening when the hearer has more as opposed to less power (e.g., asking for assistance from one's boss as opposed to a coworker), when the hearer is distant rather than close (e.g., asking to borrow a dollar from an acquaintance rather than a friend), and when the request is large rather than small (asking to borrow $100 vs. $1.00).

When performing an FTA, speakers in any culture have five options: perform it baldly, without redress; with positive politeness (i.e., language that communicates approval or closeness); with negative politeness (i.e., language that doesn't presume); off-record (i.e., in a way that makes the request deniable); or not at all (Brown & Levinson, 1987). Each of these

"super strategies" can be enacted in many ways. Negative politeness, for example, is communicated by hedging ("I was wondering whether you might . . ."), minimizing imposition ("I was *just* calling to see if . . ."), apologizing (e.g., "I hate to ask this, but . . ."), and expressing gratitude ("I'd really be grateful if you'd . . ."). Politeness theory presumes that the five super strategies are rank ordered from least to most polite and predicts that speakers in any culture will use more polite forms as the weightiness of an FTA increases. Differences in politeness may occur if speakers from different cultures have different perceptions regarding the factors influencing the weightiness of an FTA (power, distance, rank).

In a cross-cultural analysis, Holtgraves and Yang (1992) found support for several of these predictions. Korean and American college students rated three situations in terms of perceived power, distance, and request size and then wrote what they would say to gain the target's compliance in each situation. Messages were broken into three components: address forms, the request itself, and supporting moves. Address forms were coded as informal (positive politeness), formal (negative politeness), or missing; the request was coded into one of the five super strategies; and supporting talk was coded for the presence of negative politeness (e.g., apologies) as well as positive politeness (e.g., jokes, small talk). The entire message also was rated for overall politeness by two bilingual coders based on all three message components. As predicted, Korean and American students varied the overall politeness of their written messages based on their perceptions of power, distance, and rank. Cultural differences in message politeness occurred, in part, because Koreans varied their politeness more than Americans did depending on the hearer's relative power. In sum, much of what participants wrote could be understood as striking a balance between asking for what they wanted and attempting to maintain the target's (and perhaps their own) face.

Critics of politeness theory argue that (a) two types of face do not tap the diverse meanings of face across cultures (Lim & Bowers, 1991; Ting-Toomey & Kurogi, 1998); (b) the analysis of face threats pays insufficient attention to goals pursued via speech acts, institutional and cultural contexts, and act sequencing (Fitch & Sanders, 1994; Goldsmith, 2000; Tracy & Baratz, 1994; Wilson et al., 1998); and (c) the five super strategies are not mutually exclusive, and their rank ordering is contextually bound (Craig, Tracy, & Spisak, 1986; Dillard, Wilson, Tusing, & Kinney, 1997). Still, critics concur that face is key to understanding how people seek or resist compliance.

## GOALS

Goals are future states of affairs that individuals want to attain or maintain (Wilson, 2002). We seek and resist other people's compliance to elicit desired behaviors, but we almost always have other concerns too (Clark & Delia, 1979). Dillard (1990, 2004) proposed a goal-plan-action (GPA) model that highlights how people manage multiple, conflicting goals.

The GPA model distinguishes primary and secondary goals. At any point in a conversation, the *primary goal* is the objective that for the moment defines the situation or answers the question, "What is going on here?" The primary goal "brackets the situation" and "helps segment the flow of behavior into a meaningful unit; it says what the interaction is about" (Dillard et al., 1989, p. 21). Primary goals also play a motivational function: They energize the actor, stimulate planning, and push the actor toward engaging the target person. Several studies have investigated primary goals related to influence (Cody, Canary, & Smith, 1994; Kipnis, Schmidt, & Wilkinson, 1980; Schrader & Dillard, 1998). Among common

reasons for seeking compliance in personal and professional relationships are asking for assistance, giving advice, obtaining permission, and enforcing obligations. Rather than viewing themselves as seeking compliance, people conceive of their actions in terms of more specific goals.[3]

*Secondary goals* are concerns that arise in a wide range of situations and shape and constrain how individuals pursue their primary goal. Dillard et al. (1989) propose five categories of secondary goals: (a) identity goals, or desires to act consistently with one's beliefs, morals, and values; (b) conversation management goals, or desires to maintain a positive self-image, maintain other people's face, and say things that are relevant and coherent; (c) relational resource goals, or desires to maintain valued relationships; (d) personal resource goals, or desires to avoid unnecessarily risking or wasting one's time, money, or safety; and (e) arousal management goals, or desires to avoid or reduce anxiety or nervousness. Hample and Dallinger (1987), Kellermann (2004), and Kim (2002) have identified similar sets of secondary goals. Although these lists are fairly comprehensive, participants sometimes report other goals when trying to influence others. If the target person has failed to fulfill an obligation, then people often report conflicting desires to attack and support the target's face (Wilson, 1990; Wilson et al., 1998).

The GPA model outlines cognitive processes involved as speakers produce influence messages (Dillard, 1990). Goal assessment refers to an individual evaluating the importance of primary and secondary goals when facing a concrete situation. When concern about the primary goal outweighs secondary goals, the actor decides to engage the other person, which results in plan generation and editing. Sometimes people recall "stock plans" (i.e., mental representations of actions relevant to pursuing goals) from the past, but in other cases, they adapt plans to unique elements of the current situation. When primary and secondary goals are weighted about equally, the decision about whether to engage the other may depend on whether a means can be found for pursuing the primary goal without interfering with secondary goals, and hence plan generation and editing may precede the decision to engage. If suitable means are found, the speaker attempts to put the plan into action (tactic implementation) while monitoring the target person's response, which provides continuous feedback for ongoing goals assessment. Newer research suggests that these processes occur much faster, at more levels of abstraction, and with less coordination than the GPA model seems to imply (Greene, 2000; Meyer, 2007).

The GPA model's distinction between primary and secondary goals suggests two broad behavioral dimensions: the intensity with which the actor pursues the primary goal and the manner in which secondary goals shape such attempts. For example, Dillard et al. (1989) had participants recall a compliance-gaining episode and rate how much time if any they spent consciously planning what to say as well as how much effort they put into accomplishing the primary goal. Participants' conversations were rated by trained coders for how explicit participants were about what they wanted (directness), how many reasons they gave to justify their request (argument), and whether they emphasized positive consequences if the target complied or negative consequences if the target refused (positivity). Importance ratings for the primary goal were the best predictor of planning and effort, whereas importance ratings for secondary goals were the best predictor of message directness and positivity.

The GPA model helps explain Hample and Dallinger's (1998) observation that "when an initial message is rebuffed, follow-up persuasive messages are ruder, more aggressive, and more forceful than the first one" (p. 305). As an example, King (2001) observed college students trying to persuade confederates to participate in a campus cleanup campaign. Students typically started with direct requests and explanations about when or why help was needed, then stressed how complying would benefit the target or make the target feel good about himself or herself, and finally, if they continued to persist, tried to make the target feel guilty or stressed how the target would be hurt by not complying. Hample and Dallinger found that students who chose to persist after encountering resistance from a hypothetical target reduced the importance they initially placed on conversation management, relational resource, and arousal management goals.

Goals perspectives have been criticized for trying to explain dyadic processes from within the individual (Bavelas, 1991) and for embracing a view of communication that is mechanistic and ahistorical (Shepherd, 1998; for replies, see Dillard & Schrader, 1998; Wilson, 2002). Researchers recently have begun to investigate dyadic and dynamic aspects of goals, such as how individuals make inferences about their conversational partner's goals (Palomares, 2008) and adjust their own goals over time in response to their partner's emotions and behavior (Keck & Samp, 2007). Besides goals, the concept of "obstacles" also highlights the unfolding nature of compliance-gaining interactions.

## OBSTACLES

Compliance-gaining interactions usually entail more than a request followed by a grant or refusal (Sanders & Fitch, 2001), and much of what else occurs can be analyzed in terms of obstacles. Obstacles refer to "the message [targets'] beliefs that cause them to be unwilling or unable to respond immediately in the way the [message source] desires" (Clark & Delia, 1979, p. 200). Before asking for a target person's assistance, for example, we might inquire about the target's plans (checking on the person's ability to help, a potential obstacle). If hesitant to help us, the target likely will disclose obstacles; whether we persist likely will depend on the nature of those obstacles. Weiner's (1986, 1995) attribution theory offers a useful framework for understanding people's responses to obstacles.

Attributions are personal judgments about the causes of actions or events, such as why someone did well on an exam or failed to do his or her share of the work on a group project. Causes for events vary in the degree to which they are *controllable* (i.e., the degree to which they can be willfully affected by the actor); for example, a college student might receive a poor grade on an exam because he went out drinking rather than studying (controllable) or because he works long hours to pay for school (less controllable). Causes also vary in the degree to which they are *stable* (usually present or not); for instance, the student might have gone out drinking because it was his 21st birthday (unstable) or because he does not take school seriously (stable). Attributions in turn influence judgments of *responsibility,* or the degree to which the actor should be held accountable for the outcomes of the event. People typically feel anger when they judge others as responsible for negative outcomes (e.g., a student chooses not to do her part of a group project, even though it will adversely affect other members) but sympathy when they judge others as not responsible for negative outcomes (e.g., a student does not complete her part of a group project because her mother was just diagnosed with cancer). Emotions affect people's motivation to help versus to avoid or punish the other.

MacGeorge (2001) reported findings consistent with these assumptions in a study of support situations. Students read one of six scenarios in which a close friend was distressed about a problem and rated the importance of multiple goals. When they judged their friend as responsible for the problem, students rated the goal of getting their friend to take responsibility as more important and providing emotional support as less important. Responsibility judgments were not associated with the goal of providing problem support, perhaps because students felt obligated to advise and assist their friend even if the friend was responsible for the problem (Roloff et al., 1988). Students' feelings of sympathy and anger moderated some, though not all, of the impact of responsibility judgments on goals.

Because responsibility judgments are so salient, people tend to disclose uncontrollable rather than controllable reasons for resisting compliance (Folkes, 1982; Weiner, Figueroa-Munoz, & Kakihara, 1991). Weiner et al. (1991) asked undergraduates to describe a situation in which they gave an excuse to someone that was "not the truth," including the reasons they told the other person, the real reasons they withheld, and what they hoped to accomplish by giving the false excuse. Most disclosed excuses were uncontrollable and unstable, whereas more than 90% of withheld reasons were controllable. Participants reported that they withheld their "real" reasons to avoid complying with unwanted requests, hurting the other's feelings, making the other person angry, or making themselves look bad.

People also vary whether and how they persist at seeking compliance based on obstacles. In one of my own studies (Wilson et al., 1993), undergraduates telephoned other students (actually confederates) with a reminder to show up for an appointment; some confederates gave reasons for not keeping their appointment that varied in controllability and stability. For example, a controllable, unstable reason was that the person had decided to go to a special happy hour instead, whereas an uncontrollable, stable reason was that the person was taking 21 credit hours and did not have time to keep the appointment. Participants persisted longer, used more antisocial strategies, and addressed the obstacle more directly (e.g., suggesting a way around it) with targets who disclosed unstable and controllable reasons as opposed to stable or uncontrollable reasons. This tendency to differentiate between types of obstacles begins early. As they move from preschool to elementary school, children become increasingly adept at distinguishing obstacles that will be easy versus difficult to overcome (Marshall & Levy, 1998).

Although Weiner's (1986, 1995) theory sheds light on people's emotional and behavioral reactions to obstacles, questions have been raised about the assumption that attributions always mediate people's emotional reactions to influence success and failure (Segrin & Dillard, 1991) as well as about which elements of the theory extend across culture (Choi, Nisbett, & Norenzayan, 1999; J. G. Miller, 1996). These questions highlight important avenues for future research.

Since the late 1980s, scholars have grounded compliance-gaining research in theoretical frameworks that highlight directives, face, goals, and obstacles. More recently, researchers have shown how theoretically grounded analyses can address issues of social importance.

◆ *Doing Socially Relevant Work*

Several recent programs of research apply theoretical perspectives on seeking and resisting compliance to issues of social importance, including Lannutti and Monahan's (2007) research on the impact of alcohol on women's goals and messages when refusing unwanted sexual advances, LePoire and Dailey's (2006) inconsistent nurturing as social control explanation for how significant others inadvertently reinforce their partner's drug use, Hecht and Miller-Day's (2007) "keepin it REAL" program for teaching drug resistance strategies to middle school students, and my own work on parent-child relational dynamics in families at risk for child abuse or neglect (Morgan & Wilson, 2007; Wilson, Shi, Tirmenstein, Norris, & Rack, 2006; Wilson et al., 2008). Several motives may be responsible for this trend,

including a genuine desire to address socially significant issues, pressures to seek external funding and participate in interdisciplinary research, and wanting to extend beyond college student samples and scenario-based methods. Each of these research programs is informed by concepts reviewed in the prior section, as I will illustrate briefly with my own work.

Child abuse and neglect are pressing problems (United Nations Children's Fund [UNICEF], 2007; U.S. Department of Health and Human Services [USDHHS], 2007) that arise from the interplay of individual, family, community, and cultural-level factors (Belsky, 1993). Despite this complexity, research on parent-child interaction is critical for understanding child maltreatment. Child physical abuse occurs at predictable moments that arise out of larger interactions (Reid, 1986); child neglect involves a lack of care and nurturance manifested through family interaction (Hildyard & Wolfe, 2002).

Oldershaw, Walters, and Hall (1986) offer insight about compliance gaining in families with a history of child maltreatment. The researchers compared 10 physically abusive mothers and 10 comparison mothers as they completed a 45-minute interaction with one of their children (2–4 years old). Mothers' compliance-seeking strategies were coded into 12 categories and grouped into power-assertive strategies (e.g., threat, negative physical touch, humiliation) and positively oriented strategies (e.g., reasoning, bargaining, modeling). Abusive mothers issued significantly more commands during the play period and used all of the power-assertive compliance-seeking strategies more frequently than comparison mothers. Regarding sequential differences, abusive mothers issued a larger percentage of their initial requests and commands with no rationale (88% vs. 64%) and without a positive tone of voice (0% vs. 51%) relative to comparison mothers. Abused children failed to comply immediately with a larger percentage of their mothers' requests (58%) than nonmaltreated children (28%).

Following noncompliance, abusive mothers were more likely than comparison mothers to repeat commands with no rationale or with only power-assertive strategies. When their children did comply, abusive mothers were just as likely to criticize (e.g., "It's about time you did that") as praise, whereas control mothers invariably praised. Other studies also find that abusive parents respond inconsistently to child compliance (Borrego, Timmer, Urquiza, & Follette, 2004; Cerezo & D'Ocon, 1995). As would be expected from these patterns, our meta-analysis of 11 studies shows that maltreated children display higher rates of noncompliance than nonmaltreated children ($d$ = .45; Wilson et al., 2006).

Each theoretical framework discussed earlier suggests explanations for these patterns. Regarding obstacles, physically abusive parents are more likely than nonmaltreating parents to attribute child noncompliance to stable and controllable causes (e.g., their child's personality) and to view their child's actions as intentional (Bauer & Twentyman, 1985; Dopke & Milner, 2000; Larrance & Twentyman, 1983). Abusive parents also are more likely to discount their children's positive behavior (e.g., compliance) by attributing it to uncontrollable and unstable causes. As Weiner's (1986, 1995) theory would predict, such attributions lead abusive parents to feel more anger when their children resist compliance (Reid, 1986); anger in turn is associated with using power-assertive strategies (Dix, 1991).

Regarding face and directives, physically abusive parents often perceive interaction as a power struggle where their children, rather than they, drive interactions with negative outcomes (Bradley & Peters, 1991; Bugental, Blue, & Cruzcosa, 1989). Such "low-power" parents are exceptionally reactive to any behavior that could be interpreted as challenging their authority and rely on power assertion and verbal degradation to regain power (Bugental & Happaney, 2000). In the language of politeness theory, abusive parents may use threats or humiliation to emphasize that they need not attend to their child's face (i.e., they are powerful). From the perspective of speech act theory, abusive parents may assume that the conditions for their requests exist simply because they are "the parent" and hence view questions as challenges to their authority. Aside from power, relational intimacy also may filter interpretations. Nonmaltreated children are more likely than abused or neglected children to be securely attached to their parents (Morton & Browne, 1998); hence, nonmaltreating parents may be less likely to view their children's noncompliance as face threatening because the parent-child relationship is secure.

Regarding goals, abusive and non-maltreating parents may hold different ideas about what is "going on" (i.e., the primary goal) when interacting with their children. In a recent analysis of mothers high versus low in trait verbal aggressiveness (VA) during playtime interactions with their children, we found that high-trait VA mothers issued significantly more commands and suggestions than did low-trait VA mothers (Wilson et al., 2008). High-trait VA mothers appeared to view play as something to be controlled, in that they used directives to dictate what activities they and their child performed, at what speed, and for what duration. Low-trait VA mothers appeared to view the situation as "play for play's sake," in that they were more likely to follow their child's lead and used directives to organize shared activities.

These insights are embedded within parent-child interaction therapy (PCIT), a short-term intervention for families with children between the ages of 2 and 6 with proven efficacy at preventing the (re)occurrence of child abuse and neglect (Chaffin et al., 2004; Herschell, Calzada, Eyberg, & McNeil, 2002). PCIT entails two distinct phases (child-directed interaction and parent-directed interaction) that are taught through instruction, modeling, role-playing, and coaching. During the first phase, parents learn PRIDE skills (praise, reflection, imitation, description, and enthusiasm). Within free play sessions, children choose the toy(s) they want to play with, and parents are coached to follow their child's lead, demonstrate interest, and avoid commands or criticism. By altering their own behavior and seeing their child's reactions change in response, parents may be less likely to conceptualize play as a power struggle or make attributions that lead to anger. Once PRIDE skills are mastered, the second phase begins, during which parents are taught to issue clear, developmentally appropriate commands and provide consistent responses to both child compliance (e.g., praise) and non-compliance (e.g., warning and time-out). PCIT reduces negative parent-child interactions that put children at immediate risk of injury and damage their self-esteem and social competence in the longer run (Chaffin et al., 2004).

◆ *Summary*

"Compliance gaining" as an area of study has been traced in three parts: an initial flurry of research modeled on a ground-breaking study; a move toward developing theories that coalesce around the concepts of directives, face, goals, and obstacles; and a transition toward applying theory to problems of social importance. The newest phase of research highlights how compliance-gaining interactions both reflect and define participants' ongoing relationship, thereby linking questions about message processing (effects) and production (choices). Much has been learned so far, but much important work also remains to be done.

◆ *Notes*

1. A search of the Social Science Citation Index (December 31, 2007) revealed that the Marwell and Schmitt (1967) article has been cited by 132 subsequent articles; however, only 3 of the 132 citations predate the G. R. Miller et al. (1977) study.

2. Scholars in other disciplines also developed typologies of compliance-seeking strategies and investigated predictors of strategy choice. Management scholars tend to use a typology developed by Kipnis et al. (1980), while social psychologists typically use Falbo and Peplau's (1980) typology. Although these programs of research were not influenced directly by the MBRS study, they share many of the same limitations, including a lack of theoretical conceptualization and problems with the validity of the strategy selection procedure.

3. The label *primary* refers to which goal helps participants understand what is going on rather than to goal importance. Even when people frame a situation as being about "giving advice" or "asking a favor," they often rate "secondary" goals such as conversation management or relational resources as more important than the primary goal (Schrader & Dillard, 1998; Wilson et al., 1998).

◆ *References*

Austin, J. L. (1962). *How to do things with words*. Oxford, UK: Clarendon.

Bauer, W. D., & Twentyman, C. T. (1985). Abusing, neglectful, and comparison mothers' responses to child-related and non-child-related stressors. *Journal of Consulting and Clinical Psychology, 53,* 335–343.

Bavelas, J. (1991). Some problems with linking goals to discourse. In K. Tracy (Ed.), *Understanding face-to-face interaction: Issues linking goals to discourse* (pp. 119–130). Hillsdale, NJ: Lawrence Erlbaum.

Belsky, J. (1993). Etiology of child maltreatment: A developmental-ecological analysis. *Psychological Bulletin, 114,* 413–434.

Borrego, J., Timmer, S. G., Urquiza, A. J., & Follette, W. C. (2004). Physically abusive mothers' responses following episodes of child noncompliance and compliance. *Journal of Consulting and Clinical Psychology, 72,* 897–903.

Boster, F. J. (1988). Comments on the utility of compliance-gaining message selection tasks. *Human Communication Research, 15,* 169–177.

Boster, F. J., Stiff, J. B., & Reynolds, R. A. (1985). Do persons respond differently to inductively-derived and deductively-derived lists of compliance gaining message strategies? *Western Journal of Speech Communication, 49,* 177–187.

Bradley, E. J., & Peters, R. D. (1991). Physically abusive and nonabusive mothers' perceptions of parenting and child behavior. *American Journal of Orthopsychiatry, 61,* 455–460.

Brown, P., & Levinson, S. C. (1987). *Politeness: Some universals in language usage.* Cambridge, UK: Cambridge University Press.

Bugental, D. B., Blue, J., & Cruzcosa, M. (1989). Perceived control over caregiving outcomes: Implications for child abuse. *Developmental Psychology, 25,* 532–539.

Bugental, D. B., & Happaney, K. (2000). Parent-child interaction as a power contest. *Journal of Applied Developmental Psychology, 21,* 267–282.

Burleson, B. R., & Wilson, S. R. (1988). On the continued undesirability of item desirability: A reply to Boster, Hunter, & Seibold. *Human Communication Research, 15,* 178–191.

Burleson, B. R., Wilson, S. R., Waltman, M. S., Goering, E. M., Ely, T. K., & Whaley, B. B. (1988). Item desirability bias effects in compliance-gaining research: Seven studies documenting artifacts in the strategy selection procedure. *Human Communication Research, 14,* 429–486.

Caughlin, J. P., & Scott, A. M. (2009). Toward a communication theory of the demand/withdraw pattern of interaction in interpersonal relationships. In S. W. Smith & S. R. Wilson (Eds.), *New directions in interpersonal communication research* (pp. 201–221). Thousand Oaks, CA: Sage.

Cerezo, M. A., & D'Ocon, A. D. (1995). Maternal inconsistent socialization: An international pattern with maltreated children. *Child Abuse Review, 4,* 14–31.

Chaffin, M., Silovsky, J. F., Funderburk, B., Valle, L. A., Brestan, E. V., Balachova, T., et al. (2004). Parent-child interaction therapy with physically abusive parents: Efficacy for reducing future abuse reports. *Journal of Consulting and Clinical Psychology, 72,* 500–510.

Choi, I., Nisbett, R. E., & Norenzayan, A. (1999). Causal attributions across cultures: Variation and universality. *Psychological Bulletin, 125,* 47–63.

Cialdini, R. (2001). *Influence: Science and practice* (4th ed.). Glenview, IL: Scott Foresman.

Clark, R. A., & Delia, J. G. (1979). Topoi and rhetorical competence. *Quarterly Journal of Speech, 65,* 187–206.

Cody, M. J., Canary, D. J., & Smith, S. W. (1994). Compliance-gaining goals: An inductive analysis of actors' goal types, strategies, and successes. In J. A. Daly & J. M. Wiemann (Eds.), *Strategic interpersonal communication* (pp. 33–90). Hillsdale, NJ: Lawrence Erlbaum.

Cody, M. J., Greene, J. O., Marston, P. J., O'Hair, H. D., Baaske, K. T., & Schneider, M. J. (1986). Situation perception and message strategy selection. In M. L. McLaughlin (Ed.), *Communication yearbook 9* (pp. 390–420). Beverly Hills, CA: Sage.

Cody, M. J., & McLaughlin, M. L. (1980). Perceptions of compliance-gaining situations: A dimensional analysis. *Communication Monographs, 47,* 132–148.

Craig, R. T., Tracy, K., & Spisak, F. (1986). The discourse of requests: Assessment of a politeness approach. *Human Communication Research, 12,* 437–468.

Dillard, J. P. (1988). Compliance-gaining message selection: What is our dependent variable? *Communication Monographs, 55,* 162–183.

Dillard, J. P. (1990). A goal-driven model of interpersonal influence. In J. P. Dillard (Ed.), *Seeking compliance: The production of interpersonal influence messages* (pp. 41–56). Scottsdale, AZ: Gorsuch Scarisbrick.

Dillard, J. P. (2004). The goals-plans-action model of interpersonal influence. In J. S. Seiter & R. H. Gass (Eds.), *Perspectives on persuasion, social influence, and compliance gaining* (pp. 185–206). Boston: Allyn & Bacon.

Dillard, J. P., & Burgoon, M. (1985). Situational influences on the selection of compliance-gaining messages: Two tests of the predictive utility of the Cody-McLaughlin typology. *Communication Monographs, 52,* 289–304.

Dillard, J. P., & Schrader, D. (1998). On the utility of the goals-plans-action sequence. *Communication Studies, 49,* 300–304.

Dillard, J. P., Segrin, C., & Harden, J. M. (1989). Primary and secondary goals in the production of interpersonal influence messages. *Communication Monographs, 56,* 19–38.

Dillard, J. P., Wilson, S. R., Tusing, K. J., & Kinney, T. A. (1997). Politeness judgments in personal relationships. *Journal of Language and Social Psychology, 16*, 297–325.

Dix, T. (1991). The affective organization of parenting: Adaptive and maladaptive processes. *Psychological Bulletin, 110*, 3–25.

Dopke, C. A., & Milner, J. S. (2000). Impact of child noncompliance on stress appraisals, attributions, and disciplinary choices in mothers at high and low risk for child physical abuse. *Child Abuse & Neglect, 24*, 493–504.

Ellis, D. G. (1999). *From language to communication* (2nd ed.). Mahwah, NJ: Lawrence Erlbaum.

Falbo, T., & Peplau, L. A. (1980). Power strategies in intimate relationships. *Journal of Personality and Social Psychology, 38*, 618–628.

Fitch, K. L. (1998). *Speaking relationally: Culture, communication, and interpersonal connection.* New York: Guilford.

Fitch, K. L., & Sanders, R. E. (1994). Culture, communication, and preference for directness in expression of directives. *Communication Theory, 3*, 219–245.

Folkes, V. S. (1982). Communicating the reasons for social rejection. *Journal of Experimental Social Psychology, 18*, 235–252.

Goei, R., & Boster, F. J. (2005). The roles of obligation and gratitude in explaining the effectiveness of favors on compliance. *Communication Monographs, 72*, 284–300.

Goffman, E. (1967). *Interaction ritual: Essays on face-to-face behavior.* Chicago: Aldine.

Goldsmith, D. J. (2000). Soliciting advice: The role of sequential placement in mitigating face threat. *Communication Monographs, 67*, 1–19.

Greene, J. O. (2000). Evanescent mentation: An ameliorative conceptual foundation for research and theory on message production. *Communication Theory, 10*, 139–155.

Hample, D., & Dallinger, J. M. (1987). Individual differences in cognitive edition standards. *Human Communication Research, 14*, 123–144.

Hample, D., & Dallinger, J. M. (1998). On the etiology of the rebuff phenomenon: Why are persuasive messages less polite after rebuffs? *Communication Studies, 49*, 305–321.

Hecht, M. L., & Miller-Day, M. (2007). The drug resistance strategies project as translational research. *Journal of Applied Communication Research, 35*, 343–349.

Herschell, A. D., Calzada, E. J., Eyberg, S. M., & McNeil, C. B. (2002). Parent-child interaction therapy: New directions in research. *Cognitive and Behavioral Practice, 9*, 9–16.

Hildyard, K. L., & Wolfe, D. A. (2002). Child neglect: Developmental issues and outcomes. *Child Abuse & Neglect, 26*, 679–695.

Holtgraves, T., & Yang, J. N. (1992). Interpersonal underpinnings of request strategies: General principles and differences due to culture and gender. *Journal of Personality and Social Psychology, 62*, 246–256.

Hunter, J. E., & Boster, F. J. (1987). A model of compliance-gaining message selection. *Communication Monographs, 54*, 63–84.

Ifert, D. (2000). Resistance to interpersonal requests: A summary and critique of recent research. In M. Roloff (Ed.), *Communication yearbook 23* (pp. 125–161). Thousand Oaks, CA: Sage.

Jacobs, S., & Jackson, S. (1989). Building a model of conversational argument. In B. Dervin, L. Grossberg, B. J. O'Keefe, & E. Wartella (Eds.), *Rethinking communication: Vol. 2. Paradigm exemplars* (pp. 172–187). Newbury Park, CA: Sage.

Johnson, D. I., Roloff, M. E., & Riffee, M. A. (2004). Politeness theory and refusals of requests: Face threat as a function of expressed obstacle. *Communication Studies, 55*, 227–238.

Keck, K. L., & Samp, J. A. (2007). The dynamic nature of goals and message production as revealed in a sequential analysis of conflict interactions. *Human Communication Research, 33*, 27–47.

Kellermann, K. (2004). A goal-directed approach to compliance gaining: Relating differences among goals to differences in behavior. *Communication Research, 31*, 397–445.

Kellermann, K., & Cole, T. (1994). Classifying compliance-gaining messages: Taxonomic disorder and strategic confusion. *Communication Theory, 4*, 3–60.

Kelley, H. H., Berscheid, E., Christensen, A., Harvey, J. H., Huston, T. L., Levinger, G., et al. (1983). Analyzing close relationships. In H. H. Kelley, E. Berscheid, A. Christensen, J. Harvey, T. L. Huston, G. Levinger, et al.

(Eds.), *Close relationships* (pp. 20–67). New York: W. H. Freeman.

Kim, M. S. (2002). *Non-Western perspectives on human communication: Implications for theory and practice.* Thousand Oaks, CA: Sage.

King, P. E. (2001). Automatic responses, target resistance, and the adaptation of compliance-seeking requests. *Communication Monographs, 68,* 386–399.

Kipnis, D., Schmidt, S. M., & Wilkinson, I. (1980). Intraorganizational influence tactics: Explorations in getting one's way. *Journal of Applied Psychology, 65,* 440–452.

Knobloch, L. K., & Solomon, D. H. (2004). Interference and facilitation from partners in the development of interdependence within romantic relationships. *Personal Relationships, 11,* 115–130.

Kunkel, A. D., Wilson, S. R., Olufowote, J., & Robson, S. (2003). Identity implications of influence goals: Initiating, intensifying, and ending romantic relationships. *Western Journal of Communication, 67,* 382–412.

Labov, W., & Fanshel, D. (1977). *Therapeutic discourse: Psychotherapy as conversation.* New York: Academic Press.

Lannutti, P. J., & Monahan, J. L. (2007). Social cognition under the influence: Drinking while communicating. In D. R. Roskos-Ewoldsen & J. L. Monahan (Eds.), *Communication and social cognition: Theories and methods* (pp. 217–243). Mahwah, NJ: Lawrence Erlbaum.

Larrance, D. T., & Twentyman, C. T. (1983). Maternal attributions and child abuse. *Journal of Abnormal Psychology, 92,* 449–457.

LePoire, B. A., & Dailey, R. M. (2006). Inconsistent nurturing as social control theory: A new theory in family communication. In D. O. Braithwaite & L. E. Baxter (Eds.), *Engaging theories in family communication: Multiple perspectives* (pp. 82–98). Thousand Oaks, CA: Sage.

Lim, T. W., & Bowers, J. W. (1991). Facework: Solidarity, approbation, and tact. *Human Communication Research, 17,* 415–450.

MacGeorge, E. L. (2001). Support providers' interaction goals: The influence of attributions and emotions. *Communication Monographs, 68,* 72–97.

MacGeorge, E. L., Feng, B., Butler, G. L., & Budarz, S. K. (2004). Understanding advice in supportive interactions: Beyond the facework and message evaluation paradigms. *Human Communication Research, 30,* 42–70.

Marshall, L. J., & Levy, V. M., Jr. (1998). The development of children's perceptions of obstacles in compliance-gaining interactions. *Communication Studies, 49,* 342–358.

Marwell, G., & Schmitt, D. R. (1967). Dimensions of compliance-gaining behavior: An empirical analysis. *Sociometry, 30,* 350–364.

McLaughlin, M. L., Cody, M. J., & Robey, C. S. (1980). Situational influences on the selection of strategies to resist compliance-gaining attempts. *Human Communication Research, 7,* 14–36.

McQuillen, J. S. (1986). The development of listener-adapted compliance-resisting strategies. *Human Communication Research, 12,* 359–375.

Metts, S., Cupach, W. R., & Imahori, T. T. (1992). Perceptions of sexual compliance-resisting messages in three types of cross-sex relationships. *Western Journal of Communication, 56,* 1–17.

Meyer, J. R. (2007). Compliance gaining. In D. R. Roskos-Ewoldsen & J. L. Monahan (Eds.), *Communication and social cognition: Theories and methods* (pp. 399–416). Mahwah, NJ: Lawrence Erlbaum.

Millar, F. E., & Rogers, L. E. (1987). Relational dimensions of interpersonal dynamics. In G. R. Miller & M. E. Roloff (Eds.), *Interpersonal processes: New directions in communication research* (pp. 117–138). Newbury Park, CA: Sage.

Miller, G. R. (1987). Persuasion. In C. R. Berger & S. H. Chaffee (Eds.), *Handbook of communication science* (pp. 446–483). Newbury Park, CA: Sage.

Miller, G. R., Boster, F. J., Roloff, M. E., & Seibold, D. (1977). Compliance-gaining message strategies: A typology and some findings concerning situational differences. *Communication Monographs, 44,* 37–51.

Miller, G. R., Boster, F. J., Roloff, M. E., & Seibold, D. (1987). MBRS rekindled: Some thoughts on compliance-gaining in interpersonal settings. In M. E. Roloff & G. R. Miller (Eds.), *Interpersonal processes: New directions in communication research* (pp. 89–116). Newbury Park, CA: Sage.

Miller, J. G. (1996). Culture as a source of order in social motivation: Comment. *Psychological Inquiry, 7,* 240–243.

Mills, J., & Clark, M. S. (1994). Communal and exchange relationships: Controversies and research. In R. Erber & R. Gilmour (Eds.), *Theoretical frameworks for personal relationships* (pp. 29–42). Hillsdale, NJ: Lawrence Erlbaum.

Morgan, W., & Wilson, S. R. (2007). Explaining child abuse as a lack of safe ground. In B. H. Spitzberg & W. R. Cupach (Eds.), *The dark side of interpersonal communication* (2nd ed., pp. 327–362). Mahwah, NJ: Lawrence Erlbaum.

Morton, N., & Browne, K. D. (1998). Theory and observation of attachment and its relation to child maltreatment: A review. *Child Abuse & Neglect, 22,* 1093–1104.

O'Keefe, B. J. (1988). The logic of message design: Individual differences in reasoning about communication. *Communication Monographs, 55,* 80–103.

Oldershaw, L., Walters, G. C., & Hall, D. K. (1986). Control strategies and noncompliance in abusive mother-child dyads: An observational study. *Child Development, 57,* 722–732.

Palomares, N. A. (2008). Toward a theory of goal detection in social interaction: Effects of contextual ambiguity and tactical functionality on goal inferences and inference certainty. *Communication Research, 35,* 109–148.

Reid, J. B. (1986). Social-interactional patterns in families of abused and nonabused children. In C. Zahn-Waxler, E. M. Cummings, & R. Iannotti (Eds.), *Altruism and aggression: Biological and social origins* (pp. 238–255). New York: Cambridge University Press.

Roloff, M. E., Janiszewski, C. A., McGrath, M. A., Burns, C. S., & Manrai, L. A. (1988). Acquiring resources from intimates: When obligation substitutes for persuasion. *Human Communication Research, 14,* 364–396.

Sanders, R. E., & Fitch, K. L. (2001). The actual practice of compliance seeking. *Communication Theory, 11,* 263–289.

Schrader, D. C., & Dillard, J. P. (1998). Goal structures and interpersonal influence. *Communication Studies, 49,* 276–293.

Searle, J. R. (1969). *Speech acts: An essay in the philosophy of language.* Cambridge, UK: Cambridge University Press.

Searle, J. R. (1976). A classification of illocutionary acts. *Language in Society, 5,* 1–25.

Segrin, C., & Dillard, J. P. (1991). (Non)depressed persons' cognitive and affective reactions to (un)successful interpersonal influence. *Communication Monographs, 58,* 115–134.

Seibold, D. R. (1988). A response to "Item desirability in compliance-gaining research." *Human Communication Research, 15,* 152–161.

Seibold, D. R., Cantrill, J. G., & Meyers, R. A. (1985). Communication and interpersonal influence. In M. L. Knapp & G. R. Miller (Eds.), *Handbook of interpersonal communication* (pp. 551–611). Beverly Hills, CA: Sage.

Shepherd, G. J. (1998). The trouble with goals. *Communication Studies, 49,* 294–299.

Streeck, J. (1980). Speech acts in interaction: A critique of Searle. *Discourse Processes, 3,* 133–154.

Ting-Toomey, S., & Kurogi, A. (1998). Facework competence in intercultural conflict: An updated face-negotiation theory. *International Journal of Intercultural Relations, 22,* 187–225.

Tracy, K., & Baratz, S. (1994). The case for case studies of facework. In S. Ting-Toomey (Ed.), *The challenge of facework: Cross-cultural and interpersonal issues* (pp. 287–306). Albany, NY: SUNY Press.

Tracy, K., Craig, R. T., Smith, M., & Spisak, F. (1984). The discourse of requests: Assessment of a compliance-gaining approach. *Human Communication Research, 10,* 513–538.

United Nations Children's Fund (UNICEF). (2007). *Facts on children.* Retrieved November 10, 2007, from http://www.unicef.org/media/media_35903.html

U.S. Department of Health and Human Services (USDHHS). (2007). *Child maltreatment 2005.* Retrieved November 10, 2007, from http://www.acf.hhs.gov/programs/cb/pubs/cm05/cm05.pdf

Weiner, B. (1986). *An attributional theory of motivation and emotion.* New York: Springer-Verlag.

Weiner, B. (1995). *Judgments of responsibility: A foundation for a theory of social conduct.* New York: Guilford.

Weiner, B., Figueroa-Munoz, A., & Kakihara, C. (1991). The goals of excuses and communication strategies related to causal perceptions. *Personality and Social Psychology Bulletin, 17,* 4–13.

Wheeless, L. R., Barraclough, R., & Stewart, R. (1983). Compliance-gaining and power in persuasion. In R. Bostrom (Ed.), *Communication yearbook 7* (pp. 105–145). Beverly Hills, CA: Sage.

Wilson, S. R. (1990). Development and test of a cognitive rules model of interaction goals. *Communication Monographs, 57,* 81–103.

Wilson, S. R. (2002). *Seeking and resisting compliance: Why people say what they do when trying to influence others.* Thousand Oaks, CA: Sage.

Wilson, S. R., Aleman, C. G., & Leatham, G. B. (1998). Identity implications of influence goals: A revised analysis of face-threatening acts and application to seeking compliance with same-sex friends. *Human Communication Research, 25,* 64–96.

Wilson, S. R., Cruz, M. G., Marshall, L. J., & Rao, N. (1993). An attributional analysis of compliance-gaining interactions. *Communication Monographs, 60,* 352–372.

Wilson, S. R., Roberts, F., Rack, J. J., & Delaney, J. (2008). Mothers' trait verbal aggressiveness as a predictor of maternal and child behavior during play-time interactions. *Human Communication Research, 34,* 392–402.

Wilson, S. R., Shi, X., Tirmenstein, L., Norris, A., & Rack, J. (2006). Parental physical negative touch and child noncompliance in abusive, neglectful, and comparison families: A meta-analysis of observational studies. In L. Turner & R. West (Eds.), *Family communication: A reference for theory and research* (pp. 237–258). Thousand Oaks, CA: Sage.

Wiseman, R. L., & Schenk-Hamlin, W. (1981). A multidimensional scaling validation of an inductively-derived set of compliance-gaining strategies. *Communication Monographs, 48,* 251–270.

# 14

# SOCIAL INFLUENCE IN GROUPS AND ORGANIZATIONS

◆ David R. Seibold, Renee A. Meyers, and Mirit Devorah Shoham

O ur purpose in this chapter is to review theoretical perspectives on group and organizational influence. We view influence as instrumental goals and related individual, subgroup, and system effects that are constituted in communicative exchanges among group and organizational members who interact face-to-face or can readily do so. Our focus on influence as a communicative accomplishment offers a basis for the theories we select and a standpoint from which to critique the communication and interdisciplinary perspectives we treat.

The chapter is divided into two parts: influence in groups and influence in organizations, respectively. In the first part, we first survey four traditions on social influence from across disciplines that study group behavior. We then examine four prominent theories of group communication: functional theory, symbolic convergence theory, the socio-egocentric model, and structuration theory. Our emphasis is different from that of Boster and Cruz (2002), who surveyed the literature concerning persuasion and group communication. We suggest that their excellent review be read in tandem with the first part of this chapter. In the second part, we adumbrate organizational social influence perspectives and theorists, highlighting areas linked to communication research. In the main portion of the second part, we examine three prominent perspectives on organizational influence: social information processing, diffusion of innovations theory, and network theories of influence. In both parts of this chapter, we explicate each theoretical perspective, focus on the role of influence, review empirical support, note controversies and critiques, and offer directions for future research.

As a framework for describing how influence is conceived within each perspective and for comparing the conceptions, we structure our review around two tensions that characterize influence interactions (Meyers, Seibold, & Shoham, 2007). These tensions relate to our definition of group influence as *instrumental goals* and related *effects* and are central concepts in social action theories (e.g., Bourdieu, 1977; de Certeau, 1984; Sahlins, 1987). The first tension concerns whether the source of influence attempts is constituted in individual/group agency, is determined by institutional structures, or both. The second tension is whether individual, subgroup, or system effects that accrue from influence attempts are intentional, unintentional, or both. These two tensions provide the scaffolding for our analysis of influence in the four group and three organizational perspectives (see Table 14.1).

## ◆ Communication and Group Influence

### GROUP INFLUENCE FOUNDATIONS

At least four identifiable bodies of theory are germane to social influence in groups. First, prominent theorists whose work has informed our understanding of influence in groups, as well as its interdisciplinary nature, include Asch (1951) on conformity processes, Festinger's (1954) theory of social comparison processes, Zajonc's (1965) social facilitation perspective, and French and Raven's (1968) distinctions among the bases of social power, among others (e.g., Hopkins, 1964).

Second, there are theoretical perspectives concerning interpersonal influence from other disciplines that have not been integrated into studies of communicative influence in groups. Among the most prominent of these are perspectives on minority influence, especially those stemming from Tajfel (1974) and social identity theory (Martin & Hewstone, 2007); Latané's (1981) social impact theory; and Jackson's (1987) social forces model of influence.

Third, there are theoretical frameworks in communication that acknowledge influence

**Table 14.1**

| Source of Influence Goals | | |
|---|---|---|
| Agency | Group theory | |
| | Organizational theory | |
| Institutional structural factors | Group theory | |
| | Organizational theory | |
| Types of Influence Effects | | |
| *Intentional* | *Unintentional* | |
| Functional theory Structuration argument theory | Symbolic convergence theory | |
| Social information processing | Theories of network influence | |
| Adaptive structuration theory | Socio-egocentric model | |
| Diffusion of innovations | Theories of network influence | |

in groups but whose proponents have not been centrally focused on communicative influence. These include development models (Poole & Baldwin, 1996), Fisher and Hawes's (1971) interact system model, and the mediational perspective (Hirokawa & Salazar, 1997) on group decision making.

Finally, there are social influence perspectives from outside the field that communication scholars *have* drawn upon. These include Price, Cappella, and Nir's (2002) use of Deutsch and Gerard's (1955) perspective for their work on normative and information influences in online political discussions; Propp's (1997) use of Stasser's work in her evaluative interaction model; Boster's (Boster, Fryrear, Mongeau, & Hunter, 1982) reliance on French's (1956) communication discrepancy model; and Bonito's (2007) critique of hidden profiles (Stasser & Titus, 2003) in his local management model of information sharing in groups.

## GROUP COMMUNICATION THEORIES AND INFLUENCE

### Functional Theory and Influence

One of the most prominent theories of communication and group decision making is the functional theory (FT) of group decision making (Gouran & Hirokawa, 1996). FT proposes five communicative functions as prerequisites to effective decision making (Hirokawa, 1990; Hollingshead et al., 2005): (a) garnering a complete and thorough understanding of the problem, (b) recognizing the specific standards or criteria needed for an acceptable solution, (c) generating a range of feasible solutions, (d) assessing thoroughly and accurately the positive consequences of each solution, and (e) assessing thoroughly and accurately the negative consequences of each solution. Laboratory studies provide general support for FT (e.g., Hirokawa, 1985, 1988). Case study analyses of failed decisions underscore factors that impair effective production of the five functions,

resulting in either no influence or ineffective influence on final outcomes (e.g., Gouran, Hirokawa, & Martz, 1986). There also may be contingency variables that moderate the influence of the five functions (such as the nature of the task; Hirokawa, 1990). A meta-analysis revealed that assessment of negative consequences was the most influential communicative function for producing effective decisions (Orlitzky & Hirokawa, 2001).

In terms of our framework, the FT view of group influence is one in which (a) individuals and groups have agency to influence instrumental goals through communication related to the five functions, and (b) influence effects in group decision making are generally intentional in nature (hence its placement in the upper left quadrant of Table 14.1). Functional theorists believe that individual group members (and, ultimately, the group as a whole) have the ability to influence decision-making outcomes through effective use of the five requisite functions (Gouran & Hirokawa, 1996).

In the FT perspective, group members are capable of influencing each other and the final group outcome. Although group members may draw on institutional structures (status, gender, expertise) to produce influence, functional theorists have not been particularly interested in identifying those resources or how they might be employed. Of greater interest are the micro-interaction behaviors that group members produce as they seek to influence decision proposals (Hirokawa, 1985, 1988). Gouran and Hirokawa (1996) also analyze how group members might *counteract* cognitive, affiliative, and egocentric constraints in decision-making interactions (i.e., those communicative influences that are not exacerbated by cognitive and social influences; see Gouran, 2007). Members' counteractive influence strategies include questioning members' evidence, heightening awareness of relationships, engaging powerful members in reflection and examination, and clarifying the facilitative role of argument.

Influence *effects* are primarily conceived as intentional within FT; group members are aware and motivated to bring about a desired outcome. For example, Gouran and Hirokawa (1996) suggest that group members can "take steps to minimize and counteract sources of influence that limit prospects for adequately fulfilling fundamental task requirements" (p. 75). In addition, as Hirokawa and Salazar (1997) explain, "Interaction is a social tool that group members use to perform or satisfy various prerequisites for effective decision making" (p. 169).

In sum, FT views social influence as produced by group members who are capable of intentionally affecting group outcomes through the use of diverse communicative strategies. Less attention is paid to the ways that macro-structures might determine influence or the unintentional effects of various tactics. The result is a view that accords strong agency to individual group members to bring about intended influence for the production of high-quality decisions.

*Critique and Agenda.* Stohl and Holmes (1993) note the extensive reliance on zero-history laboratory groups in tests of FT (but see Propp & Nelson, 1996). Furthermore, as Waldeck, Shepard, Teitelbaum, Farrar, and Seibold (2002) summarize, conceptual ambiguities and operational disparities surrounding group "functions" and "effectiveness" undermine the ability to track influence and assess effects and thus to draw comparisons about influence across studies. Especially problematic, proponents of FT assume that members have all the relevant information needed to enact the functions specified in the theory. Little attention is accorded to varying representations of that information (or to representational gaps; Cronin & Weingart, 2007), to its distribution across members, and to the criteria used to assess that information vis-à-vis the functions specified by FT. All are likely to involve communicative influence and therefore should be part of future research. Similarly, Gouran and Hirokawa (1996) have acknowledged the salience of cognitive,

affiliative, and egocentric constraints on members' ability to make appropriate choices, and Gouran (1998) has posited interactional manifestations of these constraints on group decision making, but it will be important to assess them empirically.

### Symbolic Convergence Theory and Influence

Symbolic convergence theory (SCT) posits a view of influence different from that of FT. In terms of our framework, SCT falls in the upper right quadrant (see Table 14.1), where group members have agency but the effects tend to be unintentional. This perspective examines how groups create a shared consciousness that binds group members together as a cohesive unit: Members develop symbolic convergence through the sharing of group fantasies. Bormann (1996) defines fantasies as "the creative and imaginative shared interpretation of events that fulfill a group psychological or rhetorical need" (p. 88). They include messages that do not refer to the "here and now" of a group, such as jokes, anecdotes, fables, analogies, or imagined futures. As members converge around a symbolic representation, the shared fantasy influences and guides actions and unifies. Symbolic convergence can create a sense of common identity, foster creativity, affect assumptions, and suggest ways of coping with problems (Bormann, 1996).

SCT posits that group members are active agents in creating and maintaining fantasies, which then have an instrumental influence on group outcomes. Bormann (1996) suggests that the influential impact of fantasies often rests with the rhetorical skills of group participants. As members share their interpretations, and as other members elaborate these dramatizations, the group comes to experience similar emotions and develop similar experiences. In time, some of these shared interpretations become fantasy types that influence the group's outlook, identity, and actions. Research has focused on identifying how SCT is manifested in a variety of communicative contexts (Bormann, 1985, 1996). In addition, SCT researchers have revised the theory in response to criticisms and have worked to expand the theory to encompass the impact of SCT in both rhetorical and group contexts (e.g., Bormann, Cragan, & Shields, 1994).

Unlike FT, SCT does not view the effects of these influence attempts as intentional. Bormann (1996) suggests that group members respond positively to some fantasies, are indifferent to some, and reject others. It is unclear which fantasies will be central to group influence. The way in which two or more symbolic worlds come to overlap is more accidental than not, and outcomes of fantasies often have unintended consequences. In short, SCT provides an account of influence in which actors are actively involved in sharing fantasies through communicative discourse. The effect of these fantasies, however, is more typically accidental and unplanned. They can thus be facilitative or inhibitive in shaping a group's decision-making process (Bormann, Pratt, & Putnam, 1978).

*Critique and Agenda.* SCT studies yield intriguing descriptions of fantasy chaining and the unfolding of rhetorical visions but are less helpful as theoretical accounts for how these processes influence group outcomes. This is not surprising given the resistance by SCT proponents to calls for specification of process-product linkages (e.g., Bormann et al., 1994). Waldeck et al. (2002) offered nearly a dozen predictions, nested within three overarching propositions, but more work is needed to formalize and test the theory. In addition, although SCT investigations afford rich accounts of communicative influence in groups in a broad sense (i.e., messages that contribute to fantasy chains, rhetorical vision, and ultimately symbolic convergence), they are incomplete in terms of the structure of member-to-member(s) communicative influence. Just as we need to know more

about the specific communicative functions necessary for symbolic convergence to occur, as well as functions that specific master analogs fulfill within groups (Waldeck et al., 2002), more knowledge is needed about the forms and functions of members' verbal exchange and their interdependent nature as communicative influence in those processes.

### Socio-Egocentric Model and Influence

In proposing the socio-egocentric model (SEM), Hewes (1986, 1996) argues that there is little evidence that communicative influence has any impact on decision outcomes. His approach "is based on the assumption that much, if not all, small group communication is epiphenomenal; that is, identifiable non-interactive factors can explain observed patterns of group communication, and it is these non-interactive inputs that produce decision outputs" (Hewes, 1996, p. 193). Hence, SEM explains influence without recourse to group members' interactions. SEM assumes that groups are sets of people who act individualistically, and members' communication is generated by, and reflective of, input factors and members' previous behavior. Interaction is governed by larger structures—such as turn-taking rules and norms about vacuous comments—that make it appear the group is working collectively, but no influence is actually occurring. Members are merely engaged in a process that unfolds identically for each person so as to produce the appearance of coherence and influence.

We locate SEM in the lower right quadrant of Table 14.1, although its placement is debatable. The sources of influence in this model are noninteractive input factors—broader institutional structures that determine interaction patterns. Group members employ "a structural norm of conversation (turn taking) and a cosmetic bid toward meaningful extension of the conversation (vacuous acknowledgments)" (Hewes, 1996, p. 195) to produce collective discourse. Hence, members have little agency in this model; norms of language and communicative practice structure the flow of interaction.

We propose that influence *effects* in the SEM are largely unintentional. Interaction patterns accrue from individuals' internalization of rules and norms that allow them to produce a form of patterned discourse (Bourdieu, 1977). The fact that groups produce coherent decision-making discourse has little to do with the intentions or agency of the members themselves.

Hewes (1996) conceives of influence—in contrast to SEM—as a linear, strictly sequential process that is best captured by "temporally systematic lags between the occurrence of an action and the action that triggered it" (p. 206). Influence is best understood as individual-to-individual, act-to-act dependencies. We would place this alternative model of influence in the upper left quadrant of Table 14.1 since it both posits individual agency and assumes intentional effects.

*Critique and Agenda.* Beyond a view of group communication as information sharing and a mere conduit for preference displays, the theoretical importance and predictive utility of *communicative influence processes* in groups—relative to input-output models—can be found in Jarboe (1999), Meyers and Brashers (1999), and Pavitt (1993). Furthermore, Hoffman and Kleinman (1994) found that the valence of group members' statements concerning decision choices exerted an influence on decision outcomes in particular, but those outcomes could not be adequately predicted by the distribution of those members' choice preferences before they interacted.

However, as we have seen, Hewes (1986, 1996) offers an alternative view: (a) if communication influence is said to exist in groups, it must be found in member-to-member, act-to-act sequential structures (i.e., influence occurs when a group member's communication behaviors are demonstrated to be contingent upon another's immediately preceding message acts), and (b) since no unambiguous evidence exists for the same to date, it must be found if there is to be any value for communication-based explanations of group processes and outcomes. Poole (1999) astutely offers three criticisms of Hewes's first, pivotal proposition. First, Hewes's conceptualization of group communication as individual-to-individual influence is overly restrictive and precludes influence as member convergence surrounding a common viewpoint. This is consistent with SCT and the empirical evidence for it.

Second, Hewes's insistence on act-to-act influence tied to conditional probabilities precludes the influence(s) of critical communication events whose effects are found in much later parts of the group's interactional history and in lagged, nondyadic, or broken interactional chains. This is what is proposed by structuration theory and is reported in studies of tag-team subgroup argument influence (Seibold, McPhee, Poole, Tanita, & Canary, 1981). Working from a non–structuration theory perspective, Corman and Kuhn (2005) applied a quasi-Turing test to determine if group members could distinguish simulated socio-egocentric speech from speech generated by real human groups. Their results suggest that "people may employ different criteria as evidence of influence in group interaction than the linked content of utterances proposed by Hewes" (p. 140). In short, influence in group discussion is more complex than individual-to-individual, act-to-act dependencies.

Third, Hewes's emphasis on communicative influence as changes in subsequent behaviors in the direction advocated ignores other influences that may occur in response to individual acts (e.g., reactance effects). Indeed, support for the valence model (Hoffman & Kleinman, 1994) and distributed valence model (McPhee, Poole, & Seibold, 1982; Meyers, Brashers, & Hanner, 2000) may involve precisely such influences. Notwithstanding these critiques and findings consistent with them, empirical evidence for Hewes's restrictive conception of communicative influence should be sought.

### Structuration Theory and Influence

Structuration theory (ST; Giddens, 1984; Poole, Seibold, & McPhee, 1996) addresses the production and reproduction of groups and the factors that are implicated in that process. Much of the work on communicative *influence* within this realm has focused on group argument (see Seibold & Meyers, 2007, for a review). Within structuration argument theory (SAT), arguments are both systems (observed patterns of interaction) and structures (the unobservable generative rules and resources enabling argument) that are mutually constitutive. "Argument systems are produced in interaction through interactants' knowledgeable and skillful (but perhaps unreflective and unarticulated) use of particular rules and resources—a process that in turn reproduces those structures and makes them available as future resources" (Seibold & Meyers, 1986, p. 148). Arguments are both a medium and an outcome of group interaction.

SAT research has investigated argument patterns and structures (Canary, Brossmann, & Seibold, 1987; Meyers, Seibold, & Brashers, 1991), compared cognitive and interactional accounts of argument (Meyers, 1989; Meyers & Seibold, 1989), revealed group members' joint production of argument (Seibold et al., 1981), explored majority and minority subgroup differences (Meyers et al., 2000) in group argument, investigated argument in computer-mediated groups (Lemus, Seibold, Flanagin, & Metzger, 2004), and assessed argument process-outcome relationships (Meyers & Brashers, 1998).

SAT acknowledges both individual/group agency and institutional structural factors in the production of instrumental goals. It also allows for both intentional and unintentional effects or consequences (Giddens, 1984). Theoretically, the SAT conception of social influence encompasses all four quadrants in Table 14.1. Practically, however, most work on group argument-as-influence has focused on the left half of Table 14.1. Most descriptive studies of group argument in face-to-face and computer-mediated groups have explored how individuals or groups produce argumentative interaction. The work on argument effects assumes intentional consequences; group members are viewed as producing arguments to intentionally influence a decision proposal (see Lemus et al., 2004; Meyers et al., 2000). Less evident is research on the structural or institutional factors that are implicated in group argument. Early work investigated if and how group members insinuate cognitive arguments in actual discussion interaction (Meyers, 1989). Canary et al. (1987) illustrated how various rules and resources serve to generate predictable argument structures (see Table 14.1).

*Critique and Agenda.* Critiques of ST centered on two facets of group structuration studies. First, overemphasis on structuring processes, rather than process-outcome linkages, meant that the predictive potential of ST had not been exploited (Gouran, 1990). This concern has been addressed (Lemus & Seibold, 2007; Meyers et al., 2000), but much more work is needed. Second, empirical demonstrations of the theoretical tenet of action-structure recursivity have been scant (Contractor & Seibold, 1993). We have little insight into their dual influences in groups and their unintended effects.

In the second part, our exploration of three *organizational* theories extrapolates these layered complexities of influence in social systems—including roles, meanings, relationships, and communication structures—constituted in verbal exchanges that move members toward instrumental goals. Maintaining the lens of the individual/structural and intentional/unintentional framework in Table 14.1, we move on to social information processing, diffusion, and network perspectives on influence in organizations.

## ◆ Communication and Organizational Influence

### ORGANIZATIONAL INFLUENCE FOUNDATIONS

Prominent organizational areas and *theorists* are foundational to understanding social influence in organizations. Theoretical work on decision making (Cyert & March, 1963), leadership and motivation (see Miner, 2005), organizing and sensemaking (Weick, 1995), socialization (Van Maanen & Schein, 1979), culture (Schein, 1984), and systems (Katz & Kahn, 1966) have been historical bases for work on organizational influence.

More than 340 articles published since 1980 have reported findings concerning influence strategies or tactics (Barbuto & Moss, 2006), the majority of those studies in management and psychology. A meta-analysis reported by Barbuto and Moss (2006) revealed that each of six intra-organizational influence tactics (ingratiation, rationality, exchanges, upward appeals, assertiveness, and coalitions) demonstrated significant effects with at least one of seven dispositional antecedents (Machiavellianism, locus of control, self-monitoring, impression management, social identity, intrinsic/internal motivation, and extrinsic/external motivation). In another meta-analysis of outcomes associated with influence tactics, Higgins, Judge, and Ferris (2003) reported that particular strategies (ingratiation and rationality) employed in organizational influence processes had positive effects on work outcomes (performance assessments and extrinsic success). They summarized, "Individuals who exhibit ingratiatory behaviors, and who use logic and data to justify their requests, appear to have a greater chance of succeeding in their careers than individuals who use these tactics to a lesser degree" (p. 100). Other influence tactics (self-promotion, assertiveness, exchange, and upward appeals) had significant effects in certain situations and on specific work outcomes. Porter, Angle, and Allen (2003) provide a major compendium of conceptual and empirical articles on downward, lateral, and upward influence in organizational settings.

In a review of individual, relational, and organizational antecedents and outcomes of upward influence in communication, Waldron (1999) found important consequences for individual members and for leader-follower relationships associated with this form of communication. Communication scholars' reviews of managerial influence (Seibold, Cantrill, & Meyers, 1994), message exchanges (Stohl & Redding, 1987), and organizational competence (Jablin & Sias, 2001) highlight other foundational lines of research and studies.

Below we focus on influence-related *theories* that have been most used in *organizational communication*: social information processing, diffusion of innovation theory, and network theory that emphasizes relational influence as opposed to positional influence. We explicate each theory briefly and emphasize communication scholars' utilization of—and findings about—the perspective. As with the group influence theories above, we assess each of these frameworks in terms of the research support for the theory and controversies that surround it.

### ORGANIZATIONAL COMMUNICATION THEORIES AND INFLUENCE

#### Social Information Processing and Influence

The social information processing (SIP) framework (Salancik & Pfeffer, 1978) highlights the social environment in shaping organizational members' beliefs, attitudes, and behaviors related to task design. Individuals, motivated to reduce uncertainty and assimilate to their "immediate environment" (p. 226), rely on existing schema based on previous experiences with and current understanding of the task at hand and integrate social information collected from peers into a general interpretation of the task. SIP depicts socially constructed realities that are mediated by "socially relevant others" (Shaw, 1980, p. 45). These referents serve to filter information and channel interpersonal influence about the expectations of the larger environment (Salancik & Pfeffer, 1978). Empirical studies have explored employees' perceptions of fairness at work/organizational justice (Lamertz, 2002), technological innovation (Rice & Aydin, 1991; Rice, Grant, Schmitz, & Torobin, 1990), and general work tasks (O'Reilly & Caldwell, 1985; Stanton & Julian, 2002). Organizationally relevant information is processed socially, and it is this focus on local socialization that situates SIP in the upper left quadrant of Table 14.1. SIP treats individual needs and attitudes as socially derived; workers make sense of jobs in response to norms and the expectations of immediate others (Salancik & Pfeffer, 1977).

*Critique and Agenda.* SIP has been met with contradictory results (Pollock, Whitbred, & Contractor, 2000; Rice et al., 1990), eliciting several methodological and theoretical critiques. Methodological constraints imposed by researchers may contribute to the mixed results found in SIP studies. Zalesny and Ford (1990) found a tendency to test SIP in laboratory experiments (although more recent applications test SIP in bona fide groups and organizations) involving manipulation of task design and social cues available to subjects (Thomas & Griffin, 1983), who are often college students in zero-history groups. Individual differences among subjects are

ignored, so the "reality of their own past" (Salancik & Pfeffer, 1978, p. 226) is neglected. Mixed results in SIP research may be the product of misappropriating the model's original intentions.

Critiques of the underspecified SIP model highlight its lack of theoretical explication of the precise influence processes involved in integrating social information into personal cognitive schema (Johanson, 2000). The incorporation of network-analytic tools (e.g., Meyer, 1994; Rice & Aydin, 1991) has helped identify relational influences in one's social landscape. Before elaborating on the network approach, diffusion of innovations is first explored—justifying the necessity for systemwide consideration and the importance of looking at not only individual-level relational dynamics but also the larger structural context of influence.

*Diffusion of Innovations and Influence*

Diffusion of innovations theoretically underpins actors' decisions to adopt an innovation—any idea or object perceived as new (Rogers, 1995)—by integrating complementary levels of individual, (sub)group, and systemic influence that clarify organizational change and reduce uncertainty (Burkhardt & Brass, 1990; Krassa, 1988). Diffusion is the "process by which an innovation is communicated through certain channels over time among the members of a social system" (Rogers, 1995, p. 5), ultimately tracing the momentum of adoption (acceptance) as the innovation spreads across a community of actors. Rogers's (1995) ultimate interest in systemic factors positions the theory in the lower left quadrant of Table 14.1.

Communication is the primary conduit for diffusion, intimating a route to adoption that relies more on social influence mechanisms than objective features of the innovation itself. Organizational scholars (Flanagin, 2000; Manross & Rice, 1986) predominantly focus on the diffusion of technological innovations in the workplace—often in health service contexts (Greenhalgh,

Robert, MacFarlane, Bate, & Kynakidou, 2004)—from inception to mass saturation and transcending levels of sociality by uncovering both relational and systemic influences on individual agency.

Rogers (1995) categorizes five classes of individuals who rely on relational and systemic cues to varying degrees and consequently adopt an innovation at various stages of the diffusion process. Initial stages of adoption reflect pure individual agency (innovators, early adopters), while adoption decisions thereafter are increasingly prone to the social influence of peers (early majority) and the collective at large (late majority, laggards). However, adoption does not imply that actors merely conform to their surroundings; they complement the subjective assessments of their peers with more objective deliberations of compatibility (Rice et al., 1990; Scott, Fuller, & Hardin, 2007) or relative advantage (Schwartz & Schwartz, 2007; Scott et al., 2007).

An innovation initially is adopted by a select group of individuals, or innovators, who tend to be venturesome, cosmopolite, financially stable, and technically savvy, and they have a high tolerance for uncertainty (Rogers, 1995). Although serving a gate-keeping function, innovators are often perceived as deviants and do not influence the trajectory of diffusion for the collective. A second wave of socially integrated and respected peers and early adopters influences adoption. Early adopters are opinion leaders, serving to ameliorate innovation-related uncertainties for nonadopters by offering advice or other "subjective evaluations" (Rogers, 1995, p. 18) through their local interpersonal networks. Romm and Pliskin (1999), for example, attribute the successful diffusion of e-mail across a university to a charismatic leader. The ability of early adopters to reduce uncertainty for others recursively reinforces their own power in the social system, distinguishing them as experts sought out by organizational peers (Burkhardt & Brass, 1990). The relational influence of opinion leaders heralds a third wave of adopters, the early majority, who

constitute approximately one third of the system. The early majority's decision to adopt an innovation narrowly *before* the average member is contingent on personal deliberation as well as subjective evaluations by respected peers. Remaining members of the system, the late majority and laggards, demand more reliable assurances of benefits relative to costs. Adoption decisions are delayed until both relational and systemic influences minimize potential threats and uncertainties. A sizable group of adopters (one third of the total population) make up the late majority. Due to inherent skepticism about innovation or minimal resources, this fourth wave adopts just *after* the average member. Succumbing to relational and increasing systemic pressures, late majority members concede to standards that come to characterize the social system. Studies (Manross & Rice, 1986; Romm & Pliskin, 1999) reveal that political bases of systemic influence can culminate in adverse (non)adoption behaviors, empowering discontented employees at the expense of the organizations' implementation goals of systemwide adoption. Widespread adoption occurs once saturation of the innovation convinces the final wave of adopters—the laggards—to approve it. The typical laggard is exceedingly skeptical of change or possesses limited resources. As a result, the eventual adoption decision of a laggard derives from systemic influence—a response to assurance by members across the collective rather than any one peer.

*Critique and Agenda.* Collective verification is at the heart of threshold models that depict adoption decisions submitting to systemic, normative influence (Valente, 1995). Individuals with low thresholds adopt early, offering increasing validation to more hesitant peers, while individuals with high thresholds adopt later after waiting for saturation in the network to reduce their innovation-related uncertainties. Individuals' thresholds, therefore, affect the entire collective's ability to reach critical mass

(Monge & Contractor, 2001). Threshold models have been critiqued because they assume equal influence across members, thus failing "to capture the full dynamic involved by ignoring the fact that individuals weigh the actions and opinions of others differently" (Krassa, 1988, p. 117). In addition, scholars observing divergent behaviors across groups suggest more localized influence in subsystems (Rice et al., 1990). Thus, critical mass may be reconceptualized as a quasi-systemic force delimited by divisions, work teams, or other collectives.

Systemic pressures may prescribe innovation adoption at the group (quasi-systemic) level or at the interorganizational (suprasystemic) level. Flanagin (2000) surveyed 200 top-level executives who reported both systemic influence (normative competition across the institutional landscape) and relational influence (comparative assessments across particular contenders) shaping their decisions to adopt organizational Web sites. Adoption decisions reveal the situatedness of human agency in social context. An innovation may be accepted, rejected, or reinvented to the extent that it is normatively appropriate to the group. Nevertheless, diffusion studies are criticized for assuming an innovation should diffuse without reinvention or rejection (Rogers, 1995). This pro-innovation bias can be overcome with the acknowledgment that innovations are reinvented or rejected to accommodate the values and needs of adopters and to ensure a proper fit between the social context and the innovation (Lewis & Seibold, 1996; Romm & Pliskin, 1999). Manross and Rice (1986) argue that "mutual adaptation" (p. 163) is ideal, whereby an innovation is reinvented and adapted to accommodate its users while the users themselves simultaneously adapt to the innovation.

### Network Theory and Influence

In mapping organizations, network scholars traverse from individual to group to systemic structures that influence constituents (e.g., revealing access to social information). Delineating the contextually situated interrelationships of a social system, network nodes represent social actors that are linked in unique ways, demarcated by patterns of communication or relations that define and are simultaneously defined by the larger structural context. This social map allows researchers to infer information about its members based on the access to resources (including other members) awarded by their position in the network. These structural properties and connections predict network influence—the convergence of perceptions among actors (Ibarra & Andrews, 1993)—and delineate such social dynamics as opinion change (Friedkin & Johnsen, 1999), polarization (Friedkin, 1999), or norm formation (Friedkin, 2001). A social system becomes an opportune site for empirical study when situational contexts, such as organizational change, elevate actors' levels of uncertainty and consequent sensemaking efforts (Burkhardt, 1994). Network-analytic tools seek to unearth, from the multiple strata of sociality, relevant others that influence network peers.

Because connectivity can be operationalized in numerous ways, scholars contrast the effects of different types of network associations—especially influence in formal work-prescribed interactions versus informal, emergent relationships (Ibarra & Andrews, 1993). The divergent contexts of these structures facilitate individual-level (Tushman & Romanelli, 1983) or group-level (Bienenstock, Bonacich, & Oliver, 1990) analyses that situate unique layers of influence within a social system (placing network-analytic approaches as descriptors of unintentional influence at both the individual and systemic levels; see Table 14.1). Two classes of relevant others—relationally and positionally relevant peers—influence the network environment. The *relational* approach (Bienenstock et al., 1990; Pollock et al., 2000) emphasizes cohesive associations that involve frequent communication as a source of direct influence, while the *positional* approach (Burt, 1987) posits indirect influence through the occupation of similar (and often competing) network positions or roles.

The primary underlying mechanism of relational influence is cohesion: "frequent and empathic communication" (Meyer, 1994, p. 1016) that serves to socialize and integrate members. Cohesion is amplified within densely knit subgroups ("cliques"), where concentrated communication and relational influence result in members' convergence to one another and the collective (Bienenstock et al., 1990). Close relational peers in the immediate social environment influence via communication.

Departing from a cohesion-based rationale for homogeneity, positional models identify attitudinal and behavioral uniformities across actors who share comparable social positions or roles (Burt, 1987). From this perspective, relevant others influence more distant peers situated in comparable social environments/ structures who must adapt to comparably localized contexts. A notable positional referent is the structurally equivalent (SE) actor, whose influence over "alters" stems from shared network connections or an identical type of social arrangement (Johanson, 2000). Burt (1987) illustrates how the positional similarity of SE physicians influenced perceptions of role-specific normative practice, resulting in behavioral convergence and medical innovation.

Empirical studies typically test relational and positional models against each other to unravel influence in cohesion or SE, and they propose an interdependent relationship between types of relevant others and types of influence outcomes. Johanson's (2000) delineation of health employees' advice-seeking networks reveals how structural equivalence best predicts job-related attitudes while organization-wide attitudes are shaped by cohesive peers. Rice and Aydin (1991) assessed employees' attitudes about new technology (related to worth, utility, ease of use, etc.) and found stronger effects of SIP as proximity changes from spatial to structural to relational. The idiosyncrasies

of organizational contexts constrain the generalizability of empirical findings, posing a challenge for network scholars (Ibarra & Andrews, 1993).

Actors also discriminate among similarly situated and relationally significant peers. Burkhardt (1994) unravels an underlying motivation for employees' reliance on cohesive or SE referents: High self-monitors, adjusting behavior in response to social cues, rely more on cohesive ties in forming personal attitudes about organizational change, while low self-monitors focus more on cues from SE others. The influence of relevant peers also may be moderated by formal status in the organizational hierarchy (Tushman & Romanelli, 1983), boundary-spanning roles that gain influence by interacting with relational partners that cross group or organizational boundaries, highly/strategically connected individuals identified by measures of relative centrality (access to resources; Ibarra & Andrews, 1993), and macro-level systemic conditions— namely, critical mass— that influence attitudinal and behavioral orientations to innovation (Rice et al., 1990). In sum, unique structural roles, personal dispositions, and the situational and relational context of our social environment all serve to orient individuals to relevant others in their midst and vary their susceptibilities to network influence.

## ◆ Conclusion

We framed this discussion of social influence in groups and organizations around two tensions—individual agency versus institutional determination and intentional versus unintentional effects. This has enabled us to more clearly illustrate some of the similarities and differences in these seven theoretical conceptions of social influence and to highlight major findings associated with each perspective.

The seven group and organizational theories of influence are contrasted in the corresponding quadrants of Table 14.1.

Because social influence is ubiquitous in social situations, the empirical applications of these theories also have been ubiquitous. Scholars' divergent yet complementary perspectives uncover numerous layers of influence: for example, a phenomenon that occurs simultaneously at the individual and systemic levels (illuminating goals of agency and structure) and yielding both intended and unintended results for members. Moreover, by limiting our discussion to these two tensions, we have been forced to bypass other factors that define these views of social influence. We recognize that all seven perspectives offer a view of communicative influence in groups that is more complex and far richer than we have been capable of illustrating here.

◆ **References**

Asch, S. E. (1951). Effects of group pressure upon the modification and distortion of judgments. In H. S. Guetzkow (Ed.), *Groups, leadership, and men: Research in human relations* (pp. 177–190). Pittsburgh, PA: Carnegie Press.

Barbuto, J. E., Jr., & Moss, J. A. (2006). Dispositional effects in intra-organizational influence tactics: A meta-analysis. *Journal of Leadership & Organizational Studies, 12,* 30–33.

Bienenstock, E. J., Bonacich, P., & Oliver, M. (1990). The effect of network density and homogeneity on attitude polarization. *Social Networks, 12,* 153–172.

Bonito, J. A. (2007). A local model of information sharing in small groups. *Communication Theory, 17,* 215–280.

Bormann, E. G. (1985). Symbolic convergence theory: A communication formulation based on *homo narrans. Journal of Communciation, 35*(4), 128–139.

Bormann, E. G. (1996). Symbolic convergence theory and communication in group decision making. In R. Y. Hirokawa & M. S. Poole (Eds.), *Communication and group decision making* (2nd ed., pp. 81–113). Thousand Oaks, CA: Sage.

Bormann, E. G., Cragan, J. F., & Shields, D. C. (1994). In defense of symbolic convergence theory: A look at the theory and its criticism after two decades. *Communication Monographs, 44,* 259–294.

Bormann, E. G., Pratt, J., & Putnam, L. (1978). Power, authority, and sex: Male response to female leadership. *Communication Monographs, 45,* 317–329.

Boster, F. J., & Cruz, M. G. (2002). Persuading in the small group context. In J. P. Dillard & M. Pfau (Eds.), *The persuasion handbook: Developments in theory and practice* (pp. 477–494). Thousand Oaks, CA: Sage.

Boster, F. J., Fryrear, J. E., Mongeau, P. A., & Hunter, J. E. (1982). An unequal speaking linear discrepancy model: Implications for the polarity shift. In M. Burgoon (Ed.), *Communication yearbook 6* (pp. 395–418). Beverly Hills, CA: Sage.

Bourdieu, P. (1977). *Outline of a theory of practice.* Cambridge, UK: Cambridge University Press.

Burkhardt, M. E. (1994). Social interaction effects following a technological change: A longitudinal investigation. *Academy of Management Journal, 37,* 869–898.

Burkhardt, M. E., & Brass, D. J. (1990). Changing patterns or patterns of change: The effects of a change in technology on social network structure and power. *Administrative Science Quarterly, 35,* 104–127.

Burt, R. S. (1987). Social contagion and innovation: Cohesion versus structural equivalence. *American Journal of Sociology, 92,* 1287–1335.

Canary, D. J., Brossmann, B. G., & Seibold, D. R. (1987). Argument structures in decision-making groups. *Southern Speech Communication Journal, 53,* 18–37.

Contractor, N. S., & Seibold, D. R. (1993). Theoretical frameworks for the study of structuring processes in group decision support systems: Comparison of adaptive structuration theory and self-organizing systems theory. *Human Communication Research, 19,* 528–563.

Corman, S. R., & Kuhn, T. (2005). The detectability of socio-egocentric group speech: A quasi-Turing test. *Communication Monographs, 72,* 117–143.

Cronin, M. A., & Weingart, L. R. (2007). Representational gaps, information processing, and conflict in functionally diverse groups. *Academy of Management Review, 32,* 761–773.

Cyert, R. M., & March, J. G. (1963). *A behavioral theory of the firm.* Englewood Cliffs, NJ: Prentice Hall.

de Certeau, M. (1984). *The practice of everyday life*. Berkeley: University of California Press.

Deutsch, M., & Gerard, H. G. (1955). A study of normative and informational social influence upon individual judgment. *Journal of Abnormal and Social Psychology, 51*, 629–636.

Festinger, L. (1954). A theory of social comparison processes. *Human Relations, 7*, 117–140.

Fisher, B. A., & Hawes, L. C. (1971). An interact system model: Generating a grounded theory of small groups. *Quarterly Journal of Speech, 57*, 444–453.

Flanagin, A. J. (2000). Social pressures on organizational Website adoption. *Human Communication Research, 26*, 618–646.

French, J. R. P., Jr. (1956). A formal theory of social power. *Psychological Review, 63*, 181–194.

French, J. R. P., Jr., & Raven, B. (1968). The bases of social power. In D. Cartwright & A. Zander (Eds.), *Group dynamics* (pp. 259–269). New York: Harper & Row.

Friedkin, N. E. (1999). Choice shift and polarization. *American Sociological Review, 64*, 856–875.

Friedkin, N. E. (2001). Norm formation in social influence networks. *Social Networks, 23*, 167–189.

Friedkin, N. E., & Johnsen, E. C. (1999). Social influence networks and opinion change. *Advances in Group Processes, 16*, 1–29.

Giddens, A. (1984). *The constitution of society: Outline of the theory of structuration*. Berkeley: University of California Press.

Gouran, D. S. (1990). Exploiting the predictive potential of structuration theory. In J. A. Anderson (Ed.), *Communication yearbook 13* (pp. 313–322). Newbury Park, CA: Sage.

Gouran, D. S. (1998). The signs of cognitive, affiliative, and egocentric constraints in patterns of interaction in decision-making and problem-solving groups and their potential outcomes. In J. S. Trent (Ed.), *Communication: Views from the helm for the 21st century* (pp. 98–102). Boston: Allyn & Bacon.

Gouran, D. S. (2007, August). *Potential cognitive and social influences on communication behavior implicit in rational models of collective choice*. Paper presented at the National Communication Association/ American Forensics Association Summer Conference on Argumentation, Alta, UT.

Gouran, D. S., & Hirokawa, R. Y. (1996). Functional theory and communication in decision-making and problem-solving groups: An expanded view. In R. Y. Hirokawa & M. S. Poole (Eds.), *Communication and group decision making* (2nd ed., pp. 55–80). Thousand Oaks, CA: Sage.

Gouran, D. S., Hirokawa, R. Y., & Martz, A. E. (1986). A critical analysis of factors related to decisional processes involved in the *Challenger* disaster. *Central States Speech Journal, 37*, 119–135.

Greenhalgh, T., Robert, G., MacFarlane, F., Bate, P., & Kynakidou, O. (2004). Diffusion of innovations in service organizations: Systematic review and recommendations. *Milbank Quarterly, 82*, 581–629.

Hewes, D. E. (1986). A socio-egocentric model of group decision-making. In R. Y. Hirokawa & M. S. Poole (Eds.), *Communication and group decision making* (pp. 265–312). Beverly Hills, CA: Sage.

Hewes, D. E. (1996). Small group communication may not influence decision making: An amplification of socio-egocentric theory. In R. Y. Hirokawa & M. S. Poole (Eds.), *Communication and group decision making* (2nd ed., pp. 179–212). Thousand Oaks, CA: Sage.

Higgins, C., Judge, T. A., & Ferris, G. R. (2003). Influence tactics and work outcomes: A meta-analysis. *Journal of Organizational Behavior, 24*(1), 89–106.

Hirokawa, R. Y. (1985). Discussion procedures and decision making performance: A test of a functional perspective. *Human Communication Research, 12*, 203–224.

Hirokawa, R. Y. (1988). Group communication and decision-making performance: A continued test of the functional perspective. *Human Communication Research, 18*, 487–515.

Hirokawa, R. Y. (1990). The role of communication in group decision-making efficacy: A task-contingency perspective. *Small Group Research, 21*, 190–204.

Hirokawa, R. Y., & Salazar, A. J. (1997). An integrated approach to communication and group decision making. In L. R. Frey & J. K. Barge (Eds.), *Managing group life: Communicating in decision-making groups* (pp. 156–181). Boston: Houghton-Mifflin.

Hoffman, L. R., & Kleinman, G. B. (1994). Individual and group in group problem solving: The valence model redressed. *Human Communication Research, 21,* 36–59.

Hollingshead, A. B., Wittenbaum, G. M., Paulus, P. B., Hirokawa, R. Y., Ancona, D. G., Peterson, R. S., et al. (2005). A look at groups from the functional perspective. In M. S. Poole & A. B. Hollingshead (Eds.), *Theories of small groups: Interdisciplinary perspectives* (pp. 21–62). Thousand Oaks, CA: Sage.

Hopkins, T. K. (1964). *The exercise of influence in groups.* Totowa, NJ: Bedminster Press.

Ibarra, H., & Andrews, S. B. (1993). Power, social influence, and sense making: Effects of network centrality and proximity on employee perceptions. *Administrative Science Quarterly, 38,* 277–304.

Jablin, F. M., & Sias, P. M. (2001). Communication competence. In F. M. Jablin & L. L. Putnam (Eds.), *The new handbook of organizational communication* (pp. 819–864). Thousand Oaks, CA: Sage.

Jackson, J. M. (1987). Social impact theory: A social forces model of influence. In B. Mullen & G. R. Goethals (Eds.), *Theories of group behavior* (pp. 111–124). New York: Springer-Verlag.

Jarboe, S. (1999). Group communication and creativity processes. In L. R. Frey, D. S. Gouran, & M. S. Poole (Eds.), *The handbook of group communication theory and research* (pp. 335–368). Thousand Oaks, CA: Sage.

Johanson, J. E. (2000). Intraorganizational influence: Theoretical clarification and empirical assessment of intraorganizational social influence. *Management Communication Quarterly, 13,* 393–425.

Katz, D., & Kahn, R. L. (1966). *The social psychology of organizations.* New York: John Wiley.

Krassa, M. A. (1988). Social groups, selective perception, and behavioral contagion in public opinion. *Social Networks, 10,* 109–136.

Lamertz, K. (2002). The social construction of fairness: Social influence and sense making in organizations. *Journal of Organizational Behavior, 23,* 19–37.

Latané, B. (1981). The psychology of social impact. *American Psychologist, 36,* 343–356.

Lemus, D. R., & Seibold, D. R. (2007, August). *Argument structures and decision outcomes in computer-mediated groups.* Paper presented at the National Communication Association/American Forensics Association Summer Conference on Argumentation, Alta, UT.

Lemus, D. R., Seibold, D. R., Flanagin, A. J., & Metzger, M. J. (2004). Argument in computer-mediated groups. *Journal of Communication, 54,* 302–320.

Lewis, L. K., & Seibold, D. R. (1996). Communication during intra-organizational innovation adoption: Predicting users' behavioral coping responses to innovations in organizations. *Communication Monographs, 63,* 131–157.

Manross, G. G., & Rice, R. E. (1986). Don't hang up: Organizational diffusion of the intelligent telephone. *Information & Management, 10,* 161–175.

Martin, R., & Hewstone, M. (2007). Social-influence processes of control and change: Conformity, obedience to authority, and innovation. In M. A. Hogg & J. Cooper (Eds.), *The SAGE handbook of social psychology* (pp. 312–333). Thousand Oaks, CA: Sage.

McPhee, R. D., Poole, M. S., & Seibold, D. R. (1982). The valence model unveiled: Critique and alternative formulation. In M. Burgoon (Ed.), *Communication yearbook 5* (pp. 259–278). New Brunswick, NJ: International Communication Association/Transaction Books.

Meyer, G. W. (1994). Social information processing and social networks: A test of social influence mechanisms. *Human Relations, 47,* 1013–1047.

Meyers, R. A. (1989). Testing persuasive arguments theory's predictor model: Alternative interactional accounts of group argument and influence. *Communication Monographs, 56,* 112–132.

Meyers, R. A., & Brashers, D. E. (1998). Argument and group decision-making: Explicating a process model and investigating the argument-outcome link. *Communication Monographs, 65,* 261–281.

Meyers, R. A., & Brashers, D. E. (1999). Influence processes in group interaction. In L. R. Frey, D. S. Gouran, & M. S. Poole (Eds.), *The handbook of group communication theory and research* (pp. 288–312). Thousand Oaks, CA: Sage.

Meyers, R. A., Brashers, D. E., & Hanner, J. (2000). Majority/minority influence: Identifying argumentative patterns and predicting argument-outcomes links. *Journal of Communication, 50,* 3–30.

Meyers, R. A., & Seibold, D. R. (1989). Assessing number of cognitive arguments as a predictor of group shifts: A test and alternative interactional explanation. In B. Gronbeck (Ed.), *Spheres of argument: Proceedings of the sixth SCA/AFA conference on argumentation* (pp. 576–583). Annandale, VA: Speech Communication Association.

Meyers, R. A., Seibold, D. R., & Brashers, D. (1991). Argument in initial group decision-making discussions: Refinement of a coding scheme and a descriptive quantitative analysis. *Western Journal of Speech Communication, 55,* 47–68.

Meyers, R. A., Seibold, D. R., & Shoham, M. (2007, July). *Communicative influence in groups: A review and critique of theoretical perspectives and models.* Paper presented at the Second Annual Conference of the Interdisciplinary Network for Group Research, East Lansing, MI.

Miner, J. B. (2005). *Organizational behavior 1: Essential theories of motivation and leadership.* Armonk, NY: M. E. Sharpe.

Monge, P. R., & Contractor, N. S. (2001). Emergence of communication networks. In F. M. Jablin & L. L. Putnam (Eds.), *The new handbook of organizational communication: Advances in theory, research, and methods* (pp. 137–160). Thousand Oaks, CA: Sage.

O'Reilly, C. A., & Caldwell, D. F. (1985). The impact of normative social influence and cohesiveness on task perceptions and attitudes: A social information processing approach. *Journal of Occupational Psychology, 58,* 193–206.

Orlitzky, M., & Hirokawa, R. Y. (2001). To err is human, to correct for it divine: A meta-analysis of research testing the functional theory of group decision-making effectiveness. *Small Group Research, 32,* 313–343.

Pavitt, C. (1993). Does communication matter in social influence during small group discussion? Five positions. *Communication Studies, 44,* 216–227.

Pollock, T. G., Whitbred, R. C., & Contractor, N. S. (2000). Social information processing and job characteristics: A simultaneous test of two theories with implications for job satisfaction. *Human Communication Research, 26,* 292–330.

Poole, M. S. (1999). Group communication theory. In L. R. Frey, D. S. Gouran, & M. S. Poole (Eds.), *The handbook of group communication theory and research* (pp. 37–70). Thousand Oaks, CA: Sage.

Poole, M. S., & Baldwin, C. L. (1996). Developmental processes in group decision making. In R. Y. Hirokawa & M. S. Poole (Eds.), *Communication and group decision making* (2nd ed., pp. 215–241). Thousand Oaks, CA: Sage.

Poole, M. S., Seibold, D. R., & McPhee, R. E. (1996). The structuration of group decisions. In R. Y. Hirokawa & M. S. Poole (Eds.), *Communication and group decision making* (2nd ed., pp. 114–146). Thousand Oaks, CA: Sage.

Porter, L. W., Angle, H. L., & Allen, R. W. (Eds.). (2003). *Organizational influence processes* (2nd ed.). Armonk, NY: M. E. Sharpe.

Price, V., Cappella, J. N., & Nir, L. (2002). Does disagreement contribute to more deliberative opinion? *Political Communication, 19,* 95–112.

Propp, K. M. (1997). Information utilization in small group decision making: A study of the evaluative interaction model. *Small Group Research, 28,* 424–453.

Propp, K. M., & Nelson, D. (1996). Problem-solving performance in naturalistic groups: The ecological validity of the functional perspective. *Communication Studies, 47,* 127–139.

Rice, R. E., & Aydin, C. (1991). Attitudes toward new organizational technology: Network proximity as a mechanism for social information processing. *Administrative Science Quarterly, 36,* 219–244.

Rice, R. E., Grant, A. E., Schmitz, J., & Torobin, J. (1990). Individual and network influences on the adoption and perceived outcomes of electronic messaging. *Social Networks, 10,* 27–55.

Rogers, E. M. (1995). *Diffusion of innovations* (4th ed.). New York: Free Press.

Romm, C., & Pliskin, N. (1999). The role of charismatic leadership in diffusion and implementation of e-mail. *Journal of Management Development, 18,* 273–286.

Sahlins, M. (1987). *Islands of history.* Chicago: University of Chicago Press.

Salancik, G. R., & Pfeffer, J. (1977). An examination of need-satisfaction models and job attitudes. *Administrative Science Quarterly, 22*, 427–456.

Salancik, G. R., & Pfeffer, J. (1978). A social information processing approach to job attitudes and task design. *Administrative Science Quarterly, 23*, 224–253.

Schein, E. H. (1984). Coming to a new awareness of organizational culture. *Sloan Management Review, 25*, 71–81.

Schwartz, A., & Schwartz, C. (2007). The role of latent beliefs and group cohesion in predicting group decision support systems success. *Small Group Research, 38*, 195–229.

Scott, C. L., Fuller, M. A., & Hardin, A. M. (2007). Diffusion of virtual innovation. *The DATABASE for Advances in Information Systems, 38*, 40–44.

Seibold, D. R., Cantrill, J. G., & Meyers, R. A. (1994). Communication and interpersonal influence. In M. L. Knapp & G. R. Miller (Eds.), *Handbook of interpersonal communication* (2nd ed., pp. 542–588). Newbury Park, CA: Sage.

Seibold, D. R., McPhee, R. D., Poole, M. S., Tanita, N. E., & Canary, D. J. (1981). Argument, group influence, and decision outcomes. In C. Ziegelmueller & J. Rhodes (Eds.), *Dimensions of argument: Proceedings of the second SCA/AFA summer conference on argumentation* (pp. 663–692). Annandale, VA: Speech Communication Association.

Seibold, D. R., & Meyers, R. A. (1986). Communication and influence in group decision-making. In R. Y. Hirokawa & M. S. Poole (Eds.), *Communication and group decision making* (pp. 133–155). Beverly Hills, CA: Sage.

Seibold, D. R., & Meyers, R. A. (2007). Group argument: A structuration perspective and research program. *Small Group Research, 38*, 312–336.

Shaw, J. B. (1980). An information-processing approach to the study of job design. *Academy of Management Review, 5*, 41–48.

Stanton, J. M., & Julian, A. L. (2002). The impact of electronic monitoring on quality and quantity of performance. *Computers in Human Behavior, 18*, 85–101.

Stasser, G., & Titus, W. (2003). Hidden profiles: A brief history. *Psychological Inquiry, 14*, 304–313.

Stohl, C., & Holmes, M. E. (1993). A functional perspective for bona fide groups. In S. A. Deetz (Ed.), *Communication yearbook 16* (pp. 601–614). Newbury Park, CA: Sage.

Stohl, C., & Redding, W. C. (1987). Messages and message exchange processes. In F. M. Jablin, L. L. Putnam, K. H. Roberts, & L. W. Porter (Eds.), *Handbook of organizational communication: An interdisciplinary perspective* (pp. 451–502). Newbury Park, CA: Sage.

Tajfel, H. (1974). Social identity and intergroup behavior. *Social Science Information, 13*, 65–93.

Thomas, J., & Griffin, R. (1983). The social information processing model of task design: A review of the literature. *Academy of Management Review, 8*, 672–682.

Tushman, M. L., & Romanelli, E. (1983). Uncertainty, social location and influence in decision making: A sociometric analysis. *Management Science, 29*, 12–23.

Valente, T. W. (1995). *Network models of the diffusion of innovations*. Cresskill, NJ: Hampton.

Van Maanen, J., & Schein, E. H. (1979). Toward a theory of organizational socialization. In B. M. Staw & L. L. Cummings (Eds.), *Research in organizational behavior* (Vol. 1, pp. 209–264). Greenwich, CT: JAI.

Waldeck, J. J., Shepard, C. A., Teitelbaum, J., Farrar, W. J., & Seibold, D. R. (2002). New directions for functional, symbolic convergence, structurational, and bona fide groups perspectives of group communication. In L. R. Frey (Ed.), *New directions in group communication* (pp. 3–23). Thousand Oaks, CA: Sage.

Waldron, V. (1999). Communication practices of followers, members, and protégés: The case of upward influence tactics. In M. Roloff (Ed.), *Communication yearbook 22* (pp. 251–299). Thousand Oaks, CA: Sage.

Weick, K. E. (1995). *Sensemaking in organizations*. Thousand Oaks, CA: Sage.

Zajonc, R. B. (1965). Social facilitation. *Science, 149*, 269–274.

Zalesny, M. D., & Ford, J. K. (1990). Extending the social information processing perspective: New links to attitudes, behaviors, and perceptions. *Organizational Behavior and Human Decision Processes, 47*, 205–246.

# 15

# MASS MEDIA EFFECTS

◆ Robin L. Nabi
and Mary Beth Oliver

T he study of mass media effects has a long and storied history that predates the existence of the communication discipline itself. Yet, its breadth and scope have made it challenging for the area to gain coherence. This chapter's goal is to review the historical roots of media effects research and the most popular theoretical perspectives that have emerged to date. After discussing the state of the literature, including the limitations or controversies within each tradition, we identify some potentially fruitful avenues for future theory development.

## ◆ Historical Roots

Although interest in the effects of mediated messages can arguably be traced to long before the 20th century, it was the advent of technologies allowing for mass production and distribution of messages, electronic media in particular, that stimulated more systematic interest in the production, content, and selection of such messages and, of course, the effects they have on the audiences that consume them (Schramm, 1997). This interest was generated from a range of academic disciplines, including journalism, sociology, political science, psychology, and advertising, that converged to form the foundation of current academic interest in the study of mass media. First, we discuss general schools of thought that have influenced the development of the modern-day study of media effects and then turn to particular scholars whose works raise conceptual ideas fundamental to the most widely examined media effects paradigms.

## INFLUENTIAL SCHOOLS OF THOUGHT

Four broad schools of thought have been frequently referenced in mass communication research (see Bryant & Miron, 2004). The Chicago school of sociology emphasized notions of pragmatism and humanism. The Vienna Circle focused on logical positivism and thus motivated the emphasis on logical reasoning and empirical evidence to validate theory. British cultural studies and the Frankfurt school's critical theory both focus on issues related to the role of cultural products (such as media messages) in creating and perpetuating social and political ideologies. They are distinguished in that critical theory emphasizes the conveyance of the dominant ideology, whereas cultural studies emphasizes negotiated meaning on the part of audiences. Although each of these four approaches has greatly influenced lines of media effects research, as we will soon see, the logical positivist approaches have become increasingly emphasized in more contemporary media effects research. Indeed, as we look at the more influential scholars' works in the 20th century, we see the roots of some of the most influential theories from the past several decades.

## INFLUENTIAL SCHOLARS

As Wilbur Schramm (1997) describes in his posthumously published memoir, there are a few notable scholars whose work may be viewed as foundational to the modern study of media effects. He begins with Harold Lasswell, a product of (and later contributor to) the Chicago school. By affiliation, Lasswell was a political scientist perhaps most famous for his summary of the communication process as "*who* says *what* to *whom* through *what channel* and with *what effect*" (Lasswell, 1948). His contributions might be summarized as helping to understand how to assess media content (e.g., via more thoughtful content analyses), propaganda (and more specifically the use and effects of symbols), and consideration of the role of mass communication in informing and socializing audiences and influencing society's response to that information.

Paul Lazarsfeld, a sociologist in the famed Columbia Bureau of Applied Social Research, engaged in extensive audience-centered research. His interests focused on audience attention and selectivity. That is, who listens to what messages, why they listen, and what they do with that information. In addition to his contributions in advancing social science research, he expanded media research to consider effects of radio, film, and TV in addition to print media and interpersonal communication. Thus, beyond looking at news and information, he opened the investigations into more entertainment-based media.

Kurt Lewin, the German social psychologist who spent much of his career at Iowa, is perhaps best known for his notion of "lifespace" or the complete psychological environment (including needs, goals, beliefs, memories, unconscious influences, etc.) in which people operate and, by extension, the influence of groups on individual behavior. His ideas that these forces invariably conflict laid the foundation for research relating to dissonance, frustration and aggression, and especially group dynamics.

In sharp contrast to Lewin's methodological approach, Carl Hovland, a psychologist central to the Yale School for Communication, focused on experimental work related to the persuasive effect of specific message and audience characteristics, including message argument, source credibility, personality traits, and fear arousal.

Thus, his work on propaganda is the foundation for the contemporary study of persuasion. As Schramm (1997) characterizes it, Hovland approached communication from a learning theory perspective with an ultimate interest in understanding not simply human cognition and attitudes but, more important, human behavior.

Surely there are other scholars we could point to as influential in the field, but what is interesting about the set that Schramm (and editors Chaffee and Rogers) highlighted is that although their names might not be directly attached to central theories of media effects, their ideas were clearly influential to those theories' development. The notions of learning, socialization, attention, selectivity, consistency, and group dynamics, in addition to the methods of content analysis, survey research, and experimental approaches, are central to the research to which we now turn.

◆ *Influential Theoretical Paradigms in the Study of Media Effects*

With the literally hundreds of theoretical perspectives applied to the study of media effects, it is a daunting task to identify those that are most influential. Fortunately, recent analyses of the extant literature aid us greatly in this task, and despite different sampling strategies, they arrive at very similar conclusions.

## CONTENT ANALYSES OF THE EXTANT LITERATURE

In their content analysis of 1,806 articles published in the three leading mass communication journals between 1956 and 2000 (*Journalism and Mass Communication Quarterly, Journal of Communication*, and *Journal of Broadcasting & Electronic Media*), Bryant and Miron (2004) document

that despite the fact that more than 600 theories, models, paradigms, and schools of thought were noted, only 26 were referenced 10 or more times, and only 5 were referenced more than 30 times. These 5 include uses and gratifications, agenda setting, cultivation, social learning, and Marxism. In their follow-up content analysis of every issue of six journals between January 2001 and May 2004, they found similar results, with framing, agenda setting, cultivation, mediation models, the third-person effect, uses and gratifications, selective exposure, and social cognitive/ learning theory as the top 8 "theories," each cited at least 10 times. Particularly noteworthy, across both content analyses, nearly half of all articles merely referenced theory (48% and 47%, respectively), and 26% simply used theory as the framework for empirical study. About 12% to 13% involved theoretical critique or comparison, and only the remaining 13% to 14% involved theory construction.

These results were largely echoed in Potter and Riddle's (2007) more recent content analysis of effects articles in 16 journals in the odd years between 1993 and 2005. In their sample, they identified 144 different theories referenced across the 336 articles. Similar to Bryant and Miron (2004), Potter and Riddle found that a substantial portion of the research—65%—failed to be guided by theory. Within the studies that mentioned theory, only 12 theories were mentioned in more than 5 articles, and of these, the most commonly cited were the third-person effect (cited in 7.4% of the articles), agenda setting (7.1%), and uses and gratifications (5.7%).

These studies paint a somewhat discouraging picture of the media effects research landscape—one that is at best as likely to mention any theory as not, one that uses theory as a framework only a quarter of the time, and one with little attention to theoretical development. Even for the most commonly studied theories, there is little systematic attention and critical examination.

Indeed, many of the "theories" that Bryant and Miron (2004) and Potter and Riddle (2007) identify may be better characterized as interesting phenomena, replicable relationships among variables, or models of effects rather than theories per se (see Pavitt, Chapter 3, this volume).

Because these studies suggest a set of paradigms arguably most worthy of our attention, our focus will be so directed, and in the interest of simplicity, we will refer to them as media effect theories throughout the chapter, with the above caveats in mind. Rather than simply discussing these theories, though, we will concentrate on the previously noted concepts that reflect critical components in the process of mediated communication and then match them to the most commonly referenced theories in the extant literature. Thus, we divide the literature into five categories, with prototypical theories offered for each: learning (social cognitive theory), socialization (cultivation analysis), selective exposure (uses and gratifications), selective presentation/perception (framing, agenda setting), and perceived effects (e.g., third-person effect). In discussing these theoretical approaches, we address the essence of each perspective's predicted effects, the mechanisms that explain the effects process, and limitations or controversies raised within each domain.

## LEARNING THEORIES

Learning theories refer to those processes by which media consumers acquire knowledge, information, and behaviors. Social learning theory (Bandura, 1977; later extended and renamed social cognitive theory) is perhaps the most widely known and cited in media research, although other examples include the knowledge gap hypothesis (Tichenor, Donohue, & Olien, 1970) and Piaget's (1921) stage theory of cognitive development, both of which made it onto Bryant and Miron's (2004) "top 26" theories list.

*Social Cognitive Theory.* Social cognitive theory (SCT) revolves primarily around the functions and processes of observational learning (Bandura, 1986, 2002). That is, by observing others' behaviors, including those of media figures, one may develop rules to guide one's own subsequent actions or be prompted to engage in previously learned behavior. According to Bandura (1986, 2002), observational learning is guided by four processes, which are moderated by observers' cognitive development and skills. First, *attention* to certain models and their behavior is affected by source and contextual features, such as attractiveness, relevance, functional need, and affective valence. Second, *retention* processes focus on the ability to symbolically represent the behavior observed and its consequences, along with any rehearsal of that sequence. *Production* focuses on translating the symbolic representations into action, reproducing the behavior in seemingly appropriate contexts, and correcting for any errors based on the feedback received. Finally, *motivational* processes influence which symbolically represented behaviors are enacted based on the nature or valence (positive or negative) of the reinforcement. As observational learning occurs via symbolic representations, the effects are potentially long lasting, and self-efficacy is believed to be central to behavioral performance.

SCT, as applied to media contexts (Bandura, 2002; Stiff, 1986), suggests that for viewers' behaviors to be positively affected, the audience must pay attention to attractive models who are displaying relevant behaviors. To the extent that positive behaviors are portrayed (e.g., practicing safe sex), the model's behavior should be positively reinforced (e.g., through displays of positive outcomes, such as greater interest by the sexual partner or enhanced self-respect). To the extent that negative behaviors are portrayed (e.g., practicing unsafe sex), the model's behavior should be negatively reinforced (e.g., through displays of negative outcomes or experiencing negative affect, such as guilt or regret).

*Limitations and Critique.* SCT has received extensive support in numerous interpersonal contexts and is frequently cited to explain the effects of both positive and negative media depictions. For example, SCT is invoked as the theoretical explanation for the success of entertainment-education, or the embedding of prosocial messages into entertainment programming to influence the attitudes and behaviors of resistant audiences (Singhal & Rogers, 1999). Conversely, studies of violence often reflect the assumption that the way in which violence is portrayed (e.g., with or without consequences, performed by heroes or villains) will influence viewers' acceptance of violence and the likelihood of using violence to solve problems in their own lives.

Despite the support for SCT, it has some notable limitations. First, it is rather complex, incorporating an array of concepts and variables. As a result, SCT is not easily tested. Indeed, although many scholars reference SCT in their media effects work, very few actually test it via manipulating attraction to behavioral models, positive and negative rewards, self-efficacy, and so on. Also, measuring some of the theory's key constructs is challenging. Thus, although it is intuitively appealing and social learning is well supported, SCT is frequently not tested directly. In fact, there is some reason to believe that it may not be as readily transferable to the media environment as is often assumed, as audiences' expectations about how events unfold in fictional realms versus in reality may differ (see Nabi & Clark, 2008). Thus, future research that attempts to model the process of media influence according to SCT and to determine appropriate concept operationalizations and measurement would be most welcome.

## SOCIALIZATION THEORIES

Socialization theories focus on the acquisition of the norms and values of one's social group. Along with parents, peers, and schools, the media are considered one of the foremost agents of socialization. Although critical/cultural theories arguably focus extensively on issues of socialization, the most popularly cited theory in this domain is cultivation analysis, which offers a more social scientific approach to the phenomenon.

*Cultivation Analysis.* Cultivation analysis, or cultivation theory as many now call it, asserts that common conceptions of reality are cultivated by overall patterns of TV programming to which communities are exposed regularly over long periods of time (Gerbner, 1969; Gerbner, Gross, Morgan, Signorielli, & Shanahan, 2002). Gerbner and his colleagues propose that compared with light TV viewers, heavy viewers are more likely to perceive the world in ways that mirror reality as presented on TV rather than more objective measures of social reality. Researchers have tested and found support for the cultivation hypothesis in a range of contexts, including racism, gender stereotypes, alienation, and so on (see Morgan & Shanahan, 1997). However, a substantial proportion of cultivation research has focused on TV violence and its effects on perceptions of real-world incidences of crime and victimization (see Potter, 1993, for a review). Numerous content analyses have documented that the number of violent acts on American network TV greatly exceeds the amount of real-world violence. In turn, heavy TV viewers (a) overestimate the incidence of serious crime in society (i.e., first-order effects, or prevalence estimates) and (b) are more likely to believe that the world is a mean place where people cannot be trusted and are just looking out for themselves (i.e., second-order effects, or attitudes; Gerbner et al., 2002; Gerbner, Gross, Morgan, & Signorielli, 1980).

Beyond these basic effects, moderators of the cultivation effect have been identified. Most notable among them is personal experience (Doob & Macdonald, 1979; Shrum & Bischak, 2001; J. B. Weaver & Wakshlag, 1986), which has been proposed to have two possible effects. *Resonance* suggests that cultivation effects may be amplified in situations where viewers have more real-world experience, whereas *mainstreaming* suggests that TV exposure might override differences in perspectives that might ordinarily result from personal experiences (e.g., Gerbner et al., 2002). In addition to personal experience, the cultivation literature has revealed several other moderators of the cultivation effect, including viewing motivations (e.g., Carveth & Alexander, 1985), attention level, need for cognition (Shrum, Burroughs, & Rindfleisch, 2005), elaboration styles (Shrum, 2001), and personality traits (Nabi & Riddle, 2008).

Although originally a more sociologically based theory, cultivation theorizing has taken a decidedly psychological turn in recent years. In particular, Shrum and his colleagues offer evidence that overestimates of crime prevalence are likely the result of heuristic processing, which allows TV-based constructs to enjoy higher accessibility in the minds of heavy viewers (e.g., Shrum, 1995, 2001). That is, because heavy viewers are recently and frequently exposed to certain common images and themes on TV, those themes become more accessible in memory and thus more influential in making judgments (e.g., violence prevalence estimates).

*Limitations and Critique.* Although cultivation theory has generated a wealth of data, and though meta-analyses suggest a small but consistent cultivation effect on social reality beliefs ($r = .09$; Morgan & Shanahan, 1997), this theory has also generated a great deal of debate within the academic community. Some of the criticisms include the assumption of uniformity in media portrayals, the assumed linear relationship between

TV viewing and beliefs, lack of clarity regarding the relationship between first- and second-order beliefs, potential problems with nonfalsifiability, difficulty in establishing causal relationships, and difficulty in accounting for selectivity in exposure and interpretation of media content (Doob & Macdonald, 1979; Hirsch, 1980, 1981; Potter, 1993). In addition, cultivation analysis, as originally conceptualized by Gerbner and his colleagues, has been criticized for not clearly specifying the theoretical mechanisms that would account for television's influence on attitudes and beliefs (e.g., Hawkins & Pingree, 1990).

Many of the prior criticisms of cultivation have been addressed or acknowledged in more current research. For example, authors now routinely employ multiple controls in their analyses, many studies test for the linearity of relationships, and a great deal of research now examines cultivation as a function of exposure to specific types of media content (rather than TV content generally). In addition, Shrum's (2002) heuristic processing model of cultivation effects has made great advances in explaining the mechanisms that may account for how media exposure can influence first-order beliefs.

With these advances in mind, cultivation researchers continue to struggle with some important theoretical issues. For example, although Shrum's (2002) model provides a parsimonious explanation for media's cultivation of first-order beliefs, it does not address how media may influence second-order beliefs. Recently, Shrum and colleagues have suggested that in contrast to first-order beliefs that may be conceptualized as memory-based judgments, second-order beliefs are cultivated "on line," or during viewing itself (Shrum, 2007; Shrum et al., 2005). Thus, high levels of involvement *while viewing* may predict greater influence on viewers' attitudes. This reasoning is similar to that of other scholars who suggest that greater immersion into media narratives should lead to greater persuasion (Green &

Brock, 2000; Slater & Rouner, 2002) and will undoubtedly be very useful as researchers begin to examine the influence of media content that *under*represents certain issues (e.g., poverty) or demographic groups (e.g., Asians, Latinos).

## SELECTIVE EXPOSURE/ATTENTION THEORIES

Building from Lazarsfeld's interest in the active audience, this set of theories take as its premise the idea that audiences choose to expose themselves to or attend to messages that consciously or unconsciously meet their various psycho-logical, social, and instrumental needs. Although some media theories may touch on issues of selectivity in exposure and attention in more or less obvious ways (e.g., mood management theory, Zillmann, 1988; limited capacity model, Lang, 2000), the prototypical theory in this general domain is uses and gratifications.

*Uses and Gratifications.* The uses and gratifications (U & G) paradigm is frequently referenced as a framework through which to understand media selection and use and has evolved to include five primary tenets. In sum, they suggest that individuals are aware of their social, psychological, and biological needs; evaluate various media channels and content; assess functional alternatives; and select the media or interpersonal channel that they believe will provide the gratifications they seek to meet their various needs (e.g., Katz, Blumler, & Gurevitch, 1974; Palmgreen, Wenner, & Rosengren, 1985; Rubin, 2002; Rubin & Rubin, 1985). Such needs include those related to diversion (e.g., escapism, arousal), personal relationships (e.g., social utility), personal identity (e.g., reality exploration), and surveillance (e.g., news gathering; McQuail, Blumler, & Brown, 1972; see review by Rubin, 2002). The U & G perspective is grounded in the conceptualization of

audience members as active, in control of their own media consumption, and able to provide accurate self-reports about the gratifications they seek and receive from the media.

In the 1980s, the evidence suggesting inconsistent associations between gratifications sought and gratifications obtained led to more serious efforts to conceptually flesh out the theory. Applying an expectancy value orientation, Palmgreen (1984) laid out what he called an integrative gratifications model that captured cultural, social, and psychological variables—the most critical of which is beliefs or expectations about media and nonmedia alternatives—all of which might affect gratifications sought, media choices, and resulting gratifications. Further, Levy and Windahl (1984) identified three time periods (before, during, and after message exposure) and three audience orientation dimensions (selectivity, involvement, and utility) to help explicate audiences' needs from, uses of, and gratifications received from mass media. These conceptual advances, however, arguably failed to take hold in that most subsequent research reverted to using U & G as a generic framework to describe why people use new media forms (e.g., the Internet; Papacharissi & Rubin, 2000) or why they choose to watch certain types of programming (e.g., reality TV; Nabi, Biely, Morgan, & Stitt, 2003).

*Limitations and Critique.* Although the U & G paradigm has enjoyed sustained scholarly interest, it is also one of the most heavily criticized as being in desperate need of theoretical elaboration, specificity, and clarity. Critiques assert that the theory is overly individualistic in focus, lacks coherent typologies of people's motives for media use, and needs greater clarity of its central concepts (e.g., Conway & Rubin, 1991; Finn, 1997; Ruggiero, 2000). Further, and particularly problematic given the vague predictions derived from the U & G perspective, it is difficult to falsify and thus assess support for the theory.

Perhaps one of the most fundamental criticisms of U & G approaches reflects one of the paradigm's most basic assumptions— that audiences are active consumers of their media selections. Although it is undoubtedly true that almost all behaviors reflect, at some basic level, individuals' needs and desires, it is unclear that this observation necessarily translates into evidence for the claim that media use is as active, autonomous, or goal driven as U & G supposes. Characterizations of some media use as reflecting addictive or compulsive behaviors and research pointing to the passivity and lack of cognitive effort involved in many media behaviors, such as TV viewing, capture this criticism well (Kubey & Csikszentmihalyi, 2002; LaRose, Lin, & Eastin, 2003; McIlwraith, 1998), as does U & G's own identification of ritualistic viewing motives (i.e., to pass the time, habit).

A related criticism of U & G research is its assumption that viewers are able and willing to articulate their motivations for media consumption. For media that may be considered personal or sensitive (e.g., pornography) or perhaps simply socially undesirable (e.g., some forms of reality TV), individuals might not be willing to disclose their use or motivations for use, especially in research settings. In addition, some scholars have questioned the assumption that individuals are necessarily aware of their viewing motivations (Zillmann, 1985, 1988; Zillmann & Bryant, 1985), and extensive research on preconscious processing (see Bargh & Morsella, 2008, and Wilson & Dunn, 2004) supports this challenge. Consequently, experimental procedures and behavioral measures may be more accurate and informative indicators of some media use motivations than the self-report methods typically employed by U & G researchers.

In sum, despite the popularity and heuristic value of the U & G paradigm, the descriptive nature of much of its related research, coupled with the host of criticisms launched against it, has made it a popular target of derision by media effects scholars. However, were future research to (a) identify more clearly the boundaries of U & G, (b) provide greater specificity in the linkages between particular psychological needs and message features, or (c) consider U & G as a broad orientation under which more specific theories might be generated, this approach might shed the current disdain in which it is held in the eyes of many and emerge as a more legitimate theoretical guide for media research.

## THEORIES OF SELECTIVE PRESENTATION/PERCEPTION

Beyond theories of selective exposure are those related to selective presentation/ perception. These theories suggest that as a result of exposure to particular message content, one would view the world differently and in ways that may not necessarily accurately reflect reality. Although this may sound similar to socialization theories, the difference is that the former effects are more likely to be short, rather than long term, and shift with changing patterns of media content. Here we discuss two theories that fit these parameters—framing and agenda setting— given they are often discussed in relation to one another in the literature.

*Framing and Agenda Setting.* The notion of framing posits that the way in which information is presented, or the perspective taken in the message, influences the responses individuals have to the issue at hand (see Benoit & Holbert, Chapter 25, this volume; McLeod, Kosicki, & McLeod, Chapter 11, this volume). As Entman (1993) argues, "[t]o frame is to select some aspects of a perceived reality and make them more salient in a communicating text in such a way as to promote a particular problem definition, causal interpretation, moral evaluation, and/or treatment recommendation" (p. 52). Based on this definition, then, a frame is a perspective infused into a message that promotes the salience of selected pieces of information over others. When adopted by receivers, frames may influence individuals' views of problems and their necessary solutions.

Framing research is widespread in academe, with roots in numerous disciplines, including psychology, sociology, economics, political science, linguistics, and, of course, communication. Indeed, framing has become an extremely popular topic of media effects research, taking either of two forms that meaningfully intersect: content studies of the frames used to present various topics and the effects of various presentations on audience impression formation and decision making (see Scheufele, 1999).

In comparison, agenda setting is more closely rooted in the discipline of communication and suggests that the weight ascribed to issues in the news media is transferred to audiences such that the audience will view as more important the issues that are covered more heavily (Benoit & Holbert, Chapter 25, this volume; McCombs, 2004; McCombs & Shaw, 1972; McLeod et al., Chapter 11, this volume). Thus, this research involves assessing the amount of an issue's coverage in the media and its association with how important the public believes that issue to be. As the theory has evolved, McCombs and his colleagues have argued for two levels of agenda setting. First-level agenda setting is captured by the initial agenda setting hypothesis—amount of coverage predicts perception of importance. Second-level agenda setting is argued to focus on attributes of issues such that emphasis on certain object attributes will lead people to weight those attributes more heavily, leading to their disproportionate influence on subsequent evaluations (e.g., Ghanem, 1997; McCombs, 2004; McCombs & Ghanem, 2001).

As to the processes through which these effects occur, it is generally argued that both are, to some extent, a consequence of information accessibility biases (Scheufele & Tewksbury, 2007). However, whereas agenda setting may be more a function of

mere exposure to an issue and thus not as dependent on attention to or processing of message content per se, framing effects are fundamentally a function of message content as they involve recall of applicable information made accessible via multiple exposures (see Cappella & Jamieson, 1997; Iyengar, 1991; Price & Tewksbury, 1996, for various related perspectives). As Scheufele and Tewksbury (2007) say, the difference between the two may be summarized as "*whether* we think about an issue and *how* we think about it" (p. 14).

*Controversies and Criticisms.* There is extensive evidence supporting both framing and agenda-setting effects (see Iyengar, 1991; Wanta & Ghanem, 2007). A main controversy, however, resides in how the two effects relate to one another. Agenda-setting scholars have argued, in light of the concept of second-level agenda setting, that framing is actually a subset of agenda setting. However, given the accessibility/applicability distinction noted above in terms of the cognitive processes by which each effect occurs, others suggest that they are, in fact, different phenomena. Indeed, given the broad and varied definitions of framing, it might be argued that framing is the superordinate concept (see Scheufele & Tewksbury, 2007; D. H. Weaver, 2007). Nevertheless, this debate, on its surface, is not particularly compelling in that the answer will not fundamentally change the way in which we view these effects. To the extent the debate generates close attention to the nature of these processes, however, it is worth continued discussion (see Benoit & Holbert, Chapter 25, this volume).

Ultimately, though, it is far more important that the study of framing in particular move beyond demonstrating the effect and toward greater precision in conceptualizing the notion of framing as it applies to media research, deeper consideration of the cognitive processes that underlie these effects, and, in turn, development of a true media effects framing theory. Despite the existence of framing-based theories in other disciplines (e.g., prospect theory, Kahneman & Tversky, 1984) and numerous calls to advance theory in the media domain (e.g., Scheufele, 1999), the field has seen very limited progress on this front. The same may be argued for agenda setting. However, were scholars to expend greater effort illuminating the processes of effects by focusing on, for example, potential moderators (such as the need for orientation for agenda setting and personal relevance for framing) and effect mechanisms (e.g., accessibility, emotional arousal), we would move more rapidly toward satisfying the urgent need for theoretical development in this domain (see Nabi, 2007).

## THEORIES OF PERCEIVED MEDIA INFLUENCE

Theories of perceived media influence focus not on how media actually influence viewers' attitudes, beliefs, or behaviors but rather on individuals' *perceptions* of such influence and how those perceptions, in turn, influence audience reactions (Gunther & Storey, 2003). There are a variety of presumed influence effects noted in the literature, such as hostile media perceptions (Gunther & Schmitt, 2004; Vallone, Ross, & Lepper, 1985), which suggest that individuals who are partisan on a given issue tend to perceive news coverage as biased and thus hostile (or at least unsympathetic) to their position (see also the persuasive press phenomenon; Gunther, 1998; Gunther & Chia, 2001). However, the most heavily researched media-based perceptual bias is the third-person effect.

*The Third-Person Effect.* The perceptual component of the third-person effect (TPE) refers to the general tendency for individuals to believe that others are more (negatively) influenced by the media than they are (Davidson, 1983). The TPE's behavioral component refers to the behavioral or attitudinal implications of differential perceptions on self versus others. For example, perceptions that others will be more heavily influenced by depictions of sex or violence on television might lead to greater support for content censorship. Meta-analyses confirm the robustness of TPEs (e.g., Sun, Pan, & Shen, 2008), and although the effect itself is well established, the bulk of research now focuses on identifying the best theoretical explanation for the effect.

Multiple explanations for TPEs have been offered, including self-enhancement, exposure to harmful messages, and self-categorization, among others. The self-enhancement hypothesis suggests that people are motivated to maintain or enhance positive self-images (e.g., Gunther & Mundy, 1993). Thus, if being influenced by a message (i.e., persuasive appeals, violent content) is seen as socially undesirable, audiences are expected to assume that others are more vulnerable to and thus more influenced by that message than they. Conversely, if message yielding might be viewed as positive (e.g., prosocial appeals for donations), audiences might expect that they would be more influenced than others (also called the first-person effect; for exemplar evidence, see Duck, Hogg, & Terry, 1999; Reid, Byrne, Brundidge, Shoham, & Marlow, 2007).

The media exposure explanation for TPEs suggests that individuals assume that others are more influenced by harmful media messages in part because they are more likely to be exposed to such messages. For example, McLeod, Detenber, and Eveland (2001) found that whereas individuals' estimates of the influence of violent or misogynistic music on the self depended on their assessment of their own level of "common sense," estimates for others were predicted by the extent to which they were thought to be exposed to such content. These authors interpreted their findings as indicating that people perceive media influence on others in "magic bullet" terms but have a more nuanced model of media influence for the self.

A third explanation for TPEs rests on the categorization of self and others in relation to the message's content. That is, when a message is perceived as *appropriate* or *valued* by the target group (for the self or for others), perceptions of media influence are heightened. So, if message content is seen as normative for the in-group, first-person effects are heightened, whereas if message content is seen as normative for the out-group, third-person effects are enhanced (e.g., Duck, Hogg, & Terry, 1995; Meirick, 2004; Reid & Hogg, 2005).

*Limitations and Future Directions.* Despite the extensive evidence supporting the TPE and the range of explanations offered, there is still much uncertainty regarding the theoretical mechanism that drives this effect. Perloff (2002) suggested that self-enhancement motivations have received the preponderance of support. Yet, the evidence is inconsistent (see Tal-Or & Tsfati, 2007, for supportive evidence, and Meirick, 2005, for a counterexample). Indeed, in their critical test of the three explanations noted above, Reid et al. (2007) found strong support for the self-categorization explanation, although self-enhancement could not be ruled out for many (but not all) of the findings.

Further, judgments of differential media influence on the self versus others in the enhancement of self-image can take many forms, including perceptions that others are less critical or literate media consumers, are simply more vulnerable or susceptible to media influence, or are more frequent consumers of media content that may cause harm, among others (for reviews, see Perloff, 1999, 2002). Moreover, although numerous scholars have speculated that individuals may possess "media effects schemas" that lead to differential perceptions of media influence, research that has attempted to directly assess such schemas has obtained limited support (Meirick, 2006; Price, Huang, & Tewksbury, 1997). Consequently, although numerous potential mechanisms have been identified, stronger evidence for their viability and a

parsimonious integration of these mechanisms into a clear theoretical framework are both needed.

# ◆ Avenues for Future Theory Development

The above discussion has exposed a healthy list of theoretical limitations, including fuzzy conceptualizations of boundaries (framing/agenda setting; social cognitive theory), underdeveloped explanatory mechanisms (uses and gratifications; third-person effect), and seemingly contradictory effects of moderators (cultivation). Despite the progress made in recent years, much work remains to move these cornerstone paradigms of mass media effects research onto surer conceptual ground.

Apart from developing already prominent theoretical frameworks, we would like to consider domains of mass communication that we think would particularly benefit from scholarly attention—all of which arguably connect to areas or fill in gaps identified by our mass media forebears. The three areas we choose to focus on here include (a) the nexus of interpersonal/group and mass communication, (b) issues of emotion and media, and (c) new media contexts.

## EXAMINING THE NEXUS OF INTERPERSONAL/GROUP AND MASS COMMUNICATION

*Impression Formation.* The idea that people form impressions of others based on others' media habits has great intuitive appeal. It is easy to imagine perceiving a self-proclaimed lover of poetry as insightful, a heavy viewer of horror films as a bit psychotic, and an avid consumer of teen comedies as somewhat juvenile. As individuals often "advertise" their media preferences to others through, for example, wall posters, T-shirts, and bumper stickers, the probability that media use will be employed in the process of impression formation is surely heightened (see Zillmann & Bhatia, 1989). Further, in some instances, such as online forums in which users create avatars and identities, media content may serve as the *only* source of information available about others. In light of these uses and functions of media in expressing identity via media choice, media customization, and media creation, the importance of media as a means of impression formation is arguably more salient now than at any point in history (Gill, Oberlander, & Austin, 2006; Gosling, Gaddis, & Vazire, 2007) and is fertile territory for future research.

*Interpersonal Discussion and Media.* Despite early attention to the intersection of media and interpersonal communication (e.g., two-step flow, Katz & Lazarsfeld, 1955, and Lewin's influence of groups), these issues have largely faded to the background of the media effects research landscape, although they have not disappeared completely (see Benoit & Holbert, Chapter 25, this volume). Research on parental mediation of children's TV viewing is a notable example of research that integrates interpersonal discussion and media use (Nathanson, 2001), yet there are numerous gaps in the literature. For example, we might ask this very basic question: How much does media content form the basis for interpersonal discussion between friends, children and parents, coworkers, or strangers? Building from this question, what role does discussion of media play in relationship development and maintenance? One might imagine that issues of impression management would be relevant here, but so too might issues of relational closeness and satisfaction. At a perceptual level, we might ask: How does interpersonal discussion, either during or after media exposure, possibly reframe media messages in the minds of viewers? What effects might group viewing contexts have on message processing, perceptions, and effects? How does group identity influence media selection and, in turn, shape or reinforce group norms? There are an abundance of questions about how media and media content influence interpersonal and group discussion and relationships that present exciting opportunities for research in the upcoming years, and future media scholarship will certainly benefit from greater integration of interpersonal and mass communication theories.

## THE ROLE OF EMOTION IN MEDIA EFFECTS RESEARCH

In general, there appears to be a strong bias toward cognitively based processes and effects such that emotion-based issues are minimized in the context of the dominant media effects paradigms. This is not to suggest that no domains of media research focus on emotion. Indeed, several prominent lines of research emphasize the importance of affect-based constructs, such as emotion and persuasion research (e.g., Hovland, Janis, & Kelley, 1953; Nabi, 2002), fright reactions and children (e.g., Cantor, 2002), mood management (Zillmann, 1988), and limited capacity models of media processing that focus on valence and arousal (Lang, 2000). However, when compared with the extensive literature in which cognition is highlighted, this area of research appears rather anemic. Research in which the role of emotion is considered more fully as either the source or outcome of media exposure as well as the theoretical mechanism that might explain various media effects (e.g., TPEs, SCT) would be most welcome. This would involve looking at a range of affects beyond fear, the structure or content of media messages and emotional response, and the interplay between emotion and cognition in various media contexts (see Planalp, Metts, & Tracy, Chapter 21, this volume).

## NEW MEDIA CONTEXTS

Today's media outlets are characterized by a dizzying array of choices—hundreds of cable channels and on-demand programming are readily available and commonplace, and users now have access to a limitless diversity of content on the Internet. Further, and perhaps more important, newer media technologies now afford individuals the opportunity to customize, personalize, and create media content such as blogs, Facebook pages, YouTube video diaries, and portals (e.g., Kalyanaraman & Sundar, 2006). This media environment not only opens up virtually limitless research opportunities in terms of issues related to what individuals choose to include in their media diets but also raises the question of whether the media effects theories that have been developed in a very different era of message distribution still apply and, if so, how predictions might change in these newer contexts. We have little doubt that the issues we raised above in terms of impression management, interpersonal and group dynamics, and emotional response will be as important, if not more so, in this new era of media effects research.

## ◆ Conclusions

In this chapter, we hoped to offer some historical context to the study of media effects and to highlight the domains and theories that have received the greatest attention in the extant literature. At this point, though, we might ask: Why these theories? Of the hundreds that have purportedly been advanced over the past 60 years, why have these risen to the fore? There is no one explanation, and although we cannot assert the following with absolute certainty, it seems likely that the following three explanations may play some role. First, these theories tend to be widely applicable, and in important contexts. Second, they are often intuitively appealing and easy to understand, test, and apply, although interestingly, when they get more complicated, simpler approaches tend to once again emerge (e.g., U & G, social cognitive

theory, framing). Third, in some cases, we are virtually guaranteed to find effects and thus produce potentially publishable work.

We do not judge whether or not these reasons are appropriate, but we note that the pattern of relying on the same paradigms with minimal theoretical growth will likely continue without some change in circumstance. As we reflect on why media effects theorizing has been somewhat stunted, we might consider that one of the strongest motivations for studying the media, that is, its great practical appeal, may also serve as our greatest stumbling block in that once effects are demonstrated, the lure of issues of application becomes stronger than those related to illumination of process (see Berger, Roloff, & Roskos-Ewoldsen, Chapter 1, this volume). Perhaps the new media environment might serve as a catalyst to encourage media effects scholars to reassess our theoretical explorations, and we hope chapters such as this might help to encourage scholars to continue to build on the key lessons from our forebears that have guided theoretical developments to this point, most notably, the integration of interdisciplinary thinking with practical experience to shed light on issues of social significance.

## ◆ References

Bandura, A. (1977). *Social learning theory*. Englewood Cliffs, NJ: Prentice Hall.

Bandura, A. (1986). *Social foundations of thought and action: A social cognitive theory*. Englewood Cliffs, NJ: Prentice Hall.

Bandura, A. (2002). Social cognitive theory of mass communication. In J. Bryant & D. Zillmann (Eds.), *Media effects: Advances in theory and research* (pp. 43–67). Mahwah, NJ: Lawrence Erlbaum.

Bargh, J. A., & Morsella, E. (2008). The unconscious mind. *Perspectives on Psychological Science, 3*, 73–79.

Bryant, J., & Miron, D. (2004). Theory and research in mass communication. *Journal of Communication*, 662–704.

Cantor, J. (2002). Fright reactions to mass media. In J. Bryant & D. Zillmann (Eds.), *Media effects: Advances in theory and research* (2nd ed., pp. 287–306). Mahwah, NJ: Lawrence Erlbaum.

Cappella, J. N., & Jamieson, K. H. (1997). *Spiral of cynicism: The press and the public good.* New York: Oxford University Press.

Carveth, R., & Alexander, A. (1985). Soap opera viewing motivations and the cultivation process. *Journal of Broadcasting & Electronic Media, 29,* 259–273.

Conway, J. C., & Rubin, A. M. (1991). Psychological predictors of television viewing motivation. *Communication Research, 18,* 443–464.

Davidson, W. P. (1983). The third-person effect in communication. *Public Opinion Quarterly, 47,* 1–15.

Doob, A. N., & Macdonald, G. E. (1979). Television viewing and fear of victimization: Is the relationship causal? *Journal of Personality and Social Psychology, 37,* 170–179.

Duck, J. M., Hogg, M. A., & Terry, D. J. (1995). Me, us and them: Political identification and the 3rd-person effect in the 1993 Australian federal election. *European Journal of Social Psychology, 25,* 195–215.

Duck, J. M., Hogg, M. A., & Terry, D. J. (1999). Social identity and perceptions of media persuasion: Are we always less influenced than others. *European Journal of Social Psychology, 29,* 1879–1899.

Entman, R. M. (1993). Framing: Toward clarification of a fractured paradigm. *Journal of Communication, 43*(4), 51–58.

Finn, S. (1997). Origins of media exposure: Linking personality traits to TV, radio, print, and film use. *Communication Research, 24,* 507–529.

Gerbner, G. (1969). Toward "cultural indicators": The analysis of mass mediated message systems. *AV Communication Review, 17,* 137–148.

Gerbner, G., Gross, L., Morgan, M., & Signorielli, N. (1980). The "mainstreaming" of America: Violence profile No. 11. *Journal of Communication, 30,* 10–29.

Gerbner, G., Gross, L., Morgan, M., Signorielli, N., & Shanahan, J. (2002). Growing up with television: Cultivation processes. In J. Bryant & D. Zillmann (Eds.), *Media effects: Advances in theory and research* (pp. 43–67). Mahwah, NJ: Lawrence Erlbaum.

Ghanem, S. (1997). Filling in the tapestry: The second level of agenda setting. In M. McCombs, D. L. Shaw, & D. Weaver (Eds.), *Communication and democracy: Exploring the intellectual frontier in agenda-setting theory* (pp. 3–14). Mahwah, NJ: Lawrence Erlbaum.

Gill, A. J., Oberlander, J., & Austin, E. (2006). Rating e-mail personality at zero acquaintance. *Personality and Individual Differences, 40,* 497–507.

Gosling, S. D., Gaddis, S., & Vazire, S. (2007, March). *Personality impressions based on facebook profiles.* Paper presented at the International Conference on Weblogs and Social Media, Boulder, CO.

Green, M. C., & Brock, T. C. (2000). The role of transportation in the persuasiveness of public narratives. *Journal of Personality and Social Psychology, 79,* 701–721.

Gunther, A. C. (1998). The persuasive press inference: Effects of mass media on perceived public opinion. *Communication Research, 25,* 486–504.

Gunther, A. C., & Chia, S. C. Y. (2001). Predicting pluralistic ignorance: The hostile media perception and its consequences. *Journalism & Mass Communication Quarterly, 78,* 688–701.

Gunther, A. C., & Mundy, P. (1993). Biased optimism and the third person effect. *Journalism Quarterly, 70,* 58–67.

Gunther, A. C., & Schmitt, K. (2004). Mapping boundaries of the hostile media effect. *Journal of Communication, 54,* 55–70.

Gunther, A. C., & Storey, J. D. (2003). The influence of presumed influence. *Journal of Communication, 53,* 199–215.

Hawkins, R. P., & Pingree, S. (1990). Divergent psychological processes in constructing social reality from mass media content. In N. Signorielli & M. Morgan (Eds.), *Cultivation analysis: New directions in media effects research* (pp. 35–50). Newbury Park, CA: Sage.

Hirsch, P. (1980). The "scary world" of the non viewer and other anomalies: A reanalysis of Gerbner et al.'s findings on cultivation analysis, Part I. *Communication Research, 7,* 403–456.

Hirsch, P. (1981). On not learning from one's own mistakes: A reanalysis of Gerbner et al.'s findings on cultivation analysis. *Communication Research, 8,* 3–37.

Hovland, C. I., Janis, I. L., & Kelley, H. H. (1953). *Communication and persuasion.* New Haven, CT: Yale University Press.

Iyengar, S. (1991). *Is anyone responsible? How television frames political issues.* Chicago: University of Chicago Press.

Kahneman, D., & Tverksy, A. (1984). Choices, values, and frames. *American Psychologist, 28,* 107–128.

Kalyanaraman, S., & Sundar, S. S. (2006). The psychological appeal of personalized content in Web portals: Does customization affect attitudes and behavior? *Journal of Communication, 56,* 110–132.

Katz, E., Blumler, J. G., & Gurevitch, M. (1974). Utilization of mass communication by the individual. In J. G. Blumler & E. Katz (Eds.), *The uses of mass communications: Current perspectives on gratifications research* (pp. 19–32). Beverly Hills, CA: Sage.

Katz, E., & Lazarsfeld, P. (1955). *Personal influence.* New York: Free Press.

Kubey, R., & Csikszentmihalyi, M. (2002). Television addiction is no mere metaphor. *Scientific American, 286,* 74–78.

Lang, A. (2000). The limited capacity model of mediated message processing. *Journal of Communication, 50,* 46–70.

LaRose, R., Lin, C. A., & Eastin, M. S. (2003). Unregulated Internet usage: Addiction, habit, or deficient self-regulation? *Media Psychology, 5,* 225–253.

Lasswell, H. D. (1948). The structure and function of communication in society. In L. Bryson (Ed.), *The communication of ideas: A series of addresses* (pp. 37–51). New York: Harper.

Levy, M. R., & Windahl, S. (1984). Audience activity and gratifications: A conceptual clarification and exploration. *Communication Research, 11,* 51–78.

McCombs, M. E. (2004). *Setting the agenda: The mass media and public opinion.* Malden, MA: Blackwell.

McCombs, M., & Ghanem, S. I. (2001). The convergence of agenda setting and framing. In R. D. Reese, O. H. Gandy, & A. E. Grant (Eds.), *Framing public life: Perspectives on media and our understanding of the social world* (pp. 67–81). Mahwah, NJ: Lawrence Erlbaum.

McCombs, M. E., & Shaw, D. L. (1972). The agenda-setting function of mass media. *Public Opinion Quarterly, 36,* 176–187.

McIlwraith, R. D. (1998). "I'm addicted to television": The personality, imagination, and TV watching patterns of self-identified TV addicts. *Journal of Broadcasting & Electronic Media, 42,* 371–386.

McLeod, D. M., Detenber, B. H., & Eveland, W. P. (2001). Behind the third-person effect: Differentiating perceptual processes for self and other. *Journal of Communication, 51,* 678–695.

McQuail, D., Blumler, J. G., & Brown, J. R. (1972). The television audience: A revised perspective. In D. McQuail (Ed.), *Sociology of mass communication* (pp. 135–165). Middlesex, England: Penguin.

Meirick, P. C. (2004). Topic-relevant reference groups and dimensions of distance: Political advertising and first- and third-person effects. *Communication Research, 31,* 234–255.

Meirick, P. C. (2005). Self-enhancement motivation as a third variable in the relationship between first- and third-person effects. *International Journal of Public Opinion Research, 17,* 473–483.

Meirick, P. C. (2006). Media schemas, perceived effects, and person perceptions. *Journalism & Mass Communication Quarterly, 83,* 632–649.

Morgan, M., & Shanahan, J. (1997). Two decades of cultivation research: An appraisal and meta-analysis. In B. R. Burleson (Ed.), *Communication yearbook* (Vol. 20, pp. 1–45). Thousand Oaks, CA: Sage.

Nabi, R. L. (2002). Discrete emotions and persuasion. In J. Dillard & M. Pfau (Eds.), *Handbook of persuasion* (pp. 289–308). Thousand Oaks, CA: Sage.

Nabi, R. L. (2007). Emotion and persuasion: A social cognitive perspective. In D. R. Roskos-Ewoldsen & J. Monahan (Eds.), *Social cognition and communication: Theories and methods* (pp. 377–398). Mahwah, NJ: Lawrence Erlbaum.

Nabi, R. L., Biely, E. N., Morgan, S. J., & Stitt, C. (2003). Reality-based television programming and the psychology of its appeal. *Media Psychology, 5,* 303–330.

Nabi, R. L., & Clark, S. (2008). Testing the limits of social cognitive theory: Why negatively-reinforced behaviors may be modeled anyway. *Journal of Communication, 58,* 407–427.

Nabi, R. L., & Riddle, K. (2008). Personality traits as moderators of the cultivation effect. *Journal of Broadcasting & Electronic Media, 52,* 327–348.

Nathanson, A. I. (2001). Mediation of children's television viewing: Working toward conceptual clarity and common understanding. In W. B. Gudykunst (Ed.), *Communication yearbook 25* (pp. 115–151). Mahwah, NJ: Lawrence Erlbaum.

Palmgreen, P. (1984).Uses and gratifications: A theoretical perspective. In R. N. Bostrom (Ed.), *Communication yearbook 8* (pp. 20–55). Beverly Hills, CA: Sage.

Palmgreen, P., Wenner, L. A., & Rosengren, K. E. (1985). Uses and gratifications research: The past ten years. In K. E. Rosengren, L. A. Wenner, & P. Palmgreen (Eds.), *Media gratifications research: Current perspectives* (pp. 11–37). Beverly Hills, CA: Sage.

Papacharissi, Z., & Rubin, A. (2000). Predictors of Internet use. *Journal of Broadcasting & Electronic Media, 44,* 175–196.

Perloff, R. M. (1999). The third-person effect: A critical review and synthesis. *Media Psychology, 1,* 353–378.

Perloff, R. M. (2002). The third-person effect. In J. Bryant & D. Zillmann (Eds.), *Media effects: Advances in theory and research* (2nd ed., pp. 489–506). Mahwah, NJ: Lawrence Erlbaum.

Piaget, J. (1921). Essai sur quelques aspects du developpment de la notion de partie chez l'enfant [Essays on some aspects of the development of the notion of part in infants]. *Journal de Psychologie, 18,* 449–480.

Potter, W. J. (1993). Cultivation theory and research: A conceptual critique. *Human Communication Research, 4,* 564–601.

Potter, W. J., & Riddle, K. (2007). A content analysis of the media effects literature. *Journalism & Mass Communication Quarterly, 84,* 90–104.

Price, V., Huang, L. N., & Tewksbury, D. (1997). Third-person effects of news coverage: Orientations toward media. *Journalism & Mass Communication Quarterly, 74,* 525–540.

Price, V., & Tewksbury, D. (1996). News values and public opinion: A theoretical account of media priming and framing. In G. Barnett & F. Boster (Eds.), *Progress in communication sciences* (pp. 173–212). New York: Ablex.

Reid, S. A., Byrne, S., Brundidge, J. S., Shoham, M. D., & Marlow, M. L. (2007). A critical test of self-enhancement, exposure, and self-categorization explanations for first- and third person perceptions. *Human Communication Research, 33,* 143–162.

Reid, S. A., & Hogg, M. A. (2005). A self-categorization explanation for the third-person effect. *Human Communication Research, 31,* 129–161.

Rubin, A. M. (2002). The uses-and-gratifications perspective of media effects. In J. Bryant & D. Zillmann (Eds.), *Media effects: Advances in theory and research* (pp. 525–548). Hillsdale, NJ: Lawrence Erlbaum.

Rubin, A. M., & Rubin, R. B. (1985). Interface of personal and mediated communication: A research agenda. *Critical Studies in Mass Communication, 2,* 36–53.

Ruggiero, T. (2000). Uses and gratifications theory in the 21st century. *Mass Communication & Society, 3,* 3–37.

Scheufele, D. A. (1999). Framing as a theory of media effects. *Journal of Communication, 49,* 103–122.

Scheufele, D. A., & Tewksbury, D. (2007). Framing, agenda setting, and priming: The evolution of three media effects models. *Journal of Communication, 57,* 9–20.

Schramm, W. (1997). *The beginnings of communication study in America.* Thousand Oaks, CA: Sage.

Shrum, L. J. (1995). Assessing the social influence of television. *Communication Research, 22,* 402–429.

Shrum, L. J. (2001). Processing strategy moderates the cultivation effect. *Human Communication Research, 27,* 94–120.

Shrum, L. J. (2002). Media consumption and perceptions of social reality: Effects and underlying processes. In J. Bryant & D. Zillmann (Eds.), *Media effects: Advances in theory and research* (2nd ed., pp. 69–95). Mahwah, NJ: Lawrence Erlbaum.

Shrum, L. J. (2007). Social cognition and cultivation. In D. Roskos-Ewoldsen & J. Monahan (Eds.), *Communication and social cognition* (2nd ed., pp. 245–272). Mahwah, NJ: Lawrence Erlbaum.

Shrum, L. J., & Bischak, V. D. (2001). Mainstreaming, resonance, and impersonal impact: Testing moderators of the cultivation effect for estimates of crime risk. *Human Communication Research, 27,* 187–215.

Shrum, L. J., Burroughs, J. E., & Rindfleisch, A. (2005). Television's cultivation of material values. *Journal of Consumer Research, 32,* 473–479.

Singhal, A., & Rogers, E. M. (1999). *Entertainment-education: A communication strategy for social change.* Mahwah, NJ: Lawrence Erlbaum.

Slater, M. D., & Rouner, D. (2002). Entertainment-education and elaboration likelihood: Understanding the processing of narrative persuasion. *Communication Theory, 12,* 173–191.

Stiff, J. B. (1986). *Persuasive communication.* New York: Guilford.

Sun, Y., Pan, Z., & Shen, L. (2008). Understanding the third-person perception: Evidence from a meta-analysis. *Journal of Communication, 58,* 280–300.

Tal-Or, N., & Tsfati, Y. (2007). On the substitutability of the third-person perception. *Media Psychology, 10,* 231–249.

Tichenor, P. J., Donohue, G. A., & Olien, C. N. (1970). Mass media flow and differential growth in knowledge. *Public Opinion Quarterly, 34,* 159–170.

Vallone, R. P., Ross, L., & Lepper, M. R. (1985). The hostile media phenomenon: Biased perception and perceptions of media bias in coverage of the Beirut massacre. *Journal of Personality and Social Psychology, 49,* 577–585.

Wanta, W., & Ghanem, S. (2007). Effects of agenda setting: Mass media effects research: Advances through meta-analysis. In R. W. Preiss, B. M. Gayle, N. Burrell, M. Allen, & J. Bryant (Eds.), *Mass media effects research: Advances through meta-analysis* (pp. 37–51). Mahwah, NJ: Lawrence Erlbaum.

Weaver, D. H. (2007). Thoughts on agenda setting, framing, and priming. *Journal of Communication, 57,* 142–147.

Weaver, J. B., & Wakshlag, J. (1986). Perceived vulnerability to crime, criminal victimization experience, and television viewing. *Journal of Broadcasting & Electronic Media, 30,* 141–158.

Wilson, T. D., & Dunn, E. W. (2004). Self-knowledge: Its limits, value and potential for improvement. *Annual Review of Psychology, 55,* 493–518.

Zillmann, D. (1985). The experimental exploration of gratifications from media entertainment. In K. E. Rosengren, L. A. Wenner, & P. Palmgreen (Eds.), *Media gratifications research: Current perspectives* (pp. 225–239). Beverly Hills, CA: Sage.

Zillmann, D. (1988). Mood management through communication choices. *American Behavioral Scientist, 31,* 327–340.

Zillmann, D., & Bhatia, A. (1989). Effects of associating with musical genres on heterosexual attraction. *Communication Research, 16,* 263–288.

Zillmann, D., & Bryant, J. (1985). Selective exposure phenomena. In D. Zillmann & J. Bryant (Eds.), *Selective exposure to communication* (pp. 1–10). Hillsdale, NJ: Lawrence Erlbaum.

# 16

# INTERPERSONAL CONFLICT

♦ Alan L. Sillars

**B**owers (1974) once spoke of several initiatives by members of the (then) Speech Communication Association to encourage the interests of young scholars in a neglected area—the role of communication in conflict. The encouragement may have worked—conflict is now one of the most studied communication phenomena.

Early commentaries expressed dissatisfaction with an objectivist bias in conflict literature, at that time referring to game-theoretic research (Rubin, 1978; Simons, 1974). Rubin (1978) called for research into symbolic processes of labeling, categorizing, and abstracting experience, or what he called "para conflict" (conflict as conceived). Ironically, much of the conversation about communication since then has followed the lead of researchers in management/organizational psychology, who conceptualize communication as a trait (or "style"), and others in clinical psychology, who regard it as objective behavior (or "behavioral exchange"). These metaphors seem appropriate in the context of personality psychology and behavioral family therapy, respectively, but they are not very helpful for talking about *meaning*. This is a serious limitation for those whose primary interest lies with communication itself. It is an especially serious limitation with respect to communication in conflict, where meaning is apt to be contested perhaps more so than in any domain of communication study.

To be sure, there is a great deal of interesting research on subjective processes in interpersonal conflict (see Roloff & Miller, 2006), but this work tends to be juxtaposed with a view of communication as the behavioral component of conflict, thus reproducing an old duality. A theoretical challenge for those approaching conflict from a communication perspective is to integrate the things people say and do in conflict with the sensemaking activities that place these things in context. The emerging theory of conflict frames is a promising development in this respect.

This chapter reviews an extensive literature, highlighting fundamental properties of communication in conflict, ways of conceptualizing communicative acts and outcomes, and framing processes. This review follows a number of other summaries, including an entire handbook on conflict communication with several chapters on interpersonal conflict (Oetzel & Ting-Toomey, 2006). With so many definitive research summaries to turn to, the main objectives here are to provide commentary on how we conceptualize core communication processes and to suggest a potentially integrative perspective.

## ◆ Fundamental Properties

### WHAT IS FUNDAMENTAL ABOUT CONFLICT?

Although there are many ways of defining conflict (Canary, Cupach, & Messman, 1995), definitions offered within communication tend to say essentially the same thing—that conflict is a struggle between two or more interdependent parties, who have or perceive incompatible goals (see Putnam, 2006). It is rare to see consensus among scholars when defining anything about communication, so it may be of interest to ask why this one is so appealing. Unpacking the above definition reveals a few widely held assumptions.

*Interdependence and the Inevitability of Conflict.* First, definitions of conflict highlight the idea that conflict is an inherent possibility in human relationships to the extent that people are interdependent in achieving objectives. Given that conflict is a function of interdependence, it follows that the potential for conflict should be greatest in the most interdependent relationships, such as intimate couples and families. Studies confirm that this is where people typically experience the most frequent and intense conflicts, at least within U.S. samples (Sillars, Canary, & Tafoya, 2004). The significance of conflict in close relationships has not been lost on marital interaction researchers, who have focused on conflict perhaps more than any topic (Bradbury, Rogge, & Lawrence, 2001).

Interdependence relates to the claim that conflict is normal/continuous, not aberrant/episodic (Hawes & Smith, 1973). That is, all interdependent relationships are assumed to experience conflict, especially where there are pressures for change. A corollary to the inevitability of conflict is the belief that the occurrence of conflict is neither good nor bad; rather, the response to conflict is what counts (Deutsch, 1973). Quite obviously, such a perspective foregrounds the significance of communication.

*Conflict Goals and Levels of Conflict.* The reference to goal incompatibility, both actual and perceived, suggests that conflict is not strictly about objective circumstances so much as subjective definitions and desires. This assumption is quite clear, for example, in the applied dispute resolution literature. The essential idea behind *integrative negotiation* and *interest-based bargaining* is that apparent incompatibilities often mask integrative solutions that could be revealed through joint problem solving (e.g., Pruitt & Lewis, 1977; Ury, Brett, & Goldberg, 1988). Even when there are structural causes of conflict (e.g., competition over scarce resources), there may be solutions that respect the interests of each side and prove acceptable to all parties. Thus, apparent incompatibilities reflect the manner in which people frame conflict.

The discussion of goals implies something else quite basic—that there are different levels to conflict, reflecting different types of goals. Most often, authors distinguish *instrumental, relational,* and *identity* goals, which refer respectively to concern over a specific problem, the nature of the relationship, and self-presentation or "face" (Canary & Lakey, 2006). Sometimes, a fourth type of goal, *process,* is also distinguished, reflecting concern over the way conflict is handled.[1]

There is obvious overlap between the treatment of goals in the conflict literature and the analytic separation of multiple levels of meaning throughout the interpersonal communication literature. This refers to the distinction between *content* versus *relationship* levels of meaning (Watzlawick, Beavin, & Jackson, 1967) and analogous concepts (see Sillars & Vangelisti, 2006), which reference the propositional meaning of a message versus the pragmatic meaning and context that serve as implicit communication about the relationship. Just as Watzlawick et al. (1967) suggest that there is relational meaning in all messages, conflict authors assume there is a relational/identity dimension to all conflicts.

## WHAT IS FUNDAMENTAL ABOUT COMMUNICATION IN CONFLICT?

The standard definition of conflict seems a suitable starting point for investigating communication, as long as *perceived goal incompatibility* is regarded in a very flexible way; that is, people are not fully aware of their goals, goals emerge and change during interaction, and retrospective accounts of goals may be entirely different than prospective goals (Caughlin & Vangelisti, 2006; Hawes & Smith, 1973). In addition, the usual definition is only vaguely instructive about critical features of communication during conflict. I will suggest two such features—goal complexity and ambiguity/selectivity.

*Goal Complexity.* Since people have multiple goals, conflict may be about several things simultaneously. Thus, one key characteristic of human conflict is that the issues are potentially diffuse. Although a certain primary goal may dominate talk about conflict, unarticulated secondary goals (typically, relational and identity) also shape interaction (Hample, 2005; Roloff & Miller, 2006) and may in some sense be said to represent the "real issues" driving conflict, as opposed to those that are mostly symptomatic. A common observation, for example, is that people act out relational disputes through concrete, "picky" issues (Roloff & Johnson, 2002). Furthermore, abstract relational and identity issues (e.g., core issues of power, trust, equity, affection) are said to spawn or inflame recurring conflicts over concrete peripheral issues since the latter are easier to isolate and discuss (Sillars & Weisberg, 1987). The implication here is that there are multiple issues in conflicts, including ones that are not explicitly on the table.

A further aspect of goal complexity is goal (in)compatibility. Conflict situations often invoke multiple, incompatible goals, such as a desire to criticize but also to contain conflict and appear reasonable (Caughlin & Scott, 2009). The most skillful communicators may construct integrated messages that reconcile multiple goals (Hample, 2005; Jacobs, 2002); however, this is especially challenging in the stressful and cognitively demanding environment of ongoing argument. Thus, conflicts may be characterized by incoherent and paradoxical lines of action, such as "hit-and-run" conflict (Sillars & Wilmot, 1994), "hostile avoidance" (Roberts, 2000), and various forms of demand-withdraw (Caughlin & Scott, 2009). Because of the diffuse and contradictory nature of communicative goals, relational conflicts often violate conventional maxims governing orderly conversation (Sillars & Weisberg, 1987). This is seen, for example, in escalating arguments where speakers produce a string of topic shifts and countercomplaints (Gottman, 1979) that disrupt the other's arguments and assert alternative definitions of conflict (Sillars & Weisberg, 1987).

*Ambiguity and Selectivity.* Another distinctive feature of communication during conflict is the extent to which coordination of perspectives and meaning can become problematic. I am not speaking merely about direct disagreement over issues (or perceived goal incompatibility) but, more fundamentally, different conceptions about what is going on in the situation—whether conflict exists, what the conflict "is," what one's actions signify, and so forth. Conflict presumes differences in perspective, which seem to increase in depth and scope as conflicts intensify. Some of this can be explained by social cognitive biases (see Roloff & Miller, 2006), but inherent complexities of communication contribute to the environment in which such biases operate.

Participation in interpersonal communication presents a demanding cognitive environment: one that requires drastic selection of relevant cues from an extremely complex stimulus field and an unquestioning stance toward most inferences, simply to maintain the pace of interaction (Kellermann, 1992). Conflict interactions, especially those that are contentious and angry, are further compounded by (a) high stress, which narrows attention and reduces the complexity of thought, and (b) persuasive and defensive goals, which focus cognitive efforts on construction and rehearsal of personal arguments and direct attention to memories and interpretations that assist these efforts (Sillars & Wilmot, 1994; Sillars, Roberts, Leonard, & Dun, 2000). The consequences are illustrated by a study of couple conflict using video-assisted recall (Sillars et al., 2000). Analysis of moment-to-moment thoughts revealed that spouses were typically thinking about quite different things at any time in the interactions, made little spontaneous attempt to take the partner's perspective, and showed little hesitation or

uncertainty when making strong inferences about the partner's intentions and actions.

Selectivity and subjective certainty play upon the ambiguity of conflict and communication. Since the members of any system are interdependent (each affects the other), blame is ambiguous, except in extreme cases (Watzlawick et al., 1967). Yet, even in well-adjusted marriages, spouses may talk about conflicts in one-sided terms—each emphasizing his or her own hurt feelings, blaming the partner, and describing the partner's behavior as irrational (Schutz, 1999).

These molar attributions for conflict have a counterpart in attributions about communication. A simple illustration comes from a study in which executives from a federal agency were asked to recall a conflict and describe how it was handled (Thomas & Pondy, 1977). Predictably, individuals attributed the most cooperative conflict modes to self while attributing competition to the other party. Individuals also selected descriptive phrases for their own communication that suggested reasonableness (e.g., *pointed out, advised, suggested*) and used language to characterize the other's communication that implied arbitrariness (e.g., *demanded, refused, ordered*). Sillars et al. (2000) found much the same thing in the way spouses spontaneously "coded" one another's communication during video-assisted recall; that is, spouses attributed constructive speech acts to self more than the partner and attributed confrontational acts almost exclusively to the partner.

There are a number of similar illustrations of biased processing of communication, particularly in unhappy relationships (see Roloff & Miller, 2006; Sillars et al., 2004). Biased processing of communication is sustained partly through the inherent ambiguity of messages (see Jacobs, 2002; Sillars & Vangelisti, 2006), especially at the level of abstraction that conflict researchers are most concerned with—for example, whether a statement represents "criticism," "withdrawal," "validation," or even "cooperation" versus "competition." The same utterance (e.g., a critical comment about a coworker's report) can be taken in a number of ways (e.g., one-upmanship, an insult, helpful feedback), depending on the assumed intent (Thomas & Pondy, 1977). Much the same has been said about all communication—any speech act can be expressed in an indeterminate number of ways, and to resolve this ambiguity, one must infer the speaker's intent based on noncoded, contextual information (Jacobs, 2002). However, given the face-threatening nature of communication in conflict, there is increased potential for individuals to define speaker intent on uneven terms.

We next consider how the conflict literature characterizes communicative acts and their consequences (outcomes). While these things are essential to the overall picture, I do not consider the fact that a person, dyad, or system engages in "cooperative" or "competitive" communication to be a complete explanation for what happens subsequently. One implication of the discussion of goal complexity and ambiguity is that message effects are mediated by disputant sensemaking, such that ostensibly cooperative or competitive communication does not always have the impact one might assume.

## ◆ Describing Communication During Conflict

### STYLES, STRATEGIES, AND TACTICS

The communicative moves that people make during conflict episodes are most often conceptualized according to a *five-styles model* or according to typologies of speech acts, sometimes called *strategies/ tactics* (see Canary et al., 1995; Nicotera & Dorsey, 2006). The distinction between styles and strategies should not be taken too literally since authors often mix these terms and others. Furthermore, there is nothing

especially strategic about the usual list of "strategies" (e.g., cooperative, competitive, avoidant); that is, they do not represent coherent plans of action so much as clusters of functionally similar acts. Nonetheless, there are some basic differences between the two general approaches. Much of the research based on the five-styles model is concerned with broad individual styles comparable to traits. Styles are assessed according to self-report measures that emphasize communicative intentions at a relatively high level of abstraction (e.g., "I am nearly always concerned with satisfying all our wishes," Thomas & Kilmann, 1974; "I use my influence to get my ideas accepted," Rahim, 1983). By contrast, other typologies provide a more descriptive breakdown of communicative acts absent the presumption of enduring styles.

The *styles* approach is especially prominent in literature on workplace conflict, based originally on the two-dimensional model proposed by Blake and Mouton (1964) (*concern for people* vs. *concern for production*). The dimensions were reconceptualized by Thomas and Kilmann (1974) as *attempting to satisfy own concerns* (or assertiveness) versus *attempting to satisfy other's concerns* (or cooperativeness) and the styles (or "modes") as *competition, collaboration, compromise, avoiding*, and *accommodation*. Other two-dimensional style models are, at first glance, virtually identical (e.g., Hall, 1969; Rahim, 1983). In a later commentary, however, Thomas (1988) noted that researchers had used the models as if they were only taxonomies, without considering the assumptions that go with them. In most models, the dimensions represent stable value orientations that causally affect styles in the manner of independent to dependent variables (Thomas, 1988). Thus, such models foreground stable individual differences in conflict orientations. In contrast, Thomas considers the extent and nature of individual differences to be an open, empirical question; therefore, he substitutes the term *mode* for *style* and prefers to think of the modes as a taxonomy of intentions (to compete, etc.) without making any supposition about their origin.

The above comments anticipate the primary criticism of conflict styles—the research assumes a simplified trait model that neglects relational and situational variables (Knapp, Putnam, & Davis, 1988). From a systems perspective, conflict patterns are emergent properties of relationships, not a straightforward manifestation of pre-dispositions (Knapp et al., 1988; Sillars & Wilmot, 1994). Some authors address this point by reconceptualizing conflict style as a property of dyads or groups. Kuhn and Poole (2000) analyzed videotaped meetings of organizational teams and found that most had a characteristic style of conflict that was stable over several meetings, presumably reflecting the development of group norms. Similarly, Raush, Barry, Hertel, and Swain (1974) observed that most young couples had a mutual style—for example, a conjoint style of avoidance or shared tendency to engage in conflict through escalation and defense. These styles were generally stable across laboratory observations averaging 2 years apart.

It is also possible to conceptualize individual differences in a way that distinguishes orientations toward conflict from modes of enactment, thus allowing for a more complex relationship between the two. A good example is Hample's (1999) work on Taking Conflict Personally (TCP). TCP is an individual's predisposition to frame conflicts in personal terms and thereby to see conflicts as "potentially punishing, humiliating, stressful, and hurtful" (Hample, 1999, p. 177). However, TCP can play out differently depending on events within interactions. Although TCP predicts pre-conflict expectations, observed arguing seems to have less relation to trait TCP than to emergent properties of interaction, such as the aggressiveness of the partner and state TCP (Hample, 1999).

Other taxonomies are concerned less with enduring styles and more with speech acts performed during conflict (e.g., Gottman, 1979; Sillars & Wilmot, 1994; Weiss, 1993). These typologies identify relatively specific actions (although a conversational analyst would not think so) that fold into more abstract categories (e.g., *criticism* and *negative mind reading* nest under the broader category of *blame* in Weiss, 1993; *acceptance of responsibility* and *concessions* nest under *conciliatory remarks* in Sillars & Wilmot, 1994; see Canary et al., 1995). It is especially common to collapse across three macro-categories—for example, *cooperative* (or *integrative*), *competitive* (or *distributive*), and *avoidance* (see Nicotera & Dorsey, 2006)—but others find these categories to be too heterogeneous (Nicotera & Dorsey, 2006; Roloff & Ifert, 2000). Some find it useful to separate avoidance into hostile and friendly forms (Roberts, 2000). Canary (Canary & Lakey, 2006; Sillars et al., 2004) devised a table along these lines that organizes more than 100 categories from several conflict coding schemes into four categories, paralleling van de Vliert and Euwema's (1994) distinction between *negotiation, direct fighting, nonconfrontation,* and *indirect fighting.*

## CONFLICT PATTERNS

People do not make a simple choice between one type of message and another in conflict but instead create combinations of messages as they interact over time. Mostly what has been studied in this regard is the sequential (act-to-act) structure of conflict within individual episodes—how one action elicits a characteristic response. The dominant tendency is to respond in kind; for example, when one person speaks in an evasive or confrontative fashion, the odds of the next speaker doing likewise increase (Sillars & Wilmot, 1994). When the response is highly predictable, the interaction may assume a "static" quality characterized by recurring petty arguments or escalating denial (Raush et al., 1974).

This pattern is reflected, for example, in the high rate of negative reciprocity characteristic of distressed couples (Caughlin & Vangelisti, 2006). In effect, unhappy couples may initially contain conflict if an interaction begins on polite terms, but once there is a felt provocation, these couples tend to construct extended chains of negative and competitive messages, such that negativity becomes an "absorbing state" (Gottman, 1994). In contrast, systems characterized by greater variety may control escalation while maintaining engagement, for example, by counterbalancing small provocations with questions and jokes or returning to an issue following an interlude of avoidance (Sillars & Wilmot, 1994).

A common asymmetrical pattern is called the "demand-withdraw" pattern, whereby one person raises an issue and the other person avoids it. Most studies show that demand-withdraw is related to dissatisfaction and other negative outcomes in marriage and parent-adolescent relationships (see Caughlin & Scott, 2009). Consistent with stereotypes, women are more often seen as demanding (or "nagging") in marriage and men as withdrawing (or "stonewalling"); however, this pattern sometimes reverses, especially when it is the man who wants change. Caughlin and Scott (2009) argue that demand-withdraw patterns reflect conflicting goals during communication (e.g., wanting to end discussion while appearing reasonable and avoiding an angry response) and that there are different types of demand-withdraw (e.g., complaints followed by denial vs. leading questions followed by perfunctory answers) that result from particular goal configurations.

Most research on conflict patterns does not look beyond individual episodes, but the work on "serial arguments" is an interesting exception. Roloff and Johnson (2002) note that many everyday disputes end without resolution—people leave the scene, refuse to discuss an issue further, or simply stop arguing. Thus, the same issue may become the basis for recurring arguments. Many serial arguments consist of dispersed clusters of episodes, with several occurring within a short time frame but with clusters dispersed over longer periods (Trapp & Hoff, 1985). Trapp and Hoff (1985) identified a recurring pattern of "flare-up" and "cool down," whereby individuals become more verbally aggressive within episodes, until they disengage to cool off. After a break, the partners then reengage the argument. Serial arguments may be kept alive and episodes linked through "mulling" (mentally replaying the conflict; Cloven & Roloff, 1991) and "imagined interactions" (Honeycutt & Ford, 2001), whereby people covertly rehearse dialogue, thus priming themselves for future conflict episodes.

## WHAT DO CONFLICT CODES REPRESENT?

Whereas the term *strategy* carries too much cognitive baggage for the kinds of acts and patterns discussed here, the common phrase *communication behavior* is misleading in an opposite sense. Even when applied to direct observation of conflict, the categories used to code communication do not reference "behavior" in the sense of a constant set of linguistic or nonverbal cues. Rather, conflict codes are standardized inferences about communication from the perspective of (relatively) neutral observers. Inevitably, the observer/coder must go beyond explicit information and formal coding rules to infer the presumed intent of a remark based on implicit cultural and contextual knowledge. Although this exercise can be useful in providing an "objective" (standardized, observer-defined) perspective on communication, it is misleading to regard the standardized, outsider meanings as "actual behavior" and insider meanings as "perception" since each reflects different biases. Whereas the participants' perspective is biased by direct involvement in interaction, observers lack access to implicit context and relational history that informs the meaning of an utterance or gesture from the perspective of disputants.

# ◆ Conflict Outcomes

Recurring negative conflict can be debilitating to people and relationships—it erodes satisfaction and commitment in relationships, undermines workgroup cohesion and performance, contributes to anxiety and depression, and weakens immune systems (see Miller, Roloff, & Malis, 2007). While the negative effects of conflict are well documented, we often hear that conflict can be functional; for example, it can prevent stagnation, stimulate interest, air and solve problems, contribute to identity, and allow change (Deutsch, 1973). The two sides to conflict are reflected in the classic distinction between productive versus destructive conflict (Deutsch, 1973), which suggests that it is not conflict per se but the type of conflict that determines whether outcomes are good or bad. Much of the research on interpersonal conflict can be characterized as an effort to isolate those aspects of communication that represent productive versus destructive conflict, based on associations with good-bad outcomes.

Conflict research has gradually (but not entirely) moved away from what we might call a simple, direct effects (or main effects) model of communication to one that is more contingent, stressing moderator variables and the like. A simple direct-effects model would be reflected in a question such as the following: "How does conflict avoidance impact marital satisfaction (or task performance, etc.)?" There may be no way to respond to the question intelligibly since the answer can depend on who the people are, what they are dealing with, the history behind the precipitating event, and so forth.

It is not difficult to intuit where simple direct-effects reasoning leads; that is, direct and cooperative communication should predict positive outcomes over competitive/ hostile communication or conflict avoidance. This reasoning is not wrong so much as incomplete. As we might expect, research mostly supports the value of direct/ cooperative communication over the alternatives (Caughlin & Vangelisti, 2006; Kuhn & Poole, 2000). By itself, however, this observation does not yield a very complex understanding of the way communication works.

The most extensive research examining outcomes of communication is in the area of intimate and family conflict. Caughlin and Vangelisti (2006) and Sillars et al. (2004) organize this literature under the dimensions of avoidance-engagement (or directness) and valence (or cooperativeness/competitiveness). With respect to avoidance-engagement, studies of self-reported communication mostly indicate that conflict avoidance is associated with relationship dissatisfaction (Caughlin & Vangelisti, 2006). This finding should come as no surprise since the typical North American and Western sample idealizes directness in communication. Other research suggests, however, that avoidance has a different meaning and impact in the context of mutual positive regard and as a preferred pattern of relating versus avoidance that reflects hostility, resistance, or fear. At one extreme, avoidance may represent a coerced response to anticipated hostility, as in the case of the "chilling effect," where relational grievances and negative information are withheld because the other person is seen as having aggressive potential, either symbolic/verbal or physical (Afifi & Olson, 2005; Cloven & Roloff, 1993). On the other hand, certain subgroups of satisfied couples, such as highly autonomous spouses ("separate" couples) and some long-married couples, seem to minimize and avoid conflict by choice (Sillars et al., 2004).

Raush et al. (1974) noted that spouses who avoided confrontation in their research often colluded by supporting one another's denial and externalization of conflict. This collusion seemed to provide for stable and compatible relationships, provided it occurred in a context of mutual affection and clearly differentiated roles, as opposed to a context in which avoidance masked latent hostility that was communicated in paradoxical ways (e.g., overtly denying the need to discuss a problem while implying fault in the other). Similarly, Roberts (2000) found that a husband's angry withdrawal was associated with a wife's dissatisfaction, but other conflict avoidance by the husband was not.

Avoidance is sometimes a response to problems that are not considered important enough to bother with; at other times, it can be a way to cordon off issues that are effectively irresolvable or too costly to confront (Roloff & Ifert, 2000). Roloff and Ifert (2000) suggest several conditions under which avoidance might reduce unproductive argument while mitigating the potential harms of not talking about a problem. For example, "successful" avoidance might require mutual tolerance, alternative coping mechanisms, and an empathic ability to intuit the other's dissatisfactions and adapt without direct discussion.

Message valence or competitiveness has been operationalized in terms of verbally competitive acts and nonverbal affect (Caughlin & Vangelisti, 2006). This research is somewhat more straightforward than that on directness. Abundant evidence indicates that negative and competitive communication predicts relational dissatisfaction (both concurrently and longitudinally) and instability. Both verbal and nonverbal codes predict satisfaction, but nonverbal communication tends to be the stronger predictor (Fincham, 2004). Negative communication has been a more consistent predictor of satisfaction and stability than positivity, although there is evidence of the latter's importance as well (Caughlin & Vangelisti, 2006).

The general association between negativity and relational outcomes is clear enough. One of the questions that continues to drive research is whether specific aspects of negativity are more important predictors of relational outcomes than others (Caughlin & Vangelisti, 2006; Gottman, 1994). However, this question assumes that the same key predictors will emerge across different studies. Thus far, that has not been the case. For example, Gottman, Coan, Carrere, and Swanson (1998) replicated some elements of Gottman's (1994) "Four Horsemen of the Apocalypse"—the observation that specific negative acts (*complaint/ criticism, defensiveness, contempt*, and *stonewalling*) contribute to a process cascade that portends declining satisfaction and eventual marital breakup. However, Gottman et al. based their analysis on a revised set of "horsemen" (*defensiveness, contempt*, and *belligerence*), and milder forms of negativity also predicted divorce in this study (among wives). Negative reciprocity, which has been one of the most robust predictors of marital outcomes, was not related to either satisfaction or marital stability in Gottman et al. (1998).

Thus, it is clear that *some* manifestations of negativity/positivity are likely to predict relational outcomes in a given study; however, it is not yet apparent that certain ways of being negative or competitive have unique effects that are consistent across independent samples. Of course, intense, frequent, and prolonged negativity—deep sadness and contempt that lie close to the surface or bitter arguments that flare up inevitably with the slightest provocation— can be expected to have worse outcomes than milder and more occasional negativity balanced by positive forms of interaction (Gottman, 1994).

Aside from chronic negativity, the impacts of negative and competitive communication are likely modified by relational and cultural context. For example, Gottman (1994) describes some couples ("volatiles") who fight bitterly without undermining the marriage, reflecting the dramatic and passionate demeanor they bring to the relationship generally. Furthermore, several cultural replications indicate that observed negativity has a weaker connection to marital dissatisfaction among cultural groups who express negative emotions more freely (Orbuch & Veroff, 2002; Sillars et al., 2004,

p. 435). Presumably, these findings reflect the fact that negativity does not mean the same thing to people with different norms for confrontation and emotional expression.

## ◆ Conflict Frames

The notion that messages have simple, direct effects is captured by the "archer-target" metaphor, suggesting that archers shoot arrows (send messages) that impact targets (Bowers, 1974). One of the subtler challenges for those who study communication and conflict is to explain how people come to understand this exchange when the "arrows" are indirect or tacit. For example, Bowers (1974) notes that threats are rarely spoken, yet people often react as if they were explicit. Furthermore, nearly any gesture or utterance could be understood as a threat when certain conditions are met (i.e., the target believes that the other has both the ability and the will to impose sanctions). Rubin (1978) expands on the complexity of the archer-target relationship by noting that, even if we could document a connection between arrow and response, there is no way to know whether the response was to that arrow alone or to a thousand past arrows.

Disputants identify "arrows" by supplying implicit context; moreover, they often do so in an idiosyncratic fashion, as suggested by Watzlawick et al.'s (1967) idea that people *punctuate* relational disputes in opposing terms. Thus, to gain a better handle on the way communication contributes to conflict, we need to consider how disputing parties place messages in context. This brings us to the literature on conflict frames.

### CONCEPTUALIZING FRAMES

Although having less currency in personal relationships and family conflict literatures, frames have been discussed extensively in conjunction with negotiation, mediation, environmental conflict, political conflict, and other areas (see Nabi & Oliver, Chapter 15, this volume). This literature does not yield a unified theory so much as a collection of mini-theories with similar assumptions, and even the meaning of a *frame* varies among researchers with different agenda (Brummans et al., 2008; Putnam & Holmer, 1992). Nonetheless, there are commonalities. In the most inclusive sense, frames represent individual or collective definitions of the situation—an answer to the question, "What is going on here?" (Goffman, 1974), whereas *framing* is the process by which people "define and assign meaning to a class of objects, persons, and/or events" (Rogan, 2006, p. 158).

The above definitions highlight the holistic nature of frames, which is much of the concept's appeal. That is, frames integrate events, actions, and meanings so as to suggest a coherent understanding of interaction. This is achieved, in part, by evoking meta-labels or root metaphors (implicit or explicit) that characterize the mode of interaction, such as Bateson's (2000) example of implicit meta-communication to indicate "this is play" (not real fighting). Thus, frames are often conceptualized as alternative categories for defining what conflict "is"—for example, a win-lose struggle versus a process calling for compromise or a substantive disagreement versus relationship conflict (Pinkley, 1990).

In the most holistic sense, frames also have a narrative structure that extends beyond the immediate episode, as suggested by Weick's (1995) conception of frames as storytelling. Expanding on this notion, Brummans et al. (2008) characterize a frame as a "repertoire" of categories and labels used to construct a coherent story—for example, the "story of victimhood" told by some stakeholders in environmental disputes versus the story of "power and powerlessness" told by others. Although multiple specific frames operate within and across conflict episodes, these are integrated by the grand narrative.

Some approaches regard frames as relatively stable cognitive structures, such as social scripts that underlie conflict. However, communication scholars typically prefer a more fluid and interactive conception, in which frames serve as implicit meta-communication that assists the interpretation of messages and is, in turn, evoked and modified through interaction (Bateson, 2000; Rogan, 2006). Drake and Donohue (1996) go further in conceptualizing frames as discursive (vs. psychological) structures that disputants build around conflict issues through successive turns at talk. While this approach provides a highly interactive perspective on framing, talk does not always reveal an individual's conception of conflict (as in the case of withdrawal, deception, diplomatic or "edited" speech, etc.). Thus, it seems appropriate to recognize both interpretive and discursive/interaction frames (Rogan, 2006), with the caveat that analytic separation of the two is somewhat artificial. As Weick (1995) says, "A cue in a frame is what makes sense, not the cue alone or the frame alone" (p. 110).[2]

Next, I offer an assessment of what the key theoretical properties of conflict frames are and speculate about their importance to interpersonal conflict.

## FRAME PROPERTIES

*Bracketing.* Frames serve a *bracketing function* by highlighting aspects of experience deemed relevant to matters at hand over those set aside. The bracketing function invokes the metaphor of a picture frame—the frame around a picture says, "Attend to what is within and do not attend to what is outside" (Bateson, 2000, p. 187). Frames also bracket interpretive principles (or "premises") that apply to relevant cues—the picture frame tells the viewer not to use the same sort of thinking in interpreting the picture as the wallpaper (Bateson, 2000).

This aspect of conflict frames—the way they direct attention to particular issues and

operative principles over other potential issues—is perhaps the greatest common point of emphasis across various conceptions of frames. For example, in the "frame categories" perspective (Putnam & Holmer, 1992), frames are implicit conceptions of conflict issues that may achieve prominence at a given time, such as substantive concerns, identities/roles, conflict processes, relationship issues, or moral judgments. In Drake and Donohue's (1996) approach, language choice frames a topic by highlighting certain qualities (e.g., featuring fairness and equity over other potential issues), and an implicit negotiation occurs through successive proposing, accepting, and rejecting of interaction modes. For example, a wife's framing of child support during divorce mediation in terms of fairness serves as a proposal to discuss value aspects of the settlement.

A key insight that follows from the bracketing function is that conflicts may be as much (or more) a struggle to define the issues driving conflict as they are a direct clash over how to resolve those issues. Even if there is coordination over the ostensive topic of conflict (e.g., allocation of child care, completing a group report), individuals may construct alternative frames for identifying issues upon which the conflict is presumed to turn (e.g., as a matter of necessity, equity, authority, or process).

The significance of bracketing partly rests on the complexity of communication noted earlier—the idea that multiple goals and levels of meaning underlie any message. That is, frames direct attention to some aspects of messages over others. Furthermore, the extreme selection of relevant cues makes coordination of frames potentially problematic. A seemingly commonplace example is where one party applies a "content" frame—that is, interpreting conflict as a negotiation of overt, instrumental issues—whereas the other party applies a frame that highlights relational issues. Elsewhere, my colleagues and I labeled this situation *process-content confusion;* for example, when discussing time conflicts, a husband reported thinking that his band could only practice on Tuesdays and Fridays, whereas the wife was thinking at the same time that he was not listening to her (Sillars et al., 2000). A related phenomenon is that disputants may conceptualize issues at different levels of generality—for example, as isolated behavior (not listening) or as a broader pattern (e.g., not listening relates to general insensitivity; Roloff & Johnson, 2002). Alternative framings have implications for the ease with which issues are negotiated: Conflict is more easily discussed and managed when framed as a disagreement over specific behaviors or decisions versus abstract relational and identity issues (Deutsch, 1973). Furthermore, when these frames are invoked unevenly—one party frames a disagreement in concrete terms; the other regards it as symbolic of a general relational pattern—issue negotiation may be especially difficult to coordinate.

*Hierarchy.* Hample (2005) conceptualizes arguing frames as existing simultaneously on three levels of abstraction.[3] At the first level, people frame arguments in terms of their primary goal, which is usually one's immediate instrumental objective but is sometimes a relational or identity goal. At the second level, argument frames reflect coordination of one's own goals with those of other parties—that is, framing the relationship as cooperative or competitive and identifying and adapting to the other's specific goals. Conflict predispositions relate to framing at the first two levels; for example, those who score high on core dimensions of TCP tend to describe arguing using identity and incivility frames, whereas verbally aggressive individuals emphasize dominance and competition frames (Hample, 2005).

At the third level of abstraction, people may develop a reflective theory of arguing by abstracting principles for having good arguments, which in turn may affect a shift

in primary and secondary frames. Hample (2005) does not assume that all arguers engage the third or even second level of framing, as these represent increasing levels of sophistication. Ickes (2003) suggests, in fact, that people mostly lack meta-awareness of interpretive frames, that is, they "look *through* them rather than at them" and seldom look *at* them with critical detachment (p. 213). However, reflective framing has at least the *potential* to promote flexibility over self-initiated tendencies and reactive impulses shaped by primary and secondary frames. This is essentially Canary and Lakey's (2006) point when they suggest that mindfulness about goals is a central component of conflict competence. That is, realistic self-reflection may help one to anticipate and understand conflict episodes and thereby modify problematic responses in the heat of the moment.

There is a second sense of hierarchy that reflects the time dimension of frames. As noted above, conflict frames exist on both local and global levels—as categories that serve as implicit meta-communication for interpreting an act or event and as narratives. There is interplay between these levels since stories evolve as people work to make sense of conflict episodes, and these stories, in turn, suggest interpretive frames for immediate communication. For example, in the research on in vivo thoughts during couple conflict (Sillars et al., 2000), a recently unemployed husband was critical of his wife for not seeking work more aggressively and saw her casual approach to their pending crisis as naive and irresponsible. Consequently, he framed the wife's comments as excuses and topic shifts since her explanations failed to square with the unfolding story as he saw it. The wife put her actions in the context of a young mother trying to provide a good home for her family; therefore, she framed his assertions and pointed questions as verbal attacks on her identity motivated by his own insecurity. As Ickes (2003) notes, such frames tend to be applied to interaction in a self-confirming fashion: In the above example, the husband's framing of the wife's comments as evasive led him to conclude that he had to "keep pressing" to "drive it into her head," thus providing further confirmation for the wife's sense of being made a scapegoat and reinforcing her own passive resistance. Thus, the grand narrative provides a frame for assimilating and reacting to specific cues within face-to-face interaction.

*Storytelling and Rehearsal.* A further implication of narrative structure is that conflict frames are shaped by the process of storytelling. Since conflicts are highly salient and troubling, they are especially likely to motivate storytelling, in the sense of either covert rehearsal of dialogue (Honeycutt & Ford, 2001) or actual sharing of the story with others. As people retell the story, the narrative is likely to be transformed as it is edited to meet the requirements of a good story (Weick, 1995). That is, elements may be dropped and others embellished that make the story more plausible, succinct, coherent, and dramatic. Since each party to a dispute is likely to embellish and drop details in ways that favor their own self-presentation, separate storytelling can be expected to exaggerate initial differences in conflict frames. Indeed, when assigned to tell a transgression story from the perspective of perpetrator or victim, individuals characteristically provided one-sided accounts that became even more so upon repeated telling of the story (Baumeister & Catanese, 2001).

Storytelling also transforms conflict frameworks through narrative "closure"—the manner in which stories seal off alternative explanations. Within the context of divorce mediation, conflict narratives represent an integrated "theory of responsibility," including plot, character roles, and moral framework (Cobb, 1994). Since a challenge at any of these sites is potentially destabilizing to the

narrative as a whole, individuals engage in discursive work to close off alternative interpretations, such as elaborating a subplot to account for a contested event. Cobb (1994) suggests that much of this stabilization takes place before the mediation session, as spouses rehearse the story with others. The effect is generally to reinforce antagonistic frames, in which each party's positive position (as "victim") is contingent upon the other's negative position (as "victimizer"). Thus, mediation may require undoing discursive work of participants to open narratives to alternative interpretations that allow a positive position for the other (Cobb, 1994).

*Convergence/Divergence.* When disputants converge on a particular way of talking about conflict (i.e., as an issue of fact, interest, value, or relationship), this can be seen as an implicitly negotiated limit on the topic of discussion during some phase of interaction (Drake & Donohue, 1996). As such, simply maintaining a shared focus on a particular discursive frame represents an element of cooperation that may allow negotiation of issues to progress. Drake and Donohue (1996) tested this reasoning by examining frame convergence over successive speaking turns during divorce mediation. As expected, the number of interim agreements forged by divorcing spouses was related to their convergence on common frames and the stability of convergent phases.

Several factors discussed in this chapter make the coordination of frames potentially problematic; moreover, these factors have increased significance as conflicts escalate. With conflict escalation, motivated storytelling is likely to increase, processing of communication is increasingly directed by defensive goals, and conflict issues may become more diffuse and abstract. The latter point is suggested by the common observation that, as conflicts intensify or continue over time, there tends to be a proliferation of new issues, and the bases of conflict shift from concrete disagreements to generalized conflicts that reflect core relational and identity concerns (e.g., Raush et al., 1974). Therefore, with conflict escalation, it becomes increasingly likely that disputing parties will consider the dispute to be about fundamentally different things. Mismatched frames, in turn, promote fragmented discussion in which each speaker tends to be irrelevant and inarticulate in addressing the other's voiced concerns.

## ◆ Conclusion

Coordination of meaning tends to be especially problematic in the context of interpersonal conflict, perhaps uniquely so. Furthermore, the impacts of messages are mediated by disputant sensemaking, which may occur on uneven terms. These characteristics of conflict should command the attention of communication scholars. Moreover, what is needed is not a parallel literature on cognition versus behavior or discourse versus sensemaking but rather an integrated approach to actions performed and framing processes through which actions come to be constituted, reproduced, or transformed.

## ◆ Notes

1. Charles Berger (personal communication, 2007) asks whether conflicts are strictly about goals versus plans adopted to achieve goals. I do not mean to advocate a goals-based definition of conflict, but here is a potential response. Certainly, people do experience conflict over plans (e.g., how to write a job description for a new hire), but they do so because they see alternative plans as accomplishing incompatible goals, including instrumental goals (e.g., increasing expertise in one domain at the expense of another) as well as relational, identity, and

process goals (e.g., ensuring equity, respect, "voice"). Again, the applied dispute resolution literature assumes that conflicts are driven by apparent incompatibilities in expressed positions (or "plans"), whereas underlying interests (goals) may accommodate new alternatives acceptable to all parties. Thus, the perception of incompatible goals drives conflict even though conflicts are acted out over concrete plans.

2. Bateson (2000) states that every metacommunicative message both defines the frame and assists the receiver in understanding messages within the frame. Thus, messages evoke and modify interpretive frames, which provide a further basis for understanding messages.

3. Although concerned with "arguing" (i.e., what happens when people exchange reasons), this analysis extends to conflict since naive theories of argument mostly conflate the two activities (Hample, 2005).

## ◆ References

Afifi, T. D., & Olson, L. (2005). The chilling effect in families and the pressure to conceal secrets. *Communication Monographs, 72,* 192–216.

Bateson, G. (2000). *Steps to an ecology of mind.* Chicago: University of Chicago Press.

Baumeister, R. F., & Catanese, K. (2001). Victims and perpetrators provide discrepant accounts: Motivated cognitive distortions about interpersonal transgressions. In J. P. Forgas, K. D. Willimas, & L. Wheeler (Eds.), *The social mind: Cognitive and motivational aspects of interpersonal behavior* (pp. 274–293). Cambridge, UK: Cambridge University Press.

Blake, R. R., & Mouton, J. S. (1964). *The managerial grid.* Houston, TX: Gulf.

Bowers, J. W. (1974). Guest editor's introduction: Beyond threats and promises. *Speech Monographs, 41,* ix–xi.

Bradbury, T., Rogge, R., & Lawrence, E. (2001). Reconsidering the role of conflict in marriage. In A. Booth, A. C. Crouter, & M. Clements (Eds.), *Couples in conflict* (pp. 59–81). Hillsdale, NJ: Lawrence Erlbaum.

Brummans, B., Putnam, L., Gray, L., Hanke, R., Lewicki, R., & Wiethoff, C. (2008).

Making sense of intractable multiparty conflict: A study of framing in four environmental disputes. *Communication Monographs, 75,* 25–51.

Canary, D. J., Cupach, W. R., & Messman, S. J. (1995). *Relationship conflict.* Thousand Oaks, CA: Sage.

Canary, D. J., & Lakey, S. G. (2006). Managing conflict in a competent manner: A mindful look at events that matter. In J. G. Oetzel & S. Ting-Toomey (Eds.), *The Sage handbook of conflict communication: Integrating theory, research, and practice* (pp. 185–210). Thousand Oaks, CA: Sage.

Caughlin, J. P., & Scott, A. M. (2009). Toward a communication theory of the demand/withdraw pattern of interaction in interpersonal relationships. In S. Smith & S. R. Wilson (Eds.), *New directions in interpersonal communication.* Thousand Oaks, CA: Sage.

Caughlin, J. P., & Vangelisti, A. L. (2006). Conflict in dating and marital relationships. In J. G. Oetzel & S. Ting-Toomey (Eds.), *The Sage handbook of conflict communication: Integrating theory, research, and practice* (pp. 129–157). Thousand Oaks, CA: Sage.

Cloven, D. H., & Roloff, M. E. (1991). Sense-making activities and interpersonal conflict: Communicative cures for the mulling blues. *Western Journal of Speech Communication, 55,* 134–158.

Cloven, D. H., & Roloff, M. E. (1993). The chilling effect of aggressive potential on the expression of complaints in intimate relationships. *Communication Monographs, 60,* 198–219.

Cobb, S. (1994). A narrative perspective on mediation: Toward the materialization of the "storytelling" metaphor. In J. P. Folger & T. S. Jones (Eds.), *New directions in mediation: Communication research and perspectives* (pp. 48–63). Thousand Oaks, CA: Sage.

Deutsch, M. (1973). *The resolution of conflict: Constructive and destructive processes.* New Haven, CT: Yale University Press.

Drake, L. E., & Donohue, W. A. (1996). Communicative framing theory in conflict resolution. *Communication Research, 23,* 297–322.

Fincham, F. D. (2004). Communication in marriage. In A. L. Vangelisti (Ed.), *Handbook of family communication* (pp. 83–103). Mahwah, NJ: Lawrence Erlbaum.

Goffman, E. (1974). *Frame analysis: An essay on the organization of experience.* New York: Harper & Row.

Gottman, J. M. (1979). *Marital interactions: Experimental investigations.* New York: Academic Press.

Gottman, J. M. (1994). *What predicts divorce? The relationship between marital processes and marital outcomes.* Hillsdale, NJ: Lawrence Erlbaum.

Gottman, J. M., Coan, J., Carrere, S., & Swanson, C. (1998). Predicting marital happiness and stability from newly wed interactions. *Journal of Marriage and the Family, 60,* 5–22.

Hall, J. (1969). *Conflict management survey.* Conroe, TX: Telemetrics.

Hample, D. (1999). The life space of personalized conflicts. In M. E. Roloff (Ed.), *Communication yearbook 22* (pp. 171–207). Thousand Oaks, CA: Sage.

Hample, D. (2005). *Arguing: Exchanging reasons face to face.* Mahwah, NJ: Lawrence Erlbaum.

Hawes, L., & Smith, D. H. (1973). A critique of assumptions underlying the study of communication in conflict. *Quarterly Journal of Speech, 59,* 423–435.

Honeycutt, J. M., & Ford, S. G. (2001). Mental imagery and intrapersonal communication: A review of research on imagined interactions (IIs) and current developments. In W. B. Gudykunst (Ed.), *Communication yearbook 25* (pp. 315–345). Thousand Oaks, CA: Sage.

Ickes, W. (2003). *Everyday mind reading: Understanding what other people think and feel.* Amherst, NY: Prometheus.

Jacobs, S. (2002). Language and interpersonal communication. In M. L. Knapp & J. A. Daly (Eds.), *Handbook of interpersonal communication* (pp. 213–239). Thousand Oaks, CA: Sage.

Kellermann, K. (1992). Communication: Inherently strategic and primarily automatic. *Communication Monographs, 59,* 288–300.

Knapp, M. L., Putnam, L. L., & Davis, L. J. (1988). Measuring interpersonal conflict in organizations: Where do we go from here? *Management Communication Quarterly, 1,* 414–429.

Kuhn, T., & Poole, M. S. (2000). Do conflict management styles affect group decision making? Evidence from a longitudinal field study. *Human Communication Research, 26,* 558–590.

Miller, C. W., Roloff, M. E., & Malis, R. S. (2007). Understanding interpersonal conflicts that are difficult to resolve: A review of literature and presentation of an integrated model. In C. S. Beck (Ed.), *Communication yearbook 31* (pp. 118–173). Mahwah, NJ: Lawrence Erlbaum.

Nicotera, A. M., & Dorsey, L. K. (2006). Individual and interactive processes in organizational conflict. In J. G. Oetzel & S. Ting-Toomey (Eds.), *The Sage handbook of conflict communication: Integrating theory, research, and practice* (pp. 293–325). Thousand Oaks, CA: Sage.

Oetzel, J. G., & Ting-Toomey, S. (Eds.). (2006). *The Sage handbook of conflict communication: Integrating theory, research, and practice.* Thousand Oaks, CA: Sage.

Orbuch, T. L., & Veroff, J. (2002). A programmatic review: Building a two-way bridge between social psychology and the study of the early years of marriage. *Journal of Social and Personal Relationships, 19,* 549–568.

Pinkley, R. L. (1990). Dimensions of conflict frame: Disputant interpretations of conflict. *Journal of Applied Psychology, 75,* 117–126.

Pruitt, D. G., & Lewis, S. A. (1977). The psychology of integrative bargaining. In D. Druckman (Ed.), *Negotiations: Social-psychological perspectives* (pp. 161–192). Beverly Hills, CA: Sage.

Putnam, L. (2006). Definitions and approaches to conflict and communication. In J. G. Oetzel & S. Ting-Toomey (Eds.), *The Sage handbook of conflict communication: Integrating theory, research, and practice* (pp. 1–32). Thousand Oaks, CA: Sage.

Putnam, L. L., & Holmer, M. (1992). Framing, reframing, and issue development. In L. L. Putnam & M. E. Roloff (Eds.), *Communication and negotiation* (pp. 128–155). Newbury Park, CA: Sage.

Rahim, M. A. (1983). A measure of styles of handling interpersonal conflict. *Academy of Management Journal, 26,* 368–376.

Raush, H. L., Barry, W. A., Hertel, R. K., & Swain, M. A. (1974). *Communication, conflict, and marriage.* San Francisco: Jossey-Bass.

Roberts, L. J. (2000). Fire and ice in marital communication: Hostile and distancing behaviors as predictors of marital distress. *Journal of Marriage and the Family, 62,* 693–707.

Rogan, R. G. (2006). Conflict framing categories revisited. *Communication Quarterly, 54,* 157–173.

Roloff, M. E., & Ifert, D. E. (2000). Conflict management through avoidance: Withholding complaints, suppressing arguments, and declaring topics taboo. In S. Petronio (Ed.), *Balancing the secrets of private disclosures* (pp. 151–163). Mahwah, NJ: Lawrence Erlbaum.

Roloff, M. E., & Johnson, K. L. (2002). Serial arguing over the relational life course: Antecedents and consequences. In A. L. Vangelisti, H. T. Reis, & M. A. Fitzpatrick (Eds.), *Stability and change in relationships* (pp. 107–128). New York: Cambridge University Press.

Roloff, M. E., & Miller, C. W. (2006). Social cognition approaches to understanding interpersonal conflict and communication. In J. G. Oetzel & S. Ting-Toomey (Eds.), *The Sage handbook of conflict communication: Integrating theory, research, and practice* (pp. 97–128). Thousand Oaks, CA: Sage.

Rubin, B. D. (1978). Communication and conflict: A system-theoretic perspective. *Quarterly Journal of Speech, 64,* 202–210.

Schutz, A. (1999). It was your fault! Self-serving biases in autobiographical accounts of conflicts in married couples. *Journal of Social and Personal Relationships, 16,* 193–208.

Sillars, A., Canary, D. J., & Tafoya, M. (2004). Communication, conflict, and the quality of family relationships. In A. L. Vangelisti (Ed.), *Handbook of family communication* (pp. 413–446). Mahwah, NJ: Lawrence Erlbaum.

Sillars, A., Roberts, L. J., Leonard, K. E., & Dun, T. (2000). Cognition during marital conflict: The relationship of thought and talk. *Journal of Social and Personal Relationships, 17,* 479–502.

Sillars, A., & Vangelisti, A. L. (2006). Communication: Basic properties and their relevance to relationship research. In A. L. Vangelisti & D. Perlman (Eds.), *The Cambridge handbook of personal relationships* (pp. 331–351). New York: Cambridge University Press.

Sillars, A. L., & Weisberg, J. (1987). Conflict as a social skill. In M. E. Roloff & G. R. Miller

(Eds.), *Interpersonal processes: New directions in communication research* (pp. 140–171). Newbury Park, CA: Sage.

Sillars, A. L., & Wilmot, W. W. (1994). Communication strategies in conflict and mediation. In J. Wiemann & J. A. Daly (Eds.), *Communicating strategically: Strategies in interpersonal communication* (pp. 163–190). Hillsdale, NJ: Lawrence Erlbaum.

Simons, H. (1974). Prologue. In G. R. Miller & H. W. Simons (Eds.), *Perspectives on communication in social conflict* (pp. 1–13). Englewood Cliffs, NJ: Prentice Hall.

Thomas, K. W. (1988). The conflict-handling modes: Toward more precise theory. *Management Communication Quarterly, 1,* 430–436.

Thomas, K. W., & Kilmann, R. H. (1974). *Thomas-Kilmann conflict MODE instrument.* Tuxedo, NY: Xicom.

Thomas, K. W., & Pondy, L. R. (1977). Toward an "intent" model of conflict management among principal parties. *Human Relations, 30,* 1089–1102.

Trapp, R., & Hoff, N. (1985). A model of serial argument in interpersonal relationships. *Journal of the American Forensic Association, 22,* 1–11.

Ury, W. L., Brett, J. M., & Goldberg, S. B. (1988). Three approaches to resolving disputes: Interests, rights, and power. In W. L. Ury, J. M. Brett, & S. B. Goldberg (Eds.), *Getting disputes resolved* (pp. 3–19). San Francisco: Jossey-Bass.

van de Vliert, E., & Euwema, M. C. (1994). Agreeableness and activeness as components of conflict behaviors. *Journal of Personality and Social Psychology, 66,* 674–687.

Watzlawick, P., Beavin, J., & Jackson, D. D. (1967). *Pragmatics of human communication: A study of interactional patterns, pathologies, and paradoxes.* New York: Norton.

Weick, K. (1995). *Sensemaking in organizations.* Thousand Oaks, CA: Sage.

Weiss, R. L. (1993). *Marital Interaction Coding System-IV (MICS-IV).* Unpublished coding manual, University of Oregon, Eugene.

# 17

# INTERGROUP CONFLICT

◆ Donald G. Ellis

Sunni-Shiite violence, political acrimony between Israeli-Jews and Palestinians, prejudice, discrimination, religious differences, labor-management disputes, and the different moral universes of pro-choice and pro-life groups in the United States are all the subject matter of intergroup conflict. Intergroup conflict is a subset of the more general study of intergroup relations, which has its origins in social psychology. Intergroup relations, as defined by Taylor and Moghaddam (1994), is the study of "any aspect of human interaction that involves individuals perceiving themselves as members of a social category, or being perceived by others as belonging to a social category" (p. 6). Interaction predicated on *social category* membership is central to this definition. One research tradition in communication focuses on personal interactions that involve perceiving and treating another person as an individual with a unique identity and set of traits. Another tradition, the one most pertinent to intergroup relations, concerns *social identity* or the fact that as group members, individuals are defined by all of the perceptions and associations relevant to those groups. The most common group category identities are ethnicity, religion, gender, nationality, and categories of sexual orientation, political sensibilities, and various cultural identities. The study of intergroup relations is a vast topic with an

AUTHOR'S NOTE: This chapter was completed while the author was a Scholar in Residence at New York University. He would like to thank NYU and the Faculty Resource Network for their time and resources.

entire journal devoted to its development (i.e., *Group Processes and Intergroup Relations*). Almost every study of Black–White relations, diversity, political conflict, discrimination, stereotypes, minority-majority relations, ethnic or religious bias, or bullying on the playground is related to intergroup conflict. It would be impossible to review such an array of literature; thus, only a subset of issues will be covered. The following review focuses on the social scientific and empirical literature addressing key issues in communication, psychology, and intergroup conflict.

## SOME DEFINITIONAL DISTINCTIONS

Although the distinction between *intergroup relations* and *intergroup conflict* is relatively minor, it is defensible nonetheless. Groups can relate to one another in a nonconflictual manner, thus establishing intergroup conflict as a special subprocess of intergroup relations. Moreover, the cognitive processes subserving intergroup relations such as categorizing, stereotyping, attitudes, and attributions have different implications for conflict. And most important, issues in intergroup conflict—including their causes, management, and resolution—are practical and relevant. However, a few additional qualifiers are necessary.

First, not all social actors are required to be actively aware of the intergroup nature of the communication. This fact poses complex perceptual and methodological problems but does not obviate those instances when interaction is informed by social categories that are outside the awareness of the participants. Minority group members regularly report being treated as members of a social category even if others are unaware of it. For example, African Americans who have strong racial identification are more likely to hold negative attitudes toward Whites than are those who do not show strong

identification with their race (Stephan et al., 2002). African Americans who have strong racial identification are more likely to view Whites as a realistic threat to their well-being as well as a symbolic threat to the value systems they believe that African Americans hold than are those who do not strongly identify with their race (Stephan et al., 2002). Minorities who have strong racial identification are more likely to believe that discrimination occurs in their own life than are those who do not strongly identify with their race (Operario & Fiske, 2001). Individuals with strong racial identification are more likely to believe that discrimination will prevent them from succeeding than are individuals who less strongly identify with their race (Major, Quinton, & McCoy, 2002).

Moreover, the perpetrator of a group prejudicial comment might be completely ignorant of its social effects or, in turn, the recipient could be accused of excessive sensitivity or misinterpretation. Another important point is illustrated in a study of racially mixed health care work teams (Dreachslin, Hunt, & Sprainer, 2000). Results demonstrated that some African Americans viewed team conflict and miscommunication through a frame that attributed such problems to race, whereas other African Americans and Whites attributed the same difficulties to status differences and team roles. Dreachslin et al. (2000) note that group processes played a significant role in maintaining the frames; specifically, they assert, "Social isolation by race reinforces both overarching themes, i.e., different perspectives and alternative realities, because perceptual filters, shared beliefs and social reality are reinforced through interaction in social networks" (p. 1409). And individuals with strong ethnic identity are more likely to attribute ambiguous actions by out-group members toward in-group members to race than are those who identify less strongly (Operario & Fiske, 2001).

Second, intergroup conflict interactions are most characterized by cognitive and linguistic attributes evocative of category membership and not mutual attitudes among individual members of a group. It is not necessary for all members of a group to be acquainted or express mutual attraction. It is, for example, possible to be a member of an ethnic group (e.g., Italian, African American, Arab) and have very few personal relations with other group members, share little in common other than category membership, and have a personal category identity that ranges from low to high.

Third, the relationship between inter-personal and intergroup interactions is a continuum. Harwood and Giles (2005) explain that interactions can be high or low on either dimension, thus yielding a 2 × 2 space defined by interpersonal and intergroup interactions. An interracial couple facing problems resulting from public stereotypes would be an example of interaction high on both dimensions. Even though the couple's interpersonal relationship is highly salient, they must deal with each individual's racial category membership. Purely interpersonal communication (low on the intergroup dimension) might take place between friends or acquaintances while chatting about something in their past or their personal relationship. The opposite quadrant—or the one predominately intergroup in nature—would involve encounters between two or more people defined solely on the basis of group membership such as gender or ethnicity. These interactions might entail expressions of group biases and stereotypes or involve dialogue sessions devoted to exploring or solving problems between groups. Finally, routine service encounters during commercial exchanges would be typical of interactions low on both dimensions.

Although this scheme is a useful heuristic for categorizing interactions, the research literature is most concerned with inter-actions that have high intergroup salience. Clearly, one type of interaction rarely occurs to the exclusion of the other, and "real" interactions display a complex fluc-tuation between interpersonal and intergroup

exchanges. And personal relations in the form of cross-group friendships facilitate intergroup contact and help individuals generalize more positively to a target out-group (N. Miller, 2002; Wright & Tropp, 2005); moreover, everyday encounters with out-groups can form strong negative attitudes toward them (Stephan et al., 2002).

Intergroup researchers' practical concerns direct their attention to contact between competing groups that is structured to enhance positive group outcomes (Allport, 1954; Pettigrew, 1998). Moreover, the salience of various group identities is so ubiquitous that most interactions cannot escape intergroup perceptions. Some scholars have argued that in-group identity and intergroup conflict is evolutionarily based (cf. Gil-White, 2001) and impossible to circum-vent. As will become apparent, longitudinal (Levin, van Laar, & Sidanius, 2003) and meta-analytic (Pettigrew & Tropp, 2000, 2006) studies provide converging and convincing evidence that controlled commu-nicative contact between conflicting groups influences a variety of cognitive, linguistic, and emotional processes that reduces prejudice. After considering theoretical issues in intergroup relations, literature concerning the causes, consequences, and resolution of conflict between identity groups will be presented.

## ◆ History and Theory of Intergroup Conflict

Muzafer Sherif is credited with pioneering work in intergroup conflict (Sherif, 1951; Sherif, Harvey, White, Hood, & Sherif, 1961; cf. Taylor & Moghaddam, 1994). In Sherif's classic study (Learnpeace, n.d.), a group of boys was unwittingly cast in an experiment conducted at a summer camp in the 1950s. Although they were unaware of it, Sherif had divided them into two groups and arranged experiences that would amplify and then resolve destructive conflict between them. The groups quickly came into conflict, displaying in-group and out-group biases, prejudicial evaluations, and distorted decision making. The experimenters then induced cooperation by creating shared goals that required their working together. For example, they had to join forces to start a truck that had broken down and repair a faulty water pipe. By the end of the camp, the boys had become reconciled and even asked to return to the city on the same bus. Significantly, it was not enough merely to bring people together to talk; rather, positive interdependence and controlled interaction were necessary to ameliorate group conflict.

Sherif's experiment prompted decades of research examining the role of intergroup contact in reducing prejudice. Most of the research has been informed by efforts to identify the consequences of intergroup conflict and find ways to reduce prejudice and judgmental distortions. The bulk of this research supports the conclusion that contact reduces prejudice and encourages other positive group outcomes (Pettigrew & Tropp, 2000, 2006; Tropp, 2003). Taylor and Moghaddam (1994) describe five broad theories of intergroup relations (realistic conflict theory, equity theory, social identity theory, relative deprivation, and a five-stage model of intergroup relations), and Harwood and Giles (2005) pose a perspective on intergroup communication. Of the five broad theories, social identity theory is most pertinent to intergroup conflict and how psychological and communication processes are influenced. Realistic conflict theory capitalizes on the assumptions of economic models and assumes that conflict is the result of incompatible group interests. Real conflicts of interest are the cause of group hostility, and engendering compatible goals that induce cooperation, as in the Sherif (1951) studies, is the solution to conflict. Equity theory is based on principles of justice and finds group conflict in situations where

there is the perception of unfairness (Walster, Walster, & Berscheid, 1978). It argues that the restoration of equity (e.g., affirmative action) between advantaged and disadvantaged groups restores psychological balance and is an antidote to group retaliation. The key issue in relative deprivation theory is that conflict is signaled when one group feels "relatively" disadvantaged, even if objective circumstances suggest otherwise (cf. Crosby, 1976). Finally, the five-stage model describes stages of intergroup behavior and locates conflict in the antagonism between high- and low-status groups (Taylor & McKirnan, 1984). Social identity theory is considered below in detail because it is a major theory of intergroup conflict.

## SOCIAL IDENTITY THEORY

Social identity theory (Tajfel & Turner, 1979) and self-categorization theory (Turner, 1985) make an important distinction for intergroup conflict between personal identity and group identity (Hogg & Reid, 2006). This distinction is based on principles of categorization. Evolutionary psychologists (cf. Gil-White, 2001) have claimed that the human species evolved to process ethnic groups as distinct species because it was adaptive in the ancestral environment. Humans needed to distinguish between their own and dangerous others; consequently, the human brain evolved the capacity to sort and classify people and objects. Moreover, this was not simple learning: If humans were required in evolutionary history to approach other species (e.g., lions) and "test" whether they were truly dangerous, they would not have survived the testing period. This is related to the research noted earlier that negative everyday experiences with another group leads to anxiety about interacting with them and avoidance. Accordingly, the ability to categorize evolved as the result of cognitive (not physical) machinery selected for processing information about species. All species develop processes that make possible the recognition and preference for their own group to facilitate reproduction, security, and need fulfillment. This recognition results in the perception of norm boundaries that assist in recognizing one's own group as distinct from others. Thus, visual symbols of physical differences and interactional norms become important information for group membership. Humans are evolutionarily endowed with the ability to identify differences based on descent and inclusion in a group whose members have physiological, interactional, and normative properties in common. This is not an essentialist argument. The argument is not that we are composed of "essential" ethnic properties but that there is a psychological tendency to essentialize others (Haslam, Bastian, Bain, & Kashima, 2006). Some of the most vicious intergroup conflict is the result of one group essentializing what it considers to be the dangerous characteristics of another group. These processes evolved in a particularly salient way for "ethnic" groups but apply to groups in general. Still, the depth and legitimacy of in-group bias vary as a function of the centrality of the group identity. Not all social groups are the same. People do not fight and die for their management group at work or their book club because such groups are not related to species survival.

Thus, identities are crucially shaped by group membership—that is, their social identity. And the drive to enhance positive self-concept and maintain status motivates people to view their own in-group more favorably than out-groups. When the distinctiveness of the in-group is not apparent or fades in comparison to other groups, then group members will seek comparisons that favor their own group to regain distinctiveness. This can take the form of increasing negative attitudes toward other groups, enhancing allegiance to one's own group (ethnocentrism), distorting one's perceptions of in-groups and out-groups, or directly attacking out-groups to gain advantage. In their analysis

of lay attributions about conflict, Cargile, Bradac, and Cole (2006) found that social identity corresponded with explanations for group conflict.

Theories of intergroup conflict have sought to tease out the differences between personal and group identity. Self-categorization theory (Turner, Hogg, Oakes, Reicher, & Wetherell, 1987) makes this fundamental distinction and focuses on the variety of cognitive processes underlying intergroup conflict. When personal identity is salient, an individual is motivated by his or her own needs, beliefs, and standards; by contrast, when a social identity is activated, individuals see themselves as group members, even interchangeable with other members, and not as unique individuals. Activated social identity elevates collective needs and interests over individual ones. This dynamic implies very different predictions about the causes and reasons for certain behaviors hostile to intergroup cooperation. When a social (group) identity is salient, it intensifies cues about the typicality or atypicality of other groups and potentiates unfavorable comparisons that can stimulate conflict (Miller, 2002). Also, in-group stereotypes about out-groups are used to make judgments about them. When individual identities are salient, out-group perceptions and judgments are dependent solely on individual cognitive variations. The various lines of research discussed below will demonstrate how this distinction between individual and group identity plays an important role in intergroup conflict and its resolution.

## PREJUDICE AND INTERGROUP CONFLICT

Prejudice in the classic sense is an antipathy based on faulty and inflexible generalization (Allport, 1954). It may be felt or expressed. It may be directed toward a group or an individual of that group. With respect to intergroup conflict, prejudice refers to a negative or hostile attitude toward another social group. It is a distorted, biased, or inaccurate attitude toward a group based on defective or incomplete interpretations of information acquired through either direct or indirect experience with a group. This leads naturally to the question of how to reverse or eliminate the processes of prejudice and in-group/out-group conflict. One, deceptively simple answer is that people must assemble under favorable conditions and communicate in such a way as to facilitate cooperation, reconciliation, mutual understanding, or whatever serves the goals of conflict resolution (Allport, 1954).

Before the past decade, research on prejudice and intergroup conflict sought to explain how and why groups held biases toward one another. Researchers looked for situational factors that caused bias. However, recent research has focused on processes that mediate the relationship between groups and intergroup bias (Molina, Wittig, & Giang, 2004). Situations are moderators of intergroup bias, and cognitive processes are mediators between contact conditions and bias (Wittig & Molina, 2000). People *assimilate* into their own group by assigning the same characteristics to themselves as they do the groups to which they belong (Clement & Krueger, 2000). Cognitive representations of one's own group and groups to which one does *not* belong are theoretically and empirically foundational to the study of prejudice and intergroup conflict. Consistent with both social categorization theory and evolutionary psychology, these cognitive representations promote in-group/out-group contrasts, and these contrasts affect bias and judgments about conflict.

In-group/out-group contrasts can be explained by different theories. Cadinu and Rothbart's (1996) differentiation model assumes that as a result of ascribing in-group characteristics to themselves, individuals will ascribe the opposite to the out-group. This is understood as an exaggeration of categories designed to assist with the task of "understanding" the other group. A second theory (Greenwald et al., 2002) uses balance theory predictions to explain that in-groups resist forming links with out-groups to remain cognitively consistent. Thus, there is additional motivation to "balance" the in-group/out-group relationship with ascribing different characteristics to the two groups. Yet a third theory, termed *optimal distinctiveness theory* (Brewer, 1991), argues that people seek a balance between interpersonal affiliation and uniqueness. During intergroup conflict, they satisfy affiliation needs by assimilation to the in-group and uniqueness needs by contrasting with the out-group, thereby aggravating conflict. Although somewhat different, these theories all predict ascription of positive self and in-group characteristics and different (often negative) characteristics to out-groups.

Intergroup conflict intensifies out-group contrasts. The conflict between the Israelis and Palestinians, for example, has exaggerated and intensified the stereotypes that each group holds about the other. One explanation is that individuals selectively choose information about the other group that is indicative of dissimilarities (Blanton, 2001). Moreover, consistent with optimal distinctiveness theory described above, conflict with an out-group is an attractive opportunity for distinctiveness. Israeli-Jews continue to see themselves as democratic and peaceful in contrast to their images of Palestinian terrorism. Conversely, harmony between groups causes group members to see out-groups as more similar to themselves to achieve cognitive balance. In the absence of conflict, assimilation is the default cognitive process that is overruled by contrast during conflict. One mediating variable is the strength of group identification (Spears & Manstead, 1990). High group identification makes contrasts easier and more natural. Riketta (2005) finds strong support for these relationships between conflict and the intensity of in-group/out-group contrasts. The tendency to essentialize other groups is one of the particularly pernicious consequences of intergroup conflict.

## PSYCHOLOGICAL ESSENTIALISM

An important line of intergroup conflict research concerns lay theories of group perception (Cargile et al., 2006; Demoulin, Leyens, & Yzerbyt, 2006; Levy, Stroessner, & Dweck, 1998). Lay theories refer to informal, commonsense explanations that people have for individual and group behavior. In the intergroup conflict literature, *subjective essentialism* is one of the most important lay beliefs. Subjective essentialism is the notion that members of a group have numerous surface similarities, but all share a belief in the deep underlying features that describe themselves and differentiate them from others. These deep underlying features are assumed to capture the "essence" of individuals and groups and their underlying nature. Individuals who score high on lay principles of essentialism can be characterized as racist, sexist, or homophobic. Psychological essentialism is common and begins at a young age (Gelman & Wellman, 1991).

Essentialism influences relations between groups that are in conflict in numerous ways. Demoulin et al. (2006) explain how essentialist theories affect prejudice and accentuate contrast effects because people with strong essentialist beliefs uphold the immutability of categories such as race, ethnicity, and gender. Traditionally stigmatized groups such as homosexuals, Jews, or Africans are assumed to represent a social category equivalent to a biological species. Essentialism also leads to infra-humanization or the tendency to see out-groups as less human than a comparative in-group (Demoulin et al., 2006). This makes intergroup forgiveness more difficult and exacerbates conflict. Finally, essentialism promotes dispositional attributions to justify differences and inequalities between groups rather than situational or historical ones. This again confounds conflict resolution because solutions to conflict are unavailable; to wit, individuals are responsible for the conflict and cannot change their nature. From another perspective, the more a group is considered an "entity"—that is, perceived as a coherent unit with clear boundaries—the more observers attribute stable dispositions to the group (Yzerbyt, Rogier, & Fiske, 1998) and the more observers are likely to essentialize the group. Again, this process thwarts conflict resolution.

## EMOTIONS AND INTERGROUP CONFLICT

The study of emotions is increasingly influencing accounts of prejudice and intergroup conflict. Intergroup emotion theory extends the idea that group membership is an important part of the self-concept (Mackie, Devos, & Smith, 2000). When individuals categorize themselves as group members, they may feel deep comradeship with the other group members. Consequently, the group takes on emotional attachments and characteristics such that individuals react emotionally to in-groups and out-groups. For example, when an out-group is judged to be threatening, intergroup emotions such as anger or hostility are aroused. And the converse is true; positive judgments for the out-group garner positive intergroup emotions (Miller, Smith, & Mackie, 2004).

One practical consequence of this line of theorizing is that dominant groups (e.g., White Americans) often report that they avoid contact with minority groups (e.g., African Americans) not because they dislike them or because they hold aggressive stereotypes but because interaction produces discomfort or anxiety. They are uncertain about how to act, conversational topics, and the possibility of unintentional offense. Contact with an out-group can reduce prejudice by reducing anxiety with no attendant change in beliefs or attitudes (Voci & Hewstone, 2003). D. A. Miller et al. (2004) found no improvement of intergroup relations when working with stereotype reduction but considerable success when trying to instill positive emotions. Emotions apparently overrode cognitive factors when changing attitudes on the basis of group contact. And there is some research that suggests contact is exhausting to in-group members (Richeson & Shelton, 2003).

Anger and infrahumanization, which involves the attribution of more human emotions to the in-group, have been shown to play important roles in the intergroup conflict processes. Tam et al. (2007) note the importance of community forgiveness in permitting groups formerly in conflict to move forward in a positive way. Forgiveness means changing feelings toward the other group and adopting prosocial behaviors. They found clear evidence that anger has impeded forgiveness in the Northern Ireland conflict. Moreover, forgiveness requires that one group see the humanity in the other; seeing the out-group as less human is very detrimental to forgiveness (Tam et al., 2007). It is very common and easy to infrahumanize a group during violent conflict, and these emotions linger long after the violence has stopped. Later in the chapter, we consider how "contact" or interaction can help manage these emotions and increase forgiveness.

What perceptual and symbolic distortions result from intergroup conflict? In addressing this question, Maoz, Ward, Katz, and Ross (2002) found that peace proposals were devalued when they were thought to have originated from the other side. Among Jewish respondents, an Israeli peace proposal was devalued when it was attributed to a Palestinian author. Even "hawkish" Jews were critical of a proposal they thought came from "dovish" Jews. Another relevant line of research recognizes the perceptual distinction between individual attitudes and attitudes about one's own group (Eidelson & Eidelson, 2003). In other words, group members (say, Israeli-Jews) may not feel personally vulnerable but believe that their in-group (the collective of Israeli-Jews) is vulnerable. This research has documented how beliefs concerning vulnerability, injustice, distrust, superiority, and helplessness operate at the group level and as important individual difference variables. The perception that one's group is threatened by any of these variables predicts attitudes and policy positions. One study found that stronger beliefs about in-group vulnerability, injustice, distrust, and superiority were associated with greater support for the coercive and morally problematic policy decisions in the Israeli–Palestinian conflict (Maoz & Eidelson, 2007). The study shows how shared cultural beliefs create an ethos of conflict, influence decision making, and mobilize ethnocentric agenda. In a similar vein, some have argued that fear of harm to one's group is more related to willingness to compromise than is personal fear (Maoz & McCauley, 2005). Understanding the development of group-level norms and cultural beliefs as apart from individual beliefs is becoming increasingly important in intergroup conflict research. Future research should examine how political leaders and ethnic entrepreneurs use rhetorical appeals to vulnerability, mistrust, injustice, superiority, and helplessness to arouse passion and justify violence.

## ◆ Communication Issues and Intergroup Conflict

Communication issues have received scant attention in the academic study of intergroup conflict. Some have observed that communication scholars have been "slower to address intergroup issues" (Harwood & Giles, 2005, p. 1) than social psychologists. Ellis (2006) has organized some literature around social psychology, communication, and ethnopolitical conflict. He locates and describes communication and media issues that are germane to intergroup conflict. But much of the work in communication that refers to itself as "intergroup" avoids direct engagement with intergroup "conflict" issues. Although communication scholars make many references to identity and social categorization, their analysis of *actual* communication is sometimes highly attenuated. Communication scholars often focus on social construction and symbolic interaction explanations of how group members negotiate and acquire identities but do little to explain how those identities are implicated in actual intergroup conflicts. For example, communication scholars easily embrace identity as "fluid" and "socially constructed" (cf. Hajek, Abrams, & Murachver, 2005) but have failed to confront realistic concepts such as essentialism and the intractability of identities in actual conflicts. Identities are indeed socially constructed, but identity groups do not behave as if their identity were a flimsy concept capable of easy manipulation. Below I review the various strands of research in the area of communication and intergroup conflict. The special issue of *Group Processes and Intergroup Relations* (2005), edited by Reid and Giles, provides a useful presentation of communication issues and intergroup relations with some articles emphasizing conflict more than others. A special issue of *Journal of Social Issues* also contains an excellent overview of social psychological issues in intergroup conflict (Nagda, Tropp, & Paluck, 2006).

## COMMUNICATION ACCOMMODATION THEORY

Clearly, the most significant communication development related to intergroup relations is communication accommodation theory (CAT). This work has been described in numerous places (cf. Gallois, Ogay, &

Giles, 2004; Harwood & Giles, 2005, for reviews). CAT built on social categorization theory to include how language is used to establish social identities. It is less cognitively oriented than most of the social psychology research reviewed above. For example, individuals use accents or lexical choices to signal their group membership and stress particular identities (Giles & Powesland, 1975). Low-status English might evoke group solidarity and camaraderie for one group and social stigma for another, but both mark the individuals as members of a group with all the attendant traits, attributes, and biases of that group. How linguistic and stylistic choices shift and promote identity convergence and divergence between groups is also an important area of inquiry for CAT. CAT's claim is that social identity theory speaks to identity maintenance and in-group/out-group contrasts, but CAT explains how this works during the communication process. By using language to demonstrate group distinctiveness or similarity, individuals either encourage or discourage intergroup relations.

The majority of the research literature focuses on the development and recognition of various group identities. It refers to tensions, difference, and in-group/out-group dichotomies, but direct and galvanized conflict is relatively absent from the work in CAT. Social groups are identified along with the language that assimilates or contrasts groups. For example, Hajek and Giles (2002) examine identities between different groups of gay men (e.g., younger men and older men) and how they (younger gay men) make reference to such topics as physical attractiveness to distinguish themselves as a group. This is a form of intragroup discrimination. The core research concern is prejudice and discrimination. Communication research foci include health (Harwood & Sparks, 2003), age (Williams & Nussbaum, 2001), disability (Ryan, Bajorek, Beaman, & Anas, 2005), and others (see Harwood & Giles, 2005). Communication accommodation theory suffers, along with intergroup relations research in general, from the composition fallacy or drawing conclusions at the macro level from individual data (Pettigrew, 2006). Groups and social systems have properties of their own and are constituted by an assembly effect that is different than the sum of their parts. Group norms are more influential than most researchers recognize. A minority group's experience in school is different from that of the majority. The norms that these groups develop have different impacts on the groups. Intergroup contact has positive effects, but these effects are significantly diminished for minority groups (Pettigrew & Tropp, 2000), probably because minority groups develop norms that counteract normal contact effects.

Social identity theory originally described macro-patterns of group differences to explain intergroup conflict on the basis of power, status, and competition for resources. To that end, it was more narrowly focused on intergroup conflict. But CAT and other theories in communication have broadened the work to a more encompassing social identity perspective.

## MESSAGE VARIABLES

Recent research has examined message variables and their role in categorization and moderation of attitudes. One important message attribute is language abstractness. Some researchers have suggested that minorities are more influential if they are communicatively consistent (Sigall, Mucchi-Faina, & Mosso, 2006). These researchers found that abstract language enhances the perception of consistency for minorities; however, this was not true for majorities. It may be that audiences listening to majority messages direct their attention to other things. Researchers have examined how stereotypes are communicatively passed from one person to another (Wigboldus, Spears, & Semin, 2005). They propose that categorization processes activate stereotypes

that are brought to the foreground of consciousness. Stereotypes must then be made salient on the basis of the situation and the audience. This research showed that stereotype-consistent information is communicated at a higher level of linguistic abstraction. Stereotypes are not fixed images in people's minds but dependent on both communicative contexts and perceivers. Abstract language allows stereotypes to be activated and thus reproduced in a more socially sensitive manner. Abstract language is assumed to be more consistently true than concrete language.

Findings from Maass, Cadinu, Boni, and Borini (2005) nicely parallel the Wigboldus et al. (2005) work and the linguistic expectancy bias. Maass et al. (2005) found that when individuals communicate in a stereotypically expected manner, that information is communicated abstractly. The concrete qualities of another person are transformed into traits, especially when they are consistent with stereotypes. This cognitive mechanism is responsible for the maintenance of stereotypes and suggests that stereotypes and language abstraction are linked by cognitive processes and interpersonal communication. Clarifying the relationship between stereotypes and interpersonal relations, Ruscher, Cralley, and O'Farrell (2005) found a relationship between initial interactions in an interpersonal relationship and stereotypes. Close dyads that were especially inclined to get along shared more common stereotypes. Apparently, the transmission of out-group stereotypes is facilitated by friendship formation.

The effect of audiences on the interpretation of messages is apparent in a study by Elder, Sutton, and Douglas (2005). They reported that group members make strategic considerations, on the basis of in-group/out-group membership, with respect to how certain communications will be understood. Self-esteem is maintained by retaining a distinction between in-group and out-group members. Thus, when negative information is communicated to an out-group, it elicits greater in-group sensitivity. The in-group is aware of the potential threat of giving critical information to an out-group. Moreover, taking the criticism public was equally objectionable whether the criticism came from an in-group or out-group member. An in-group critic speaking to an in-group audience is acceptable, but the same critic speaking to an out-group is perceived to be embarrassing the group. The strategic use of communication and its group identity consequences should be a focal point for future research.

◆ *Communication, the Contact Hypothesis, and the Resolution of Intergroup Conflict*

Both the contact hypothesis (Allport, 1954) and conflict resolution are more naturally aligned with issues in communication. The contact hypothesis holds that assembling people from different identity groups to talk about issues can reduce stereotypes and increase friendliness. At some point in the intergroup conflict process, contact is inevitable; there is simply no escaping the importance of communication. It is communication that manages incommensurability. The idea of contact seems simple but in actuality is not. Contrasting group identities are a powerful basis for conflict, and reducing the effects of group identity and social categorization is very difficult; nevertheless, contact works. Meta-analytic evidence convincingly demonstrates that contact reduces prejudice for ethnic and racial groups as well as elderly groups, the disabled, and those with different sexual orientations (Pettigrew & Tropp, 2006). But there are also some who question the way such research has been conducted (Dixson, Durrheim, & Tredoux, 2005).

However, contact is not effective unless structured under certain conditions; in fact, uncontrolled contact can exacerbate stereotypes and prejudice. The contact hypothesis recognizes the importance of communicative context for encounter experiences between conflicting groups by insisting on situational conditions that optimize controlled communication designed to maximize successful outcomes (Pettigrew, 1998). The most critical ingredients of successful communicative contact are (a) an environment of equality and diminished status differences, (b) cooperative interdependence and pursuit of common goals, and (c) social norms supporting intergroup contact and affiliative relations (cf. Allport, 1954; Pettigrew, 1998). Ellis (2006) explains that the contact hypothesis and its general implications form a conceptual basis for the role of communication in managing and ameliorating difficult conflicts. The formal theory of contact has been amended, with authors proposing nuanced distinctions among situations and arrangements. Moreover, timing is important. When two groups have communicative contact, it is related to successful conflict resolution (Zartman, 1989). Forbes (2004) warns against the tendency to think of communicative contact in the naive, liberal sense of the term, where the magic elixir of friendly personal relations will somehow dissolve deeply ingrained prejudices. Unstructured contact between individuals often does improve particular relationships but little beyond that. Moreover, contact between conflicting group members can exacerbate conflict as the groups compete even more because each is trying to avoid adaptation costs (Forbes, 2004).

The communication that characterizes conflicting groups is highly disfigured, consisting of blame, accusation, stereotypes, delegitimation, prejudice, and various biases. Nonetheless, groups must have contact to overcome these patterns; how-ever, it is the type of communication during contact that matters. Currently, the world can be characterized by the seeming paradox of increased contact via new technologies, such as the Internet, migration, and increased cultural contact, yet substantial group conflict. Indeed, there was considerable contact between Blacks and Whites in the southern United States before 1960 but with a great deal of prejudice and discrimination. Contact involving focused and goal-oriented intergroup conflict resolution requires beginning with encounters between the two groups designed to reduce prejudices and improve interpersonal relations, followed by macro-strategies involving linguistic, commercial, and structural interdependence. Three lines of research that address core issues in communication, contact, and the resolution of intergroup conflict will now be considered.

In the first of these, Tropp and Pettigrew (2005) note that while some research concludes that intergroup contact leads to reductions in prejudice, other research finds no effect on prejudice reduction. In reconciling these disjunctions, they begin with the distinction between the affective and cognitive dimensions of prejudice. Affective ties such as intercultural friendships, liking, and feelings of closeness are inversely correlated with prejudice. Moreover, measures of prejudice based on affective issues such as sympathy, admiration, and intimacy were particularly influenced by positive interpersonal contact. In contrast, cognitive aspects of prejudice (e.g., stereotypes) are more resistant to change through positive contact. Tropp and Pettigrew (2005) found that contact can produce positive results, but this is principally true for the affective dimension. Most early work on contact focused on the cognitive dimension of prejudice, that is, stereotype reduction and realignments of attitudes and beliefs. But more recent thinking concludes that developing closer friendships, intimate relationships, and trust is most effective in reducing prejudice. These findings are consistent with previously cited work by Voci and Hewstone (2003) on the importance of contact in anxiety reduction.

This research underscores the importance of interpersonal communication to the entire experience of contact and resolution of intergroup conflict. It suggests a different orientation to improving the likelihood of positive contact outcomes. Out-group members who are confronted on the basis of cognitive differences in judgments, beliefs, or ideological positions are treated more objectively. This tendency creates distance between the groups that makes assimilation even more difficult. Orienting toward the other on the basis of affect and quality interpersonal relations makes emotions and feelings more relevant and increases the potential for moving closer interpersonally. Indeed, research has shown that emotions and empathy are particularly effective at reducing prejudice (Finlay & Stephan, 2000). Narratives have also been shown to increase positive relations for intractable conflicts and peace education (Sunwolf & Frey, 2000). In all likelihood, as affective ties between in-group members and out-groups increase, the motivation to reduce stereotypes and to confront cognitive prejudices increases. Generalizing from individuals to groups is enhanced when group membership is salient. Consequently, the type of interaction that is high on both the interpersonal and group dimensions will most likely promote generalization from individuals to out-groups.

The second line of research concerns the importance of the communication process in explaining how the effectiveness of intergroup contact varies (Nagda, 2006). Within this purview, intergroup contact experience can be meaningful and enriching, leading to significant relational improvement, or characterized by resentment and judgmentalism that fuels estrangement. The question becomes one of how meaningful encounters are sustained. The answer lies in the intergroup dialogue experience, which allows for the collective exploration of identities in a context that promotes respect and change (cf. Ellis, 2006; Maoz & Ellis, 2001, 2005). The key communication issues in intergroup contact designed to manage conflict are (a) alliance building or a willingness to work through problems; (b) engaging the self or a willingness to bring one's own ideas and practices to the encounter through a willingness to work, share, and inquire; (c) critical self-reflection, which requires an examination of one's own ideas; and (d) appreciating differences in others, including hearing their personal histories and points of view. Not only do these dimensions not differ across racial and ethnic groups, but these communication processes lead to increased motivation to reduce differences. They are highly implicated in a sequence that begins with the appreciation of difference and leads to critical analysis and alliance building. Intergroup conflict theorists must continue to explore not only the affective and interpersonal dimensions of contact but the cognitive and realistic dimensions as well. Nagda (2006) makes the distinction between friendship and alliances. Friendship implies personal interest and liking, and alliances are more practical and problem oriented. They are about conjoint commitment to change and solutions. Friendships and alliances reflect the dual track of conflict resolution, that is, the necessity of change and development on personal and pragmatic levels. This is mirrored in work on dialogue groups versus problem-solving groups. Dialogue groups engage people to learn about others, widen identities, develop visions of justice, and promote democratic sensibilities. Dialogue is a means of public deliberation for critical engagement and mobilization for change (McCoy & Scully, 2002; Stephan & Stephan, 2001). Problem-solving groups concentrate on realistic political policy and solutions to material problems (Kelman, 1997). Together, these two tracks represent a commitment to alliances that solve problems and undo prejudice in the process. The dialogic experience has to be purposeful and connected to pragmatic issues. The concept of "dialogue" is not an ethereal process inculcated with abstractions and spirituality; rather, dialogue is the

practice of working through difficult issues together. Democracies, in particular, construct common ground; hence, the goal of dialogue is not so much to manage or control conflict by jointly producing policies and solutions as it is to work through problems and differences that foster new realities and relationships. These new relationships can then form a foundation for future efforts to resolve differences.

The third research program has applied close analysis of communication methods to contact experiences between Israeli-Jews and Palestinians (Ellis & Maoz, 2002, 2003, 2007; Maoz & Ellis, 2001, 2005). Although traditional work in social psychology reviewed previously retains a rigorous variable-analytic research tradition, there is very little work that focuses on the actual communication processes that characterize intergroup contact. Ellis and Maoz (2003) have developed such a communication perspective in their work on patterns of communication and argument between Israeli-Jews and Palestinians. Within this perspective, conflict, by definition, is inter-active and results from interdependent people who perceive incompatible goals. Interdependence cannot be separated from communication. All behavior in an inter-active situation has message value and is therefore communicative. A communicative relationship is a frame that defines how the parties perceive each other (e.g., friend or foe; dominant or subordinate; friendly or unfriendly) and defines what can be said within the frame. Certain moves or messages can be considered appropriate or inappropriate because of the nature of the relationship.

Interactional approaches to conflict postulate that messages form sequences and patterns of exchange. Communication exists through time. Patterns of message exchanges over time constitute the defining characteristics of the conflicting parties. To describe an individual, group, or culture as having a communication style (e.g., competitive, accommodating, democratic, integrative) is to say that they engage in a recurring communication pattern. Interaction between conflicting groups takes the form of "He said A and he said B and she said C and so on"—a series of moves and countermoves. Every message in a sequence is both a response to something previous and a stimulus for something in the future. These ongoing interchanges constitute a chain of overlapping links.

The Ellis and Maoz studies revealed that the arguments during political dialogues between Israeli-Jews and Palestinians were not necessarily consistent with expectations from work on cultural speech codes (Katriel, 1986; Philipsen, 1997). In other words, the Israeli-Jews do not necessarily use more assertive arguments, and the Arabs are not necessarily less overtly aggressive. It appears that the dialogue context of communication does provide an environment for more equal status discussion and thus alters speech codes. Palestinians are more assertive during these dialogues than speech code theory, but not theories based on minority relations, would suggest. They speak more and engage in more reasoning and elaboration. This means that they state propositions and then support them with evidence in the classic tradition of argument. This dialogue context may also strengthen the sense of unity for groups with minority status. And the communication patterns reflect this. More recent studies that extend the analysis of argument to the Internet (Ellis & Maoz, 2007) further explore contexts for intergroup contact. Analysis of communication characteristics during intergroup contact is one of the best ways to uncover the context-depen-dent group norms that become meaningful prototypes for similarities and differences between groups (Hogg & Reid, 2006). If groups develop their own norms, and individuals categorize and define themselves on that basis, then these context-dependent norms become standards for perceptions, attitudes, and feelings that must be understood.

## ◆ Conclusion

Much theoretical work must be done to integrate communication studies with the tradition of intergroup relations in general. Hogg and Reid (2006) have made a very good start at this by locating the social identity perspective within communication research. Their primary insight is that group norms are context dependent but, more important, group norms are produced, reproduced, maintained, and changed through communication. Group norms, or collective cognitive images that represent the group, rely on communication to reduce uncertainty and regulate perceptions. Two lines of research should be pursued. One is to integrate further the social categorization work with persuasion. Influentials and opinion leaders in groups probably attend most to the group norms and encourage their endorsement. Persuading someone to behave in accordance with group prototypes is a matter of internalizing relevant in-group properties. Some work has begun (cf. Lapinski & Rimal, 2005) in this area, but there seems to be much potential for effective applications. Common category membership provides the semantic intersubjectivity that persuaders seek. How this might work in the political, health, advertising, or business arena suggests an interesting research agenda. A second line of future research pertaining to media effects is suggested by Reid and Hogg (2005). The studies by Eidelson and Eidelson (2003) dovetail nicely with third-person media effects (Reid & Hogg, 2005) by attending to the distinction between first-person and third-person perceptions. Self-categorization theory helps explain third-person effects by noting that people make judgments about the extent to which media are normative for in-groups and out-groups. Normative media for out-groups produce third-person effects; that is, out-groups are more influenced by such media than are in-groups. There are many implications for media effects by recognizing the group-specific, differential impact of media. The contact hypothesis is fundamentally democratic and provides a public space and safe environment for critical engagement. There is strong evidence that programs of intergroup conflict reduction show positive results in the educational and political arenas and need to be promoted continuously.

## ◆ References

Allport, G. W. (1954). *The nature of prejudice.* Reading, MA: Addison-Wesley.

Blanton, H. (2001). Evaluating the self in the context of another. In G. B. Moskowitz (Ed.), *Cognitive social psychology* (pp. 75–87). Mahwah, NJ: Lawrence Erlbaum.

Brewer, M. B. (1991). The social self: On being the same and different at the same time. *Personality and Social Psychology Bulletin, 17,* 475–482.

Cadinu, M. R., & Rothbart, M. (1996). Self-anchoring and differentiation process in the minimal group paradigm. *Journal of Personality and Social Psychology, 70,* 661–677.

Cargile, A. C., Bradac, J. J., & Cole, T. (2006). Theories of intergroup conflict: A report of lay attributions. *Journal of Language and Social Psychology, 25,* 47–63.

Clement, R. W., & Krueger, J. (2000). The primacy of self-referent information in perceptions of social consensus. *British Journal of Social Psychology, 39,* 279–299.

Crosby, F. J. (1976). A model of egoistical relative deprivation. *Psychological Review, 83,* 85–113.

Demoulin, S., Leyens, J., & Yzerbyt, V. (2006). Lay theories of essentialism. *Group Processes and Intergroup Relations, 9,* 25–42.

Dixson, J., Durrheim, K., & Tredoux, C. (2005). Beyond the optimal contact strategy: A reality check for the contact hypothesis. *American Psychologist, 60,* 697–711.

Dreachslin, J. L., Hunt, P. L., & Sprainer, E. (2000). Workforce diversity: Implications for the effectiveness of health care delivery teams. *Social Science and Medicine, 50,* 1403–1414.

Eidelson, R. J., & Eidelson, J. I. (2003). Dangerous ideas: Five beliefs that propel groups toward conflict. *American Psychologist, 58,* 182–192.

Elder, T. J., Sutton, R. M., & Douglas, K. M. (2005). Keeping it to ourselves: Effects of audience size and composition on reactions to criticisms of the ingroup. *Group Processes & Intergroup Relations, 8,* 231–244.

Ellis, D. G. (2006). *Transforming conflict: Communication and ethnopolitical conflict.* Lanham, MD: Rowman & Littlefield.

Ellis, D. G., & Maoz, I. (2002). Cross-cultural argument interactions between Israeli-Jews and Palestinians. *Journal of Applied Communication Research, 30,* 181–194.

Ellis, D. G., & Maoz, I. (2003). A communication and cultural codes approach to ethnonational conflict. *International Journal of Conflict Management, 14,* 255–272.

Ellis, D. G., & Maoz, I. (2007). Online argument between Israeli Jews and Palestinians. *Human Communication Research, 33,* 291–309.

Finlay, K., & Stephan, W. G. (2000). Reducing prejudice: The effects of empathy on intergroup attitudes. *Journal of Applied Social Psychology, 30,* 1720–1737.

Forbes, H. D. (2004). Ethnic conflict and the contact hypothesis. In Y. T. Lee, C. McCauley, F. Moghaddam, & S. Worchel (Eds.), *The psychology of ethnic and cultural conflict* (pp. 69–88). Westport, CT: Praeger.

Gallois, C., Ogay, T., & Giles, H. (2004). Communication accommodation theory: A look back and a look ahead. In W. B. Gudykunst (Ed.), *Theorizing about intercultural communication* (pp. 121–148). Thousand Oaks, CA: Sage.

Gelman, S. A., & Wellman, H. M. (1991). Insides and essences: Early understandings of the non-obvious. *Cognition, 38,* 213–244.

Giles, H., & Powesland, P. F. (1975). *Speech style and social evaluation.* London: Academic Press.

Gil-White, F. (2001). Are ethnic groups biological species to the human brain? Essentialism in human cognition of some social groups. *Current Anthropology, 42,* 515–554.

Greenwald, A. G., Banaji, M. R., Rudman, L. A., Farnham, S. D., Nosek, B. A., &

Mellott, D. S. (2002). A unified theory of implicit attitudes, stereotypes, self-esteem, and self-concept. *Psychological Review, 109,* 3–25.

Hajek, C., Abrams, J. R., & Murachver, T. (2005). Female, straight, male, gay, and worlds betwixt and between: An intergroup approach to sexual and gender identities. In J. Harwood & H. Giles (Eds.), *Intergroup communication* (pp. 43–64). New York: Peter Lang.

Hajek, C., & Giles, H. (2002). The old man out: An intergroup analysis of intergenerational communication among gay men. *Journal of Communication, 52,* 698–714.

Harwood, J., & Giles, H. (Eds.). (2005). *Intergroup communication.* New York: Peter Lang.

Harwood, J., & Sparks, L. (2003). Social identity and health: An intergroup communication approach to cancer. *Health Communication, 15,* 145–159.

Haslam, N., Bastian, B., Bain, P., & Kashima, Y. (2006). Psychological essentialism, implicit theories, and intergroup relations. *Group Processes and Intergroup Relations, 9,* 63–76.

Hogg, M. A., & Reid, S. A. (2006). Social identity, self-categorization, and the communication of group norms. *Communication Theory, 16,* 7–30.

Katriel, T. (1986). *Talking straight: Dugri speech in Israeli sabra culture.* Cambridge, UK: Cambridge University Press.

Kelman, H. C. (1997). Group processes in the resolution of international conflicts. *American Psychologist, 52,* 212–220.

Lapinski, M. K., & Rimal, R. N. (2005). An explication of social norms. *Communication Theory, 15,* 127–147.

Learnpeace. (n.d.). www.ppu.org.uk/learn/peaceed/pe_robbers_cave.html. Retrieved June 4, 2007.

Levin, S., van Laar, C., & Sidanius, J. (2003). The effects of ingroup and outgroup friendship on ethnic attitudes in college: A longitudinal study. *Group Processes and Intergroup Relations, 6,* 76–92.

Levy, S. R., Stroessner, S. J., & Dweck, C. S. (1998). Stereotype formation and endorsement: The role of implicit theories. *Journal of Personality and Social Psychology, 74,* 1421–1436.

Maass, A., Cadinu, M., Boni, M., & Borini, C. (2005). Converting verbs into adjectives:

Asymmetrical memory distortions for stereotypic and counterstereotypic information. *Group Processes & Intergroup Relations, 8,* 271–290. Retrieved June 12, 2007, from Psychology: A SAGE Full-Text Collection database.

Mackie, D. M., Devos, T., & Smith, E. R. (2000). Intergroup emotions: Explaining offensive action tendencies in an intergroup context. *Journal of Personality and Social Psychology, 79,* 602–616.

Major, B., Quinton, W., & McCoy, S. (2002). Antecedents and consequences of attributions to discrimination: Theoretical and empirical advances. In M. P. Zanna (Ed.), *Advances in experimental social psychology* (Vol. 34, pp. 251–329). San Diego: Academic Press.

Maoz, I., & Eidelson, R. J. (2007). Psychological bases of extreme policy preferences: How the personal beliefs of Israeli-Jews predict their support for population transfer in the Israeli-Palestinian conflict. *American Behavioral Scientist, 50,* 1476–1497.

Maoz, I., & Ellis, D. G. (2001). Going to ground: Argument in Israeli-Jewish and Palestinian encounter groups. *Research on Language and Social Interaction, 34,* 399–419.

Maoz, I., & Ellis, D. G. (2005). Facilitating groups in severe conflict: The case of transformational dialogue between Israeli-Jews and Palestinians. In L. Frey (Ed.), *Facilitating group communication in context: Innovations and applications with natural groups* (pp. 123–143). Cresskill, NJ: Hampton.

Maoz, I., & McCauley, R. (2005). Psychological correlates of support for compromise: A polling study of Jewish-Israeli attitudes towards solutions to the Israeli-Palestinian conflict. *Political Psychology, 26,* 791–807.

Maoz, I., Ward, A., Katz, M., & Ross, L. (2002). Reactive devaluation of an "Israeli" vs. "Palestinian" peace proposal. *Journal of Conflict Resolution, 46,* 515–546.

McCoy, M. L., & Scully, P. L. (2002). Deliberative dialogue to expand civic engagement: What kind of talk does democracy need? *National Civic Review, 91,* 117–135.

Miller, D. A., Smith, E. R., & Mackie, D. M. (2004). Effects of intergroup contact and political predispositions on prejudice: Role of intergroup emotions. *Group Processes and Intergroup Relations, 7,* 221–237.

Miller, N. (2002). Personalization and the promise of contact theory. *Journal of Social Issues, 58,* 387–410.

Molina, L. E., Wittig, M. A., & Giang, M. T. (2004). Mutual acculturation and social categorization: A comparison of two perspectives on intergroup bias. *Group Processes and Intergroup Relations, 7,* 239–265.

Nagda, B. A. (2006). Breaking barriers, crossing borders, building bridges: Communication processes in intergroup dialogues. *Journal of Social Issues, 62,* 553–576.

Nagda, B. A., Tropp, L. R., & Paluck, E. L. (2006). Looking back as we look ahead: Integrating research, theory, and practice on intergroup relations. *Journal of Social Issues, 62,* 439–451.

Operario, D., & Fiske, S. T. (2001). Ethnic identity moderates perceptions of prejudice: Judgments of personal versus group discrimination and subtle versus blatant bias. *Personality and Social Psychology Bulletin, 27,* 550–561.

Pettigrew, T. F. (1998). Intergroup contact theory. *Annual Review of Psychology, 49,* 65–85.

Pettigrew, T. F. (2006). The advantages of multilevel approaches. *Journal of Social Issues, 62,* 615–620.

Pettigrew, T. F., & Tropp, L. R. (2000). Does intergroup contact reduce prejudice? Recent meta-analytic findings. In S. Oskamp (Ed.), *Reducing prejudice and discrimination* (pp. 93–114). Mahwah, NJ: Lawrence Erlbaum.

Pettigrew, T. F., & Tropp, L. R. (2006). A meta-analytic test of intergroup contact theory. *Journal of Personality and Social Psychology, 90,* 751–783.

Philipsen, G. (1997). A theory of speech codes. In G. Philipsen & T. L. Albrecht (Eds.), *Developing communication theories* (pp. 119–156). Albany: State University of New York Press.

Reid, S. A., & Giles, H. (Eds.). (2005). Intergroup relations: Its linguistic and communicative parameters [Special issue]. *Group Processes and Intergroup Relations, 8.*

Reid, S. A., & Hogg, M. A. (2005). A self-categorization explanation of the third-person effect. *Human Communication Research, 31,* 129–161.

Richeson, J. A., & Shelton, J. N. (2003). When prejudice does not pay: Effects of interracial contact on executive function. *Psychological Science, 14,* 287–290.

Riketta, M. (2005). Cognitive differentiation between self, ingroup, and outgroup: The roles of identification and perceived intergroup conflict. *European Journal of Social Psychology, 35,* 97–106.

Ruscher, J. B., Cralley, E. L., & O'Farrell, K. J. (2005). How newly acquainted dyads develop shared stereotypic impressions through conversation. *Group Processes & Intergroup Relations, 8,* 259–270. Retrieved June 12, 2007, from Psychology: A SAGE Full-Text Collection database.

Ryan, E. B., Bajorek, S., Beaman, A., & Anas, A. P. (2005). I just want you to know that them is me: Intergroup perspectives on communication and disability. In J. Harwood & H. Giles (Eds.), *Intergroup communication* (pp. 117–137). New York: Peter Lang.

Sherif, M. (1951). A preliminary experimental study of inter-group relations. In J. H. Rohrer & M. Sherif (Eds.), *Social psychology at the crossroads* (pp. 388–424). New York: Harper.

Sherif, M., Harvey, O. J., White, B. J., Hood, W. R., & Sherif, C. W. (1961). *Intergroup conflict and cooperation: The Robber's Cave experiment.* Norman: University of Oklahoma Book Exchange.

Sigall, H., Mucchi-Faina, A., & Mosso, C. (2006). Minority influence is facilitated when the communication employs linguistic abstractness. *Group Processes and Intergroup Relations, 9,* 443–451.

Spears, R., & Manstead, A. S. R. (1990). Consensus estimation in social context. *European Review of Social Psychology, 1,* 81–109.

Stephan, W. G., Boniecki, K. A., Ybarra, O., Bettencourt, A., Ervin, K. S., Jackson, L. A., et al. (2002). The role of threats in the racial attitudes of Blacks and Whites. *Personality and Social Psychology Bulletin, 28,* 1242–1254.

Stephan, W. G., & Stephan, C. W. (2001). *Improving intergroup relations.* Thousand Oaks, CA: Sage.

Sunwolf & Frey, L. R. (2000). Storytelling: The power of narrative communication and interpretation. In W. P. Robinson & H. Giles (Eds.), *The new handbook of language and social psychology* (pp. 119–135). London: John Wiley.

Tajfel, H., & Turner, J. C. (1979). An integrative theory of intergroup conflict. In W. G. Austin & S. Worchel (Eds.), *The social psychology of intergroup relations* (pp. 33–48). Monterey, CA: Brooks/Cole.

Tam, T., Hewstone, M., Cairns, E., Tausch, N., Maio, G., & Kenworthy, J. (2007). The impact of intergroup emotions on forgiveness in Northern Ireland. *Group Processes and Intergroup Relations, 10,* 119–135.

Taylor, D. M., & McKirnan, D. J. (1984). A five-stage model of intergroup relations. *British Journal of Social Psychology, 23,* 291–300.

Taylor, D. M., & Moghaddam, F. M. (1994). *Theories of intergroup relations.* Westport, CT: Praeger.

Tropp, L. R. (2003). The psychological impact of prejudice: Implications for intergroup contact. *Group Processes and Intergroup Relations, 6,* 131–149.

Tropp, L. R., & Pettigrew, T. F. (2005). Differential relationships between intergroup contact and affective and cognitive dimensions of prejudice. *Personality and Social Psychology Bulletin, 31,* 1145–1158.

Turner, J. C. (1985). Social categorization and the self-concept: A social cognitive theory of group behavior. In E. J. Lawler (Ed.), *Advances in group processes* (Vol. 2, pp. 77–122). Greenwich, CT: JAI.

Turner, J. C., Hogg, M. A., Oakes, P. J., Reicher, S. D., & Wetherell, M. S. (1987).

*Rediscovering the social group: A self-categorization theory.* Oxford, UK: Blackwell.

Voci, A., & Hewstone, M. (2003). Intergroup contact and prejudice toward immigrants in Italy: The mediational role of anxiety and the moderational role of group salience. *Group Processes and Intergroup Relations, 6,* 37–54.

Walster, E., Walster, G. W., & Berscheid, E. (1978). *Equity: Theory and research.* Boston, MA: Allyn & Bacon.

Wigboldus, D. H. J., Spears, R., & Semin, G. R. (2005). When do we communicate stereotypes? Influence of the social context on the linguistic expectancy bias. *Group Processes & Intergroup Relations, 8,* 215–230. Retrieved June 12, 2007, from Psychology: A SAGE Full-Text Collection database.

Williams, A., & Nussbaum, J. F. (2001). *Intergenerational communication across the lifespan.* Mahwah, NJ: Lawrence Erlbaum.

Wittig, M. A., & Molina, L. (2000). Moderators and mediators of prejudice reduction. In S. Oskamp (Ed.), *Reducing prejudice and discrimination* (pp. 295–318). Mahwah, NJ: Lawrence Erlbaum.

Wright, S. C., & Tropp, L. R. (2005). Language and intergroup contact: Investigating the impact of bilingual instruction on children's intergroup attitudes. *Group Processes and Intergroup Relations, 8,* 309–328.

Yzerbyt, V. Y., Rogier, A., & Fiske, S. (1998). Group entitativity and social attribution: On translating situational constraints into stereotypes. *Personality and Social Psychology Bulletin, 24,* 1090–1104.

Zartman, I. W. (1989). *Ripe for resolution.* Oxford, UK: Oxford University Press.

# BARGAINING AND NEGOTIATION

◆ Michael E. Roloff and Shu Li

Cushman and Craig (1976) observed that negotiation was becoming the primary means of managing differences. With regard to research, their words were prophetic, as the negotiation literature rapidly grew throughout that last quarter of the 20th century and continues to expand in the new millennium. Communication is one of several disciplines whose researchers have contributed to this expansion. Although the original *Handbook of Communication Science* did not include a chapter focused on negotiation research, the chapter on communication and conflict reviewed some of it (Roloff, 1987). The links between negotiation and interpersonal (Sillars, Chapter 16, this volume) and intergroup conflict (Ellis, Chapter 17, this volume) remain strong, but the negotiation literature has formed an independent critical mass. Our goal is to examine the theoretical perspectives and approaches that have been used to study communication and negotiation. We first provide a brief history of this research corpus, after which we will examine approaches used to study key questions. We will end with an overall assessment of theory and proposals for future directions.

## ◆ History

Negotiation research has always been multidisciplinary. Historical, game-theoretic, social psychological, and cognitive learning approaches were represented in the early literature. The emergence of a communication approach occurred much later. In their classic review of the negotiation literature, Rubin and Brown (1975) did not include a chapter specifically focused on communication. This lack of focus on communication is surprising. Scholars have long acknowledged the inherent connection between communication and negotiation (e.g., Morley & Stephenson, 1977). Because negotiation has been used as a means of creating exchange agreements or managing conflicts, researchers interested in negotiation contexts such as collective bargaining and international diplomacy had a dominant influence on the development of negotiation research. These scholars were from fields and disciplines such as economics, psychology, and political science and brought with them the questions, theories, and methods common to investigators in their academic homes. Although their theoretical perspectives and research sometimes included communication, their characterization of communication was quite limited, often focusing on issues such as the opportunity to communicate.

Putnam and Jones (1982b) reviewed the early negotiation and communication literature and found it scattered and limited in scope. They identified three approaches. The mechanistic approach examined the direct effect of communication on negotiation outcomes (e.g., communication modality). The psychological approach focused on the effects of information acquisition and message strategies, and the pragmatic approach examined the sequences or phases characterizing negotiations. Few theories were discussed within each of the three approaches, and none of the frameworks were used across the three approaches. In addition, Putnam and Jones noted that most schemes for coding negotiation interaction were not firmly grounded in theory.

During the following decade, during which research increased dramatically, several trends became evident. First,

researchers conducted more theory-driven research. Some researchers continued to import perspectives from allied disciplines, but they more fully investigated the role of communication implied by these frameworks (e.g., Putnam & Jones, 1982a; Tutzauer & Roloff, 1988). Not all theoretical perspectives were imported. Donohue (1981b) created a communication-based rules perspective that highlights how negotiators can use communication to gain relative advantage and thereby increase their individual outcomes. In addition, several researchers employed perspectives on argumentation (e.g., Putnam, Wilson, Waltman, & Turner, 1986) and rhetoric (Putnam, Van Hoeven, & Bullis, 1991) to study negotiation discourse.

The second trend reflected refinement and diversification of methods and samples. Researchers created interaction coding schemes that were more sophisticated and tied to negotiation processes (e.g., Donohue, 1981a). Alternative statistical methods were proposed (Tutzauer, 1987), and conversation-analytic methods were used to examine micro-patterns within negotiation discourse (e.g., Neu, 1988). And although the use of experimental methods continued, researchers began to study transcripts of actual negotiations (e.g., Hinkle, Stiles, & Taylor, 1988) or conducted field studies of ongoing negotiations (e.g., Putnam et al., 1986).

The third trend was increased specialization. Rather than taking a holistic approach to understanding negotiation, researchers focused on specific features. For example, Putnam and Roloff (1992) edited a volume on communication and negotiation that contained chapters focused on a wide array of research areas such as planning, argumentation, framing, and negotiation relationships. Some of the research cited in the chapters was grounded in theory, but few cited the same theoretical perspectives.

Chatman, Putnam, and Sondak (1991) conducted a new literature review and noted the emergence of a communication approach.

This perspective was distinguishable from others in its focus on how the meanings attached to micro-levels of talk are constructed by negotiators during their interactions. Researchers continued to study the direct effect of communication on outcomes or treated communication as a mediating factor between antecedent conditions and outcomes. Some researchers were conducting descriptive studies of negotiation discourse and adopted a systems interaction approach that examined communication patterns evident in the discourse or an interpretive-symbolic perspective that focused on the meanings that negotiators attached to their communication. Although Chatman et al. noted a number of research programs, they characterized the literature on communication and negotiation as being in its "infancy." It is now more than a decade and a half since Chatman et al. reviewed the literature, and it is appropriate to see if research on communication and negotiation has matured. Hence, we investigate the approaches researchers have taken when answering the key research questions and whether they are making progress toward answering them.

We adopted an organizational pattern roughly derived from research questions used by Cappella (1987) to understand social interaction research. Because scholars agree that negotiation is a form of interaction, Cappella's framework is an appropriate way to organize the negotiation literature. Cappella noted four levels of questions associated with interaction research. Zero-order questions focus on identifying the types and structures of variables to be studied. First-order questions examine psychological and social factors that influence the baseline frequency with which individuals encode and decode communication. Second-order questions require identification of patterns of communication. Third-order questions investigate how interaction influences relational states.

## ◆ Zero-Order Questions

Zero-order questions are focused on generating descriptions and often involve developing schemes for identifying or coding features of discourse. When developing descriptions, negotiation researchers use two approaches. The metaphorical approach treats negotiation as though it is like another form of communication; consequently, the schemes researchers use are not designed for studying negotiation. Some researchers treat negotiation as a form of group decision making (see Poole & Dobosh, Chapter 22, this volume) and use Bale's interaction process analysis to code negotiation transcripts (e.g., Theye & Seiler, 1979). Other researchers treat negotiation as a rhetorical event and use rhetorical methods to identify themes, rituals, and tropes (e.g., Putnam, 2004a). Negotiation has also been approached as a type of argument, and methods used to analyze types and sequences of arguments have been applied to negotiation transcripts (e.g., Putnam & Geist, 1985). Still others have approached negotiation as a conversation and used conversation-analytic techniques to examine micro-sequences (e.g., Neu, 1988) or speech acts (Hinkle et al., 1988). And some have viewed negotiation as a form of influence and have used linguistic typologies to identify directives in negotiation transcripts (Donohue & Diez, 1985) or to code influence tactics (e.g., Galinat & Muller, 1988). Although the metaphorical approach can provide insights into negotiation, it can be problematic. Because the perspectives and schemes were not devised for understanding negotiation, they may ignore its unique features. Moreover, metaphorical approaches may highlight features that are of little consequence in negotiation.

The second approach involves developing schemes specifically related to negotiation. There are two forms. The first is weakly derived from theory. In some cases, the schemes are based on common notions of what occurs during negotiations (e.g., Morley & Stephenson, 1977) or informal observations of negotiations (Osterberg, 1950). In other cases, researchers develop coding schemes to reflect processes consistent with a particular conceptualization of negotiation as well as those that have been discovered by researchers (Donohue, 1981b). Finally, some schemes arise from the desire to overcome deficiencies in existing negotiation schemes (e.g., Putnam & Jones, 1982a) or to adapt schemes created for other forms of interaction to negotiation (Walcott & Hopmann, 1975).

The second form is theory driven, and the coding schemes are linked to a theory of negotiation and subsequent research that investigates the theory. Donohue (1981a) created a rule-based negotiation theory that highlighted a variety of communication moves that lead to gaining relative advantage in a negotiation (attacking, defending, and integrating). He then created a coding scheme to assess those moves that was later modified (Donohue, Diez, & Hamilton, 1984). One of the most commonly used schemes is associated with Pruitt's (1981) program of research on integrative bargaining. Although initially focused on logrolling (multi-issue offers containing issues of different priorities), the scheme expanded and was modified as specific projects identified new forms of communication (e.g., information sharing, heuristic trial and error, contentiousness). Perhaps the most complex scheme was derived from Taylor's (2002) cylindrical model of communication behavior in crisis negotiations. He differentiated messages according to level (avoidance, distributive, integrative), theme (identity, instrumental, relational), and intensity. An exhaustive coding scheme was initially applied to transcripts, and through replication, the categories were refined and some removed. The frequencies of the behavioral categories were then subjected to a form of nonmetric multidimensional scaling that verified the existence of the behavioral levels, themes, and intensity.

Although these approaches have generated considerable research and demonstrated the diverse content that characterizes negotiation discourse, they have not produced an integrated view of communication in negotiation. Taylor's (2002) cylindrical model comes closest to an integrated perspective in that it highlights several features of communication, but it has little to say about the micro-processes identified through conversation analysis, and the model was generated to study only one form of negotiation. In part, the absence of an integrated framework stems from the different perspectives on negotiation or the divergent theories and experiences of the researchers who develop the coding schemes. Certainly, such diversity has not impeded research activity, and standards for improving schemes enhance the quality of the scholarship (Putnam, 2005; Weingart, Olekalns, & Smith, 2005). However, the absence of an integrated framework leaves open the question of how the various features might independently or in combination influence negotiation processes and outcomes, and by and large, the diversity and separation of schemes reduce the coherency of the area.

## ◆ First-Order Questions

First-order questions are focused on the psychological and social factors that influence the frequency with which communication behaviors are enacted and how these actions are interpreted.

### PSYCHOLOGICAL FACTORS

As noted earlier, negotiation researchers have often adopted a psychological orientation when studying communication and negotiation, and this approach continues (Bazerman, Curhan, Moore, & Valley, 2000). Researchers representing this orientation have investigated four psycho-logical influences on negotiation commu-nication: individual differences, cognition, motivation, and affect.

*Individual Differences.* The study of indi-vidual differences has been a traditional approach to negotiation research (Rubin & Brown, 1975). A great deal of this research is focused on the degree to which individual differences are related to negotiation moti-vations and outcomes with much less exploring the influence of individual differ-ences on communication during negotia-tion. Forgas (1998) discovered that high Machiavellians were more likely to report using competitive negotiation strategies than low Machiavellians, but high Machiavellians reported using more com-petitive strategies when in a bad relative to a good mood. In addition, men are often more active during negotiation and achieve greater individual profits than women (e.g., Neu, Graham, & Gilly, 1988). However, Kray, Thompson, and Galinsky (2001) found that when gender stereotypes about negotiation effectiveness were explicitly activated (i.e., telling negotiators that men typically outperform women), women reacted negatively to them, made initial offers more to their advantage, and outper-formed men. Finally, Jordan and Roloff (1997) found that self-monitoring was pos-itively related to achieving individual nego-tiation goals largely through the plans that were formed and enacted.

Although individual difference perspec-tives have yielded some useful insights, the utility of this approach for researching communication and negotiation is limited. There are a large number of individual difference variables from which to choose, making it difficult to create a coherent picture of their collective influence; hence, one is often left with a laundry list of possible predictors. Furthermore, the influ-ence of individual differences is often moderated by a host of situational vari-ables, not all of which can be specified

in advance. Thus, after establishing an initial relationship between an individual difference characteristic and negotiation, the program of research reduces to an ongoing search for moderators. Finally, because individual difference perspectives are inherently focused on describing traits, their links to specific forms of commu-nication are typically underdeveloped.

*Cognition.* Cognitive approaches are con-cerned with how individuals think about negotiation. Although negotiators strive for rationality, they are only quasi-rational, and their decision making is often im-plicit, nonsequential, and nonrecoverable (Hammond & Brehmer, 1973). These factors lead to cognitive conflict during a negotiation, and various stakeholders in a negotiation often have different cognitive models of the issues (Bolland & Redfield, 1988). Even when their views of possible agreements are similar, negotiators have difficulty describing their preferences and are inconsistent when evaluating them (Brehmer, 1976), and these differences remain even after months of negotiation (Balke, Hammond, & Meyer, 1973). Evidence suggests that communication may actually exacerbate cognitive conflict (Brehmer & Hammond, 1977), although some tactics may be helpful (Alexander, 1979).

During the late 1980s and 1990s, cognitive perspectives emerged that focused on the judgment biases that undercut effective negotiation (Neale & Bazerman, 1991). These biases included framing effects, overconfidence, reactive devaluation, fixed pie, perspective taking, moods, and nonrational escalation. The limited amount of research examining the relationship between cognitive biases and communica-tion has demonstrated that communication can both reinforce and attenuate cognitive biases such as the fixed pie and framing (see Roloff & Van Swol, 2008). Thompson and Nadler (2002) also observed that communication media can create cognitive biases.

Other researchers have adopted a framing approach. A frame constitutes a cognitive device by which individuals understand the issues that are being negotiated. Such frames may be apparent in a person's cognitions such as his or her mental maps (Olekalns & Smith, 2005) or in discourse (Drake & Donohue, 1996). Some research suggests that frames are derived from social motivations such as cooperation and motivation (Olekalns & Smith, 2005), and other perspectives suggest that they result from a conscious selection among frames based on their situational prominence and utility (e.g., Esser, 2004). Putnam (2004b) argues that frames may be transformed during negotiations by shifting language such as specific to general, general to specific, part to whole, individual to system, and literal to symbolic.

Another recent cognitive approach has examined the impact of tactical knowledge on negotiation communication and outcomes. Tactical knowledge refers to the degree to which a person is aware of negotiation tactics. When accessed from memory or primed through instructions, tactical knowledge can guide behavior and facilitate reaching agreements. Providing descriptions of negotiation tactics increases the use of integrative strategies (e.g., making multiple issue offers) but has no effect on distributive ones (e.g., making single-issue offers, making arguments that substantiate individual positions; Weingart, Hyder, & Prietula, 1996). Furthermore, the impact of tactical knowledge on outcomes is constrained by the complexity of the issues under consideration (Hyder, Prietula, & Weingart, 2000), and the use of tactical knowledge may be moderated by self-confidence (Sullivan, O'Connor, & Burris, 2006).

The cognitive approaches have provided useful insights into negotiation behavior and outcomes; however, they do not constitute a unified theory. For example, the study of cognitive biases suffered from an extensive list of largely unconnected biases (Carnevale & Pruitt, 1992). Furthermore, none of the cognitive perspectives explains how cognition

is transformed into action. For example, tactical knowledge includes actions such as "making a multi-issue offer," but that belief provides little insight into the process by which individuals identify and prioritize issues, package them, and modify them during negotiation. Research has been conducted on the plans negotiators develop (e.g., Roloff & Jordan, 1991), but these investigations do not provide a detailed account of the cognitive processes that produced the specific features of plans.

*Motivation.* Motivational approaches have a long tradition in negotiation research (e.g., Schelling, 1960) and are focused on the motives that guide a negotiator's behavior. Two general motivations influence negotiation behavior and outcomes (De Dreu & Carnevale, 2003). Social motivations constitute the desire to see the outcomes of negotiation distributed in a certain manner, and epistemic motivations reflect a desire to hold an accurate view of events.

Using research conducted on conflict management styles, Pruitt and Rubin (1986) proposed the dual-concern theory of conflict, which highlights social motivations. Concerns reflect a negotiator's desires for outcomes and, when focused on one's own outcomes, reflect an egoistic motivation and, when focused on a partner's outcomes, reflect a prosocial motivation. The strength of each concern combines to suggest different methods of negotiating. When unconcerned about their own and their partners' outcomes, individuals are avoidant and unlikely to enter into negotiation. When concerned about their partners' outcomes and unconcerned about their own outcomes, negotiators are willing to make concessions or compromise. When they are focused on their own outcomes and unconcerned about their partners, they are tough and contentious. Finally, when they are concerned with their own and others' outcomes, they are integrative.

Pruitt (1981) posited that integrative agreements are most likely to be discovered when individuals are highly committed to achieving their aspirations but are flexible as to the means of achieving them. Hence, negotiators must stubbornly pursue their interests while adjusting their proposals so that their partners' interests are served. This principle is reflective of dual concern for own and partners' outcomes and promotes communication behaviors such as sharing priority information, logrolling (i.e., package offers in which concessions are offered on low-priority issues while demands are advanced on high-priority ones), and controlling contentious behavior (e.g., substantive argumentation, threats). If negotiators are more concerned about their partners' outcomes than they are about their own, they engage in rapid concession making and sacrifice their own benefits. If they are primarily concerned about their own outcomes, they engage in single-item offers and are contentious, which can lead to a one-sided victory or deadlock.

The dual-concern theory prompted a great deal of research, and a meta-analysis was conducted on their results (De Dreu, Weingart, & Kwon, 2000). Consistent with the theory, negotiators who are prosocially motivated (i.e., are concerned about their partners' outcomes) but are unwilling to yield (i.e., are committed to achieving their own outcomes) are more likely to engage in problem-solving actions and reach integrative agreements while avoiding contentiousness than are negotiators who are prosocially motivated but willing to yield or are egoistically motivated (i.e., are only concerned with achieving their own outcomes).

De Dreu and Carnevale (2003) advanced a motivated information-processing model of negotiation that combines features of the dual-concern theory and cognitive perspectives on heuristics and biases. They argue that conflict management is impeded by naive realism and ego-defensiveness. Naive realism is the tendency to assume the world is as one perceives it and produces cognitive biases such as fixed pie assumptions and confirmatory information search.

Ego-defensiveness is the desire to uphold a positive self-image and produces cognitive biases such as self-serving evaluations and reactive devaluation. De Dreu and Carnevale also note that individuals have epistemic motivations that reflect a desire to hold an accurate and rich view of the world. When epistemic motivation is high, individuals engage in a systematic analysis of negotiation issues and more information seeking, which undercut naive realism and ego-defensiveness and facilitate finding integrative agreements.

By combining social motivations from the dual-concern theory with epistemic motivations, De Dreu and Carnevale (2003) identified negotiator archetypes. Egoistic social motivations focus on finding ways to enhance one's own outcomes, whereas prosocial motivations direct information search toward identifying the means to benefit both self and partner. Epistemic motivations influence the level of effort involved in information processing and gathering such that when epistemic motivations are high, individuals will systematically process and seek information (i.e., they are thinkers), and when low, individuals will rely on heuristics to understand the negotiation (i.e., they are cognitive misers). Hence, a prosocially motivated negotiator who also is high in epistemic motivation may engage in active information sharing and searching for alternative solutions, whereas a prosocially motivated negotiator may make unilateral concessions or will seek a compromise. Although we are unaware of a meta-analysis of research testing this perspective, individual studies seem supportive of many of its features (e.g., De Dreu, Beersma, Stroebe, & Euwema, 2006; De Dreu & Van Kleef, 2004).

In some respects, the motivational approaches have provided useful insights into communication and negotiation. They cast motivations as a cause of specific types of communication and note that the impact of motivations on negotiation outcomes is mediated by communication. De Dreu and Carnevale (2003) posited that motivations are not fixed and that communication enacted during a negotiation may influence them; hence, rather than merely being a mediator, communication may change motivations. The greatest limitation of motivational approaches stems from their lack of attention to cognitive factors associated with message design (see Berger, Chapter 7, this volume). Although De Dreu and Carnevale's perspective incorporates cognitive approaches to negotiation and does consider particular types of communication (e.g., information seeking, multi-issue offers), it does not explicate the processes that create message features (e.g., the types of questions that are asked; the types of issues contained in a package).

## AFFECT

Although often acknowledged as important, few perspectives have examined how a person's feelings, moods, or emotions are related to negotiation processes and outcomes. One such model was advanced by Barry and Oliver (1996). Their model focuses on affect at three points in time: anticipated, experienced, and postsettlement. Based on the relational history, negotiators experience prenegotiation affect, which prompts them to form expectations about the upcoming negotiation and to enact certain tactics at the beginning of the negotiation, which may be reciprocated. The initial tactics may confirm or violate expectations, which can alter subsequent tactics. Tactics enacted toward the end of the negotiation influence outcomes and satisfaction, which in turn influences the negotiators' desire to implement the agreement and their wish to negotiate in the future.

Although the affective model examines genuine affect, some models have studied the tactical use of emotion. This approach assumes that negotiators can manage their emotional displays and use them to gain advantage by signaling priorities or serving

as a form of persuasion (Kopelman, Rosette, & Thompson, 2006). Moreover, negotiators track each other's emotional displays during negotiation and respond to them, but these effects are complicated. At an emotional level, there is emotional contagion such that an opponent's affect is reciprocated (anger yields anger), but at a behavioral level, individuals appear to mismatch their strategies and concede more to an angry than to a happy opponent (Van Kleef, De Dreu, & Manstead, 2004a, 2004b). However, the advantage of acting angry only occurs when the opponent is in a rather weak position (Sinaceur & Tiedens, 2006; Van Kleef, De Dreu, Pietroni, & Manstead, 2006). Other emotions such as guilt and disappointment influence concession making but primarily among individuals who are trusting and had a cooperative motivation (Van Kleef et al., 2006).

Theory and research focused on affect and negotiation have grown in volume. However, although studies address the reactions negotiators have to their emotional displays (e.g., concession making), they tell us little about how emotion is enacted. Indeed, in some research, individuals are prompted to enact an emotion or emotional displays are manipulated within a scenario, but there is no analysis of the different manner in which a given emotion might be expressed during negotiation.

## SOCIAL FACTORS

Negotiation researchers have studied two types of social factors: constituency pressure and culture.

*Constituency Pressure.* Often, individuals negotiate on behalf of others; consequently, representatives may be engaged in simultaneous negotiations with an opponent and their own constituency. Constituencies may exert pressure on their representatives to bargain aggressively to achieve their interests, which McGrath (1966) characterized as R-forces. Walton and McKersie (1965) noted that constituency pressures are manifested in intraorganizational negotiation.

R-forces can influence negotiation processes and outcomes. Meta-analysis indicates that accountability to a constituency generally increases a representative's competitiveness (Druckman, 1994), and field research indicates that difficult intraorganizational bargaining can limit the use of integrative bargaining (McKersie et al., 2008). Moreover, constituency pressure in the form of goal congruence and trust influences the communication enacted during negotiation with an opponent and negotiations during caucuses with constituency members (Turner, 1990). However, O'Connor (1997) found that accountability pressures were attenuated when negotiations involved teams rather than individuals largely because of the ability of team negotiators to diffuse responsibility.

Although traditional theories have usefully guided research, their focus is limited. First, they view constituencies as homogeneous groups that send a single message to their representatives. In some cases, constituencies may be composed of factions with different agenda who try to influence the issues on the table and how they are approached. If so, representatives must develop a negotiation strategy for managing these differences. In some cases, representatives may try to create consensus among the various groups or at least minimize infighting. In others, they try to aggregate the perspectives into a single one (Kotzian, 2007). At the same time, the various factions enact an intraorganizational negotiation strategy that will make sure that their interests are part of the negotiation mix. At present, theories provide little guidance as to these issues.

## CULTURE

As intercultural theory and research has grown (see Kim, Chapter 26, this volume), negotiation researchers have relied on cultural dimensions such as individualism-collectivism, vertical and horizontal cultures, high- and low-context communication, and power distance (Hofstede, 1980; Triandis, 2000) and self-construals (Markus & Kitayama, 1991) to guide their research. For example, information exchange patterns vary with cultural factors, such as high- versus low-context mode of communication (Brett, 2000; Brett & Gelfand, 2005; Gelfand & Dyer, 2000). Collectivist cultures tend to use high-context communication, which is indirect, implicit, and heavily dependent on the situation and relationship. Individualist cultures use low-context communication, which is direct, is explicit, and relies more on surface meaning. Negotiators from these two types of cultures, operating in their conventional mode of communication, often resort to different information exchange strategies. For example, in low-context cultures such as the United States, negotiators use more direct questions and answers in information sharing than their counterparts from high-context cultures such as Japan and Hong Kong (Adair & Brett, 2004; Adair, Okumura, & Brett, 2001). Culture also influences the interpretation and use of power in negotiations (Hofstede, 1980). People from high–power distance cultures (e.g., countries such as China, Japan, Turkey) are less likely to negotiate with their superiors but are more likely to use their position power when negotiating with those lower in the hierarchy.

Although cultural approaches to negotiation have enriched cross-cultural negotiation practice, a potential problem arises: The classical culture categorizations (e.g., individualism and collectivism) may become less predictive of negotiation behavior as the forces of globalization gradually blur cultural boundaries. For example, well-educated young people in traditionally collectivist Asian cultures who are exposed to Western culture are converging with their counterparts in individualist cultures in surveys on cultural values and communication behaviors (Nisbett, 2003), and the way they negotiate may also become similar.

Although theory focused on first-order questions has been extensive and useful, it ignores the communication patterns that emerge during the course of a negotiation. As we will note in the following section, these perspectives provide limited information about the sequence of communication.

## ◆ Second-Order Questions

Although studying the base rate at which communication occurs provides useful information, it ignores the patterns of communication that arise during a negotiation as individuals react to each other's actions and how these patterns may change as negotiation goes through phases.

### COMMUNICATION PATTERNS

Researchers have identified both reciprocal and nonreciprocal sequences within negotiation (Olekalns & Smith, 2000). Reciprocal sequences can be integrative, such as mutual logrolling, or distributive, such as mutual threats. Nonreciprocal patterns can be complementary, during which negotiators engage in similar but not identical actions, such as when positional arguments prompt threats or during which negotiators respond with completely different tactics, such as when a negotiator responds to a counterpart's threat (distributive action) by suggesting a change in procedures (procedural suggestion).

Olekalns and Smith (2003) argued that reciprocal and nonreciprocal patterns reflect three sequences. Reciprocal sequences constitute actions in which negotiators exactly match each other's strategies (e.g., attacks prompt counterattacks). Complementary sequences involve nonreciprocated patterns in which a similar but not identical

response occurs (e.g., attacks prompt defensive reactions). Some sequences are transformational, in which negotiators send mixed messages often aimed at changing the course of a negotiation, such as when a negotiator responds to another's positional arguments (distributive action) by logrolling (integrative actions).

Researchers have also studied the number of communication acts that characterize a sequence. Some research indicates that negotiators typically engage in a two-part sequence (Weingart, Prietula, Hyder, & Genovese, 1999), such as when attacks prompt defensive reactions, while some have argued that negotiations can best be characterized by a four-part sequence (Taylor & Donald, 2003), such as when attack-and-defend patterns are repeated twice. Research on communication sequences demonstrates their usefulness for understanding negotiation. Communication sequences predict the likelihood of deadlocks (e.g., Putnam & Jones, 1982a) and the degree to which their agreements are integrative (e.g., Olekalns & Smith, 2000). Furthermore, research indicates that these patterns may vary during the course of a negotiation (e.g., Galinat & Muller, 1988; Goering, 1997; Olekalns & Smith, 2000). Finally, negotiators often use strategies in sequences, even though the overall occurrence of the strategies is relatively infrequent (Olekalns & Smith, 2003). This latter finding suggests that research conducted on first-order questions may overlook key information contained in sequences.

Several theories have been used to understand communication patterns. Putnam and Jones (1982a) employed a role-based perspective based in part on Walton and McKersie's (1965) framework and prior research on collective bargaining as a framework. They argued that the roles of labor and management create role expectations that may prompt strategic sequences. In a collective bargaining simulation, they discovered that the likelihood of an impasse was characterized by patterns of attack-attack and defend-defend, which typically were initiated by management negotiators. However, Goering (1997) was unable to replicate some of these patterns in actual negotiations.

Some researchers have used Kelly's (1979) perspective on interdependency to understand sequences. Kelly argues that individuals decide how to behave based on the outcomes associated with their behavioral options. In some cases, the options and outcomes are not desirable, and individuals psychologically transform them. Olekalns and Smith (1999) suggest that individuals globally transform a negotiation by engaging in specific strategies and sustain or modify transformations by locally enacting behavior sequences. In their study, dyads composed of prosocial individuals were relationally focused and engaged in actions associated with integrative bargaining, whereas dyads composed of individualistic and cooperatively motivated individuals engaged in action typically associated with distributive bargaining. They also found that prosocial dyads used accommodative sequences to prevent conflict escalation.

Two theories used for understanding first-order questions have been applied to second-order questions with limited success. Weingart et al. (1999) found that negotiators who had tactical knowledge engaged in longer chains of integrative behaviors but only if integrative actions had been initially reciprocated, but reciprocity of distributive behavior occurred regardless of tactical knowledge. Olekalns and Smith (2003) used a motivational approach similar to the dual-concern theory to study sequences. Contrary to the theory, they found that both individualistic and cooperative dyads could find integrative agreements but in different ways. Individualistic dyads reached integrative agreements by making multi-issue offers, positional arguments, and nonreciprocated exchange of priority information. In some ways, the methodological sophistication

of research on communication patterns exceeds that of theorizing. The methods are in some ways more complex and rigorous than those used for exploring other questions. However, the theories are only loosely connected to hypotheses, and more often than not, they prove to be less than adequate predictors.

## NEGOTIATION PHASES

Scholars have long noted that negotiations seem to go through a variety of phases or stages. Some scholars suggest that negotiations consist of a dominant strategy (either integrative or distributive) that occurs throughout negotiations, whereas others note that negotiations may go through phases of integrative and distributive strategies (Putnam, 1990). Moreover, models vary in the degree to which they identify phases in which negotiations will go through long periods of a dominant strategy, with a few transitions between them, and those that are episodic, in which there are short phases of a dominant strategy with many transitions (Putnam, 1990). Regardless of form, these models are typically prescriptive or descriptive and lack detailed information about the causal factors that produce phases (Holmes, 1992). Current theory attempts to address these shortcomings.

Olekalns, Brett, and Weingart (2003) argue that communication actions can vary in strategic orientation (distributive and integrative) as well as function (information or action). These dimensions create four strategy clusters: distributive information, integrative information, claiming value (i.e., distributive actions), and creating value (integrative actions). On the basis of Morley and Stephenson's (1977) rational model of stages in negotiation, Olekalns et al. note that negotiators often transition from distributive to integrative orientations and, based on a script analysis of negotiation (O'Connor & Adams, 1999), from informational functions to actions. Also, negotiators often redirect negotiations through smooth transitions between strategies or explicit interruptions of ongoing strategic moves. They predicted that negations initially involve transitions in strategy or in both function and strategy while interruptions tend to shift negotiations from distributive to integrative strategies. Research confirmed that negotiators often begin with distributive strategies and information exchange and shift to integrative strategies and actions. However, negotiators typically change their strategy or functional orientation rather than both.

Recently, Olekalns and Weingart (2008) advanced a theory of emergent negotiations that provides the most detailed account of negotiation dynamics. Their analysis is based on two assumptions. First, negotiation is a goal-directed activity; second, at the outset of negotiations, contextual factors increase the saliency of individualistic or cooperative orientations factors. However, to reach integrative agreements, negotiators must balance their desire to claim value for themselves and their desire to create value for the partner. Hence, their strategies shift back and forth between distributive and integrative as they discover that their current actions are not likely to reach their goals or as their goals change. Consequently, negotiations may go through periods of process maintenance (stable communication patterns) and process shifts (unstable communication patterns), which can occur at the interindividual level (i.e., communication is mutually contingent) or is negotiation-wide (i.e., dominant forms of communication over a time period). Goal congruency (shared vs. unshared goals), goal type (individualistic vs. cooperative), and goal strength (strong vs. weak commitment) influence stability and the type of instability. Although the perspective is too new for research to be reported, it provides a useful framework for understanding both patterns and phases.

Theory development on phases shows progress. It has gone from prescriptive and descriptive approaches to those that provide an explanatory basis on which to predict changes in communication.

## ◆ Third-Order Questions

Third-order questions focus on the association between communication and relationships. Some relational perspectives on negotiation have emerged. For example, Rubin and Brown (1975) argued that negotiators vary in their interpersonal orientation or responsiveness to their relationships. Donohue and Ramesh (1992) noted that negotiators often use relational distance to signal their relational intentions. Evans, Jacobson, Greenhalgh, and Gilkey (1993) posited that relational orientations influence negotiators' cognitions and tactics.

Recently, a larger relational perspective has emerged that incorporates earlier perspectives (Gelfand, Major, Raver, Nishii, & O'Brien, 2006). This perspective argues that individuals have a relational self-construal that is composed of relational cognition, emotion, and motivation. When activated, this construal can influence prenegotiation psychological states, although its strength can be moderated by a variety of situational features. These states influence the type of initial tactics (e.g., concession making, mimicry) that are enacted and, depending on the congruency between the negotiator's relational self-construals, may influence later tactics (e.g., claiming and creating value). The later strategies influence the type of agreements, which, in turn, determine the postsettlement compliance and desire for future interaction.

The relational construal approach takes into account within-dyad similarities in relational construal. When two negotiators have highly accessible relational self-construals, they may engage in relational satisficing in which they are unwilling to strenuously argue for individual gains, and they may not reach integrative economic agreements. However, they do gain relational capital (i.e., mutual liking, knowledge, trust, relational commitment) that may help them achieve long-term economic benefits. When both negotiators have inaccessible relational self-construals, their negotiations are very task oriented (e.g., logrolling), and they may find integrative economic agreements. However, their relationship is not especially strong. When both negotiators have moderately accessible relational self-construals, they are most likely to find integrative agreements and form strong relationships. Rather than focusing primarily on the relationship or the outcomes, they focus on both. When relational self-construals are incongruent (one negotiator's is accessible and the other's is not), then the model predicts that negotiators will engage in relational distancing. As a result, integrative agreements will not be found, and the quality of their relationship will be low. The relational self-construal approach integrates the prior research into a single perspective from which predictions about negotiation outcomes and consequences can be deduced. Its greatest weakness stems from the limited discussion of tactics and how they are constructed.

## ◆ Assessment and Future Directions

As noted earlier, Chatman et al. (1991) characterized communication and negotiation research as being in its infancy. Although we are unaware of any benchmarks for identifying academic maturity, our analysis suggests that the area has moved far beyond infancy, perhaps even to young adulthood. Research has addressed each of the four orders of questions associated with interaction, and theories have emerged that guide it. Indeed, research is more theory driven than it was a decade and a half ago. Furthermore, rather than merely importing and adapting theories, theories

are being crafted that are specifically focused on communication. Also, we see greater mutual exchange and fertilization of ideas across allied fields and disciplines than ever before.

However, some issues require attention. First, there is little theorizing that addresses multiple levels of questions. In our view, a useful theory addresses questions of each order. For example, frameworks should provide an exhaustive list of the relevant forms of communication (zero order), the psychological and social factors that influence their use (first order), the patterns they form (second order), and the degree to which they are associated with relationships (third order). We found no such theorizing, and theories were primarily focused on one order of question. However, when reviewing research on negotiation and information technology, Thompson and Nadler (2002) noted that electronic media can affect information exchange (first-order question), social contagion (first-order question), coordination (second-order question), and rapport building (third-order question) enacted during negotiation. However, it is necessary that we move beyond acknowledgment to constructing theory.

Second, most theories provide limited insights into the specific processes that produce messages. Although providing insights into the communication strategies that are enacted, neither the cognitive or motivational approaches explain how messages are constructed before or during a negotiation. For example, we are unsure whether communication constitutes formulaic statements or a spontaneous construction of linguistic elements.

Finally, we also found that the links to theory are loose. Often, a theory is cited but instead of using the logic of the theory, researchers rely on prior research or intuition to deduce hypotheses. Unfortunately, theories do not always spell out their logic, and when developing hypotheses, researchers are left to their own devices. However, it is our hope that future theorizing will provide a more elaborated and formal analysis of negotiation and communication.

# ◆ References

Adair, W. L., & Brett, J. M. (2004). Culture and negotiation processes. In M. J. Gelfand & J. M. Brett (Eds.), *The handbook of negotiation and culture: Theoretical advances and cultural perspectives* (pp. 158–176). Palo Alto, CA: Stanford University Press.

Adair, W. L., Okumura, T., & Brett, J. M. (2001). Negotiation behavior when cultures collide: The United States and Japan. *Journal of Applied Psychology, 86,* 371–385.

Alexander, E. R., III. (1979). The reduction of cognitive conflict: Effects of various types of communication. *Journal of Conflict Resolution, 23,* 120–138.

Balke, W. M., Hammond, K. R., & Meyer, G. D. (1973). An alternate approach to labor-management relations. *Administrative Science Quarterly, 18,* 311–327.

Barry, B., & Oliver, R. L. (1996). Affect in dyadic negotiation: A model and propositions. *Organizational Behavior and Human Decision Processes, 67,* 127–143.

Bazerman, M. H., Curhan, J. R., Moore, D. A., & Valley, K. L. (2000). Negotiation. *Annual Review of Psychology, 51,* 279–314.

Bolland, M., & Redfield, K. D. (1988). The limits to citizen participation in local education: A cognitive interpretation. *Journal of Politics, 50,* 1033–1046.

Brehmer, B. (1976). Social judgment theory and the analysis of interpersonal conflict. *Psychological Bulletin, 83,* 985–1003.

Brehmer, B., & Hammond, K. R. (1977). Cognitive factors in interpersonal conflict. In D. Druckman (Ed.), *Negotiation: Social psychological perspectives* (pp. 79–103). Beverly Hills, CA: Sage.

Brett, J. M. (2000). Culture and negotiation. *International Journal of Psychology, 35,* 97–104.

Brett, J. M., & Gelfand, M. (2005). A cultural analysis of the underlying assumptions of negotiation theory. In L. L. Thompson (Ed.), *Frontiers of social psychology: Negotiations* (pp. 173–202). New York: Psychology Press.

Cappella, J. N. (1987). Interpersonal communication: Definition and fundamental questions. In C. R. Berger & S. H. Chaffee (Eds.), *Handbook of communication science* (pp. 184–238). Newbury Park, CA: Sage.

Carnevale, P. J., & Pruitt, D. G. (1992). Negotiation and mediation. *Annual Review of Psychology, 43,* 531–582.

Chatman, J. A., Putnam, L. L., & Sondak, H. (1991). Integrating communication and negotiation research. In M. H. Bazerman, R. J. Lewicki, & B. H. Sheppard (Eds.), *Research on negotiation in organizations* (pp. 139–164). Greenwich, CT: JAI.

Cushman, D. P., & Craig, R. T. (1976). Communication systems: Interpersonal implications. In G. R. Miller (Ed.), *Explorations in interpersonal communication* (pp. 37–58). Beverly Hills, CA: Sage.

De Dreu, C. K. W., Beersma, B., Stroebe, K., & Euwema, M. C. (2006). Motivated information processing, strategic choice, and the quality of negotiated agreement. *Journal of Personality and Social Psychology, 90,* 927–943.

De Dreu, C. K.W., & Carnevale, P. J. (2003). Motivational bases of information processing and strategy in conflict and negotiation. In M. P. Zanna (Ed.), *Advances in experimental social psychology* (Vol. 35, pp. 235–291). New York: Academic Press.

De Dreu, C. K. W., & Van Kleef, G. A. (2004). The influence of power on information search, impression formation, and demands in negotiation. *Journal of Experimental Social Psychology, 40,* 303–319.

De Dreu, C. K.W., Weingart, L. R., & Kwon, S. (2000). Influence of social motives on integrative negotiation: A meta-analytic review and test of two theories. *Journal of Personality and Social Psychology, 78,* 889–905.

Donohue, W. A. (1981a). Analyzing negotiation tactics: Development of a negotiation interact system. *Human Communication Research, 7,* 273–287.

Donohue, W. A. (1981b). Development of a model of rule use in negotiation interaction. *Communication Monographs, 48,* 106–120.

Donohue, W. A., & Diez, M. E. (1985). Directive use in negotiation interaction. *Communication Monographs, 52,* 305–318.

Donohue, W., Diez, M., & Hamilton, M. (1984). Coding naturalistic negotiation interaction. *Human Communication Research, 10,* 403–425.

Donohue, W. A., & Ramesh, C. (1992). Negotiator-opponent relationships. In L. L. Putnam & M. E. Roloff (Eds.), *Communication and negotiation* (pp. 209–232). Newbury Park, CA: Sage.

Drake, L. A., & Donohue, W. A. (1996). Communicative framing theory in conflict resolution. *Communication Research, 23,* 297–322.

Druckman, D. (1994). Determinants of compromising behavior in negotiation: A meta-analysis. *Journal of Conflict Resolution, 38,* 507–556.

Esser, H. (2004). The "logic" of the understanding: To debate on "arguing" and "bargaining" in international negotiations. In F. U. Pappi, E. Riedel, P. W. Thurner, & R. Vaubel (Eds.), *The institutionalization of international negotiations* (pp. 33–68). Frankfurt, Germany: Campus Verlag.

Evans, P. B., Jacobson, H. K., Greenhalgh, L., & Gilkey, R. W. (1993). The effect of relationship orientation on negotiators' cognitions and tactics. *Group Decision and Negotiation, 2,* 103–118.

Forgas, J. P. (1998). On feeling good and getting your way: Mood effects on negotiator cognition and bargaining strategies. *Journal of Personality and Social Psychology, 74,* 565–577.

Galinat, W. H., & Muller, G. F. (1988). Verbal responses to different bargaining strategies: A content analysis of real-life buyer-seller interaction. *Journal of Applied Social Psychology, 18,* 160–178.

Gelfand, M. J., & Dyer, N. (2000). A cultural perspective on negotiation: Progress, pitfalls, and prospects. *Applied Psychology: An International Review, 49,* 62–99.

Gelfand, M. J., Major, V. S., Raver, J. L., Nishii, L. H., & O'Brien, K. (2006). Negotiating relationally: The dynamics of the relational self in negotiations. *Academy of Management Review, 31,* 427–451.

Goering, E. M. (1997). Integration versus distribution in contract negotiations: An interaction analysis of strategy use. *Journal of Business Communication, 34,* 383–400.

Hammond, K. R., & Brehmer, B. (1973). Quasi-rationality and distrust: Implications for international conflict. In L. Rappoport & D. Summers (Eds.), *Human judgment and*

*social interaction* (pp. 338–389). New York: Holt, Rinehart & Winston.

Hinkle, S., Stiles, W. B., & Taylor, L. A. (1988). Verbal processes in a labour/management negotiation. *Journal of Language and Social Psychology, 7,* 123–136.

Hofstede, G. H. (1980). *Culture's consequences: International differences in work-related values.* Beverly Hills, CA: Sage.

Holmes, M. E. (1992). Phases structures in negotiations. In L. L. Putnam & M. E. Roloff (Eds.), *Communication and negotiation* (pp. 83–105). Newbury Park, CA: Sage.

Hyder, E. B., Prietula, M. J., & Weingart, L. R. (2000). Getting to best: Efficiency versus optimality in negotiation. *Cognitive Science, 24,* 169–204.

Jordan, J. M., & Roloff, M. E. (1997). Planning skills and negotiator goal accomplishment: The relationship between self-monitoring and plan generation, plan enactment, and plan consequences. *Communication Research, 24,* 31–64.

Kelly, H. H. (1979). *Personal relationships: Their structures and process.* Hillsdale, NJ: Lawrence Erlbaum.

Kopelman, S., Rosette, A. S., & Thompson, L. (2006). The three faces of Eve: Strategic displays of positive, negative, and neutral emotions in negotiations. *Organizational Behavior and Human Decision Processes, 99,* 81–101.

Kotzian, P. (2007). Arguing and bargaining in international negotiations: On the application of the frame-selection model and its implications. *International Political Science Review 28,* 79–99.

Kray, L. J., Thompson, L., & Galinsky, A. (2001). Battle of the sexes: Gender stereotype confirmation and reactance in negotiations. *Journal of Personality and Social Psychology, 80,* 942–958.

Markus, H. R., & Kitayama, S. (1991). Culture and the self: Implications for cognition, emotion, and motivation. *Psychological Review, 98,* 224–253.

McGrath, J. E. (1966). A social psychological approach to the study of negotiation. In R. Bowers (Ed.), *Studies of behavior in organizations: A research symposium* (pp. 101–134). Athens: University of Georgia Press.

McKersie, R. B., Sharpe, T., Kochan, T. A., Eaton, A. E., Strauss, G., & Morgenstern, M.

(2008). Bargaining theory meets interest-based negotiations: A case study. *Industrial Relations, 47,* 66–96.

Morley, L., & Stephenson, G. (1977). *The social psychology of bargaining.* London: Allen & Unwin.

Neale, M. A., & Bazerman, M. H. (1991). *Cognition and rationality in negotiation.* New York: Free Press.

Neu, J. (1988). Conversation structure: An explanation of bargaining behaviors in negotiations. *Management Communication Quarterly, 2,* 23–45.

Neu, J., Graham, J. L., & Gilly, M. C. (1988). The influence of gender on behaviors and outcomes in a retail buyer-seller negotiation simulation. *Journal of Retailing, 64,* 427–452.

Nisbett, R. E. (2003). *The geography of thought: How Asians and Westerners think differently . . . and why.* New York: Free Press.

O'Connor, K. M. (1997). Groups and solos in context: The effects of accountability on team negotiation. *Organizational Behavior and Human Decision Processes, 72,* 384–407.

O'Connor, K. M., & Adams, A. A. (1999). What novices think about negotiation: A content analysis of scripts. *Negotiation Journal, 15,* 135–147.

Olekalns, M., Brett, J. M., & Weingart, L. R. (2003). Phases, transitions and interruptions: Modeling processes in multiparty negotiations. *International Journal of Conflict Management, 14,* 191–211.

Olekalns, M., & Smith, P. L. (1999). Social value orientations and strategy choices in competitive negotiations. *Personality and Social Psychology Bulletin, 25,* 657–668.

Olekalns, M., & Smith, P. L. (2000). Understanding optimal outcomes: The role of strategy sequences in competitive negotiations. *Human Communication Research, 26,* 527–557.

Olekalns, M., & Smith, P. L. (2003). Testing the relationships among negotiators' motivational orientations, strategy choices and outcomes. *Journal of Experimental Social Psychology, 39,* 101–117.

Olekalns, M., & Smith, P. L. (2005). Cognitive representations of negotiation. *Australian Journal of Management, 30,* 57–76.

Olekalns, M., & Weingart, L. R. (2008). Emergent negotiations: Stability and shifts in negotiation dynamics. *Negotiation and Conflict Management Research, 1,* 135–160.

Osterberg, W. H. (1950). A method for the study of business conferences. *Personnel Psychology, 3,* 169–178.

Pruitt, D. G. (1981). *Negotiation behavior.* New York: Academic Press.

Pruitt, D. G., & Rubin, J. Z. (1986). *Social conflict: Escalation, stalemate, and settlement.* New York: Random House.

Putnam, L. L. (1990). Reframing integrative and distributive bargaining: A process perspective. In B. H. Sheppard, M. Bazerman, & R. J. Lewicki (Eds.), *Research on negotiation in organizations* (Vol. 2, pp. 3–30). Greenwich, CT: JAI.

Putnam, L. L. (2004a). Dialectical tensions and rhetorical tropes in negotiations. *Organization Studies, 25,* 35–53.

Putnam, L. L. (2004b). Transformations and critical moments in negotiations. *Negotiation Journal, 20,* 275–295.

Putnam, L. L. (2005). Discourse analysis: Mucking around with negotiation data. *International Negotiation, 10,* 17–32.

Putnam, L. L., & Geist, P. (1985). Argument in bargaining: An analysis of the reasoning process. *Southern Speech Communication Journal, 50,* 225–245.

Putnam, L. L., & Jones, T. S. (1982a). Reciprocity in negotiations: An analysis of bargaining interaction. *Communication Monographs, 49,* 171–191.

Putnam, L. L., & Jones, T. S. (1982b). The role of communication in bargaining. *Human Communication Research, 8,* 262–280.

Putnam, L. L., & Roloff, M. E. (Eds.). (1992). *Communication and negotiation.* Newbury Park, CA: Sage.

Putnam, L. L., Van Hoeven, S. A., & Bullis, C. A. (1991). The role of rituals and fantasy themes in teachers' bargaining. *Western Journal of Speech Communication, 55,* 85–103.

Putnam, L. L., Wilson, S. R., Waltman, M. S., & Turner, D. (1986). The evolution of case arguments in teachers' bargaining. *Journal of the American Forensic Association, 23,* 63–81.

Roloff, M. E. (1987). Communication and conflict. In C. R. Berger & S. H. Chaffee (Eds.), *Handbook of communication science* (pp. 484–534). Newbury Park, CA: Sage.

Roloff, M. E., & Jordan, J. M. (1991). The influence of effort, experience and persistence on the elements of bargaining plans. *Communication Research, 18,* 306–332.

Roloff, M. E., & Van Swol, L. M. (2008). Shared cognition and communication within group decision making and negotiation. In D. R. Roskos-Ewoldsen & J. L. Monahan (Eds.), *Communication and social cognition: Theories and methods* (pp. 171–196). Mahwah, NJ: Lawrence Erlbaum.

Rubin, J. A., & Brown, B. (1975). *The social psychology of bargaining and negotiation.* New York: Academic Press.

Schelling, T. C. (1960). *The strategy of conflict.* Cambridge, MA: Harvard University Press.

Sinaceur, M., & Tiedens, L. Z. (2006). Get mad and get more than even: When and why anger expression is effective in negotiations. *Journal of Experimental Social Psychology, 42,* 314–322.

Sullivan, B. A., O'Connor, K. M., & Burris, E. R. (2006). Negotiator confidence: The impact of self-efficacy on tactics and outcomes. *Journal of Experimental Social Psychology, 42,* 567–581.

Taylor, P. J. (2002). A cylindrical model of communication behavior in crisis negotiations. *Human Communication Research, 28,* 7–48.

Taylor, P. J., & Donald, I. (2003). Foundations and evidence for an interaction-based approach to conflict negotiation. *International Journal of Conflict Management, 14,* 213–232.

Theye, L. D., & Seiler, W. J. (1979). Interaction analysis in collective bargaining: An alternative approach to the prediction of negotiated outcomes. In D. Nimmo (Ed.), *Communication yearbook 3* (pp. 375–392). New Brunswick, NJ: Transaction Press.

Thompson, L., & Nadler, J. (2002). Negotiating via information technology: Theory and application. *Journal of Social Issues, 58,* 109–124.

Triandis, H. C. (2000). Culture and conflict. *International Journal of Psychology, 35,* 145–152.

Turner, D. B. (1990). Intraorganizational bargaining: The effect of goal congruence and trust on negotiator strategy use. *Communication Studies, 41,* 54–75.

Tutzauer, F. (1987). Exponential decay and damped harmonic oscillation as models of the bargaining process. In M. L. McLaughlin (Ed.), *Communication yearbook 10* (pp. 217–240). Newbury Park, CA: Sage.

Tutzauer, F., & Roloff, M. E. (1988). Communication processes leading to integrative agreements: Three paths to joint benefits. *Communication Research, 15,* 360–380.

Van Kleef, G. A., De Dreu, C. K. W., & Manstead, A. S. R. (2004a). The interpersonal effects of anger and happiness in negotiations. *Journal of Personality and Social Psychology, 86,* 57–76.

Van Kleef, G. A., De Dreu, C. K. W., & Manstead, A. S. R. (2004b). The interpersonal effects of emotions in negotiations: A motivated information processing approach. *Journal of Personality & Social Psychology, 87,* 510–528.

Van Kleef, G. A., De Dreu, C. K. W., Pietroni, D., & Manstead, A. S. R. (2006). Power and emotion in negotiation: Power moderates the interpersonal effects of anger and happiness on concession making. *European Journal of Social Psychology, 36,* 557–581.

Walcott, C., & Hopmann, P. (1975). Interaction analysis and bargaining behavior. *Experimental Study of Politics, 4,* 1–19.

Walton, R. E., & McKersie, R. B. (1965). *A behavioral theory of labor negotiations: An analysis of a social interaction system.* New York: McGraw-Hill.

Weingart, L., Olekalns, M., & Smith, P. L. (2005). Quantitative coding negotiation processes. *International Negotiation, 9,* 441–456.

Weingart, L. R., Hyder, E. B., & Prietula, M. J. (1996). Knowledge matters: The effect of tactical descriptions on negotiation behavior and outcomes. *Journal of Personality and Social Psychology, 70,* 1205–1217.

Weingart, L. R., Prietula, M. J., Hyder, E. B., & Genovese, C. R. (1999). Knowledge and the sequential processes of negotiation: A Markov chain analysis of response-in-kind. *Journal of Experimental Social Psychology, 35,* 366–393.

# 19

# ESTABLISHING AND MAINTAINING RELATIONSHIPS

◆ Denise Haunani Solomon
and Anita L. Vangelisti

The reflexive nature of communication and relationships is accepted by communication scholars as both inherent and axiomatic. People draw upon their understanding of an association to enact relationally appropriate behaviors, to interpret a partner's actions, and to select communication strategies (Planalp, 1985). Reciprocally, people define and come to understand their relationships based on the meanings they derive from interaction (Duck & Pond, 1989). Communication functions to establish relationships when messages are produced or processed in ways that suggest the formation or escalation of a personal bond between interaction partners. Communication functions to maintain relationships when message production or processing reinforces and sustains preexisting levels of involvement. Scholarly efforts to understand these communication functions focus on how thoughts and words create, define, modify, and maintain interpersonal relationships.

This chapter highlights theory and research that clarifies how communication establishes and maintains interpersonal relationships. Although all interpersonal communication episodes have implications for the relationships between participants, we focus on research traditions that specifically address communication's role in the initiation, development, and maintenance of intimacy within personal relationships. In doing so, we feature theory and research by communication scholars, as well as prominent contributions made by researchers in other disciplines. This review also privileges bodies of work that are unified within a theoretical framework because these perspectives both organize empirical research on interpersonal communication and provide a platform for future endeavors.

To begin, we recount the emergence of relationship development as an area of sustained scholarship. Then, we examine lines of inquiry that focus on communication during the initiation and development of interpersonal relationships, and we review theories and programs of research that address communication and relationship maintenance. To conclude this chapter, we suggest directions for future research on communication and the establishment or maintenance of personal relationships.

## ◆ The Emergence of Research on Relationship Development

The study of communication and relationship development was fueled in the 1970s by increasingly sophisticated conceptions of interpersonal communication. Watzlawick, Beavin, and Jackson (1967) described communication as a process through which interactants define their association, such that every utterance conveys information about and enacts the relationship. Communication scholars recognized a symbiotic association between communication and relationships, wherein changes in relationships both prompt and reflect changes in communication (e.g., Miller, 1978). Advances in cognitive psychology also provided a foundation for incorporating cognition into perspectives on communication and relationships (Berger & Roloff, 1982). These developments allowed scholars to conceptualize communication at the heart of relationship escalation and maintenance.

In its infancy, research on establishing relationships was dominated by perspectives that focused on people's traits as predictors of attraction and relationship escalation (see Huston, Surra, Fitzgerald, & Cate, 1981). These perspectives suggested that people seek out partners who are similar to themselves, compare their social characteristics during the initiation of relationships, assess the similarity of their values as relationships escalate, and evaluate the complementarity of their needs within intimate associations (e.g., Kerckhoff & Davis, 1962; Murnstein, 1970). Characteristics that individuals bring into a relationship were considered central to the development of that association, and the ways partners use communication to negotiate compatibility and incompatibility were largely neglected.

Theoretical perspectives on relationship maintenance prominent in the 1970s also emphasized intrapersonal and cognitive processes. In particular, social exchange theories addressed how rewards and costs contribute to the stability and satisfaction of ongoing associations. These approaches emphasized how people make decisions about social relationships to maximize personally profitable experiences (Roloff, 1981). People tend to continue relationships that have provided rewards in the past, and relationships are stable when partners can maintain self-interested exchange patterns that are mutually fulfilling. Furthermore, people experience dissatisfaction with a relationship when they judge social exchange to be unfair, rewards do not meet their expectations, or the resources they possess fall outside an optimal range. In these ways, individual expectations, needs, and evaluations were considered the foundation for relationship maintenance.

As communication perspectives on relationship development gained momentum, research on establishing and maintaining relationships became increasingly focused on messages produced and interpreted in the context of relationships. Scholars began to theorize about the relational messages exchanged between partners (e.g., Rogers & Farace, 1975). This work laid a foundation for thinking about how messages vary according to the nature of the relationship between communication partners (Knapp, Ellis, & Williams, 1980). Corresponding theoretical advancements addressed the cognitive structures required to process relational messages, track changes in relationship states, and transcend lapses in interaction (Planalp, 1985).

Questions about the link between relationship characteristics and communication continue to inspire research; however, the 1990s witnessed an important change in research on communication in relationships. Exemplifying this shift, twin volumes on the dark side of interpersonal communication (Cupach & Spitzberg, 1994) and interpersonal relationships (Spitzberg & Cupach, 1998) brought together research on a host of specific relationship phenomena. Consistent with the framework put forth by these volumes, much of the contemporary research on establishing and maintaining relationships is focused on specific communication quandaries, rather than more general trends in everyday interaction that correspond with relationship development, escalation, or stability.

Over the past 40 years, research on establishing and maintaining relationships has grown to encompass a variety of intrapersonal and interpersonal processes that unfold within interpersonal associations. Perhaps because the roots of this scholarship are in social and cognitive psychology, many theoretical perspectives privilege individuals' personality traits, perceptions and motivations, and sensemaking processes. At the same time, relationships begin, develop, and exist when two individuals exchange messages, create shared meanings, and use communication to sustain their association. The theories that we discuss in the remainder of this chapter represent efforts to conceptualize, predict, and explain the variegated processes that establish and maintain interpersonal relationships.

## ◆ Theorizing About Establishing Relationships

As noted previously, theories about communication and establishing relationships grew out of a research tradition focused on individual qualities as the force behind the initiation and development of relationships. From this foundation, we trace the emergence of theories and programs of research that embraced interpersonal communication and dyadic processes as key to understanding how people establish relationships.

### SOCIAL PENETRATION THEORY

Social penetration theory explains the development of personal relationships as rooted in self-disclosure. The theory suggests that increases in relational intimacy are a consequence of individuals sharing increasingly personal information about themselves with each other (Altman & Taylor, 1973). When people first meet, they tend to exchange information that is relatively impersonal, and they restrict the range of topics they discuss. As time passes and individuals learn more about each other, they increase the *depth* of their disclosure by revealing more personal information, and they increase the *breadth* of disclosure by discussing a greater variety of topics. Based on the principles of social exchange noted previously, Altman and Taylor (1973) suggested that relationship development continues as long as the rewards that partners perceive to be associated with their relationship are greater than the costs they believe they incur.

Consistent with social penetration theory, research reveals a positive association between disclosure and the degree to which partners are emotionally involved in their relationships (Rubin, Hill, Peplau, & Dunkel-Schetter, 1980), and partners who disclose more to each other report greater relational satisfaction (Hendrick, 1981) and stability (Sprecher, 1987). At the same time, researchers have noted a number of qualifications to the idea that there is a linear association between disclosure and intimacy. For instance, Altman, Vinsel, and Brown (1981) argued that relational partners experience dialectical tensions between being open and closed about what they discuss with each other (see also Baxter & Montgomery, 1996). Despite these qualifications, social penetration theory anchors research on communication and establishing relationships because it positions communication as the foundation for intimacy.

## UNCERTAINTY REDUCTION THEORY

Like social penetration theory, uncertainty reduction theory recognizes that initial interactions between strangers involve an exchange of public information, and these interactions change in predictable ways as they progress. Whereas social penetration theory elaborates on changes in self-disclosure that occur over time, uncertainty reduction theory focuses on mechanisms that motivate communication behaviors.

A core assumption of uncertainty reduction theory is that people are driven to increase the predictability of their own and their communication partner's behavior. The theory specifies that communication allows people to reduce uncertainty, which promotes intimacy (Berger & Calabrese, 1975). Tests of the theory in terms of relationship development have focused on how the effects of uncertainty change as relationships progress. For example, people's confidence in their ability to predict a partner's attitudes and behaviors is positively correlated with initial attraction to that partner (see Berger, 1987). Within initial interactions, partners exchange demographic information that allows them to locate each other within social and cultural realms; friends, in contrast, ask questions that elicit more evaluative and

attitudinal information (see Berger, 1988). Although the relevant types of information change as relationships develop, these studies suggest that uncertainty reduction is an important part of establishing interpersonal relationships.

## PREDICTED OUTCOME VALUE THEORY

Sunnafrank (1986) questioned the primacy of uncertainty reduction in relationship development and offered predicted outcome value theory as an alternative explanation for communication during initial interactions and relationship development. As with social penetration theory, predicted outcome value theory proposes that people pursue relationships with others based on their perceptions of future rewards and costs. Hence, the concern during initial interactions is gathering information that allows individuals to predict future outcomes.

Predicted outcome value theory is formalized in four propositions: (a) Attraction increases as the predicted value of future outcomes increases, (b) predicting positive future outcomes promotes messages that extend conversations and encourage future interactions, (c) predicting negative future outcomes promotes messages that end conversations and preclude future interactions, and (d) people try to discuss topics that render the most positive predicted outcomes (Sunnafrank, 1986). The implications for relationship development are straightforward: When the future promises to be rewarding, people communicate to develop the relationship; when the future is perceived as unrewarding, people refrain from advancing the relationship.

Empirical tests of the theory are consistent with its claims. In studies of initial interactions between classmates, predicted outcome value was positively associated with the amount of verbal communication, the intimacy level of messages, and nonverbal affiliative expressiveness (Sunnafrank, 1988), as well as asking questions and using nonverbal cues to encourage the partner to talk (Sunnafrank, 1990). In addition, predicted outcome value after an initial interaction has been linked to the amount of communication, magnitude of long-term attraction, and degree of relationship development 9 weeks later (Sunnafrank & Ramirez, 2004). The tenets of predicted outcome value have also been supported by research on computer-mediated communication (Ramirez & Burgoon, 2004). Although its body of empirical work is not expansive, the theory's premise that assessments of the potential for future rewards influence relationship development is robust.

## STAGE MODELS OF RELATIONAL DEVELOPMENT

Whereas uncertainty reduction theory and predicted outcome value theory emphasize initial interactions, stage models of relational development describe the behaviors and interaction patterns that occur over the full trajectory of relationship development and deterioration. With respect to establishing relationships, stage models provide insight into the communication processes that typically occur from the moment potential partners first meet to the time they present themselves to others as a "couple." The stage model put forth by Knapp (1984) illustrates how this perspective characterizes relationship development (see also Levinger, 1983).

Knapp's (1984) model includes five stages that portray how partners communicate as they begin their relationship and become more intimate with each other. The first stage, *initiating*, involves messages that instigate communication and typically portray individuals as pleasant and likeable. The second stage, *experimenting*, is conceived as a period when relational partners become acquainted and try to reduce their uncertainty about each other. *Intensifying* is the third stage; after people become acquainted, they may opt to escalate their relationship by

engaging in more personal disclosures, developing private symbols, and expressing more commitment to their relationship. When partners begin to see and portray themselves as a "couple," Knapp suggested they are *integrating*; this stage may be characterized by increased similarity in verbal behavior or by decisions to share property. Finally, *bonding* involves the institutionalization of the relationship, often through the couple's participation in a public ritual.

Stage models have been criticized for characterizing relational development as a relatively simple, linear process; however, both Knapp (1984) and Levinger (1983) make explicit statements to the contrary (see Poole & Dobosh, Chapter 22, this volume). Rather than being conceived as simple, linear descriptions of relationship development, stage models are best regarded as general frameworks that researchers can use to explore communication as people establish relationships.

## RELATIONAL SCHEMAS

Stage models that focus on patterns of interaction between partners are complemented by research explicating the knowledge structures that organize information about interpersonal relationships. Planalp (1985) defined relational schemas as "coherent frameworks of relational knowledge that are used to derive relational implications of messages and are modified in accord with ongoing experience with relationships" (p. 9; see also Baldwin, 1992). A relational schemas perspective highlights how relationships develop as people compare communication experiences with their knowledge about interpersonal relationships.

Different programs of research have emphasized the different types of knowledge contained within relational schemas. For example, Planalp (1985) examined patterns of recall for a generic student-professor interaction and concluded that relational schemas specify the behavioral rights and obligations that characterize types of relationships. Davis and Todd (1985) identified nine characteristics within prototypes for friendships and found that variations in friendship (e.g., best friends vs. close friends) were distinguished by the perceived viability, support, intimacy, enjoyment, spontaneity, success, and stability within those associations. Likewise, relationships can be distinguished by the type of love that is present (e.g., romantic love, motherly love, brotherly love; Fehr, 1988).

Relational schemas also encompass cognitive models of relationship trajectories and social scripts. People conceptualize relational escalation in terms of six phases: (a) meeting and making small talk; (b) dating, displaying physical affection, and sharing informal activities; (c) self-disclosing; (d) having sexual intercourse; (e) meeting parents, exchanging gifts, talking about the other, and stating a commitment; and (f) marrying (Honeycutt, Cantrill, & Greene, 1989). People also have scripts for performing more specific routines that occur within interpersonal relationships. For example, typical scripts for a first date include (a) preparing for the date, (b) meeting the date, (c) engaging in shared activities, and (d) ending the date (Rose & Frieze, 1989).

Although relational schemas can be useful for understanding how people make sense of communication events and draw inferences about developing relationships, most research in this tradition emphasizes stable and culturally shared expectations for relationships. As a consequence, research on relational schemas has tended to neglect the ways in which knowledge structures develop to guide people's evolving expectations within particular associations.

## THE TURNING POINTS PERSPECTIVE

An alternative to perspectives that emphasize stages of relationship development is one focused on critical events within social relationships. These turning points are defined as "any event or occurrence that is associated with change in a relationship" (Baxter & Bullis, 1986, p. 470). Identifying relational turning points not only provides a way to describe the developmental course of relationships but also reveals the meanings that partners associate with particular events and how they conceptualize their relationship.

Most of the turning points research has used the *retrospective interview technique* (Huston et al., 1981). This procedure requires participants to report the turning points that have occurred in their relationships, typically from the time of first meeting until another point in time relevant to the study (e.g., marriage). As they identify each of these turning points, participants are asked to plot them on a graph; the units on the horizontal axis usually reflect time increments (e.g., monthly intervals), and the vertical axis typically depicts changes in relational quality (e.g., commitment, chance of marriage). After participants plot their turning points, they draw lines representing the path between those events, and they answer probing questions relevant to the specific investigation.

Studies using the retrospective interview technique have revealed that partners tend to follow four different trajectories from initial meeting to marriage (Huston et al., 1981; Surra, 1985). Research also indicates that couples experience different types of turning points, that a substantial portion of turning points involve explicit communication about the relationship, and that turning points viewed by partners as negative are inversely associated with satisfaction (Baxter & Bullis, 1986). Turning point data were used to identify two trajectories in partners' commitment to marriage (Surra & Hughes, 1997): *Relationship-driven* partners reported changes in commitment that were mostly positive, moderate in rate, and reflective of positive beliefs about their relationship, whereas *event-driven* partners described changes that were relatively negative, rapid, and characterized by negative beliefs about the relationship.

Of course, the retrospective interview technique brings with it all of the strengths and weaknesses of other self-report methods. Given this, research on relational turning points reveals how people construct the history of their relationship, perhaps more so than the actual course of a relationship's development.

## THE RELATIONAL TURBULENCE MODEL

The relational turbulence model focuses on one particular turning point—the transition from casual to serious involvement in dating relationships. The formation of mutual commitments within a romantic association requires partners to coordinate and integrate their identities, roles, and behaviors. According to the theory, achieving an intimate, mutually committed relationship requires partners to survive intense and often negative experiences as they move their relationship from casual to serious (Solomon & Knobloch, 2001, 2004).

The theory identifies two relationship qualities that are sparked by relationship changes. *Relational uncertainty* is the degree of confidence people have in their perceptions of their own involvement within a relationship, their partner's involvement, and the nature of the relationship itself (Knobloch & Solomon, 1999). *Interference from a partner* indexes how much being interdependent with another person disrupts the performance of goal-directed routines (Knobloch & Solomon, 2004). The theory further specifies that increases in relational uncertainty and experiences of goal interference cause people to be more reactive to events that occur in their relationship (Solomon & Knobloch, 2004).

Empirical tests do not, as a set, indicate that relational uncertainty and experiences of interference peak during the transition from casual to serious involvement in

dating relationships (e.g., Knobloch & Solomon, 2004; Solomon & Knobloch, 2001). In contrast, ample evidence links relational uncertainty and interference from a partner to heightened reactivity, including more negative appraisals of relationship irritations, more negative evaluations of social networks, perceptions of more relational turbulence, and more extreme emotional reactions to a variety of events (Solomon, Weber, & Steuber, 2009). Given the evidence, recent instantiations of the relational turbulence model focus on the impact of transitions, in general, on communication and experiences of stress within ongoing romantic associations (Solomon et al., 2009).

## SUMMARY AND SYNTHESIS

Whereas early work on attraction and relationship development emphasized personal traits as the impetus for establishing an interpersonal association, the theories discussed in this section appreciate the complexities, nuances, and dynamics that unfold as partners embark on a relationship with each other. As we might expect, however, these theories vary in the extent to which they illuminate communication patterns and dyadic forces during the formation and escalation of relationships.

Communication behaviors are explicitly the focus of several theories previously reviewed. Social penetration theory considers self-disclosure as the essence of intimacy, uncertainty reduction theory positions information exchange as a key mechanism in resolving questions and ambiguities, predicted outcome value theory states that communication allows people to promote and discover the likelihood of rewarding experiences, and stage models of relationship development feature changing patterns of interaction as the basis of escalating intimacy. Other theories we have discussed are less clearly focused on communication per se. Relational schemas encompass expectations for communication, as well as other types of experiences; turning points may reflect or prompt communication events, but they include a broader variety of experiences that can transform relationships; and the relational turbulence model considers communication alongside emotions and cognitions as experiences that are exacerbated during the transition from casual to serious involvement in a relationship. Thus, the centrality of communication varies within the theories we have discussed.

These theories also vary in the extent to which they represent dyadic processes. Within social penetration theory and stage models of relationship development, the mutuality of self-disclosure and participation in patterns of interaction are prerequisites for increased involvement in a relationship. Uncertainty reduction theory and predicted outcome value theory imply that decreased ambiguity and favorable projections must be mutual for relationships to progress, but these theories do not emphasize dyadic processes. Likewise, relational schemas and accounts of turning points may or may not contain details shared between relationship partners. Relational turbulence model research has also focused exclusively on how individuals perceive their relationships and react to events that unfold within them. Although all of these theories and programs of research are purported to explain the inherently dyadic process of forming interpersonal relationships, their focus—to varying degrees—tends to emphasize the experiences of individuals within those relationships.

## ◆ Theorizing About Maintaining Relationships

Whereas research on communication and establishing relationships traces back to the 1970s, the emergence of relationship maintenance as an area of inquiry is relatively recent (Perlman, 2001). Dindia and Canary (1993) identified four definitions of relationship maintenance: (a) continuing a relationship or keeping it in existence; (b) keeping a relationship in a specified state, such as at a particular level of intimacy; (c) keeping a relationship in a satisfactory condition; and (d) preventing or correcting relationship problems. Empirical efforts to study relationship maintenance include studies of strategies (Stafford & Canary, 1991) and cognitive and behavioral activities (e.g., Rusbult, Van Lange, Wildschut, Yovetich, & Verette, 2000) that sustain relationships. Because early work on the stability and satisfaction of relationships was informed by social exchange theories, we begin our discussion of relational maintenance theories with perspectives closely tied to that tradition.

### EQUITY THEORY

Equity theory is grounded in the assumption that individuals are motivated to maximize the rewards they receive and minimize their costs but that they also understand that certain norms and rules guide social relationships. Consequently, people are most satisfied when they believe that the outcomes both partners receive from the relationship are proportional to what each puts into the relationship (Hatfield, Pillemer, Sprecher, Utne, & Hay, 1984). Individuals who perceive that they are *underbenefited* (i.e., getting less than they should) are likely to feel angry, whereas people who believe that they are *overbenefited* (i.e., getting more than they deserve) may feel guilty (Hatfield, 1983). When people perceive their relationship to be inequitable, they try to eliminate their distress by restoring equity.

Consistent with the theory, romantic partners tend to be less satisfied when they perceive that their relationships are inequitable (Sprecher, 1986, 1992; Walster, Walster, & Traupmann, 1978). More specifically, people who believe they are underbenefited typically are less happy with their relationships than those who believe they are treated equitably by their partner.

Individuals who perceive they are over-benefited also tend to be somewhat dissatisfied, but this effect is not as strong as the effect of being underbenefited. Sprecher (2001) found that people who perceived they were overbenefited were relatively happy with their relationship, and being overbenefited did not have the same deleterious influence on satisfaction as being underbenefited.

Although equity theory has a great deal of explanatory power, scholars have raised issues that point to its limitations. For instance, some studies have demonstrated that the benefits partners receive are more important in predicting their satisfaction than their perceived equity (Cate, Lloyd, Henton, & Larson, 1982). Others have found that people vary in the extent to which they are concerned with equity (Buunk & Van Yperen, 1991) and that they have particular ideas about the extent to which behavior in different relationships should be guided by equity principles (e.g., Clark & Mills, 1979).

## THE INVESTMENT MODEL

The investment model is an expansion of Kelley and Thibaut's (1978) interdependence theory, which specifies that satisfaction is a function of the reward value of a relationship, relative to expectations, and that commitment stems from the superiority of a relationship, compared with viable alternatives. Rusbult (1980) reformulated interdependence theory to incorporate the value of resources gained through involvement in a relationship (e.g., a larger social network) and those resources that have been devoted to developing the association (e.g., time or emotional involvement). Because ending a relationship would lead to the loss or waste of these resources, the theory specifies that investments increase commitment to a relationship. Consistent with the theory, studies of individuals in romantic relationships, including a 15-year longitudinal study (Bui, Peplau, & Hill,

1996) and a meta-analysis (Le & Agnew, 2003), indicate that people are more committed to a relationship when they are satisfied with rewards and costs, they perceive alternatives to be low quality, and they are invested in the association.

The investment model further specifies that people committed to their relationship maintain the association by (a) focusing on how their relationship compares favorably with others, (b) derogating the attractiveness of potential alternative relationships, (c) engaging in accommodative behavior when faced with dissatisfying experiences, and (d) sacrificing their own self-interests for the good of the relationship or partner (Rusbult & Buunk, 1993; Rusbult, Drigotas, & Verette, 1994). The substantial empirical evidence in support of these claims speaks to the investment model's heuristic value in efforts to understand the maintenance of ongoing relationships.

## AFFECT-EXCHANGE RESEARCH

Whereas equity theory and the investment model emphasize general perceptions of rewards and costs in relationships, several scholars have examined how rewarding and costly experiences are manifest in interactions between partners. Studies in this tradition suggest that partners who are unhappy with their relationship, compared with happy partners, demonstrate more negative affect and less positive affect (Notarius & Johnson, 1982), display more negative nonverbal behaviors (Noller, 1982), and engage in fewer supportive behaviors (Pasch & Bradbury, 1998) toward each other. Individuals' positive behaviors and relational satisfaction are correlated (Weiss & Heyman, 1990), and partners' negative behaviors and expressions of negative affect predict relational satisfaction over time (Markman, 1981), even when initial levels of satisfaction are controlled (Gottman & Krokoff, 1989).

Although expressions of positive and negative affect are both assumed to be relevant to relationship maintenance, individuals' negative behaviors are more strongly associated with satisfaction than are their positive behaviors (Jacobson, Waldron, & Moore, 1980; Wills, Weiss, & Patterson, 1974). This finding, however, does not suggest that expressions of positive affect are unrelated to relationship outcomes. Gottman and Levenson (1992) reported that couples' satisfaction was more strongly influenced by the ratio of positive to negative behaviors than by the absolute frequency of either positive or negative behaviors, and Huston and Chorost (1994) found that the association between negativity and relational quality was buffered by partners' expressions of positive affect. Generally, these studies suggest that negative behaviors may be the more sensitive gauge of how people feel about their romantic relationships but that expressions of positivity during interactions serve important relationship maintenance functions.

The link between romantic partners' negative behaviors and their satisfaction has emerged in the literature as a consistent finding; however, it is complicated by at least two factors. First, research points to gender differences both in the expression of negative affect and in the influence of negative affect on relational outcomes (Gottman & Krokoff, 1989; Huston & Vangelisti, 1991; Notarius & Johnson, 1982). Second, the majority of research on couples' affective behavior has been done in the context of conflict or problem-solving interactions, which may highlight the importance of partners' negativity and restrict the influence of their positive behaviors (Cutrona, 1996). These complications point to the need for further research on how positive and negative behaviors contribute to relationship maintenance.

## RELATIONAL DIALECTICS THEORY

Relational dialectics theory is a perspective on relationship maintenance that emphasizes the trade-offs and conflicting desires that create tension within close relationships (Baxter & Montgomery, 1996). The theory characterizes relationships as in a constant state of flux as inherent contradictions emerge through discourse (Baxter, 2004b). It specifies three core tensions—*expression-privacy*, *stability-change*, and *integration-separation*—which can be manifested within the relationship or between the relationship as a unit and people outside the relationship (Baxter & Montgomery, 1996). More generally, the theory suggests that manifestations of and responses to relational dialectics are central to experiences within ongoing relationships (see Baxter & DeGooyer, 2001).

Early research on relational dialectics identified the prevalence of tensions within romantic associations and coworker friendships (Baxter, 1990; Bridge & Baxter, 1992) and the strategies or rituals that people use to manage dialectical tensions (Baxter & Simon, 1993; Braithwaite & Baxter, 1995). In more recent research, relational dialectics has emerged as an interpretive theory that illuminates how partners create meanings through the interpenetration of different perspectives (Baxter, 2006).

One question that has been raised about relational dialectics theory concerns whether it is, in fact, a theory. Baxter (2004a) clarified that relational dialectics theory is a sensitizing theory, which advances assumptions and concepts to frame inquiry, rather than a predictive theory. The heuristic value of relational dialectics theory is evident in the variety of relationship types it has been used to study, the way it reveals fundamental tensions that emerge in the discourse of relationships, and how it points to a complex and impalpable aspect of relationship maintenance.

## INFORMATION MANAGEMENT THEORIES

One particular dialectical tension revolves around revealing and concealing private information. Until the 1980s, disclosure was viewed as having benefits for relationships, whereas its counterparts (e.g., avoidance, secrecy, and deception) were seen as harmful or socially unacceptable. In the early 1980s, several scholars challenged the notion that complete openness always has positive consequences (e.g., Bochner, 1982; Parks, 1982). Most researchers now agree that disclosing and withholding information are associated with both positive and negative outcomes. This consensus spawned a body of research on how information management—strategic revelation and concealment—contributes to the maintenance of interpersonal relationships.

Information management in ongoing relationships can be indexed by the extent to which partners avoid topics or keep information secret. A number of studies have revealed a negative association between keeping secrets and relational satisfaction (e.g., Vangelisti, 1994; Vangelisti & Caughlin, 1997). There also is evidence that individuals' perceptions of others' secrecy are associated with feelings of rejection and avoidance (Caughlin & Golish, 2002). Afifi, Caughlin, and Afifi (2007) suggested that the effects of avoidance and secrecy on relationships are moderated by (a) the extent to which avoidance or secrecy is explicitly recognized in conversation, (b) perceptions of the extent of avoidance and secrecy, (c) individuals' privacy rules and communication standards, (d) the perceived reasons for avoidance or secrecy, and (e) the larger relational and cultural context. As such, the relationship maintenance consequences of information management may be quite complex.

Information management research has also examined factors that predict or motivate avoidance and secrecy. Caughlin and Afifi (2004) identified a variety of reasons underlying topic avoidance, including self-protection, relationship protection, partner unresponsiveness, conflict avoidance, privacy, and a lack of closeness (see also Guerrero & Afifi, 1995a, 1995b). By contrast, the reasons that people reveal a family secret to a relationship partner include perceiving that the relationship with that partner is intimate,

the partner will be accepting of the secret, and the relationship can survive sharing the secret (Vangelisti, Caughlin, & Timmerman, 2001). In general, these studies show that information management is one way that people use communication to maintain relationships that they value.

## SUMMARY AND SYNTHESIS

Relationship maintenance as an area of inquiry was formalized more recently than scholarly work on relationship development; nonetheless, a variety of theories and programs of research exist to guide studies of how communication functions to maintain relationships. As we saw with respect to theories focused on establishing relationships, these efforts represent varying degrees of emphasis on communication behavior and dyadic processes.

Perhaps not surprisingly, theories grounded in social psychological perspectives on exchange—namely, equity theory and the investment model—attend only incidentally to communication. Relational dialectics theory positions communication more centrally as one source of tension between openness and privacy. Within scholarship related to affect exchange or information management, the affect and information that people do—or do not—express to partners is conceptualized as a key aspect of relationship maintenance.

Likewise, theories and research related to relationship maintenance vary in the degree to which they address dyadic patterns within interpersonal associations. In the case of equity theory, people's view of their own outcomes relative to a partner's outcomes is the basis for perceptions of being over-benefited or underbenefited. The investment model, on the other hand, focuses more exclusively on how an individual's perceptions of a relationship lead to cognitions and behaviors that promote relationship maintenance. Information management research also tends to privilege the perceptions and communication behaviors of individuals within relationships, rather than the ways that partners collaboratively negotiate information-sharing boundaries. In contrast, affect exchange research focuses squarely on messages and sequences of messages exchanged during dyadic interactions. In a more abstract way, relational dialectics theory also emphasizes how tensions within individuals and between partners are manifest within the discourse of relationships.

## ◆ *Future Directions for Theorizing About Establishing and Maintaining Relationships*

As we observed previously, communication functions to establish and maintain interpersonal relationships because the messages people exchange can create, define, modify, or reinforce the bonds between them. In synthesizing theories addressing relationship formation and those focused on relationship maintenance, we noted that these frameworks vary in the extent to which they grapple with communication behavior per se and dyadic processes. Indeed, virtually all of the theories that we discussed prominently feature intrapersonal or cognitive processes, while the dynamics of interpersonal interaction are often less well developed. Consequently, the corpus of work tends to portray relationships as two individuals coming together, rather than an evolving dyadic social unit. We see five avenues for advancing research on communication and relationship development beyond the current emphasis on individuals within relationships.

### THINKING DYADICALLY ABOUT INTERPERSONAL COMMUNICATION

We believe there is ample room for theories that address the dynamics of interaction between partners. Although affect exchange research demonstrates that the communication between partners is associated with concurrent and subsequent relationship quality, other theories considered neglect the ways in which messages and sequences within interactions are diagnostic or consequential for relationships. What are the patterns of information exchange that allow partners to co-construct their association as one in which uncertainty is being reduced, positive outcomes are being promoted, relationship stages are being performed, or a turning point is unfolding? What interaction patterns prompt perceptions of equity or inequity, reveal or resolve relational dialectics, or coordinate privacy boundaries? Whether a complaint grows into an intense conflict depends on whether the target of that complaint accepts or rejects the criticism (Dersley & Wootton, 2000). In the same way, gaining a better understanding of how communication establishes or maintains relationships requires researchers to look beyond what people perceive and how they act to how they co-create meaning and interact.

### THEORIZING ABOUT PHYSIOLOGY

Cognitive structures and processes have a prominent place in research on relationship formation and maintenance, whereas physiological variables have been largely ignored. Like any other animal, humans have physiological systems that alert them to threats and a stress-response system that helps them to manage those threats. As especially social creatures, humans may be uniquely affected by other people as sources of stress and resources for stress management. Research demonstrates that expressing and receiving affection from personal relationship partners attenuates people's physiological stress reactions (e.g., Floyd et al., 2007). By extension, we consider it fruitful to examine how physiological reactions to communication with another person might be an impetus for escalating or maintaining a bond with that partner.

## CONTEXTUALIZING RELATIONSHIPS

People establish and maintain interpersonal relationships within the web of bonds that form their social network, and communication with social network members both reflects and affects the quality of a particular relationship (e.g., Julien et al., 2000). Moreover, the cultural context represents an important scope condition to theories of relationship development because it affects the mechanisms featured by these theories (e.g., norms for self-disclosure, tolerance for uncertainty, conceptions of rewards and costs, standards for equity, perceptions of investments, and privacy rules). The study of interpersonal relationships emerged during a unique historical moment—between the availability of birth control pills and the spread of HIV and while the divorce rate in the United States escalated dramatically—leaving an indelible mark on theories of interpersonal relationships (Fitzpatrick, 1993). More recent technological advances have also changed the context for relationships by creating opportunities for relationship initiation (Whitty, 2004) and maintenance (Stafford, 2005) that transcend physical, temporal, and geographic boundaries (Katriel, 1999). Scholars would do well to incorporate these influential aspects of context into theories about interpersonal relationships.

## EXAMINING RELATIONSHIPS ACROSS THE LIFE SPAN

Another avenue for future research addresses the evolving experiences of communication and relationships over the life span. Burleson (1995, p. 577) described interpersonal relationships as "doubly developmental" because both relationships and the individuals within them change and evolve over time. Theories featured in this chapter attend to the development of relationships, rather than the ways in which individuals change over the course of a lifetime. A life span perspective on interpersonal relationships appreciates that the cognitive and physical resources that people bring to a relationship, the motives and priorities people have for interpersonal relationships, the personal demands and opportunities that compete with relationships for attention, and the norms or values that shape communication all change as people progress from adolescence through stages of adulthood (Pecchioni, Wright, & Nussbaum, 2005). For the most part, the research informing the theories we have discussed was conducted on people in *emerging adulthood*—a stage of life wherein individuals live without either the protective constraints of adolescence or the demanding responsibilities of adulthood (Arnett, 2000). When older and typically married populations are studied, stages of adulthood and their implications for relationship maintenance are usually unspecified. Thus, understanding how phenomena that evolve over the life span may qualify and extend theories of relationship development is an untapped area of inquiry ripe for theoretical innovations.

## INTEGRATING CONCEPTIONS OF ESTABLISHING AND MAINTAINING RELATIONSHIPS

We offer one final direction for future research. In conceptualizing and organizing this chapter, we attended to the distinction that is often drawn between theory and research about relationship initiation and escalation and scholarship that focuses on the maintenance of previously established relationships. This distinction has merit because the issues salient in an interaction between new acquaintances are different from those that dominate long-standing associations. At the same time, we wonder if this division implies that communication operates in fundamentally different ways within developing and established relationships. As we reflect on the conceptions of communication offered by the field's intellectual forebears (e.g., Miller, 1978; Watzlawick et al., 1967), we are reminded of the fundamental symbiotic bond between communication and relationships. In other words, communication instantiates a relationship between two individuals (Duck & Pond, 1989), irrespective of whether the exchange is a first encounter or one that occurs after many years of involvement. We are hopeful that continued theorizing about establishing and maintaining relationships will illuminate the fundamental role of communication in giving form to interpersonal relationships.

## ◆  References

Afifi, T. D., Caughlin, J., & Afifi, W. A. (2007). The dark side (and light side) of avoidance and secrets. In B. H. Spitzberg & W. R. Cupach (Eds.), *The dark side of interpersonal communication* (pp. 61–92). Mahwah, NJ: Lawrence Erlbaum.

Altman, I., & Taylor, D. A. (1973). *Social penetration.* New York: Holt, Rinehart, & Winston.

Altman, I., Vinsel, A., & Brown, B. H. (1981). Dialectic conceptions in social psychology: An application to social penetration and privacy regulation. In L. Berkowitz (Ed.), *Advances in experimental social psychology* (Vol. 14, pp. 107–160). New York: Academic Press.

Arnett, J. J. (2000). Emerging adulthood: A theory of development from the late teens through the twenties. *American Psychologist, 55,* 469–480.

Baldwin, M. W. (1992). Relational schemas and the processing of social information. *Psychological Bulletin, 112,* 461–484.

Baxter, L. A. (1990). Dialectical contradictions in relationship development. *Journal of Social and Personal Relationships, 7,* 69–88.

Baxter, L. A. (2004a). Relationships as dialogues. *Personal Relationships, 11,* 1–22.

Baxter, L. A. (2004b). A tale of two voices: Relational dialectics theory. *Journal of Family Communication, 4,* 181–192.

Baxter, L. A. (2006). Relational dialectics theory: Multivocal dialogues of family communication. In D. O. Braithwaite & L. A. Baxter (Eds.), *Engaging theories in family communication* (pp. 130–145). Thousand Oaks, CA: Sage.

Baxter, L. A., & Bullis, C. (1986). Turning points in developing romantic relationships. *Human Communication Research, 12,* 469–493.

Baxter, L. A., & DeGooyer, D., Jr. (2001). Perceived aesthetic characteristics of interpersonal conversations. *Southern Communication Journal, 67,* 1–18.

Baxter, L. A., & Montgomery, B. M. (1996). *Relating: Dialogues and dialectics.* New York: Guilford.

Baxter, L. A., & Simon, E. P. (1993). Relationship maintenance strategies and dialectical contradictions in personal relationships. *Journal of Social and Personal Relationships, 10,* 225–242.

Berger, C. R. (1987). Communicating under uncertainty. In M. E. Roloff & G. R. Miller (Eds.), *Interpersonal processes* (pp. 39–62). Newbury Park, CA: Sage.

Berger, C. R. (1988). Uncertainty and information exchange in developing relationships. In S. W. Duck (Ed.), *Handbook of personal relationships* (pp. 239–255). New York: John Wiley.

Berger, C. R., & Calabrese, R. J. (1975). Some explorations in initial interaction and beyond: Toward a developmental theory of interpersonal communication. *Human Communication Research, 1,* 99–112.

Berger, C. R., & Roloff, M. E. (1982). Thinking about friends and lovers: Social cognition and relational trajectories. In M. E. Roloff & C. R. Berger (Eds.), *Social cognition and communication* (pp. 151–192). Beverly Hills, CA: Sage.

Bochner, A. P. (1982). On the efficacy of openness in close relationships. In M. Burgoon (Ed.), *Communication yearbook 6* (pp. 109–123). Beverly Hills, CA: Sage.

Braithwaite, D. O., & Baxter, L. A. (1995). "I do" again: The relational dialectics of renewing marriage vows. *Journal of Social and Personal Relationships, 12,* 177–198.

Bridge, D., & Baxter, L. A. (1992). Blended relationships: Friends as work associates. *Western Journal of Communication, 56,* 200–225.

Bui, K. T., Peplau, L. A., & Hill, C. T. (1996). Testing the Rusbult model of relationship commitment and stability in a 15-year study of heterosexual couples. *Personality and Social Psychology Bulletin, 22,* 1244–1257.

Burleson, B. R. (1995). Personal relationships as a skilled accomplishment. *Journal of Social and Personal Relationships, 12,* 575–581.

Buunk, B. P., & Van Yperen, N. W. (1991). Referential comparisons, relational comparisons, and exchange orientation: Their relation to marital satisfaction. *Personality and Social Psychology Bulletin, 17,* 709–717.

Cate, R. M., Lloyd, S. A., Henton, J. M., & Larson, J. (1982). Fairness and reward level as predictors of relationship satisfaction. *Social Psychology Quarterly, 45,* 177–181.

Caughlin, J. P., & Afifi, T. D. (2004). When is topic avoidance unsatisfying? A more complete investigation into the underlying links between avoidance and dissatisfaction in parent-child and dating relationships. *Human Communication Research, 30,* 479–513.

Caughlin, J. P., & Golish, T. D. (2002). An analysis of the association between topic avoidance and dissatisfaction: Comparing perceptual and interpersonal explanations. *Communication Monographs, 69,* 275–296.

Clark, M. S., & Mills, J. R. (1979). Interpersonal attraction in exchange and communal relationships. *Journal of Personality and Social Psychology, 37,* 12–24.

Cupach, W. R., & Spitzberg, B. H. (1994). *The dark side of interpersonal communication.* Hillsdale, NJ: Lawrence Erlbaum.

Cutrona, C. (1996). *Social support in couples.* Thousand Oaks, CA: Sage.

Davis, K. E., & Todd, M. J. (1985). Assessing friendship: Prototypes, paradigm cases and relationship description. In S. Duck & D. Perlman (Eds.), *Understanding personal relationships* (pp. 17–37). Beverly Hills, CA: Sage.

Dersley, I., & Wootton, A. (2000). Complaint sequences within antagonistic argument. *Research on Language and Social Interaction, 33,* 375–406.

Dindia, K., & Canary, D. J. (1993). Definitions and theoretical perspectives on maintaining relationships. *Journal of Social and Personal Relationships, 10,* 163–173.

Duck, S., & Pond, K. (1989). Friends, Romans, countrymen, lend me your retrospections: Rhetoric and reality in personal relationships. In C. Hendrick (Ed.), *Close relationships* (pp. 17–38). Newbury Park, CA: Sage.

Fehr, B. (1988). Prototype analysis of the concepts of love and commitment. *Journal of Personality and Social Psychology, 55,* 557–579.

Fitzpatrick, M. A. (1993). Communication and the new world of relationships. *Journal of Communication, 43,* 119–126.

Floyd, K., Mikkelson, A. C., Tafoya, M. A., Farinelli, L., La Valley, A. G., Judd, J., et al. (2007). Human affection exchange: XIV. Relational affection predicts resting heart rate and free cortisol secretion during acute stress. *Behavioral Medicine, 32,* 151–156.

Gottman, J. M., & Krokoff, L. J. (1989). Marital interaction and satisfaction: A longitudinal view. *Journal of Consulting and Clinical Psychology, 57,* 47–52.

Gottman, J. M., & Levenson, R. W. (1992). Marital processes predictive of later dissolution: Behavior, physiology, and health. *Journal of Personality and Social Psychology, 63,* 221–233.

Guerrero, L. K., & Afifi, W. A. (1995a). Some things are better left unsaid: Topic avoidance in family relationships. *Communication Quarterly, 43,* 276–296.

Guerrero, L. K., & Afifi, W. A. (1995b). What parents don't know: Topic avoidance in parent-child relationships. In T. Socha & G. Stamp (Eds.), *Parents, children, and communication* (pp. 219–247). Mahwah, NJ: Lawrence Erlbaum.

Hatfield, E. (1983). Equity theory and research: An overview. In H. H. Blumberg, A. P. Hare, V. Kent, & M. Davies (Eds.), *Small groups and social interaction* (Vol. 2, pp. 401–412). Chichester, England: John Wiley.

Hatfield, E., Pillemer, J., Sprecher, S., Utne, M., & Hay, J. (1984). Equity and intimate relations: Recent research. In W. Ickes (Ed.), *Compatible and incompatible relationships* (pp. 1–27). New York: Springer-Verlag.

Hendrick, S. S. (1981). Self-disclosure and marital satisfaction. *Journal of Personality and Social Psychology, 40,* 1150–1159.

Honeycutt, J. M., Cantrill, J. G., & Greene, R. W. (1989). Memory structures for relational escalation: A cognitive test of the sequencing of relational actions and stages. *Human Communication Research, 16*, 62–90.

Huston, T. L., & Chorost, A. F. (1994). Behavioral buffers on the effect of negativity on marital satisfaction: A longitudinal study. *Personal Relationships, 1*, 223–239.

Huston, T. L., Surra, C. A., Fitzgerald, N. M., & Cate, R. (1981). From courtship to marriage: Mate selection as an interpersonal process. In S. Duck & R. Gilmour (Eds.), *Personal relationships 2: Developing personal relationships* (pp. 53–88). New York: Academic Press.

Huston, T. L., & Vangelisti, A. L. (1991). Socioemotional behavior and satisfaction in marital relationships. *Journal of Personality and Social Psychology, 61*, 721–733.

Jacobson, N. S., Waldron, H., & Moore, D. (1980). Toward a behavioral profile of marital distress. *Journal of Consulting and Clinical Psychology, 48*, 696–703.

Julien, D., Tremblay, N., Bélanger, I., Dubé, M., Bëgin, J., & Bouthillier, D. (2000). Interaction structure of husbands' and wives' disclosure of marital conflict to their respective best friend. *Journal of Family Psychology, 14*, 286–303.

Katriel, T. (1999). Rethinking the terms of social interaction. *Research on Language and Social Interaction, 32*, 95–101.

Kelley, H. H., & Thibaut, J. E. (1978). *Interpersonal relations: A theory of interdependence.* New York: John Wiley.

Kerckhoff, A. C., & Davis, K. E. (1962). Value consensus and need complementarity in mate selection. *American Sociological Review, 27*, 295–303.

Knapp, M. L. (1984). *Interpersonal communication and human relationships.* Boston: Allyn & Bacon.

Knapp, M. L., Ellis, D. G., & Williams, B. A. (1980). Perceptions of communication behavior associated with relationship terms. *Communication Monographs, 47*, 262–278.

Knobloch, L. K., & Solomon, D. H. (1999). Measuring the sources and content of relational uncertainty. *Communication Studies, 50*, 261–278.

Knobloch, L. K., & Solomon, D. H. (2004). Interference and facilitation from partners in the development of interdependence within romantic relationships. *Personal Relationships, 11*, 115–130.

Le, B., & Agnew, C. R. (2003). Commitment and its theorized determinants: A meta-analysis of the investment model. *Personal Relationships, 10*, 37–57.

Levinger, G. (1983). Development and change. In H. H. Kelley, E. Berscheid, A. Christensen, J. H. Harvey, T. L. Huston, G. Levinger, et al. (Eds.), *Close relationships* (pp. 315–359). New York: W. H. Freeman.

Markman, H. J. (1981). Prediction of marital distress: A five-year follow-up. *Journal of Consulting and Clinical Psychology, 49*, 760–762.

Miller, G. R. (1978). The current state of theory and research in interpersonal communication. *Human Communication Research, 4*, 164–177.

Murnstein, B. I. (1970). Stimulus-value-role: A theory of marital choice. *Journal of Marriage and the Family, 32*, 465–481.

Noller, P. (1982). Channel consistency and inconsistency in the communications of married couples. *Journal of Personality and Social Psychology, 43*, 732–741.

Notarius, C. I., & Johnson, J. S. (1982). Emotional expression in husbands and wives. *Journal of Marriage and the Family, 45*, 483–489.

Parks, M. R. (1982). Ideology in interpersonal communication: Off the couch and into the world. In M. Burgoon (Ed.), *Communication yearbook 6* (pp. 79–107). Beverly Hills, CA: Sage.

Pasch, L. A., & Bradbury, T. N. (1998). Social support, conflict, and the development of marital dysfunction. *Journal of Consulting and Clinical Psychology, 66*, 219–230.

Pecchioni, L. L., Wright, K. E., & Nussbaum, J. F. (2005). *Life-span communication.* Mahwah, NJ: Lawrence Erlbaum.

Perlman, D. (2001). Maintaining and enhancing personal relationships: Concluding commentary. In J. H. Harvey & A. Wenzel (Eds.), *Close romantic relationships* (pp. 357–377). Mahwah, NJ: Lawrence Erlbaum.

Planalp, S. (1985). Relational schemata: A test of alternative forms of relational knowledge as guides to communication. *Human Communication Research, 12*, 3–29.

Ramirez, A., Jr., & Burgoon, J. K. (2004). The effect of interactivity on initial interactions: The influence of information valence and modality and information richness on computer-mediated interaction. *Communication Monographs, 71,* 422–447.

Rogers, L. E., & Farace, R. V. (1975). Analysis of relational communication in dyads: New measurement procedures. *Human Communication Research, 1,* 222–239.

Roloff, M. E. (1981). *Interpersonal communication: The social exchange approach.* Beverly Hills, CA: Sage.

Rose, S., & Frieze, I. H. (1989). Young singles' scripts for a first date. *Gender & Society, 3,* 258–268.

Rubin, Z., Hill, C. T., Peplau, L. A., & Dunkel-Schetter, C. (1980). Self-disclosure in dating couples: Sex roles and the ethic of openness. *Journal of Marriage and the Family, 42,* 305–317.

Rusbult, C. E. (1980). Commitment and satisfaction in romantic associations: A test of the investment model. *Journal of Experimental Social Psychology, 16,* 172–186.

Rusbult, C. E., & Buunk, B. P. (1993). Commitment processes in close relationships: An interdependence analysis. *Journal of Social and Personal Relationships, 10,* 175–204.

Rusbult, C. E., Drigotas, S. M., & Verette, J. (1994). The investment model: An interdependence analysis of commitment processes and relationship maintenance phenomena. In D. J. Canary & L. Stafford (Eds.), *Communication and relational maintenance* (pp. 115–132). San Diego: Academic Press.

Rusbult, C. E., Van Lange, P. A. M., Wildschut, T., Yovetich, N. A., & Verette, J. (2000). Perceived superiority in close relationships: Why it exists and persists. *Journal of Personality and Social Psychology, 79,* 521–545.

Solomon, D. H., & Knobloch, L. K. (2001). Relationship uncertainty, partner interference, and intimacy within dating relationships. *Journal of Social and Personal Relationships, 18,* 804–820.

Solomon, D. H., & Knobloch, L. K. (2004). A model of relational turbulence: The role of intimacy, relational uncertainty, and interference from partners in appraisals of irritations. *Journal of Social and Personal Relationships, 21,* 795–816.

Solomon, D. H., Weber, K. M., & Steuber, K. R. (2009). Turbulence in relational transitions. In S. W. Smith & S. R. Wilson (Eds.), *New directions in interpersonal communication research.* Thousand Oaks, CA: Sage.

Spitzberg, B. H., & Cupach, W. R. (1998). *The dark side of close relationships.* Mahwah, NJ: Lawrence Erlbaum.

Sprecher, S. (1986). The relation between inequity and emotions in close relationships. *Social Psychology Quarterly, 49,* 309–321.

Sprecher, S. (1987). The effects of self disclosure given and received on affection for an intimate partner and stability of the relationship. *Journal of Social and Personal Relationships, 4,* 115–128.

Sprecher, S. (1992). How men and women expect to feel and behave in response to inequity in close relationships. *Social Psychology Quarterly, 55,* 57–69.

Sprecher, S. (2001). A comparison of emotional consequences of and changes in equity over time using global and domain-specific measures of equity. *Journal of Social and Personal Relationships, 18,* 477–501.

Stafford, L. (2005). *Maintaining long-distance and cross-residential relationships.* Mahwah, NJ: Lawrence Erlbaum.

Stafford, L., & Canary, D. J. (1991). Maintenance strategies and romantic relationship type, gender, and relational characteristics. *Journal of Social and Personal Relationships, 8,* 217–242.

Sunnafrank, M. (1986). Predicted outcome value during initial interactions: A reformulation of uncertainty reduction theory. *Human Communication Research, 13,* 3–33.

Sunnafrank, M. (1988). Predicted outcome value in initial conversations. *Communication Research Report, 5,* 169–172.

Sunnafrank, M. (1990). Predicted outcome value and uncertainty reduction theories: A test of competing perspectives. *Human Communication Research, 17,* 76–103.

Sunnafrank, M., & Ramirez, A., Jr. (2004). At first sight: Persistent relational effects of get-acquainted conversations. *Journal of Social and Personal Relationships, 21,* 361–379.

Surra, C. A. (1985). Courtship types: Variations in interdependence between partners and social networks. *Journal of Personality and Social Psychology, 49,* 357–375.

Surra, C. A., & Hughes, D. K. (1997). Commitment processes in accounts of the development of premarital relationships. *Journal of Marriage and the Family, 59,* 5–21.

Vangelisti, A. L. (1994). Family secrets: Forms, functions, and correlates. *Journal of Social and Personal Relationships, 11,* 113–135.

Vangelisti, A. L., & Caughlin, J. P. (1997). Revealing family secrets: The influence of topic, function, and relationships. *Journal of Social and Personal Relationships, 14,* 679–705.

Vangelisti, A. L., Caughlin, J. P., & Timmerman, L. (2001). Criteria for revealing family secrets. *Communication Monographs, 68,* 1–17.

Walster, E., Walster, G. W., & Traupmann, J. (1978). Equity and premarital sex. *Journal of Personality, 36,* 82–92.

Watzlawick, P., Beavin, J. H., & Jackson, D. D. (1967). *Pragmatics of human communication.* New York: Norton.

Weiss, R. L., & Heyman, R. E. (1990). Observation of marital interaction. In F. D. Fincham & T. N. Bradbury (Eds.), *The psychology of marriage* (pp. 87–117). New York: Guilford Press.

Whitty, M. T. (2004). Cyber-flirting: An examination of men's and women's flirting behavior both offline and on the Internet. *Behaviour Change, 21,* 115–126.

Wills, T. A., Weiss, R. L., & Patterson, G. R. (1974). A behavioral analysis of the determinants of marital satisfaction. *Journal of Consulting and Clinical Psychology, 42,* 802–811.

# 20

# MEDIA ENTERTAINMENT

◆ Christoph Klimmt
and Peter Vorderer

Media entertainment has become an established field of communication science. Despite the pervasiveness of entertainment media and audiences, as well as their social, economic, and even political relevance, the amount of published research regarding the phenomenon was small for several decades. Interestingly, Katz and Foulkes criticized the lack of entertainment research as early as 1962. Today, the importance of media entertainment within modern societies is no longer debated (Wolf, 1999), and thematic research has grown considerably, beginning in the 1970s and booming since the late 1990s (Zillmann & Vorderer, 2000). The prosperity of entertainment research is fuelled mainly by two key characteristics of this research domain: Entertainment media and their consumption experiences are (a) highly diverse and (b) developing rapidly (e.g., Bryant & Vorderer, 2006), which creates a wide range of questions for and social relevance of entertainment research. The demand for theory construction, as well as empirical research, replication, and application, is high, driven both by fundamental research's mission to describe and explain relevant phenomena and by dynamic industries calling for applied studies on ever-new platforms, forms, and content of media entertainment.

## ◆ Historical Roots and Early Developments

The first waves of mediated mass entertainment, such as low-cost novels in the second half of the 19th century or picture-rich newspapers in the early 20th century (Engel, 1997), did not stimulate much scientific concern. The advent of radio entertainment and cinemas showing films revealed the importance of entertainment in mass societies to elites (e.g., Carey, 1993). We may consider the minimal scientific activity that occurred during this era to be the beginning of systematic entertainment research, especially Herzog's (1944) surveys on the motives of American women to listen to radio soap operas. These radio shows were probably the most popular entertainment product of the 1930s and 1940s. Produced in an industrialized manner and implementing advanced business models such as product placement, they regularly reached huge audiences. This study of the motivations driving selective exposure to one important genre of media entertainment was pioneering work for the field. It first introduced the issue of media enjoyment to scientific consideration instead of ignoring the entertainment factor in favor of issues of (undesired) media effects.

Katz and Foulkes (1962) elaborated a motivational framework for entertainment consumption. Their concept of "escapism" explained the preference for entertainment media as the desire to contrast negative experiences of everyday life, which is accomplished through "identification" with the world of entertainment media and temporary withdrawal from stressful real-life circumstances (see also Pearlin, 1959). The foundational contribution of this work to early entertainment research is the psychological-theoretical perspective on people's motivation to select media entertainment repeatedly. In addition, the discussion of experiential processes such as "identification," which underlie enjoyment experiences, paved the way for one of the most important branches of contemporary entertainment research (Vorderer, Klimmt, & Ritterfeld, 2004).

These and a few other pieces of early entertainment research remained isolated and unique within communication science for at least another decade, partly because mass entertainment was not considered academically relevant or deserving of intellectual analysis (e.g., Munch-Petersen, 1973). Especially in Europe, elite preferences for traditional, "classic," and "serious" literature and arts were reflected in scientific ignorance concerning entertainment media (Bark, 1973). The opportunities for entertainment research finally appeared in the 1970s for two main reasons. Outside of the academic system, societal change following political movements in the late 1960s stimulated research explicitly devoted to overcoming elitist attitudes regarding "quality" literature and media ("ideology-critical research"; cf. Groeben & Vorderer, 1988). Within academia, entertainment consumption was discovered to be a relevant topic to the psychology of emotion (Planalp, Metts, & Tracy, Chapter 21, this volume). Affective experiences triggered by comedy, pornography, mediated sports, and other modes of media entertainment attracted the attention of psychologists, especially Percy Tannenbaum (1980) and his mentee, Dolf Zillmann. Building on general foundations from the psychology of emotion and applying experimental methods from psychology to the study of users of media entertainment, Zillmann and his early collaborators—most important, Joanne Cantor and Jennings Bryant—formed and shaped the beginnings of systematic, theory-driven inquiry on media entertainment, which still guides and informs contemporary approaches (Bryant, Roskos-Ewoldsen, & Cantor, 2003).

## ◆ Universal Theories of Media Entertainment

### TERMINOLOGICAL TROUBLES

While the importance of media entertainment has been acknowledged in the communication discipline, the definition of media entertainment remains problematic. A substantial variety of message genres, forms, and contents can be classified as "entertaining," both from the perspective of communicators (e.g., authors of novels, TV stations that broadcast comedy) and from the perspective of audiences. Bosshart and Macconi (1998) list six characteristics of entertaining media messages. Entertainment is

- psychological relaxation—It is restful, refreshing, light, distracting;

- change and diversion—It offers variety and diversity;

- stimulation—It is dynamic, interesting, exciting, thrilling;

- fun—It is merry, amusing, funny;

- atmosphere—It is beautiful, good, pleasant, comfortable;

- joy—It is happy, cheerful. (p. 4)

These components can certainly serve as building blocks for a definition of media entertainment, albeit they are neither semantically nor conceptually distinct from each other. They reflect the diversity problem of entertainment researchers very well, however. An exciting, highly suspenseful sports broadcast is media entertainment, just as are a hilarious and intelligent television comedy, a spectacular action movie, a puzzle-rich adventure video game, a sad-romantic novel, and many more media genres and offerings. These few examples already indicate the large range of experiential qualities that media audiences (can) consider entertainment (Vorderer et al., 2004).

Consequently, simple, unidimensional concepts or processes can neither define nor scientifically explain media entertainment (Bryant & Vorderer, 2006). Rather, a multilevel structure is required for definitions and theories of media entertainment (see Figure 20.1): On a more abstract level, universal theories that cover the shared characteristics of all manifestations of media entertainment can connect entertainment to other large-scale domains of social science (e.g., psychological well-being, cf. Kahneman,

**Figure 20.1**    Multilevel Structure of Entertainment Theories in Communication Science

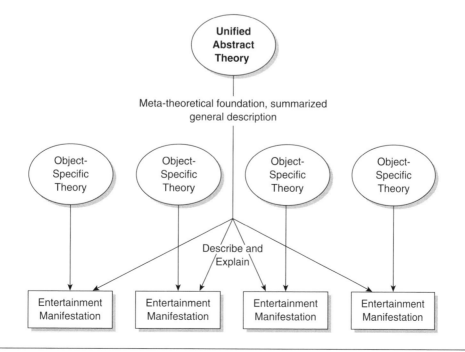

Diener, & Schwarz, 1999, or evolutionary psychology, cf. Steen & Owens, 2001). At a more specific level, object-related theories describe and explain the determinants and dimensions of individual experiential qualities definable as entertainment. For example, theories of suspense (Vorderer, Wulff, & Friedrichsen, 1996) address one major class of entertaining media messages and their effect on audiences; they do so without referring to other manifestations of media entertainment, such as melancholy or pride. Such object-level theories can vary concerning the description of the entertainment experience itself and the underlying psychological processes that trigger the experience. They can compete with each other and can undergo empirical testing (e.g., Mares & Cantor, 1992). So far, entertainment researchers have focused mostly on one of two levels of theory construction, that is, either suggested overarching frameworks (universal theories) or elaborated and tested object-specific theories (e.g., concerning the entertainment manifestation of suspense; cf. Zillmann, 1994).

## ENTERTAINMENT AS EMOTION MACHINE: ZILLMANN'S FRAMEWORK

An important framework of media entertainment has grown out of Zillmann's experimental research (Zillmann, 2003). His view of people's responses to entertaining media messages focused on affective processes, and he applied his theory of human emotion to various modes of entertainment (cf. Bryant & Miron, 2003). According to Zillmann's framework, affect regulation drives people's motivational system, and external stimuli—including mass media messages—are useful tools either to sustain desired emotional states or to enter new states that differ from one's current emotional condition. Grounded in biological and psychophysiological considerations (e.g., Zillmann & Zillmann, 1996), this framework models the use of media

entertainment as an unmediated type of behavior that is motivated by natural hedonistic preferences (Zillmann, 1988).

Key processes within the framework are the desire for mood regulation ("mood management": Zillmann, 1988), empathic emotions that agents of mass media elicit (e.g., heroes of crime drama or players in sports broadcasts; cf. Zillmann, 1996a), and euphoria that results from excitatory relief during confrontation with rapidly changing situational characteristics such as the "happy ending" in suspense movies (Zillmann, 1996b). The framework includes cognitive processes only as components of emotional states. For instance, emotions of fear and hope are driven by empathy for a likeable movie character, and the consequent suspense is theorized to result from moral judgments about the character (Raney, 2005). In general, however, Zillmann's framework of entertainment theory primarily emphasizes the *emotional* dimension of media entertainment and explains people's strong and sustainable demand for entertainment by biological-hedonistic, unmediated behavioral tendencies to enter or sustain pleasurable mood states (Zillmann, 2000).

## ENTERTAINMENT AS PLAYFUL COMMUNICATION: AN ACTION-THEORETICAL FRAMEWORK

An alternative universal theory conceptualizes the use and experience of media entertainment as a playful mode of human communication (Vorderer, 2001, 2003; Vorderer et al., 2004). By highlighting the commonalities between entertainment use and playful action, this framework expands the view of entertainment beyond issues of emotion and affect regulation and addresses the complex network of motivational (needs, motives, volitions affecting media selection), cognitive (expectations toward media messages, information processing, top-down knowledge activated during message reception), emotional (appraisals, arousal processes), and behavioral variables involved in enjoyable media experiences. Moreover, it highlights the overall relevance of media entertainment to people's daily lives and well-being (Vorderer et al., 2004; see Figure 20.2). Two classes of motivations are argued to energize exposure to entertainment media (Klimmt, 2008):

• Following Katz and Foulkes (1962), one class of motivations relates to contrasting stressful or otherwise unpleasant real-life experience with pleasant, novel, unusual, or otherwise positive mediated experiences (escapism; see Henning & Vorderer, 2001). This escape type of motivation includes emotion regulation (Salovey, Hsee, & Mayer, 1993; Zillmann, 1988) as well as underlying or connected cognitive states. For instance, a real-world experience of frustration due to powerlessness in the workplace may foster a young employee's motivation to play a strategy video game after work, which facilitates an (enjoyable) experiential state of governing a (virtual) country with armies at his command and citizens obeying to his regime.

• Drawing from developmental psychology (e.g., Oerter, 1999; Sutton-Smith, 1997), the second class of motivations for using media entertainment involves work on developmental tasks (Havighurst, 1981) such as identity formation or gender role socialization.

The as-if quality of play—that is, play's location between reality and fantasy—allows individuals to test actions, emotions, and identities without risking failure or social rejection ("it is only a game"; cf. Sutton-Smith, 1997). In a similar way, the fictional or quasi-real worlds of media entertainment provide information relevant to developmental tasks: Video games offer young boys (emotional) experiences of masculinity (Jansz, 2005), telenovelas teach (female) adolescents about relationship formation and maintenance (Mayer, 2003), and crime drama assures adults about the

morality and functionality of society at large. Working on developmental tasks is thus a very "serious" class of motivations behind entertainment use. In this sense, the action-theoretical framework argues that the role of media entertainment in daily life and across the life span is much more central and complex than generally thought to be the case. As in human play, all processes involved in entertaining media use—motivations, cognitions, emotions—depend on developmental changes and personological variables, which render entertainment research still more multifaceted and diverse.

The "entertainment as play" paradigm is based on a broader concept of motivation than Zillmann's framework. Following views from the philosophy and psychology of human action (Gollwitzer & Bargh, 1996; Groeben, 1986; Heckhausen, 1991; Oerter, 1999) and self-determination theory (Deci & Ryan, 2000), the pursuit and use of media entertainment can be motivated by processes that range from complex, reflective decision making to quick, impulsive, situation-bound choices energized by spontaneous preferences for mood regulation. In contrast to Zillmann's perspective, however, this framework does not suggest that selection of media entertainment that is not thoughtfully planned (such as zapping behavior when watching TV) is necessarily driven by biological forces and hedonistic mood optimization. Rather, it may also be the consequence of automaticity (Bargh, 1997). That is, thoughtful-reflective selection of entertainment fare that is frequently repeated becomes automatic over time, and the associated goals are stored as "chronic" motivations in memory such that both the entertainment-related goals (e.g., escapist relaxation after the workday) and media selection (e.g., searching for a mildly suspenseful crime drama on TV) can be processed with little deliberate thought.

The action-theoretical framework also proposes that the motivational processes involved in selecting entertainment media are highly diverse. In this sense, the framework is compatible with the uses and

**Figure 20.2**　A Complex, Action-Theoretical Model of Media Entertainment

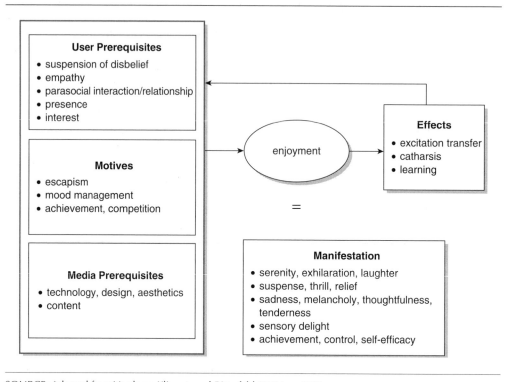

SOURCE: Adapted from Vorderer, Klimmt, and Ritterfeld (2004, p. 393).

gratifications perspective, which is frequently applied in entertainment research (e.g., Nabi & Oliver, Chapter 15, this volume; Nabi, Stitt, Halford, & Finnerty, 2006) but adopts more variants of human action (e.g., impulsive, automatized, and reflected media choice) and is more specific in terms of the origins of motivations to use media entertainment (by rooting back to self-determination theory and evolutionary psychology; cf. Steen & Owens, 2001; Vorderer, Steen, & Chan, 2006).

#### ◆ Object Theories of Media Entertainment

While the conceptual frameworks introduced above represent general approaches to media entertainment, much thematic research addresses specific questions such as the user experience with certain genres or the psychological processes underlying a particular

mode of media enjoyment. These more focused formulations and the empirical studies they stimulate result in theories and models that capture parts of the abstract concept of entertainment such as suspense, exhilaration, or melancholy (Bosshart & Macconi, 1998; Bryant & Miron, 2003). In this section, we introduce three prominent examples of such specialized, limited-scope entertainment theories and briefly review thematic empirical work. This section intends to illustrate different perspectives and strategies employed in theoretical-empirical entertainment research to provide a broader understanding of the field.

#### SUSPENSE: THE EXPERIENCE OF DISPOSITION-BASED EMPATHIC EMOTIONS

One important experiential state that most media users and communication researchers count as entertainment is suspense (Vorderer et al., 1996). Although suspense is an unpleasant affective state that largely consists of stress and fear, the enormous popularity of suspenseful media messages such as crime drama, action movies, and live sports broadcasts suggests that suspenseful experiences contain a substantial portion of pleasure as well. Zillmann (1994, 1996a) has developed the most prominent theory of suspense in communication science. He argues that suspense is an affective response of media users to specific attributes and behaviors of characters displayed by the media message (for instance, a novel or a movie). Suspense is thus construed as a *social*-emotional process. Zillmann's theory proposes that emotional reactions to media characters result from the dispositions users form toward these characters. Positive dispositions lead to empathic emotions, whereas negative dispositions foster resentful or even hostile emotions. The attitudes toward media characters thus determine the affective responses toward the characters and their fate, as narrated by the media message. Dispositions, in turn, follow from moral evaluations of the characters. For example, viewers judge a protagonist's behavior in terms of moral integrity. "Good" characters will receive positive evaluations, but people behaving badly (e.g., criminals, arrogant characters) will garner negative evaluations. Morality thus affects dispositions, which then determine media users' affective responses.

According to Zillmann's theory, suspense may be construed as a specific $2 \times 2$ configuration of disposition-based emotional reactions: If media users fear negative story developments for characters they empathize with (that is, morally "good" characters) and hope for positive outcomes for these characters, this mixture of hope and fear marks the experience of suspense. The complementary emotional state results from concerns that disliked characters (those receiving users' negative moral judgment) may face positive outcomes (that

they "simply do not deserve") or hopes that negative events, which seem to be morally appropriate, such as punishment, will befall them (Raney, 2005). Hopes for specific outcomes and fears that the opposite outcomes may occur are thus the affective substance of suspense (Zillmann, 1996a). Therefore, suspense results from social-emotional *relevance*: If media users care about what happens to characters (because they like them or because they strongly dislike them), entertainment media may trigger emotional responses (e.g., by presenting morally good characters in threatening circumstances) that are construed as suspense. Moreover, suspense is a result of *uncertainty*: Future-related emotions such as hope and fear can emerge only if users are unsure of a character's fate. Directors and authors can thus trim suspense experiences by adding or removing uncertainty about what will happen to likeable and nonlikeable characters.[1]

Zillmann and his collaborators have reported ample empirical evidence for this theory. Their experiments demonstrate the key roles of moral judgment, dispositions toward the media characters, and outcome probabilities for suspense experiences. For example, Comisky and Bryant (1982) manipulated a video displaying a car chase sequence. In line with Zillmann's theory, they found that the less likely a positive outcome was for the hero (as long as the outcome probability was not zero), and the more positive dispositions held toward the protagonist, the more suspense viewers experienced. Recent conceptual reviews (Raney, 2004; Raney & Bryant, 2002) and experimental evidence (Raney, 2005) suggest some additions and clarifications to Zillmann's original model. Specifically, the process of moral judgment seems to be more complex: First, morality is relevant in viewer evaluations of both characters' actions (e.g., the crimes of the "bad guys") *and* the punishment they (may or may not) receive. Punishment of perpetrators in suspense movies needs to be morally appropriate in order to be enjoyable for viewers;

excessive punishment of "bad guys" causes moral concern and undermines enjoyment. Second, individual attitudes toward justice moderate the morality-based enjoyment process (Raney, 2005).

Overall, suspense is one of the few well-explored domains of entertainment research, and communication scholars have accumulated considerable theoretical-explanatory substance. Nevertheless, various questions and challenges remain: For instance, the cognitive processes that lead to disposition formation may be more diverse than Zillmann's focus on morality suggests (Raney, 2004). Viewer expectations (e.g., knowledge about a movie genre) may also moderate suspense processes (de Wied, Hoffman, & Roskos-Ewoldsen, 1997). Moreover, personality factors, such as sensation seeking (Zuckerman, 2006), have not been introduced systematically as an audience-based element in suspense models. Consequently, the domain of suspense holds more complexity for theoretical-empirical communication, although the basic mechanics of this entertaining experiential state are well understood.

## PARASOCIAL RELATIONSHIPS: LONG-TERM INVOLVEMENT WITH MEDIA CHARACTERS SHAPES ENJOYMENT

Many genres of media entertainment center on people, including actors, musicians, talk show hosts, sports stars, and other kinds of celebrities that regularly appear in the media. Television, in particular, displays famous people with high frequency and in multiple contexts. Several communication theories address audience responses to people in (entertainment) media, including the disposition-based theories introduced by Zillmann (see above). Parasocial relationship theory takes a broader stance on media characters and pertains to issues of long-term involvement with characters that affects people's selection of entertainment fare, their enjoyment experiences during exposure, and

entertainment effects (Klimmt, Hartmann, & Schramm, 2006).

The fundamental assumption of parasocial relationship theory is that (fictional or nonfictional) characters who appear regularly in the media trigger social information processing in users (Giles, 2002; Horton & Wohl, 1956). People observe, categorize, and evaluate characters on the screen and store their impressions in memory. Perceptions of familiarity and social attitudes evolve with repeated "parasocial contact" (Schiappa, Gregg, & Hewes, 2005). For instance, protagonists of a crime series such as *CSI: Miami* can increase social involvement (parasocial relationships) throughout the course of one season if a given viewer watches most or all of the season's shows. "Meeting" such characters on television again will then evoke experiences of familiarity, and eventually, viewers will hold mental representations of well-known and likeable characters who are potentially comparable to those of real-life friends or neighbors (Gleich, 1997).

Such relationships vary not only in intensity but also in terms of quality. Viewers' parasocial bond to a media celebrity can be dominated by admiration (e.g., a young boy's relationship to Arnold Schwarzenegger), strong emotional sympathy (e.g., a woman's relationship to Diana, Princess of Wales; cf. Brown, Basil, & Bocarnea, 2003), erotic desire (e.g., an adolescent male's relationship to Beyoncé), or envious disdain (e.g., an adult woman's relationship to Paris Hilton). Relationship quality determines the experiences media users go through when they see a media character on-screen. Therefore, both relationship intensity and quality are crucial to understanding the implications of parasocial relationships for media entertainment.

The first set of implications from this research refers to entertainment *selection*. If a media user holds a strong, positive parasocial relationship with a character who is supposed to be featured in a particular entertainment offering, the user will be more likely to select that message due to the parasocial relationship (e.g., Chory-Assad & Yanen, 2005). In turn, strong-negative parasocial relationships increase the motivation to avoid the message.

Second, watching messages that feature characters one holds strong parasocial relationships with will shape the *quality and intensity of enjoyment*. For instance, talk shows featuring a well-liked movie star may render viewers' experience particularly entertaining because viewing such shows evokes as-if impressions of being together with an old friend, states of deep admiration, and a sense of intimacy (Horton & Wohl, 1956). Older viewers who rediscover their favorite rock band from 30 years ago on TV may remember positive experiences of fandom and concert atmosphere, which then contribute to the entertainment experience as "emotion memories" (Oatley, 1994). In an empirical example, Hartmann, Stuke, and Daschmann (2008) found that intensity of a parasocial relationship to racing driver Michael Schumacher affected the level of suspense experienced during broadcasts of a Formula One race.

Third, parasocial relationships may also affect the postexposure effects of media entertainment. For instance, the persuasive impact of fictional entertainment messages (Appel & Richter, 2007; Green & Brock, 2000) is likely to be larger and more sustainable if the audience holds strong-positive parasocial relationships to media characters (e.g., Jackson & Darrow, 2005; Papa et al., 2000). In turn, if the medium no longer fosters the parasocial relationship, viewers may have a strong negative response. Cohen (2004; Eyal & Cohen, 2006) reports remarkably strong and aversive emotional responses to a favorite character's disappearance from television shows ("parasocial break-ups").

Overall, the parasocial relationships concept applies to many manifestations of media entertainment and can describe and explain numerous cognitive and emotional processes involved in selection, experience, and effects of entertainment fare. It is connected to theories on social cognition and person perception from social psychology (Giles, 2002; Klimmt et al., 2006) and thus illustrates the importance of grounding concepts for entertainment research on fundamental work from various branches of the social sciences.

## INTERACTIVE ENTERTAINMENT THEORY: MODELING THE ENJOYMENT OF VIDEO GAMES

Video games are probably the most rapidly growing and most dynamically evolving segment of the entertainment landscape (Vorderer & Bryant, 2006). Their main characteristic—interactivity—poses new challenges for entertainment theory, as the more traditional concepts developed for noninteractive ("linear") entertainment media such as novels, movies, or sports broadcasts failed to cover the experiential implications of interactivity. Exploring the dimensions and determinants of interactive entertainment experiences is thus a growing subdomain of the field (Vorderer & Bryant, 2006). The conceptual strategy for developing theories of interactive entertainment is to adopt concepts from conventional entertainment research and critically question their viability in the domain of the video game experience (e.g., Klimmt, 2003). Additional conceptual input comes from empirical explorations, mostly survey results (e.g., Sherry, Lucas, Greenberg, & Lachlan, 2006; Wood, Griffiths, Chappell, & Davies, 2004). Experimental theory testing with video games had been difficult until recently, as the theory-based manipulation of game content required programming work that was much more complicated and knowledge intensive than, for instance, editing a movie. With better tools for game modification available, theory-driven experimental tests mark the latest step in the communication science of interactive entertainment (e.g., Hefner, Klimmt, & Vorderer, 2007; Klimmt, Hartmann, & Frey, 2007; Ravaja, Saari, Salminen, Laarni, & Kallinen, 2006).

The state of the art in interactive entertainment theory is multidimensional explications (and explanations) of video game enjoyment (e.g., Klimmt, 2003; Ryan, Rigby, & Przybylski, 2006; Sherry et al., 2006). One group of game enjoyment concepts focuses on interactive use and thus refers to the experiential consequences of players' own activity. These concepts propose feelings of effectance (Klimmt & Hartmann, 2006), mastery, control (Grodal, 2000), competence, and success (Klimmt, 2003) as elements of game enjoyment. Another group of approaches highlights similarities between game enjoyment and conventional modes of entertainment. For instance, suspense seems to contribute to game enjoyment in the same way that it adds to linear entertainment experiences (e.g., Schneider, Lang, Shin, & Bradley, 2004) because suspense is the experiential manifestation of *challenging* situations, which occur frequently in most types of games. Another concept game researchers have imported from traditional entertainment research is identification with a character or role (Hefner et al., 2007). Game enjoyment thus stems in part from vicarious or simulated experiences of "being" an interesting person, such as a war hero (Jansz, 2005) or a race car driver.

As the number of concepts and empirical results on video game enjoyment continues to grow, a key challenge of interactive entertainment theory is to organize the different drivers of game enjoyment into structural models and to elaborate potential links among those facets of game enjoyment. Klimmt (2003) has proposed a model of game enjoyment that explicitly argues for synergistic interactions of different enjoyment components. For example, in this model, interactivity enables efficacy experiences (first element of game enjoyment) that foster self-attributions about positive game events, which leads to pride (second element of game enjoyment) as a consequence of one's own perceived competence ("I have achieved the positive game event"; see also Klimmt & Hartmann, 2006).

With the rapid development of the video game landscape, however, new questions concerning interactive entertainment regularly emerge: Differences between playing against computer-directed versus human opponents, particular enjoyment processes in players of "Massively Multiplayer Online Role Playing Games" such as *World of Warcraft* (Chan & Vorderer, 2006; Yee, 2006), or the theoretical implications of new input devices such as the motor-sensor systems of Nintendo's Wii add to the long list of issues for interactive entertainment theory to resolve. Thus, video games are an excellent example of the continuous pressure on entertainment research both to keep up with rapid changes in the objects of research and to reconnect with the various existing theories on older entertainment media or related branches of fundamental theory.

## ◆ A Vision for Entertainment Research

The previous two sections have illustrated that the field of media entertainment is highly dynamic and rich in theories. It is an especially attractive field for young researchers, given its high relevance for people's everyday lives, the numerous subdomains of inquiry, and the large number of unexplored research issues. In regard to the philosophy of science and to interdisciplinary collaboration, entertainment research is an interesting field of communication because it relates to virtually all disciplines of the social sciences and even beyond: *Psychological* perspectives are key to explaining individual entertainment experiences. They drive most of the empirical entertainment research, as the individual processes of selection, experience, and effects mark the center of the field (Bryant & Vorderer, 2006; Shrum, 2004). *Sociology* and *cultural studies* contribute to our understanding of the form and content as well as the habitualized and ritualized use of media entertainment at the level of groups and societies (e.g., Schulze,

1992), and indicate the strong dependence of psychological processes of entertainment on culture and socialization: What is enjoyable in Western societies is not necessarily fun in Asian or Middle Eastern societies (e.g., Acland, 2003). On the other hand, physiology and neuroscience allow the sensory and biological underpinnings of individual entertainment experiences to be understood (e.g., Ravaja et al., 2006).

Thus, the future of entertainment research requires a great deal of work. Theory development and empirical entertainment studies need to continue in light of almost infinite numbers of entertainment media, genres, and formats. In addition to this operative continuation of today's work, the even more challenging issues for the future are (a) the systematic cross-cultural foundation of entertainment research and (b) the nano-micro-meso-macro integration of conceptual elements that affect the selection, experience, and effects of media entertainment.

Concerning the cross-cultural dimension of entertainment research, communication science needs to acknowledge that entertainment media have evolved as a significant export, and today's entertainment economy is a truly global business (Havens, 2003; Wolf, 1999). For instance, the *Harry Potter* books and movies attract audiences worldwide, whereas many other entertainment media only succeed at national levels: For example, a special kind of strategy video game ("build-up games," which require much player effort and time to establish economic structures before actual war strategies become accessible) are extremely popular in Germany but are largely unsuccessful in American markets. For entertainment research, these cultural and cross-cultural issues imply new challenges to describing and explaining how media enjoyment "works."

Liebes and Katz (1986) have published a highly informative study on culturally different audiences' construal of the same entertainment format (*Dallas*). Much more of this kind of work lies ahead for future entertainment research in order for the

research enterprise to stay abreast of the dynamic development of entertainment media and their reception worldwide (Trepte, 2007; Valkenburg & Janssen, 1999). These tasks can be accomplished with effective international networking among entertainment research laboratories, which is as necessary as defining common conceptual grounds of media enjoyment that can assist in the development of transnational methodological-procedural standards (e.g., how to operationalize specific manifestations of enjoyment cross-culturally).

While the cross-cultural orientation calls for broader perspectives on media entertainment, the other major challenge ahead arises from the interdisciplinary modeling of specific enjoyment experiences across the different levels of human functioning. Perspective integration is especially appropriate for complex modes of enjoyment, such as the pleasant state of exhilaration in consumers of an irony-based comedy program like *The Simpsons* (Gray, 2007). The psychological approach to this kind of media enjoyment will include both a strong cognitive (knowledge retrieval, elaboration, and comprehension) and a strong affective (increased arousal, pleasant emotion of joy) dimension. Their complete modeling needs to incorporate neuroscientific construals as well, for example, the patterns of brain activation for elaborative memory processes and pleasant affective states (e.g., Damasio, 2004). Physiological approaches equally contribute to full descriptions of the enjoyment experience. Organismic responses to surprise, for instance, are well documented in physiological research (Ravaja et al., 2006) and may turn out to be an important building block for a multilevel construal of the *Simpsons* experience because the format frequently uses surprises to foster (irony-based) exhilaration. The scientific disciplines concerned with human biological functioning should thus play a crucial role in future entertainment research to understand the "nano" level of enjoyment experiences on which conscious-individual manifestations of entertainment are grounded.

The "micro" level, which is the classic research from psychology and communication, will still play the lead role in future entertainment research, as it investigates those processes (e.g., knowledge, person perception, attribution, social comparison, recognition of the mediation of experience, suspension of disbelief) that determine the experiential quality of entertainment accessible to the individual media user (Bryant & Vorderer, 2006; Zillmann & Vorderer, 2000). To contribute effectively to multilevel models of enjoyment experiences, the traditional lines of entertainment research will need to further exploit the rich reservoirs of theory of the social sciences (e.g., much work in social psychology is important to analyze audience responses to people-centered entertainment messages; see the sections on suspense and on parasocial relationships above).

Entertainment research so far has neglected the importance of the social situations that surround media consumption and group processes involved in media enjoyment. Television consumption often occurs while other family members are present (Bryant & Bryant, 2001). The fun of horror movies in the cinema "works" much better if the viewer is part of a group (Tamborini, 2003). Many video game players prefer online games that connect them to a few or (extremely) many other people (Pena & Hancock, 2006). Research on media entertainment should integrate input from social psychology and sociology to better understand the experiential implications that follow from group situations of media consumption and from the entertainment's relevance in ongoing social interaction. Thus, theorizing the "meso" level of entertainment experiences—that is, social situations and group processes—is also an important task ahead for multilevel models of media entertainment in communication science.

Finally, future entertainment research must cap the combined contributions of nano-, micro-, and meso-aspects with a macro-perspective on popular culture and history, as well as cultural (see above) and life span dimensions (see McLeod, Kosicki, & McLeod, Chapter 11, this volume). Socialization through media in Western societies is a complex process with remarkable impact on individual communication patterns and entertainment experiences. Consider, for example, the collective importance of Disney's main characters and the way they affected audience preferences and expectations toward media entertainment (Watts, 2001). Germany's television system, which had been limited to very few channels until the mid-1980s, has shaped national audience habits and entertainment preferences for today's older generations in very specific ways. Such system-level factors are frequently set as constant in individual-based entertainment research, but a full-spectrum account of entertainment experiences should consider the variability and influence of relevant macro-aspects as well.

The core of the challenge for future entertainment described here is to model *synergistic interactions of determinants and dimensions of media entertainment across levels of analysis.* While it is intuitively clear that (complex) modes of media entertainment such as the *Simpsons* experience relate to all levels mentioned, from neurological functioning to cultural and societal framing, it is most important to theorize how the different components relate to each other and how specific interactions among the components contribute to variance in media enjoyment. The need for nano-micro-meso-macro integration therefore relates to both theory connectivity and methodological compatibility.

Communication science is definitely the discipline that is best suited to master the enormous challenges outlined here because (a) communication research on media entertainment and beyond already addresses several levels mentioned above (e.g., research in information systems, mass communication, and popular communication, to name some thematically relevant divisions of the International Communication Association), and (b) the discipline has a strong and successful tradition of adopting and translating concepts and methods from other (social) sciences (Bryant & Miron, 2004). Therefore, we conclude the present chapter on a very optimistic note: Entertainment research will be central in the communication science of the future because it is already rich in theories and still offers numerous opportunities for theoretical-empirical expansion. It also offers great chances to improve the connections among the various academic traditions within the communication discipline (Craig, 1999). From an applied perspective, entertainment research is a significant part of communication's contribution to address societal problems. Some of these problems *stem* from the popularity of media entertainment (e.g., the effects of violent entertainment media; see Nabi & Oliver, Chapter 15, this volume), while society may *resolve* other problems by using media entertainment (e.g., "entertainment education"; cf. Singhal, Cody, Rogers, & Sabido, 2004). Thus, entertainment research deserves its place among the established fields of communication science, and we argue that entertainment research will become one of the discipline's major realms in the future.

## ◆ Note

1. Interestingly, users who already know about the outcome of an entertaining media message (e.g., because they have been exposed to it before) are capable of suppressing their knowledge to actively keep up a subjective uncertainty about the outcome and thus to maintain a pleasant level of suspense (suspension of disbelief; cf. Böcking, 2008; Brewer, 1996).

## ◆ References

Acland, C. R. (2003). *Screen traffic: Movies, multiplexes, and global culture*. Durham, NC: Duke University Press.

Appel, M., & Richter, T. (2007). Persuasive effects of fictional narratives increase over time. *Media Psychology, 10*, 113–134.

Bargh, J. (1997). The automaticity of everyday life. In R. S. Wyer (Ed.), *The automaticity of everyday life: Advances in social cognition* (pp. 1–61). Mahwah, NJ: Lawrence Erlbaum.

Bark, J. (1973). Research in popular literature and praxis-related literary scholarship: A report. *New German Critique, 1*, 133–141.

Böcking, S. (2008). *Grenzen der Fiktion? Von Suspension of Disbelief zu einer Toleranztheorie für die Filmrezeption* [Limits of fictionality? From suspension of disbelief toward a theory of tolerance in movie appreciation]. Cologne: Halem.

Bosshart, L., & Macconi, I. (1998). Defining "entertainment." *Communication Research Trends, 18*(3), 3–6.

Brewer, W. F. (1996). The nature of narrative suspense and the problem of rereading. In P. Vorderer, H. J. Wulff, & M. Friedrichsen (Eds.), *Suspense: Conceptualizations, theoretical analyses, and empirical explorations* (pp. 107–127). Mahwah, NJ: Lawrence Erlbaum.

Brown, W. J., Basil, M. D., & Bocarnea, M. C. (2003). Social influence of an international celebrity: Responses to the death of Princess Diana. *Journal of Communication, 53*, 587–605.

Bryant, J., & Bryant, J. A. (Eds.). (2001). *Television and the American family*. Mahwah, NJ: Lawrence Erlbaum.

Bryant, J., & Miron, D. (2003). Excitation-transfer theory and three-factor theory of emotion. In J. Bryant, D. R. Roskos-Ewoldsen, & J. Cantor (Eds.), *Communication and emotion: Essays in honor of Dolf Zillmann* (pp. 31–60). Mahwah, NJ: Lawrence Erlbaum.

Bryant, J., & Miron, D. (2004). Theory and research in mass communication. *Journal of Communication, 54*, 662–704.

Bryant, J., Roskos-Ewoldsen, D. R., & Cantor, J. (Eds.). (2003). *Communication and emotion: Essays in honor of Dolf Zillmann*. Mahwah, NJ: Lawrence Erlbaum.

Bryant, J., & Vorderer, P. (Eds.). (2006). *Psychology of entertainment*. Mahwah, NJ: Lawrence Erlbaum.

Carey, J. (1993). *The intellectuals and the masses: Pride and prejudice among the literary intelligentsia, 1880–1939*. New York: St. Martin's.

Chan, E., & Vorderer, P. (2006). Massively multiplayer online games. In P. Vorderer & J. Bryant (Eds.), *Playing video games:*

*Motives, responses, and consequences* (pp. 77–90). Mahwah, NJ: Lawrence Erlbaum.

Chory-Assad, R., & Yanen, A. (2005). Hopelessness and loneliness as predictors of older adults' involvement with favorite television performers. *Journal of Broadcasting and Electronic Media, 49,* 182–201.

Cohen, J. (2004). Parasocial break-up from favorite television characters: The role of attachment styles and relationship intensity. *Journal of Social and Personal Relationships, 21,* 187–202.

Comisky, P., & Bryant, J. (1982). Factors involved in generating suspense. *Human Communication Research, 9,* 49–58.

Craig, R. T. (1999). Communication theory as a field. *Communication Theory, 9,* 119–161.

Damasio, A. R. (2004). *Looking for Spinoza: Joy, sorrow and the feeling brain.* London: Vintage.

Deci, R. M., & Ryan, E. L. (2000). Self-determination theory and the facilitation of intrinsic motivation, social development, and well-being. *American Psychologist, 55,* 68–78.

de Wied, M., Hoffman, K., & Roskos-Ewoldsen, D. R. (1997). Forewarning of graphic portrayal of violence and the experience of suspenseful drama. *Cognition & Emotion, 11,* 481–494.

Engel, M. (1997). *Tickle the public: 100 years of the popular press.* London: Indigo.

Eyal, K., & Cohen, J. (2006). When good friends say goodbye: A parasocial breakup study. *Journal of Broadcasting and Electronic Media, 50,* 502–523.

Giles, D. (2002). Parasocial interaction: A review of the literature and a model for future research. *Media Psychology, 4,* 279–305.

Gleich, U. (1997). *Parasoziale Interaktionen und Beziehungen von Fernsehzuschauern mit Personen auf dem Bildschirm: Ein theoretischer und empirischer Beitrag zum Konzept des aktiven Rezipienten* [Parasocial interactions and relationships of TV viewers with people on the screen: A theoretical and empirical contribution to the concept of the active viewer]. Landau: Verlag Empirische Paedagogik.

Gollwitzer, P. M., & Bargh, J. A. (Eds.). (1996). *The psychology of action: Linking cognition and motivation to behavior.* New York: Guilford.

Gray, J. (2007). Imagining America: The Simpsons go global. *Popular Communication, 5,* 129–148.

Green, M. C., & Brock, T. C. (2000). The role of transportation in the persuasiveness of public narratives. *Journal of Personality and Social Psychology, 79,* 701–721.

Grodal, T. (2000). Video games and the pleasures of control. In D. Zillmann & P. Vorderer (Eds.), *Media entertainment: The psychology of its appeal* (pp. 197–212). Mahwah, NJ: Lawrence Erlbaum.

Groeben, N. (1986). *Handeln, Tun, Verhalten als Einheiten einer verstehend-erklärenden Psychologie: Wissenschaftstheoretischer Überblick und Programmentwurf zur Integration von Hermeneutik und Empirismus* [Action, "doing," behavior as units of an understanding and explaining psychology: Metatheoretical overview and conceptual draft of the integration of hermeneutics and empiricism. Tübingen: Francke.

Groeben, N., & Vorderer, P. (1988). *Leserpsychologie: Lesemotivation—Lektürewirkung* [Psychology of readers: Motivation to read—effects of reading]. Münster: Aschendorff.

Hartmann, T., Stuke, D., & Daschmann, G. (2008). Parasocial relationships with drivers affect suspense in racing sport spectators. *Journal of Media Psychology, 20,* 24–34.

Havens, T. J. (2003). On exhibiting global television: The business and cultural functions of global television fairs. *Journal of Broadcasting & Electronic Media, 47,* 18–35.

Havighurst, R. J. (1981). *Developmental tasks and education.* New York: Longman.

Heckhausen, H. (1991). *Motivation and action.* Berlin: Springer.

Hefner, D., Klimmt, C., & Vorderer, P. (2007). Identification with the player character as determinant of video game enjoyment. In L. Ma, R. Nakatsu, & M. Rauterberg (Eds.), *International Conference on Entertainment Computing 2007* (Lecture Notes in Computer Science 4740, pp. 39–48). Berlin: Springer.

Henning, B., & Vorderer, P. (2001). Psychological escapism: Predicting the amount of television viewing by need for cognition. *Journal of Communication, 51,* 100–120.

Herzog, H. (1944). What do we really know about daytime serial listeners? In P. F. Lazarsfeld,

B. Berelson, & F. N. Stanton (Eds.), *Radio research, 1942–43* (pp. 3–33). New York: Duell, Sloan and Pearce.

Horton, D., & Wohl, R. R. (1956). Mass communication and para-social interaction: Observation on intimacy at a distance. *Psychiatry, 19,* 185–206.

Jackson, D. J., & Darrow, T. I. A. (2005). The influence of celebrity endorsements on young adults' political opinions. *Harvard International Journal on Press/Politics, 10,* 80–89.

Jansz, J. (2005). The emotional appeal of violent video games for adolescent males. *Communication Theory, 15,* 219–241.

Kahneman, D., Diener, E., & Schwarz, N. (Eds.). (1999). *Well-being: The foundations of hedonic psychology.* New York: Russell Sage Foundation.

Katz, E., & Foulkes, D. (1962). On the use of mass media for escape: Clarification of a concept. *Public Opinion Quarterly, 26,* 377–388.

Klimmt, C. (2003). Dimensions and determinants of the enjoyment of playing digital games: A three-level model. In M. Copier & J. Raessens (Eds.), *Level Up: Digital Games Research Conference* (pp. 246–257). Utrecht, The Netherlands: Faculty of Arts, Utrecht University.

Klimmt, C. (2008). Enjoyment/entertainment seeking. In W. Donsbach (Ed.), *The Blackwell encyclopedia of communication* (Vol. 4, pp. 1539–1543). London: Blackwell.

Klimmt, C., & Hartmann, T. (2006). Effectance, self-efficacy, and the motivation to play video games. In P. Vorderer & J. Bryant (Eds.), *Playing video games: Motives, responses, and consequences* (pp. 132–145). Mahwah, NJ: Lawrence Erlbaum.

Klimmt, C., Hartmann, T., & Frey, A. (2007). Effectance and control as determinants of video game enjoyment. *CyberPsychology & Behavior, 10,* 845–847.

Klimmt, C., Hartmann, T., & Schramm, H. (2006). Parasocial interactions and relationships. In J. Bryant & P. Vorderer (Eds.), *Psychology of entertainment* (pp. 291–313). Mahwah, NJ: Lawrence Erlbaum.

Liebes, T., & Katz, E. (1986). Patterns of involvement in television fiction: A comparative analysis. *European Journal of Communication, 1,* 151–171.

Mares, M. L., & Cantor, J. (1992). Elderly viewers' responses to televised portrayals of old age:

Empathy and mood management vs. social comparison. *Communication Research, 19,* 459–478.

Mayer, V. (2003). Living telenovelas/telenovelizing life: Mexican American girls' identities and transnational telenovelas. *Journal of Communication, 53,* 479–495.

Munch-Petersen, E. (1973). Trivial literature and mass reading. *Orbis Litterarum, 27,* 157–178.

Nabi, R. L., Stitt, C. R., Halford, J., & Finnerty, K. L. (2006). Emotional and cognitive predictors of the enjoyment of reality-based and fictional television programming: An elaboration of the uses and gratifications perspective. *Media Psychology, 8,* 421–447.

Oatley, K. (1994). A taxonomy of the emotions of literary response and a theory of identification in fictional narrative. *Poetics, 23,* 53–74.

Oerter, R. (1999). *Psychologie des Spiels: Ein handlungstheoretischer Ansatz* [The psychology of play: An action-theoretical approach]. Weinheim: Beltz.

Papa, M. J., Singhal, A., Law, S., Pant, S., Sood, S., Rogers, E. M., et al. (2000). Entertainment-education and social change: An analysis of parasocial interaction, social learning, collective efficacy, and paradoxical communication. *Journal of Communication, 50,* 31–55.

Pearlin, L. I. (1959). Social and personal stress and escape television viewing. *Public Opinion Quarterly, 23,* 255–259.

Pena, J., & Hancock, J. T. (2006). An analysis of socioemotional and task communication in online multiplayer video games. *Communication Research, 33,* 92–109.

Raney, A. A. (2004). Expanding disposition theory: Reconsidering character liking, moral evaluations, and enjoyment. *Communication Theory, 14,* 348–369.

Raney, A. A. (2005). Punishing media criminals and moral judgment: The impact on enjoyment. *Media Psychology, 7,* 145–163.

Raney, A. A., & Bryant, J. (2002). Moral judgment and crime drama: An integrated theory of enjoyment. *Journal of Communication, 52,* 402–415.

Ravaja, N., Saari, T., Salminen, M., Laarni, J., & Kallinen, K. (2006). Phasic emotional reactions to video game events: A psychophysiological investigation. *Media Psychology, 8,* 343–367.

Ryan, R. M., Rigby, C. S., & Przybylski, A. (2006). The motivational pull of video games: A self-determination theory approach. *Motivation and Emotion, 30,* 347–363.

Salovey, P., Hsee, C. K., & Mayer, J. D. (1993). Emotional intelligence and the self-regulation of affect. In D. M. Wegner & W. Pennebaker (Eds.), *Handbook of mental control* (pp. 258–277). Englewood Cliffs, NJ: Prentice Hall.

Schiappa, E., Gregg, P. B., & Hewes, D. E. (2005). The parasocial contact hypothesis. *Communication Monographs, 72,* 92–115.

Schneider, E. F., Lang, A., Shin, M., & Bradley, S. D. (2004). Death with a story: How story impacts emotional, motivational, and physiological responses to first-person shooter video games. *Human Communication Research, 30,* 361–375.

Schulze, G. (1992). *Die Erlebnisgesellschaft: Kultursoziologie der Gegenwart* [The experience-driven society: Cultural sociology of the present]. Frankfurt am Main: Campus-Verlag.

Sherry, J., Lucas, C., Greenberg, B., & Lachlan, K. (2006). Video game uses and gratifications as predictors of use and game preference. In P. Vorderer & J. Bryant (Eds.), *Playing video games: Motives, responses, consequences* (pp. 213–224). Mahwah, NJ: Lawrence Erlbaum.

Shrum, L. J. (Ed.). (2004). *Blurring the lines: The psychology of entertainment media.* Mahwah, NJ: Lawrence Erlbaum.

Singhal, A., Cody, M., Rogers, E., & Sabido, M. (Eds.). (2004). *Entertainment education and social change: History, research and practice.* Mahwah, NJ: Lawrence Erlbaum.

Steen, F. F., & Owens, S. A. (2001). Evolution's pedagogy: An adaptionist model of pretense play and entertainment. *Journal of Cognition and Culture, 1,* 289–321.

Sutton-Smith, B. (1997). *The ambiguity of play.* Cambridge, MA: Harvard University Press.

Tamborini, R. (2003). Enjoyment and social functions of horror. In J. Bryant, D. R. Roskos-Ewoldsen, & J. Cantor (Eds.), *Communication and emotion: Essays in honor of Dolf Zillmann* (pp. 417–444). Mahwah, NJ: Lawrence Erlbaum.

Tannenbaum, P. H. (Ed.). (1980). *The entertainment functions of television.* Hillsdale, NJ: Lawrence Erlbaum.

Trepte, S. (2007). Cultural proximity in media entertainment: An eight-country study on the relationship of nationality and the evaluation of U.S. prime-time fiction. *Communications: The European Journal of Communication Research, 32,* 349–371.

Valkenburg, P., & Janssen, S. C. (1999). What do children value in entertainment programs? A cross-cultural investigation. *Journal of Communication, 49,* 3–21.

Vorderer, P. (2001). It's all entertainment, sure. But what exactly is entertainment? Communication research, media psychology, and the explanation of entertainment experiences. *Poetics, 29,* 247–261.

Vorderer, P. (2003). Entertainment theory. In J. Bryant, D. R. Roskos-Ewoldsen, & J. Cantor (Eds.), *Communication and emotion: Essays in honor of Dolf Zillmann* (pp. 131–154). Mahwah, NJ: Lawrence Erlbaum.

Vorderer, P., & Bryant, J. (Eds.). (2006). *Playing video games: Motives, responses, consequences.* Mahwah, NJ: Lawrence Erlbaum.

Vorderer, P., Klimmt, C., & Ritterfeld, U. (2004). Enjoyment: At the heart of media entertainment. *Communication Theory, 14,* 388–408.

Vorderer, P., Steen, F. F., & Chan, E. (2006). Motivation. In J. Bryant & P. Vorderer (Eds.), *Psychology of entertainment* (pp. 3–18). Mahwah, NJ: Lawrence Erlbaum.

Vorderer, P., Wulff, H. J., & Friedrichsen, M. (Eds.). (1996). *Suspense: Conceptualizations, theoretical analyses, and empirical explorations.* Mahwah, NJ: Lawrence Erlbaum.

Watts, S. (2001). *The magic kingdom: Walt Disney and the American way of life.* Columbia: University of Missouri Press.

Wolf, M. J. (1999). *The entertainment economy: The mega-media forces that are re-shaping our lives.* London: Penguin.

Wood, R. T. A., Griffiths, M. D., Chappell, D., & Davies, M. N. O. (2004). The structural characteristics of video games: A psychostructural analysis. *CyberPsychology & Behavior, 7,* 1–10.

Yee, N. (2006). The psychology of massively multiplayer online role playing games: Motivations, emotional investment, relationships, and problematic use. In R. Schroeder & A. Axelson (Eds.), *Avatars at work and play: Collaboration and interaction in shared virtual environments* (pp. 187–207). London: Springer.

Zillmann, D. (1988). Mood management through communication choices. *American Behavioral Scientist, 31,* 327–340.

Zillmann, D. (1994). Mechanism of emotional involvement with drama. *Poetics, 23,* 33–51.

Zillmann, D. (1996a). The psychology of suspense in dramatic exposition. In P. Vorderer, H. J. Wulff, & M. Friedrichsen (Eds.), *Suspense: Conceptualizations, theoretical analyses, and empirical explorations* (pp. 199–231). Mahwah, NJ: Lawrence Erlbaum.

Zillmann, D. (1996b). Sequential dependencies in emotional experience and behavior. In R. D. Kavanaugh, B. Zimmerberg, & S. Fein (Eds.), *Emotion: Interdisciplinary perspectives* (pp. 243–272). Mahwah, NJ: Lawrence Erlbaum.

Zillmann, D. (2000). Mood management in the context of selective exposure theory. In M. E. Roloff (Ed.), *Communication yearbook 23* (pp. 123–145). Thousand Oaks, CA: Sage.

Zillmann, D. (2003). Theory of affective dynamics: Emotions and moods. In J. Bryant, D. R. Roskos-Ewoldsen, & J. Cantor (Eds.), *Communication and emotion: Essays in honor of Dolf Zillmann* (pp. 533–568). Mahwah, NJ: Lawrence Erlbaum.

Zillmann, D., & Vorderer, P. (Eds.). (2000). *Media entertainment: The psychology of its appeal.* Mahwah, NJ: Lawrence Erlbaum.

Zillmann, D., & Zillmann, M. (1996). Psychoneuroendocrinology of social behavior. In E. T. Higgins & A. W. Kruglanski (Eds.), *Social psychology: Handbook of basic principles* (pp. 39–71). New York: Guildford.

Zuckerman, M. (2006). Sensation seeking in entertainment. In J. Bryant & P. Vorderer (Eds.), *Psychology of entertainment* (pp. 367–387). Mahwah, NJ: Lawrence Erlbaum.

# 21

# THE SOCIAL MATRIX
# OF EMOTION EXPRESSION
# AND REGULATION

◆ Sally Planalp, Sandra Metts,
and Sarah J. Tracy

E motional expression and regulation are integrally tied to the dynamics of interaction and serve important functions for individuals, dyads, organizations, and cultures. In this chapter, we summarize theories and empirical research that illustrate the intersection among emotion experience, expression, and regulation and the ways in which this intersection is manifested in and shaped by communication processes. We begin with two fundamental questions: What do we mean by emotion, expression, and regulation, and what are the theoretical approaches that frame their analysis?

◆ *Emotion, Expression, and
Regulation: Definitional and Theoretical Issues*

*DEFINITIONS*

Scholars disagree about definitions of emotion and even debate whether such discussions are worthwhile (Bard & Cornelius, 2007).

They generally agree, however, that emotions are complicated phenomena whose workings, especially in the social world, are best captured by studying them from a variety of theoretical perspectives. Most researchers either posit working definitions or proceed with implicit definitions they believe will be palatable to readers and work well enough to advance the research.

For our purposes, we draw on Keltner and Gross's (1999) definition of emotions as "episodic, relatively short-term biologically based patterns of perception, experience, physiology, action, and communication that occur in response to specific physical and social challenges and opportunities" (p. 468). Intuition and empirical research offer joy, love, surprise, fear, anger, sadness, disgust, and shame as examples but exclude enduring mood states such as depression and dis-positions such as social anxiety (Sedikides, 1992; Watson & Clark, 1992). Emotion expression refers to the outward manifestations of emotional states. However, expression is sometimes used in the limited sense of nonverbal "displays" of emotional states (primarily in facial patterns) as well as in the broader sense of communicative behaviors that reference emotions that have no characteristic display pattern. Emotion regulation refers to the processes by which individuals control the intensity and quality of emotional experience and the degree to which this experience is fully expressed, if at all (Gross, 1998). Indeed, there may be no such thing as a truly spontaneous emotion untouched by regulation. The ubiquitous shaping forces of language and cultural learning are inherent constraints on both the content of emotional experience (Barrett, Mesquita, Ochsner, & Gross, 2007) and its expression and regulation (Davidson, 2003).

## THEORETICAL APPROACHES TO EMOTIONAL EXPRESSION AND REGULATION

Although the broad conceptual landscape of emotional expression and regulation (hereafter EER) is difficult to map, several theoretical approaches emerge as useful, albeit with substantial overlap among them. We offer a brief description of each perspective as it guides research on EER and informs the discussions of EER at the four levels of analysis that follow.

*Functional.* In his essays on the evolutionary advantages of emotions in man and (other) animals, Darwin (1872/1965) was first to recognize that emotions are functional responses to environmental cues. More recently, scholars have extended the notion of survival to include the protection and continuation of the collective (i.e., social and cultural groups) as well as the individual (e.g., Cosmides & Tooby, 2000). Thus, Darwin's theory of evolution as applied to emotion is now reflected in theories clustered within functional approaches to EER.

Darwin's most direct scholarly progeny are the extensive programs of research on facial expression and recognition by Ekman, primarily with adults, and Izard, primarily with children (Ekman, 1973, 2003; Izard, 1977; Izard & Ackerman, 2000). In addition, these approaches to EER reveal the variety of functions served at the individual and social levels, including managing priorities; guiding action; guiding distribution of resources; providing information; forming, reinforcing, and protecting social bonds; negotiating goals; and socializing shared values and norms. Lazarus's (1991) theory based on the person-in-environment relationship and Izard and colleagues' differential emotions theory (DET; Izard & Ackerman, 2000) provide the most explicit articulations. Keltner and Haidt (1999) have also provided a broad sweep of functions of EER across four levels of analysis: the individual, dyad, group, and culture.

*Process/Componential.* Analyzing emotion as an unfolding process made up of components operating at several levels (psychological, neurological, physiological, and behavioral) is perhaps the most comprehensive and inclusive approach to characterizing the complex processes of EER (Frijda, 1986). For example, neuroimaging studies of the brain confirm the central role of the amygdala in recognizing affectively loaded stimuli and then activating higher order systems associated with physiological/behavioral responses and with processing the meaning/content of the stimulus (LeDoux & Phelps, 2000). Thus, cognition (whether consciously attended or not) quickly enters the process. Several lines of research on the appraisal process indicate that emotional arousal is processed psychologically, based on situational cues and social norms (Roseman & Smith, 2001; Scherer, Schorr, & Johnstone, 2001). Regulation may operate through all stages of appraisal—primary, secondary, and reappraisal—although it is most consciously employed during secondary appraisal and reappraisal (Gross, 1998). During these stages, preliminary response patterns may be moderated or exaggerated, and the nature of the emotion experience may be defined and redefined.

*Linguistic and Textual.* Communication scholars are particularly drawn to approaches that highlight the ways people talk about and with emotion. Studies range from micro-indicators of emotion—such as language intensity and verbal immediacy—to emotion vocabularies and more macro-level analyses of metaphor, euphemisms, and imagery (Bowers, Metts, & Duncanson, 1985; Fussell, 2002). Linguistic work across cultures is notable, including analysis of emotion words in many languages (Hupka, Lenton, & Hutchison, 1999), analysis of metaphors (Kövecses, 2000), and cross-cultural comparisons of emotion words (Wierzbicka, 1994). Larger texts have also been analyzed with a political lens, from the pioneering work of Lutz and Abu-Lughod (1990) to more recent work by Ahmed (2004).

*Skills Based.* A number of scholars have recently focused attention on the skills necessary to recognize emotions and appropriately regulate their expression. Ekman's research originally focused on accuracy of facial recognition by adults, and that concern has evolved over the decades into a much broader effort to understand how emotion cues and knowledge are used skillfully or unskillfully to varying degrees. These goals led Ekman and Friesen (1975) to formulate the system of emotion display rules (simulation, inhibition, intensification, deintensification, and masking) that guide the expression of emotion (even when not felt) according to social norms. Grounded in the scholarly work of Salovey, Mayer, and colleagues (e.g., Salovey, Bedell, Detweiler, & Mayer, 2000) and popularized (some would say distorted) by Goleman (1995), *emotional intelligence* has become almost a household phrase. The construct includes an array of abilities broadly clustered into those associated with recognizing emotions in self and others, expressing emotions appropriately, and responding effectively to expressions of others (see Mathews, Zeidner, & Roberts, 2004). Saarni (1999) and others (see Lewis & Haviland-Jones, 2000) have expanded Izard's work with infants into an impressive body of literature on the development of EER skills and capabilities across the life span, with emphasis on childhood but even extending to the elderly (Labouvie-Vief, Devoe, & Bulka, 1990).

*Therapeutic.* Therapeutic aspects of EER date back to the ancient Greek notion of catharsis, entered the 20th century with Freud's "talking cure," and persist in scholarly debates today about the when's, how's, what for's, pros, and cons of expressing, suppressing, and regulating emotions (Kennedy-Moore & Watson, 1999). The therapeutic nature of talking or writing about difficult emotions has been made testable through somatic indicators of health such as immune responses (Booth & Pennebaker, 2000). The EER of trauma, in particular, has received considerable attention (e.g., Kirmayer, Lemelson, & Barad, 2007), as has work on posttraumatic growth (Calhoun & Tedeschi, 2006).

*Interactional and Self-Presentational.* Two millennia ago, Aristotle addressed the role of EER in impression management, enactment of social roles, persuasion, credibility, friendships and enmity, justice, and other social issues that occupy scholars today (Cooper, 1932). More recently, Goffman's (1959, 1967) dramaturgical model linked emotions to social performance (as both cause and effect) and to smooth interactions among actors and audience members. One well-known descendant of Goffman's work is Hochschild's (1983) notion of the "managed heart," applied most often but not exclusively to workplaces with sensitivity to the commodification and transmutation of emotion. Other scholars have engaged EER from ritual, symbolic interactionist, exchange, structural, and other perspectives (Turner & Stets, 2005). Indeed, emotion serves as a resource as individuals enact, negotiate, adjust, and change social roles whether at home (Hochschild, 1989), at work (Tracy, 2000), or in the community (Flam & King, 2005).

*Social Constructionist and Poststructuralist.* The dominant theme of the social constructionist perspective is that we feel, express, and regulate emotions that fit within a particular catalog of linguistic choices, historical forces, and social activities (Harré, 1986; Harré & Parrott, 1996). A strong constructionist position denies that emotion has any fixed biological underpinnings, but most scholars recognize that both relatively immutable biology and relatively flexible social constructions influence EER (Oatley, 1993). From this point of view, the thoughts and physical reactions associated with emotion are constantly changing, culturally sensitive, and dependent on local norms and discourses (Averill, 1994).

Communication scholars have also borrowed from poststructuralist theories that frame emotion as an ongoing subjective and interactional process, constructed through multiple, contradictory, and overlapping discourses (Foucault, 1980). A poststructural

approach views the self and emotions as overdetermined and fragmented. Feelings are not "real" or "fake." Rather, emotions as well as feelings of (in)authenticity are embedded in and moderated by multiple discourses of power (Tracy, 2005).

## ◆ EER at Four Levels of Analysis

In this section, we review the research, following Keltner and Haidt (1999), at the individual, dyadic, organizational, and cultural levels of analysis. As with theoretical perspectives, it is common for lines of research to cross levels. After all, emotion is expressed and regulated by individuals in their interactions in dyads, groups, and organizations against a backdrop of culture. So even though we may place research at one level (perhaps somewhat arbitrarily), more often than not it will "bleed over" into other levels of analysis.

### INDIVIDUALS

Research on EER within individuals is dominated by the therapeutic approach. The goals are to enhance mental health by addressing the pros and cons of expression and suppression and by offering and assessing strategies for regulation (interfacing here with a skills perspective). Developments in neurology and genetics and the search for effective regulation strategies have also implicated the process/component view to a great extent. Even at the level of individual EER, the social interactionist perspective plays a role as well.

*Modes of Expression.* Descriptive analyses of modes of expressing emotion have been going on for decades, reaching their zenith in Ekman's muscle-by-muscle facial affect coding system (FACS; Ekman & Friesen, 1975). Nevertheless, it is clear that a more complete picture of emotional expression must include vocal (Johnstone & Scherer, 2000), verbal (e.g., Fussell, 2002), body, and movement cues, actions, and even context (Planalp, 1998). How those cues are generated in combination or interpreted as a gestalt is anybody's guess (Planalp & Knie, 2002). Although much work on modes of expression assumes that expression is the same regardless of social circumstances, Kraut and Johnston (1979) noted that bowlers smiled more when looking at or talking to others than when they made strikes, Fridlund (1991) demonstrated that even the belief that a friend was watching a funny video increased smiling, and Scherer (1994) writes convincingly of "push" (from the biological process) and "pull" (toward social expectations) as both influencing expression.

*Suppression Versus Expression.* Many researchers have analyzed the pros and cons of expressing versus suppressing emotion for the individual. Suppressing a felt emotion takes effort and memory capacity (Richards & Gross, 2000) and may backfire as "post suppression rebound" (Wegner, 1992), whereas expression may help individuals reach helpful insights, especially about traumatic events (Pennebaker, 1997). Other scholars argue, however, that venting aggression without reflection may lead to more aggressive behavior (Bushman, Baumeister, & Stack, 1999), and extreme and prolonged expression may intensify or prolong arousal (Kennedy-Moore & Watson, 1999).

The suppression/expression debate quickly moves beyond the individual to dyadic, social, and cultural concerns. As Tavris (1989) puts it, "If expressed anger causes another person to shoot you, it won't matter that you die with very healthy arteries" (p. 129). Kennedy-Moore and Watson (1999) raise additional issues such as how too much or too little expression affects support, relationship maintenance, and rejection if norms are violated, as well as differing gender, family, and cultural

norms of expression. By now, the debate has moved to questions of what should be expressed when, how, to whom, under what circumstances, and with what goals; thus it slides into the realm of regulation, which has burgeoned recently (e.g., Gross, 2007; Philippot & Feldman, 2004).

*Strategies for Regulation.* Process or component models help to organize the broad repertoire of emotion management options (e.g., Planalp, 1999). Reappraisal is widely studied and clearly influenced by messages from dyads, organizations, and cultures. Techniques may target maladaptive beliefs, mental biases, or explanatory styles (Peterson & Park, 2007; Segrin, 1998; Wilson & Gilbert, 2003) or implement more productive thinking patterns such as mindfulness (interfacing with the skills approach). Physiological reactions can be addressed with deep breathing, exercise, or alcohol and drugs. Of course, expression can also be used in the service of regulation, as discussed above. Recent work has turned this array of strategies toward special populations and problems, where the skills and therapeutic perspectives founded in developmental work come into play.

## DYADS AND CLOSE RELATIONSHIPS

Several of the theoretical approaches to EER described previously are useful for analyzing dyadic and relational interaction. Undoubtedly, a few discrete emotions have hardwired or innate facial displays (e.g., fear, anger, sadness, and joy). However, these basic emotions are now embedded within complex derivative emotion families, and their expression is largely symbolic rather than spontaneous (Buck, Losow, Murphy, & Costanzo, 1992). Thus, evolutionary theory necessarily interfaces with sociological theories of emotional experience and the functions served by emotion expression.

*Emotion Expression.* Most scholars agree that emotional expressivity is a fundamental aspect of social attraction (Sabatelli & Rubin, 1986). Evolutionary theory accounts for this phenomenon as a logical mechanism in ensuring social survival. Boone and Buck (2003) argue that emotional expressivity (i.e., moderate levels of expressiveness that are easy for receivers to interpret accurately) facilitates social coordination because it signals that the sender is cooperative and trustworthy. Presumably, such signals allow others to select associates, friends, and mates who will not exploit them and will therefore be socially and reproductively beneficial. Even sex differences in the relatively more frequent and acceptable expressions of anger for men compared with women have been explained as the manifestation of early males' competitive environment. Similarly, the tendency to say "I love you" first in a developing relationship and to respond more assertively to feelings of romantic jealousy are attributed to the early male prerogative in mating sequences (Cosmides & Tooby, 2000).

Dramatism and related sociological perspectives also recognize the utility of emotion expression but characterize it in terms of role enactment and social performance. Both the experience and expression of emotion are linked to the successful or unsuccessful maintenance of face during social performance (Goffman, 1959, 1967). Loss of face results in guilt, embarrassment, or shame and disrupts the role performance for all interactants. The inept performer is expected to express the concomitant displays of these social emotions and enact remedial behaviors that restore social order (Goffman, 1959).

A central aspect of successful public performance is the ability to follow socially defined display rules—the "socially learned, often culturally different, rules about the management of expression, about who can show which emotion to whom and when they can do so" (Ekman, 2003, p. 4). In Western cultures, these rules mandate expressing positive emotions (e.g., interest or happiness), which facilitate "benign" interaction, and restraining expression of negative emotions (e.g., anger or sadness), which might induce conflict or distress for others through emotional contagion (Malatesta & Izard, 1984). This norm is so pervasive that even when research participants are instructed to act as though they do not like the person with whom they are interacting, they still begin the conversation with displays of liking such as smiling and forward lean, only slowly decreasing them during the course of the conversation (Ray & Floyd, 2006). Similarly, respondents rate individuals in videotapes and photographs as more likeable when they are laughing than when they are not, even though the respondents can easily distinguish the fake laughter from the genuine laughter (Reysen, 2006).

Of course, violations of the normative preference for positive emotion expression are a functional alternative, in some cases. Confiding in a close other when feeling sad, hurt, or disappointed is usually productive in alleviating initial distress (Kennedy-Moore & Watson, 2001) and facilitating the coping process through reappraisal (Bartsch & Hubner, 2005; Burleson & Goldsmith, 1998). However, it only functions effectively when the situation frames its appropriateness, the dyad has the expectation of intimate sharing, and the expression is limited in duration. Inappropriate, excessive, or continued expressions of sadness tend to shift listeners' attributions from unfortunate circumstances to personal dispositions of the expresser (Karasawa, 1995). Violations of the positivity bias may also be used strategically to facilitate self-presentational goals (Garner, 1996). This is evident when people strategically intensify the display of anger to achieve the self-presentational goal of intimidation and control (Clark, Pataki, & Carver, 1996).

Awareness of emotion display rules and their social consequences are acquired early in life (Misailidi, 2006). Zeman and Garber (1996) analyzed the responses of first-, third-, and fifth-grade children to scenarios in which a child felt anger, sadness, and physical pain. Regardless of the emotion, children reported that they would exert significantly more expressive control in the presence of peers than in the presence of mother or father or when alone. These children had already learned to appraise the potential costs of expressing negative emotions (Manstead & Fischer, 2001) and to assume that parental acceptance moderates the potential for negative dispositional attributions.

*EER in the Development and Maintenance of Romantic Relationships.* To recognize the relatively greater emotional openness characteristic of close relationships does not mean that emotion regulation and strategic expression are irrelevant. Indeed, they are fundamental elements in both the formation and maintenance of close relationships, especially romantic relationships (Guerrero & Andersen, 2000). Romantic relationships in Western cultures are crafted, more or less strategically, from the array of possible associations encountered in the social matrix. Central to the developmental process is the adaptation of cultural display norms to the more emotionally open climate of close relationships. This transition can be a challenge because during the initiation stage, displays of positive affect are necessary to attract potential partners; however, as individuals become more interdependent and interact in more varied contexts, the positivity bias is difficult to maintain. Disagreements and "bad" behavior are inevitable. Thus, negative emotional expression tends to increase during the turbulent middle stages of relationship development (Knobloch, Miller, & Carpenter, 2007) and decrease over time as relational partners reduce uncertainty and establish interaction norms, trust, and acceptance.

Murray and Holmes (1996) propose that romantic couples who successfully navigate the transition phases of relationship formation are able to balance the dialectic of "hope and doubt." Hope that this will be the "right person" is fostered during the initiation phase; however, doubt begins to emerge when a potential partner's negative behaviors can no longer be explained away as situational anomalies. In relationships that continue to be satisfying, partners balance this dialectic by embedding anomalies within positive emotional schemas known as *positive illusions* (Murray & Holmes, 1996), and in relationships with high commitment, divergent behaviors will be accommodated through benign attributions and positive emotional responses (Rusbult, Yovetich, & Verette, 1996).

Although appraisal theory is not explicitly incorporated into this line of research, it provides a useful theoretical framework. Gross and colleagues' model of emotion regulation (Richards, Butler, & Gross, 2003; Richards & Gross, 2000) distinguishes two types of emotion regulation: cognitive reappraisal (interpreting an event in positive terms at the time of the emotional arousal) and suppression (concealing overt signs of emotional arousal). We speculate that positive illusions and benign attributions shape the appraisal process in relationally productive ways. Specifically, in satisfying relationships, emotional arousal is recognized and motivates open discussion of the problem; however, because cognitive reappraisal is positive, the discussion is less likely to escalate into conflict. In troubled relationships, cognitive reappraisal is not employed and arousal is intense, unfocused, or negative. The only options seem to be uncontrolled expression or suppression of overt expression. Support for this speculation is evident in Gottman and Levenson's (2002) analysis of marital conflict. They identified two expressive patterns that predicted divorce over a 14-year period. Early divorce was predicted by "unregulated volatile positive and negative affect," whereas later divorce was predicted by high emotional neutrality or suppression of felt emotion (i.e., physiological measures recorded high arousal, but facial coding showed little expression).

Research that moves beyond the couple as the unit of analysis indicates that emotional regulation has implications for children as well. For example, Katz and Gottman (1993) found that mutually hostile or demand/withdrawal patterns in the conflict of parents influenced children's social competence and emotional well-being over time. Likewise, studies of emotional contagion and emotional transmission indicate that the emotions experienced by parents outside of the home are often transmitted to the children. Typically, the pattern involves negative emotions experienced by fathers that are transmitted to mothers and subsequently from mothers to their children (Larson & Almeida, 1999).

*Relationship-Specific Emotions.* EER is also relevant to close relationships because certain emotions are definitively embedded within a relational frame that determines their functions. For example, we can become angry with a rude driver, a disorganized store clerk, or even our computer, but only relational partners can make us feel hurt or jealous. Hurt is experienced when a close other diminishes a partner's worth or the value of the relationship. Although sometimes difficult to express because it is a blend of sadness, fear, and anger, controlled expression of hurt functions to inform (remind) a partner about areas of vulnerability and gives him or her an opportunity to apologize and reconfirm personal/relational worth (Vangelisti, 2007). We experience jealousy when a close relationship is threatened by a rival. Like hurt, jealousy is a blend of other emotions (fear, anger, sadness, love) and is sometimes difficult to express. When appropriately expressed, however, it serves personal and relational functions, such as strengthening the primary relationship, confirming self-esteem, and reducing uncertainty about the primary relationship as well as the rival relationship (Guerrero & Andersen, 1998).

Finally, romantic love is perhaps the most popularized exemplar of a relationship-specific emotional state. In a developing relationship, expressions of love not only signal an emotional state but also a desired relational definition. Thus, Tolhuizen (1989) includes the expression of love as a relationship intensification strategy (rather than a relationship initiation strategy), and Baxter and Bullis (1986) include it within the passion turning point. However, the expression of love is also risky if not reciprocated by one's partner. The cautious distance between first feelings of love and their expression is evident in the research by Flora and Segrin (2000). They found that a euphoric state of "felt like you were walking on cloud nine" was experienced within only 2.76 months of dating; however, the statement "I love you" was spoken after 3.63 months. Apparently, these respondents continued to (re)appraise their own feelings and the situational cues from their partner before explicitly making the relational definition bid.

Of course, expressions of love can also be used to meet a variety of self-presentational and interactional goals. Booth-Butterfield and Trotta (1994) analyzed dating couples' descriptions of the circumstances surrounding the first expression of love. Although half of the sample linked the expression to true feelings, about 20% attributed the expression to situational or normative expectations (e.g., a delightful evening or "made love" for the first time), and about 13% attributed it to a specific motive (e.g., gaining sexual compliance or testing the other person's response).

## ORGANIZATIONS

Organizational practitioners and researchers have historically undervalued emotionality, viewed it as antithetical to rationality, or treated it as a commodity to be channeled and commercialized. Communication scholars have been central in critiquing this notion. Mumby and Putnam (1992) offer the concept of "bounded emotionality" as an "alternative mode of organizing in which nurturance, caring, community, supportiveness, and inter-relatedness are fused with individual responsibility to shape organizational experiences" (p. 474). Organizational communication scholars have examined the ways that emotion is constructed, constrained, and moderated through micro-practices and macro-discourses. Such research is clustered around the topics of burnout and stress, emotion labor, emotional intelligence, humor and moods, and emotional abuse/bullying.

*Stress and Burnout.* Given that early research framed emotion as problematic and something that needed to be regulated and constrained, it is not surprising that much organizational research is focused on emotional "burnout." Presumably, workers experience a general "wearing out" from the pressures of work and experience emotional exhaustion, depersonalization of coworkers and clients, and diminished feelings of personal accomplishment (Maslach, 1982). Burnout is especially common among "helping" and caring professionals (e.g., nurses, teachers, social workers) who have intense social contact with others.

The concept of emotional contagion is central to burnout research (Hatfield, Cacioppo, & Rapson, 1994). For example, Miller, Stiff, and Ellis (1988) introduced a two-pronged conceptualization of empathy consisting of (a) emotional contagion, in which the caregiver experiences emotional responses parallel to the client's emotion, and (b) empathic concern, or a concern about the welfare of another without feeling parallel emotions. While empathic concern leads to increased satisfaction and decreased burnout, emotional contagion can encourage depersonalization of clients and lead to burnout for the worker.

The preponderance of literature suggests that stress and burnout are personal pathologies best combated through individual techniques such as deep breathing,

biofeedback, and therapy (Newton, 1995). In contrast to this individualistic approach, organizational communication scholars have identified a number of structural factors that mitigate burnout and stress. These include social support, strong superior-subordinate relationships, participation in decision making, and organizational identification (Tracy, 2005). Alternatively, the conservation of resources model (Brotheridge & Lee, 2002; Hobfoll, 1989) suggests that burnout is not directly tied to a specific task or high level of workload. Rather, it is based on the supposition that stress depends on the immediate rewards of the task and that people feel stress when valuable resources are threatened.

*Emotional Labor.* Emotional labor is among the most common themes of emotion study in organizations. It draws heavily from the social constructionist and dramaturgical perspectives, suggesting that employees regulate and express emotions in accord with the face they are expected to present on the organizational stage. Given the general cultural mandate to appear likeable and pleasant, most members of an organization tend to express positive emotions more freely and control the expression of negative emotions more carefully (Kramer & Hess, 2002). Different rules exist in different arenas, and public or "front stage" areas (e.g., serving patrons at their table in a restaurant) have stricter rules regarding performance than private "back stage" areas (e.g., the kitchen). Hochschild (1983) initiated the study of instrumental emotional display in her study of Delta flight attendants. *Emotion management* is the routine practice of aligning emotion displays with social norms, such as looking happy when given a gift. *Emotion labor* is the commercialization of this process, when the emotional fronts of employees are co-opted and controlled by management for reasons of increased profit.

Communication researchers have examined the way employees work to construct a variety of emotional demeanors, ranging from inflated cheeriness, to neutrality and calm, to the repression of fear and anger. Most studies have been qualitative and interpretive, investigating the costs and rewards of emotion labor of a variety of professions, including 911 call takers (Shuler & Sypher, 2000), cruise staff (Tracy, 2000), teachers (McPherson, Kearney, & Plax, 2003), and firefighters (Scott & Myers, 2005), among others.

*Emotional Intelligence.* Emotional intelligence is the most commercialized emotion concept in the organizational realm, producing consultants, corporate training sessions, and popular press books. The core assumption of emotional intelligence is that good business practice requires competencies associated with EER. The concept is closely associated with transformational leadership—a style in which leaders respond to the emotional needs of employees, develop trust and cooperation, and engender enthusiasm for the organizational task at hand (Fineman, 2006). Although the study of emotional intelligence has a longstanding tradition in the academic world, the publication of Goleman's popular press books, *Emotional Intelligence* (1995) and *Working With Emotional Intelligence* (1998), brought the concept to the general public and introduced two domains of competence: *personal* and *social.* Personal competence includes self-awareness, self-regulation, and motivation. Social competence includes empathy and social skills (such as leadership and influence).

Goleman's contribution is something of a mixed blessing. His model may have little to offer those who take seriously the construct of emotional competencies. The only direct reference to emotional competencies is "emotional self-awareness," "empathy," and perhaps "optimism." On the other hand, the management skills and professional competencies included in his model are useful tools within any organization. Goleman's work may not be theoretically and empirically grounded; however, its popularity suggests that organizational members and researchers alike recognize the importance of emotional skills, particularly in coping with occupational stress and managing problematic relationships (Mathews et al., 2004).

*Organizational Humor and Morale.* A strain of research that aligns with the functional approach to emotion is the examination of positive moods, morale, and humor in groups and organizations. Employees in negative moods are less satisfied, experience more burnout, and are more likely to leave their job. However, they are also likely to better process cognitive information and make finer judgments (Weiss & Cropanzano, 1996). Thus, good moods are linked to rasher decisions but also to increased creativity, satisfaction, and resilience. A key way organizations attempt to tap into the benefits of good moods is through humor. While managerial attempts to control humor are difficult and can backfire (Collinson, 2002), a number of studies find workplace humor to be functional. Humor can enhance job satisfaction; provide in-group solidarity; manage the emotions of others; help employees cope with low-level work; construct organizational culture; provide opportunities to strategically avoid certain topics, issues, or people; reduce burnout and job stress; reveal organizational values and beliefs; help employees adjust to change; and provide avenues for organizational sensemaking (Tracy, Myers, & Scott, 2006).

*Workplace Emotional Abuse.* Emotional communication also has a dark side, as typified by workplace transgressions or misbehaviors, including incivility, bullying, and emotional abuse (Metts, Cupach, & Lippert, 2006). Incivility includes various forms of rude behavior inconsistent with norms of respect and cooperation. Bullying is long-term, persistent harassment that feels intentional to the target. Emotional abuse comes in the form of insults, threats, intimidation, signs of contempt, isolation, and discounting the target's worth or competence, often from a superior. Communication scholars have examined the prevalence, harm, and cycle of workplace misbehavior, the emotional pain of abuse, and resistance to bullying (Lutgen-Sandvik, 2006; Lutgen-Sandvik, Tracy, & Alberts, 2007; Tracy, Lutgen-Sandvik, & Alberts, 2006). Consistent with emotion theory, the three families of emotions experienced in response to workplace misbehaviors are anger, hurt, and insecurity-related emotions (Metts et al., 2006). Employees may respond to bullying and emotional abuse through seeking social support and constructing narratives that may be credible to power holders who might initiate change. Employees may also move beyond the occasions of abuse compassion (Miller, 2007) as well as forgiveness—transforming initial negative emotions into positive regard, which facilitates reconstruction of workplace harmony (Metts et al., 2006).

## CULTURES

At the cultural level, EER is studied from several theoretical lenses with contributions from many disciplines. Although arguments can be made for the universality of certain expressions, the bulk of research has explored variation in EER across cultures, including linguistic variation and, to a much lesser extent, historical contexts. A new contribution for communication scholars is to study how culturally shared media resources are used in EER.

*Universality and Cultural Variability.* Ekman (1993) used an evolutionary perspective and extensive data to argue that the face is the most likely locus of universally recognizable emotional expressions. Russell (1994) reinterpreted Ekman's data, however, as indicating little better than chance recognition, except

for discriminating positive and negative emotions. No other modalities such as the voice, body, or language have been suggested as universal, although some specific cues such as blushing may be.

Cultural variability in EER is so widely observed that summarizing the evidence is challenging, although the process model of emotion provides a useful organizing scheme (Mesquita & Albert, 2007). The richest pictures of EER come from anthropologists working from social interaction or social constructionist perspectives to describe the emotional worlds of diverse cultures, especially those most removed from Western influence. By contrast, variability within European-based cultures is much subtler (Scherer, 1988). Notable ethnographies with much to say about regulation have been done for the Inuit of northern Canada (Briggs, 1970), the Ifaluk of the western Pacific (Lutz, 1988), the Ilongots of the Philippines (Rosaldo, 1980), the Balinese (Wikan, 1990), and others (see, e.g., Heelas, 1986). Emotional expression is often addressed (e.g., Irvine, 1990), but regulation is a dominant theme because of its many manifestations in childhood socialization, collective rituals, conflict negotiations, philosophies of emotion control, and intercultural misunderstandings.

Although the EER skills that are needed to function as adult members of each culture are rarely addressed directly, they can often be inferred. Briggs (1970), for example, describes in detail how Inuit children are encouraged and coerced into skillfully regulating their anger so that it is almost completely suppressed in adulthood. The therapeutic approach can also be found in discussions of what different cultures consider emotionally healthy, how imbalance or emotional illness can be remedied (Georges, 1995), and how trauma can be transformed socially (Bloom, 1998).

*Linguistic and Historical Influences.* The structure of emotion words in different languages has been analyzed, often as a complement to ethnographic work (e.g., Shaver, Wu, & Schwartz, 1992). The basic distinction between positive and negative emotion words is common, but further distinctions are highly variable across cultures. Historians also analyze written texts to give accounts of EER during different historical periods. For example, W. I. Miller (1993) used the Icelandic sagas to provide a compelling account of Viking negotiations of honor and humiliation. Stearns's edited volumes (e.g., Stearns & Lewis, 1998) and books reveal EER in etiquette and advice manuals, personal letters, written accounts of sermons, song lyrics, newspaper articles, advertising, and the like. From that work, one gets the sense of EER being as variable historically as it is culturally.

It would be a mistake, however, to assume uniformity within geographically or historically defined cultures without considering social positions based on gender, status, age, ethnicity, social roles, and other factors. Shields (2002) criticizes the tendency to study gender and emotion in terms of similarities and differences and proposes instead to consider how emotion is gendered (e.g., "Emotional = female; angry = male?"; Shields, 2002, pp. 139–168) and how we "do" gendered emotion through EER. Although she focuses on the United States, her perspective is consistent with evidence from other cultures. One does not do Balinese EER but rather low-status, young, female Balinese EER, so a great deal of knowledge beyond general cultural expectations is needed to tune EER performances to social niches. Of course, those who haven't quite "melted" into melting pot cultures or into new social roles may experience tensions between competing EER expectations (Diner, 1998).

A relatively new domain of inquiry that holds promise for communication researchers is the role of the mass media in EER. Research on emotion and the media is well established, with most work focusing on emotional responses to media content (e.g., Bryant, Roskos-Ewoldsen, & Cantor, 2003). More relevant to EER is the use of media (video, music, television) as a culturally shared resource for managing emotion or mood. Obviously, individuals may manage feelings by making choices to read pleasant or unpleasant news (Knobloch-Westerwick & Alter, 2006) or to watch TV programming relevant to specific feelings such as regret (Nabi, Finnerty, Domschke, & Hull, 2006). Similarly, collective responses to shared emotionally charged or traumatic events are undoubtedly shaped by media responses, as either a direct result of seeking solace or an indirect result of seeking information (Buttny & Ellis, 2007). In addition, ample opportunities exist to study expressions of emotion in public media channels such as blogs or YouTube.

## ◆ Conclusion

Emotions are an important interface between the personal and the public, the self, and the social world. Our goal in this chapter has been to illustrate the complex but systematic nature of this interface by reviewing theoretical and empirical accounts of emotion at the individual, dyadic/relational, organizational, and cultural levels. We close with an invitation for scholars to continue to explore the domains of inquiry that we have summarized here. The ubiquitous and influential nature of emotional experience, expression, and regulation merits the attention of communication scholars interested in both the mundane and extraordinary aspects of social life.

## ◆ References

Ahmed, S. (2004). *The cultural politics of emotion.* New York: Routledge.

Averill, J. R. (1994). Emotions unbecoming and becoming. In P. Ekman & R. J. Davidson (Eds.), *The nature of emotion* (pp. 265–269). New York: Oxford University Press.

Bard, K., & Cornelius, R. (2007). Emotion researcher: The definition issue. *International Society for Research on Emotion, 22,* 2–15.

Barrett, L. F., Mesquita, B., Ochsner, K. N., & Gross, J. J. (2007). The experience of emotion. *Annual Review of Psychology, 58,* 373–403.

Bartsch, A., & Hubner, S. (2005). Towards a theory of emotional communication. *Comparative Literature and Culture: A WWWeb Journal, 7.*

Baxter, L. A., & Bullis, C. (1986). Turning points in developing romantic relationships. *Human Communication Research, 12,* 469–493.

Bloom, S. L. (1998). By the crowd they have been broken, by the crowd they shall be healed. In R. G. Tedeschi, C. L. Park, & L. G. Calhoun (Eds.), *Posttraumatic growth* (pp. 179–213). Mahwah, NJ: Lawrence Erlbaum.

Boone, R. T., & Buck, R. (2003). Emotional expressivity and trustworthiness. *Journal of Nonverbal Behavior, 27,* 163–182.

Booth, R. J., & Pennebaker, J. W. (2000). Emotions and immunity. In M. Lewis & J. M. Haviland-Jones (Eds.), *Handbook of emotion* (2nd ed., pp. 558–570). New York: Guilford.

Booth-Butterfield, M., & Trotta, M. R. (1994). Attributional patterns for expressions of love. *Communication Reports, 7,* 119–129.

Bowers, J. W., Metts, S. M., & Duncanson, W. T. (1985). Emotion and interpersonal communication. In M. L. Knapp & G. R. Miller (Eds.), *Handbook of interpersonal communication* (pp. 502–559). Beverly Hills, CA: Sage.

Briggs, J. L. (1970). *Never in anger.* Cambridge, MA: Harvard University Press.

Brotheridge, C. B., & Lee, R. T. (2002). Testing a conservation of resources model of the dynamics of emotional labor. *Journal of Occupational Health Psychology, 7,* 57–67.

Bryant, J., Roskos-Ewoldsen, D., & Cantor, J. (Eds.). (2003). *Communication and emotion.* Mahwah, NJ: Lawrence Erlbaum.

Buck, R., Losow, J. I., Murphy, M. M., & Costanzo, P. (1992). Social facilitation and inhibition of emotional expression and communication. *Journal of Personality and Social Psychology, 63,* 962–968.

Burleson, B. R., & Goldsmith, D. J. (1998). How the comforting process works. In P. A. Andersen & L. K. Guerrero (Eds.), *The handbook of communication and emotion* (pp. 245–280). Orlando, FL: Academic Press.

Bushman, B. J., Baumeister, R. F., & Stack, A. D. (1999). Catharsis, aggression, and persuasive influence. *Journal of Personality and Social Psychology, 76,* 367–376.

Buttny, R., & Ellis, D. G. (2007). Accounts of violence from Arabs and Israelis on *Nightline. Discourse and Society, 18,* 139–161.

Calhoun, L. G., & Tedeschi, R. G. (Eds.). (2006). *Handbook of posttraumatic growth.* Mahwah, NJ: Lawrence Erlbaum.

Clark, M. S., Pataki, S. P., & Carver, V. J. (1996). Some thoughts and findings on self-presentation of emotions in relationships. In G. J. O. Fletcher & J. Fitness (Eds.), *Knowledge structures in close relationships* (pp. 247–274). Mahwah, NJ: Lawrence Erlbaum.

Collinson, D. (2002). Managing humor. *Journal of Management Studies, 39*(3), 269–288.

Cooper, L. (Trans.). (1932). *The rhetoric of Aristotle.* Englewood Cliffs, NJ: Prentice Hall.

Cosmides, L., & Tooby, J. (2000). Evolutionary psychology and the emotions. In M. Lewis & J. M. Haviland-Jones (Eds.), *Handbook of emotion* (2nd ed., pp. 91–115). New York: Guilford.

Darwin, C. (1965). *The expression of the emotions in man and animals.* Chicago: University of Chicago Press. (Original work published 1872)

Davidson, R. J. (2003). Darwin and the neural bases of emotion and affective style. *Annals of the New York Academy of Sciences, 1000,* 316–336.

Diner, H. R. (1998). Ethnicity and emotion in America. In P. N. Stearns & J. Lewis (Eds.), *An emotional history of the United States* (pp. 197–217). New York: NYU Press.

Ekman, P. (1973). Cross-cultural studies of facial expression. In P. Ekman (Ed.), *Darwin and facial expression* (pp. 169–222). New York: Academic Press.

Ekman, P. (1993). Facial expression and emotion. *American Psychologist, 48,* 384–392.

Ekman, P. (2003). *Emotions revealed.* New York: Henry Holt & Co.

Ekman, P., & Friesen, W. V. (1975). *Unmasking the face.* Englewood Cliffs, NJ: Prentice Hall.

Fineman, S. (2006). Emotion and organizing. In S. R. Clegg, C. Hardy, T. Lawrence, & W. Nord (Eds.), *The Sage handbook of organizational studies* (pp. 675–700). London: Sage.

Flam, H., & King, D. (Eds.). (2005). *Emotions and social movements.* New York: Routledge.

Flora, J., & Segrin, C. (2000). Relationship development in dating couples. *Journal of Social and Personal Relationships, 17,* 811–825.

Foucault, M. (1980). *Power/knowledge* (C. Gordon, L. Marshall, J. Mepham, & K. Soper, Trans.). New York: Pantheon.

Fridlund, A. J. (1991). Sociality of solitary smiling. *Journal of Personality and Social Psychology, 60,* 299–240.

Frijda, N. H. (1986). *The emotions.* Cambridge, UK: Cambridge University Press.

Fussell, S. R. (2002). *The verbal communication of emotion.* Mahwah, NJ: Lawrence Erlbaum.

Garner, P. W. (1996). The relations of emotional rule taking, affective/moral attributions, and emotional display rule knowledge to low-income school-age children's social competence. *Journal of Applied Developmental Psychology, 17,* 19–36.

Georges, E. (1995). A cultural and historical perspective on confession. In J. W. Pennebaker (Ed.), *Emotion, disclosure and health* (pp. 11–22). Washington, DC: American Psychological Association.

Goffman, E. (1959). *The presentation of self in everyday life.* New York: Doubleday.

Goffman, E. (1967). *Interaction ritual.* New York: Pantheon.

Goleman, D. (1995). *Emotional intelligence.* New York: Bantam.

Goleman, D. (1998). *Working with emotional intelligence.* New York: Bantam.

Gottman, J. M., & Levenson, R. W. (2002). A two-factor model for predicting when a couple will divorce. *Family Process, 41,* 83–96.

Gross, J. J. (1998). Antecedent- and response-focused emotion regulation. *Journal of Personality and Social Psychology, 74,* 224–237.

Gross, J. J. (Ed.). (2007). *Handbook of emotion regulation.* New York: Guilford.

Guerrero, L. K., & Andersen, P. A. (1998). The experience and expression of romantic jealousy. In P. A. Andersen & L. K. Guerrero (Eds.), *The handbook of communication and emotion* (pp. 155–188). San Diego: Academic Press.

Guerrero, L. K., & Andersen, P. A. (2000). Emotion in close relationships. In C. Hendrick & S. S. Hendrick (Eds.), *Close relationships* (pp. 171–183). Thousand Oaks, CA: Sage.

Harré, R. (1986). An outline of the social constructionist viewpoint. In R. Harré (Ed.), *The social construction of emotions* (pp. 2–14). Oxford, UK: Basil Blackwell.

Harré, R., & Parrott, W. G. (1996). *The emotions.* London: Sage.

Hatfield, E., Cacioppo, J. T., & Rapson, R. L. (1994). *Emotional contagion.* New York: Cambridge University Press.

Heelas, P. (1986). Emotion talk across cultures. In R. Harré (Ed.), *The social construction of emotions* (pp. 234–266). Oxford, UK: Basil Blackwell.

Hobfoll, S. E. (1989). Conservation of resources: A new attempt at conceptualizing stress. *American Psychologist, 44,* 513–524.

Hochschild, A. R. (1983). *The managed heart.* Berkeley: University of California Press.

Hochschild, A. R. (1989). *The second shift.* New York: Avon Books.

Hupka, R. B., Lenton, A. P., & Hutchison, K. A. (1999). Universal development of emotion categories in natural language. *Journal of Personality and Social Psychology, 77,* 247–278.

Irvine, J. T. (1990). Registering affect. In C. A. Lutz & L. Abu-Lughod (Eds.), *Language and the politics of emotion* (pp. 126–161). Cambridge, UK: Cambridge University Press.

Izard, C. E. (1977). *Human emotions.* New York: Plenum.

Izard, C. E., & Ackerman, B. P. (2000). Motivational, organizational, and regulatory functions of discrete emotions. In M. Lewis & J. M. Haviland-Jones (Eds.), *Handbook of emotion* (2nd ed., pp. 253–264). New York: Guilford.

Johnstone, T., & Scherer, K. R. (2000). Vocal communication of emotion. In M. Lewis & J. M. Haviland-Jones (Eds.), *Handbook of emotion* (2nd ed., pp. 220–235). New York: Guilford.

Karasawa, K. (1995). An attributional analysis of reactions to negative emotions. *Personality and Social Psychology Bulletin, 21,* 456–467.

Katz, L. F., & Gottman, J. J. (1993). Patterns of marital conflict predict children's internalizing and externalizing behaviors. *Developmental Psychology, 29,* 940–950.

Keltner, D., & Gross, J. J. (1999). Functional accounts of emotions. *Cognition and Emotion, 13,* 467–480.

Keltner, D., & Haidt, J. (1999). Social functions of emotions at four levels of analysis. *Cognition and Emotion, 13,* 505–521.

Kennedy-Moore, E., & Watson, J. C. (1999). *Expressing emotion.* New York: Guilford.

Kennedy-Moore, E., & Watson, J. C. (2001). How and when does emotional expression help? *Review of General Psychology, 5,* 187–212.

Kirmayer, L. J., Lemelson, R., & Barad, M. (2007). *Understanding trauma.* New York: Cambridge University Press.

Knobloch, L. E., Miller, L. E., & Carpenter, K. E. (2007). Using the relational turbulence model to understand negative emotion within courtship. *Personal Relationships, 14,* 91–112.

Knobloch-Westerwick, S., & Alter, S. (2006). Mood adjustment to social situations through mass media use. *Human Communication Research, 32,* 58–73.

Kövecses, Z. (2000). *Metaphor and emotion.* Cambridge, UK: Cambridge University Press.

Kramer, M. W., & Hess, J. A. (2002). Communication rules for the display of emotions in organizational settings. *Management Communication Quarterly, 16,* 66–80.

Kraut, R. E., & Johnston, R. E. (1979). Social and emotional messages of smiling. *Journal of Personality and Social Psychology, 37,* 1539–1553.

Labouvie-Vief, G., Devoe, M., & Bulka, D. (1990). Speaking about feelings. *Psychology and Aging, 4,* 425–437.

Larson, R. W., & Almeida, D. M. (1999). Emotional transmission in the daily lives of families: A new paradigm for studying family process. *Journal of Marriage and the Family, 61,* 5–20.

Lazarus, R. S. (1991). *Emotion and adaptation.* New York: Oxford University Press.

LeDoux, J. E., & Phelps, E. A. (2000). Emotional networks in the brain. In M. Lewis & J. M. Haviland-Jones (Eds.), *Handbook of emotion* (2nd ed., pp. 157–172). New York: Guilford.

Lewis, M., & Haviland-Jones, J. M. (Eds.). (2000). *Handbook of emotion* (2nd ed.). New York: Guilford.

Lutgen-Sandvik, P. (2006). Take this job and. . . . *Communication Monographs, 73,* 406–433.

Lutgen-Sandvik, P., Tracy, S. J., & Alberts, J. K. (2007). Burned by bullying in the American workplace: Prevalence, perception, degree, and impact. *Journal of Management Studies, 44,* 837–862.

Lutz, C. A. (1988). *Unnatural emotions.* Chicago: University of Chicago Press.

Lutz, C. A., & Abu-Lughod, L. (1990). *Language and the politics of emotion.* Cambridge, UK: Cambridge University Press.

Malatesta, C. Z., & Izard, C. E. (1984). Conceptualizing emotional development in adults. In C. Z. Malatesta & C. E. Izard (Eds.), *Emotion in adult development* (pp. 13–21). Beverly Hills, CA: Sage.

Manstead, A. S. R., & Fischer, A. H. (2001). Social appraisal. In K. R. Scherer, A. Schorr, & T. Johnstone (Eds.), *Appraisal processes in emotion* (pp. 221–232). New York: Oxford University Press.

Maslach, C. (1982). *Burnout.* Englewood Cliffs, NJ: Prentice Hall.

Mathews, G., Zeidner, M., & Roberts, R. D. (2004). *Emotional intelligence.* Cambridge: MIT Press.

McPherson, M. B., Kearney, P., & Plax, T. G. (2003). The dark side of instruction. *Journal of Applied Communication Research, 31,* 76–90.

Mesquita, B., & Albert, D. (2007). The cultural regulation of emotions. In J. J. Gross (Ed.), *Handbook of emotion regulation* (pp. 486–503). New York: Guilford.

Metts, S., Cupach, W. R., & Lippert, L. (2006). Forgiveness in the workplace. In J. M. Harden Fritz & B. L. Omdahl (Eds.), *Problematic relationships in the workplace* (pp. 249–278). New York: Peter Lang.

Miller, K. I. (2007). Compassionate communication in the workplace. *Journal of Applied Communication Research, 35,* 223–245.

Miller, K. I., Stiff, J. B., & Ellis, B. H. (1988). Communication and empathy as precursors to burnout among human service workers. *Communication Monographs, 55,* 250–265.

Miller, W. I. (1993). *Humiliation.* Ithaca, NY: Cornell University Press.

Misailidi, P. (2006). Young children's display rule knowledge. *Social Behavior and Personality, 34,* 1285–1296.

Mumby, D. K., & Putnam, L. L. (1992). The politics of emotion. *Academy of Management Review, 17*, 465–486.

Murray, S. L., & Holmes, J. G. (1996). The construction of relationship realities. In G. J. O. Fletcher & J. Fitness (Eds.), *Knowledge structures in close relationships* (pp. 91–120). Mahwah, NJ: Lawrence Erlbaum.

Nabi, R. L., Finnerty, K., Domschke, T., & Hull, S. (2006). Does misery love company? *Journal of Communication, 56*, 689–706.

Newton, T. (1995). *"Managing" stress.* Thousand Oaks, CA: Sage.

Oatley, K. (1993). Social construction in emotions. In M. Lewis & J. M. Haviland (Eds.), *Handbook of emotions* (pp. 341–352). New York: Guilford.

Pennebaker, J. W. (1997). *Opening up* (Rev. ed.). New York: Guilford.

Peterson, C., & Park, N. (2007). Explanatory style and emotion regulation. In J. J. Gross (Ed.), *Handbook of emotion regulation* (pp. 159–179). New York: Guilford.

Philippot, P., & Feldman, R. S. (Eds.). (2004). *The regulation of emotion.* Mahwah, NJ: Lawrence Erlbaum.

Planalp, S. (1998). Communicating emotion in everyday life. In P. A. Andersen & L. K. Guerrero (Eds.), *Handbook of communication and emotion* (pp. 29–48). San Diego: Academic Press.

Planalp, S. (1999). *Communicating emotion.* New York: Cambridge University Press.

Planalp, S., & Knie, K. (2002). Verbal and nonverbal cues to emotion. In S. Fussell (Ed.), *The verbal communication of emotions* (pp. 55–77). Mahwah, NJ: Lawrence Erlbaum.

Ray, G. B., & Floyd, K. (2006). Nonverbal expressions of liking and disliking in initial interaction: Encoding and decoding perspectives. *Southern Communication Journal, 71*, 45–65.

Reysen, S. (2006). A new predictor of likeability. *North American Journal of Psychology, 8*, 373–382.

Richards, J. M., Butler, E. A., & Gross, J. J. (2003). Emotion regulation in romantic relationships. *Journal of Social and Personal Relationships, 20*, 599–620.

Richards, J. M., & Gross, J. J. (2000). Emotion regulation and memory. *Journal of Personality and Social Psychology, 79*, 410–424.

Rosaldo, M. Z. (1980). *Knowledge and passion.* New York: Cambridge University Press.

Roseman, I. J., & Smith, C. A. (2001). Appraisal theory. In K. R. Scherer, A. Schorr, & T. Johnstone (Eds.), *Appraisal processes in emotion* (pp. 3–19). New York: Oxford University Press.

Rusbult, C. E., Yovetich, N. A., & Verette, J. (1996). An interdependence analysis of accommodation processes. In G. J. O. Fletcher & J. Fitness (Eds.), *Knowledge structures in close relationships* (pp. 63–90). Mahwah, NJ: Lawrence Erlbaum.

Russell, J. A. (1994). Is there universal recognition of emotion from facial expression? *Psychological Bulletin, 115*, 102–141.

Saarni, C. (1999). *The development of emotional competence.* New York: Guilford.

Sabatelli, R. M., & Rubin, M. (1986). Nonverbal expressiveness and physical attractiveness as mediators of interpersonal perceptions. *Journal of Nonverbal Behavior, 10*, 120–133.

Salovey, P., Bedell, B. T., Detweiler, J. B., & Mayer, J. D. (2000). Current directions in emotional intelligence research. In M. Lewis & J. M. Haviland-Jones (Eds.), *Handbook of emotion* (2nd ed., pp. 504–520). New York: Guilford.

Scherer, K. R. (Ed.). (1988). *Facets of emotion.* Hillsdale, NJ: Lawrence Erlbaum.

Scherer, K. R. (1994). Affect bursts. In S. H. M. van Goozen, N. E. Van de Poll, & J. A. Sergeant (Eds.), *Emotions* (pp. 161–193). Hillsdale, NJ: Lawrence Erlbaum.

Scherer, K. R., Schorr, A., & Johnstone, T. (Eds.). (2001). *Appraisal processes in emotion.* New York: Oxford University Press.

Scott, C., & Myers, K. K. (2005). The socialization of emotion. *Journal of Applied Communication Research, 33*, 67–92.

Sedikides, C. (1992). Changes in the valence of the self as a function of mood. In M. S. Clark (Ed.), *Emotion and social behavior* (pp. 271–311). Newbury Park, CA: Sage.

Segrin, C. (1998). Interpersonal communication problems associated with depression and loneliness. In P. A. Andersen & L. K. Guerrero (Eds.), *The handbook of communication and emotion* (pp. 215–242). San Diego: Academic Press.

Shaver, P. R., Wu, S., & Schwartz, J. C. (1992). Cross-cultural similarities and differences in emotion and its representation. In M. S. Clark (Ed.), *Emotion* (pp. 175–212). Newbury Park, CA: Sage.

Shields, S. A. (2002). *Speaking from the heart.* New York: Cambridge University Press.

Shuler, S., & Sypher, B. D. (2000). Seeking emotional labor. *Management Communication Quarterly, 14,* 50–89.

Stearns, P. N., & Lewis, J. (1998). *An emotional history of the United States.* New York: New York University Press.

Tavris, C. (1989). *Anger.* New York: Simon & Schuster.

Tolhuizen, J. H. (1989). Communication strategies for intensifying dating relationships. *Journal of Social and Personal Relationships, 6,* 413–434.

Tracy, S. J. (2000). Becoming a character for commerce. *Management Communication Quarterly, 14,* 90–128.

Tracy, S. J. (2005). Locking up emotion. *Communication Monographs, 72,* 261–283.

Tracy, S. J., Lutgen-Sandvik, P., & Alberts, J. K. (2006). Nightmares, demons and slaves. *Management Communication Quarterly, 20,* 148–185.

Tracy, S. J., Myers, K. K., & Scott, C. (2006). Cracking jokes and crafting selves. *Communication Monographs, 73,* 283–308.

Turner, J. H., & Stets, J. E. (2005). *The sociology of emotions.* New York: Cambridge University Press.

Vangelisti, A. L. (2007). Communicating hurt. In B. H. Spitzberg & W. R. Cupach (Eds.), *The dark side of interpersonal communication* (2nd ed., pp. 121–142). Mahwah, NJ: Lawrence Erlbaum.

Watson, D., & Clark, L. A. (1992). On traits and temperament. *Journal of Personality, 60,* 441–476.

Wegner, D. M. (1992). You can't always think what you want. In M. P. Zanna (Ed.), *Advances in experimental social psychology* (Vol. 25, pp. 193–224). New York: Academic Press.

Weiss, H. M., & Cropanzano, R. (1996). Affective events theory. In B. M. Staw & L. L. Cummings (Eds.), *Research in organizational behavior* (Vol. 19, pp. 1–74). Greenwich, CT: JAI.

Wierzbicka, A. (1994). Emotion, language, and cultural scripts. In S. Kitayama & H. R. Markus (Eds.), *Emotion and culture* (pp. 133–196). Washington, DC: American Psychological Association.

Wikan, U. (1990). *Managing turbulent hearts.* Chicago: Chicago University Press.

Wilson, T. D., & Gilbert, D. T. (2003). Affective forecasting. In M. P. Zanna (Ed.), *Advances in experimental social psychology* (Vol. 35, pp. 345–411). San Diego: Academic Press.

Zeman, J., & Garber, J. (1996). Display rules for anger, sadness, and pain. *Child Development, 67,* 957–973.

# 22

# GROUP DECISION MAKING

◆ Marshall Scott Poole
and Melissa A. Dobosh

Decision making is the primal act of a small group. When a group of people make a decision, they constitute the group as a unit whose members can act mindfully and in concert. Decisions are often consequential far beyond the boundaries of the group, setting in motion invasions, investigations, new products and programs, and major investments. While groups do many things, decision making is the epitome of group communication, an activity in which reasoning, argument, influence, collaboration, representation, and other communicative practices are enacted.

Group decision making is a complex construct. Most group communication textbooks define *decision making* relatively narrowly as the process of evaluating and choosing among alternatives (Beebe & Masterson, 2006; Keyton, 2002), reserving the term *problem solving* for a comprehensive, multistage process that begins with a problem and ends with selection of a solution. For the purposes of this review, however, we will take a more comprehensive view and refer to the entire process, from problem identification to implementation planning, as decision making. All of the following activities may fall within the scope of the term *decision making* as it will be used in this chapter: problem formulation, problem analysis, criteria development, solution development, solution evaluation and selection, and implementation planning.

Decision making is a multilevel process, with smaller decisions typically nested within larger decisions, which may themselves be part of larger group projects (McGrath & Tschan, 2004). "Every decision involves a series of activities and choices nested in choices of broader scope, rather than a single simple choice" (Poole & Hirokawa, 1996, p. 9). Moreover, it is often difficult to understand a single decision without considering larger issues and prior decisions and without grappling with relatively fuzzy boundaries of the larger issues (Tracy & Standerfer, 2002).

◆ **Historical Roots**

Theory and research on communication and group decision making stem from the scholarship of group discussion, which flourished from about 1920 to the 1960s. An excellent history of this subject by Keith (2007; see also Frey, 1996) recounts how pioneering scholars such as O'Neill, Baird, Cowperthwaite, McBurney, Hance, and Sheffield, following the lead of the philosopher John Dewey (1910), advanced discussion as a tool of democracy. For Dewey, discussion was a method of inquiry that could promote reasoned action and, more important, the knowledge, attitudes, motivations, and skills required to participate in a democratic society.

Dewey (1910) articulated "reflective thinking" as a pattern for solving complex problems based on inquiry. Reflective thinking consisted of five steps: "(1) a felt difficulty; (2) its location and definition; (3) suggestion of possible solutions; (4) development by reasoning of the bearing suggestions; (5) further observation and experiment leading to its acceptance or rejection" (p. 72). Discussion scholars adopted this pattern as a method of democratic decision making in early textbooks (McBurney & Hance, 1939; Sheffield, 1927). Group discussion scholars attributed a moral force to discussion as an instrument of enlightenment and democracy. They advocated training in

principles of discussion to enable citizens to become informed participants in democratic governance, a bulwark against the power of the few.

Scholars in speech took a primarily theoretical and practical orientation toward group discussion and did not conduct much formal research until the 1950s. Influenced by social psychology and sociology, scholars began to pursue scientific study of group communication during the 1940s and 1950s (Frey, 1996; Keith, 2007). As Frey (1996) recounts, from 1945 to 1970, communication scholars studied patterns of interaction during group decision making, communicative differences between groups able to reach consensus and those that could not, and breakdowns in group decision making. During this period, group communication research established firm foundations in the discipline.

The 1970s have been characterized as a "decade of discontent" in group research (Frey, 1996). This decade began with a number of critiques of group communication research, including (a) that it was generally atheoretical or borrowed theory from other disciplines; (b) that it focused largely on artificial laboratory groups rather than on real groups in their natural contexts; (c) that is was too embedded within traditional positivist social scientific approaches; (d) that it did not sufficiently include study of communication, interaction, and messages in groups; and (e) that it neglected group processes in favor of static variables (see more detailed treatments in Frey, 1996; Poole, 1999).

Responses to these critiques in the 1980s resulted in the development of several theories of group communication. During the last part of the 1980s and the 1990s, interpretive and qualitative approaches to the study of groups became prominent (Frey, 1996). Putnam and Stohl (1996) articulated the bona fide group perspective, which theorized groups within their contexts and guided a number of studies (e.g., Frey, 2002). In the first decade of the 21st century, group research is quite diversified in terms of theoretical orientation, method, and topic.

Since 1995, there has been a decrease in studies of group decision making by communication scholars. Calls for the study of natural groups have led many scholars to investigate aspects of groups other than decision making. Perhaps the most notable countertrend has been the growth of interest in computer-supported groups. Since much computer support is designed to facilitate group decision making, most of these studies have focused on decision making explicitly or implicitly (Scott, 1999).

The democratic roots of group communication have imparted a moral momentum to this area that persists today, though group discussion has largely passed from attention. Most theories of groups incorporate implicit normative assumptions. While not often acknowledged, notions of the desirability of democratic participation, thorough and logical decision making, and healthy respect for members' points of view underpin theories that are couched in more neutral terms.

## ◆ Theories of Communication and Group Decision Making

This chapter is organized around five major theoretical positions: the functional theory of decision making, theories of decision development, perspectives on argumentation and influence in group decision making, structurational theories of group decision making, and perspectives on deliberation and democracy in group decision making.

### FUNCTIONAL THEORY OF GROUP DECISION MAKING

The goal of the functional theory of group decision making is to understand why some groups are more successful or effective than others. The theory strives to explain, predict, and improve group decision making by focusing on the communication that precedes choice making in a group (Hirokawa, 1983). The functional perspective takes a normative approach to describing and predicting group performance based on the functions of inputs or processes (Hollingshead, Wittenbaum, Paulus, Hirokawa, Ancona, Peterson, Jehn, & Yoon, 2005).

Functional theory advances an input-process-output (IPO) model that focuses on instrumental functions of communication during decision making (see Pavitt, Chapter 3, this volume). Three types of communication occurring in groups were identified during early functional decision-making research (Gouran & Hirokawa, 1986): Promotive communication advances the group toward accomplishing its task, disruptive communication distracts the group or puts up barriers to task accomplishment, and counteractive communication refocuses the group and includes behaviors that group members take to get the group back on track.

Functional theory of group decision making is based on several assumptions (Gouran & Hirokawa, 1996). First, groups are oriented toward task, group, or social emotional goals. Second, group behavior and performance vary and can be evaluated. Third, interaction processes have utility and can be regulated. Finally, internal and external factors influence group performance through interaction. These assumptions inform the following five requisite functions that are essential to satisfactory group decision making (Hirokawa, 1988; Hollingshead et al., 2005; Orlitzky & Hirokawa, 2001):

1. Developing an understanding of the problematic situation (problem analysis)

2. Achieving understanding of the requirements for an acceptable choice (establishment of evaluation criteria)

3. Developing a range of realistic and acceptable alternatives (generation of alternative solutions)

4. Assessing the positive qualities of alternative choices (evaluation of positive consequences of a solution)

5. Assessing the negative qualities of alternative choices (evaluation of negative consequences of a solution)

A group that enacts these five functions maximizes its chance of making an effective decision.

Enactment of requisite functions is threatened by constraints on effective decision making (Gouran & Hirokawa, 1996). Cognitive constraints affect group process when members face a task where little information is known, time is limited, and task complexity is beyond what they normally face. Affiliative constraints affect group process when relationships among members become a dominant concern. This concern can emerge from fear of relationship deterioration, overt influence of one member, and deviance. Finally, egocentric constraints affect group process when one member is driven by personal needs or motivations. Through the use of preventive and counteractive measures, these constraints can be diminished or overcome during group interactions. Some example counteractive measures include making salient the potential costs of an inappropriate decision, calling for genuine critical evaluation, and shifting focus to self-examination (Gouran & Hirokawa, 1996).

In a meta-analysis of studies testing functional theory, factors identified by functional theory could account for about 60% of the total variance in decision-making effectiveness (Orlitzky & Hirokawa, 2001). Of the five prerequisites, understanding the problem and evaluating positive and negative qualities of alternatives accounted for 52% of the variance. In this analysis, they also identified several contingencies, including task structure, information requirements, and evaluation demands. Specifically, fulfilling the requisite functions has a greater impact on decision-making effectiveness when the group has a complex task with many pos-sible solutions but unclear and unverifiable criteria, as well as unequal distribution of information among members.

Several directions for future research on functional theory are evident. First, other factors than functions, such as operating procedures or the nature of the group's task (Orlitzky & Hirokawa, 2001), should be investigated for their moderating impact on group decision making. Second, functional theory emphasizes task-oriented functions and outcomes, virtually ignoring other types of functions (Hollingshead et al., 2005). Study of groups whose major focus is social-emotional goals, such as therapy and support groups, might yield insight into relational outcomes such as maintenance and satisfaction.

Finally, the functional theory posits a linear view of group decision making based on the IPO model. While it may seem logical that group interaction has causal effects on group outcomes, there lies the possibility of reverse causality where prior group performance affects future group performance (Wittenbaum, Hollingshead, & Botero, 2004). Thus, groups could be studied at multiple time points (Hollingshead et al., 2005), allowing better understanding of the factors that shape decision making effectiveness.

## THEORIES OF DECISION DEVELOPMENT

There are two major classes of theories of decision development: phase models and the punctuated equilibrium model. Both advance a unique description of the decision process, and both explain decision development differently.

### Phase Models

The most common theory of decision development posits that groups pass through a series of *phases* that culminate in a choice. A phase is a period of coherent activity that serves some function in the decision process. The original phase models posited that a single, set sequence of phases led to a decision. These unitary sequence models typically explain decision making in terms of an ordered sequence of problems or requirements groups must satisfy to make a decision. For instance, Bales and Strodtbeck's (1951) classic model posits that groups must work through three phases—a period of orientation in which members define the nature of the decision task and explore the problem tentatively, followed by a period of evaluation in which members critically analyze the problem and possible solutions and sometimes get into conflicts, followed by a final phase of control in which the group narrows down their options and makes the decision. The sequence seems to have a sort of logical inevitability in which earlier phases set the groundwork for later ones. Other unitary sequence models of group decision-making communication were derived by Fisher (1970) and Mabry (1975).

Another class of phase models argues that groups may follow different sequences of phases, depending on various factors such as the complexity of the decision task and the climate of the group. Poole (1981) argued that most studies that found evidence for unitary sequence models had problems with design and analysis that included (a) dividing discussions into the same number of segments as expected phases, thereby hiding more complex developmental paths, and (b) summarizing data across groups, thereby hiding between-group differences in developmental paths. In a series of studies, Poole and colleagues (summarized in Poole & Baldwin, 1996) found multiple sequences in group decision making. Their studies and prior literature indicated that one quarter of groups follow the unitary sequence, about a third follow a solution-oriented sequence in which the group primarily focuses on solutions, and about 40% follow a complex path consisting of multiple series of complete and partial unitary sequences in which the groups seem to iterate through the phases in the unitary model, often in complicated orders. Poole's

studies also showed that significant periods in many groups did not have coherent phases, suggesting that other types of activity or periods of disorganization were occurring.

The multiple-sequence theory of group decision development was advanced to explain these findings (Poole, 1983). This model posited that phases are constructed through the intertwining of three aspects of communication: task functions, relational functions, and the substantive content of the discussion. A phase represents a combination of coherent task and relational functions around a specific topic that is stabilized for a period of time. For example, a critical problem analysis phase would consist of a period in which acts functioned to define the problem and its roots, relationships among members were marked by disagreement and debate, and topics related to the problem were discussed. This leaves room for periods that are less coherent or even incoherent, the "nonphases" observed in earlier studies.

Members' attempts to fulfill what they believe to be the functional prerequisites of the decision influence which phases are generated and their sequencing. For example, if the group is agreed that they understand the problem from the outset, then members are likely to launch into solutions, generating a solution-oriented sequence. The complexity of the decision path is determined by two factors: the degree to which members' beliefs about prerequisites match actual task requirements and the degree of consensus among members about decision prerequisites. If members are not accurate about the demands of the task or if they are in conflict about prerequisites, a more complex path will result.

Factors that influence members' beliefs about prerequisites for decisions include (a) task characteristics such as goal clarity and task novelty and (b) internal structural variables such as group cohesiveness, concentration of power, and group size. Members' implicit theories of decision making, such as whether decisions are best made through rational discussion or political bargaining, also should influence beliefs about prerequisites (Poole, Seibold, & McPhee, 1996).

The final factors that shape decision paths are breakpoints, events that represent discontinuities in interaction and may complicate decision paths, including *normal* topic shifts and short breaks; *delays,* during which the group cycles back to previously completed work to reinterpret or rework it; and *disruptions,* such as a major conflict, failure, or crisis in the group.

Poole and Roth (1989a, 1989b) tested the multiple-sequence model on a sample of 47 group decisions that varied in terms of task characteristics and internal group structure and found general support for the model. They discovered relationships between the contingency variables and the decision paths groups followed. Honeycutt and Poole (1994; see also Pavitt & Johnson, 2001) reported evidence for members' implicit theories; they found three types of individual procedural schemata for group decision making—rational, political, and information sharing, two of which correspond to the three posited in the multiple-sequence model.

Phase models have several advantages. Phases correspond to a natural perceptual unit for social interaction—the episode—and so are likely to depict decision making in a way meaningful to researchers and practitioners alike. They represent the process of decision making, rather than only its inputs and outputs, and they go beyond synoptic views such as those presented in qualitative summaries of decision processes. Finally, they have practical implications, especially when linked with normative models such as reflective thinking. The multiple-sequence phase model has an advantage of unitary phase models in that it better captures the complexities of decision making. On the other hand, the unitary sequence model is more parsimonious and can be more clearly linked to normative models at this point in time.

One disadvantage of phase models is that they are "messy": Their depiction of the decision process is complicated, and they do not reduce to simple but powerful principles or constructs, such as groupthink. A second problem is that phase models tend to ignore behaviors or processes that do not fit within their specified functions; hence, they are always subject to limitations due to the types of interaction codes they are based on. Finally, more research is needed on the relationship of developmental sequences and outcomes (Poole & Baldwin, 1996).

## PUNCTUATED EQUILIBRIUM MODEL

Gersick (1989, 1991) advanced the punctuated equilibrium model based on studies of project teams. The model specifies five significant events or periods that occur during a decision process: (1) In a newly formed group's first meeting, the group rapidly settles on an approach to its task, (2) which it follows for the first phase of its work. (3) Then, at the midpoint of the group's work, the group reassesses its initial approach and abandons it, reorienting on a new approach to the task, (4) which governs work in the second phase of the group project. (5) In the group's final meeting, members make a push to finish their work and finalize the decision. This typically involves a last-minute rush as the group hurries to tie up loose ends.

The punctuated equilibrium model posits that the major directions of the group are set at critical junctures (punctuations) and that the group then settles into steady phases of work (equilibrium) until the next punctuation occurs. The group's effectiveness depends on several characteristics of this process. If the group's initial approach is deeply flawed, then it may render the first phase of work useless, at least in terms of contributing to the final solution. If the first phase enables the group to develop a foundation for its more calibrated activities after the midpoint transition, then the group is more likely to be effective. And it is not only ideas that can be built during the first phase but also the group's ability to work as a group, if the members can work through conflicts or develop good working relationships.

Another important determinant is the nature of the group's midpoint transition. Gersick found that it was important for the group to look outward to its context (e.g., communicate with its managers or clients, gather more data) for information regarding how it needed to reorient its efforts. Generally, during the first phase, the group draws in on itself and isolates itself from its environment. Opening up to its context during the transition and the second phase of work is critical to effectiveness because it maximizes the possibility that the group's new approach is a sound one.

The punctuated equilibrium model is more parsimonious than multiple-sequence phase models. It specifies a basic script for group decision making that is consistent with a good deal of evidence from previous research and from Gersick's studies. As formulated, it is limited to project groups, short-term teams that dissolve on completion of their task, and it is not clear whether it applies to ongoing groups. That the transition occurs at the midpoint of the group's work is probably in part a function of the nature of project teams. For a group with a limited life span, it is logical to assume that some reevaluation would occur at the halfway point and that this would lead to adjustments in strategy. For ongoing groups, there may be more than one transition point, corresponding to various milestones that might be set to guide decision making.

## PERSPECTIVES ON ARGUMENT AND INFLUENCE IN GROUP DECISION MAKING

Argumentation and analysis and accompanying influence processes exercise a strong influence on group decision making. As we have seen, the functional theory of group decision making holds that sound argumentation and reasoning processes are vital to effective decision making. In Chapter 14, Seibold, Meyers, and Shoham summarize how various group theories, functional theory, symbolic convergence theory, socio-egocentric theory, and structuration theory conceptualized argument and influence in groups. We will not repeat their insights here but instead will focus on some additional lines of thought.

### Information Exchange in Group Decision Making

Over the past two decades, a body of theory and research has developed on information sharing in groups and its impact on group decision making. Stasser and Titus's (1985) seminal study showed that groups tend to discuss and base their decision on information shared by all or most members at the expense of information known only to a single member (unshared information). For tasks structured as "hidden profiles," in which the correct answer is based on unshared information and shared information points to a suboptimal decision, groups have been shown to favor suboptimal choices. This troubling result sparked more than 20 studies in psychology and communication.

Wittenbaum et al.'s (2004) summary of research in this area indicates that unshared information tends to come out later in the discussion and that negative information is discussed more than positive information. Overall, information pooling and group decision quality are improved when unshared information is salient and abundant and when there is disagreement on the best option. If members are told to remember information and contribute it in the following discussion, there is more discussion of unshared information. There is also a tendency for more unshared information to come out if members know one another's areas of expertise. A study by Henningsen and Henningsen (2007) suggests that groups may deal with information that is missing by trying to infer it or by employing a diminished information set. Procedures and norms also influence information sharing. There is more discussion of unshared information if members are asked to rank alternatives rather than make a single decision (Hollingshead, 1996). Groups that follow a norm of critical evaluation discuss more unshared information, but there were mixed results from using various other procedures (Wittenbaum et al., 2004).

Several explanations for the preference for shared information have been advanced. Stasser (1992) offered a statistical explanation. If the probability of all pieces of information coming out is equally likely, then shared information is more likely to be discussed since it is duplicated across members, creating more pieces of the same information. Another explanation is that there is an association between prediscussion preferences and shared information. Preferences formed on the basis of shared information are reinforced when that information is mentioned, thus creating a self-reinforcing cycle that favors the alternative the shared information supports. Finally, social comparison has been advanced as an explanation. Faced with an ambiguous task for which there is no apparent correct answer, members look to others for validation. When others mention shared information, it may make that information seem more valuable, relevant, and accurate. Positive reactions then reinforce repetition of shared information. Together, the three explanations offer a plausible account.

In an insightful review and critique, Wittenbaum et al. (2004) outline several limitations in the assumptions of the collective information-sharing paradigm. The paradigm assumes that (a) communicators are unbiased, (b) they work cooperatively, (c) information is shared as given to the members, (d) unshared information is more important than shared information, (e) information is shared with the entire group, and (f) decision quality is the primary outcome.

Contrary to these assumptions, Wittenbaum et al. (2004) argue that in most groups, (a) communicators share information to further their own goal; (b) they may be cooperative but they also may be competitive; (c) members may elaborate on information, frame it in certain ways that serve their goals, or even misrepresent it; (d) unshared information may be less important than shared information, depending on the goal of the group and its members; (e) not all tasks are hidden profiles; (f) information may be shared only with select members; and (g) other outcomes than quality are important to members, including building relationships with other members and influencing the group to make decisions consistent with the members' goals. This more realistic set of assumptions may enable this new paradigm to address anomalies in results for more traditional collective information-sharing research.

Bonito (2007) advances a model that accounts for information sharing in terms of local interaction coherence and activation of information in memory as a function of ongoing discussion. This model has the potential to subsume information sharing under a more general formulation that could link it to other phenomena such as information seeking.

## DECISIONAL REGRET THEORY

Decisional regret theory (Sunwolf, 2006) is based on the premise that argumentation in groups reflects attempts by members to reduce their anxiety about uncertain outcomes. When faced with an important and complex decision, members often face dissonance because there are advantages and disadvantages to all options. In this situation, members anticipate regret if they make the wrong choice and direct their interaction to reducing the possibility of decisional regret.

"The basic communicative dynamic of Decisional Regret Theory (DERT) is the production, sharing, and reconstruction of predecisional imaginary narratives that allow possible alternative outcomes to be anticipated and considered" (Sunwolf, 2006, p. 122). These imaginary narratives take the form of counterfactuals that pose questions about alternative interpretations of the evidence and alternative choices. For instance, a juror might put himself in the place of the victim and imagine how she would feel if they do not convict her assailant. These counterfactual stories initially tend to increase the shared anxiety over the decision by the group. This anxiety is often contagious and may lead to inaction or deadlock. However, if the group uses the counterfactual to further its thinking and to rule out some alternatives, it will contribute to a developing decision. Other members' responses to these counterfactual stories—confirming and reinforcing them, altering them, rejecting them, offering alternative counterfactual stories—influence the impact they have on members' thinking. Sunwolf (2006) documented the prevalence and some effects of counterfactual narratives in a study of four juries.

Decisional regret theory links communication with the growing literature on regret and counterfactual thinking in social psychology. It points to a type of argument that has been largely neglected and, in so doing, underscores the complexity of argument and influence in groups. The theory would benefit from greater specification of the possible responses to counterfactual narratives—not just the immediate response but how the narrative is treated in subsequent interaction and in members' thinking—and their effects on decision making. Also needed is more research on this nascent theory. At this point, the jury is out, so to speak, on decisional regret theory.

### Argument and Deliberation in Groups

Tracy and Standerfer (2002) present a useful perspective on group decision making that underscores the complexity of decision making and its embeddedness in context. Based on micro-level discourse analysis of political decision making, they concluded that no group decision can be considered in isolation but must be considered as part of a larger deliberative process. In addition to its functions related to analyzing the issues and advancing and advocating courses of action, deliberative discourse also serves to formulate the decision itself—for instance, by opening up a consent agenda item that had already been determined into a broader discussion. Prior decisions show up as points of contestation as a by-product of this formulation process. Also involved in formulating the decision is discussion about the process of making the decision.

As the deliberation unfolds, previously decided matters are pulled back onto the table, partly in bids to reconsider and partly as means of assessing the competence and legitimacy of those members who made the previous decision. Discourse not only serves to help make the current decision but also often pertains to the future, registering issues that will be visited, setting up challenges of the existing structure of the group and other matters. The deliberative frame asserts that decisions are not necessarily neat, isolable acts but have complex connections to context and to past and future actions of the group.

One major challenge faced by the deliberative perspective is bounding the decision process. If we seriously consider the prior and future issues and decisions any current decision is linked to, then any delimitation of the decision by deciding on a bounded set of concerns can ultimately be challenged as arbitrary because there are always other linkages and implications that can be drawn. Its very openness can be a liability for this perspective.

### STRUCTURATIONAL THEORY OF GROUP DECISION MAKING

The structurational theory of group decision making (DeSanctis & Poole, 1994;

Poole & DeSanctis, 1990; Poole, Seibold, & McPhee, 1985, 1996) is concerned with how group decisions are constituted through members' actions, explores the processes by which the production and reproduction of group decisions occur, and identifies the factors that influence these processes.

The theory draws on the thought of Anthony Giddens (1984), who made a distinction between *system,* the observable pattern of relations in a group, and *structure,* the rules and resources members use to generate and sustain the group system. Giddens (1984) characterizes structures as "recipes" for acting that are composed of a configuration of rules and material and social resources used to bring about the action. Structuration theory construes the observable group system as a set of practices constituted by members' structuring behavior. The key to understanding this system lies not in surface-level behaviors or functions but in the structures and structuring processes that support these.

The central concept in the theory is *structuration,* the processes by which systems are produced and reproduced through members' use of rules and resources. This definition assumes structures are dualities. Not only is a system produced and reproduced through structuration, but so too are the structures themselves. Structures are both the medium and outcome of action. They are the medium of action because group members draw on structures to interact, but they are also its outcome because rules and resources exist only by virtue of being used in a practice. For instance, when a group takes a vote, it is employing the rules behind voting to act, but it is also reminding itself that these rules exist, working out a way of using the rules, and perhaps creating a special version of them. Hence, structures have a virtual existence; they exist in a continuous process of structuration.

Structures are sometimes generated by the group, but more often, groups appropriate them from existing institutions. Majority voting schemes, for example, are a key institution of democratic societies, so it is not surprising that groups often employ votes to make decisions. The appropriation process, which adapts structural features to specific groups and circumstances and may lead to structural innovation and change, is an important focus of research in structuration theory. A vote, for instance, could be used to ensure fair participation or to browbeat minority members into line, depending on how the group structures voting into its process.

Two general classes of factors influence structuration. The first class includes direct influences: characteristics of the group such as the group's tasks; contextual features such as the structures available in relevant institutions; members' degree of insight into how the structuring process works; differential distributions of resources, which create power and status distinctions; and the unintended consequences of action, which arise as a result of the complexity of group systems and their environments. The second set of influences on structuration is more indirect and hinges on the dynamics through which different structural features mediate and interact with each other. For example, numerous investigators have reflected on the contradiction between the collective nature of group action and members' individualistic striving for control and personal position in groups (Poole et al., 1996).

Structuration theory has been applied in the study of argument and influence in groups (Seibold, Meyers, & Shoham, Chapter 14, this volume), impacts of group decision support systems (GDSSs; Contractor & Seibold, 1993; DeSanctis, Poole, & Zigurs, 2008; DeSanctis & Poole, 1994), and jury decision making (Sunwolf & Seibold, 1998). Poole et al. (1996) summarized evidence regarding the nature of the structuring process and its impacts in groups. DeSanctis et al. (2008) summarized more than 40 studies in a research program on structuration of group decision support systems.

Collectively, this research provides evidence that (a) interaction mediates the impact of structures such as decision rules, information and arguments brought to the group by members, and procedures provided by a GDSS; (b) groups vary in how they appropriate structures, the degree of consensus they have on appropriations, and control over appropriation, among other things; and (c) there are relationships between mode of appropriation and decision-making outcomes such as consensus change, perceived decision quality, and satisfaction with the decision. This research addresses, in part, Gouran's (1990) criticism that structuration theory has neglected the prediction of outcomes.

Several schemes for classifying structural features and modes of appropriating them have been developed (Poole et al., 1996; Seibold & Meyers, 2007). These schemes have facilitated the identification of micro-level patterns of argumentation (Seibold et al., Chapter 14, this volume) and also of longitudinal patterns in the structuration of GDSSs. The classification schemes have also divulged general patterns of appropriations of structures embedded in technologies, ranging from autonomous control to counterdependent rejection.

The structurational approach attempts to acknowledge and mediate the tensions in group research between action and structure, micro- and macro-levels of analysis, and the group and its environment. Its focus on structuring processes and appropriation allows the theory to account for variations in group processes and explains variance that cannot be accounted for by theories that focus primarily on deterministic regularities. The structurational theory of group decision making offers an account of the social construction of the decision process, a central and often neglected topic of communication research.

There are both conceptual and empirical challenges for the structurational perspective. At the conceptual level, there is the difficulty of representing and modeling a duality that continuously and instantaneously produces and reproduces itself. The sheer number and variety of structures at the local, group, and higher levels pose the challenge of sorting out which are operative and explaining how they interact (see McLeod, Kosicki, & McLeod, Chapter 11, this volume). There has been little systematic theoretical development related to this problem. Kontopoulos (1993) argues that structuration-based theories need much more detailed specification than Giddens provides to be useful. Adaptive structuration theory (DeSanctis & Poole, 1994; Poole & DeSanctis, 1990) represents one attempt to move in this direction.

Another conceptual problem is the issue of how structures persist over time. In principle, they are instantaneous and synchronous, so their temporal extension is problematic. Giddens (1984) argues that they exist in actors' "memory traces," but this does not account for the intersubjective nature of structures since each memory trace would capture different aspects of the structure and how it enters into practice. Most group researchers employing structuration theory presume that structures or traces of them can be preserved in artifacts such as books, media, or technologies, like GDSSs, waiting to be activated through appropriation. Orlikowski (2000) argues that structures exist only in actors' practices and that artifacts such as books or GDSSs are "interpretively flexible." There is at this point no consensus on the ontological status of structures, and so the foundations of structuration theory are still being worked out.

At the empirical level, it is literally impossible to gain access to the duality of structuration. Studies must focus on only one side of structuration—either the constraining effects of structure or strategic interaction—with the hope that a series of studies can yield the full picture. This is by nature reductive and poses a problem of maintaining continuity and consistency in a long series of studies. Moreover, it does not allow a direct test of the theory. Structuration theory is tested through investigation of its implications—for example, if structuring processes are operating as the theory supposes, we will observe meaningful variations in how a group uses procedures and technologies. Results consistent with this hypothesis, however, are amenable to alternative explanations. There is also always the danger of self-fulfilling, circular studies. Structuration is quite complex, and aspects of it can be seen in all social life. Its very ubiquity makes it easy to read into (or force fit onto) any phenomenon. Many studies simply use structurational concepts without trying to test whether they provide a good template and thus add little to our basic knowledge. One cure for this is systematic research with large samples.

## PERSPECTIVES ON DELIBERATION AND DEMOCRACY IN GROUPS

Several scholars have articulated views of group decision making that restore an emphasis on democratic processes. Barge (2002) argued that most decision-making theory and research is premised on a problem-centered viewpoint that emphasizes identifying and "fixing" deficiencies or gaps in the current situation. This viewpoint privileges debate and controversy as the primary form of interaction for solving problems and making decisions. This entails dissecting problems into their components and developing solutions through systematic and critical analysis.

Barge (2002) critiqued traditional approaches to decision making on the grounds that these assumptions are based on a narrow view of communication that assumes (a) that actors know what the ideal state of things is (and hence can recognize and define problems or gaps) and (b) that there is one right way to promote change—solving problems. Problem-centered approaches can lead to an over-emphasis on the negative and to blaming certain groups or individuals as the source of the problem. Debate presupposes that parties are

able to understand each other and that there is common ground for action. However, in many cases—from major intransigent problems such as climate change to local disagreements over community development—parties have remarkably different world-views and very little common understanding or common ground (see Ellis, Chapter 17, this volume; Sillars, Chapter 16, this volume).

Barge (2002) suggests that we also consider an alternative approach to decision making as dialogue in addition to the traditional view of problem solving. A dialogic approach would start not with problems but with communicating to understand and to set the stage for building common ground. Rather than debate, dialogue involves seeing the whole among the parts, seeing the connections between the parts, inquiring into assumptions, learning through inquiry and disclosure, and creating shared meaning among many people (Barge, 2002, p. 168). Models for this alternative view of decision making include appreciative inquiry (Cooperrider & Srivastva, 1987), which identifies current strengths and then tries to build on them in desired directions, and community dialogue, which emphasizes open discussion of different viewpoints in a safe environment to gradually build under-standing and (potential) grounds for action.

Gastil (1993a, 1993b; Gastil, Burkhalter, & Black, 2007) argued that an important and neglected aspect of group decision making is its legitimacy in the eyes of group members and outside stakeholders. A legitimate decision is one that emerges from a fair or just process and is consistent with the normative groundings of society. Legitimacy fosters the commitment of the group and strengthens its willingness to implement or follow through on the decision. A legitimate decision also validates the norms under-girding it and ultimately the larger institu-tions that encompass the group. For example, in the U.S. jury system, certain norms should be followed, and when these are violated, the jury's decision becomes illegitimate, regardless of the strength of its reasoning or the power vested in it by the judicial system.

Gastil articulated a model of democracy in small groups in which democratic group members' relations are premised on equal sharing of power, which is ultimately vested in the group as a whole, rather than individual members. Gastil (1993b) identified several barriers to enacting this democratic model, including long and unorganized meetings, unequal levels of involvement and commitment, strong cliques within the group, unequal communication skills, markedly different communication styles, and intense personal conflicts.

The dialogic and democratic models stress the importance of the nature of the decision process rather than outcomes per se. Both models reconnect group decision making to its normative base in democracy and public participation that was emphasized in early group research. This return to explicit normative considerations is a useful corrective for the tendency to approach group communication research as an objective, scientific enterprise concerned with what is, rather than what should be.

The emphasis placed on legitimacy, understanding, commitment, action, and satisfaction with the decision process by these models tends to crowd out concerns with decision-making effectiveness or efficiency. More research is needed on this topic. Another assumption of these models is that participants will regard democratic or participatory modes of decision making as the legitimate approaches. This, too, is an empirical question. In view of the finding cited above that members may hold implicit theories of decision making that include political logics, it is possible that members will grant legitimacy to other approaches than democracy or participation.

## ◆ Discussion

Group decision making has been a major preoccupation of communication scholars for more than 80 years. Scholarship has moved from a normative and prescriptive treatment through a long period of primarily scientific inquiry, ending today with a combination of scientific and normative emphases that are hoped to be an admixture and not a farrago. In this section, we will venture several comments and suggestions for future directions.

There is a need for contemporary group communication scholars to accord more attention to decision making. Calls for the study of natural or bona fide groups have led many scholars to investigate aspects of groups other than decision making, including dialectics in theater groups, symbolic convergence in covens, children's groups, and classroom groups. These are worthy subjects, but so too is group decision making, through which many of the most consequential actions of groups are taken, such as the decision to launch *Challenger*, the U.S. adventure in Iraq, and the issuance of complex financial instruments that led to the housing meltdown of the past few years.

Recent research has underscored the importance of context in group decision making, and two aspects should be on the agenda for future research. First, there is a need to consider the relationships among decisions over time and level. Any single decision is clearly influenced by prior and anticipated decisions and actions, and it is important to understand better the dynamics of this influence. Second, the bona fide group perspective underscores the importance of context in group decision making. How groups find and process information; how they are influenced by their members' multiple, overlapping, ever-changing memberships in other groups; how interrelationships among groups affect decision making; and how boundary issues influence decisions are all intriguing and important topics.

Much has been learned about the development of decisions in groups, but other questions press. First, how does decision making correlate with other temporal processes in groups, such as coordination of activities, norm formation, fluctuations in group cohesion, socialization of members, and conflict management

(Arrow, Henry, Poole, Wheelan, & Moreland, 2005)? Kuhn and Poole (2000) found that norms for conflict management formed early in a group's life influenced subsequent decision-making effectiveness. More research on interconnections among group processes seems likely to yield useful insights. Second, how does decision making relate to correlative processes such as problem finding, problem framing, and creativity? These have all been the subject of research in communication and other disciplines, but seldom have they been studied in relation to each other. Third, how does general group development relate to decision making? It seems likely that decision making during the group's formative period would differ from processes during the group's work period. In groups "stuck" in certain stages (e.g., those that cannot get past their initial conflicts), developmental processes should have strong impacts on decision making. Finally, there has been relatively little attention to the content of decision making, that is, the particular substantive decisions that are made. With the exception of the work on collective information sharing, this subject remains largely unexplored.

The recent trend toward studies of groups in their natural contexts has yielded important insights into groups and group decision making; however, it is important that this work be balanced by laboratory studies. In line with the critiques of the 1970s and 1980s, many of today's scholars argue that laboratory groups are artificial and cannot yield valid knowledge. However, this criticism ignores a key strength of laboratory research: its ability to establish causal influences that are difficult, if not impossible, to establish in the field due to lack of control. Laboratory researchers, for their own part, have too often set their bars too low and established conditions in the lab that do not resemble those under which natural groups operate. Witness the recent cogent critique of collective information-sharing research by Wittenbaum et al. (2004), which provides a recipe for more realistic laboratory studies in this area. A program of research on group support systems by the first author and colleagues went to some lengths to ensure that they embodied more realistic conditions (see the summary by DeSanctis et al., in press).

Research on democracy and deliberation in groups has reminded many more traditional scholars of the normative roots of group communication research and expanded our view of group decision making. The well-known research on concertive and unobtrusive control in groups (Barker, 1993) should also give us pause. While participation in groups can promote truly democratic openness, it may also hide control and hegemony under the appearance of democracy. The struggle to implement democratic values in the face of control and the possibility of false, illusory democracy are worthy subjects for future research.

If it does anything, this review shows the multifaceted nature of group decision making and the multiple theoretical frameworks that have been advanced to encompass it. The next few decades of research seem poised to work out the connections among the different aspects of decision making and the theories that attempt to explain them.

## ◆ References

Arrow, H., Henry, K. B., Poole, M. S., Wheelan, S., & Moreland, R. (2005). Traces, trajectories, and timing: The temporal perspective on groups. In M. S. Poole & A. B. Hollingshead (Eds.), *Theories of small groups: Interdisciplinary perspectives* (pp. 313–368). Thousand Oaks, CA: Sage.

Bales, R. F., & Strodtbeck, F. L. (1951). Phases in group problem solving. *Journal of Abnormal and Social Psychology, 46,* 485–495.

Barge, J. K. (2002). Enlarging the meaning of group deliberation: From discussion to dialogue. In L. R. Frey (Ed.), *New directions in group communication* (pp. 159–177). Thousand Oaks, CA: Sage.

Barker, J. R. (1993). Tightening the iron cage: Concertive control in self-managing teams. *Administrative Science Quarterly, 38,* 408–437.

Beebe, S., & Masterson, J. T. (2006). *Communication in small groups* (8th ed.). Boston: Pearson/Allyn & Bacon.

Bonito, J. A. (2007). A local model of information sharing in small groups. *Communication Theory, 17,* 252–280.

Contractor, N. S., & Seibold, D. R. (1993). Theoretical frameworks for the study of structuring processes in group decision support systems: Adaptive structuration theory and self-organizing systems theory. *Human Communication Research, 19,* 528–563.

Cooperrider, D. L., & Srivastva, S. (1987). Appreciative inquiry in organizational life. In R. W. Woodman & W. A. Passmore (Eds.), *Research in organizational change and development* (Vol. 1, pp. 129–169). Greenwich, CT: JAI.

DeSanctis, G., & Poole, M. S. (1994). Capturing the complexity in advanced technology use: Adaptive structuration theory. *Organization Science, 5,* 121–147.

DeSanctis, G., Poole, M. S., & Zigurs, I. (2008). The Minnesota GDSS project: Group support systems, group processes, and group outcomes. *Journal of the Association for Information Systems, 9,* 551–608.

Dewey, J. (1910). *How we think.* Boston: D. C. Heath.

Fisher, B. A. (1970). Decision emergence: Phases in group decision-making. *Communication Monographs, 7,* 53–66.

Frey, L. R. (1996). Remembering and "remembering": A history of theory and research on communication and group decision making. In R. Y. Hirokawa & M. S. Poole (Eds.), *Communication and group decision making* (pp. 19–51). Thousand Oaks, CA: Sage.

Frey, L. R. (2002). *Group communication in context: Studies of bona fide groups* (2nd ed.). Thousand Oaks, CA: Sage.

Gastil, J. (1993a). *Democracy in small groups: Participation, decision-making, and communication.* Philadelphia: New Society Publishers.

Gastil, J. (1993b). Identifying obstacles to small group democracy. *Small Group Research, 24,* 5–27.

Gastil, J., Burkhalter, S., & Black, L. W. (2007). Do juries deliberate? A study of deliberation, individual difference, and group member satisfaction at a municipal courthouse. *Small Group Research, 38,* 337–359.

Gersick, C. J. (1989). Marking time: Predictable transitions in work groups. *Academy of Management Journal, 32,* 274–309.

Gersick, C. J. (1991). Revolutionary change theories: A multilevel exploration of the punctuated equilibrium paradigm. *Academy of Management Review, 16,* 10–36.

Giddens, A. (1984). *The constitution of society: Outline of the theory of structuration.* Berkeley: University of California Press.

Gouran, D. S. (1990). Exploiting the predictive potential of structuration theory. In J. A. Anderson (Ed.), *Communication yearbook 13* (pp. 313–322). Newbury Park, CA: Sage.

Gouran, D. S., & Hirokawa, R. Y. (1986). Counteractive functions of communication in effective group decision-making. In R. Y. Hirokawa & M. S. Poole (Eds.), *Communication and group decision making* (pp. 81–90). Beverly Hills, CA: Sage.

Gouran, D. S., & Hirokawa, R. Y. (1996). Functional theory and communication in decision-making and problem-solving groups: An expanded view. In R. Y. Hirokawa & M. S. Poole (Eds.), *Communication and group decision making* (2nd ed., pp. 55–80). Thousand Oaks, CA: Sage.

Henningsen, D. D., & Henningsen, M. (2007). Do groups know what they don't know? Dealing with missing information in decision making groups. *Communication Research, 34,* 507–525.

Hirokawa, R. Y. (1983). Group communication and problem solving effectiveness: An investigation of group phases. *Human Communication Research, 9,* 291–305.

Hirokawa, R. Y. (1988). Group communication and decision-making performance: A continued test of the functional perspective. *Human Communication Research, 14,* 487–515.

Hollingshead, A. B. (1996). The rank-order effect in group decision making. *Organizational Behavior and Human Decision Processes, 68,* 181–193.

Hollingshead, A. B., Wittenbaum, G. M., Paulus, P. B., Hirokawa, R. Y., Ancona, D. G., Peterson, R. S., et al. (2005). A look at groups from the functional perspective. In M. S. Poole & A. Hollingshead (Eds.), *Theories of small groups: Interdisciplinary perspectives* (pp. 21–63). Thousand Oaks, CA: Sage.

Honeycutt, J. M., & Poole, M. S. (1994, November). *Procedural schemata for group decision making.* Paper presented at the 80th annual meeting of the National Communication Association, New Orleans, LA.

Keith, W. M. (2007). *Democracy as discussion: Civic education and the American forum movement.* Lanham, MD: Lexington.

Keyton, J. (2002). *Communicating in groups* (2nd ed.). New York: Oxford University Press.

Kontopoulos, K. M. (1993). *The logics of social structure.* Cambridge, UK: Cambridge University Press.

Kuhn, T., & Poole, M. S. (2000). Do conflict management styles affect group decision-making? Evidence from a longitudinal field study. *Human Communication Research, 26,* 558–590.

Mabry, E. A. (1975). An exploratory analysis of a developmental model for task-oriented small groups. *Human Communication Research, 2,* 66–74.

McBurney, J. H., & Hance, K. (1939). *The principles and methods of discussion.* New York: Harper & Bros.

McGrath, J. E., & Tschan, F. (2004). Dynamics in groups and teams: Groups as complex action systems. In M. S. Poole & A. H. Van de Ven (Eds.), *Handbook of organizational change and innovation* (pp. 50–72). New York: Oxford University Press.

Orlikowski, W. J. (2000). Using technology and constituting structures: A practice lens for studying technology in organizations. *Organization Science, 11,* 404–428.

Orlitzky, M., & Hirokawa, R. Y. (2001). To err is human, to correct for it divine: A meta-analysis of research testing the functional theory of group decision-making effectiveness. *Small Group Research, 32,* 313–341.

Pavitt, C., & Johnson, K. K. (2001). The association between group procedural MOPs and group discussion procedure. *Small Group Research, 32,* 595–623.

Poole, M. S. (1981). Decision development in small groups I: A test of two models. *Communication Monographs, 48,* 1–24.

Poole, M. S. (1983). Decision development in small groups III: A multiple sequence theory of decision development. *Communication Monographs, 50,* 321–341.

Poole, M. S. (1999). Theories of group communication. In L. Frey, D. Gouran, & M. S. Poole (Eds.), *Handbook of group communication theory and research* (pp. 37–70). Thousand Oaks, CA: Sage.

Poole, M. S., & Baldwin, C. L. (1996). Developmental processes in group decision-making. In R. Y. Hirokawa & M. S. Poole (Eds.), *Communication and group decision making* (2nd ed., pp. 215–241). Thousand Oaks, CA: Sage.

Poole, M. S., & DeSanctis, G. (1990). Understanding the use of group decision support systems: The theory of adaptive structuration. In J. Fulk & C. Steinfield (Eds.), *Organizations and communication technology* (pp. 175–195). Newbury Park, CA: Sage.

Poole, M. S., & Hirokawa, R. Y. (1996). Introduction: Communication and group decision making. In R. Y. Hirokawa & M. S. Poole (Eds.), *Communication and group decision making* (2nd ed., pp. 3–18). Thousand Oaks, CA: Sage.

Poole, M. S., & Roth, J. (1989a). Decision development in small groups IV: A typology of decision paths. *Human Communication Research, 15,* 323–356.

Poole, M. S., & Roth, J. (1989b). Decision development in small groups V: Test of a contingency model. *Human Communication Research, 15,* 549–589.

Poole, M. S., Seibold, D. R., & McPhee, R. D. (1985). Group decision-making as a structurational process. *Quarterly Journal of Speech, 71,* 74–102.

Poole, M. S., Seibold, D. R., & McPhee, R. D. (1996). The structuration of group decisions. In R. Y. Hirokawa & M. S. Poole (Eds.), *Communication and group decision making* (2nd ed., pp. 114–146). Thousand Oaks, CA: Sage.

Putnam, L. L., & Stohl, C. (1996). Bona fide groups: An alternative perspective for communication and small group decision-making. In R. Y. Hirokawa & M. S. Poole (Eds.), *Communication and group decision making* (2nd ed., pp. 147–178). Thousand Oaks, CA: Sage.

Scott, C. R. (1999). Communication technology and group communication. In L. R. Frey, D. S. Gouran, & M. S. Poole (Eds.), *The handbook of group communication theory and research* (pp. 432–474). Thousand Oaks, CA: Sage.

Seibold, D. R., & Meyers, R. A. (2007). Group argument: A structuration perspective and research program. *Small Group Research, 38,* 312–336.

Sheffield, A. D. (1927). *Creative discussion: A statement of method for leaders and members of discussion groups and conferences.* New York: The Inquiry.

Stasser, G. (1992). Pooling of unshared information during group discussion. In S. Worchel, W. Wood, & J. Simpson (Eds.), *Group process and productivity* (pp. 48–57). Newbury Park, CA: Sage.

Stasser, G., & Titus, W. (1985). Pooling of unshared information in group decision making: Biased information sampling during discussion. *Journal of Personality and Social Psychology, 48,* 1448–1467.

Sunwolf. (2006). Decisional regret theory: Reducing the anxiety about uncertain outcomes during group decision making through shared counterfactual storytelling. *Communication Studies, 57,* 107–134.

Sunwolf & Seibold, D. R. (1998). Jurors' intuitive rules for deliberation: A structurational approach to the study of communication in jury decision making. *Communication Monographs, 65,* 282–307.

Tracy, K., & Standerfer, C. (2002). Selecting a school superintendent: Sensitivities in group deliberation. In L. R. Frey (Ed.), *Group communication in context: Studies of bona fide groups* (2nd ed., pp. 109–134). Thousand Oaks, CA: Sage.

Wittenbaum, G. W., Hollingshead, A. B., & Botero, I. C. (2004). From cooperative to motivated information sharing in groups: Moving beyond the hidden profile paradigm. *Communication Monographs, 71,* 286–310.

# PART 5

# COMMUNICATION CONTEXTS

# 23

# INTERPERSONAL DIMENSIONS OF HEALTH COMMUNICATION

◆ Donald J. Cegala and Richard L. Street, Jr.

Health communication occurs daily in a variety of interpersonal contexts (Welch Cline, 2003) and among people in various relationships (e.g., health care providers, patients, family members, intimate couples, friends, and strangers), making it impossible to address adequately in one chapter, or even one book, all of the relevant theory, concepts, and research that might comprise "interpersonal dimensions of health communication." Consequently, this chapter's focus has been narrowed considerably. We have opted to direct our attention to selected aspects of physician-patient communication in part because our expertise lies in that realm and in part because systematic study of physician-patient communication has a longer research tradition than health communication in other interpersonal contexts. Even so, this chapter is not an in-depth review of physician-patient communication research. Several such reviews are readily available (e.g., Hall, Roter, & Katz, 1988; Ley, 1988; Ong, DeHaes, Hoos, & Lammes, 1995; Pendleton, 1982; Roter & Hall, 2006), as are summaries of research on the effects of communication skills interventions for physicians and patients (e.g., Anderson & Sharpe, 1991; Cegala, 2003; Cegala & Lenzmeier Broz, 2002, 2003; Harrington, Noble, & Newman, 2004; Hulsman, Ros, Winnubst, & Bensing, 1999). We have chosen to focus on theory guiding physician-patient communication inquiry and some avenues for future theory development. However, to set a context for what follows, we provide a brief historical perspective on the 35 years of research concerning physician-patient communication.

## ◆ A Brief History of Physician-Patient Communication

Historically, physician-patient communication research can be placed along two dimensions, quantitative versus qualitative/critical and perceptual versus behavioral studies.

*Quantitative-Qualitative/Critical* Quantitative and outcome-related research on physician-patient communication had its origins in the late 1960s and early 1970s with the work of Korsch, Gozzi, and Francis (1968); Davis (1968); Ley (1982; Ley, Bradshaw, Eaves, & Walker, 1973); Byrne (1976); and Roter (1977). Typically, these researchers segmented the physician's (and sometimes the patient's) communication into specific units (e.g., utterances) and then categorized these units by their function (e.g., information giving, directives, negative affect) using coding schemes they created or borrowed from other verbal analysis work (e.g., Bales, 1950). The very popular Roter Interaction Analysis System (RIAS) is an example of such a coding method. With this system, coders listen to an audio recording or watch a video recording to identify specific types of verbal behaviors (e.g., biomedical question asking, counseling, provision of psychosocial information) by the physician and patient. The unit of analysis is the utterance, typically defined as the oral analog of a sentence. Each utterance is then assigned to a discourse category whereby frequency or proportional indices of that form of verbal behaviors are computed and analyzed relative to variables of interest (e.g., physician gender, patient satisfaction). While such studies provided correlational evidence linking aspects of communication to demographic variables (e.g., gender, social class) or to postconsultation outcomes, they offered limited theoretical explanations for these relationships.

Interpretive/critical studies of physician-patient communication examine the discourse through the lens of critical theory or the patient's or researcher's personal experiences and perspective. Regarding the former, two exemplars are Waitzkin's (1991) *The Politics of Medical Encounters* and Todd's (1989) *Intimate Adversaries*. For example, Waitzkin's analysis of communication in medical encounters adopts a critical theory perspective on the way physicians marginalize and medicalize patients' concerns to maintain control and reinforce societal values such as family, work, and individual responsibility. Todd offers a feminist critique of physician–women patient interactions and argues that women's perspectives often are muted because of their lower social standing as both patients and women. Rather than adopting a theoretical frame a priori, interpretive approaches derive conceptual themes from careful analysis of discourse garnered from ethnographic, observational, and interview data collection methods. Typically, the goal is to represent the differences in patients' and physicians' perspectives in the medical encounter with a focus on power differences and how these differences might create misunderstanding and lower quality of care. Fadiman (1998), Kleinman (1980), and Sharf, Stelljes, and Gordon (2005) offer excellent examples of this type of research.

*Behavioral Versus Perceptual Measures of Communication.* Quantitative approaches to physician-patient communication can be broken down by the manner in which communication is measured. Some studies assess patients' perceptions of the physician's and their own communication (e.g., Gordon, Street, Sharf, Kelly, & Souchek, 2006; Lerman et al., 1990; Street, 1991). These approaches have the advantage of incorporating the patients' perspective on such issues as the degree to which physicians were informative and supportive and the degree to which the patients believed they participated in the consultation and in making decisions. On one hand, measurement of others' perceptions provides little information on specific physician and patient behaviors that led to the perceptions. Conversely, other studies have coders examine transcripts or audio-video recordings of medical consultations and either rate or categorize physician and patient communication behaviors into certain categories such as information giving, positive affect, question asking, or counseling (e.g., Roter & Larson, 2002; Stewart et al., 2000; Street & Millay, 2001). Frequency or proportional measures of communication are then computed. While these approaches identify specific communicative acts that occurred in the consultation, they often do not correlate well with perceptual measures of related behaviors (e.g., Saba et al., 2006; Street, 1992a). In other words, a speech act may be coded as "information giving," but the patient may not perceive it as "informative" because, by definition, a behavior may satisfy a criterion to count as a certain speech act, yet the patient may not perceive it as a particular salient act. For example, a doctor gives information when offering a diagnosis ("you have a virus"), yet the patient may not view the statement as informative because it is a repetition of what he or she has been told before and does not alleviate the uncertainty associated with persistent symptoms. Or, a physician's comment, "You appear to have a pulled muscle in your back," is coded as an act of information giving using a discourse coding scheme, but it may be perceived as very informative by a patient worried about a serious disease but perceived as immaterial by a patient aware of this diagnosis but more interested in symptom relief.

In summary, physician-patient communication has been studied from a variety of perspectives and approaches. While there are rich descriptions of the discourse of medical encounters, factors related to variability in physician-patient communication, and

correlations between certain behaviors and postconsultation outcomes, much remains to be done with respect to providing meaningful, theoretical accounts of processes affecting communication and outcomes as well as creating measures that integrate behavioral and perceptual features of communication.

## ◆ State of Physician-Patient Communication Theory

Several scholars have noted the lack of theory concerning physician-patient communication (e.g., Frederikson, 1993; Ong et al., 1995; Roter & Hall, 1989; Thompson, 1984). The validity of this observation, of course, depends on one's view of what theory is. However, there is probably universal agreement that no overarching theory of physician-patient communication exists. Some of the reasons for the absence of a general theory parallel those for the lack of a general theory of communication. There are numerous processes and variables operating at multiple levels (e.g., individual, situational, cultural) in complex ways. In addition, the systematic study of physician-patient communication is relatively new, and much of the research has been conducted by scholars whose primary interest or training is not in communication. Also, those who do research on physician-patient communication typically approach it from a pragmatic viewpoint, focusing more on ways to improve communication than on explaining how it works. Thus, key features of the very essence of communication (e.g., as a process of mutual influence, affective-cognitive factors affecting communicative performance and perceptions) are often ignored.

The lack of an overarching theory of physician-patient communication is not particularly surprising or disturbing, although more serious attention to theory development is clearly needed if explanations for observed effects are sought. We discuss avenues for future theory development and research later in the chapter. Despite the absence of a general theory, the literature in physician-patient communication is abundant with models and concepts. Although much of the early research on physician-patient communication was atheoretical and descriptive, the literature over the past 20 or so years has been largely model or concept guided rather than theory driven (see Pavitt, Chapter 3, this volume, for distinctions between models and theories). Below, we focus on selected aspects of this literature to provide an overview of current conceptualizing and research in physician-patient communication.

## MODELS AND CONCEPTS

Over the past three decades, numerous models of the physician-patient relationship have been developed and advocated with varying degrees of enthusiasm (see Emanuel & Emanuel, 1992; Leopold, Cooper, & Clancy, 1996; Perry, 1993). Many of the models were developed and offered as alternatives to paternalistic approaches to the physician-patient relationship (see Emanuel & Emanuel, 1992) that were largely an outgrowth or reflection of Parsons's (1951) articulation of the sick role. Other models were influenced by ideas consistent with Engel's (1977, 1978) biopsychosocial approach to health care.

Several key concepts associated with these models of the physician-patient relationship serve as cornerstones for current views of ideal physician-patient communication. Interestingly, however, an examination of models developed from about 1951 to the 1990s reveals many instances of "reinventing the wheel" rather than a steady progression in the development of key concepts about physician-patient communication. For example, Szasz and Hollender (1956) discussed the importance of partnership and mutual participation as characterizing a preferred physician-patient relationship early on in the development of physician-patient

models, but 40 years later, Leopold et al. (1996) reintroduced these same ideas in calling for an ideal form of physician-patient communication. Similarly, Balint (1955) introduced the concept of patient centeredness in the mid-1950s, and Engel's (1978) presentation of the biopsychosocial approach to medicine contained many key ideas that have since been discussed in several versions of patient-centered medicine (e.g., Silverman, Kurtz, & Draper, 1998; Smith, 2002; Stewart et al., 1995). Certainly, part of this repetition and recycling of key concepts relevant to physician-patient communication is due to a typical time lag for new ideas to be widely disseminated and accepted. Changing social, political, and economic conditions (e.g., managed care, laws governing patients' rights) also have sparked renewed interest in ideas as they become more relevant to the social/cultural fabric.

Probably another factor contributing to recycling or reinvention is that few concepts in the physician-patient communication literature are initially presented in a clear, unambiguous manner. Despite attempts to disambiguate or integrate literature on several key concepts (e.g., Cahill, 1996; R. M. Epstein et al., 2005; Makoul & Clayman, 2005; Mead & Bower, 2000), there is still confusion about what key terms mean and how they may best be operationalized. It is not entirely clear why there is such confusion at the conceptual level. One possible contributing factor may be the pragmatic nature of research in this area (e.g., there is a tendency to move quickly to apply concepts before they are adequately developed and examined). As for the lack of adequate operational definitions, confusion at the conceptual level almost always leads to inadequate measurement. In addition, measurement and psychometrics are typically not a strength of many scholars who do research in this area. Below, we identify and discuss key concepts that significantly influence current views of ideal, or what we might call competent, physician-patient communication.

## ◆ Underlying Concepts of Competent Physician-Patient Communication

There is variance in current views of ideal physician-patient communication, but virtually all are grounded in one or more key concepts that have evolved and recycled over the past 50 or so years. In addition, one of the characteristics of research into physician-patient communication is that most of it has adopted a perspective that is decidedly noninteractive. In particular, virtually all of the research, with the exception of conversation-analytic studies (e.g., Robinson, 2003), has examined either physicians' communication or, far less often, patients' communication. Few researchers have examined the interaction of physicians and patients simultaneously or have attempted to develop models integrating research on physicians' and patients' communication. Thus, it is not surprising that the key concepts guiding this research have been associated with either physicians' communication or patients' communication. Accordingly, we first discuss physician communication followed by an examination of patient communication.

### COMPETENT PHYSICIAN COMMUNICATION

With respect to physicians, the concept of *patient-centeredness* has guided most current research into ideal physician communication. There are multiple views of what patient-centeredness is (e.g., Bensing, 2000; R. M. Epstein et al., 2005; Stewart et al., 1995), and there is even less agreement on how to operationalize it. Mead and Bower (2000), among others, attempted to synthesize and integrate the literature on patient centeredness, suggesting that it is composed of five dimensions: a biopsychosocial perspective, the patient-as-person, sharing power and responsibility, a

therapeutic alliance, and doctor-as-person. Together, these dimensions imply that patient centeredness consists of physician communication that is patient focused (as opposed to disease or physician focused). Among other things, this includes eliciting the patient's perspective (e.g., concerns, preferences, feelings), understanding and treating the patient as an individual with a unique psychosocial context, negotiating treatment options that are consistent with the patient's values, and encouraging the patient to become involved in his or her health care, including participating in treatment decisions to the degree he or she wishes (see A. M. Epstein & Street, 2007).

An example of basic research that reflects a small part of patient centeredness is work on agenda setting (Beckman & Frankel, 1984; Marvel, Epstein, Flowers, & Beckman, 1999) and its translation into communication skills applied during the first 3 minutes of a medical interview (e.g., Cegala, 2005; Silverman et al., 1998). These skills essentially involve the physician allowing and encouraging the patient to talk about his or her medical complaints free of interruptions or closed questioning that may circumvent the patient's entire agenda from being articulated. Such skills allow the patient to "tell his or her story" (Mishler, 1984) and provide initial information about his or her psychosocial context. Another example is from the vast literature on physician-patient information exchange (Thompson, 2000), which Silverman et al. (1998) and others have translated into physician communication skills for improving the clarity, amount, and quality of information provided about such matters as diagnosis, treatment options, and prognosis.

Despite wide endorsement of patient-centered principles as a guide for medical education (Association of American Medical Colleges, 1984) and the ethical/legal treatment of patients (Commission for the Study of Ethical Problems in Medicine and Biomedical and Behavioral Research, 1982), controversy remains about the components of patient-centered communication and its practical value (e.g., de Haes, 2006). In our view, most of the disagreement ultimately focuses on two issues, the degree of empirical support for the benefits of patient-centered communication and the extent to which one may expect universal preference for patient-centered communication.

*Empirical Support for the Benefits of Patient-Centered Communication.* There is a clear distinction in the literature between empirical support for the benefits of effective physician-patient communication and the benefits of patient-centered communication. There is virtually universal agreement that the quality of physician-patient communication can influence postconsultations with respect to such factors as patient satisfaction and adherence, reduced malpractice claims, and better health outcomes (e.g., Ley, 1988; Ong et al., 1995; Pendleton, 1982; Roter, 1989; Stewart et al., 1995). Literature reviews reveal mixed to reasonably good support for the effectiveness of physician communication skills training interventions designed to enhance patient-centered communication (Lewin, Skea, Entwistle, Zwarenstein, & Dick, 2001; Griffin et al., 2004). The majority of studies demonstrate some degree of success in getting physicians to apply patient-centered principles of communication, although virtually no study is 100% successful in this endeavor (i.e., only some portion of patient-centered skills is employed significantly more in intervention vs. control groups). Yet, there is a difference between measured success in teaching patient-centered communication skills and measured benefits derived from such application. Examination of the latter across numerous studies indicates reasonably good support for increased patient satisfaction following interviews in which physicians apply patient-centered communication principles. However, the results concerning other health outcomes that are often viewed as the gold standard of measured effectiveness

(e.g., clinical outcomes of better health such as reduced blood pressure, increases in compliance with medication, or enhancement of physical or mental functioning) are far less clear. Many studies of patient-centered communication do not incorporate measures of such health outcomes, and those that do are characterized by mixed findings (i.e., comparisons between intervention and control groups sometimes reveal positive effects, other times negative effects, and often no differences). Interestingly, the Griffin et al. (2004) review finds that studies with patient communication skills interventions (as opposed to physician interventions) have far more significantly positive health outcome results. These outcomes will be examined when we consider the literature on competent patient communication.

Some scholars argue that there are clear moral reasons for endorsing patient-centered communication, despite a lack of consistent empirical support for its benefits (e.g., Duggan, Geller, Cooper, & Beach, 2006). Although this position may have some merit, it lacks a necessary persuasive element for convincing funding agencies to invest in a continued research effort. Part of the difficulty in addressing this aspect of physician-patient communication is that most of the research on patient-centered communication is physician focused. This, unfortunately, is typical of the literature in physician-patient communication in general. There are, of course, good reasons for scholars to have dedicated their research effort to the study of physicians' communication. But, despite their power position, physicians are only half of the physician-patient dyad. We know from research on natural language use (e.g., Levinson, 1983) and studies showing that a power position does not necessarily translate into a communication control position (e.g., Watzlawick, Beavin, & Jackson, 1967) that communication participants have many options for shaping and influencing interaction. These observations will have continued relevance in the section on patient communication.

*Preference for Patient-Centered Communication.* A second major concern about patient-centered communication is the extent to which it has universal appeal and benefit to patients (e.g., de Haes, 2006). Perhaps one of the key values of this observation is that it indirectly recognizes the need for research that better contextualizes physician-patient communication within individual, dyadic, organizational, societal, and cultural parameters. We will address this matter to some extent in the section on avenues for future physician-patient communication research and theory.

There is a rather large and confusing literature on patients' preferences for different styles of physician-patient communication, especially with respect to involvement in medical decision making (Say, Murtagh, & Thomson, 2006). The various styles are keyed to differences in models of the physician-patient relationship (Perry, 1993) and concepts derived from those models. For example, consumer-based models suggest a preference for maximum information from physicians (e.g., about diagnosis, prognosis, treatment options) so patients can select the course of treatment that best meets their needs. Similarly, several studies reveal that patients' education, age, and socioeconomic status often determine a preference for more paternalistic approaches to health care (e.g., Beisecker, 1988; Kaplan, Gandek, Greenfield, Rogers, & Ware, 1995; Makoul, 1998; Say et al., 2006; Street, Voigt, Geyer, Manning, & Swanson, 1995), with older, less educated, and poorer patients preferring a less active role. Overall, the literature on patient preferences for various physician-patient relationships and communication styles has prompted several scholars to question the universal acceptance and desire for patient-centered communication and, consequently, its universal value and benefit. This may in part be due to the fact that what "counts as" patient-centered communication may vary among patients.

Although concerns about universal applicability of patient-centered communication principles are worthy of attention and continued monitoring, they seem to be less valid as criticisms of patient-centered communication per se than as criticisms of specific applications of it. We are not aware of anyone who has advocated blind, universal application of patient-centered communication. Indeed, many formulations of patient-centered communication principles include physicians' skills for assessing patients' preferences for the kind and amount of information desired and the degree to which patients want involvement in decision making (e.g., Silverman et al., 1998). This sort of communication skill is within the patient-centered purview of treating the patient as an individual with a unique history as well as unique goals and needs. It seems that much of the controversy regarding patient preferences and patient-centered communication ignores this aspect of patient-centered communication models.

Another fundamental aspect of this apparent controversy is ambiguity about what is meant by involvement in decision making. Considerable literature indicates that virtually all patients say they want information about their medical condition (e.g., Beisecker & Beisecker, 1990; DiMatteo, Reiter, & Gambone, 1994; Guadagnoli & Ward, 1998; Joos, Hickman, & Borders, 1993; Ong et al., 1995; Williams, Weinman, Dale, & Newman, 1995). The controversial aspect of involvement comes into play when patients are asked about their desire for participation in decision making (e.g., selecting a treatment). Data relevant to this query are often the source of conflicting results and questioning about patients' preference for involvement with their health care. Much of this confusion is likely related to how questions about decision making are formulated and interpreted (Entwistle et al., 2004). For example, W. Levinson, Kao, Kuby, and Thisted (2005) conducted a survey of a large, representative sample of U.S. citizens and found that 96% of the respondents preferred to be offered choices about treatment and to be asked their opinions, while 52% preferred to leave final decisions to their physicians. From these results, the authors concluded that people vary substantially in their preferences for participation in decision making and that health care providers and organizations should not assume all patients wish to participate in clinical decision making.

A fundamental question here is the following: What exactly is medical decision making, and to what extent can typical patients be expected to want to participate in such decision making? The fact that 96% of the sample expressed a preference for choices to be offered and their opinions sought when making medical decisions clearly indicates a desire for patient-centered communication and an interest in being involved in decisions about health care. The fact that 52% of the sample preferred to leave the final decision to their physician seems to reflect that many patients realize they do not have the technical expertise to make fine discriminations among medical diagnoses and medical procedures. Fundamentally, this is no different from people trusting in their financial advisers to make final decisions about where to invest money, once the advantages and risks of options have been discussed. Yet, such circumstances would not likely be viewed as noninvolvement in financial decision making. In short, it is important to separate patients' desire to be involved in the decision-making process (e.g., information exchange, discussing/evaluating alternatives) from who assumes *responsibility* for the decision. Similarly, the fact that such a huge percentage of respondents in the W. Levinson et al. (2005) study preferred to be informed of options and to have an opportunity to express their views about them says that they indeed preferred the sort of involvement in decision making that is consistent with principles of patient-centered communication.

Finally, the most reasonable criticism regarding patient preference is the notion that physicians should seek input about patients' preferences and adapt their communication style accordingly, rather than assume all patients desire or should be involved in decision making. In this sense, patient-centered communication is less a specific set of behaviors and more the physician's skill at adapting behavior and making appropriate, patient-centered choices from a repertoire of communicative actions. Yet, with some exceptions, little work has been done on developing communication models that integrate complementary physician and patient communication skills (Towle & Godolphin, 1999). Such models would likely provide guidance to physicians for adapting to varying patient preferences and other contextual circumstances.

## COMPETENT PATIENT COMMUNICATION

Far less attention has been given to patients' communication than to physicians' communication. This is probably largely due to early research revealing considerable problems in physicians' communication (then, virtually no attention was given to communication training in medical schools) and a view that focusing on physicians would be a more practical approach to solving communication problems. There are probably fewer than 30 studies devoted to patients' communication in comparison to several hundred studies of physician communication. Nevertheless, several related concepts in the literature have guided research on patient communication, and although little effort has been made to systematically integrate these concepts with patient-centered approaches, the concepts suggest communication skills that parallel physicians' ideal patient-centered communication.

The overarching term that is currently most used in the literature to identify competent patient communication with health care providers is *patient participation*. However, there is far from universal agreement on the particular meaning of this term. Patient participation has been viewed by various constituencies as comprising other behavior instead of, or in addition to, communicating effectively with health care providers (e.g., searching for medically related information, learning and applying self-administered tests and procedures, navigating the health care system). Cahill (1996) has provided perhaps the most comprehensive analysis of the patient participation concept. Her literature review and analysis reveal defining attributes of patient participation that underscore the centrality of communication with the health care provider, suggesting this is the most common meaning for the term (Cahill, 1998).

Despite Cahill's often-cited construct explication, she did not provide specific guidance for operationalizing the concept in terms of patient communication skills. Most of the direction for operationalizing the concept has come from patient communication skills training research (Anderson & Sharpe, 1991; Cegala & Lenzmeier Broz, 2003; Harrington et al., 2004; Haywood, Marshall, & Fitzpatrick, 2006), which has been succinctly summarized by Kaplan, Greenfield, Gandek, Rogers, and Ware (1996):

> Patients who ask questions, elicit treatment options, express opinions, and state preferences about treatment during office visits with physicians have measurably better health outcomes than patients who do not. (p. 497)

Of course, the fact that such inquisitive patients experience better outcomes may have little to do with their communication during interactions with doctors. Such highly inquisitive people may tend to be more obsessive-compulsive and thus prone to adhere to treatment regimens than those who are less inquisitive (the third variable problem).

Our individual (Cegala, 2006b; Cegala, McClure, Marinelli, & Post, 2000; Street, 2001; Street & Millay, 2001) and collective (Cegala, Street, & Clinch, 2007) work on patient participation has also been influenced by this literature. We define patient participation as consisting of information seeking (e.g., asking questions, verifying accuracy of information obtained), information provision (e.g., presenting detailed, organized information about symptoms), assertive utterances (e.g., stating preferences, opinions), and expressing concerns (e.g., stating emotional states such as worry, fear).

Another source that has influenced views about patient participation is the large literature on shared decision making (Makoul & Clayman, 2005). Some scholars have argued that the central feature of patient participation is engaging in shared decision making with health care providers (Eldh, Ekman, & Ehnfors, 2006), while others have simply treated the concepts as equivalent (Guadagnoli & Ward, 1998), but overall, the lack of conceptual and operational clarity associated with shared decision making (Makoul & Clayman, 2005) appears to have resulted in less influence on definitions of patient participation than has the literature on patient communication skills training.

*Empirical Support for the Benefits of Patient Participation.* There is some evidence that patient participation is associated with better health outcomes, such as greater compliance, improved health (e.g., reduction of hypertension), and better physical and mental functioning, but reviewers of this literature emphasize that the evidence is meager and more research is needed (e.g., Anderson & Sharpe, 1991; Harrington et al., 2004).

On the other hand, in reviewing research into communication skills interventions for both physicians and patients, Griffin et al. (2004) conclude that there is more evidence for the positive effects of health-related outcomes for patient interventions than for physician interventions. We can speculate on some of the reasons for this trend. First, it is easier to influence patients' communication

410 PART 5: Communication Contexts

than it is to change physicians' communication (Anderson & Sharpe, 1991; Haywood et al., 2006; Hulsman et al., 1999), and the resulting effect sizes appear to be much larger for patients than for physicians. Second, there is considerable variance across studies in the communication skills taught to physicians (Cegala & Lenzmeier Broz, 2002), and there is some evidence to suggest that key skills involving provision of treatment information and shared decision making about treatment selection either are not taught or are taught in a limited way (Lewin et al., 2001). This is an important limitation, as research on compliance suggests that patients are much more likely to follow recommended treatment regimens if they have been involved in selecting a treatment (e.g., Alexander, Sleath, Golin, & Kalinowski, 2006; Donovan & Blake, 1992; Erraker, Kirscht, & Becker, 1984). In addition, following a recommended treatment regimen is likely to result in either cure or some degree of control over a medical problem (e.g., reduced blood sugar, hypertension), thus further connecting treatment adherence with positive health outcomes. Thus, to the extent that communication skills interventions for physicians do not adequately include content relevant to negotiated treatment options, it is likely that there will be fewer positive effects on adherence and physical and mental health outcomes. Third, some evidence indicates that patients who participate actively in a medical interview shape and influence the way physicians communicate (Cegala et al., 2007; Kravitz et al., 2005; Maly, Umezawa, Leake, & Silliman, 2004; Street, 1992b; Street, Gordon, Ward, Krupat, & Kravitz, 2005). The Cegala et al. (2007) results are particularly relevant here because they suggest that highly active patients influence physicians to communicate in a more patient-centered manner with respect to treatment decision making. Thus, interventions to enhance patient communication skills may indirectly affect health outcomes by their influence in shaping physicians' communication about shared treatment decision making.

Overall, there is reasonably good support for the value of patient participation, although more research is needed in linking the communicative components of patient participation to health outcomes. More research is also needed on the ways in which the discourse of active patients shapes and influences physicians' discourse. This in part entails research designs that assess the effects of various components of patient communication skills interventions. Continued patient communication skills interventions research should attend carefully to the literature on patients' preferences. There is a need for patient communication skills interventions to address differences in patients' preferences for involvement and participation in the medical interview and in medical decision making. For example, one important factor is discriminating among the reasons for patients' lack of interest in participation. There are clear differences and implications for reasons based on communication reticence/apprehension or ignorance of the potential benefits of participation versus genuine, informed desire for a less participatory model of physician-patient communication. Along these lines, it is especially important for researchers to be mindful of how questions about participation preferences are phrased and presented to patients (Entwistle et al., 2004). Finally, somewhat related to patients' preferences issues is research showing that racial/ethnic minorities do not respond as well to patient communication skills interventions as do White patients (Cegala & Post, 2006). In addition, most of the research on patient communication skills training does not even examine potential differences in effects among White versus minority participants. Thus, considerable research is needed to examine the barriers minorities experience in communicating with physicians and how to develop culturally sensitive communication skills interventions to address such barriers. For additional discussion of other issues about needed research into patient communication skills interventions, see reviews by Cegala (2003, 2006a).

◆ **Directions for Future Research in Physician-Patient Communication**

We conclude this chapter with suggestions for future research into physician-patient communication. Discussion is limited to three areas that appear especially important to the advancement of theory.

### CONTEXTUALIZING MODELS

Earlier, we indicated that one reason for the lack of a general theory about physician-patient communication is its complexity. The literature reveals several findings at the individual level indicating that such factors as sex, age, ethnicity, socioeconomic status, severity of illness, attitudes, health beliefs, and numerous other variables potentially affect physician-patient communication (Ley, 1988; Ong et al., 1995; Pendleton, 1982; Roter, 1989; Thompson, 1990). This complexity is further compounded by contextualizing factors at organizational, societal, and cultural levels (e.g., types of health insurance, social class, language/cultural barriers). While it is unlikely that any model or theory will be able to integrate all of the possible factors that shape physician-patient communication, more work is needed in developing and testing such approaches (e.g., Street, 2003). One approach might include reviewing and integrating existing research, particularly on key factors known to affect physician-patient communication. Say et al.'s (2006) attempt to sort out the key factors affecting patient preference is a good example of this approach. More work along these lines may result in each study of physician-patient communication including a minimum number of key individual and contextualizing variables. Advances in statistical analyses now provide researchers

with the necessary tools for examining the effects of variables at several different levels (Hayes, 2007; Slater, Snyder, & Hayes, 2007). More complex research designs and application of multilevel statistical analysis would likely provide a database for meta-analyses to access multilevel effects across studies.

### MICRO-LEVEL ANALYSIS

Despite the abundance of physician-patient communication research, most of it says very little about communication as an interactive, sequential process. Hence, we may know, for example, that physicians' information provision typically has a positive influence on patients' satisfaction and adherence, but we know very little about what information provision looks like and what sorts of messages lead to perceptions of being informed. We know very little about the sequential development of talk within the physician-patient dyad. Most of the research assessing actual talk is content analytic based and reports overall frequencies or percentages of talk in various categories. While this sort of research has been important and helpful in understanding aspects of physician-patient communication, it does not reveal how physicians and patients interact over the course of an interview. Much more sequential analysis of talk is needed.

Along similar lines, more conversation-analytic research is needed to further understand the sequential development of talk and identify "moments of significance" within the stream of the medical interview. Here, the idea of "moments of significance" refers to the phenomenon whereby a single sequence of talk within an interview may be the most significant factor in shaping participants' perceptions or behavior. Although there are clear limitations in doing so, employment of stimulated recall procedures (e.g., Cegala, McNeilis, Socha McGee, & Jonas, 1995) in conjunction with sequential or conversation analysis may provide added insight into the interactive process of medical interviews. More attention to the interactive process of medical interviews, especially in research designs that include key contextualizing variables as discussed above, is likely to provide the sort of database that will lead to more advanced theory in physician-patient communication.

## INTEGRATION OF WHAT IS KNOWN

Although there are limitations in studies of physician-patient communication, there is an abundant database that is in need of synthesis and integration. We have identified one way this literature should be synthesized and integrated above in discussing the need to develop contextualizing models. Another way the literature can be integrated is with respect to physician and patient communication skills. Very little of the physician or patient communication skills intervention research has examined the effects of training both physicians and patients. Even fewer studies have been based on an integrative model of complementary physician-patient skills. It is evident from the literature reviewed in this chapter that ample models and concepts have guided physician-patient communication research, but this research has largely ignored physician-patient communication as a process. Models are needed that incorporate complementary physician and patient communication skills, and more research is needed in testing these models as guides and applications in research into communication skills interventions.

## ◆ Conclusion

Although there is no widely accepted general theory of physician-patient communication, the literature is abundant with models and key concepts that have guided researchers'

investigations of communication phenomena within the medical interview. We have organized this chapter around selected key concepts derived from various models of physician-patient communication. Our selection of concepts and related research is, in our view, a reasonably good reflection of the current state of conceptual and empirical work in physician-patient communication. Although the concepts examined here have generated exciting and useful research on physician-patient communication, much work is needed in sharpening and refining concepts and their operational definitions, as well as integrating related concepts into a broader theoretical framework. We have offered some suggestions for future research that we believe may move the literature on physician-patient communication in this direction.

Before concluding this chapter on interpersonal dimensions of health communication, we would be remiss in not revisiting earlier comments about our decision to focus on physician-patient communication. Current and continued physician-patient communication research is vital to the goal of improving health care. But the physician-patient dyad is only one component within a complex, multileveled system of elements that influence and shape the experience of individuals' illness (and wellness). Within this complex are numerous and frequent communications about health among people in a variety of interpersonal relationships and settings, and these interactions in part shape the perceptions, interpretations, and communication in physician-patient dyads. Indeed, the most significant interpersonal health communication experiences (e.g., those that influence health beliefs, fears, beliefs, and attitudes about physicians, abundance, or lack of social support) ideally would be included as contextualizing variables in multilevel analyses of physician-patient communication (e.g., health beliefs acquired through family communication about illness/wellness, the degree of social support one has from one's spouse).

There is a growing body of research exploring various interpersonal contexts outside of the physician's office that has potential in contextualizing physician-patient communication but also broadening and deepening our understanding of the role of interpersonal communication in health. For example, some research into genetic counseling (Wilson et al., 2004) and family communication (Morgan, 2004; Powell & Segrin, 2004; Zhang & Siminoff, 2003) provides insight into how communication shapes and influences individuals' health beliefs, experience of illness, and decisions about health-risky behavior. There is a growing body of research directed to understanding the cultural influences on health beliefs and other aspects of health communication. The extensive research into social support in various interpersonal contexts provides understanding of how supportive communication, or the lack of it, affects individuals' health (e.g., Albrecht & Goldsmith, 2003). Similarly, research on health narratives (e.g., Harter, Japp, & Beck, 2005) shows, sometimes in surprising ways, how the telling or hearing of stories about health and illness affects people's lives, often in profound ways. In short, we believe this chapter has addressed important concepts and research relevant to health and interpersonal communication between physicians and patients. But we would be remiss in not recognizing the growing and rich body of research into other contexts that also in part comprise interpersonal dimensions of health communication.

◆ **References**

Albrecht, T. L., & Goldsmith, D. J. (2003). Social support, social networks, and health. In A. D. T. L. Thompson, K. Miller, & R. Parrott (Eds.), *Handbook of health communication* (pp. 263–284). Mahwah, NJ: Lawrence Erlbaum.

Alexander, S. C., Sleath, B., Golin, C. E., & Kalinowski, C. T. (2006). Provider-patient communication and treatment adherence. In H. B. Bosworth, E. Z. Oddone, & M. Weinberger (Eds.), *Patient treatment adherence concepts, interventions, and measurement* (pp. 329–372). Mahwah, NJ: Lawrence Erlbaum.

Anderson, L. A., & Sharpe, P. A. (1991). Improving patient and provider communication: A synthesis and review of communication interventions. *Patient Education and Counseling, 17,* 99–134.

Association of American Medical Colleges. (1984). *Physicians for the 21st century: Report of the project panel on the general professional for medicine (GPEP Report).* Washington, DC: Association of American Medical Colleges.

Bales, R. F. (1950). *Interactional process analysis: A method for the study of small groups.* Cambridge, MA: Addison-Wesley.

Balint, M. (1955). The doctor, his patient and the illness. *Lancet, 1,* 683–688.

Beckman, H., & Frankel, R. (1984). The effect of physician behavior on the collection of data. *Annals of Internal Medicine, 101,* 692–696.

Beisecker, A. E. (1988). Aging and the desire for information and input in medical decisions: Patient consumerism in medical encounters. *The Gerontologist, 28,* 330–335.

Beisecker, A. E., & Beisecker, T. D. (1990). Patient information-seeking behaviors when communicating with doctors. *Medical Care, 28,* 19–28.

Bensing, J. (2000). The separate worlds of evidence-based medicine and patient-centered medicine. *Patient Education and Counseling, 39,* 17–25.

Byrne, P. S. (1976). Racial and cultural factors of relevance for the general practitioner. *Proceedings of the Royal Society of Medicine, 69,* 857.

Cahill, J. (1996). Patient participation: A concept analysis. *Journal of Advanced Nursing, 24,* 561–571.

Cahill, J. (1998). Patient participation: A review of the literature. *Journal of Clinical Nursing, 7,* 119–128.

Cegala, D. J. (2003). Patient communication skills training: A review with implications for cancer patients. *Patient Education and Counseling, 50,* 91–94.

Cegala, D. J. (2005). The first three minutes. In E. Berlin Ray (Ed.), *Health communication in practice: A case study approach* (pp. 3–10). Mahwah, NJ: Lawrence Erlbaum.

Cegala, D. J. (2006a). Emerging trends and future directions in patient communication skills training. *Health Communication, 20,* 123–129.

Cegala, D. J. (2006b). Patient participation, health information, and communication skills training: Implications for cancer patients. In G. Kreps, D. O'Hair, & L. Sparks (Eds.), *The handbook of communication and cancer care* (pp. 383–394). Cresskill, NJ: Hampton.

Cegala, D. J., & Lenzmeier Broz, S. (2002). Physician communication skills training: A review of theoretical backgrounds, objectives, and skills. *Medical Education, 36,* 1–13.

Cegala, D. J., & Lenzmeier Broz, S. (2003). Provider and patient communication skills training. In A. T. L. Thompson, K. Miller, & R. Parrott (Eds.), *Handbook of health communication* (pp. 95–119). Mahwah, NJ: Lawrence Erlbaum.

Cegala, D. J., McClure, L., Marinelli, T. M., & Post, D. M. (2000). The effects of communication skills training on patients' participation during medical interviews. *Patient Education and Counseling, 41,* 209–222.

Cegala, D. J., McNeilis, K. S., Socha McGee, D., & Jonas, A. P. (1995). A study of doctors' and patients' perceptions of information processing and communication competence during the medical interview. *Health Communication, 7,* 179–203.

Cegala, D. J., & Post, D. M. (2006). On addressing racial and ethnic health disparities: The potential role of patient communication skills interventions. *American Behavioral Scientist, 49,* 853–867.

Cegala, D. J., Street, R. L., Jr., & Clinch, C. R. (2007). The impact of patient participation on physicians' information provision during a primary care medical interview. *Health Communication, 21,* 177–185.

Commission for the Study of Ethical Problems in Medicine and Biomedical and Behavioral Research. (1982). *Making health care decisions: The ethical and legal implications of informed consent in the patient-practitioner relationship.* Washington, DC: Author.

Davis, M. S. (1968). Variations in patients' compliance with doctors' advice: An empirical analysis of patterns of communication. *American Journal of Public Health and the Nation's Health, 58,* 274–288.

de Haes, H. (2006). Dilemmas in patient centeredness and shared decision making: A case for vulnerability. *Patient Education and Counseling, 62,* 291–298.

DiMatteo, M. R., Reiter, R. C., & Gambone, J. C. (1994). Enhancing medication adherence through communication and informed collaboration choice. *Health Communication, 6,* 253–265.

Donovan, J. L., & Blake, D. R. (1992). Patient non-compliance: Deviance or reasoned decision-making? *Social Science and Medicine, 34,* 507–513.

Duggan, P. S., Geller, G., Cooper, L. A., & Beach, M. C. (2006). The moral nature of patient-centeredness: Is it "just the right thing to do"? *Patient Education and Counseling, 62,* 271–276.

Eldh, A. C., Ekman, I., & Ehnfors, M. (2006). Conditions for patient participation and non-participation in health care. *Nursing Ethics, 13,* 503–514.

Emanuel, E. J., & Emanuel, L. L. (1992). Four models of the physician-patient relationship. *Journal of the American Medical Association, 267,* 2221–2226.

Engel, G. L. (1977). The need for a new medical model: A challenge for biomedicine. *Science, 196,* 129–136.

Engel, G. L. (1978). The biopsychosocial model and the education of health professionals. *New York Academy of Sciences, 310,* 169–181.

Entwistle, V. A., Watt, I. S., Gilhooly, K., Bugge, C., Haites, N., & Walker, A. E. (2004). Assessing patients' participation and quality of decision-making: Insights from a study of routine practice in diverse settings. *Patient Education and Counseling, 55,* 105–113.

Epstein, A. M., & Street, R. L., Jr. (2007). *Patient-centered communication in cancer care: Promoting healing and reducing suffering* (NIH Pub. No. 07-6225). Bethesda, MD: National Cancer Institute.

Epstein, R. M., Franks, P., Fiscella, K., Shields, C. G., Meldrum, S. C., Kravitz, R. L., et al. (2005). Measuring patient-centered communication in patient-physician consultations: Theoretical and practical issues. *Social Science and Medicine, 61,* 1516–1528.

Erraker, S. A., Kirscht, J. P., & Becker, M. H. (1984). Understanding and improving patient compliance. *Annals of Internal Medicine, 108,* 258–268.

Fadiman, A. (1998). *The spirit catches you and you fall down: A Hmong child, her American doctors, and the collision of two cultures.* New York: Farrar, Straus, and Giroux.

Frederikson, L. G. (1993). Development of an integrative model for medical consultation. *Health Communication, 5,* 225–237.

Gordon, H. S., Street, R. L., Jr., Sharf, B. F., Kelly, P. A., & Souchek, J. (2006). Racial differences in trust and lung cancer patients' perceptions of physician communication. *Journal of Clinical Oncology, 24,* 904–909.

Griffin, S. J., Kinmonth, A. L., Veltman, M. W., Gillard, S., Grant, J., & Stewart, M. (2004). Effect on health-related outcomes of interventions to alter the interaction between patients and practitioners: A systematic review of trials. *Annals of Family Medicine, 2,* 595–608.

Guadagnoli, E., & Ward, P. (1998). Patient participation in decision-making. *Social Science and Medicine, 47,* 329–339.

Hall, J. A., Roter, D. L., & Katz, N. R. (1988). Meta-analysis of correlates of provider behavior in medical encounters. *Medical Care, 26,* 657–675.

Harrington, J., Noble, L. M., & Newman, S. P. (2004). Improving patients' communication with doctors: A systematic review of intervention studies. *Patient Education and Counseling, 52,* 7–16.

Harter, L. M., Japp, P. M., & Beck, C. S. (Eds.). (2005). *Narratives, health, and healing: Communication theory, research, and practice.* Mahwah, NJ: Lawrence Erlbaum.

Hayes, A. F. (2007). A primer on multilevel modeling. *Human Communication Research, 32,* 385–410.

Haywood, K., Marshall, S., & Fitzpatrick, R. (2006). Patient participation in the consultation process: A structured review of intervention strategies. *Patient Education and Counseling, 63,* 12–23.

Hulsman, R. L., Ros, W. J., Winnubst, J. A., & Bensing, J. M. (1999). Teaching clinically experienced physicians' communication skills: A review of evaluation studies. *Medical Education, 33,* 655–668.

Joos, S. K., Hickman, O. H., & Borders, L. M. (1993). Patients' desires and satisfaction in general medicine. *Public Health Reports, 108,* 751–759.

Kaplan, S. H., Gandek, B., Greenfield, S., Rogers, W., & Ware, J. E. (1995). Patient and visit characteristics related to physicians' participatory decision-making style. *Medical Care, 33,* 1176–1187.

Kaplan, S. H., Greenfield, S., Gandek, B., Rogers, W. H., & Ware, J. E. (1996). Characteristics of physicians with participatory decision-making styles. *Annals of Internal Medicine, 124,* 497–504.

Kleinman, A. (1980). *Patients and healers in the context of culture.* Berkeley: University of California Press.

Korsch, B. M., Gozzi, E. K., & Francis, V. (1968). Gaps in doctor-patient communication: 1. Doctor-patient interaction and patient satisfaction. *Pediatrics, 42,* 855–871.

Kravitz, R. L., Epstein, R. M., Feldman, M. D., Franz, C. E., Azari, R., Wilkes, M. S., et al. (2005). Influence of patients' requests for direct-to-consumer advertised antidepressants: A randomized controlled trial. *Journal of the American Medical Association, 293,* 1995–2002.

Leopold, N., Cooper, J., & Clancy, C. (1996). Sustained partnership in primary care. *Journal of Family Practice, 42,* 129–137.

Lerman, C. E., Brody, D. S., Caputo, G. C., Smith, D. G., Lazaro, C. G., & Wolfson, H. G. (1990). Patients' Perceived Involvement in Care Scale: Relationship to attitudes about illness and medical care. *Journal of General Internal Medicine, 5,* 29–33.

Levinson, S. C. (1983). *Pragmatics.* Cambridge, UK: Cambridge University Press.

Levinson, W., Kao, A., Kuby, A., & Thisted, R. A. (2005). Not all patients want to participate in decision making: A national study of public preferences. *Journal of General Internal Medicine, 20,* 531–535.

Lewin, S. A., Skea, Z. C., Entwistle, V., Zwarenstein, M., & Dick, J. (2001). *Interventions for providers to promote a patient-centered approach in clinical consultations* (Review, No. CD003267). Chichester, UK: Cochrane Database of Systematic Reviews.

Ley, P. (1982). Satisfaction, compliance and communication. *British Journal of Clinical Psychology, 21*(Pt. 4), 241–254.

Ley, P. L. (1988). *Communicating with patients: Improving communication, satisfaction and compliance.* New York: Croon Helm.

Ley, P., Bradshaw, P. W., Eaves, D., & Walker, C. M. (1973). A method for increasing patients' recall of information presented by doctors. *Psychological Medicine, 3,* 217–220.

Makoul, G. (1998). Perpetuating passivity: Reliance and reciprocal determinism in physician-patient interaction. *Journal of Health Communication, 3,* 233–259.

Makoul, G., & Clayman, M. L. (2005). An integrative model of shared decision making in medical encounters. *Patient Education Counseling, 60,* 301–312.

Maly, R. C., Umezawa, Y., Leake, B., & Silliman, R. A. (2004). Determinants of participation in treatment decision-making by older breast cancer patients. *Breast Cancer Research and Treatment, 85,* 201–209.

Marvel, M. K., Epstein, R. M., Flowers, K., & Beckman, H. B. (1999). Soliciting the patient's agenda: Have we improved? *Journal of the American Medical Association, 281,* 283–287.

Mead, N., & Bower, P. (2000). Patient-centredness: A conceptual framework and review of the empirical literature. *Social Science and Medicine, 51,* 1087–1110.

Mishler, E. G. (1984). *The discourse of medicine.* Norwood, NJ: Ablex.

Morgan, S. E. (2004). The power of talk: African Americans' communication with family members about organ donation and its impact on the willingness to donate. *Journal of Social and Personal Relationships, 21,* 112–124.

Ong, L. M. L., DeHaes, J. C. J. M., Hoos, A. M., & Lammes, F. B. (1995). Doctor-patient communication: A review of the literature. *Social Science and Medicine, 40,* 903–918.

Parsons, T. (1951). *The social system.* New York: Free Press.

Pendleton, D. A. (1982). Doctor-patient communication: A review of the literature. In D. A. Pendleton & J. C. Hasler (Eds.), *Doctor-patient communication* (pp. 5–53). London: Academic Press.

Perry, C. A. (1993). Models of physician-patient interaction: Paternalism to mutual participation. In B. D. Rubin & N. Guttman (Eds.), *Caregiver patient communication* (pp. 23–39). Dubuque, IA: Kendall/Hunt.

Powell, H. L., & Segrin, C. (2004). The effect of family and peer communication on college students' communication with dating partners about HIV and AIDS. *Health Communication, 16,* 427–450.

Robinson, J. D. (2003). An interactional structure of medical activities during acute visits and its implications for patients' participation. *Health Communication, 15,* 27–57.

Roter, D. L. (1977). Patient participation in the patient-provider interaction: The effects of patient question asking on the quality of interaction, satisfaction and compliance. *Health Education Monographs, 5,* 281–310.

Roter, D. L. (1989). Which facets of communication have strong effects on outcome: A meta analysis. In M. Stewart & D. Roter (Eds.), *Communicating with medical patients* (pp. 183–196). Newbury Park, CA: Sage.

Roter, D. L., & Hall, J. A. (1989). Studies of doctor-patient interaction. *Annual Review of Public Health, 10,* 163–180.

Roter, D. L., & Hall, J. A. (2006). *Doctors talking with patients/patients talking with doctors: Improving communication in medical visits* (2nd ed.). Westport, CT: Praeger.

Roter, D., & Larson, S. (2002). The Roter Interaction Analysis System (RIAS): Utility and flexibility for analysis of medical interactions. *Patient Education and Counseling, 46,* 243–251.

Saba, G. W., Wong, S. T., Schillinger, D., Fernandez, A., Somkin, C. P., Wilson, C. C., et al. (2006). Shared decision making and the experience of partnership in primary care. *Annals of Family Medicine, 4,* 54–62.

Say, R., Murtagh, M., & Thomson, R. (2006). Patients' preference for involvement in medical decision making: A narrative review. *Patient Education and Counseling, 60,* 102–114.

Sharf, B. F., Stelljes, L. A., & Gordon, H. S. (2005). "A little bitty spot and I'm a big man": Patients' perspectives on refusing diagnosis or treatment for lung cancer. *Psychooncology, 14,* 636–646.

Silverman, J., Kurtz, S., & Draper, J. (1998). *Skills for communicating with patients.* Abingdon, UK: Radcliff Medical Press.

Slater, M. D., Snyder, L., & Hayes, A. F. (2007). Thinking and modeling at multiple levels. *Human Communication Research, 32,* 375–384.

Smith, R. C. (2002). *Patient-centered interviewing: An evidence-based method* (2nd ed.). New York: Lippincott Williams & Wilkins.

Stewart, M. A. (1995). Effective physician-patient communication and health outcomes: A review. *Canadian Medical Association Journal, 152,* 1423–1433.

Stewart, M., Brown, J. B., Donner, A., McWhinney, I. R., Oates, J., Weston, W. W., et al. (2000). The impact of patient-centered care on outcomes. *Journal of Family Practice, 49,* 796–804.

Stewart, M., Brown, J. B., Weston, W. W., McWhinney, I. R., McWilliam, C. L., & Freeman, T. R. (1995). *Patient-centered medicine.* Thousand Oaks, CA: Sage.

Street, R. L., Jr. (1991). Physicians' communication and parents' evaluations of pediatric consultations. *Medical Care, 29,* 1146–1152.

Street, R. L., Jr. (1992a). Analyzing communication in medical consultations: Do behavioral measures correspond to patients' perceptions? *Medical Care, 30,* 976–988.

Street, R. L., Jr. (1992b). Communication styles and adaptations in physician-patient conversation. *Social Science and Medicine, 34,* 1155–1164.

Street, R. L., Jr. (2001). Active patients as powerful communicators. In W. P. Robinson & H. Giles (Eds.), *The new handbook of language and social psychology* (pp. 541–560). Chichester, UK: John Wiley.

Street, R. L., Jr. (2003). Communication in medical encounters: An ecological perspective. In T. L. Thompson, A. M. Dorsey, K. I. Miller, & R. Parrott (Eds.), *Handbook of health communication* (pp. 63–89). Mahwah, NJ: Lawrence Erlbaum.

Street, R. L., Jr., Gordon, H. S., Ward, M. M., Krupat, E., & Kravitz, R. L. (2005). Patient participation in medical consultations: Why some patients are more involved than others. *Medical Care, 43,* 960–969.

Street, R. L., Jr., & Millay, B. (2001). Analyzing patient participation in medical encounters. *Health Communication, 13,* 61–73.

Street, R. L., Jr., Voigt, B., Geyer, C., Jr., Manning, T., & Swanson, G. P. (1995). Increasing patient involvement in choosing treatment for early breast cancer. *Cancer, 76,* 2275–2285.

Szasz, T. S., & Hollender, M. C. (1956). The basic models of the doctor-patient relationship. *Archives of Internal Medicine, 97,* 585–592.

Thompson, T. L. (1984). The invisible helping hand: The role of communication in the health and social service programs. *Communication Quarterly, 32,* 148–163.

Thompson, T. L. (1990). Patient health care: Issues in interpersonal communication. In E. B. Ray & L. Donohew (Eds.), *Communication and health: Systems and applications* (pp. 27–50). Hillsdale, NJ: Lawrence Erlbaum.

Thompson, T. L. (2000). The nature and language of illness explanations. In B. B. Whaley (Ed.), *Explaining illness: Research, theory, and practice* (pp. 3–40). Mahwah, NJ: Lawrence Erlbaum.

Todd, A. D. (1989). *Intimate adversaries: Cultural conflict between doctors and women patients.* Philadelphia: University of Pennsylvania Press.

Towle, A., & Godolphin, W. (1999). Framework for teaching and learning informed shared decision making. *British Medical Journal, 319,* 766–771.

Waitzkin, H. (1991). *The politics of medical encounters: How doctors and patients deal with social problems.* New Haven, CT: Yale University Press.

Watzlawick, P., Beavin, J. H., & Jackson, D. D. (1967). *Pragmatics of human communication.* New York: W. W. Norton.

Welch Cline, R. J. (2003). Everyday interpersonal communication and health. In A. D. T. Thompson, K. Miller, & R. Parrott (Eds.), *Handbook of health communication* (pp. 285–317). Mahwah, NJ: Lawrence Erlbaum.

Williams, S., Weinman, J., Dale, J., & Newman, S. (1995). Patient expectations: What do primary care patients want from the GP and how far does meeting expectations affect patient satisfaction? *Family Practice, 12,* 193–201.

Wilson, B. J., Forrest, K., van Teijlingen, E. R., McKee, L., Haites, N., Matthews, E., et al. (2004). Family communication about genetic risk: The little that is known. *Community Genetics, 7,* 15–24.

Zhang, A. Y., & Siminoff, L. A. (2003). Silence and cancer: Why do families and patients fail to communicate? *Health Communication, 15,* 415–429.

# 24

# COMMUNICATION CAMPAIGNS

◆ Charles Atkin
and Charles T. Salmon

The term *campaign* is derived from the military domain, representing a distinct phase of a war designed to accomplish specific objectives. Applications have broadened considerably to encompass communication strategies devised to produce a wide variety of social, political, health, and commercial effects on the population. The overview of communication campaigns by Rogers and Storey (1987) yielded 11 definitions from which four essential elements were extracted: (1) A campaign intends to generate specific outcomes or effects (2) in a relatively large number of individuals, (3) usually within a specified period of time and (4) through an organized set of communication activities.

Researchers have assessed the impact of media-based campaigns using survey and experimental designs over the past several decades. The findings from many key studies are summarized in literature reviews by Backer, Rogers, and Sopory (1992); Atkin (2001); and Rice and Atkin (2009). The preponderance of the evidence shows that conventional campaigns typically have only limited direct and immediate effects on most health behaviors. For example, Snyder's (2001) comprehensive meta-analysis of 48 media health campaigns shows that behavior change typically occurs among approximately 7% to 10% more people in the campaign sites than those in control communities; the average effects are 12% for adoption of a new behavior, 7% for promotion of detection and treatment behaviors, and 5% for cessation of current habits.

## ◆ *Approaching Campaign Design*

The campaign as process is fairly universal across topics and venues, using a systematic framework and fundamental strategic principles developed over the past few decades. Campaign planners perform a thorough situational analysis, develop a coherent set of strategies, and execute the creation and placement of messages in accordance with effective media campaign practices.

The starting point in campaign design is a conceptual analysis of the situation comprising several forms of assessment. The initial step is to analyze the behavioral aspects of the communication problem to determine which actions should be performed by which people to attain the goal. The design team specifies *focal segments* of the population whose practices are to be changed and the bottom-line *focal behaviors* that the campaign ultimately seeks to influence. The next step is to trace backwards from the focal behaviors to identify the proximate and distal determinants and then create *models* of the pathways of influence via attitudes, beliefs, knowledge, social influences, and environmental forces. In most cases, the model will differ somewhat for each topic, as it varies according to focal behaviors and population segments. The next phase is to examine the model from a communication perspective, specifying *target audiences* and *target behaviors* that can be directly influenced by campaign messages. The communication campaign can then be designed to affect the most promising pathways, guided by a comprehensive plan for combining manifold strategic components subject to manipulation by the campaigner.

The campaign plan prioritizes prospective pathways, focal behaviors, channels, and dissemination options. Should the campaign seek to change fundamental behaviors or chip away at more readily altered peripheral actions? Should the most resistant or the most receptive segments be the focus of campaign efforts? Should resources be devoted to attaining direct influence on the focal segment or reallocated to using indirect pathways of influence (e.g., by stimulating interpersonal influencers and by leveraging or combating environmental determinants)? Which influencers should be targeted? Should messages primarily attack the *competition* (e.g., unhealthful, antisocial, or ecologically detrimental behavior) or promote the desired alternative? Which channels are most effective and accessible given the purposes and resources of the campaign? Should the campaign messages be scheduled in concentrated bursts or spread out over a lengthy period of time?

Audience response to the campaign stimuli typically proceeds through the basic stages of exposure and processing before effects can be achieved at the learning, yielding, and action levels. *Exposure* includes the simple reception of a message and the degree of attention to its content. *Processing* encompasses mental comprehension, interpretive perceptions, pro/counterarguing, and cognitive connections and emotional reactions produced by the campaign message. The strategic guidelines presented in this chapter draw upon models, processes, generalizations, and recommendations in the voluminous research literature on campaigns, persuasive communication, and social change, including theoretical perspectives and reviews by Atkin (2001); Atkin and Silk (2008); Atkin and Wallack (1990); Backer et al. (1992); Kotler, Roberto, and Lee (2002); Hale and Dillard (1995); Hornik (2002); Maibach and Parrott (1995); McGuire (1994); Salmon (1989); Salmon and Atkin (2003); and Slater (1999).

Among the notable frameworks are the Ajzen and Fishbein (1980) theory of reasoned action, which combines attitudes and norms along with belief expectancies and values to predict behavioral intentions; several components of the theory can be influenced by campaign messages. Likewise, individuals tend to exhibit behavior similar to credible role models who receive negative or positive reinforcements in message depictions, according to Bandura's (1986) social cognitive learning theory. As with other persuasive messages, the influence of campaign stimuli may operate via central and peripheral routes to persuasion, as outlined in the elaboration likelihood model (Petty & Cacioppo, 1986) or the heuristic systematic model (Eagly & Chaiken, 1993).

The campaign-oriented integrative theory of behavior change (Cappella, Fishbein, Hornik, Ahern, & Sayeed, 2001) combines the health belief model, social cognitive theory, and the theory of reasoned action. The transtheoretical model (Prochaska & Velicer, 1997) identifies subgroups based on their current stage in the process of behavior change (precontemplation, contemplation, preparation, action, or maintenance). Over time, campaigns target specific audience segments at different stages of progression, which is now more feasible with new technology such as interactive Web sites. Diffusion theory (Rogers, 2003) describes how new ideas and practices spread through interpersonal networks and the influential role played by opinion leaders. Reflecting more environmental approaches to social change, theory on community-based interventions (Bracht, 1999) highlights the importance of integrating micro- and macro-level change efforts. Through mobilization and participation of a wide variety of social institutions, communities can serve as actual *mechanisms* of change as well as *sites* of change.

## ◆ Formative Research

The applicability of general campaign design principles depends on the specific context (especially types of audiences to be influenced and type of product being promoted), so effective design usually requires extensive formative evaluation inputs (Atkin & Freimuth, 2001; Salmon & Jason, 1992). In the early stages of campaign development, designers collect background information about the focal segments and interpersonal influencers,

using statistical databases and custom surveys to learn about audience predispositions (e.g., what they already know about the topic, what values and attitudes they hold, what behaviors they are currently practicing), channel usage patterns, stylistic preferences, and evaluations of prospective messengers and appeals. Designers of community-based campaigns conduct specialized formative research involving extensive analysis of communication networks, patterns of opinion leadership, and relationships among businesses and government agencies (Bracht, 2001).

As message concepts are being refined and rough executions are created, qualitative reactions are obtained in focus group discussion sessions, and supplemental quantitative ratings can be measured in message testing laboratories. Formative research helps bridge the gap between topical specialists and their target audiences in knowledge, values, priorities, and level of involvement. Gathering pretest feedback prior to final production and dissemination is particularly helpful in assessing whether the audience regards the message content and style as informative, believable, motivating, convincing, useful, on-target, and enjoyable . . . and not too preachy, disturbing, confusing, irritating, or dull. Research is crucial in resolving disputes between sponsoring organization officials, communication strategists, and creative professionals. Feedback from the audience can reveal whether the campaign's tone is too righteous (admonishing people about their incorrect behavior), the recommendations too extremist (rigidly advocating unpalatable ideals), the executions too politically correct (staying within tightly prescribed boundaries of propriety to avoid offending overly sensitive authorities and interest groups), and the executions too self-indulgent (attempting sophisticated executions where creativity and style overwhelm substantive content considerations). In particular, pretesting can detect problematic elements that may produce psychological reactance on the part of the audience, which can actually result in boomerang effects where the counter-productive behaviors are reinforced.

# ◆ Audience Segmentation

There are two major strategic advantages of subdividing the population along multiple dimensions related to demographic charac-teristics, predispositions, personality traits, and social context. First, message efficiency can be improved if subsets of the audience are prioritized according to their centrality in attaining the campaign's objectives as well as receptivity to being influenced. Second, effectiveness can be increased if message content, form, and style are tailored to the attributes and abilities of the sub-groups (Atkin & Freimuth, 2001; Dervin & Frenette, 2001). Three distinct types of audi-ences are targeted in media campaigns. Most messages are aimed directly to the *focal segments* whose behavior is to be changed. A supplemental approach is to ini-tiate a multistep flow by disseminating mes-sages to various types of *influencers* who are in a position to personally influence focal individuals. Third, the campaign may seek to alter the environment by aiming certain messages at societal and organizational policy makers responsible for devising constraints and creating opportunities that shape individuals' decisions and behaviors.

The nature of the substantive problem dictates the broad parameters of the focal audience to be influenced. Because audience receptivity is also a significant determinant of campaign effectiveness, campaign designers tend to pick off the easier targets. A fundamental factor is stage of readiness to perform the practice. Campaigns tend to achieve the strongest impact with triggering or reinforcing messages designed for people who are already favorably predisposed. A more important but less receptive target is the segment of people who have not yet tried the

undesirable behavior but whose background characteristics suggest they are "at risk" in the near future. On the other hand, those committed to unsuitable practices are not readily influenced by directly targeted campaigns, so a heavy investment of re-sources to induce immediate discontinuation is likely to yield only a marginal payoff. Campaigners also need to consider other demographic, social, and psychological-based subgroups such as the higher versus lower income strata or high versus low sensation seekers (see Palmgreen, Donohew, & Harrington, 2001). Influencing these varied population segments requires a complex mix of narrowly customized messages and broadly applicable multitargeted messages that use diverse appeals and optimally ambiguous recommended actions.

# ◆ Problem Prevention Versus Positive Promotion

Campaigns usually seek to influence an enduring discrete act or a recurring behav-ioral practice. The two fundamental ap-proaches are to promote a positive behavior (e.g., eat fruit, recycle paper, donate blood) and to prevent problematic behavior (e.g., fat consumption, unlocked doors, campfires in a dry forest). Promoting desirable behav-ior works best if attractive "products" can be offered, such as tasty fruit, the designated driver arrangement, or staircase exercising; the negatively oriented prevention approach is most potent in cases where harmful out-comes are genuinely threatening.

Prevention campaigns focus primarily on the harmful consequences of the undesirable practice rather than promoting a positive alternative to compete with it. Messages typically attack the "competition" by threat-ening dire consequences of performing a proscribed behavior. Although threats can be effective if handled skillfully, the narrow reliance on negatively attacking the competition unduly restricts the strategic arsenal. A softer tactic is to discount the perceived benefits of the practice. In campaign messages that promote a positive product, there is a continuum of prospective target responses that can be explicitly recommended for adoption. These actions can vary in the acceptability to the audience, based primarily on effort and sacrifice required to perform the behavior and monetary expense. This barrier can be overcome with smaller or softer products that demand lower investment and generate fewer drawbacks. In creating a "product line" menu, the designer weighs receptivity versus resistance of the audience and the potency of the incentives associated with each product. With resistant audiences, it may be fruitless to advocate a sizable degree of change that is beyond the recipients' latitude of acceptability; for certain behaviors, the initial series of product representations may profitably use the incremental "foot in the door" strategy. In certain cases, the campaign may initially promote modestly demanding products such as prebehaviors (e.g., sign pledge card, state intentions publicly, wear red ribbon) or undemanding forms of sacrifice (e.g., trial adoption, brief abstinence, token donation). The prolonged nature of campaigns enables the use of gradually escalating sequential approaches over a period of months or years. In addition, numerous intermediate responses might be targeted, such as awareness, knowledge, images, salience priorities, beliefs, expectancies, values, and attitudes; campaigns may seek to change key variables along the pathways leading to the focal behavior. Other types of target responses come into play when campaigns are aiming at influencers and societal policy makers.

### ◆ Types of Messages

Depending on the most promising mechanisms of influence, campaigns use three basic communication processes by which messages move the target audience toward the desired response: awareness, instruction,

and persuasion. *Awareness* messages tell people what to do, specify who should do it, and provide cues about when and where it should be done. Although this type of message may be superficial, it can stimulate the audience to seek richer content from elaborated informational resources such as Web pages, books, and opinion leaders. A key role of awareness messages is to arouse interest or concern and to prompt further information seeking on the subject. In addition, awareness messages employ sensitization strategies that leverage the rich array of pertinent but unrecognized influences present in the everyday environment experienced by focal individuals. In the mass media, there typically are numerous news stories, advertisements, entertainment portrayals, and other public service campaigns that present content consistent with campaign goals. Similarly, individuals may not be conscious of certain social norms, interpersonal influences, behavioral models, or societal conditions that might contribute to performance of the focal behavior. Thus, some campaign messages can serve a priming function to cue the audience to available pro-campaign stimuli.

The *instruction* messages present "how to do it" information in campaigns emphasizing knowledge gain and skills acquisition. If the components of the recommended behavior are elaborate or complex, messages can educate the audience with a detailed blueprint. If certain individuals lack confidence to carry out the behavior, messages can provide encouragement or training to enhance personal efficacy. If the focal segment is subject to peer pressure or exposed to counterproductive media portrayals, instruction messages can teach *peer resistance* and *media literacy skills*. To overcome potentially corruptive effects of commercial advertising or entertainment media portrayals, a small portion of messages may be devoted to *inoculating* viewers and listeners against these influences that might undermine the campaign.

Most campaigns also present messages featuring *persuasive* reasons why the audience should adopt the advocated action or avoid the proscribed behavior. The classic case involves the mechanism of attitude creation or change, usually via knowledge gain and belief formation. For audiences that are favorably inclined, the campaign has the easier persuasive task of reinforcing existing predispositions: strengthening a positive attitude, promoting postbehavior consolidation, and motivating behavioral maintenance over time. Because a lengthy campaign generally disseminates a broad array of persuasive messages, strategists often marshal a variety of appeals built around motivational incentives designed to influence attitudes and behaviors; the selection and organization of persuasive appeals is described in detail in subsequent sections.

The relative emphasis on the three types of messages varies at different stages of the campaign and for different target audiences because the pathways to impact depend on the existing pattern of knowledge and attitudes of the audience.

# ◆ Qualitative Message Factors

The central element of the overall campaign is the content, form, and style of individual messages. Sophisticated message design includes strategic selection of substantive material, mechanical construction of message components, and creative execution of stylistic features.

There are five key qualitative attributes in campaign messages. The first factor encompasses motivational *incentives*, which are fundamental to persuasive messages. For most pathways of influence, several additional message qualities increase effectiveness. *Credibility* is the extent to which the message content is believed to be accurate and valid; this is primarily conveyed by the trustworthiness and competence of the source and the provision of convincing evidence. The style and ideas should be *engaging*, by using stylistic features that are superficially attractive and entertaining (as well as less pleasing components that are nevertheless arresting or refreshing) and substantive content that is interesting, mentally stimulating, or emotionally arousing. To influence behavior, the presentation must be personally *involving* and *relevant*, such that the receivers regard the recommendation as applicable to their situation and needs. Finally, the *understandability* of the message contributes to recipient processing and learning via presentation of material in a comprehensive and comprehensible manner that is simple, explicit, and sufficiently detailed.

# ◆ Diverse Incentive Appeals

The most elaborate and influential messages feature persuasion. The promoting and attacking approaches used in persuasive campaign messages are generally accompanied by corresponding positive or negative incentive appeals. Messages for high-involvement practices tend to emphasize substantive incentives, presenting persuasive arguments supported by credible messengers or evidence to move the audience through a lengthy hierarchy of output steps such as attention, attitude change, and action (McGuire, 1994). The most widely used frameworks (theory of reasoned action, protection motivation theory, and health belief model) draw upon a basic expectancy-value mechanism where messages primarily influence an array of beliefs regarding the subjective likelihood of each outcome occurring; attitudinal and behavioral responses are contingent upon each individual's valuation of these outcomes.

Although many campaigns simply exhort individuals to act in a specified way, it is usually more effective to present message content that links the desired behavior to valued attributes or consequences that serve as positive incentives (or content linking the undesirable behavior to negative incentives). The incentive appeals for complying with a recommendation often build on existing values of the target audience.

For campaigns in the ubiquitous health domain, the basic dimensions of incentives include physical health, time/effort, economic, moral, legal, social, psychological, and aspirational aspects (each with possible positive and negative value predispositions). Due to the overly narrow emphasis on negative health threats (e.g., death, illness, injury), it is important to consider diversifying the negative incentive strategies to include appeals not directly related to physical health per se (e.g., psychological regret, social rejection) and to give greater emphasis to reward-oriented positive incentives (e.g., valued states or consequences such as well-being, altruism, attractiveness).

Persuasive appeals emphasize the two basic components in the expectancy-value formulation: the subjective probability of a consequence's occurring and the degree of positive or negative valence of that outcome. The operational formula for preventing undesirable behaviors is *vulnerability × severity,* positing that the audience is maximally motivated by a high likelihood of suffering a very painful consequence. The most common communication strategy is to change beliefs regarding the probability component.

*Positive Appeals.* One way that campaigns can diversify appeals is by increasing the generally modest proportion of positive incentives. For each of the negative consequences of performing the proscribed practice, there is usually a mirror-image positive outcome that can be promised for performing the desired alternative. For example, positive social incentives include being "cool," gaining approval and respect, forming deeper friendships, building trust with

parents, and being a good role model. On the psychological dimension, messages might promise such outcomes as gaining control over one's life, positive self-image, attaining one's goals, feeling secure, or acting intelligently.

*Multiple Appeals.* Dozens of persuasive appeals are potentially effective in any campaign, and the degree of potency is fairly equivalent in many cases. Rather than relying on a few incentives, it is generally advantageous to use multiple appeals across a series of messages in a campaign. In selecting incentives, the key criteria are the salience of the promised or threatened consequences, the malleability of beliefs about the likelihood of experiencing these outcomes, and the potential persuasiveness of the arguments that can be advanced (see Cappella et al., 2001).

*Evidence.* In conveying certain incentive appeals, evidence is needed to support claims made in the message. This is most important when belief formation is a central mechanism and when the source or sponsor is not highly credible. The type of evidence featured varies according to each audience; for example, sophisticated and highly involved individuals tend to be more influenced by messages citing statistics, providing documentation, and quoting technical experts, whereas dramatized case examples and testimonials by famous sources may work better for less involved audience members. A message that demonstrates how the evidence is relevant to the situation experienced by the target audience helps forestall denial of applicability. In offering evidence to broad media audiences that inevitably vary in predispositions, special care should be taken with extreme claims (rare cases, implausible statistics, overly dramatic depictions of consequences) or clearly biased marshalling of supportive facts. These elements may strain credulity and trigger counterarguing among audience members and may be challenged by critics in rebuttal messages in contentious spheres of campaigning.

*Message Sidedness.* Due to the complex nature of many behaviors recommended in campaigns, compliance is impeded by a variety of disadvantages perceived by the audience (e.g., obstacles, drawbacks, and forsaken alternatives). A one-sided message strategy presents only arguments favoring the desired behavior (or contesting the competition) and ignores the disadvantageous aspects of the side being advocated. Because campaigns often involve contentious issues where messages featuring disparate positions reach the audience, the "two-sided" approach may be used; the elements of the opposing case are strategically raised and discounted to counteract current and future challenges.

The three basic techniques for addressing drawbacks are refutation, diminution, and tactical concession. First, supposed advantages of the objectionable behavior (or disadvantages of the promoted behavior) can be directly *refuted* with contrary evidence or emotional attacks. Messages can acknowledge that the competition has certain attractive aspects and then argue that each seeming positive consequence is unlikely to be experienced, not so positive after all, or relatively unimportant. Second, salient and substantive drawbacks of the focal behavior (and attractive features of alternatives) can be mentioned and then *downplayed* by arguing that these factors are relatively unimportant compared with the beneficial features. Third, minor disadvantages can simply be *conceded* as a tactic for enhancing credibility and thus increasing the believability of other arguments in the message.

## ◆ Source Messengers

The *messenger* is the model or presenter appearing in the message that delivers information, demonstrates behavior, or provides a testimonial; the presenter featured in the message is distinct from the institutional sponsor and the message creators. Messengers serve a variety of functions, particularly by enhancing qualitative factors that convey the incentives in campaign messages: They should be engaging (attractiveness, likability), credible (trustworthiness, expertise), and relevant to the audience (similarity, familiarity). A messenger high on these factors can increase attention to message content, facilitate comprehension by personalizing message concepts, elicit positive cognitive responses, heighten emotional arousal via identification or transfer of affect, and increase retention due to memorability. Careful pretesting helps avoid selection of compelling personalities who distract from the substantive content or controversial individuals who trigger source derogation and message counterarguing. The key categories of public communication campaign messengers are celebrities, public officials, topical expert specialists, professional performers, ordinary people, specially experienced individuals (e.g., victims or beneficiaries), and unique characters (e.g., animated or costumed).

The type of messenger to be featured depends on the predispositions of the target audience and the persuasion mechanism underlying the strategy (particularly the nature of the incentive). Messenger appropriateness also depends on the type of message (e.g., awareness messages tend to present celebrities, instruction messages rely on experts, persuasion messages use victims). Messengers play differing roles, depending on the communication task: For example, celebrities help draw attention to a dull topic, experts enhance response efficacy, ordinary people heighten self-efficacy, victims convey the severity of harmful outcomes, and victims who share similar characteristics of the audience augment susceptibility claims. Salmon and Atkin (2003) provide an elaborate discussion of strengths and weaknesses of various types of messengers.

## ◆ Communication Channels

In disseminating messages, most campaign designers still rely heavily on television, newspapers, Web sites, and pamphlets carrying prepackaged informational pages, public service spots, and news releases. These channels are supplemented by an array of secondary channels and vehicles: mini-media (e.g., billboards, posters, theater slides), entertainment-education placements (e.g., songs, program inserts, comics), and interactive technology (e.g., blogs, CDs, tailored messages, computer games). The integration of electronic social networks and mobile communication is transforming communication campaign design as well. Cell phones are greatly extending the reach of information dissemination and the accessibility of focal segments throughout the day.

In assessing each option for channeling campaign messages, myriad advantages and disadvantages can be taken into consideration along a number of communicative dimensions. Salmon and Atkin (2003) discuss channel differences in terms of *reach* (proportion of community exposed to the message), *specializability* (narrowly reaching specific subgroups), *intrusiveness* (capacity for surmounting selective exposure and commanding attention), *safeness* (avoiding risk of boomerang or irritation), *participation* (active receiver involvement while processing stimulus), *meaning modalities* (array of senses employed in conveying meaning), *personalization* (human relational nature of source-receiver interaction), *decodability* (mental effort required for processing stimulus), *depth* (channel capacity for conveying detailed and complex content), *credibility* (believability of material conveyed), *agenda setting* (potency of channel for raising salience priority of issues), *accessibility* (ease of placing messages in channel), *economy* (low cost for producing and disseminating stimuli), and *efficiency* (simplicity of arranging for production and dissemination).

For example, TV public service announcements (PSAs) are strong on reach, intrusiveness, and decodability but weak on accessibility, safeness, depth capacity, and participation. Among the strengths of newspaper articles are accessibility, reach, depth, credibility, agenda setting, economy,

and efficiency; major weaknesses are decodability and personalization. For pamphlets, strong features are depth and participation; weak aspects are reach, decodability, and personalization. Key strengths of interactive media are specializability, safeness, and participation.

Conceptually, channel appropriateness is determined by the usage patterns of the priority receivers and the nature of the message. Pragmatically, the limited resources for most public campaigns also play a role. It is usually more practicable to stage a pseudo-event that generates news coverage than to raise funds to purchase time or space in the ideal media vehicle, more feasible to achieve a minor product placement in an entertainment program than to capture the whole plotline, and more economical to place a PSA on a low-rated mature adult radio station than on a hot teen station.

A leading low-cost approach to placing messages is creative publicity, using public relations techniques for generating news and feature story coverage in the mass media. Certain public communication campaign domains such as health, safety, and the environment are central among journalistic priorities for newspapers, women's magazines, TV newscasts, and daytime TV talk shows. Public relations practitioners have moved beyond passive distribution of press releases to aggressively placing guests on talk shows, regularly feeding feature writers with compelling story ideas, and creatively staging pseudo-events to attract journalist attention. Gaining consistent visibility in the news media can facilitate an agenda-setting effect, whereby problems and solutions are perceived as more urgent and significant. This is particularly important in media advocacy strategies targeted to opinion leaders and policy makers in society. Moreover, publicity in the mainstream media can attract attention of key types of informal influencers, who can exert an indirect impact on the focal individuals.

The related practice of *entertainment-education* involves embedding campaign topic–related material in entertainment programming (or creating entertainment programming as a vehicle for education). Because the interesting and enjoyable style of presentation attracts large audiences and conveys information in a relevant and credible manner, this approach has proved to be quite successful in promoting prosocial and health initiatives in Africa, Asia, and South America (Singhal, Cody, Rogers, & Sabido, 2004). Entertainment-education has been used sparingly in the United States, with narrow applications in efforts to promote the designated driver, safety belts, safe sex, and drug abstinence, along with child-oriented topics such as alcohol, occupational roles, and conflict resolution. Current and potential roles of new media in advancing campaigns are described in Rice and Atkin (2009). PSAs are appearing increasingly online, typically in the form of brief banner ad messages or solicitations to visit a Web site. However, these messages have severe content capacity limitations, the sponsors have little control over placement of their banner ads, and ads are often blocked by computer software. In the health domain, the Internet is becoming a major source for online information, discussion, therapy, and access to physicians (Rice, 2006). The value of anonymity inherent in Web information search is valuable for private or sensitive topics (e.g., STD/HIV prevention).

Certain new communication media, such as voice response systems, interactive video, DVDs and CD-ROMs, and computer games, can be effective in reaching various population segments as well. Lieberman (2001) recommends that computer-mediated campaigns feature youthful genres, support information seeking, incorporate challenges and goals, use learning-by-doing, create functional learning environments, and facilitate social interaction. Another review by Lieberman (2006) describes several kinds of video game learning relevant to campaigns, including skill acquisition from interactive games, improved self-efficacy through

success in vicarious experiences, and role-playing and modeling.

Interpersonal components of campaigns might be extended through the use of e-mail, such as in the Digital Heroes Campaign (DHC), where online mentors were matched with mentees for 2 years to foster better youth development (Rhodes, Spencer, Saito, & Sipe, 2006). In addition, the medium of mobile phones is well suited to offer tailored, wide-reaching, interactive, and continuing campaign interventions. Blogs serve an important role in linking users with similar information needs and concerns to share their views and experiences, while wikis support collaboration among project members. Podcasts are another audio-based means of providing relevant information to motivated audiences at their convenience.

Central to an understanding of the role of new media in campaigns are the concepts of interactivity, narrowcasting, and tailoring. *Interactivity* has two primary dimensions—direction of communication and level of receiver control over the communication process—which yield four kinds of relationships between the user and the source (monologue, feedback, responsive dialogue, and mutual discourse); these can be associated with specific design features, such as surveys, games, purchasing products or services, e-mail, hyperlinks, and chat rooms. Rimal and Adkins (2003) suggest applying social marketing principles to *narrowcasting* via segmentation and targeting Internet users. The messages are tailored to match the theoretically relevant audience characteristics, and interactive/individualized feedback facilitates motivation to adopt behaviors. *Tailoring* involves designing customized messages that reflect the individual's predispositions and abilities (Kreuter, Farrell, Olevitch, & Brennan, 1999). Online screening questionnaires assess factors such as readiness stage, stylistic tastes, knowledge levels, and current beliefs and then direct them to narrowly targeted messages. Not only does this approach increase the likelihood of learning and persuasion, but it also decreases the possibility of boomerang effects.

New media may be useful for community-level and policy advocacy campaigns. For example, organizers seeking to generate wider participation in a civic program or greater support for a new law can use an interactive Web site coupled with e-mail to mobilize citizens. Online and CD-ROM resources are available for community campaign designers, such as Web sites providing technical information on how to develop community-based interventions and CD-ROMs detailing the steps for planning and evaluating campaigns.

◆ *Quantity of Dissemination*

Strategic dissemination encompasses the volume of messages, the amount of repetition, the prominence of placement, and the scheduling of message presentation. A substantial *volume* of stimuli helps attain adequate reach and frequency of exposure, as well as comprehension, recognition, and image formation. Moreover, message saturation conveys the significance of the problem addressed in the campaign, which heightens agenda setting and salience. A certain level of *repetition* of specific executions facilitates message comprehension and positive affect toward the product, but high repetition produces wear-out and diminishing returns.

Placement *prominence* of messages in conspicuous positions within media vehicles (e.g., prime-time network television, newspaper front page, heavily traveled billboard locations, or high-rank search engine Web sites) serves to enhance both exposure levels and perceived significance. Another quantitative consideration involves the *scheduling* of a fixed number of presentations; depending on the situation,

campaign messages may be most effectively concentrated over a short duration, dispersed thinly over a lengthy period, or distributed in intermittent bursts of "flighting" or "pulsing." There are also key "timing points" when the audience is more attentive or in an information-seeking mode. For example, these may occur during the period when electoral or policy decisions are being made, on the occasion when a problematic incident or significant progress is heavily covered in the media, on a special day or during a month when a topic is being publicized, or more routinely at a time soon after an early phase of the campaign has primed the audience to move on to a higher stage of involvement. During these defining moments, campaign messages are more likely to resonate with receptive segments of the public.

Finally, the diverse assortment of messages in a public communication campaign is typically encountered by various subgroup receivers via numerous channels at an often irregular sequence and timetable. To provide a common thread unifying the campaign stimuli, designers employ *continuity devices* (e.g., logo, slogan, jingle, messenger), which increase memorability and enable the audience to cumulatively integrate material across exposure impressions.

To maximize quantity, campaigners diligently pursue a combination of approaches to gain media access: monetary support from government and industry to fund paid placements and leveraged media slots, aggressive lobbying for free public service time or space, skillful use of public relations techniques for generating entertainment and journalistic coverage, and reliance on low-cost channels of communication such as the Internet and posters. Moreover, the limited quantity of messages disseminated in a campaign can be boosted by sensitizing audiences to appropriate content already available in the media and by stimulating information seeking from specialty sources.

The *length* of the campaign is a final consideration. The realities of public service promotion and problem prevention often require exceptional persistence of effort over long periods of time simply to attain a critical mass of exposures. In many cases, perpetual campaigning is necessary because focal segments of the population are in constant need of influence; over time, there are newcomers who are moving into the priority audience, backsliders who are reverting to prior misbehavior, evolvers who are gradually adopting the recommended practice at a slow pace, waverers who are needing regular doses of reinforcement to stay the course, and latecomers who are finally seeing the light after years of inappropriate habits.

## ◆ *Environmental Influencers and Policy Makers*

It is often valuable for campaigners to supplement the direct approach of educating and persuading the focal segment by also influencing secondary target audiences who can exert interpersonal influence on focal individuals or who can help reform environmental conditions that shape behavior. Mass media campaigns have considerable potential for producing effects on institutions and groups at the national and community levels, as well as motivating personal influencers in close contact with the focal individuals. These audiences are often more receptive to campaign messages, and their indirectly stimulated activities are more likely to be effective than campaign messages directly targeted to the focal segment. These influencers dispense positive and negative reinforcement, exercise control (by making rules, monitoring behavior, and enforcing consequences), shape opportunities, facilitate behavior with reminders at opportune moments, and serve as role models. Furthermore, influencers can customize their messages to the unique needs and values of the individual. At the interpersonal level, the campaign seeks to inspire, activate, or empower those in a

position to personally exert influence, such as parents, bosses, friends, and coworkers. In addition, individuals' decisions are strongly shaped by the constraints and opportunities in their societal environment, such as monetary expenses, laws, entertainment role models, commercial messages, social forces, and community services. Policy makers in government, business, educational, medical, media, religious, and community organizations can initiate interventions that alter the environment.

A related means of integrating media and interpersonal communication is to organize campaign activities at the community level. Community-based campaigns can engage stakeholders at all stages of process, from contributing design inputs to assisting in implementation to active involvement in consequences; some campaigns explicitly seek to empower communities and activate voluntary associations, government agencies, schools, or businesses to achieve short-term success and help attain sustainability and institutionalization of campaign initiatives. Bracht (2001) describes key stages in organizing community campaigns, including assessing assets and capacities, developing a collaborative organizational structure, generating cooperation of multiple partners and broad citizen participation, and consolidating program maintenance.

A good example is the reformers who refined techniques that combine community organizing and media publicity to advance healthy public policies via *media advocacy* (Wallack & Dorfman, 2001). Through agenda setting on health issues, news coverage can shape the public agenda and the policy agenda pertaining to new initiatives, rules, and laws. An important element involves changing the public's beliefs about the effectiveness of policies and interventions that are advanced, which leads to supportive public opinion (and direct pressure) that can help convince institutional leaders to formulate and implement societal constraints and opportunities.

◆ *Evaluating Campaign Effects and Effectiveness*

To examine the outcomes of a campaign, researchers perform summative evaluation using a variety of methods. Valente (2001) summarizes classical study designs, including field experimental, cross-sectional, cohort, panel, time-series, or event-history designs. This postcampaign research typically measures the audiences that are reached, the effects of the campaign on individual attitudes and behaviors, and the impact on organizations and communities. In addition, investigators may assess cost-effectiveness and attempt to isolate the key factors that determine positive or negative outcomes (e.g., theory *failure* due faulty conceptualization and campaign design vs. *process failure* due to inadequate implementation).

Depending on the intentions of the sponsoring organization, campaigns emphasize differing levels of effectiveness, ranging from individual to societal. Campaigns that seek to change individual-level outcomes focus on knowledge (awareness, salience, familiarity, recall), attitudes (affect, belief, opinion), or behavior (behavioral practice, trial behavior). The preponderance of evaluation data suggests that campaigns are capable of exerting moderate to powerful influences on cognitive outcomes, less influence on attitudinal outcomes, and still less influence on behavioral outcomes (Atkin, 2001; Snyder, 2001). Furthermore, behavioral outcomes tend to vary in proportion to such factors as the dose of information, duration of campaign activities, integration of mass and interpersonal communication systems, and integration of social change strategies (enforcement, education, and engineering).

There are a number of reasons why a campaign may not have a strong impact. Audience resistance barriers arise at each stage of response, from exposure to behavioral implementation. Perhaps the most elemental problem is reaching the audience and attaining attention to the messages. Other key barriers include misperception of susceptibility to negative outcomes, deflection of persuasive appeals, denial of applicability of the target behaviors to the self, rejection of unappealing recommendations, and inertial lethargy. Due to the wide variety of pitfalls, audience members are lost at each stage of message response. The messages may be regarded as offensive, disturbing, boring, stale, preachy, confusing, irritating, misleading, irrelevant, uninformative, useless, unbelievable, or unmotivating. Moreover, insufficient quantitative dissemination may render some of the campaign messages as just plain invisible. Given the many links in the effects chain necessary to lead an individual from initial exposure to sustained behavioral change, it is small wonder that expectations have become modest for the ability of campaigns to effect change.

Organizational- and societal-level outcomes tend to involve alterations in environment factors that produce improvements in society. These types of campaigns are initially evaluated according to progress in implementation of specific policies. The resultant impact on the population is typically examined via summative evaluation of aggregate changes in behavioral patterns to determine how fluctuations correspond to environmental variations.

In addition to engendering desired results that are expected by the sponsoring organizations, campaigns may also induce unanticipated and occasionally unwelcome consequences. These other types of outcomes constitute effects but are not necessarily indicators of campaign effectiveness, as the effects may actually run contrary to the goals of the campaign (Salmon & Murray-Johnson, 2001). For example, boomerang effects occur when a message elicits the opposite reaction intended by the campaign (e.g., forest fire prevention messages depicting spectacular blazes may trigger acts of arson, particularly among sensation seekers).

Salmon and Murray-Johnson (2001) make distinctions among six types of campaign effectiveness: *Definitional effectiveness* is the extent to which stakeholders succeed in having a social phenomenon defined as a social problem (e.g., getting a problem on the public agenda, notably via news media agenda setting); *ideological effectiveness* concerns whether responsibility for a problem is defined as primarily individual or societal; *political effectiveness* is the degree to which a campaign creates visibility or symbolic value for some stakeholder, regardless of other outcome measures; *contextual effectiveness* assesses how much the intervention achieved its goals within a particular context (e.g., education vs. enforcement vs. engineering approaches); *cost-effectiveness* concerns the trade-offs over time between different inputs and outputs (e.g., prevention vs. treatment, addressing certain problems over others); and *programmatic effectiveness* is the familiar concept of assessing a campaign's performance relative to its stated goals and objectives.

## ◆ Looking to the Future: Specificity and Pragmatism

Scholars in various sectors of the communication discipline have yet to define communication campaigns in terms that are sufficiently precise for the development of a system of formal propositions or theory. Consider, for a moment, two interventions that contain the four essential elements of a campaign described above and that are considered classics in the literature of campaign effectiveness: "VD Blues" (Greenberg & Gantz, 2001) and the "Stanford Three Community Study" (Flora, 2001). Although both interventions commonly are referred to as "campaigns" in standard reviews of the literature, they are hardly equivalent as scientific phenomena (see Salmon, 1989,

1992). First, they differ in the *dose* of information disseminated: The first disseminated information through a single television program, whereas the second immersed community residents in a deluge of information from a variety of mutually reinforcing sources. Second, they differ in *duration:* One lasted for 60 minutes, and the other lasted for more than a year. Third, they differ in the degree of *media richness:* One relied on television alone, and the other incorporated multiple media, print, and broadcast. Fourth, they differ in terms of degree of *vertical integration* of communication channels: One relied on mass media only, and the other incorporated interpersonal and organizational communication. Fifth, they differ in terms of degree of *horizontal integration* of approaches to social change: One relied on education (in the form of televised spots), and the other incorporated elements of engineering and enforcement (through innovative delivery systems and construction of social normative influences). Sixth, they differ in terms of *level of analysis:* One focused on individual effects, and the other examined change processes at the level of community. Given this tremendous degree of variance in two elements treated as essentially equivalent in the campaign literature, it is easy to see why scientific generalizations about campaigns tend to be rather tentative and vague and resort to the usual clichés of predicting "moderate" levels of effects.

Most of the published evaluations of campaign effects provide little useful information about which components of the campaign contribute to the impact that is measured. For example, the typical field experiment simply compares treatment communities that receive a full multifaceted campaign intervention with control communities that receive no campaign; this design typically does not permit examination and isolation of "what works."

Future research is needed to determine the following pragmatic issues pertaining to campaign design and resource allocation:

• What is the impact of various quantities of campaign messages? Research should examine the minimum volume of stimuli needed to achieve meaningful effects on key outcomes, and the quantitative point of diminishing returns from larger volumes. With respect to repetition, it would be helpful to know at what point wear-out occurs for a particular message execution.

• What is the optimum mix of message incentives? Most campaigns use multiple persuasive appeals, but little is known about the most effective combination of positive versus negative messages and fear appeals versus other negative appeals.

• What is the best ratio of direct versus indirect messages? Campaigns are increasingly relying on messages targeted to interpersonal influencers and on media advocacy approaches aimed at the general public and policy makers, but the optimum balance among these approaches has not been identified.

• What is the relative impact of various channels and modes of disseminating messages? Specifically, researchers need to assess the cost-effectiveness of paid advertisements versus public service messages, prepared messages versus news publicity versus entertainment inserts, TV versus radio versus print versus Web sites versus secondary media, and mass communication versus personal outreach. Additional research is needed as well to assess unintended effects of communication campaigns (Cho & Salmon, 2007; Guttman & Salmon, 2004). Particularly in the genre of health, campaigns that elicit confusion, anxiety, scapegoating, and stigma may do more harm than good. The potential of such outcomes once again speaks to the need for sophisticated systems of formative and summative research.

The proliferation of communication technologies is rapidly revolutionizing the campaign of the future. Evaluation research is needed to monitor opportunities in the rapidly evolving technological landscape and to assess the expanding potential of new applications for improving campaign effectiveness.

## ◆ Conclusion

Most public communication campaigns have attained rather modest impact due to meager resources, resistant audiences, and limited strategic approaches. Thus, it is advisable for campaigners to seek realistically modest outcomes, especially when attempting to influence fundamental behaviors in the short run. Be prepared for a long haul because many campaigns will take years to achieve and maintain significant impact. More emphasis should be given to relatively attainable impacts, by aiming at more receptive focal segments and by creating or promoting more palatable positive products perceived to have a favorable benefit-cost ratio.

Greater success can be attained if campaigners play to the strengths of the mass media by imparting new knowledge, enhancing salience of a problem or product, teaching new techniques, and stimulating information seeking. The relatively small collection of packaged messages can be augmented by generating publicity and by sensitizing audiences to respond to congruent content available in the media. Quantity can be increased by pursuing monetary resources to enable paid placements and by using creative and political resources to generate free publicity and engineer healthy entertainment portrayals. Finally, the limited direct effects can be overcome by shifting campaign resources to indirect pathways of facilitating and controlling the behavior of the focal segment via interpersonal, organizational, and societal influences. The focal-targeted media messages should be augmented with supplementary education, persuasion, and control, using the media campaign to shape and energize these forces.

The degree of campaign success can be improved if more effective strategies are employed in the future. This chapter has advocated greater diversification of pathways, products, incentives, and channels beyond the approaches conventionally used in campaigns. This approach requires the disciplined development of strategies based on careful analysis of the situation, sensitive application of communication theory, and regular use of evaluation research. The general principles are best implemented by collecting background information about the audiences, pretesting messages to determine potential impact, and measuring outcomes to assess overall effects and isolate key contributing factors. The formulation of a comprehensive strategic plan is needed to effectively integrate the optimum combinations of campaign components that will directly and indirectly influence behaviors. The ideas outlined in this chapter offer some promising approaches for designers to consider in developing media-based campaigns for addressing societal problems.

## ◆ References

Ajzen, I., & Fishbein, M. (1980). *Understanding attitudes and predicting social behavior.* Englewood Cliffs, NJ: Prentice Hall.

Atkin, C. (2001). Theory and principles of media health campaigns. In R. Rice & C. Atkin (Eds.), *Public communication campaigns* (pp. 49–68). Thousand Oaks, CA: Sage.

Atkin, C., & Freimuth, V. (2001). Formative evaluation research in campaign design. In R. Rice & C. Atkin (Eds.), *Public communication campaigns* (pp. 125–145). Thousand Oaks, CA: Sage.

Atkin, C., & Silk, K. (2008). Health communication. In D. Stacks & M. Salwen (Eds.), *An integrated approach to communication theory and research* (2nd ed., pp. 489–453). Hillsdale, NJ: Lawrence Erlbaum.

Atkin, C., & Wallack, L. (1990). *Mass communication and public health: Complexities and conflicts.* Newbury Park, CA: Sage.

Backer, T., Rogers, E., & Sopory, P. (1992). *Designing health communication campaigns: What works?* Newbury Park, CA: Sage.

Bandura, A. (1986). *Social foundations of thought and action: A social cognitive theory.* Englewood Cliffs, NJ: Prentice Hall.

Bracht, N. (Ed.). (1999). *Health promotion at the community level: New advances.* Thousand Oaks, CA: Sage.

Bracht, N. (2001). Community partnership strategies in health campaigns. In R. Rice & C. Atkin (Eds.), *Public communication campaigns* (pp. 323–342). Thousand Oaks, CA: Sage.

Cappella, J., Fishbein, M., Hornik, R., Ahern, R. K., & Sayeed, S. (2001). Using theory to select messages in anti-drug media campaigns: Reasoned action and media priming. In R. Rice & C. Atkin (Eds.), *Public communication campaigns* (pp. 214–230). Thousand Oaks, CA: Sage.

Cho, H., & Salmon, C. T. (2007). Unintended effects of health communication campaigns. *Journal of Communication, 57,* 293–317.

Dervin, B., & Frenette, M. (2001). Applying sense-making methodology: Communicating communicatively with audiences as listeners, learners, teachers, confidantes. In R. Rice & C. Atkin (Eds.), *Public communication campaigns* (pp. 69–87). Thousand Oaks, CA: Sage.

Eagly, A., & Chaiken, S. (1993). *Psychology of attitudes.* New York: Harcourt, Brace Jovanovich.

Flora, J. (2001). The Stanford community studies: Campaigns to reduce cardiovascular disease. In R. Rice & C. Atkin (Eds.), *Public communication campaigns* (pp. 193–213). Thousand Oaks, CA: Sage.

Greenberg, B., & Gantz, W. (2001). Singing the (VD) blues. In R. Rice & C. Atkin (Eds.), *Public communication campaigns* (pp. 269–272). Thousand Oaks, CA: Sage.

Guttman, N., & Salmon, C. T. (2004). Guilt, fear, stigma and knowledge gaps: Ethical issues in public health communication interventions. *Bioethics, 18,* 531–552.

Hale, J., & Dillard, J. (1995). Fear appeals in health promotion: Too much, too little or just right? In E. Maibach & R. Parrott (Eds.), *Designing health messages: Approaches from communication theory and public health practice* (pp. 65–80). Newbury Park, CA: Sage.

Hornik, R. (2002). *Public health communication.* Mahwah, NJ: Lawrence Erlbaum.

Kotler, P., Roberto N., & Lee, N. (2002). *Social marketing: Improving the quality of life.* Thousand Oaks, CA: Sage.

Kreuter, M., Farrell, D., Olevitch, L., & Brennan, L. (1999). *Tailoring health messages.* Mahwah, NJ: Lawrence Erlbaum.

Lieberman, D. (2001). Using interactive media in communication campaigns for children and adolescents. In R. Rice & C. Atkin (Eds.), *Public communication campaigns* (pp. 373–388). Thousand Oaks, CA: Sage.

Lieberman, D. (2006). What can we learn from playing interactive games? In P. Vorderer & J. Bryant (Eds.), *Playing video games: Motives, responses, and consequences* (pp. 379–397). Mahwah, NJ: Lawrence Erlbaum.

Maibach, E., & Parrott, R. (1995). *Designing health messages: Approaches from communication theory and public health practice.* Thousand Oaks, CA: Sage.

McGuire, W. (1994). Using mass media communication to enhance public health. In L. Sechrest, T. Backer, E. Rogers, T. Campbell, & M. Grady (Eds.), *Effective dissemination of clinical health information* (AHCPR Pub. No. 95-0015, pp. 125–151). Rockville, MD: Public Health Service, Agency for Health Care Policy and Research.

Palmgreen, P., Donohew, L., & Harrington, N. (2001). Sensation seeking in anti-drug campaign and message design. In R. E. Rice & C. K. Atkin (Eds.), *Public communication campaigns* (pp. 300–304). Thousand Oaks, CA: Sage.

Petty, R., & Cacioppo, J. (1986). *Communication and persuasion: Central and peripheral routes to attitude change.* New York: Springer-Verlag.

Prochaska, J., & Velicer, W. (1997). The transtheoretical model of health behavior change. *American Journal of Health Promotion, 12,* 38–48.

Rhodes, J., Spencer, R., Saito, R., & Sipe, C. (2006). Online mentoring: The promise and challenges of an emerging approach to youth development. *Journal of Primary Prevention, 27,* 497–513.

Rice, R. (2006). Influences, usage, and outcomes of Internet health information searching: Multivariate results from the Pew surveys. *International Journal of Medical Informatics, 75,* 8–28.

Rice, R., & Atkin, C. (2009). Public communication campaigns: Theoretical principles and practical applications. In J. Bryant & M. Oliver (Eds.), *Media effects: Advances in theory and research* (3rd ed., pp. 435–457). Hillsdale, NJ: Lawrence Erlbaum.

Rimal, R. N., & Adkins, A. D. (2003). Using computers to narrowcast health messages: The role of audience segmentation, targeting, and tailoring in health promotion. In

T. L. Thompson, A. M. Dorsey, K. I. Miller, & R. Parrott (Eds.), *Handbook of health communication* (pp. 497–513). Mahwah, NJ: Lawrence Erlbaum.

Rogers, E. (2003). *Diffusion of innovations* (5th ed.). New York: Free Press.

Rogers, E., & Storey, D. (1987). Communication campaigns. In C. Berger & S. Chaffee (Eds.), *Handbook of communication science* (pp. 817–846). Newbury Park, CA: Sage.

Salmon, C. (1989). *Information campaigns: Balancing social values and social change.* Newbury Park, CA: Sage.

Salmon, C. (1992). Building theory "of" and "for" communication campaigns: An essay on ideology and public policy. In S. A. Deetz (Ed.), *Communication yearbook 15* (pp. 312–345). Newbury Park, CA: Sage.

Salmon, C., & Atkin, C. (2003). Media campaigns for health promotion. In T. Thompson, A. Dorsey, K. Miller, & R. Parrott (Eds.), *Handbook of health communication* (pp. 472–494). Hillsdale, NJ: Lawrence Erlbaum.

Salmon, C., & Jason, J. (1992). A system for evaluating the use of media in CDC's National AIDS Information and Education Program. *Public Health Reports, 106,* 639–645.

Salmon, C., & Murray-Johnson, L. (2001). Communication campaign effectiveness. In R. Rice & C. Atkin (Eds.), *Public communication campaigns* (pp. 168–180). Thousand Oaks, CA: Sage.

Singhal, A., Cody, M., Rogers, E., & Sabido, M. (2004). *Entertainment-education and social change: History, research, and practice.* Mahwah, NJ: Lawrence Erlbaum.

Slater, M. (1999). Integrating application of media effects, persuasion, and behavior change theories to communication campaigns: A stages-of-change framework. *Health Communication, 11,* 335–354.

Snyder, L. (2001). How effective are mediated health campaigns? In R. Rice & C. Atkin (Eds.), *Public communication campaigns* (pp. 181–190). Thousand Oaks, CA: Sage.

Valente, T. (2001). Evaluating communication campaigns. In R. Rice & C. Atkin (Eds.), *Public communication campaigns* (pp. 125–145). Thousand Oaks, CA: Sage.

Wallack, L., & Dorfman, L. (2001). Putting policy into health communication: The role of media advocacy. In R. Rice & C. Atkin (Eds.), *Public communication campaigns* (pp. 389–401). Thousand Oaks, CA: Sage.

# 25

# POLITICAL COMMUNICATION

◆ William L. Benoit and R. Lance Holbert

Lazarsfeld and colleagues' work on the 1940 and 1948 U.S. presidential elections focused on how citizens made vote choices (Berelson, Lazarsfeld, & McPhee, 1954; Lazarsfeld, Berelson, & Gaudet, 1948). This project had a profound impact on the study of political communication. Two key elements of it were the limited-effects model and the relationship between mass media and interpersonal communication (in particular, the two-step flow of communication). The former holds that the mass media have little impact on public opinion. The latter argues that political information in the media is consumed largely by opinion leaders, and these opinion leaders act as mediators between media and the broader public. Thus, the impact of media is relatively small and largely indirect, with the direct effects of communication in a political context firmly rooted in interpersonal communication (Katz & Lazarsfeld, 1955). This chapter focuses on responses to the limited-effects model (agenda setting, priming, and framing; see Nabi & Oliver, Chapter 15, this volume) and political discussion (including the two-step flow).

## ◆ Background

Lazarsfeld and his colleagues focused on human decision making, primarily vote choice and attitude change (Sheingold, 1973). Although, as Chaffee and Hochheimer (1985) pointed out, the Lazarsfeld studies point to media as a potentially important source of political information for voters, their focus on attitude and behavioral change led the Columbia researchers to argue that media have only small, indirect effects on voter decision-making processes through opinion leaders. Out of this model came the broader limited-effects approach to communication research that dominated the field for several decades (Klapper, 1960).

The limited-effects purview, as used in political communication research over the past several decades, represents an "upper-middle-range" theory, a type of theory important for its organizing power (Chaffee & Berger, 1987). One of the keys to any theory of the middle range is replication and the building of empirical statements over time. Replication is central to social science research and provides greater certainty about the true nature of a relationship being studied (Rosenthal, 1991). Holbert, Benoit, Hansen, and Wen (2002) argue that replication is not well established in modern-day political communication research, and the lack of replication has weakened our understanding of fundamental political communication processes.

The introduction of graduate programs in mass communication, many housed in journalism schools, thwarted the hegemony of the Lazarsfeld paradigm (Delia, 1987). New theory was introduced that envisioned the role of the press and elections in very different terms from Lazarsfeld (e.g., McCombs & Shaw, 1972). For example, the argument underlying agenda setting is that political communication needs to shine its empirical lens earlier along the hierarchy of effects (see McGuire, 1989)—toward awareness, information processing, and salience—and away from the latter stages of attitudes and behavior. Although, as Katz (1987) argues, this "alternative institutional paradigm" was not a radical departure from the limited-effects model, this type of research opened the eyes of the discipline to the possibility of sizable media influence in the political realm (Johnston, Hagen, & Jamieson, 2000).

Political communication scholarship still wrestles with the fundamental question of whether political campaigns influence election outcomes (e.g., Holbrook, 1996). Significant roadblocks remain in place for the case that elections matter, and many of those impediments can be traced to the Lazarsfeld tradition. Political communication research is conducted primarily in two fields, communication and political science. When viewed from the perspective of the individual scholar, both communication scholars (see Katz, 1987) and political science scholars (e.g., Zaller, 1996) have made arguments against the limited-effects model. However, when viewed from the macro level of the field, the communication discipline has made greater strides away from the Lazarsfeld tradition than has political science. Support for this argument can be found in a comparison of the national data sets that define the two fields and the level of political communication scholarship found in the two fields' top journals.

The American National Election Studies (ANES), produced by the University of Michigan, the cornerstone data for the study of political science, remain bereft of well-structured communication variables. Recent work by Althaus and Tewksbury (2007) on a 2006 ANES pilot study to create a new set of media use survey measures may aid in overcoming ANES's political communication weaknesses that have been evident since the 1980s. However, the introduction of the National Annenberg Election Studies (NAES) through the Annenberg School for Communication at the University of Pennsylvania is a more immediate remedy for the ANES data limitations. The Annenberg study designs are communication driven, and several surveys focus on communication events (e.g., debates and political party conventions; Romer, Kenski, Winneg, Adasiewicz, & Jamieson, 2006). The Annenberg data sets have been useful for understanding a wide range of important political communication dynamics in elections (e.g., Kenski & Stroud, 2006; Young, 2006).

As Bennett and Manheim (2006) state, "Political science has been slow to develop a robust agenda of work on media and politics" (p. 220). A recent survey of the 2000–2003 political communication literatures validates this assertion (Graber & Smith, 2005). Although flagship journals in political science publish a relatively small percentage of articles devoted to political communication (e.g., *American Political Science Review*, 4.8%; *American Journal of Political Science*, 9%), flagship journals in communication devote significant percentages of work to political communication (e.g., *Journal of Communication*, 20%; *Journalism & Mass Communication Quarterly*, 30%). Communication has developed a robust agenda of work on media and politics and leads the study of political communication as a whole.

One of the most important consequences of the limited-effects model is to encourage scholars to vary the foci of their theoretical and empirical lenses, looking at points earlier in the process than ultimate behavior (voting) or attitudes toward a candidate or political party. Specifically, we focus the remainder of this chapter on several concepts that attempt to understand campaign effects other than voting or attitudes toward candidates or parties: agenda setting, priming, framing, the two-step flow of communication, and political discussion.

## ◆ Agenda Setting

We begin with an important assumption: Humans have limited cognitive capacity (Miller, 1956). They cannot remember every bit of information they encounter or every inference they draw. Nor can they keep all related cognitions in short-term memory when they process newly acquired information or make decisions. Downs (1957) argued that some people have little incentive to expend effort to gather and process information about a political campaign simply to improve their vote choice. Specifically, he opined, "It may be rational for a man to delegate part or all of his political decision-making to others, no matter how important it is that he make correct decisions" (p. 233). These "others" may take the form of a valued family member, a community opinion leader, a political pundit, a political candidate, or a political party. As James (1890/1983) observed, "My thinking is first and last and always for the sake of my doing, and I can only do one thing at a time" (pp. 959–960). People turn to others through face-to-face communication and various forms of mass communication to aid their political decision-making processes. These acts of delegation are grounded in a pragmatism (Fiske, 1992) that puts into perspective the role of politics relative to the other aspects of one's life (i.e., family, friends, work, hobbies). However, this process of delegation lends importance to the study of political communication in general and the potential influence of mass communication for how a citizenry functions within a democracy in particular.

Lazarsfeld and Merton (1948/1960) recognized that the mass media can "confer status on public issues, persons, organizations, and social movements." Cohen (1963) stated the basic idea of agenda setting when he wrote that the press "may not be successful much of the time in telling people what to think, but it is stunningly successful in telling its readers what to think about" (p. 13). In 1972, McCombs and Shaw coined the phrase *agenda setting* to describe this idea and outlined a theory about a process of salience transfer, predicting a positive relationship between the frequency of the discussion of a concept in the mass media and the public's perception of the importance of that concept: Increased presence of a topic in the news is expected to increase salience for the public. They reported a strong, statistically significant positive relationship between the number of times a topic (such as foreign policy) was mentioned in news articles, editorials, and broadcast news stories and the importance of that issue to undecided voters. The mass media may not have told those voters what to think about foreign policy, but the media did tell them that they should be thinking about foreign policy.

Since then, considerable research has investigated agenda setting (see McCombs, 2005). Wanta and Ghanem (2007) conducted a meta-analysis of this research, concluding that "these results show how wide ranging the agenda-setting influence of the news is. . . . Significant agenda-setting effects were found for studies using a variety of methodologies" (p. 46). A competing explanation for agenda-setting effects is that the public importance of a topic and news coverage of that topic are both related to events in the world related to that issue. However, McCombs (2004) pointed to research establishing that the news coverage of a topic and the public importance of an issue cannot be assumed to stem from circumstances in the world (e.g., stories about crime are related to importance of crime, but neither is strongly related to the actual incidence of crime). Agenda setting is one of the few political communication theories that has received worldwide attention and verification through empirical studies conducted around the globe (see Weaver, McCombs, & Shaw, 2004). Political communication through the media plays an important role in determining which public policy issues are salient to citizens.

Recent scholarship has extended the basic idea of agenda setting to the related question of which factors influence the media's agenda (McCombs, 2004). The sources of the media agenda include political campaigns, political parties, various branches of government, and public relations agencies (see Weaver et al., 2004). Agenda-setting research has also begun to investigate attribute agenda setting, or second-level agenda setting (McCombs, 2004). The idea here is that the characteristics attributed to a person, situation, or event can transfer from the media to become salient within public opinion (e.g., characterizing Senator John F. Kerry [D-MA] as a "flip-flopper" during the 2004 U.S. presidential election). The development of second-level agenda setting means that this area of research has come full circle, arguing that the mass media can, after all, influence attitudes (what to think based on negative vs. positive attributes) as well as issue importance (what to think about). Kiousis and McCombs (2004) have offered empirical support for the claim that attitude strength can serve as a mediator of the relationship between media salience and public salience and that attitude formation and change should no longer be assumed to be an outcome of salience transfer. Additional empirical work— most important, the use of experimental methods—needs to be undertaken to better address some of these core causal issues. Nonetheless, one can state with confidence that an important effect of the mass media is to influence the agenda, or the perceived importance of issues for the public. Research on second-level agenda setting is also beginning to debunk the limited-effects thesis that the media are not capable of influencing attitudes. Indeed, the issue of the role of attitudes relative to the process of salience transfer has received newfound attention within the field.

Agenda setting is vital as a response to the minimal-effects theories. It is possible that the mass media do not significantly affect attitudes or voter intentions (although as we have noted, substantial challenges have arisen to minimal effects), but there is no question that the media can affect judgments of salience through the agenda-setting process. Furthermore, we argue that the basic idea of salience transfer underlines the idea of media priming. Whereas Price and Tewksbury (1995) argue that "agenda setting—commonly thought to be a kind of basic media effect upon which priming depends—is actually but one particular variant of priming, which is itself a far more general effect" (pp. 7–8, as quoted by Weaver et al., 2004, p. 266), we see the process of influence outlined in agenda setting as the more basic and general effect relative to priming.

# ◆ Priming

Roskos-Ewoldsen, Roskos-Ewoldsen, and Carpentier (2002) explain that "priming refers to the effect of some preceding stimulus or event on how we react, broadly defined, to some subsequent stimulus" (p. 97). Again, limitations on human information processing mean that every piece of information cannot be equally important in decision making. Scheufele (2000) argues that agenda setting and priming are both based on salience transfer, or accessibility of concepts in memory:

> Both agenda-setting and priming are based on the assumption of attitude accessibility and, in particular, a memory-based model of information processing. Mass media can influence the salience of certain issues as perceived by the audience; that is, the ease with which these issues can be retrieved from memory. (p. 300)

So, priming builds on the idea of salience transfer developed in agenda setting. We want to note that some discussions of media priming reference ideas on priming from social psychology. However, the priming effect outlined in cognitive and social psychology is clearly not the same type of priming effect outlined in political communication (see Roskos-Ewoldsen et al., 2002). For example, Roskos-Ewoldsen, Klinger, and Roskos-Ewoldsen (2007) illustrate the nature of priming from a psychology perspective with a lexical decision task (Meyers & Schvaneveldt, 1971). Participants were asked to decide whether a series of letters was a word or not. When *nurse* preceded *doctor*, participants were able to recognize that *doctor* was a word much faster than when *doctor* was preceded by an unrelated word such as *bread*. Thus, being primed with one word (*nurse*) activated related words in memory, allowing a subsequent word (*doctor*) to be recognized more quickly than without the prime. However, Roskos-Ewoldsen et al. (2007) observe that the priming effect of words has a very limited duration (around

700 milliseconds). The salience transfer in agenda setting and priming outlined in political communication scholarship exists over a much longer time period (e.g., 24 hours or more; Krosnick & Kinder, 1990), so we argue that the salience transfer process identified in agenda setting is a better model for understanding media priming in the context of political communication than the concept of priming in social psychology.

Priming is important because it can concern the criteria people employ to make political judgments: "By calling attention to some matters while ignoring others, television news influences the standards by which governments, presidents, policies, and candidates for public office are judged" (Iyengar & Kinder, 1987, p. 63, emphasis omitted). Meta-analysis has established that there is "a small but significant effect of media primes on subsequent judgments or behavior" (Roskos-Ewoldsen et al., 2007, p. 65). Thus, research confirms that priming is a process that can influence people's judgments.

To illustrate how salience transfer (agenda setting) can serve the basis for media priming, consider Petrocik's theory of issue ownership. Petrocik (1996) argues that over time, the two major political parties in America have come to be associated with particular sets of issues: Republicans are thought to "own," or be better able to handle, such issues as taxes and foreign policy, whereas Democrats, in contrast, are believed to be better able to deal with such issues as education or the environment. Presidential candidates are likely to emphasize, through the mass media (e.g., news, advertising, debates, direct mail), the issues owned by their own political party more than candidates from the opposing party. Research has confirmed that in fact Republicans tend to stress Republican issues more and Democratic issues less than Democrats (Petrocik, Benoit, & Hansen, 2003–2004). This differential issue emphasis on Democratic and Republican issues matters because of the agenda-setting effect: The issues stressed most often by presidential candidates, who are key sources for the media agenda, are likely to become more important to voters. In other words, salience transfer from the presidential candidates' messages to the public's agenda occurs through their influence on the media agenda and the ability of the media agenda to affect the public's agenda. Petrocik et al. (2003–2004) explain that "candidates campaign on issues that confer an advantage in order to prime their salience in the decision calculus of the voters" (p. 599). Petrocik (1996) shows that the party that is able to make its issues salient to the public has a better chance of winning the election. So, according to issue ownership theory, presidential candidates tend to stress the issues owned by their own party, making those issues more salient to voters through media (i.e., agenda setting) and leading citizens to vote (i.e., make judgments) for candidates who are thought better at handling the problems that are most important to a given voter (i.e., long-term priming). Furthermore, priming is another argument against the limited-effects model.

## ◆ Framing

Goffman (1974) defines frames as "schemata of interpretation" (p. 20). Gamson and Modigliani (1987) explain that a frame is "a central organizing idea that provides meaning to an unfolding strip of events" (p. 143). Tversky and Kahneman's (1981) prospect theory was one influence on framing theory. Participants were given one of two sets of logically identical choices (e.g., save 72% from dying or allow 28% to die). When the choices were described as gains, people tended to be risk aversive; when the same choices were characterized as losses, people were more likely to take risks. So, frames are viewpoints or perspectives that influence how we understand events, people, or ideas in the world—and which can affect the choices we make. There are many ways one can interpret the world and the people,

events, and ideas within it. However, again, limits on human cognitive capacity mean we cannot use all possible perspectives to understand the world. In short, frames are inevitable—and the particular perspective or frame we employ is consequential.

Iyengar (1991) focused on two alternate frames, episodic and thematic: "The episodic news frame takes the form of a case study or event-oriented report and depicts public issues in terms of concrete instances. . . . The thematic frame, by contrast, places policy issues in some more general or abstract context" (p. 14). Popkin (1994, p. 87) identifies other frames that can operate during presidential campaigns, including portraying an incumbent president who is seeking a second term as either a candidate or a president; any candidate can be discussed in terms of his or her record in office or the type of person he or she is. Another type of frame that is potentially quite powerful is a metaphor: Lakoff (2002) outlines an argument about how Democrats and liberals communicate and ultimately think about "government as nurturing parent," whereas Republicans and conservatives communicate and think about "government as strict father." Notice in these examples, frames are operationalized as choices or contrasts: episodic or thematic, candidate or president, record or character, strict or nurturing. Frames are a point of view, and as such, alternate points of view are available for characterizing people, events, or ideas.

Frames can be important because, as Entman (1993) notes, they can "promote a particular problem definition, causal interpretation, moral evaluation, and/or treatment recommendation for the item described" (p. 52, emphasis omitted). Iyengar (1991) argues that choice of frame matters because "episodic framing tends to elicit individualistic rather than societal attributions of responsibility, while thematic framing has the opposite effect" (Iyengar, 1991, pp. 15–16). Similarly, people may evaluate a person and his or her actions differently if he or she is characterized as a "candidate" (who might say anything to get elected) or as a "president" (who is the leader of our nation).

Scheufele (2000) groups agenda setting and priming together and distinguishes them from framing:

> Agenda-setting and priming rely on the notion of attitude accessibility. . . . Framing, in contrast, is based on the concept of prospect theory; that is, on the assumption that subtle changes in the wording of the description of a situation might affect how audience members interpret this situation. In other words, framing influences how audiences think about issues, not by making aspects of the issue more salient, but by invoking interpretive schemas that influence the interpretation of incoming information.

As our analysis above indicates, we agree that agenda setting and priming are both based on salience or accessibility. However, we argue that priming and framing have an important commonality: Both are concerned with how cognitions (a prime, a frame) influence interpretation of the world and the people, events, and ideas in it. The principal difference between priming and framing appears to be one of complexity: A prime can be relatively simple—a person, an event, a topic. In contrast, frames have been conceptualized as a viewpoint or perspective, a way to understand the relationships between people and events in the world. Frames can include metaphors (as mentioned above), narratives (e.g., Fisher, 1987), or even fantasy themes (Bormann, 1972), which can influence interpretation of the world and events in it. Although most scholars do not stress salience when discussing framing (Chong & Druckman, 2007, are an exception), arguably, a frame presented in the media must have some salience, or it cannot survive long enough in memory to have much influence on interpretation. Thus, we are not willing to agree that salience (accessibility) is unrelated to framing. Instead, it is important to understand how basic agenda setting, priming,

and framing processes complement one another in producing democratic outcomes. Ultimately, theory building and testing should be able to bring all three of these areas of political communication under a single process of influence. It is important to study the individual processes, but our focus should also remain ever vigilant on how to seek to unite these theoretical foundations because each is at work in how elites, various social institutions, and the general population engage one another in our basic democratic processes.

## ◆ Two-Step Flow of Communication

Katz (1987) provides the most systematic summary of the communication field's critiques of the Lazarsfeld two-step flow model (i.e., limited-effects tradition): institutional, critical, and technological paradigms. The institutional paradigm is best reflected in McCombs's (2004, 2005) work on agenda setting. It is the most empirical and least radical of the critiques. Chaffee and Hochheimer's (1985) discussion of viewing political communication outlets as the providers of information (i.e., journalistic perspective) rather than as the initiator of attitude/behavioral change (i.e., marketing perspective) falls within this paradigm, and there is a rich tradition of research that has come out of this perspective (e.g., Hansen & Benoit, 2007). In particular, work by Eveland and colleagues has focused on better understanding some of the core processes at work in the influence of a variety of political communication forms on political knowledge (e.g., Eveland, Hayes, Shah, & Kwak, 2005; Eveland, Marton, & Seo, 2004). Although advances have been made in the study of the relationship between various forms of political communication and knowledge, this area of study is still wrestling with some of its most fundamental causal issues (e.g., Eveland et al., 2005).

The second paradigm—critical—is best reflected in the work of Gitlin (1978), who argues that the limited-effects model has "drained attention from the power of the media to define normal and abnormal social and political activity, to say what is politically real and legitimate and what is not" (p. 205). Additional classic works in this paradigm include Herman and Chomsky (1988) and McChesney (2000).

The third paradigm, the technological, is grounded in the work of McLuhan (1964) and his technological determinist framework. McLuhan argued that it is the form of our communication outlets (e.g., television vs. radio) that produces effects, not the content being provided through those forms of communication. The types of effects outlined by McLuhan and others in this research tradition exist across levels (but primarily macro in orientation), and they are unintended and large (e.g., Meyrowitz, 1994). This research tradition has been influential in the study of communication in general (e.g., Meyrowitz, 1985) and political communication in particular (Pfau, 1988). Each of the three paradigms criticizes Lazarsfeld, the two-step flow model, and the limited-effects paradigm, albeit from different epistemological perspectives, and argues that media can have a profound influence on a political system.

Bennett and Manheim (2006) recently offered another critique of the two-step flow of communication, arguing that modern communication campaigns are representative of a one-step flow of communication. This argument is unique in that it is not reflective of an epistemological or methodological shift (i.e., critical and technological paradigms) or a shifting in perspective away from an approach to campaigns as persuasion to campaigns as knowledge acquisition (i.e., alternative institutional paradigm). Instead, Bennett and Manheim advocate a marketing perspective, arguing that "the underlying relations between individuals, society, sources, and messages are, indeed, changing

in ways that suggest the need to formulate a new communication paradigm" (p. 217). In short, Bennett and Manheim argue that the two-step flow of communication is bounded by time, representative of a specific era that has now passed with the formation of a new media environment.

This most recent critique of the two-step flow of communication centers on changes in society, communication technologies, and individual communication habits (Bennett & Manheim, 2006). Societal changes mean that individuals are no longer as involved in group activities as in the past (Putnam, 2000), have much more control over their new digital information worlds (Tedesco, 2004), and function within multiple self-expression networks loosely defined as being reflective of lifestyle groups (e.g., Englis & Solomon, 1995). As far as technological change, many of Bennett and Manheim's (2006) arguments reflect Chaffee and Metzger's (2001) basic point that "new media are cracking the foundations of our conception of mass communication" (p. 369). Chaffee and Metzger argue that we should discard the term *mass communication*, with all its connotations, and adopt the new term of *media communication* to reflect our new media environment. Finally, as far as individual communication habits, Bennett and Manheim stress concepts such as mobility and audience members acting as not only receivers of information but also senders and creators of messages for instant mass distribution through the World Wide Web (Rheingold, 2002). Each of these changes signals a shift away from a two-step flow of media influence and toward a one-step process.

However, the one-step flow of communication, as outlined by Bennett and Manheim (2006), has as much (or more) to do with the sender of the message as the receiver. In essence, the one-step flow of communication stems from the providers of mass communication messages adapting to the new communication environments of the audience member. Bennett and Manheim argue that "the communication process [in today's media environment] is aimed at the individual or at the direct messaging of assembled networks of like demographics" (p. 215). Extending this point, Bennett and Manheim state that "to the extent that communicators are effective in achieving this objective, they will, for all practical purposes, have substituted their own audience selection and targeting skills for the role formerly assigned to peer group interaction" (pp. 215–216). These means of content distribution, in coordination with how audience members take in and use these messages, "replace the social interaction component of the two-step flow" (p. 216). This leaves us with a one-step flow of communication.

A key concept in this argument is lifestyle. More important, the notion of targeting lifestyle serves as the most direct assault on the two-step flow of communication because it is a concept that is central to Lazarsfeld's turf, marketing. Our lifestyles define our patterns of consumption, and marketing focuses on influencing consumption patterns (e.g., Michman & Mazze, 2006). Modern politics is about communicating a lifestyle and seeking to connect to voters who currently function within that lifestyle or aspire to live that lifestyle in the future. In short, politics is lifestyle and lifestyle is consumption, so politics is consumption (i.e., citizen-consumers; see Shah, McLeod, Friedland, & Nelson, 2007). Indeed, this approach to the study of communicating politics is based on a marketing perspective: As Shah et al. (2007) argue, "Political campaigns are now grounded in marketing principles, with branding of political candidates and issues, targeted political advertising, staged media events, and market segmentation strategies all commonplace" (p. 8).

The development of candidate, party, or issue as brand is where we most directly witness the marketing of politics as lifestyle. A brand embodies the characteristics that make one attitude object stand out and distinguish itself from other attitude objects that it is competing with in a competitive

marketplace (Keller & Lehmann, 2006). A brand consists of both a physiological dimension (i.e., brand tangibles) and a psychological dimension (i.e., brand intangibles; Levy, 1999). The physiological dimension is what the attitude object can do for the potential consumer, while the psychological dimension is what that attitude object *means* to the potential consumer. Public policy issues and candidates are now fully marketed as brands. Once more, specific consumer-citizens are targeted based on lifestyle to potentially connect to a brand. The ability of political campaign professionals to identify, target, and connect with multiple subpopulations as reflective of lifestyles defines the benchmarks for the effectiveness of modern political campaigns. Political campaigning is moving away from a focus on the public as mass and is increasingly moving toward a focus on a series of subpopulations that candidates' campaigns or advocacy groups feel they can connect with to garner enough support to achieve a specific goal (e.g., win an election, get a bill passed into law). This is what Bennett (1998) calls "the trend toward strategically targeted demographic communication" (p. 756).

This approach to the study of political campaigns is grounded in strategic communication, as rightfully identified by Bennett (1998). As a result, political communication scholars who take this approach can work from research in the marketing, advertising, and public relations fields on the concept of integrated marketing communication (IMC; see Kitchen, Brignell, Li, & Jones, 2004). Kitchen et al. (2004) stress that an IMC approach steps away from viewing campaigns from an inside-out approach, where messages are created inside an organization (e.g., campaign) and then pushed out at an audience. Instead, IMC is reflective of an outside-in approach, where strategic communicators take their leads from potential consumers and then form persuasive messages based on what the potential audience offers in terms of tastes, lifestyle, and receptivity. Like Lazarsfeld, this approach to the study of political campaigns is grounded in marketing. However, it is not the type of marketing of the Lazarsfeld era that established the two-step flow as a model of communication influence.

With this stated, an empirical question that is central to the Bennett and Manheim (2006) argument has not been formally addressed in extant political communication literature. The Bennett and Manheim argument is predicated on the assumption that professional political strategists are effective in isolating and connecting to various lifestyle subpopulations to such a degree as to displace the social interaction dynamics that define the two-step flow. We quite simply do not know if professional political communicators have achieved this level of effectiveness, and as a result, there needs to be formal political communication research on this very important empirical question. Until this known-unknown becomes more of a known-known, we will not be able to state definitively whether we can call a close to the two-step flow communication era and usher in the one-step communication flow era. In addition, there has been very little work completed on the rise of political operatives as a professional class. Much like the study of journalists as a professional class (e.g., Gans, 1979), there needs to be more systematic research conducted on the rise of the political communication campaign professional. We need to understand better the culture of this group, its norms, its goals, its practices, and its techniques. Political communication research needs to continue to adapt to the changing nature of the political communication environment, and formal research on the professional political communication class has become essential to understanding political campaigns.

## ◆ Political Discussion

The importance of interpersonal political communication emerged from the Lazarsfeld

tradition and remains central to the study of political communication (Kim, Wyatt, & Katz, 1999). Indeed, political discussion is seen as central to the processes of public opinion formation and change (Price, 1992). The role of political discussion networks is well established in the political communication literature (e.g., Huckfeldt & Sprague, 1995) and has received tremendous attention recently (e.g., Beck, Dalton, Greene, & Huckfeldt, 2002). Building directly from the Lazarsfeld tradition, recent research continues to explore the relationships between political talk and how it relates to both old media (e.g., McLeod, Scheufele, & Moy, 1999) and new media (e.g., Nisbett & Scheufele, 2004) in producing a range of democratic outcomes. In addition, this work remains focused on the concept of opinion leader as it relates to basic communicative processes that serve as a foundation for democracy (e.g., Shah & Scheufele, 2006). In short, although well-established research traditions break free of Lazarsfeld and colleagues, many of the same processes and concepts identified by these researchers several decades ago remain a central focus for today's communication research agenda.

The study of deliberation has become firmly situated in the field of communication (e.g., Price, Cappella, & Nir, 2002), and the single scholar who has served to push this area of study forward is Jürgen Habermas (see Communication Theory, special issue, November 2007). As Huspek (2007) argues, "Fundamental to the deliberative model are demanding communicative processes that must necessarily be in play if political decisions and courses of action are to earn legitimacy" (p. 329). Although a great deal is asked of democratic citizens in a deliberative framework, Habermas (2006) insists that the study of deliberation (at all levels) is a necessary but not sufficient condition for understanding democracy. Once more, deliberation matters relative to election outcomes. As Habermas (2006) states, "Voters do not 'naturally' grow up out of the soil of civil society. Before they pass the formal threshold of campaigns and general elections, they are shaped by the confused din of voices rising from both everyday talk and mediated communication" (p. 417). Discourse does not simply exist as interpersonal communication and among the general public. Deliberation also exists in mass communication. This point is brought to light in Zaller's (1992) R-A-S (receive, accept, sample) model of public opinion formation and change. Zaller claims that central to public opinion is the nature of elite discourse (one-sided vs. two-sided), how this elite discourse and deliberation is made available to the public through media, and then how this elite discourse is accepted and integrated by the general public.

The study of deliberation is best defined as being driven by a meta-concept, rather than formal theory. Deliberation is defined as being a host of activities involving an ever-expansive range of political discourse (Pan, Shen, Paek, & Sun, 2006). The only bounds established for defining deliberation derive from a series of normative criteria: "inclusion, equality, justice, publicity, and reason" (Pan et al., 2006, p. 316). Indeed, normative boundaries and normative concerns are central to this area of research (e.g., Guttman, 2007). Although a great many scholars stress the importance of "talk" in producing quality democratic processes (see Bohman & Rehg, 1997), questions have been raised about whether the study and improved practice of deliberation can serve to resolve all of democracy's ills (e.g., Schudson, 1997). Deliberation scholars study processes of influence (e.g., McLeod, Scheufele, Moy, Horowitz, et al., 1999), but a key question is whether the present study of process equates to formal theory building. It is clear that deliberation is connected to other meta-concepts such as community (e.g., Shah, McLeod, & Yoon, 2001) and that this area of research is dealing with an important set of relationships that speak to core democratic issues. However, formal social scientific deliberation theory needs to be constructed if this area of research is to continue to gain momentum within the communication sciences.

While on the topic of theory building in relation to the meta-concept of deliberation, there appears to be a disconnect between the study of political or democratic deliberation and formal interpersonal communication theories that exists in the broader extant communication literatures. For example, Moy and Gastil (2006) argue that "deliberative conversations embrace conflict" (p. 445). A number of interpersonal and organizational communication theories deal squarely with the issue of conflict. Roloff (1987) provides an expansive summary of the study of communication and conflict. In addition, more recent communication research on conflict in an interpersonal context (e.g., Keck & Samp, 2007; see Ellis, Chapter 17, this volume; Sillars, Chapter 16, this volume) offers a rich theoretical tradition in interpersonal com-munication that may aid the study of conflict within a political deliberation context. Although deliberation focuses on the study of conflict, there is a surprising chasm between this research and interpersonal or organizational communication theories that pertain to the study of conflict. In short, the study of political deliberation may not need to reinvent the wheel as it begins to shift from the study of a meta-concept to formal theory building.

The study of deliberation is not just about conflict. It is also about the process by which people with diverse interests and needs come together to understand one another, work out potential differences, and seek to come to a consensus about who they are as a collective and establishing courses of action to deal with matters that are affecting their shared community (McLeod, Scheufele, Moy, Horowitz, et al., 1999). For example, there is little question that the issue of uncertainty exists in citizens as they seek to engage a range of deliberative processes. Uncertainty reduction theory (URT; see Berger & Calabrese, 1975) has been applied in a number of contexts, from physician-patient interactions (e.g., Sheer & Cline, 1995) to long-distance dating relationships (e.g., Maguire, 2007). URT has also been applied to the study of political mass communication effects (e.g., Boyle et al., 2004) but can also easily be applied to political communication dynamics involving more traditional forms of interpersonal and group deliberation. There is no question that uncertainty principles are involved in democratic deliberative processes. Use of existing communication theories (e.g., URT) as a base can serve as a foundation from which to build a more coherent theory pertaining to democratic deliberation.

## ◆ Conclusion

The limited-effects model has had a tremendous influence on theory and research on political campaign communication. One of those influences has been to provoke three interrelated areas of research. Agenda setting argues that salience can transfer from the mass media to the public. Priming and framing address consequences of salience. One can prime a topic (such as the war in Iraq), increasing the salience of that topic to voters as they evaluate public policy and, during a campaign, candidates for office. As long as this issue remains salient (recall that humans have limitations on their information-processing ability), that which has been primed can influence perceptions of events and candidates. One can also provide a frame or point of view for interpreting the world, which can similarly influence perceptions as long as the frame is salient. These three processes all arise as a consequence of limitations on human information processing.

Although the two-step flow of communication has received its share of criticism from works reflective of the alternative institutional (e.g., McCombs & Shaw, 1972), critical (e.g., Gitlin, 1978), and technological (e.g., McLuhan, 1964) paradigms, and even more recently with Bennett and Manheim's (2006) one-step flow argument, this model remains influential in the study of political communication. The concept of opinion leader remains the focus of political communication research

(e.g., Scheufele & Shah, 2000), and the model's stressing of the importance of political discussion can be found in the present flurry of research on citizens' deliberative processes (e.g., Moy & Gastil, 2006). Although no one present-day political communication study would define itself as being a pure reflection of the two-step flow model of communication influence, it is undeniable that elements of the model (and reactions to the theoretical, conceptual, and empirical bases for the model) continue to shape political communication research. The media can influence the public, and we are improving our understanding of the communicative processes by which this influence occurs.

## ◆ References

Althaus, S., & Tewksbury, D. (2007). *How should we measure media exposure?* http://www.jour.unr.edu/pcr/1703_2007_a utumn/invitation.html

Beck, P. A., Dalton, R. J., Greene, S., & Huckfeldt, R. (2002). The social calculus of voting: Interpersonal, media, and organizational influences on presidential choices. *American Political Science Review, 96,* 57–73.

Bennett, W. L. (1998). The uncivic culture: Communication, identity, and the rise of lifestyle politics. *PS: Political Science & Politics, 31,* 741–761.

Bennett, W. L., & Manheim, J. B. (2006). The one-step flow of communication. *Annals of the American Academy of Political and Social Science, 608,* 213–232.

Berelson, B. R., Lazarsfeld, P. F., & McPhee, W. N. (1954). *Voting: A study of opinion formation in a presidential campaign.* Chicago: University of Chicago Press.

Berger, C. R., & Calabrese, R. J. (1975). Some explorations in initial interaction and beyond: Toward a developmental theory of interpersonal communication. *Human Communication Research, 1,* 99–112.

Bohman, J., & Rehg, W. (Eds.). (1997). *Deliberative democracy.* Cambridge: MIT Press.

Bormann, E. (1972). Fantasy and rhetorical vision: The rhetorical criticism of social reality. *Quarterly Journal of Speech, 58,* 396–407.

Boyle, M. P., Schmierbach, M., Armstrong, C. L., McLeod, D. M., Shah, D. V., & Pan, Z. (2004). Information seeking and emotional reactions to the September 11th terrorist attacks. *Journalism & Mass Communication Quarterly, 81,* 155–167.

Chaffee, S. H., & Berger, C. R. (1987). What communication scientists do. In C. R. Berger & S. H. Chaffee (Eds.), *Handbook of communication science* (pp. 99–122). Newbury Park, CA: Sage.

Chaffee, S. H., & Hochheimer, J. L. (1985). The beginnings of political communication research in the United States: Origins of the "limited effects" model. In M. Gurevitch & M. R. Levy (Eds.), *Mass communication review yearbook* (Vol. 5, pp. 75–104). Beverly Hills, CA: Sage.

Chaffee, S. H., & Metzger, M. J. (2001). The end of mass communication? *Mass Communication & Society, 4,* 365–379.

Chong, D., & Druckman, J. N. (2007). Framing theory. *Annual Review of Political Science, 10,* 103–126.

Cohen, B. C. (1963). *The press and foreign policy.* Princeton, NJ: Princeton University Press.

Delia, J. G. (1987). Communication research: A history. In C. R. Berger & S. H. Chaffee (Eds.), *The handbook of communication science* (pp. 20–98). Newbury Park, CA: Sage.

Downs, A. (1957). *An economic theory of democracy.* New York: Harper & Row.

Englis, B. G., & Solomon, M. R. (1995). To be or not to be: Lifestyle imagery, reference groups, and the clustering of America. *Journal of Advertising, 24,* 13–28.

Entman, R. (1993). Framing: Toward a clarification of a fractured paradigm. *Journal of Communication, 43,* 51–58.

Eveland, W. P., Jr., Hayes, A. F., Shah, D. V., & Kwak, N. (2005). Understanding the relationship between communication and political knowledge: A model comparison approach using panel data. *Political Communication, 22,* 423–446.

Eveland, W. P., Jr., Marton, K., & Seo, K. M. (2004). Moving beyond "just the facts": The influence of online news on the content and structure of public affairs knowledge. *Communication Research, 31,* 82–108.

Fisher, W. R. (1987). *Human communication as narration: Toward a philosophy of reason, value, and action.* Columbia: University of South Carolina Press.

Fiske, S. T. (1992). Thinking is for doing: Portraits of social cognition from daguerreotype to Laserphoto. *Journal of Personality & Social Psychology, 63,* 877–889.

Gamson, W. A., & Modigliani, A. (1987). The changing culture of affirmative action. In R. G. Braungart & M. M. Braungart (Eds.), *Research in political sociology* (Vol. 3, pp. 137–177). Greenwich, CT: JAI.

Gans, H. J. (1979). *Deciding what's news: A study of* CBS Evening News, NBC Nightly News, Newsweek *and* Time. New York: Vintage.

Gitlin, T. (1978). Media sociology: The dominant paradigm. *Theory and Society, 6,* 205–253.

Goffman, E. (1974). *Frame analysis.* New York: Harper & Row.

Graber, D. A., & Smith, J. M. (2005). Political communication faces the 21st century. *Journal of Communication, 55,* 479–507.

Guttman, N. (2007). Bringing the mountain to the public: Dilemmas and contradictions in the procedures of public deliberation initiatives that aim to get "ordinary citizens" to deliberate policy issues. *Communication Theory, 17,* 411–438.

Habermas, J. (2006). Political communication in media society: Does democracy still enjoy an epistemic dimension? The impact of normative theory on empirical research. *Communication Theory, 16,* 411–426.

Hansen, G. J., & Benoit, W. L. (2007). Communication forms as predictors of issue knowledge in presidential campaigns: A meta-analytic assessment. *Mass Communication & Society, 10,* 189–210.

Herman, E. S., & Chomsky, N. (1988). *Manufacturing consent: The political economy of the mass media.* New York: Pantheon.

Holbert, R. L., Benoit, W. L., Hansen, G. J., & Wen, W.-C. (2002). The role of communication in the formation of an issue-based citizenry. *Communication Monographs, 69,* 296–310.

Holbrook, T. M. (1996). *Do campaigns matter?* Thousand Oaks, CA: Sage.

Huckfeldt, R., & Sprague, J. (1995). *Citizens, politics, and social communication:*

*Information and influence in an election campaign.* New York: Cambridge University Press.

Huspek, M. (2007). Symposium: Habermas and deliberative democracy: Introductory remarks. *Communication Theory, 17,* 329–332.

Iyengar, S. (1991). *Is anyone responsible? How television frames political issues.* Chicago: University of Chicago Press.

Iyengar, S., & Kinder, D. R. (1987). *News that matters: Television and American opinion.* Chicago: University of Chicago Press.

James, W. (1983). *The principles of psychology.* Cambridge, MA: Harvard University Press. (Original work published 1890)

Johnston, R., Hagen, M. G., & Jamieson, K. H. (2000). *The 2000 presidential election and the foundations of party politics.* Cambridge, UK: Cambridge University Press.

Katz, E. (1987). Communication research since Lazarsfeld. *Public Opinion Quarterly, 51,* S25–S45.

Katz, E., & Lazarsfeld, P. F. (1955). *Personal influence: The part played by people in the flow of mass communications.* New York: Free Press.

Keck, K. L., & Samp, J. A. (2007). The dynamic nature of goals and message production as revealed in a sequential analysis of conflict interactions. *Communication Research, 33,* 27–47.

Keller, K. L., & Lehmann, D. R. (2006). Brands and branding: Research findings and future priorities. *Marketing Science, 25,* 740–759.

Kenski, K., & Stroud, N. J. (2006). Connections between Internet use and political efficacy, knowledge, and participation. *Journal of Broadcasting & Electronic Media, 50,* 173–192.

Kim, J., Wyatt, R. O., & Katz, E. (1999). News, talk, opinion, participation: The part played by conversation in deliberative democracy. *Political Communication, 16,* 361–386.

Kiousis, S., & McCombs, M. E. (2004). Agenda setting effects and attitude strength: Political figures during the 1996 presidential election. *Communication Research, 31,* 36–57.

Kitchen, P. J., Brignell, J., Li, T., & Jones, G. S. (2004). The emergence of IMC: A theoretical perspective. *Journal of Advertising Research, 44,* 19–30.

Klapper, J. T. (1960). *The effects of mass communication: An analysis of research on the effectiveness and limitations of mass media in influencing the opinions, values, and behavior of their audiences.* Glencoe, IL: Free Press.

Krosnick, J. A., & Kinder, D. R. (1990). Altering the foundations of support for the president through priming. *American Political Science Review, 84,* 497–512.

Lakoff, G. (2002). *Moral politics: How liberals and conservatives think.* Chicago: University of Chicago Press.

Lazarsfeld, P. F., Berelson, B., & Gaudet, H. (1948). *The people's choice: How the voter makes up his mind in a presidential campaign* (2nd ed.). New York: Columbia University Press.

Lazarsfeld, P. F., & Merton, R. (1960). Mass media, popular taste, and organized social action. In W. Schramm (Ed.), *Mass communications* (2nd ed., pp. 492–512). Urbana: University of Illinois Press. (Original work published 1948)

Levy, S. J. (1999). *Brands, consumers, symbols, and research: Sidney J. Levy on marketing.* Thousand Oaks, CA: Sage.

Maguire, K. C. (2007). "Will it ever end?" A (re)examination of uncertainty in college student long-distance dating relationships. *Communication Quarterly, 55,* 415–432.

McChesney, R. W. (2000). *Rich media, poor democracy: Communication politics in dubious times.* New York: New Press.

McCombs, M. (2004). *Setting the agenda: The mass media and public opinion.* Cambridge, UK: Polity.

McCombs, M. (2005). A look at agenda setting: past, present, and future. *Journalism Studies, 6,* 543–557.

McCombs, M. E., & Shaw, D. L. (1972). The agenda setting function of the mass media. *Public Opinion Quarterly, 36,* 176–187.

McGuire, M. J. (1989). Theoretical foundations of campaigns. In R. E. Rice & C. K. Atkin (Eds.), *Public communication campaigns* (2nd ed., pp. 43–65). Newbury Park, CA: Sage.

McLeod, J. M., Scheufele, D. A., & Moy, P. (1999). Community, communication, and participation: The role of mass media and interpersonal discussion in local political participation. *Political Communication, 16,* 315–336.

McLeod, J. M., Scheufele, D. A., Moy, P., Horowitz, E., Holbert, R. L., Zhang, W., et al. (1999). Understanding deliberation: The effects of discussion networks on participation in a public forum. *Communication Research, 26,* 743–774.

McLuhan, M. (1964). *Understanding media: The extensions of man.* New York: Mentor.

Meyers, D. E., & Schvaneveldt, R. W. (1971). Facilitation in recognizing pairs of words: Evidence of a dependence between retrieval operations. *Journal of Experimental Psychology, 90,* 227–234.

Meyrowitz, J. (1985). *No sense of place: The impact of electronic media on social behavior.* New York: Oxford University Press.

Meyrowitz, J. (1994). Medium theory. In D. Crowley & D. Mitchell (Eds.), *Communication theory today* (pp. 50–77). Stanford, CA: Stanford University Press.

Michman, R. D., & Mazze, E. M. (2006). *The affluent consumer: Marketing and selling the affluent lifestyle.* Westport, CT: Praeger.

Miller, G. A. (1956). The magic number seven plus or minus two: Some limits on our capacity to process information. *Psychological Review, 63,* 81–97.

Moy, P., & Gastil, J. (2006). Predicting deliberative conversation: The impact of discussion networks, media use, and political cognitions. *Political Communication, 23,* 443–460.

Nisbett, M. C., & Scheufele, D. A. (2004). Political talk as catalyst for online citizenship. *Journalism & Mass Communication Quarterly, 81,* 877–896.

Pan, Z., Shen, L., Paek, H., & Sun, Y. (2006). Mobilizing political talk in a presidential campaign: An examination of campaign effects in a deliberative framework. *Communication Research, 33,* 315–345.

Petrocik, J. R. (1996). Issue ownership in presidential elections, with a 1980 case study. *American Journal of Political Science, 40,* 825–850.

Petrocik, J. R., Benoit, W. L., & Hansen, G. L. (2003–2004). Issue ownership and presidential campaigning, 1952–2000. *Political Science Quarterly, 118,* 599–626.

Pfau, M. (1988). The mass media and American politics: A review essay. *Western Political Quarterly, 42,* 173–186.

Popkin, S. L. (1994). *The reasoning voter: Communication and persuasion in presidential campaigns* (2nd ed.). Chicago: University of Chicago Press.

Price, V. (1992). *Communication concepts 4: Public opinion.* Newbury Park, CA: Sage.

Price, V., Cappella, J. N., & Nir, L. (2002). Does disagreement contribute to more deliberative opinion? *Political Communication, 19,* 95–112.

Price, V., & Tewksbury, D. (1995). *News values and public opinion: A theoretical account of media priming and framing.* Presented at the annual meeting of the International Communication Association, Albuquerque, NM.

Putnam, R. D. (2000). *Bowling alone: The collapse and revival of American community.* New York: Simon & Schuster.

Rheingold, H. (2002). *Smart mobs: The next social revolution.* Cambridge, MA: Perseus.

Roloff, M. E. (1987). Communication and conflict. In C. R. Berger & S. H. Chaffee (Eds.), *Handbook of communication science* (pp. 484–536). Newbury Park, CA: Sage.

Romer, D., Kenski, K., Winneg, K., Adasiewicz, C., & Jamieson, K. H. (2006). *Capturing campaign dynamics 2000 & 2004: The national Annenberg election survey.* Philadelphia: University of Pennsylvania Press.

Rosenthal, R. (1991). Replication in behavioral research. In J. W. Neuliep (Ed.), *Replication in the social sciences* (pp. 1–30). Newbury Park, CA: Sage.

Roskos-Ewoldsen, D. R., Klinger, M. R., & Roskos-Ewoldsen, B. (2007). Media priming: A meta-analysis. In R. W. Preiss, B. M. Gayle, N. Burrel, M. Allen, & J. Bryant (Eds.), *Mass media effects research: Advances through meta-analysis* (pp. 53–81). Mahwah, NJ: Lawrence Erlbaum.

Roskos-Ewoldsen, D., Roskos-Ewoldsen, B., & Carpentier, F. R. D. (2002). Media priming: A synthesis. In J. Bryant & D. Zillman (Eds.), *Media effects: Advances in theory and research* (pp. 97–120). Mahwah, NJ: Lawrence Erlbaum.

Scheufele, D. A. (2000). Agenda-setting, priming, and framing revisited: Another look at cognitive effects of political communication. *Mass Communication & Society, 3,* 297–316.

Scheufele, D. A., & Shah, D. V. (2000). Personality strength and social capital: The role of dispositional and informational variables in the production of civic participation. *Communication Research, 27*, 107–131.

Schudson, M. (1997). Why conversation is not the soul of democracy. *Critical Studies in Mass Communication, 14*, 297–309.

Shah, D. V., McLeod, D. M., Friedland, L. A., & Nelson, M. R. (2007). The politics of consumption/the consumption of politics. *Annals of the American Academy of Political and Social Science, 611*, 6–15.

Shah, D. V., McLeod, J. M., & Yoon, S. (2001). Communication, context, and community: An exploration of print, broadcast, and Internet influences. *Communication Research, 28*, 464–506.

Shah, D. V., & Scheufele, D. A. (2006). Explicating opinion leadership: Nonpolitical dispositions, information consumption, and civic participation. *Political Communication, 23*, 1–22.

Sheer, V. C., & Cline, R. J. (1995). Testing a model of perceived information adequacy and uncertainty reduction in physician-patient interactions. *Journal of Applied Communication Research, 23*, 44–59.

Sheingold, C. A. (1973). Social networks and voting: The resurrection of a research agenda. *American Sociological Review, 38*, 712–720.

Tedesco, J. C. (2004). Changing the channel: Use of the Internet for communicating about politics. In L. L. Kaid (Ed.), *Handbook of political communication research* (pp. 507–532). Mahwah, NJ: Lawrence Erlbaum.

Tversky, A., & Kahneman, D. (1981). The framing of decisions and the psychology of choice. *Science, 211*, 453–458.

Wanta, W., & Ghanem, S. (2007). Effects of agenda setting. In R. W. Preiss, B. M. Gayle, N. Burrel, M. Allen, & J. Bryant (Eds.), *Mass media effects research: Advances through meta-analysis* (pp. 37–51). Mahwah, NJ: Lawrence Erlbaum.

Weaver, D., McCombs, M., & Shaw, D. L. (2004). Agenda-setting research: Issues, attributes, and influences. In L. L. Kaid (Ed.), *Handbook of political campaign research* (pp. 257–282). Mahwah, NJ: Lawrence Erlbaum.

Young, D. G. (2006). Late-night comedy and the salience of the candidates' caricatured traits in the 2000 election. *Mass Communication & Society, 9*, 339–366.

Zaller, J. R. (1992). *Nature and origins of mass opinion*. New York: Cambridge University Press.

Zaller, J. (1996). The myth of massive media impact revived: New support for a discredited idea. In D. C. Mutz, P. M. Sniderman, & R. A. Brody (Eds.), *Political persuasion and attitude change* (pp. 17–78). Ann Arbor: University of Michigan Press.

# 26

# INTERCULTURAL COMMUNICATION

◆ Young Yun Kim

Intercultural communication inquiry began in the 1950s and the 1960s, riding the wave of globalization (McLuhan, 1962) and the post–World War II emergence of the United States as a world power. Idealism and optimism were strong in the United States, and President Kennedy established the Peace Corps in 1961, challenging Americans to serve their country and the cause of international peace. In this historical context, early intercultural communication studies were motivated by humanistic, as well as practical, interests in the hope of generating knowledge that could help promote better understanding and effective communication between individuals of differing cultural upbringings.

This early interest in the micro-level interface of individuals across cultures and societies continues to be the focal domain of intercultural communication theory and research, while keeping it close to the area of interpersonal communication within the communication discipline. On the other hand, the domain of intercultural communication has evolved largely independently from areas of communication investigating macro-structural issues of "international communication," "global communication," and "development communication." Research in these areas primarily addresses issues pertaining to mass-mediated and other technological forms of communication (such as the Internet) involving two or more nation-states within the global communication system, such as globalization of media ownership and infrastructure, trans-border flows of media programs and contents, and their impact on traditional societies, cultures, and languages (cf. Thussu, 2006).

*Intercultural communication* is commonly defined in terms of two central concepts, culture and communication. The anthropological concept of culture has been employed as a label for the collective cultural life experiences associated with a society or a nation. Over time, the domain has expanded to include communication activities involving individuals of differing domestic sociological groups of differing backgrounds such as ethnicity, race, and other discernible social categories. Accordingly, the domain of intercultural communication is closely linked to the domains of other social science disciplines such as cultural anthropology and cross-cultural psychology, as well as sociology. Within the discipline of communication, intercultural communication can be conceptually differentiated from interpersonal communication based on the relatively high degree of difference in the communicators' internalized culturally or subculturally rooted system of meaning, knowledge, values, and worldviews.

Intercultural communication thus is broadly defined as the communication process in which individual participants of differing cultural or subcultural backgrounds come into direct contact with one another. The inclusive conception of intercultural communication allows for considering all communication encounters to be potentially "intercultural," with varying degrees of "interculturalness" in the experiential backgrounds of interactants (Ellingsworth, 1977; Sarbaugh, 1988). Gudykunst and Kim (2003) employ the concept of "stranger" (Simmel, 1908/1950) to integrate a wide range of intercultural communication contexts represented by terms such as *intergroup, interethnic,* and *interracial communication* into a continuum of varying degrees of difference, unfamiliarity, and psychological distance present between communicators. In so doing, Gudykunst and Kim characterize the distinction between intercultural communication and intracultural

communication as a matter of degree rather than of kind (p. 18).

Integral to the broad conceptualization of intercultural communication are two subdomains commonly known as *cultural communication* and *cross-cultural communication.* A significant amount of cultural communication research has been directed toward identifying unique or prevailing patterns of communication in specific cultures. Studies of cross-cultural communication, on the other hand, have compared communication-related phenomena in two or more cultural or subcultural groups, similar to the distinction between cultural and cross-cultural perspectives in psychology (see Greenfield, 1997; Van de Vijver & Leung, 1997).

## ◆ Core Theories Motivating Intercultural Communication Inquiry

Intercultural communication has enjoyed a substantial theoretical development in the past two decades or so. Three volumes of the *Handbook of International and Intercultural Communication* (Asante, Newmark, & Blake, 1979; Asante & Gudykunst, 1989; Gudykunst & Mody, 2004) have presented state-of-the-art overview articles. More important, four different volumes have been published to feature many of the notable or promising current theories of cultural, cross-cultural, and intercultural communication (Gudykunst, 1983, 2005c; Y. Y. Kim & Gudykunst, 1988; Wiseman, 1995). Collectively, these theorizing efforts present a fairly accurate picture of the overall history of theory/research development in intercultural communication as a whole, as well as the continuity and discontinuity of individual theories over time. Across these four theory volumes, more than 30 different theories at varying stages of development have been presented. Almost all of the entries in the first theory volume are exploratory discussions on the applicability of different "perspectives" on communication (e.g., rules perspective, rhetorical perspective, and the perspective of coordinated management of meaning), generating few research activities. In comparison, the majority of the entries in the three subsequent volumes offer a set of knowledge claims in the form of propositions or theorems. A number of the theories first introduced in the second volume (Y. Y. Kim & Gudykunst, 1988) appear again, updated and revised, in at least one of the two subsequent volumes. The most recent volume (Gudykunst, 2005c) features a total of 17 theories, including 10 updated versions of previously published theories.

Six of these theories are presented here as core theories that have motivated much of the intercultural communication research over the past two decades. Priority has been given to older, more enduring theories that have been subjected to extensive empirical tests while continuing to generate strong research interests today. This selection criterion ensures that the identified core theories represent some of the most prominent and productive knowledge claims to date. The six selected theories consist of one theory of cultural communication (speech code theory), two theories of cross-cultural communication (face-negotiation theory and conversational constraints theory), and three theories of intercultural communication (anxiety/uncertainty management theory, communication accommodation theory, and the integrative communication theory of cross-cultural adaptation).

## SPEECH CODE THEORY

As early as 1981, Philipsen laid the groundwork for the ethnographic study of cultural communication based on the premise that "the function of communication in cultural communication is to maintain a healthy balance between the forces of individualism and community, to provide a sense of shared identity which, nonetheless,

preserves individual dignity, freedom, and creativity" (Philipsen, 1981, p. 5).

Rooted in the phenomenological-hermeneutic tradition and applying Geertz's (1973) framework of the interpretation of culture, Philipsen and his associates (Philipsen, 1992, 1997, 2002; Philipsen, Coutu, & Covarrubias, 2005) have developed an interpretive theory of cultural communication. Whereas the neopositivist and systems methodological interests lie in theorizing about universal phenomena and making generalizable knowledge claims, this theory offers an interpretive framework for identifying, describing, and illuminating the essential features of communication unique to the particular speech community. The most recent rendition of this theory (Philipsen et al., 2005) defines "speech codes" as "constructs that observer-analysts formulate explicitly in order to interpret and explain communicative conduct in a particular speech community." The six general propositions address the principles of the inseparable connectedness of culture and speech code in a given speech community. Proposition 6, for example, stipulates, "The artful use of a shared speech code is a sufficient condition for predicting, explaining, and controlling the form of discourse about the intelligibility, prudence, and morality of communicative conduct."

Directly or indirectly, the theory has served as a significant intellectual foundation and framework for an extensive body of original field studies that commonly employ qualitative-emic research methods such as ethnographic field observations, conversational analysis, discourse analysis, and textual-rhetorical analysis. The theory and associated studies have contributed to deepening understanding of the conversation patterns and other communication practices unique to a given cultural or subcultural community. Among the notable works are an examination of the cultural meaning of the word *communication* in some American speech (Katriel & Philipsen, 1990), recognizable Indian ways of speaking in Native American communities (Pratt, 1998;

Wieder & Pratt, 1990), Russian "cultural pragmatics" in the context of Russian American encounters (Carbaugh, 1993), Finnish silence and third-party introduction (Carbaugh, 2005), the second-person pronoun *Sie* among Germans (Winchatz, 2001), and interpersonal communication and relationship patterns in Colombia (Fitch, 1998), to name only a few.

## FACE NEGOTIATION THEORY

In contrast to the insider perspective taken in emic studies of cultural communication, cross-cultural communication theorists have taken the perspective of an objective "outsider" in comparing two or more cultural groups and have sought to design their studies based on culture-general theoretical concepts. By and large, etic studies of cross-cultural communication reflect the philosophy of cultural universalism. Their main aim is to identify cross-cultural variations in communication-related phenomena along certain universal dimensions. *Individualism-collectivism* tops the list of theories guiding cross-cultural communication research. The group-level individualism-collectivism dimension has been extended to a personality equivalent, "idiocentrism-allocentrism" or "independent-interdependent self-construal" (Triandis, 1988).

Combining these etic concepts of individualism-collectivism and independent-interdependent self-construal with the concept of "facework" from Goffman's (1955, 1959) seminal ethnographic works, face negotiation theory (Ting-Toomey, 1988) was initially developed to explain cultural variations in conflict styles along individualistic-collectivistic cultural lines. Since then, the theory has undergone substantial changes. In its most recent incarnation (Ting-Toomey, 2005b), the theory integrates cultural-level dimensions and individual-level attributes to explain "face concerns," conflict styles, and

"facework" behaviors, among others. At the cultural level, there are 12 propositions (e.g., "Members of individualistic cultures tend to express a greater degree of self-face maintenance concerns than members of collectivistic cultures"; "Members of collectivistic cultures tend to express a greater degree of other face concerns than members of individualistic cultures"). At the individual level, the theory offers 10 propositions linking independent and interdependent self-construal to individual communicators' patterns of face concern and conflict style (e.g., "Independent self is associated positively with self-face concern"; "Interdependent self is associated positively with other-face/mutual-face concern"). Two additional propositions describe "facework" variations according to "in-group" and "out-group" relational-situational contexts in which conflicts occur (e.g., "Individualists or independent-self personalities tend to express a greater degree of self-face maintenance concerns and less other-face maintenance concerns in dealing with both in-group and out-group conflict situations").

Face negotiation theory has been a strong presence in the area of intercultural communication and beyond, including the applied multidisciplinary area of intercultural training (e.g., Ting-Toomey, 2004). Although some of the propositions in the revised theory await systematic empirical tests, the overall theory has grown from a relatively simple one that offers only a cultural-level comparison of "facework" to a more complex, three-layered structure adding individual and situational-relational levels of comparisons. This theoretical evolution reflects continuous and extensive research efforts largely by Ting-Toomey and her associates to test various propositions (e.g., Oetzel & Ting-Toomey, 2003; Oetzel et al., 2001; Ting-Toomey et al., 1991; Ting-Toomey & Kurogi, 1998) in a number of different countries. Furthermore, Ting-Toomey (2005a) has introduced a new area of research by proposing a related but separate identity management theory by extending the concept of facework to the context of *intercultural* encounter and relationship development.

## CONVERSATIONAL CONSTRAINTS THEORY

M. Kim's (1993) conversational constraints theory explains variations in goal-oriented behaviors of intercultural communicators. This theory initially began as an attempt to account for differences in individual communication behaviors according to the culture-level dimension of individualism and collectivism. In this original version, M. Kim posited that when pursuing goals, members of collectivistic cultures view "face-supporting behavior" (e.g., avoiding hurting the hearer's feelings) as more important than do members of individualistic cultures. In comparison, members of individualistic cultures were characterized as viewing clarity as more important than do members of collectivistic cultures when pursuing goals.

M. Kim (1995) soon moved away from this "norms-based" approach in favor of the two corresponding "culturally based" individual-level constructs, independent self-construal and interdependent self-construal. Accordingly, the revised theory presents three main propositions linking independent and interdependent self-construals to three different conversational constraints: "not hurting the hearer's feelings," "minimizing imposition to the hearer," and "clarity in the pursuit of primary goals." The theory posits, for instance, that higher levels of the need for approval result in higher levels of the perceived importance of the concern for the hearer's feelings and "perceived importance of minimizing imposition on the hearer." In contrast, higher levels of the need for dominance lead to higher levels of "the perceived importance of clarity." M. Kim adds three other psychological factors that are posited to influence conversational

constraints: "need for social approval," "need for dominance," and "psychological gender" (masculinity, femininity). Here, higher levels of masculinity are linked to higher levels of the perceived importance of clarity, whereas higher levels of femininity are linked to the perceived importance not to hurt the hearer's feelings and higher levels of avoiding imposition.

This theory has motivated, as well as has been influenced and shaped by, an extensive array of empirical data. A series of original studies carried out by M. Kim and her associates provides empirical data supporting many of the formally articulated 11 propositions (e.g., M. Kim, 1994; M. Kim et al., 1996; M. Kim, Sharkey, & Singelis, 1994; Miyahara & Kim, 1993; Singelis & Brown, 1995). This theory has served, and is likely to continue to serve, as one of the main intellectual bases for understanding cultural as well as personal variations in communication behaviors of individuals. M. Kim's (2005) recent description of this theory includes two additional conversational constraints: "concern for avoiding negative evaluation by the hearer" and "concern for effectiveness," suggesting a continuing expansion of the theoretical domain and opportunities for new research.

## ANXIETY/UNCERTAINTY MANAGEMENT THEORY

Directly and indirectly, all theories in the area of intercultural communication, including the core theories discussed here, address the question of effectiveness in communicating with culturally dissimilar individuals. Gudykunst's anxiety/uncertainty management (AUM) theory is aimed directly and specifically at explaining "communication effectiveness" defined in terms of the correspondence between the sender's intended meaning and the receiver's interpretation of it in intercultural encounters. From the early formulations (Gudykunst,

1988, 1995) to the most recently updated version (Gudykunst, 2005a), the theory maintains that the ability to manage these two psychological experiences is essential to increasing intercultural communication effectiveness. Throughout the continuing refinement of this theory over the past two decades, Berger and Calabrese's (1975) uncertainty reduction theory, along with a number of theories of intergroup psychology such as Stephan and Stephan's (1985) intergroup anxiety theory and social identity theory (Tajfel, 1981; Tajfel & Turner, 1986), have played an important foundational role.

In the latest 2005 version, the theory includes another key psychological concept, "mindfulness" (Langer, 1989), as the factor that "mediates" the effectiveness-producing functions of uncertainty management and anxiety management. It also identifies seven psychological (e.g., "motivation" and "social categorization") and situational (e.g., "informality" and "institutional support") factors as "superficial causes" that influence communication effectiveness indirectly by influencing the two "basic causes" (anxiety and uncertainty). Altogether, the theory offers 47 axioms, 41 of which link each of the two basic causes (uncertainty, anxiety), seven superficial causes, one moderating process factor (mindfulness), and one "outcome" factor (communication effectiveness). The remaining 6 axioms identify cross-cultural variability in the anxiety and uncertainty experiences of individual sojourners using some of the cross-cultural theories such as Hofstede's (1980) four cultural dimensions (individualism-collectivism, high-low power distance, high-low uncertainty avoidance need, and masculinity-femininity).

Gudykunst and his international network of associates have produced an extensive amount of empirical data in support of many of the theoretical predictions, particularly with respect to the causal relationships between each of the two core constructs, uncertainty and anxiety, and the final outcome factor, communication effectiveness (e.g., Gudykunst, 1985; Gudykunst et al.,

1992; Gudykunst & Hammer, 1988; Gudykunst & Nishida, 2001; Hammer, Wiseman, Rasmussen, & Bruschke, 1998; Kimberly, Gudykunst, & Guerrero, 1999). Gudykunst (2005b) further extended this theory by employing the same core constructs (uncertainty management, anxiety management, and mindfulness) to formulate a separate theory designed to explain the psychological adjustment of temporary sojourners in a foreign cultural environment. Over the past two decades, this theory has been a ubiquitous force driving intercultural communication inquiry and has contributed to cross-cultural psychology (e.g., Gudykunst & Bond, 1997), intergroup social psychology (e.g., Gudykunst, 1986), and intercultural training (e.g., Gudykunst, 1998).

## COMMUNICATION ACCOMMODATION THEORY

The origin of communication accommodation theory is traced back to "accent mobility" research in the 1970s by Giles and his associates (e.g., Giles, 1973, 1979) and to speech accommodation theory (Giles, Rosenthal, & Young, 1986; Street & Giles, 1982) that was designed to examine the social psychological parameters underlying the moves speakers make in their speech behaviors. A number of other social-psychological theories such as social identity theory (Tajfel, 1981; Tajfel & Turner, 1986) and ethnolinguistic identity theory (Giles & Johnson, 1987) have provided this theory some of its foundational ideas. Since its first formal presentation in propositional form in 1988 (Gallois, Franklyn-Stokes, Giles, & Coupland, 1988), communication accommodation theory has been expanded and elaborated (Gallois, Giles, Jones, Cargile, & Ota, 1995; Gallois, Ogay, & Giles, 2005; Soliz & Giles, Chapter 5, this volume).

Focusing on the individual's communication behavior ("convergent" behavior and "divergent/maintenance" behavior), communication accommodation theory offers a broadly based and multilayered explanatory system that consists of macro-level, situational, psychological, and behavioral dimensions of constructs. In its latest, streamlined version (Gallois et al., 2005), the theory identifies key factors of each dimension: (a) three factors of the sociohistorical context ("intergroup history," "interpersonal history," and "societal/cultural norms and values"), (b) two types of individual communicators' initial orientation ("intergroup" or "interpersonal"), and (c) prevailing norms governing the immediate interaction situation. The immediate situational norms, in turn, interact with each communicator's "psychological accommodation" strategies ("accommodative" or "nonaccommodative"), "behavior tactics," "perceptions/attributions," and "evaluations/future intensions" with respect to the other communicator.

Linking factors across the dimensions, the theory offers 11 sets of propositions that specify the interrelationships among the identified groups of factors. Proposition 1, for example, predicts a communicator's initial psychological orientation toward accommodation or nonaccommodation under three conditions: positive or negative intergroup history, weak or strong in-group identification, and a positive or negative prior experience with another member of the interacting partner's group.

As pointed out by Gallois et al. (2005), "a plethora of research and related theories" have contributed to the continuing development and evolution of communication accommodation theory over three decades. Given the generic concept of *group* defining the intergroup perspective, this theory can be applied to study the interface of various types of sociological and cultural groups. Indeed, many of the components identified and linked together in propositional statements have tested facets of this theory in wide-ranging situational-social contexts, including the context of intergenerational communication (Giles, Coupland, & Williams, 1992) and the "gendered workplace" (Boggs & Giles, 1999). This open-ended theoretical domain allows for additional communication contexts to which this theory can be fruitfully applied for future research, thus informing the theory in its continuing development.

## INTEGRATIVE THEORY OF CROSS-CULTURAL ADAPTATION

For more than seven decades, adapting to a new and unfamiliar environment has been one of the most salient research issues across social science disciplines. In the area of intercultural communication, this inquiry began with Y. Y. Kim's (1977) publication of a variable-analytic "path model" of "acculturation" developed in her dissertation research (1976) of Korean immigrants in the Chicago area. Subsequently, Y. Y. Kim (1988, 1995a) proposed a broader, interdisciplinary, and integrative theory, which has been updated and further refined in more recent presentations (Y. Y. Kim, 2001, 2005a).

Synthesizing and incorporating major concepts from across social science disciplines into a single integrative communication theory, Y. Y. Kim has sought to develop a "big picture"—a broadly based general theory designed to help cross-pollinate largely separate and at times divergent probes (e.g., studies of long-term immigrant acculturation and short-term sojourners). The theory is grounded in a set of "open-systems" meta-theoretic assumptions that regard cross-cultural adaptation not as an independent variable or a dependent variable but as the entirety of a natural and universal phenomenon that unfolds over time through communicative engagement of an individual with a new, unfamiliar, or changing cultural environment.

Y. Y. Kim's integrative theory presents two models. The *process model* describes and explains the "stress-adaptation-growth" dynamic that, over time, leads to a gradual transformation of the individual in the direction of greater "fitness" with respect to the new or changing environment. The *structural model* identifies four dimensions of factors as interactively working together to facilitate or impede the adaptation process described in the process model: (a) individual predisposition (adaptive personality, ethnic proximity/distance, preparedness), (b) the environment (host conformity pressure, host receptivity, ethnic group strength), (c) intercultural transformation (functional fitness, psychological health, intercultural identity development), and (d) communication (host communication competence, host interpersonal communication, host mass communication, ethnic interpersonal communication, and ethnic mass communication). The interlocking bilateral relationships between and among these constructs are specified in 21 theorems (e.g., "The greater the host communication competence, the greater the participation in host social [interpersonal, mass] communication"; "The greater the host receptivity and host conformity pressure, the greater the host communication competence"; Y. Y. Kim, 2001, pp. 91–92).

The theory was built on ample research evidence that has been made available across the social sciences. Once developed, many of the 21 theorems have been supported by empirical data from a substantial number of studies. Y. Y. Kim and her associates have carried out some of the studies in a variety of cultural and subcultural groups such as Southeast Asian refugees (Y. Y. Kim, 1990), Native Americans (Y. Y. Kim, Lujan, & Dixon, 1998), international university students in the United States (Tamam, 1993) and in Japan (Maruyama, 1998), Turkish employees of an American military organization in Germany (Y. Y. Kim & Braun, 2002), and Korean expatriates in the United States and their counterparts in South Korea (Y. S. Kim & Y.Y. Kim, 2007; Y. Y. Kim & Y. S. Kim, 2004). The many other investigators' studies that have documented empirical evidence for this theory include Haitian immigrants in the United States (Walker, 1993), Chinese immigrant children in Canada (Lee & Chen, 2000), American university exchange students overseas (e.g., Milstein, 2005; Pitts, 2007), and native-born mainstream White Australians who have undergone extensive intercultural experiences (Shearer, 2003).

With the advent of globalization, one no longer has to leave home to experience cross-cultural adaptation. People around the world are increasingly exposed to the images and sounds of once-distant cultures, while in many urban centers, local people are routinely coming in contact with foreign-born individuals. Opening a new chapter for cross-cultural adaptation research, Y. Y. Kim (1995b, 2006, 2008) has applied her integrative communication theory to addressing this rapidly unfolding phenomenon of "stay-home" cross-cultural adaptation by proposing "intercultural identity transformation" as a viable new model for human development.

## ◆ Looking Ahead

Though far from being complete, the above overview has attempted to highlight some of the primary theorizing efforts that have motivated a substantial amount of research activities over the past two decades and continue to serve as the major intellectual core of intercultural communication inquiry today.

The six theories and related research activities are clearly indicative of the steady and substantial advancements made in intercultural communication inquiry. The vast majority of the cross-cultural and intercultural communication theories are built on the representational-empirical-objectivist assumptions underpinning the methodological traditions of neopositivism and systems structure. Complementing such social scientific theories, speech code theory has served as a main intellectual guide for a host of rich ethnographic studies that have generated insights into many specific cultural and subcultural communities and their communication practices. Collectively, these works have shown a trend toward expanding conceptual domains and more comprehensive explanatory systems that integrate multiple layers of explanatory factors to help explain individual-level communication phenomena within, across, and between cultural and subcultural boundaries.

As the process of globalization continues to unfold with new technological means of communication, the systematic insights offered in these six theories will need to be reexamined and updated with new research questions. Yet, the essential ideas and patterns of relationships presented in the intercultural communication theories will continue to be relevant. This is because the knowledge claims made are not bounded by any particular communication medium (face-to-face or mediated), specific social setting (such as classrooms, health care contexts, or multinational organizations), or specific culture or cultures brought together by communicators. To the extent that substantial collective differences remain in human communities, Philipsen's speech code theory can offer a way to examine what is unique about each group. Ting-Toomey's face negotiation theory can provide a comparative insight into differing psychological responses to conflict situations, while M. Kim's conversational constraints theory points to a set of culturally rooted values that potentially help shape the priorities or goals that individual communicators seek to achieve in conversations.

Likewise, as long as individuals cross the boundaries of group differences and engage each other in communication activities, Gudykunst's anxiety/uncertainty management theory offers a systematic way to gauge and manage the universal psychological experiences of anxiety and uncertainty in the interest of maximizing intercultural effectiveness. A multilayered account provided by Gallois, Ogay, and Giles in their communication accommodation theory directs our attention to key macro-sociohistorical and situational factors and their influences on the extent to which individual communicators act to accommodate, or not to accommodate, culturally dissimilar individuals. Y. Y. Kim's integrative theory of cross-cultural adaptation provides a comprehensive and systemic understanding of the largely unconscious phenomenon of adaptive personal transformation, as individuals around the world continue to interact, face-to-face or via technologically mediated channels, with a different or changing cultural and subcultural environment.

## INTERDISCIPLINARY KNOWLEDGE INTEGRATION

In varying degrees, each of these theories is interdisciplinary in nature, using and incorporating relevant theories outside the area such as interpersonal communication (e.g., Berger & Calabrese, 1975), cultural anthropology (e.g., E. T. Hall, 1976), cross-cultural and social psychology (e.g., Hofstede, 1980; Tajfel, 1981; Triandis, 1988), and urban sociology (e.g., Simmel, 1908/1950) into a distinctively communication framework. Communication accommodation theory (Gallois et al., 2005) and the integrative theory of cross-cultural adaptation (Y. Y. Kim, 2005a) are two of the most interdisciplinary and comprehensive explanatory systems that have been produced in intercultural communication, so far.

In the case of cultural and cross-cultural communication theories in which culture and cultural variations are the focal issues (such as Philipsen's speech code theory, Ting-Toomey's face negotiation theory, and M. Kim's conversational constraints theory), the "cultural mental models" approach in cognitive anthropology (D'Andrade, 1984; D'Andrade & Strauss, 1992; Handwerker, 2002; Holland & Quinn, 1987; Keesing, 1974, 1994) provides a potentially fruitful opportunity to broaden and enrich their respective interdisciplinary knowledge bases. This approach addresses the way in which internalized (or presupposed) cultural knowledge is organized into cultural mental models from everyday language and thought and has guided much of the inquiry in a number of disciplines, including cognitive linguistics, sociolinguistics, and cognitive psychology. Among recent such studies are an investigation of the cultural basis of Chinese metaphors of thinking (Wee, 2006; Yu, 2003) and Japanese language, gender, and ideology (Takekuro, 2006).

In addition, theorizing in cultural and cross-cultural communication could benefit from an increased effort to broaden the current emphasis on cultural and cross-cultural differences by including a systematic examination of human universals in communication. Potentially useful to this effort are the ongoing studies in this area in psychology and anthropology. Traditionally, anthropological research has concerned itself with the ways in which cultures differ from one another at the supra-individual level of analysis, whereas cross-cultural psychology has maintained a focus on the individual as the unit of analysis in search of cultural differences in psychological tendencies. Despite the differing focal interests, these two disciplinary approaches have produced multiple findings that reveal cross-cultural commonalities of interest to cross-cultural communication researchers. On the basis of an extensive review of numerous anthropological field studies, for instance, Munroe and Munroe (1997) identify a number of human universals in individual-level variables (such as perceptual-cognitive needs for simplification, language and language-related behaviors, and the basic drive to adapt to one's environment) and in interpersonal-level variables (such as the principle of reciprocity, in-group solidarity and intergroup polarization, and ethnocentrism). Similar universal patterns are identified by Norenzayan and Heine (2005), whose examination of the findings from cross-cultural psychological studies reveals universal perceptual and cognitive patterns such as tendencies of stereotyping, ethnocentrism, and emotion and emotion recognition. Similar efforts could be made in cultural and cross-cultural communication research, so as to achieve a more balanced and nuanced understanding of communication systems within and across societies and groups. Such an understanding might lead to a set of new practical insights for bridging some of the challenging gaps of cultural and subcultural differences and working toward greater mutuality and cooperative relationship building.

## PHILOSOPHICAL-METHODOLOGICAL CHALLENGES

For the most part, theoretical advancements in intercultural communication inquiry have been made without major controversies. Most of the few published criticisms have been made by "critical" (or "postcolonial") researchers regarding three of the six core theories. Critical scholarship, indeed, has been a salient and productive intellectual force in intercultural communication in recent years (e.g., Collier, 2005; Gonzalez & Tanno, 1997; Nakayama & Martin, 1998; Young, 1996). Focusing on issues of power and power inequality in intercultural communication within and between cultural or subcultural groups, critical scholars have raised questions about the legitimacy of the "dominant paradigm" of representational and value-neutral social scientific theories, including traditional phenomenological-interpretive theories. Central to such criticisms is the argument that authors of social scientific theories fail to address the predicaments in which members of traditionally underprivileged groups find themselves as "victims" of systematic oppression, thereby serving to reproduce the status quo of the dominant cultural ideology (S. Hall, 1989).

In introducing an anthology of essays presented largely from a critical perspective, for example, Gonzalez, Houston, and Chen (1994) state their goal of presenting the perspective of the authors' own cultural experience "instead of writing to accommodate the voice that is culturally desirable by the mainstream Anglo standards" (p. xiv).

As such, Hedge (1998) critiques Y. Y. Kim's integrative theory of cross-cultural adaptation as being "optimistic." Based on a critical-feminist study involving interviews with a small group of Asian Indian immigrant women in the United States, Hedge reports the experiences of these women in terms of "displacement" and the "struggle" of having to deal with the contradictions between their internal identity and the external "world in which hegemonic structures systematically marginalize certain types of difference" (p. 36). Criticisms also have been directed to Gudykunst's anxiety/uncertainty management theory, including Yoshitake's (2002) argument that the theory is biased in that it is predicated on the Western cultural view that uncertainty reduction is necessary and important to be effective in intercultural communication. (See Gudykunst, 2003, for his response to this criticism.)

Similar criticisms have been made regarding Philipsen's speech code theory for not accounting for manifestations of power in discourse. Philipsen et al. (2005) have responded to such criticisms by pointing out that a cornerstone of the philosophical foundation underpinning speech code theory is "openness to the possibility that any dimension of social life, including power, be observed as manifested in discourse" (p. 64).

Criticisms such as these reflect some fundamental disagreements about the nature of "good" theories and "valid" knowledge claims between the probability-based, representational, and value-neutral (or value-inclusive) approach in social scientific inquiry and the largely interpretive, explicitly value-driven (or value-exclusive) approach in critical inquiry. The philosophical-methodological divergence presents some intellectual barriers in intercultural communication inquiry that cannot be bridged easily. Efforts have been made by some researchers to either reconcile and merge (e.g., Collier, 2005) or embrace in a dialectic relationship (e.g., Martin & Nakayama, 1999) the oppositional approaches to scholarship. It is yet to be seen whether the fundamental philosophical differences can be bridged or reconciled. For now, there is clearly a need for intercultural communication researchers to acquire deeper knowledge of differing philosophical-methodological systems. It is only through expanded methodological literacy that divergent perspectives may be better understood, so as to be able to compare and contrast differing perspectives and to seek consensus with respect to some basic requisite criteria for assessing the soundness of all knowledge claims and research practices.

## EMERGING RESEARCH ISSUES

In addition to the six core theories, a number of other theories featured in the fourth theory volume (Gudykunst, 2005c) are noteworthy for having generated a body of research activities and for providing new opportunities for investigating new research issues of importance to intercultural communication inquiry.

Burgoon (Burgoon, 1995; Burgoon & Hubbard, 2005), for example, has extended her two interpersonal communication theories, expectancy violation theory (Burgoon, 1983) and interaction adaptation theory (Burgoon, Stern, & Dillman, 1995), to cross-cultural and intercultural contexts. The theory posits that cultures vary in expectancy norms in terms of content, rigidity, and evaluations and that such cultural differences are likely to present the challenges of "asynchronicity" in intercultural communication. The theory provides a framework for cross-cultural communication researchers to examine the real-time interaction patterns within and across cultures, as well as for intercultural communication researchers to examine how communicators succeed or fail in making adaptive adjustments when interacting with others of dissimilar cultural backgrounds.

Orbe's co-cultural theory (Orbe, 1998; Orbe & Spellers, 2005) is another theory that invites new research efforts. The theory uniquely focuses on the psychological postures commonly observed among members of traditionally underrepresented groups (e.g., non-Whites and women). Grounded in a "critical" perspective and informed by "muted group theory" and "standpoint theory," this theory presents a typology of nine "communication orientations" commonly employed by co-cultural group members when interacting with dominant group members (e.g., "nonassertive separation," "assertive accommodation," and "aggressive assimilation"). Among the many research issues that can be generated from this typology are the situational and environmental conditions under which each of the eight co-cultural orientations is likely to be activated, intensified, or avoided.

Y. Y. Kim's (1994, 1997, 2005b) contextual theory of interethnic communication is yet another theory on which new sets of research are raised. This theory presents an integrative explanatory system to explain the associative and dissociative behaviors of individuals of dissimilar ethnic backgrounds. With the main aim of theoretical integration of various concepts and research findings across several social science disciplines, this theory focuses on a broad spectrum of interethnic behaviors on a continuum of "association" and "dissociation" and presents eight theorems that explain the nature of interrelationships among the associative-dissociative continuum of interethnic behavior and eight factors of three contextual layers: the communicator, the situation, and the environment. In particular, the three theorems address the role of three environmental factors in interethnic communication that rarely have been examined in the past—institutional equity/inequity, in-group strength/weakness, and environmental stress.

# ◆ Conclusion

Perhaps more than investigators in many other areas in the field of communication, intercultural communication researchers have been a heterogeneous group in terms of national origin and ethnicity. Despite and perhaps because of such diversity, intercultural communication as an area of study has been a vibrant academic home for scholars interested in a wide range of communication phenomena involving issues of culture, cultural variations, and interface of cultures. As cultures and subcultures of the world continue to come together ever more closely at the grassroots level, and given the theoretical advancements and new research opportunities described in this chapter, we may look to the future of intercultural communication inquiry with a degree of optimism and confidence. Such an outlook also requires a resolve, individually and collectively, to continue to strive for attaining knowledge claims that can withstand the test of time and, ultimately, serve humanity's survival, mutuality, and peace from the ground up—the very ideals that inspired intercultural communication inquiry in the first place.

# ◆ References

Asante, M., & Gudykunst, W. (Eds.). (1989). *Handbook of international and intercultural communication.* Newbury Park, CA: Sage.

Asante, M., Newmark, E., & Blake, C. (1979). *Handbook of intercultural communication.* Beverly Hills, CA: Sage.

Berger, C., & Calabrese, R. (1975). Some explorations in initial interactions and beyond. *Human Communication Research, 1,* 99–112.

Boggs, C., & Giles, H. (1999). "The canary in the coal mine": The nonaccommodation cycle in the gendered workplace. *International Journal of Applied Linguistics, 22,* 223–245.

Burgoon, J. (1983). Nonverbal violation of expectations. In J. Wiemann & R. Harrison (Eds.), *Nonverbal interaction* (pp. 77–111). Beverly Hills, CA: Sage.

Burgoon, J. (1995). Cross-cultural and intercultural applications of expectancy violations theory. In R. Wiseman (Ed.), *Intercultural communication theory* (pp. 194–214). Thousand Oaks, CA: Sage.

Burgoon, J., & Hubbard, A. (2005). Cross-cultural and intercultural applications of expectancy violations theory and interaction adaptation theory. In W. Gudykunst (Ed.), *Theorizing about intercultural communication* (pp. 149–171). Thousand Oaks, CA: Sage.

Burgoon, J., Stern, L., & Dillman, L. (1995). *Interpersonal adaptation: Dyadic interaction patterns.* New York: Cambridge University Press.

Carbaugh, D. (1993). Competence as cultural pragmatics: Reflections on some Soviet and American encounters. In R. Wiseman & J. Koester (Eds.), *Intercultural communication competence* (pp. 168–183). Newbury Park, CA: Sage.

Carbaugh, D. (2005). *Cultures in conversation.* Mahwah, NJ: Lawrence Erlbaum.

Collier, M. (2005). Theorizing about cultural identifications: Critical updates and continuing evolution. In W. Gudykunst (Ed.), *Theorizing about intercultural communication* (pp. 235–256). Thousand Oaks, CA: Sage.

D'Andrade, R. (1984). Cultural meaning system. In R. A. Shweder & R. A. Levine (Eds.), *Culture theory: Essays on mind, self, and emotion* (pp. 88–119). Cambridge, UK: Cambridge University Press.

D'Andrade, R., & Strauss, C. (1992). *Human motives and cultural models.* New York: Cambridge University Press.

Ellingsworth, H. (1977). Conceptualizing intercultural communication. In B. Ruben (Ed.), *Communication yearbook 2* (pp. 345–350). New Brunswick, NJ: Transaction.

Fitch, K. (1998). *Speaking relationally: Culture, communication, and interpersonal connection.* New York: Guilford.

Gallois, C., Franklyn-Stokes, A., Giles, H., & Coupland, N. (1988). Communication accommodation in intercultural encounters. In Y. Y. Kim & W. B. Gudykunst (Eds.), *Theories in intercultural communication* (pp. 157–185). Newbury Park, CA: Sage.

Gallois, C., Giles, H., Jones, E., Cargile, A., & Ota, H. (1995). Accommodating intercultural encounters: Elaborations and extensions. In R. Wiseman (Ed.), *Intercultural communication theory* (pp. 115–147). Thousand Oaks, CA: Sage.

Gallois, C., Ogay, T., & Giles, H. (2005). Communication accommodation theory. In W. Gudykunst (Ed.), *Theorizing about intercultural communication* (pp. 121–148). Thousand Oaks, CA: Sage.

Geertz, C. (1973). *The interpretation of culture.* New York: Basic Books.

Giles, H. (1973). Accent mobility: A model and some data. *Anthropological Linguistics, 15,* 87–105.

Giles, H. (1979). A new theory of the dynamics of speech. *Diogenes, 106,* 119–136.

Giles, H., Coupland, N., & Williams, A. (1992). International talk and communication with older people. *International Journal of Aging & Human Development, 34*(4), 271–297.

Giles, H., & Johnson, P. (1987). Ethnolinguistic identity theory: A social psychological approach to language maintenance. *International Journal of the Sociology of Language, 68,* 69–99.

Giles, H., Rosenthal, D., & Young, L. (1986). Speech accommodation theory. In M. McLaughlin (Ed.), *Communication yearbook 10* (pp. 13–48). Newbury Park, CA: Sage.

Goffman, E. (1955). On face-work: An analysis of ritual elements in social interaction. *Psychiatry: Journal for the Study of International Processes, 18,* 213–231.

Goffman, E. (1959). *The presentation of self in everyday life.* Garden City, NY: Doubleday.

Gonzalez, A., Houston, M., & Chen, V. (1994). *Our voices: Essays in culture, ethnicity, and communication: An intercultural anthology.* Los Angeles: Roxbury.

Gonzalez, A., & Tanno, D. (Eds.). (1997). *Politics, communication, and culture.* Thousand Oaks, CA: Sage.

Greenfield, P. (1997). Culture as process: Empirical methods for cultural psychology. In J. Berry, Y. Poortinga, & J. Pandey (Eds.), *Handbook of cross-cultural psychology: Vol. 1. Theory and method* (2nd ed., pp. 301–346). Boston: Allyn & Bacon.

Gudykunst, W. (Ed.). (1983). *Intercultural communication theory.* Beverly Hills, CA: Sage.

Gudykunst, W. (1985). The influence of cultural similarity, type of relationship, and self-monitoring on uncertainty reduction processes. *Communication Monographs, 52,* 203–217.

Gudykunst, W. (Ed.). (1986). *Intergroup communication: The social psychology of language* (Vol. 5). London: Edward Arnold.

Gudykunst, W. (1988). Uncertainty and anxiety. In Y. Kim & W. Gudykunst (Eds.), *Theories of intercultural communication* (pp. 123–156). Newbury Park, CA: Sage.

Gudykunst, W. (1995). Anxiety/uncertainty management (AUM) theory. In R. Wiseman (Ed.), *Intercultural communication theory* (pp. 8–58). Thousand Oaks, CA: Sage.

Gudykunst, W. (1998). Applying anxiety/uncertainty management (AUM) theory to intercultural adjustment training. *International Journal of Intercultural Relations, 22*(2), 227–250.

Gudykunst, W. (2003). Understanding must precede criticism: A response to Yoshitake's critique of anxiety/uncertainty (AUM) theory. *Intercultural Communication Studies, 12*(1), 25–40.

Gudykunst, W. (2005a). An anxiety/uncertainty management (AUM) theory of effective communication: Making the mesh of the net finer. In W. Gudykunst (Ed.), *Theorizing about intercultural communication* (pp. 281–322). Thousand Oaks, CA: Sage.

Gudykunst, W. (2005b). An anxiety/uncertainty management (AUM) theory of strangers' intercultural adjustment. In W. Gudykunst (Ed.), *Theorizing about intercultural communication* (pp. 419–457). Thousand Oaks, CA: Sage.

Gudykunst, W. (Ed.). (2005c). *Theorizing about intercultural communication.* Thousand Oaks, CA: Sage.

Gudykunst, W., & Bond, M. (1997). Intergroup relations across cultures. In J. Berry, M. Segall, & C. Kagitcibashi (Eds.), *Handbook of cross-cultural psychology* (2nd ed., pp. 118–161). Boston: Allyn & Bacon.

Gudykunst, W., Gao, G., Schmidt, K., Nishida, T., Bond, M., Leung, K., et al. (1992). The influence of individualism-collectivism, self-monitoring, and predicted outcome values on communication in ingroup and outgroup relationships. *Journal of Cross-Cultural Psychology, 23,* 196–213.

Gudykunst, W., & Hammer, M. (1988). The influence of social identity and intimacy of interethnic relationships on uncertainty reduction processes. *Human Communication Research, 14,* 569–601.

Gudykunst, W., & Kim, Y. Y. (2003). *Communicating with strangers: An approach to intercultural communication* (4th ed.). New York: McGraw-Hill.

Gudykunst, W., & Mody, B. (Eds.). (2004). *Handbook of international and intercultural communication* (3rd ed.). Thousand Oaks, CA: Sage.

Gudykunst, W., & Nishida, T. (2001). Anxiety, uncertainty, and perceived effectiveness of communication across relationships and cultures. *International Journal of Intercultural Relations, 25,* 55–72.

Hall, E. T. (1976). *Beyond culture.* New York: Doubleday.

Hall, S. (1989). Ideology and communication theory. In B. Dervin, L. Grossberg, B. O'Keefe, & E. Wartella (Eds.), *Rethinking communication: Vol. 1. Paradigm issues* (pp. 40–52). Newbury Park, CA: Sage.

Hammer, M., Wiseman, R., Rasmussen, J., & Bruschke, J. (1998). A test of uncertainty/anxiety reduction theory: The intercultural adaptation context. *Communication Quarterly, 46,* 309–326.

Handwerker, W. P. (2002). The construct validity of cultures: Cultural diversity, culture theory, and a method for ethnography. *American Anthropologist, 104*(1), 106–122.

Hedge, R. (1998). Swinging the trapeze: The negotiation of identity among Asian Indian immigrant women in the United States. In D. Tanno & A. Gonzalez (Eds.),

*Communication and identity across cultures* (pp. 34–55). Thousand Oaks, CA: Sage.

Hofstede, G. (1980). *Culture's consequences.* Beverly Hills, CA: Sage.

Holland, D., & Quinn, N. (1987). *Cultural models in language and thought.* New York: Cambridge University Press.

Katriel, T., & Philipsen, G. (1990). "What we need is communication": "Communication" as a cultural category in some American speech. In D. Carbaugh (Ed.), *Cultural communication and intercultural contact* (pp. 77–93). Hillsdale, NJ: Lawrence Erlbaum.

Keesing, R. (1974). Theories of culture. *Annual Review of Anthropology, 3,* 73–97.

Keesing, R. (1994). Theories of culture revisited. In R. Borofsky (Ed.), *Assessing cultural anthropology* (pp. 301–312). New York: McGraw-Hill.

Kim, M. (1993). Culture-based interactive constraints in explaining intercultural strategic competence. In R. Wiseman & J. Kolene (Eds.), *Intercultural communication competence* (pp. 132–150). Newbury Park, CA: Sage.

Kim, M. (1994). Cross-cultural comparisons of the perceived importance of conversational constraints. *Human Communication Research, 21,* 128–151.

Kim, M. (1995). Toward a theory of conversational constraints. In R. Wiseman (Ed.), *Intercultural communication theory* (pp. 148–169). Thousand Oaks, CA: Sage.

Kim, M. (2005). Culture-based conversational constraints theory. In W. Gudykunst (Ed.), *Theorizing about intercultural communication* (pp. 93–117). Thousand Oaks, CA: Sage.

Kim, M., Hunter, J., Miyahara, A., Horvath, A., Bresnahan, M., & Yoon, H. (1996). Individual- vs. culture-level dimensions of individualism and collectivism: Effects on preferred conversational styles. *Communication Monographs, 63,* 29–49.

Kim, M., Sharkey, W., & Singelis, T. (1994). The relationship between individuals' self-construal and perceived importance of interactive constraints. *International Journal of Intercultural Relations, 18,* 117–140.

Kim, Y. S., & Kim, Y. Y. (2007). Communication patterns and psychological health in the process of cross-cultural adaptation: A study of American and Korean expatriate workers. In B. Allen, L. Flores, & M. Orbe (Eds.), *Communication within/across organizations* (pp. 229–258). Washington, DC: National Communication Association.

Kim, Y. Y. (1976). *Communication patterns of foreign immigrants in the process of acculturation: A survey among Korean population in Chicago.* Unpublished doctoral dissertation, Northwestern University, Evanston, IL.

Kim, Y. Y. (1977). Communication patterns of foreign immigrants in the process of acculturation. *Human Communication Research, 4*(1), 66–77.

Kim, Y. Y. (1988). *Communication and cross-cultural adaptation: An integrative theory.* Clevedon, England: Multilingual Matters.

Kim, Y. Y. (1990). Communication and adaptation of Asian Pacific refugees in the United States. *Journal of Pacific Rim Communication, 1,* 191–207.

Kim, Y. Y. (1994). Interethnic communication: The context and the behavior. In S. Deetz (Ed.), *Communication yearbook 17* (pp. 511–538). Newbury Park, CA: Sage.

Kim, Y. Y. (1995a). Cross-cultural adaptation: An integrative theory. In R. Wiseman (Ed.), *Intercultural communication theory* (pp. 170–193). Newbury Park, CA: Sage.

Kim, Y. Y. (1995b). Identity development: From cultural to intercultural. In H. Mokros (Ed.), *Information and behavior: Vol. 5. Interaction and identity* (pp. 347–369). New Brunswick, NJ: Transaction.

Kim, Y. Y. (1997). The context-behavior interface in interethnic communication. In J. Owen (Ed.), *Context and communication behavior* (pp. 261–291). Reno, NV: Context Press.

Kim, Y. Y. (2001). *Becoming intercultural: An integrative theory of communication and cross-cultural adaptation.* Thousand Oaks, CA: Sage.

Kim, Y. Y. (2005a). Adapting to a new culture: An integrative communication theory. In W. Gudykunst (Ed.), *Theorizing about intercultural communication* (pp. 375–400). Thousand Oaks, CA: Sage.

Kim, Y. Y. (2005b). Association and dissociation: A contextual theory of interethnic communication. In W. Gudykunst (Ed.), *Theorizing about intercultural communication* (pp. 323–350). Thousand Oaks, CA: Sage.

Kim, Y. Y. (2006). From ethnic to interethnic: The case for identity adaptation and transformation. *Journal of Language and Social Psychology, 23*(3), 283–300.

Kim, Y. Y. (2008). Intercultural personhood: Globalization and a way of being. *International Journal of Intercultural Relations, 32*, 359–368

Kim, Y. Y., & Braun, V. (2002, July). *Host communication competence and psychological health: A study of Turkish workers adaptation in an American-German host environment.* Paper presented at the annual conference of the International Communication Association, Seoul, Korea.

Kim, Y. Y., & Gudykunst, W. (Eds.). (1988). *Theories in intercultural communication.* Newbury Park, CA: Sage.

Kim, Y. Y., & Kim, Y. S. (2004, March). The role of host environment in cross-cultural adaptation: A comparison of American expatriates in South Korea and their Korean counterparts in the United States. *Asian Communication Research, 1*(1), 5–25.

Kim, Y. Y., Lujan, P., & Dixon, L. (1998). "I can walk both ways": Identity integration of American Indians in Oklahoma. *Human Communication Research, 25*(2), 252–274.

Kimberly, N., Gudykunst, W., & Guerrero, S. (1999). Intergroup communication over time. *International Journal of Intercultural Relations, 22*(4), 1–34.

Langer, E. (1989). *Mindfulness.* Reading, MA: Addison-Wesley.

Lee, B., & Chen, L. (2000). Cultural communication competence and psychological adjustment. *Communication Research, 27*, 764–792.

Martin, J., & Nakayama, T. (1999). Thinking dialectically about culture and communication. *Communication Theory, 1*, 1–25.

Maruyama, M. (1998). *Cross-cultural adaptation and host environment: A study of international students in Japan.* Unpublished doctoral dissertation, University of Oklahoma, Norman.

McLuhan, M. (1962). *The Gutenberg galaxy.* New York: New American Library.

Milstein, T. (2005). Transformation abroad: Sojourning and the perceived enhancement of self-efficacy. *International Journal of Intercultural Relations, 29*, 217–238.

Miyahara, A., & Kim, M. (1993). Requesting styles among "collectivists" cultures: A comparison between Japanese and Koreans. *Intercultural Communication Studies, 6*, 104–128.

Munroe, R., & Munroe, R. (1997). A comparative anthropological perspective. In J. W. Berry, Y. H. Poortinga, & J. Pandey (Eds.), *Handbook of cross-cultural psychology: Vol. 1. Theory and method* (2nd ed., pp. 171–213). Boston: Allyn & Bacon.

Nakayama, T., & Martin, J. (Eds.). (1998). *Whiteness: The communication of social identity.* Thousand Oaks, CA: Sage.

Norenzayan, A., & Heine, S. (2005). Psychological universals: What are they and how can we know? *Psychological Bulletin, 131*, 763–784.

Oetzel, J., & Ting-Toomey, S. (2003). Face concerns in interpersonal conflict: A cross-cultural empirical test of the face-negotiation theory. *Communication Research, 30*, 599–624.

Oetzel, J., Ting-Toomey, S., Masumoto, T., Yokochi, Y., Pan, X., Takai, J., et al. (2001). Face behaviors in interpersonal conflicts: A cross-cultural comparison of Germany, Japan, China, and the United States. *Communication Monographs, 68*, 235–258.

Orbe, M. (1998). *Constructing co-cultural theory: An explication of culture, power, and communication.* Thousand Oaks, CA: Sage.

Orbe, M., & Spellers, R. (2005). From the margins to the center: Utilizing co-cultural theory in diverse contexts. In W. Gudykunst (Ed.), *Theorizing about intercultural communication* (pp. 173–191). Thousand Oaks, CA: Sage.

Philipsen, G. (1981, March). *The prospect for cultural communication.* Paper presented at the Seminar on Communication Theory from Eastern and Western Cultural Perspectives, Honolulu, HI.

Philipsen, G. (1992). *Speaking culturally: Explorations in social communication.* Albany: State University of New York Press.

Philipsen, G. (1997). A theory of speech codes. In G. Philipsen & T. Albrecht (Eds.), *Developing communication theories* (pp. 119–156). Albany: State University of New York Press.

Philipsen, G. (2002). Cultural communication. In W. Gudykunst & B. Mody (Eds.), *Handbook of international and intercultural communication* (2nd ed., pp. 51–68). Thousand Oaks, CA: Sage.

Philipsen, G., Coutu, L., & Covarrubias, P. (2005). Speech code theory: Restatement, revisions, and response to criticisms. In W. Gudykunst (Ed.), *Theorizing about intercultural communication* (pp. 55–68). Thousand Oaks, CA: Sage.

Pitts, M. J. (2007, May). *Short-term adjustment and intergroup relations among U.S. American student sojourners: Applying theory(ies) to practice.* Paper presented at the annual conference of the International Communication Association, San Francisco.

Pratt, S. (1998). Razzing: Ritualizing uses of humor as a form of identification among American Indians. In D. Tanno & A. Gonzalez (Eds.), *Communication and identity across cultures* (pp. 56–79). Thousand Oaks, CA: Sage.

Sarbaugh, L. (1988). *Intercultural communication.* New Brunswick, NJ: Transaction.

Shearer, H. (2003, December). *Intercultural personhood: A "mainstream" Australian biographical case study.* Unpublished doctoral dissertation, Griffith University, Mt. Gravatt, Queensland, Australia.

Simmel, G. (1950). The stranger. In K. Wolff (Trans. & Ed.), *The sociology of Georg Simmel* (pp. 402–408). New York: Free Press. (Original work published 1908)

Singelis, T., & Brown, W. (1995). Culture, self, and collectivist communication: Linking culture to individual behavior. *Human Communication Research, 21,* 354–389.

Stephan, W., & Stephan, C. (1985). Intergroup anxiety. *Journal of Social Issues, 41*(3), 157–175.

Street, R., & Giles, H. (1982). Speech accommodation theory: A social cognitive approach to language and speech behavior. In M. Roloff & C. Berger (Eds.), *Social cognition and communication* (pp. 193–226). Beverly Hills, CA: Sage.

Tajfel, H. (1981). *Human categories and social groups.* Cambridge, UK: Cambridge University Press.

Tajfel, H., & Turner, J. (1986). The social identity theory of intergroup behavior. In S. Worchel & W. Austin (Eds.), *Psychology of intergroup relations* (2nd ed., pp. 7–24). Chicago: Nelson-Hall.

Takekuro, M. (2006). Japanese language, gender, and ideology: Cultural models and real people. *Journal of Sociolinguistics, 10,* 679–683.

Tamam, E. (1993). *The influence of ambiguity tolerance, open-mindedness, and empathy on sojourners' psychological adaptation and perceived intercultural communication effectiveness.* Unpublished doctoral dissertation, University of Oklahoma, Norman.

Thussu, D. K. (2006). *International communication: Continuity and change* (2nd ed.). London: Hoddler Arnold.

Ting-Toomey, S. (1988). Intercultural conflict styles: A face-negotiation theory. In Y. Y. Kim & W. Gudykunst (Eds.), *Theories in intercultural communication* (pp. 213–235). Newbury Park, CA: Sage.

Ting-Toomey, S. (2004). Translating conflict face-negotiation theory into practice. In D. Landis, J. Bennett, & M. Bennett (Eds.), *Handbook of intercultural training* (3rd ed., pp. 217–248). Thousand Oaks, CA: Sage.

Ting-Toomey, S. (2005a). Identity management theory: Facework in intercultural relationships. In W. Gudykunst (Ed.), *Theorizing about intercultural communication* (pp. 195–210). Thousand Oaks, CA: Sage.

Ting-Toomey, S. (2005b). The matrix of face: An updated face-negotiation theory. In W. Gudykunst (Ed.), *Theorizing about intercultural communication* (pp. 71–92). Thousand Oaks, CA: Sage.

Ting-Toomey, S., Gao, G., Trubinsky, P., Yang, Z., Kim, H., Lin, S., et al. (1991). Culture, face maintenance, and styles of handling interpersonal conflict: A study in five cultures. *International Journal of Conflict Management, 2,* 275–295.

Ting-Toomey, S., & Kurogi, A. (1998). Facework competence in intercultural conflict: An updated face-negotiation theory. *International Journal of Intercultural Relations, 22*(2), 187–225.

Triandis, H. (1988). Collectivism vs. individualism: A reconceptualization of a basic concept in cross-cultural psychology. In G. Verman & C. Bagley (Eds.), *Cross-cultural studies of personality, attitudes and cognition* (pp. 60–95). London: Macmillan.

Van de Vijver, F., & Leung, K. (1997). Methods and data analysis of comparative research. In J. Berry, Y. Poortinga, & J. Pandey (Eds.), *Handbook of cross-cultural psychology: Vol. 1. Theory and method* (2nd ed., pp. 257–300). Boston: Allyn & Bacon.

Walker, D. (1993, March). *The role of the mass media in the adaptation of Haitian immigrants in Miami.* Unpublished doctoral dissertation, Indiana University School of Journalism, Bloomington.

Wee, L. (2006). The cultural basis of metaphor revisited. *Pragmatics & Cognition, 14*(1), 111–128.

Wieder, L., & Pratt, S. (1990). On being a recognizable Indian among Indians. In D. Carbaugh (Ed.), *Cultural communication and intercultural contact* (pp. 45–64). Hillsdale, NJ: Lawrence Erlbaum.

Winchatz, M. R. (2001). Social meanings in German interactions: An ethnographic analysis of the second-person pronoun *Sie. Research on Language and Social Interaction, 34,* 337–369.

Wiseman, R. (Ed.). (1995). *Intercultural communication theory.* Thousand Oaks, CA: Sage.

Yoshitake, M. (2002). A critical examination of the anxiety/uncertainty management (AUM) theory as a major intercultural communication theory. *Intercultural Communication Studies, 11*(2), 177–194.

Young, R. (1996). *Intercultural communication: Pragmatics, genealogy, deconstruction.* Philadelphia: Multilingual Matters.

Yu, N. (2003). Chinese metaphors of thinking. *Cognitive Linguistics, 14*(2/3), 141–165.

# 27

# THE SCIENTIFIC INVESTIGATION OF MARITAL AND FAMILY COMMUNICATION

◆ Ascan F. Koerner

T here has been a long tradition and strong interest in the scientific investigation of marriages and families in the United States from both the sociological (i.e., macro) and psychological (i.e., micro) perspectives (Koerner, 2007). The reasons for this interest are many. From the sociological perspective, these interpersonal relationships are of great interest because marriages and families can be considered to be the basic forms of social organization. Marriages and families constitute the building blocks of communities and societies, and how marriages and families function often reflects similar processes in society at large. In addition, the family is also widely accepted to be the primary socialization agent of young children and a significant socialization agent for adolescents and young adults. Thus, understanding how and what families socialize is an important aspect of understanding societies and the individuals in them.

From a psychological perspective, marriage and family relationships are no less significant. One reason for their importance is that family relationships for most people are their most enduring, most intimate, and most significant interpersonal relationships and greatly affect their mental and physiological functioning and well-being. Specifically, marriages and family relationships affect the subjective experiences of persons in them, measured by variables such as relationship satisfaction, as well as more objective outcomes, such as psychopathology, physical health, and longevity. It is no surprise, then, that the psychological interest in marriage and the family results in no small measure from clinical application. In addition, families are also the primary socializers of children and thus affect a wide variety of psychological processes in children and grown adults, including attachment, core beliefs and values, motivation, and the psychological processes underlying interpersonal relationships.

As a consequence of the general relevance of marriage and family relationships for the social sciences, the roles that marriages, families, and family relationships play both for societies at large and for individuals, as well as the impact that societal and psychological variables have on marital and family relationships and their functioning, are well researched. The impact of this tradition within both sociological and psychological research perspectives on the scientific investigation of marital and family *communication*, however, has been mixed. As far as marital communication is concerned, the most influential research has been conducted by those coming from the psychological tradition. Early in the history of this line of inquiry, many researchers recognized the interdependence of the marital couple and, as a result, focused on the interaction processes in marriages. In particular, they were concerned with identifying and distinguishing between functional and dysfunctional patterns of interaction. As a consequence, the social scientific investigation of marital communication is very well established and has reached very high levels of methodological sophistication. However, because of psychology's emphasis on hypothesis testing and experimentation, combined with clinicians' concern for treating individuals and couples, most theoretical models that stem from this tradition are fairly narrow in scope and address specific behaviors and contexts rather than aiming at providing comprehensive accounts of "the marriage."

The social scientific investigation of families and family relationships, on the other hand, has been more influenced by researchers embracing a sociological perspective. While generally recognizing that the family is a system, many of these researchers are more interested in the interactions of family systems with other social systems and institutions than in the interactions within family systems themselves. As a consequence, compared with other variables affecting families, the social scientific investigation of family communication specifically is a relatively recent endeavor, and the amount of social science research on family communication is rather modest, especially when compared with that on marital communication. In addition, even for those researchers with an interest in communication, communication was, and often still is, conceptualized in fairly simplistic terms. For example, communication might be equated with measures of relationship quality and satisfaction or reduced to simple, one-dimensional qualities, such as warmth or openness.

Another reason for the relative lack of social scientific research on family communication is that within the discipline of communication itself, the use of social scientific theories and methods to study communication is a relatively recent development. Furthermore, family communication as its own specialty within the discipline of communication is an even more recent development. Although research focusing specifically on family communication and family relationships was published in early communication journals and handbooks and has thus been part of the field from its beginning, the National Communication Association has had a Family Communication division only since 1995, and has such a division is entirely missing from the International Communication Association. Also, the first academic journal exclusively devoted to family communication (*Journal of Family Communication*) did not come into being until 2001, and the first handbook of family communication was not published until 2004 (Vangelisti, 2004).

Despite these slow beginnings, interest in social scientific research on family communication has grown tremendously over the past several years. It has brought with it a significant increase in not only more rigorous social scientific studies of family communication but also the development of several theories and models of family communication. While these models and theories do not yet rest on a depth and breadth of empirical knowledge comparable to that in marital communication, progress definitely has been made, and this area has a very bright future. In fact, as this review will show, many of the theories proposed in family communication are more ambitious, that is, of broader scope than those relating to marital communication.

Given the sheer amount of social scientific research on marital and family communication, it is impossible to summarize it or even to provide a comprehensive overview of it in a single chapter. Readers interested in such reviews are referred to edited volumes on family communication by Braithwaite and Baxter (2006) and Vangelisti (2004), as well as to reviews by Bradbury, Fincham, and Beach (2000) on marital satisfaction and Roloff and Miller (2006) on conflict in marriages and families.

The following sections focus on some of the main theories in the areas of marital and family communication as exemplars of the type of research that is taking place. In particular, theories that emerged from within the field of communication or that had a significant impact on it will be considered, including descriptions of their main assumptions and assertions as well as some of the research using them. The chapter will conclude with an outlook on future developments in these areas.

## ◆ Marital Communication

As already stated, research in marital communication has reached significant theoretical and methodological sophistication and can be considered a mature area of the discipline. Because the underlying motivation for much of the research was initially to identify what makes persons happy and satisfied in marriages and, closely related, what makes marriages stable, explaining and predicting marital satisfaction and stability (i.e., divorce) have received the lion's share of research attention (Fincham & Beach, 2006). These investigations identified the effects of factors related to cognition and affect on satisfaction and stability, such as anxiety and depression (Whisman, Uebelacker, & Weinstock, 2007), attributions (Bradbury & Fincham, 1992), empathic accuracy (Thomas, Fletcher, & Lange, 1997), expectations (Vanzetti, Notarius, & NeeSmith, 1992), and expectation accessibility (Fincham, Garnier, Gano-Phillips, & Osborn, 1995). Other research has more explicitly focused on the effects of marital communication on satisfaction and stability—in particular, research on communication related to marital conflict, on demand/withdrawal patterns of interaction, on the provisions of social support, and on the expression of positive affect in marriages.

### MARITAL CONFLICT

A prominent example of research on marital conflict is the work by Gottman and his associates (Gottman, 1993, 1994; Gottman & Krokoff, 1989; Gottman, Murray, Swanson, Tyson, & Swanson, 2002; Gottman & Levenson, 1986). Investigating which interaction processes in married couples are most relevant for relationship satisfaction and stability, Gottman found that behaviors during conflict interactions are particularly predictive of relationship satisfaction and stability, in one study with 80% accuracy for satisfaction and 83% for stability after 6 years (Gottman, Coan, Carrere, & Swanson, 1998). In particular, behaviors that expressed negative affect for the partner, such as criticism, defensiveness, contempt, and withdrawal, were predictive of dissatisfaction and divorce (Gottman, 1994). Surprisingly, expressing anger, which has been suggested by others to be a particularly corrosive behavior in marriages (e.g., Hendrix, 1988), was not only not associated with divorce but actually predicted greater marital satisfaction over time (Gottman & Krokoff, 1989).

Over the years, Gottman has sought to identify explanatory mechanisms (see Gottman et al., 2002) for the effects of the negative behaviors that involve physiological responses, such as arousal, as mediating factors. Using various measures of arousal (e.g., blood pressure, heart rate, and skin conductance), this research showed that frequently, spouses who manifest physiological arousal in response to negative affect expressed by their partners often reciprocate or escalate negative behaviors, whereas spouses who are able to sooth themselves or are soothed by their partners engage in more positive behaviors, or at least avoid reciprocation and escalation of negative behaviors. Particularly in men, arousal often leads to emotional withdrawal from the relationship, which has long-term negative effects on relationship satisfaction and stability (Gottman & Levenson, 1992).

The role of physiological arousal, however, is not necessarily the same for all individuals and couples. For example, in the case of violently abusive husbands, Coan, Gottman, Babcock, and Jacobson (1997) found two different types of batterers: (a) those who are generally more violent outside their marriages and whose heart rate slows down during marital conflict and (b) those whose violence is largely confined to their marriages and whose heart rate increases during marital conflict. Results such as these suggest not only that whether a spouse gets physiologically aroused during conflict varies between individuals, but also that the effects that arousal has on behaviors is different for different individuals. Thus, the link between physiological arousal and violent behavior in conflict is more complicated than initially assumed.

The effects of expressing affect during conflict, however, are not limited only to negative emotions. In at least one study, Gottman et al. (1998) found that only the expression of positive affect for the partner predicted marital satisfaction and stability over time. Uncharacteristically, the expression of negative affect had no predictive power in this study. This finding suggests either that the expression of positive affect has its own effects on physiology that are somewhat opposite those of negative affect or that not all effects of expressing affect during conflict communication are mediated by physiological arousal. In any event, such contradictory findings suggest that although the effects of expressing emotions have been successfully demonstrated, explaining the effects has been much less successful.

While explicating the effects of expressing affect during marital conflict, Gottman (1993) also observed that conflict does not have the same effects on all marriages and that different couples handle conflict differently with different outcomes. These observations led him to propose a marital typology based on conflict behaviors that identified three functional and two dysfunctional types. Among the functional types, the *validating* couple includes partners who openly communicated their needs and desires and are receptive of those of the other person. They are supportive of one another and engage in collaborative problem solving and, throughout the conflict, maintain largely positive affect. They are also able to repair any damage caused to the relationship as a result of expressed negative affect by apologizing, soothing the other, and expressing positive affect for one another.

Less intuitively functional are couples who represent the *volatile* type. In these couples, both partners are more competitive than collaborative, and they freely express their negative affect toward one another. These couples, however, manage to compensate for their open expression of negative affect by also expressing a surplus of positive affect, which ultimately enables them to maintain their relationship. Equally counterintuitive are *avoidant* couples, in which both partners avoid open conflict and often even fail to acknowledge their divergent interests. As a result, they neither engage in any form of problem solving nor express their negative affect. Although these couples consequently fail to resolve their differences, they individually accommodate each other, and because they do not create a lot of hurt feelings, they are able to maintain their relationships even in the absence of frequent expressions of positive affect for one another.

A characteristic all three functional types share is that for them to remain functional, they need to maintain an expressed positive to expressed negative affect ratio of at least 5:1 (Gottman et al., 1998). Thus, stable volatile couples who express a lot of negative affect express significantly more positive affect than similarly stable validating or avoidant couples. Another shared characteristic is that each conflict type contains within it particular challenges to maintaining its particular style. Thus, validating couples exert much energy in cognitive editing, avoidant couples often lack vitality, and volatiles who fail to express surplus positive affect easily transition into hostile or hostile-detached couples.

Hostile and hostile-detached couples constitute the two dysfunctional couple types identified by Gottman (1993). Conflict in these couples is characterized by the open expression of negative affect, often with the intent to hurt or denigrate the other, without the presence of surplus positive affect. Because of the significant negative emotional toll that such conflict interactions incur, couples with these conflict styles are unlikely to stay together for very long and, if married, usually divorce (see Sillars, Chapter 16, this volume).

Despite, or maybe because of, the great attention that Gottman's research has received within the discipline and the general public, his research is not without its critics, especially on methodological grounds (e.g., Heyman & Slep, 2001; Stanley, Bradbury, & Markman, 2000). Although these criticisms raise legitimate concerns about the validity of some of the more spectacular of Gottman's claims (e.g., predicting divorce with greater than 90% accuracy), they do not undermine the basic theoretical contributions of the research.

## DEMAND-WITHDRAWAL

Closely related to the study of conflict is the study of demand-withdrawal patterns in marriage. Demand-withdrawal is characterized by one partner demanding, criticizing, or otherwise calling for behavior change in the other and the partner responding with avoidance or outright refusal to change. Although this behavior sometimes occurs during conflict, when it is also conceptualized as "stonewalling" (e.g., Gottman, 1994), it is more often investigated in the context of marital problem solving or during relationship talk. Early investigations of the pattern by Christensen (1987, 1988; Christensen & Heavey, 1990) identified it generally as a gendered pattern of wife demand–husband withdrawal. More recent investigations, however, suggest that this gender-specific finding might have been the result of demand characteristics of earlier studies (couples were asked to talk about relationships, which they themselves often perceived as being the wife's topic), and patterns of husband demand–wife withdrawal have also been observed, particularly in discussions of topics chosen by the husband (Klinetob & Smith, 1996; Sillars, Chapter 16, this volume).

In either case, demand-withdrawal patterns are negatively associated with marital satisfaction (Christensen, 1987, 1988), although the explanatory mechanism for this association has not yet been fully explicated, and three alternatives have been considered. One possibility is that the demands of one partner lead to negative affect by the withdrawing partner, who feels pressured or coerced and experiences reactance or the loss of autonomy. Another possibility is that the demanding partners experience frustration because of the uncooperativeness of their spouse or because they are unable to achieve their goals in the face of partner resistance and avoidance. A third possibility is that the negative affect introduced by the demand-withdrawal escalates, and it is this escalation that has negative effects on relationship satisfaction and stability.

One communication scholar who investigated the causal processes linking demand-withdrawal to marital satisfaction and stability is John Caughlin (2002; Caughlin & Huston, 2002; Caughlin & Vangelisti, 2000). Investigating the effects of demand-withdrawal over time, Caughlin (2002) assessed 46 married couples at two times about a year apart. Results indicated that demand-withdrawal has a stable association with dissatisfaction, but also that, at least for wives, demand-withdrawal was associated with an increase in marital satisfaction. Caughlin interpreted these results as providing support for both the *enduring dynamics model,* which suggests that relationship processes develop early in marriage and remain relatively stable, and the *accommodation model,* which suggests that spouses make adjustments in their behaviors and their responses to their partners' behaviors as marriages mature. Not supported was the *disillusionment model,* which suggests that spouses become more dissatisfied in marriages because they lose some of the positive illusions they had about each other during courtship.

## SOCIAL SUPPORT

Communicating during conflict and problem solving, however, are not the only interpersonal behaviors that affect marital satisfaction and stability. Among the more positive behaviors that have been investigated in the context of marriage is social support, which is not only associated with satisfaction and stability, but also with benefits to mental and physical health (Gardner & Cutrona, 2004). Different scholars have used somewhat different definitions of social support. Some used broader definitions, such as the fulfillment of basic interpersonal needs (Kaplan, Cassel, & Gore, 1977) or communication that is responsive to another's needs and functions to comfort, encourage, reassure, and problem solve (Gardner & Cutrona, 2004). Others have used more narrow definitions, such as Burleson (1994, 2003, and Chapter 9, this volume) and his associates, who focus on emotional support, which is defined as communication intended to help another to effectively cope with emotional distress. Regardless of the definition's scope, the behaviors associated with social support are those that validate the emotional experience of the distressed person, express sympathy for and affiliation with the distressed person, and provide assistance for the person in addressing the underlying cause for the distress.

Different theoretical accounts that have emerged for the effects of social support on marriages vary mainly because they make different assumptions about the underlying causes for distress. Thus, work by Cutrona and her colleagues (Cutrona, 1990, 1996; Gardner & Cutrona, 2004) is based on the assumption that a number of unmet needs can cause psychological distress and that supportive communication is effective to the extent to which it addresses the underlying, unmet needs (*optimal matching model*). For example, targets of support who experience a need for information find communication that provides information supportive, targets who experience a lack of affiliation find affiliative communication supportive, and so forth.

In the field of interpersonal communication, most research on social support has been conducted by Burleson and his associates (Burleson, 2003; Burleson & Mortenson, 2003; Burleson et al., 2005; Jones & Burleson, 2003). This research has focused on a theoretical model based on Lazarus's (1991) theory of emotion that makes cognitive reappraisal central to the supporting process and de-emphasizes other forms of support, such as informational or instrumental support. According to this model, spouses provide emotional support by first acknowledging and legitimizing the emotional distress the target is experiencing and then helping the target alleviate the emotional distress by reappraising the situation (Burleson & Goldsmith, 1998). The latter step involves talking about the target's situation and feelings in a way that not only validates them but also suggests reinterpretations of the events, their meaning, or consequences in ways that are less emotionally distressful.

Both models of social support have garnered significant empirical support, and although they are often presented as alternatives to one another (e.g., Burleson, 2003), there are probably more similarities than differences between them. For example, while Burleson and his colleagues are probably right to emphasize that emotional distress is most likely the proximate cause for persons to seek social support, emotional distress can certainly result from frustrated needs. Thus, communication that meets those needs should be at least as effective in leading to a reappraisal of the situation as communication that focuses exclusively on cognitive reappraisals to alleviate emotional distress. Consequently, targets should perceive such communication as effective, very much as Cutrona (1990, 1996) suggests.

## EXPRESSING POSITIVE AFFECT

Another aspect of marital communication associated with positive rather than negative interactions that also has received considerable attention is the expression of positive affect, which is generally associated with increased intimacy and relationship satisfaction (Caughlin & Huston, 2002). Positive affect is particularly powerful when communicated nonverbally. The notion that positive affect is central to interpersonal relationships and that it is communicated mainly nonverbally was already articulated by the Palo Alto group (Watzlawick, Beavin, & Jackson, 1967). In the context of marriage, nonverbal communication of affect has been related to intimacy (Gottman, Markman, & Notarius, 1977) and marital satisfaction. Extensive research by Noller (1980, 1982; Noller & Gallois, 1986) found that effective nonverbal communication is associated with marital satisfaction and also that women both encode and decode nonverbal communication more accurately than men. Reasoning that for nonverbal communication to affect relationship satisfaction, it should be perceived as referring to either the partner or the relationship, Koerner and Fitzpatrick (2002a) distinguished between relationship-relevant and relationship-irrelevant nonverbal affect and found that only relationship-relevant affect was associated with marital satisfaction. Thus, at least when it is communicated nonverbally, positive affect only affects relationship satisfaction when it is attributed to a partner's feelings about the relationship or self. Whether this association also holds for the verbal communication of positive affect is as of yet undetermined.

## MARRIAGE TYPOLOGIES

Although the theories discussed thus far seem to focus on particular phenomena, modes of communication, or processes that appear to apply equally to all marriages, similar communication affects different couples differently, and different couples communicate differently in similar situations. This is not a surprise to anyone who studies human communication. Not only do individuals and their psychologies differ, but humans are also influenced by the particular cultural, historical, and relational contexts in which they live and relate to one another. Thus, to find that all humans communicate or respond exactly alike in a similar situation would be very surprising indeed.

Such variations in behaviors and outcomes, however, are not just the noise of extraneous variables and influences that can safely be ignored when building theories of marital communication. Rather, these variations are at least partially systematic and contribute to the associations between communication behaviors and outcomes and therefore cannot simply be treated as error variance. Specifically, these variations are the result of an interesting attribute of marriages—namely, that marriages create their own, unique relationship contexts that affect how couples communicate. Gottman's (1994) marital typology that identified three stable couple types that communicate very differently during conflict but that achieve similar outcomes already has been discussed. This typology was derived empirically, and Gottman never explicated why these couples communicate so differently during conflict, but his typology converges with another important marital typology, Fitzpatrick's (1988) marital types, which provides such an explanation.

Fitzpatrick's (1988) typology is one of the earliest and most influential typologies of marriages (Fincham, 2004). It is broad in scope in that it focuses neither on only specific circumstances in marriages nor on only one or two interpersonal processes. Rather, it categorizes marriages based on how spouses represent their marriages cognitively in terms of marital beliefs and values and how these beliefs are expressed through behavior. Specifically, categorization is based on spouses' reports of their *ideology* (e.g., beliefs and values relevant to marriage), behavioral *interdependence* (e.g., coordination of schedules and the sharing of space), and *communication* (e.g., whether couples engage in or avoid conflict).

On the basis of their scores on these three dimensions, individuals are categorized into one of three marital types: traditional, independent, or separate. *Traditionals* have a conventional ideology, are very interdependent, and have a moderately expressive communication style with their spouses during conflict. *Independents* have an unconventional ideology, are moderately interdependent, and report a very expressive communication style during conflict. *Separates* have a conventional ideology, are not very interdependent, and report little expressivity in their conflict communication. In about two thirds of marriages, both spouses have the same marital type; the remaining marriages fall into a mixed type, most frequently a traditional wife and a separate husband (Fitzpatrick, 1988).

In addition to being broadly applicable to investigations of marriage in a variety of circumstances and various interpersonal processes and phenomena, this typology has two additional strengths. First, it is based equally on theory (the three underlying dimensions were conceptualized based on prevailing marital theories) and empirical observation (the three types represent naturally occurring clusters in the conceptual space defined by the three dimensions). Second, it also postulates that different marriages achieve similar outcomes in different ways based on the relational context that they themselves define. That is, different types of marriages confronting the same set of challenges communicate differently to achieve similar outcomes—or communicate similarly but achieve different outcomes—because of the unique relational contexts that the marriages themselves create. Thus, in the context of conflict, for example, Fitzpatrick's traditionals behave like Gottman's validators, interdependents behave like volatiles, and separates behave like avoiders.

Another recent marital typology that also converges with Fitzpatrick's has been suggested by Caughlin and Huston (2006). On the basis of their own and others' research on affect in marriage, they concluded that positive affect and antagonism (i.e., conflict) are not mutually exclusive or the endpoints of a single continuum. Rather, these two dimensions are orthogonal to one another and define a conceptual space in which marriages with different types of emotional climate can be observed (Caughlin & Huston, 2006). *Tempestuous* marriages are high on both antagonism and affection and correspond to Fitzpatrick's and Gottman's interdependent/volatile type. *Warm* marriages are high on affection and low on antagonism and correspond to the traditional/validating type. *Bland* marriages are low on both dimensions and correspond to the separate/avoiding type. *Hostile* marriages, Caughlin and Huston's fourth type, are low on affection and high on antagonism and do not correspond to any of Fitzpatrick's types but correspond to Gottman's hostile/hostile-detached type. As Caughlin and Huston acknowledge, this is not a stable type of marriage, and these couples usually experience divorce.

To find that Fitzpatrick's typology, which is based on general cognitive representations and reported behaviors, converges with typologies of marriages that emerge in research focusing on very specific aspects of marriages (conflict in Gottman's case, emotional expression in Caughlin & Huston's case) supports the validity of the typology. In addition, this convergence also suggests that the field generally could benefit from theorizing that, rather than focusing on a single phenomenon, tries to provide a comprehensive account of marital relationships.

◆ *Family Communication*

As previously mentioned, there has been less social scientific research on family communication than on marital communication. Thus, although the overall number of phenomena and variables relevant to family communication probably exceed those of marital communication, the number of empirically established relationships between variables and thus the sum total of established empirical knowledge about family communication is smaller than the amount known about marital communication. Nonetheless, this knowledge is not insignificant, and at least in their scope, the models and theories of family communication are as impressive as those of marital communication.

*OLSON'S CIRCUMPLEX MODEL*

As already noted, family communication research is significantly more scarce than research on marital communication, mainly because researchers outside the communication discipline are more inclined to overlook communication as a variable of interest. One notable exception from this trend is Olson's circumplex model of family functioning (Olson, 1981, 1993; Olson, Russell, & Sprenkle, 1983; Olson, Sprenkle, & Russell, 1979). This model not only makes communication a central concept in family functioning, but also conceptualizes family communication in relatively sophisticated terms.

Olson argues that family systems are best described, and their functioning is best understood, by considering two fundamental attributes of families: cohesion and adaptability. Specifically, according to the circumplex model, moderate levels on both dimensions are associated with best functioning, whereas extremes on the dimensions are associated with less than optimal functioning. For cohesion, this means that families that are *separated* or *engaged* function better than families that are either *disengaged* or *enmeshed*, and for adaptation, this means that families that are *flexible* or *structured* function better than families that are *rigid* or *chaotic*. Families that are moderate on both dimensions function best, followed by families that are moderate on one but extreme on the other dimension, and families that are extreme on both dimensions are the least functional.

Family communication is identified by Olson (1981, 1993) as a third, facilitating dimension. That is, it is a family's communication that determines where the family falls along the two underlying dimensions of cohesion and adaptability. Communication is also what allows families to change their location along the dimensions, which is particularly important for the application of the circumplex model to family therapy. In such applications, once counselors have established where along the two dimensions families fall, they can suggest specific communication behaviors that move families more toward the moderate levels on the dimensions, thereby increasing or restoring family functioning. Specific communication skills identified by Olson that facilitate such movements include speaking skills such as speaking for self and avoiding speaking for others, listening skills such as active listening and empathy, and general communication skills such as self-disclosure, clarity, continuity and tracking, and showing respect and regard for others.

## FAMILY COMMUNICATION PATTERNS THEORY

A theory that emerged from within the communication discipline and that, like Olson's model, links specific communication behaviors in families to a wide range of family and child outcomes is family communication patterns theory (FCPT; Fitzpatrick & Ritchie, 1994; Koerner & Fitzpatrick, 2002b, 2002c, 2004, 2006; Ritchie & Fitzpatrick, 1990). FCPT postulates that creating a shared social reality is a basic process that is necessary for families to function and that defines family relationships. Families create a shared reality through two communication behaviors: *conversation* orientation and *conformity* orientation, which also determine families' communication patterns. Conversation orientation refers to open and frequent communication between parents and children with the purpose of co-discovering the meaning of

symbols and objects that constitute a family's social environment. It is associated with warm and supportive relationships characterized by mutual respect and concern for one another. Conformity orientation, in contrast, refers to more restricted communication between parents and children in which those in authority, typically the parents, define social reality for the family. It is associated with more authoritarian parenting and less concern for the children's thoughts and feelings.

Theoretically orthogonal, these two orientations define a conceptual space with four family types. *Consensual* families are high on both conversation orientation and conformity orientation. Their communication is characterized by a tension between an interest in open communication and in exploring new ideas, on one hand, and a pressure to agree and to preserve the existing hierarchy of the family, on the other hand. Parents resolve this tension by listening to their children and explaining their values and beliefs to their children in the hope that the children will adopt the parents' belief system. Children in these families are usually well adapted and satisfied.

*Pluralistic* families favor conversation orientation over conformity orientation. Their communication is characterized by open, unconstrained discussions that involve all family members and a wide range of topics. Parents in these families do not control their children and accept their children's different opinions, although they also explain their own values and beliefs to them. Children of these families learn to be independent and autonomous and to communicate persuasively, and they are generally satisfied with their family relationships.

*Protective* families emphasize conformity over conversation orientation. Their communication is characterized by an emphasis on obedience to parental authority and by little concern for conceptual matters. Parents in these families decide for their children and see little value in explaining their reasoning to them, although they state their beliefs and values and expect their children to subscribe to them, too. Children in protective families learn that there is little value in family conversations and to distrust their own decision-making ability.

*Laissez-faire* families are low on both conformity and conversation orientation. Their communication is characterized by few, usually uninvolving interactions. Members of laissez-faire families are emotionally distant from one another, and family members have little interest in the thoughts and feeling of other family members. Children of these families learn that there is little value in family conversation and that they have to make their own decisions. Because they do not receive much support from their parents, however, they come to question their decision-making ability and are especially susceptible to peer influence.

Family communication patterns have been associated with a number of family processes, such as conflict resolution (Koerner & Fitzpatrick, 1997), confirmation and affection (Schrodt, Ledbetter, & Ohrt, 2007), family rituals (Baxter & Clark, 1996), and understanding (Sillars, Koerner, & Fitzpatrick, 2005), as well as with child-related outcomes, such as communication apprehension (Elwood & Schrader, 1998), conflict with romantic partners (Koerner & Fitzpatrick, 2002c), resiliency (Fitzpatrick & Koerner, 2005), and children's mental and physical health (Schrodt & Ledbetter, 2007).

Not all social scientific research in family communication is conducted to test or elaborate on these more comprehensive theories of family communication. As is the case for research on marital communication, much research and theorizing is directed at more narrowly defined family communication phenomena and processes.

## FAMILY SECRETS

One example of research devoted to explicating a specific aspect of family communication is Vangelisti's work on family secrets (Vangelisti, 1994, 1997; Vangelisti, Caughlin, & Timmerman, 2001).

According to Vangelisti (1994), family secrets can be differentiated by form (i.e., who keeps information from whom), topic (what is kept secret), and function (what are the effects of keeping the secret for the family). Forms vary from *whole family* secrets (all family members know, but outsiders do not) to *intrafamily* secrets (some family members know, but others and outsiders do not) to *individual* secrets (only one family member knows, but other family members and outsiders do not). Topics vary from the *conventional* (e.g., children's grades, illness of a parent) to *rule violations* (e.g., alcohol use, out-of-wedlock pregnancy of a family member) to *taboos* (e.g., marital difficulties, physical and sexual abuse). The functions of secrets identified by Vangelisti (1994) were essentially positive for family relationships and included *bonding, evaluation, maintenance, privacy, defense,* and *communication.*

Vangelisti (1994) found associations between the form, topic, and function of secrets and their associations with satisfaction. For example, taboo secrets were most likely to be whole family secrets and least likely to be individual secrets, whereas rule violations were most likely to be individual secrets and least likely whole family secrets. There was no association between form and topic for conventional secrets. As far as the association between form and function was concerned, Vangelisti found that whole family secrets mainly served the evaluative, defense, and privacy functions; intrafamily secrets mainly served the maintenance function; and individual secrets mainly served the evaluative and privacy functions.

As far as revealing family secrets to outsiders, Vangelisti (1997; Vangelisti et al., 2001) found that a member's satisfaction with his or her family relationships was negatively associated with revealing secrets to outsiders, whereas closeness and similarity with the outsider were positively associated with revealing family secrets. These findings suggest that revealing or sharing family secrets is used to manage one's interpersonal relationships, with both family members and outsiders. Revealing secrets reduces the importance and intimacy of family relationships, and family members can use such revelations to assert greater autonomy and independence from the families. At the same time, revealing family secrets also increases the intimacy and interdependence of the family member's relationship with the outsider, and family members can use revealing secrets to increase the closeness of these relationships. How family members balance such conflicting demands in cases where they desire closeness with both family members and outsiders is an interesting question yet to be explored.

## AFFECTIVE COMMUNICATION IN FAMILIES

Another research program with a relatively narrow scope is Floyd's investigation of the expression of affection in families and his development of affective exchange theory (AET; Floyd, 2001; Floyd & Morman, 2000, 2003, 2005). Floyd's research has two attributes that distinguish it from less innovative research programs. First, unlike most other theories of human communication, which attempt to explain the effects of communication but take communication itself as given, Floyd provided a theoretical explanation for why affect is communicated in family relationships by explicitly grounding AET in the theory of evolution. He argues that humans' ability to experience and express affection was selected for because it created significant benefits in terms of survival and reproduction. Thus, rather than standing on its own, AET is tied to a larger, extremely powerful explanatory framework. Second, whereas most other scholars have studied affection in the context of romantic relationships, Floyd's investigation of AET has taken place primarily in the context of father-son relationships.

Tying AET to the theory of evolution not only places the theory into a larger,

powerful explanatory framework that is relevant to and used by a number of behavioral sciences, but also has led to the formulation of very specific and unique hypotheses. For example, because parental affection is motivated by enabling one's offspring to survive and propagate, fathers should be more affectionate with biological as opposed to stepchildren, a prediction supported by Floyd and Morman (2001). Similarly, fathers should also be more affectionate with heterosexual sons than with bisexual or homosexual sons, a prediction supported by reports from hetero- and homosexual adult men regarding their relationships with their fathers (Floyd, 2001) and replicated by Floyd, Sargent, and Di Corcia (2004). These researchers also found that fathers' knowledge of their sons' sexual orientation mediated these relationships such that fathers who knew that their sons were bisexual or homosexual were less affectionate with them than fathers who assumed that their sons were heterosexual.

By investigating AET in the context of father-son relationships, Floyd and his associates not only demonstrated the importance of affection for nonromantic relationships, but also described a family relationship in great detail that is otherwise often neglected by family communication scholars. For example, Floyd et al. (2004) found that affection in father-son relationships is expressed more through supportive behavior than through direct verbal or nonverbal expression of affection. Also, by comparing current fathers' reports on their relationships with their fathers with their and their sons' reports on their current father-son relationships, Morman and Floyd (2002) were also able to demonstrate the impact that changing cultural norms have had on this family dyad. Specifically, the researchers found that both fathers and sons in contemporary relationships report much more affectionate communication than current fathers had with their own fathers. This finding suggests that while evolved psychological processes do play a role in father-son relationships, so too do cultural forces.

## ◆ Conclusion and Future Directions

While it is difficult to predict the future, at least two common threads in the research reviewed here suggest directions in which the social scientific investigation of marital and family communication might be heading. The first common thread is that the models and theories are expanding and necessarily becoming more complex to account for the complexity of the behaviors and outcomes they are trying to explain. The second common thread is that research findings that seem to be isolated and specific to a particular context, phenomenon, or process converge into broader, more comprehensive models.

Sometimes, the increased complexity of theoretical models results from the inclusion into the models of what initially seemed to be extraneous factors to increase the precision of the models' explanations. One example of this process is the research on marital satisfaction and stability, which, in addition to conflict behaviors, started to consider expressions of positive affect as a causal factor into satisfaction and stability and also came to see affection and antagonism as orthogonal rather than as opposites.

Other times, the complexity of theoretical models increases not just because the number of variables included in the models increases but also because the models include variables of very different types that belong to very different explanatory systems. For example, Gottman's model of marital conflict includes not only the expression of different types of affect as variables but also individuals' cognitive and physiological processes. Similarly, Floyd's work on affective exchange integrates interpersonal behaviors expressing affection, heritable psychological propensities associated with

behaviors selected for by evolution, and social influences associated with historical cultural or larger societal changes.

The tendency for convergence of empirical observations and narrowly defined theoretical models into larger, more comprehensive, and complex theories of human behavior is equally apparent. Reference was made to how research on marital conflict and the emotional climate of marriages converge with, and flesh out, Fitzpatrick's (1988) marital typology. Similar processes may take place in the field of family communication as well. Because it is based on fundamental and necessary cognitive processes, FCPT is a likely candidate for a theory that will be able to integrate a number of what currently appear to be unrelated or even divergent theoretical models.

Ultimately, thanks to a well-established body of knowledge of basic empirical facts about communication in marriages and families and owing to an increase in technological and statistical sophistication, we will be able not only to construct ever more complex theoretical models of communication but also to test them empirically. These models will be complex not only horizontally—that is, in the number of variables they include—but also vertically. That is, they will integrate basic physiological and cognitive processes that have been brought about through evolution, with processes dependent on the specific relational context created by the relationship itself and with processes dependent on culture and society at large (see McLeod, Kosicki, & McLeod, Chapter 11, this volume).

If the past can be described as the painstaking assembly of empirical knowledge about the associations of variables relevant to communication and the development of theoretical explanations and models of narrowly defined processes and phenomena, the future lies in the integration of these models into theoretical explanations that do justice to the complexity of human behavior.

A final development that will affect future research is the increased attention communication researchers pay to non-traditional marriages, such as remarriages; interethnic and homosexual marriages; and complex families, such as single-parent, blended, step-, and multigenerational families; and families created through artificial reproductive technologies or adoption. At this point, the majority of research on these relationships has focused on establishing similarities and differences of these marriages and families to their more traditional counterparts. As a result, how communication is conceptualized in most of this research has not yet reached the same level of theoretical sophistication as some of the other work reviewed in this chapter. Given the interest in researching these relationships, however, combined with the general trend toward more complex theoretical explanations of human communication, suggests that our understanding of these relationships will increase dramatically in the near future.

# ◆ References

Baxter, L. A., & Clark, C. L. (1996). Perceptions of family communication patterns and the enactment of family rituals. *Western Journal of Communication, 60*, 254–268.

Bradbury, T. N., & Fincham, F. D. (1992). Attributions and behavior in marital interaction. *Journal of Personality and Social Psychology, 63*, 613–628.

Bradbury, T. N., Fincham, F. D., & Beach, S. R. H. (2000). Research on the nature and determinants of marital satisfaction: A decade in review. *Journal of Marriage and the Family, 62*, 964–980.

Braithwaite, D. O., & Baxter, L. A. (Eds.). (2006). *Engaging theories in family communication: Multiple perspectives.* Thousand Oaks, CA: Sage.

Burleson, B. R. (1994). Comforting messages: Features, functions, and outcomes. In J. A. Daly & J. M. Wiemann (Eds.), *Strategic interpersonal communication* (pp. 135–161). Hillsdale, NJ: Lawrence Erlbaum.

Burleson, B. R. (2003). Emotional support skills. In J. O. Greene & B. R. Burleson (Eds.), *Handbook of communication and social interaction skills* (pp. 551–594). Mahwah, NJ: Lawrence Erlbaum.

Burleson, B. R., & Goldsmith, D. J. (1998). How the comforting process works: Alleviating emotional distress through conversationally induced reappraisals. In P. A. Anderson & L. K. Guerrero (Eds.), *Handbook of communication and emotion: Theory, research, application and contexts* (pp. 245–280). San Diego: Academic Press.

Burleson, B. R., & Mortenson, S. R. (2003). Explaining cultural differences in evaluations of emotional support behaviors: Exploring the mediating influences of value systems and interaction goals. *Communication Research, 30*, 113–146.

Burleson, B. R., Samter, W., Jones, S. M., Kunkel, A. W., Holmstrom, A. J., Mortenson, S. T., et al. (2005). Which comforting messages really work best? A different perspective on Lemieux and Tighe's "receiver perspective." *Communication Research Reports, 22*, 87–100.

Caughlin, J. P. (2002). The demand/withdraw pattern of communication as a predictor of marital satisfaction over time. *Human Communication Research, 28*, 49–85.

Caughlin, J. P., & Huston, T. L. (2002). A contextual analysis of the association between demand/withdraw and marital satisfaction. *Personal Relationships, 9*, 95–119.

Caughlin, J. P., & Huston, T. L. (2006). The affective structure of marriage. In A. Vangelisti, & D. Perlman (Eds.), *The Cambridge handbook of personal relationships* (pp. 131–155). Cambridge, UK: Cambridge University Press.

Caughlin, J. P., & Vangelisti, A. L. (2000). An individual difference explanation of why married couples engage in the demand/withdraw pattern of conflict. *Journal of Social and Personal Relationships, 17*, 523–551.

Christensen, A. (1987). Detection of conflict patterns in couples. In K. Hahlweg & M. J. Goldstein (Eds.), *Understanding major mental disorder: The contribution of family interaction research* (pp. 250–265). New York: Family Process Press.

Christensen, A. (1988). Dysfunctional interaction patterns in couples. In P. Noller & M. A. Fitzpatrick (Eds.), *Perspectives on marital interaction* (pp. 31–52). Avon, England: Multilingual Matters.

Christensen, A., & Heavey, C. L. (1990). Gender and social structure in the demand/withdraw pattern of marital conflict. *Journal of Personality and Social Psychology, 59*, 73–82.

Coan, J., Gottman, J., Babcock, J., & Jacobson, N. (1997). Battering and the male rejection of influence from women. *Aggressive Behavior, 23*, 375–388.

Cutrona, C. E. (1990). Stress and social support: In search of optimal matching. *Journal of Social and Clinical Psychology, 9*, 3–14.

Cutrona, C. E. (1996). *Social support in couples.* Thousand Oaks, CA: Sage.

Elwood, T. D., & Schrader, D. C. (1998). Family communication patterns and communication apprehension. *Journal of Social Behavior and Personality, 13*, 493–502.

Fincham, F. D. (2004). Communication in marriage. In A. Vangelisti (Ed.), *Handbook of family communication* (pp. 83–103). Mahwah, NJ: Lawrence Erlbaum.

Fincham, F. D., & Beach, S. R. H. (2006). Relationship satisfaction. In A. Vangelisti & D. Perlman (Eds.), *The Cambridge handbook of personal relationships* (pp. 579–594). Cambridge, UK: Cambridge University Press.

Fincham, F. D., Garnier, P. C., Gano-Phillips, S., & Osborn, L. N. (1995). Preinteraction expectations, marital satisfaction, and accessibility: A new look at sentiment override. *Journal of Family Psychology, 9*, 3–14.

Fitzpatrick, M. A. (1988). *Between husbands and wives: Communication in marriage.* Newbury Park, CA: Sage.

Fitzpatrick, M. A., & Koerner, A. F. (2005). Family communication schemata: Effects on children's resiliency. In S. Dunwoody, L. B. Becker, D. McLeod, & G. Kosicki. (Eds.), *The evolution of key mass communication concepts: Honoring Jack M. McLeod* (pp. 115–139). Cresskill, NJ: Hampton Press.

Fitzpatrick, M. A., & Ritchie, L. D. (1994). Communication schemata within the family: Multiple perspectives on family interaction. *Human Communication Research, 20*, 275–301.

Floyd, K. (2001). Human affection exchange I: Reproductive probability as a predictor of men's affection with their sons. *Journal of Men's Studies, 10*, 39–50.

Floyd, K., & Morman, M. T. (2000). Affection received from fathers as a predictor of men's affection with their own sons: Testing the modeling and compensation hypotheses. *Communication Monographs, 67*, 347–361.

Floyd, K., & Morman, M. T. (2001). Human affection III: Discriminative parental solicitude in men's affectionate communication with their biological and nonbiological sons. *Communication Quarterly, 49*, 310–327.

Floyd, K., & Morman, M. T. (2003). Human affection exchange II: Affectionate communication in father-son relationships. *Journal of Social Psychology, 143*, 599–612.

Floyd, K., & Morman, M. T. (2005). Fathers' and sons' reports of fathers' affectionate communication: Implications of a naive theory of affection. *Journal of Social and Personal Relationships, 22*, 99–109.

Floyd, K., Sargent, J. E., & Di Corcia, M. (2004). Human affection exchange VI: Further tests of reproductive probability as a predictor of men's affection with their adult sons. *Journal of Social Psychology, 144*, 191–206.

Gardner, K. A., & Cutrona, C. E. (2004). Social support communication in families. In A. Vangelisti (Ed.), *Handbook of family communication* (pp. 495–512). Mahwah, NJ: Lawrence Erlbaum.

Gottman, J. M. (1993). The roles of conflict engagement, escalation or avoidance in marital interaction: A longitudinal view of five types of couples. *Journal of Consulting and Clinical Psychology, 61*, 6–15.

Gottman, J. M. (1994). *What predicts divorce?* Hillsdale, NJ: Lawrence Erlbaum.

Gottman, J. M., Coan, J., Carrere, S., & Swanson, C. (1998). Predicting marital happiness and stability from newlywed interactions. *Journal of Marriage and the Family, 60*, 5–22.

Gottman, J. M., & Krokoff, L. J. (1989). The relationship between marital interaction and marital satisfaction: A longitudinal view. *Journal of Consulting and Clinical Psychology, 57*, 47–52.

Gottman, J. M., & Levenson, R. W. (1986). Assessing the role of emotion in marriage. *Behavioral Assessment, 8*, 31–48.

Gottman, J. M., & Levenson, R. W. (1992). Marital processes predictive of later dissolution: Behavior, physiology, and health. *Journal of Personality and Social Psychology, 63*, 221–233.

Gottman, J. M., Markman, H., & Notarius, C. (1977). The topography of marital conflict:

A sequential analysis of verbal and nonverbal behavior. *Journal of Marriage and the Family, 39,* 461–477.

Gottman, J. M., Murray, J. D., Swanson, C., Tyson, R., & Swanson, K. R. (2002). *The mathematics of marriage: Dynamic nonlinear model.* Cambridge, MA: MIT Press.

Hendrix, H. (1988). *Getting the love you want: A guide for couples.* New York: Henry Holt.

Heyman, R. E., & Slep, A. M. S. (2001). The hazards of predicting divorce without crossvalidation. *Journal of Marriage and the Family, 62,* 473–479.

Jones, S. M., & Burleson, B. R. (2003). Effects of helper and recipient sex on the experience and outcomes of comforting messages: An experimental investigation. *Sex Roles, 48,* 1–19.

Kaplan, B. H., Cassel, J. C., & Gore, S. (1977). Social support and health. *Medical Care, 15,* 47–58.

Klinetob, N. A., & Smith, D. A. (1996). Demand-withdraw communication in marital interaction: Tests of interpersonal contingency and gender role hypotheses. *Journal of Marriage and the Family, 58,* 945–957.

Koerner, A. F. (2007). Social cognition and family communication. In D. R. Roskos-Ewoldsen & J. L. Monahan (Eds.), *Social cognition and communication* (pp. 197–216). Mahwah, NJ: Lawrence Erlbaum.

Koerner, A. F., & Fitzpatrick, M. A. (1997). Family type and conflict: The impact of conversation orientation and conformity orientation on conflict in the family. *Communication Studies, 48,* 59–75.

Koerner, A. F., & Fitzpatrick, M. A. (2002a). Nonverbal communication and marital adjustment and satisfaction: The role of decoding relationship relevant and relationship irrelevant affect. *Communication Monographs, 69,* 33–51.

Koerner, A. F., & Fitzpatrick, M. A. (2002b). Toward a theory of family communication. *Communication Theory, 12,* 70–91.

Koerner, A. F., & Fitzpatrick, M. A. (2002c). Understanding family communication patterns and family functioning: The roles of conversation orientation and conformity orientation. *Communication Yearbook, 26,* 37–69.

Koerner, A. F., & Fitzpatrick, M. A. (2004). Communication in intact families. In A. Vangelisti (Ed.), *Handbook of family communication* (pp. 177–195). Mahwah, NJ: Lawrence Erlbaum.

Koerner, A. F., & Fitzpatrick, M. A. (2006). Family communication patterns theory: A social cognitive approach. In D. O. Braithwaite & L. A. Baxter (Eds.), *Engaging theories in family communication: Multiple perspectives* (pp. 50–65). Thousand Oaks, CA: Sage.

Lazarus, R. S. (1991). *Emotion and adaptation.* New York: Oxford University Press.

Morman, M. T., & Floyd, K. (2002). A "changing culture of fatherhood": Effects on affectionate communication, closeness, and satisfaction in men's relationships with their fathers and their sons. *Western Journal of Communication, 66,* 395–411.

Noller, P. (1980). Gender and marital adjustment level differences in decoding messages from spouses and strangers. *Journal of Personality and Social Psychology, 41,* 272–278.

Noller, P. (1982). Channel consistency and inconsistency in the communication of married couples. *Journal of Personality and Social Psychology, 43,* 732–741.

Noller, P., & Gallois, C. (1986). Sending emotional messages in marriages. *British Journal of Social Psychology, 25,* 287–297.

Olson, D. H. (1981). Family typologies: Bridging family research and family therapy. In E. E. Filsinger & R. A. Lewis (Eds.), *Assessing marriage: New behavioral approaches* (pp. 74–89). Beverly Hills, CA: Sage.

Olson, D. H. (1993). Circumplex model of marital and family systems. In F. Wals (Ed.), *Normal family processes* (2nd ed., 104–137). New York: Guilford.

Olson, D. H., Russell, C. S., & Sprenkle, D. H. (1983). Circumplex model of marital and family systems, VI: Theoretical update. *Family Process, 22,* 69–83.

Olson, D. H., Sprenkle, D. H., & Russell, C. S. (1979). Circumplex model of marital and family systems: Cohesion and adaptability dimensions, family types, and clinical applications. *Family Process, 18,* 3–28.

Ritchie, L. D., & Fitzpatrick, M. A. (1990). Family communication patterns: Measuring interpersonal perceptions of interpersonal relationships. *Communication Research, 17,* 523–544.

Roloff, M. E., & Miller, C. W. (2006). Mulling about family conflict and communication:

What we know and what we need to know. In L. Turner & R. West (Eds.), *Family communication: A reference of theory and research* (pp. 143–164). Thousand Oaks, CA: Sage.

Schrodt, P., & Ledbetter, A. M. (2007). Communication processes that mediate family communication patterns and mental well-being: A mean and covariance structures analysis of young adults from divorced and non-divorced families. *Human Communication Research, 33,* 330–356.

Schrodt, P., Ledbetter, A. M., & Ohrt, J. K. (2007). Parental confirmation and affection as mediators of family communication patterns and children's mental well-being. *Journal of Family Communication, 7,* 23–46.

Sillars, A., Koerner, A. F., & Fitzpatrick, M. A. (2005). Communication and understanding in parent-adolescent relationships. *Human Communication Research, 31,* 103–128.

Stanley, S. M., Bradbury, T. N., & Markman, H. J. (2000). Structural flaws in the bridge from basic research on marriage to interventions for couples: Illustrations from Gottman, Coan, Carrere, and Swanson (1998). *Journal of Marriage and the Family, 62,* 256–264.

Thomas, G., Fletcher, G. J. O., & Lange, C. (1997). On-line empathic accuracy in marital interaction. *Journal of Personality and Social Psychology, 72,* 838–850.

Vangelisti, A. L. (1994). Family secrets: Forms, functions and correlates. *Journal of Social and Personal Relationships, 11,* 113–135.

Vangelisti, A. L. (1997). Revealing family secrets: The influence of topic, function, and relationships. *Journal of Social and Personal Relationships, 14,* 679–705.

Vangelisti, A. L. (Ed.). (2004). *Handbook of family communication.* Mahwah, NJ: Lawrence Erlbaum.

Vangelisti, A. L., Caughlin, J. P., & Timmerman, L. (2001). Criteria for revealing family secrets. *Communication Monographs, 68,* 1–27.

Vanzetti, N. A., Notarius, C. I., & NeeSmith, D. (1992). Specific and generalized expectancies in marital interaction. *Journal of Family Psychology, 6,* 171–183.

Watzlawick, P., Beavin, J. H., & Jackson, D. D. (1967). *Pragmatics of human communication.* New York: W. W. Norton.

Whisman, M. A., Uebelacker, L. A., & Weinstock, L. M. (2007). Psychopathology and marital satisfaction: The importance of evaluating both partners. *Journal of Consulting and Clinical Psychology, 72,* 830–838.

# 28

# COMPUTER-MEDIATED COMMUNICATION

◆ Joseph B. Walther

Computer-mediated communication is a field sufficiently new that it did not warrant a chapter in the original *Handbook of Communication Science*. The burgeoning research literature we have today was only beginning to accumulate in 1987, and with some important exceptions (e.g., Rice & Associates, 1984), the research then was published primarily outside the communication field. Now, it appears there is no social science discipline that does not study the effects of the Internet. Divisions devoted to the topic are among the largest within professional communication associations. Journals exclusively focused on the subject exist. There are few niches in which scholarship has not adopted computer-mediated communication in some form, as a research tool or form of dissemination if not as a focus. In society, new "killer apps" seem to appear with regularity, each one raising a chorus of questions about how communication is changing because of it.

Given the field's youth and explosive development, it is ironic that several commentators are already speculating about the demise of the area. Parks (in press) recently raised the question, "What will we study when the Internet disappears?" while a former editor of the *Journal of Computer-Mediated Communication,* Herring (2004), characterized the field as "slouching toward the ordinary." Both commentators note how Internet use has become second nature for many people, particularly younger generations. As a result, its study is losing the novelty and appeal it once held as something intrinsically interesting. The Internet is becoming as mundane as the telephone, television, newspaper, notepad, mail system, copy machine, fax machine, answering machine, party line, CB radio, support group, community center, adult movie gallery, directory service, encyclopedia, and library it has come to replace.

Computer-mediated communication (CMC) research has already accumulated more material and foci than one chapter can summarize. To review the whole field would include real-time dyadic chat systems such as Instant Messenger, group chat systems including conferencing as well as role-playing games, and tailored group decision support systems. It would include asynchronous systems such as dyadic or list-based e-mail and distributed bulletin board and discussion systems. It may regard the World Wide Web, including textual, graphical, photographical, audio, and video systems, as well as hyperlinking aspects. CMC is now an intrinsic component of video-sharing systems such as YouTube and social networking sites and date-finding systems such as MySpace and Facebook or Match.com and eHarmony, respectively, and may also include computer-based, graphically enhanced social interaction spaces such as Second Life or any number of massively multiplayer online role-playing games (MMORPGs). For a compact review of the progression of systems and the research topics they prompted, Herring's (2004) review is highly recommended.

But these are simply the technologies, and their enumeration belies the kinds of functional activities they support and the possible transformations of traditional communication processes they may prompt, from friendship and relationship formation, familial maintenance, identity play and sexual exploration, personal identity deception and deception of attributes or instrumental claims; information sharing and group decision making (within local or globally distributed groups and teams), community maintenance including social support, political activation and influence, and the enhancement of local social capital; distributed education, health information, and health behavioral modification, as well as other forms of persuasion and social influence from survey response facilitation to charitable donation to product and vendor reviews; and organizational communication from internal coordination and organizational structure to virtual teams and remote leadership. These interactive communication functions do not even begin to address information exchange systems that do not immediately involve human agents at both ends of information transactions, as seen in information systems such as e-commerce and online parts ordering, to virtual libraries, to search engine use and usability, all of which may include variables familiar to communication researchers as well. All of these processes, as well as others, have been alleged to be affected, for better or for worse, by CMC.

Rather than attempt to provide even a cursory review of so many domains, this chapter will instead attempt to highlight some ways that the study of CMC has raised questions for communication science. The field's growing pains are evident, and the problems they entail may highlight not only issues in CMC research but also questions in more general domains of social interaction research and ways of thinking about them.

This discussion will focus on several general issues in the development and acceptance of theories in CMC. After a brief orientation to the development of the field, the discussion focuses on several key problematics in the CMC research literature, illustrating these issues, at times, by reference to some of the theoretical models of CMC that have commanded the most research attention. These problematics include (a) the particular ways in which CMC complicates assumptions about communication; (b) issues of operationalization, when research decisions about how to employ technology variations to assess hypothetical factors necessitate incidental but potentially consequential levels on other factors; and (c) problems in theoretical derivation with respect to pro-positions and hypotheses, as represented in research designs. When approached carefully, these aspects have advanced our understanding of CMC. More often, problems in these research activities have obscured progress in the field. These issues demand attention so that we can be prepared to develop theoretical understandings of new CMC media and settings to come. Following those issues, the work examines some promising new trends and ideas for future research.

◆ *Emergence of CMC Research*

Research traditions were appropriated from other domains in early CMC research. In the 1980s, CMC became popular among relatively geographically close users in supporting online communities (for review, see Lutters & Ackerman, 2003). Interest-oriented and hobby discussions generally took place over dial-in bulletin board systems (see Rheingold, 1993). The convenience of asynchronous communication was also an advantage. CMC's use of written text alone (plus file transfers) raised certain questions about communication but was generally not problematic, given the focus on file transfers, and exchanging opinions and advice within topical discussions (see Hiltz & Turoff, 1978).

Commercial CMC networks developed, which expanded these discussions. By providing numerous local telephone numbers across countries, consumers dialed in cheaply but connected to others through networks encompassing great geographical expanses, for business or personal use. The Compuserve, Prodigy, and America Online (now AOL) networks fostered interest groups, which drew virtual community research: The virtual community was a product of shared interests rather than the accident of geographical proximity (Utne, 1995). At roughly the same time, computer networks were implemented to support distributed information systems in various corporations, within and among universities, and in military settings, and electronic mail and computer conferencing piggybacked on these systems' "backbones." Correspondingly, one major approach to CMC reflected network analytic perspectives on the connections among groups and their members (e.g., Rice, 1982). Research on community and technology continues to have dualistic foci, looking at how CMC supports dispersed communities of interest as well as its use to supplement and enhance connections within one's own geographic networks. Contemporary research focusing on the benefits and detriments of weak tie connections reflects community psychology and network-analytic traditions (see, e.g., Steinfield, Pentland, Ackerman, & Contractor, 2007; Wellman, 2001).

Accompanying the emerging Internet's ability to connect people over distances, a second research tradition was applied to CMC: teleconferencing research, which focused on the processes that support collaboration. This approach, accompanied by research on small group conversational behavior, was used to inform the computer science design of CMC systems (Turoff, 1991) and to understand CMC's effects (e.g., Hiltz, Johnson, & Agle, 1978; Johansen, Vallee, & Spangler, 1979). *The Social Psychology of Telecommunications* (Short, Williams, & Christie, 1976), which focused on audio- and teleconferencing, offered early CMC researchers predictions about the effects of CMC's relative dearth of nonverbal cues (Rice & Case, 1983). Numerous experiments, particularly small group decision making via CMC and face-to-face communication, found CMC deficient with regard to socioemotional tone and frequency of decision making while appearing to promote greater antagonism (for review, see Walther, 1996).

It was primarily from these beginnings that CMC research began to gain momentum. The deficiencies of CMC to support group and interpersonal interaction were documented under the umbrella of several related theoretical approaches. The assumptions of these approaches were examined, and theoretical alternatives emerged through explicit critique, rejection, and replacement of the assumptions and the research practices they entailed.

## ◆ Assumptions

All theories are premised on certain assumptions about communicators' agency, and CMC theories differ with respect to the nature and level of determinism exerted by individual, social, and technological influences on cognition and behavior. The identification of assumptions has, at times, been explicit in CMC research, which has helped clarify positions and identify opportunities to challenge extant models in robust ways. At other times, assumptions about media and communication have remained implicit. Unidentified, incompatible assumptions have created tensions and have made clear comparisons among various approaches more difficult.

Culnan and Markus (1987) explicated the communication assumptions underlying some of the earliest theories applied to CMC and the evidence-gathering strategies that supported them. Both social presence theory (Short et al., 1976) and information richness theory (Daft & Lengel, 1984) predated CMC but were actively applied subsequently (e.g., Daft, Lengel, & Trevino, 1987). Another approach was the "lack of social context cues" position (see, e.g., Kiesler, Siegel, & McGuire, 1984), a native CMC theory. Each of these theories (and those to follow) focused on the amount and nature of cue systems a communication system carries as causal factors driving CMC's effects. As the nonverbal cue systems become fewer due to

technological capacity, communication was posited to feature less cognizance of others and less normative behavior, civility, co-ordination, empathy, and friendliness, or less ability to reduce equivocality. Although these telecommunication and CMC models were originally articulated in the psychology and management literature, they were consistent with dominant views of "channel reliance" in nonverbal communication research as well (for review, see Burgoon et al., 2002) and referenced that literature tangentially.

Culnan and Markus (1987) referred to the approaches described above collectively as the "cues-filtered-out" framework, in that they shared these common assumptions regarding the absence of nonverbal signals in CMC: "(1) communication mediated by technology filters out many cues found in face-to-face interaction, (2) different media filter out or transmit different cues, and (3) substituting technology-mediated for face-to-face communication will result in predictable changes in intrapersonal and interpersonal variables" (p. 423). Culnan and Markus critiqued this implicit position and its related research as having failed to consider other potential causes for impersonal effects of CMC or their potential remediation, and they generally questioned the conclusions of the research up to that time.

Subsequent research has approached these assumptions in several ways and, in doing so, advanced alternative assumptions and propositions. Several critiques have attempted the serious intellectual challenge of not only specifying alternative theoretical mechanisms in CMC dynamics but simultaneously attempting to account for empirical results from previous studies that supported prior positions, as well as to explain how these seemingly contrary results could be subsumed and interpreted within the contingencies of newer perspectives.

For example, to create a more robust model of media selection and effects, Fulk, Schmitz, and Steinfield (1990) first deconstructed the assumptions of media richness theory (Daft & Lengel, 1984). Like other cues-filtered-out positions, media richness assumed that media have fixed capacities that must be matched to theoretically appropriate types of messages. Fulk et al. (1990) argued instead that the capability of a medium—CMC in particular— derives from users' observations of the overt and covert evaluations of various media that are made by members of one's social network. Indeed, empirical tests by Fulk, Schmitz, and Ryu (1995) demonstrated that users' perceptions of e-mail richness reflected their perceptions of e-mail's richness as perceived, in turn, by their closest colleagues.

Another rejoinder to cues-filtered-out assumptions about CMC's structural properties constraining the socioemotional capacity of communication, Walther's (1992) social information processing (SIP) theory of CMC espoused that users exploit communicative content and style in CMC to affect socioemotional dynamics. Likewise, the social identification/deindividuation (SIDE) model also assailed cues-filtered-out depictions of antisocial CMC (Lea & Spears, 1992). The visual anonymity of CMC leads to a loss of self- and other awareness, it claimed, and if a group identity or social category fits one's self and one's partners, CMC users respond to each other as members of in-groups or out-groups. They enact group norms, hostile or sociable, and experience attraction to the in-group that is impersonal rather than interpersonal (Reicher, Spears, & Postmes, 1995).

While each of these sets of challenges and alternative approaches has advanced thinking, a by-product has been a fragmentation of the field. Each of the models mentioned above that has arisen in reaction to the cues-filtered-out approach can and has been used to predict and explain similar sets of phenomena (including media choice, relationship dynamics, productivity and effectiveness, etc.). Writers can and do apply one theory post hoc to account for empirical results gathered in the exploration of another theory. There is no consensus about which alternative best fits particular situations or technological

applications, and almost no effort has been made to posit or test boundary conditions, contingencies, or competing theories simultaneously (for exceptions, see Sassenberg, 2002; Walther, Slovacek, & Tidwell, 2001; Wang, Walther, & Hancock, 2009). Rather, in some cases, theorists have proposed that one approach can subsume all others (Postmes & Baym, 2005), while some of the same proponents later acknowledged the need for integrated, contingent, and contextual theoretical work (Tanis & Postmes, 2008). So in one sense, we are ahead of where we were before, when there was a generally uniform paradigm promoting the view that CMC was expected to render socioemotionally defi-cient effects. In rejecting this conclusion, we have developed an embarrassment of riches: multiple models based on strongly contrasting assumptions, yet with overlapping predictions and unclear boundaries.

There is a critical need for the articulation of theoretical boundary conditions in CMC research. With CMC being a mainstream activity it is obvious that a variety of situational features affect its use, and research should conceptualize situational factors that affect different assumptions about the manner in which technology-mediated communication addresses users' goals. For instance, users may employ CMC because they are seeking social connections or they may use CMC for the very purpose of minimizing involvement with others. There may be practical alternatives to CMC or there may be none. Each of these conditions affects the applicability of any specific theoretical model to CMC usage and outcomes. CMC is used in large groups, small groups, or no groups, and these settings likely affect how people conceptualize partners, leading them to draw on different means of social influence from one context to another (E.-J. Lee, 2004). One size of theory may not fit all applications, but seldom has research explicated the boundaries within which a theory's assumptions should or should not hold, a gap that the young field should undertake to fill.

Finally, it may be precisely because researchers using both older and newer theories have not articulated clear boundary conditions that earlier cues-filtered-out assumptions about CMC remain surprisingly well entrenched in research and in popular understandings of CMC. Notions about the inherent deficiency of CMC to support meaningful communication are frequently revived and rearticulated, despite evidence supporting more contingent views. However, it is not only the issues of assumptions and boundaries that have hindered progress. It is also likely that certain problems in operationalizing the causal effects of CMC have contributed as well.

## ◆ Operationalization

Another factor making advancement of formal understanding about CMC difficult is that the causal properties being examined in any given study are not easy to isolate. Whether in field studies, field experiments, or controlled laboratory experiments, CMC involves a variety of characteristics (for review, see Eveland, 2003), some of which may be of specific theoretical interest and others that may not, but many are present in some form in any given CMC utilization. As a result, empirical conclusions that are attributed to a specific feature of CMC often cannot be definitively explained in terms of that specific attribute only.

In the case of field studies, identifying causal factors is always an issue, just as it is for other foci. CMC is no less challenged. When comparing social support over the Internet with face-to-face interaction, for example, numerous medium factors and sociometric factors probably interact. Internet social support communications may include (a) a lack of face-to-face contact and the relative loss of nonverbal expression that is inherent in text-based interaction;

(b) contacts with individuals who are unknown to the subject or to other members of the subject's personal network; (c) presentation of self and others via absolute anonymity, pseudonymity, nominal identification, or efforts to authenticate others' qualifications; (d) asynchronous composition of messages and varying time intervals before interactive replies appear; (e) a potential audience that is different in size by scales of magnitude from that which individuals traditionally can access (for review, see Walther & Boyd, 2002); and (f) the ability to "lurk" for answers without uttering a request (Nonnecke & Preece, 2001). Any of these specific attributes may drive differences in the kinds of outcomes online versus offline social support generates, and field research tends to assume that any or all of them may be the active elements.

Indeed, some CMC research offers lists of CMC and social attributes, any or all of which may explain why there may be differences between online and offline communication outcomes, and the research makes no effort to isolate any specific attribute or subset of attributes to demonstrate cause. One may ask whether it would really be very fruitful to isolate these various factors after all. Scientifically it makes sense, but phenomenologically it makes perhaps little since these attributes generally co-occur, are embedded in, and enable one another. It is likely that the persistence of older theoretical positions that might otherwise have been set aside has to do with the possible conflation of causes that quite understandably appears in CMC research. Why not focus on the first potential causal factor that comes to mind since research does not discern whether that one and not some other factor affected communication?

Although field *experiments* should offer greater precision than field *studies*, similar problems arise in CMC research. For example, seldom does research on virtual, distributed groups account for the independent or interactive effects of dissimilarity in geographic location as well as the use of CMC. This is an easy conflation to make since, obviously, geographically dispersed partners must use mediated communication. However, so may co-located partners, and rarely are these factors treated orthogonally. Thus, virtual groups' relational problems that have been attributed to the mediated communication of people separated by actual geographic distances (e.g., Cramton, 2001) may be simply the result of distance or even *presumed* distance (Bradner & Mark, 2002). Even when distance is a focal variable, the proportion of group members across locations is a factor more often taken for granted than isolated or controlled. However, the negative effect of distance among six CMC group partners in two locations dissipates somewhat when six partners are spread among three locations and dissipates further when members are evenly spread across six locations (Polzer, Crisp, Jarvenpaa, & Kim, 2006). When researchers assess multiple causal factors in the field, more complex understandings arise to counter previous expectations for the deleterious effects of mediation, distribution, and cultural heterogeneity found in more traditional settings (Mortensen & Hinds, 2001).

We would expect that laboratory experiments allow us to reduce the conflation of potential confounding factors that field research often entails, but it is in this setting that multiple causal aspects of CMC may be most invisible and pernicious. As in other research, investigators attempt to make various conditions equivalent across experimental and control conditions. In CMC, several nonhypothetical social and technical characteristics must be selected to commence research on a focal variable. Many such factors, however, do not incur random effects: Other studies demonstrate that simple contextual variables interact with CMC channel effects on various outcomes. Such factors include shorter or longer time periods (Ramirez & Zhang, 2007), whether or not

participants know each other or expect to encounter each other again (Ramirez, 2007), whether the CMC is synchronous or asynchronous (the comparison of which remains considerably undertheorized and understudied), and other such factors. Therefore, controlling these factors by selecting one level across CMC conditions embeds research findings within the context of the selected level and may not generalize to other CMC settings.

Other subtle methodological decisions also have the potential to bias results. Research on the effects of anonymity provides an example. That CMC users experience anonymity has been a frequent focus of CMC research. In early studies, the visual anonymity of communicators was imputed to cause deindividuation, leading to deregulation and normlessness, resulting in impersonal and hostile communication (Kiesler et al., 1984). SIDE theorists challenged this interpretation, arguing that visual anonymity and its consequent deindividuation (the "DE" in SIDE) impel CMC users to identify with groups (via social identification, the "SI" in SIDE), in which case impersonal and hostile behavior is better explained as reflecting a group's norm than as deregulated, individualized reactions: Visual "anonymity is likely to enhance the salience of social identity . . . by emphasizing the interchangeability of group members and obscuring interpersonal differences" (Reicher et al., 1995, p. 178). In contrast, CMC in which users see others' pictures breaks down the group identification and instantiates interpersonal relations. Interpersonal attraction is expected to be asystematic and random: We like some people more and others less, averaging out to neutral on the whole.

Operationally, the execution of most studies focusing on anonymity effects goes beyond *visual* anonymity, fixing other sociotechnical facets of the setting in ways that may inflate impersonal experiences. This includes using abstract identifiers rather than personal names online and relatively restricted interaction periods that minimize inter-personal awareness (for review, see Saunders & Ahuja, 2006). When such conditions are imposed, it is difficult to detect whether and how CMC users might attempt to overcome visual anonymity through other communi-cative mechanisms (see, e.g., McLeod, 2000). Consequently, it is unclear whether people simply cannot tell who is who in these restricted conditions (i.e., they are deperson-alized, which may be transient) or whether they do not wish to know (i.e., they are deindividuated). Such questions undermine claims that CMC is CMC because of some inherent anonymity and deindividuation accompanying users' inability to see each other online. Only sometimes has the *degree* of anonymity systematically varied within CMC settings (e.g., Hiltz, Turoff, & Johnson, 1989; Scott & Bonito, 2006), with different results accruing as anonymity takes on various dimensions.

In addition, many technical and meth-odological decisions that must be made in CMC have no direct equivalent in face-to-face interaction, further straining the ability to isolate causal factors. For instance, there are few direct analogs of anonymity in face-to-face communication (Anonymous, 1998), and anonymity in CMC cannot be isolated in an organic way from writing and other potentially causal factors. Other potential influences include the use of abbreviated or group-based on-screen identifiers rather than names (Douglas & McGarty, 2001), bogus/programmed "partner" responses rather than actual interaction (Tanis & Postmes, 2008), writing rather than speaking (Baron, 1998), and, as mentioned, the embeddedness of one's conversational partners in same or alternative locations and degrees of group member distribution across locations (Polzer et al., 2006). Any of these factors are potential active variables, and the more an experiment constrains real-world aspects of CMC usage for the sake of experimental control, the more rather than less these factors may unknowingly influence communication in ways that are typically unacknowledged.

Despite some admirable efforts to vary systematically and partial out the influences of numerous specific social and technical factors in one experiment (Burgoon et al., 2002), obviously one cannot covary all relevant attributes all the time. Just as obviously, failure to do so entails some amount of risk. Thus, it remains that subtle variations in one or another peripheral factor in a given CMC study may lead results to reflect unique or unexpected findings. Researchers and readers must take care to evaluate whether data are gathered in a manner in which nonhypothesized social and technical features were present in ways that may bias results for or against expected outcomes and replicate studies systematically by varying these potential confounds.

## ◆ Derivation

Interpreting results of CMC research theo-retically is further challenged because research designs often do not stringently reflect specific aspects of the theories they ostensibly assess. Rarely do empirical studies focus on particular propositions that dictate specific communication processes via tech-nology. It is not much of an exaggeration to characterize the dominant approach to CMC research as follows: (a) Some property (or properties) is identified that some form (or all forms) of CMC (may) have. This often includes surface features such as the lack of nonverbal cues. Properties are selected on the basis of some functional asso-ciation with some distal correlate. (b) An argument is made with respect to the rela-tionship between the property and its effect on some outcome. The relationship is often conceptualized to obtain through the activa-tion of some specified processes, although those processes are seldom empirically examined. (c) Some measure of the outcome is specified. (d) Communication via CMC takes place (or is simulated), although there is wide variety in terms of mode, duration, and interface. In some cases, it is not clear whether communication as a process has any potential causal or mediating role in the psychological responses that accrue from antecedent causes, and it is frequently the case that interaction, if it occurs, is not analyzed. (e) Measurements are gathered and compared. (f) Conclusions about the causal effects of CMC are inferred.

When research focuses on superficial causes and effects to the neglect of specific underlying processes, findings are likely to be interpreted as supporting all aspects of a model, as though all aspects must have been activated to produce expected outcomes. This is not an unreasonable approach for initial tests of a new model, but it is limited in terms of its ultimate utility in theory testing. Thus, theories that specify dynamics at micro-interaction levels have been tested using gross-level measures of distal outcomes rather than by examining the interaction processes themselves.

Research examining all of the theoretical CMC models has followed this approach at some point. For instance, SIP theory (Walther, 1992) seems to have drawn considerable support, before some of its underlying specifications were actually ever tested. SIP posits two primary arguments: First, just as individuals primarily employ nonverbal cues to express affect and social information offline, CMC users rely on other cues for the expression and detection of characteristics, attitudes, and affective expressions online. Indeed, what distinguishes SIP from cues-filtered-out positions, including SIDE, is its proposition that communicators actively seek and exploit whatever cues they can when motivated to develop interpersonal impressions and relations online. Second, because less social information traverses a written message than a multimodal face-to-face exchange, relational processes take longer in CMC to achieve parity with face-to-face communication.

Most SIP-oriented research explores the second proposition. It may involve assigning subjects to CMC (and face-to-face) conditions and measuring perceptions at several points over time (e.g., B. H. Lee, Sim, Trevor, & Detenber, 2004; Ramirez, Zhang, McGrew, & Lin, 2007). Gains in self-administered relationship scores, or reductions in conflict, are considered evidence for the underlying dynamics specified in the theory. Were findings the opposite, of course, the model would be challenged. However, even supporting results merely scratch the surface of the theory's requirements. In the case of SIP's development, recent efforts have begun examining the basic processes specified by the first proposition, with regard to translation of affect from nonverbal to verbal and other online behaviors. These efforts have included the use of cues, including self-disclosure and personal questions (Tidwell & Walther, 2002), as well as verbal style and content variations (Walther, Loh, & Granka, 2005), chronemics (Kalman & Rafaeli, 2008), and fonts and graphics, including emoticons (textual depictions of facial expressions; see, e.g., Derks, Bos, & von Grumbkow, 2007).

The reification of the gross theoretical model, without scrutiny of the constituent theoretical process, also describes many studies related to media richness theory. Media richness proposes that some messages or tasks are communicated more efficiently in one medium than in another. The more equivocal the task and the richer the medium one uses, the more efficient the exchange. When equivocality is low, a leaner medium is more efficient. Equivocality is conceptualized as the number of possible interpretations that can legitimately be made of a situation and how long it takes to reach consensus on the most effective interpretation. A medium's richness is determined by (a) the number of communicative cue systems, (b) how immediately feedback can be exchanged from receiver to sender (i.e., from concurrent to delayed), (c) message personalization (specific individual tailoring or generic), and (d) the capacity to employ natural language (conversational or formal). CMC joined the richness hierarchy as a relatively lean medium, theoretically speaking (Daft et al., 1987): It was conceived to be leaner than telephone communication on these four characteristics but richer than letters.

In one of the first tests of the theory, Daft et al. (1987) examined the performance ratings of managers who also provided responses to projective assessments asking them what media they would prefer to use for a variety of communication tasks. The results showed that better managers made more theoretically consistent match projections than did poorer performing managers. These results are not inconsistent with media richness theory, but neither do they really test the propositions of the model with respect to efficient equivocality reduction.

Empirical tests of media richness have generated notoriously inconsistent support (for review, see Fulk & Boyd, 1991; Timmerman, 2002). Research that asks respondents to *project* what media they would select under various conditions tends to support media richness. *Observational* tests that assess what media managers really choose (e.g., Markus, 1994) or what effects different media qualities bestow on task efficiency (e.g., Dennis & Kinney, 1998) typically fail.

When CMC research generates a lack of support for hypotheses, or results appear to support an alternative model, researchers often equivocate. If one takes the conclusions of previous studies at face value and does not recognize that there is—more often than not—indirect or absent testing of theoretical process variables in previous studies, a researcher may not see that the problems he or she has encountered are not inconsistent with others'. So impervious to contradictory evidence has media richness theory become that, in at least one instance, researchers disregarded their own clearly disconfirming findings rather than question the model's viability or scope (Cummings, Lee, & Kraut, 2006). As one result of these missed connections, cues-filtered-out assumptions of CMC's inability to convey affective and individuating information are still frequently employed to frame rather broad predictions about the effects of CMC, despite what is now a substantial history of critique and counterevidence with respect to these positions' scope. Such approaches appear in recent studies of persuasion (Guadagno & Cialdini, 2002; cf. Joinson & Reips, 2007), emotional expression (Byron, 2008), and the perseverance of stereotypes (Epley & Kruger, 2005), employing research methods that elsewhere have been recognized to limit ecologically valid results (see Walther, 1992).

Research on the use of the Internet for news and political information has followed the same general paradigm. People may get information from newspapers, broadcast media, and Web sites, blogs, and online discussions. Researchers may (or may not) offer a list of attributes that distinguish the Internet from traditional news sources. Research then assesses the extent to which people use Internet media in comparison to other sources but without assessing the degree to which the specific attributes are causes or corollaries (for review, see Bimber, 2000). Data reflecting that the Internet is indeed used as an information channel are taken as confirmation that those attributes must have been the driving factors. Such an approach *seems* to reflect hypothesized causal factors, and theories are considered confirmed. The research cannot discern whether subsets of causes or other unspecified causes were at play.

These problems—assumptions about communication, operationalization issues, and the degree to which research is designed to support or falsify specific theoretical processes—pertain not only to the earlier theories of CMC but to more recent theoretical rivals as well. The next parts of this discussion focus on some of the most dominant contemporary theories in CMC and examine their status and prospects in terms of these same issues.

## ◆ Emerging Ideas and Future Efforts

Other paradigms on the horizon and issues that new technologies foreground may gather research momentum in the near future.

One of the more provocative stances to appear in the field is Kock's (2004) formulation of CMC in the context of Darwinian evolution theory: CMC's existence reflects an extension of human adaptation. This position stands in interesting contrast to older prognostications that CMC, as an unnatural condition, might lead us all to treat one another as machines (e.g., Shamp, 1991), although there is compelling evidence that we treat computers as we do people rather than vice versa (for review, see E.-J. Lee & Sundar, Chapter 29, this volume). Kock (2004) argues that some species have developed the ability to communicate over distances where visual contact is occluded, which bestows survival value. Vocal shrieks and calls perform this function. So does writing, which also persists over time and can be transported. The transmission of writing across vast distance in *little* time demonstrates, according to Kock, that CMC is a natural adaptation in line with the trajectory of our species' development.

Other scholars are continuing the debate over the degree of presence that various forms of electronic communication provide, or may be made to provide, and its functional implications. Presence may include the kinds of experience typified by forgetting one's physical location, as in immersive virtual reality, or the state of flow that online computer games can provide (see Sherry, 2004). The level of presence or involvement that CMC may foster, under various circumstances, is a matter that theory and research have occasionally visited. Case studies and other accounts suggest that CMC users sometimes become strongly if not viscerally involved in their online interactions (e.g., Dibbell, 1993) and emotionally invested with individuals they have not met in person. Other accounts suggest that some users engage in CMC in quite intimate ways that are liminal or questionably connected to "real life" (Turkle, 1995). Such intimacies online, when apprehended, have become the downfall of several political leaders (e.g., Page, 2006).

The issue of CMC's potential for presence comes to the fore in research on the use of CMC by individuals with poor face-to-face social skills who prefer online relationships (Caplan, 2003, 2007). It appears that such individuals exploit the manner in which CMC's visual occlusion and physical separation affords an optimal degree of *distance* from conversation partners. Coupled with more cognizant control over message construction than face-to-face interaction provides, CMC fosters encounters that can provide a strong degree of intensity and involvement.

Caplan (2001) suggests that the hyperpersonal model of CMC (Walther, 1996) provides a framework with which to conceptualize this otherwise conflicted coupling of distance and immediacy. The hyperpersonal model identifies four simultaneous phenomena that enhance communication: CMC provides selective self-presentation, idealization of partners, exploitation of technical attributes to enhance message composition, and mutually enhancing feedback mechanisms that facilitate particularly intimate encounters through text-based interaction. The hyperpersonal model has received a good degree of attention in CMC research and remains a useful approach for some of the phenomena discussed in this chapter. Elements of the model have been applied in several settings and tests in recent years, from studies of self-presentation and idealization in student dyads (Ramirez & Wang, 2008) and online dating sites (Ellison, Heino, & Gibbs, 2006) to the micro-behaviors in keyboarding, timing, and linguistics of impression management (Walther, 2007) and online deception (Toma, Hancock, & Ellison, 2008). Questions about the theoretical integrity of the model still remain in terms of the logical necessity and interrelationship of its four components, and the extrinsic predictors of hyperpersonal or hypernegative processes (see Walther & Parks, 2002). Despite these challenges, the hyperpersonal model is useful in guiding research about how mindful and strategic

CMC may be and how these elements play a role in the intimacy and desirability that CMC sometimes facilitates where face-to-face communication may not.

New CMC platforms and applications force us to ask how well the theories and approaches we know can cover rapid developments and significant changes in technological attributes. Questions are frequently raised about the utility of theories that were developed when CMC was just plain text, now that variants include free videoconferencing and multi-modal social networking sites. Yet at times, as technology use advances, theoretically understandable dynamics from offline come into view in interesting new ways. For instance, Antheunis, Valkenburg, and Peter (2008) argue that social networking sites such as Facebook offer interpersonal information for which seekers previously had to employ a variety of strategies to glean—passive, active, and interactive strategies, according to Berger and colleagues' typology (Berger, Gardner, Parks, Schulman, & Miller, 1976). Social networking sites convey a good deal of personal information that observers obtain relatively passively (Stutzman, 2006): disclosures of personal beliefs and preferences, networks of acquaintances in common (who might share information about a target), who they befriend, and what they write in reaction to others. Whereas interactive face-to-face questions and answers are the most efficient way to gather information at this level of intimacy offline, they are also the most face-threatening approach in face-to-face interaction (Berger et al., 1976). Because users can peruse others' personal data online without the target's knowledge, searchable online databases and social networking sites mitigate the social risk associated with traditional interpersonal information-seeking strategies (Ramirez, Walther, Burgoon, & Sunnafrank, 2002). How this phenomenon affects relationships is not yet known. The point is that

technology does indeed change, but its changes often invoke constructs that communication scientists can describe and theorize.

This is not to say that applying familiar paradigms to CMC developments is always a simple matter. As the problematics discussed above should suggest, CMC environments are complicated and multifaceted, and theoretical attempts to explain their actions may have much to cover. Caplan (2001) illustrates how even a chat room setting defies analysis through the frameworks of traditional mass communication, interpersonal communication, or other conventional approaches:

> The chat room example illustrates an entirely new and different communication system.... Media organizations are sending impersonal advertisements designed for broad audiences along the bottom of the screen; some individuals are engaged in reciprocal dyadic personal conversations; at one time multiple conversations are taking place; conversational participants are not constrained by time (i.e., participants may get up and walk away for a few minutes . . . ); there are no constraints due to physical space or distance in this sort of communication; participants in the chat-room are, at the same time, both mass communication sources and audiences (i.e., there may be an audience of 10,000 other people in the chat room reading what one individual types to one particular receiver); some people sporadically participate, or sometimes never participate, but simply still observe the activity without being bound by the rules and norms that govern interpersonal interaction; additionally, and quite often, it is common that conversational participants have no idea (in a personal sense) of who they are conversing with.

At the other end of the spectrum, observers such as Lutters (2007) suggest that many CMC practices are beginning to appear much more "normal," as designers and users integrate CMC into their existing relationships and information-processing needs. According to Lutters, if CMC was once an alternative to "real life," it is now integrated with physical life; although it used to be that a person could "be anyone" online, people are now cultivating persistent identity across sites and applications; the value of online anonymity may be replaced by online reputation management concerns; and although conversation was the core data in early CMC research, there are vast data now about all kinds of online behavior such as site visits, purchase patterns, ratings, and rankings. Although we must compare CMC with face-to-face and other modalities to see how they may differ, there are fewer contexts daily in which we can apprehend communication partners through one interface alone, and our relationships with people and institutions are increasingly multimodal.

When Parks (in press) suggested that we are near the end of the study of the Internet, he did not suggest that the Internet will be an unworthy *component* of study. Rather, a more robust and enduring approach to communication will be to retract attention from technological phenomenalism and refocus on functionally oriented communication processes that include mediated communication as an important element within more holistic events. How, when, and why CMC can be a valued part of communication ecologies continues to demand research attention. As the complex, rapid evolution of existing CMC research indicates, developing new conceptual models and testing them will be quite challenging, given conflicting but strongly held assumptions about how media affect communication, the operational complications that CMC exerts, and the general challenge that confronts the analysis of process in any communication environment.

◆ *References*

Anonymous. (1998). To reveal or not to reveal: A theoretical model of anonymous communication. *Communication Theory, 8,* 381–407.

Antheunis, M. L., Valkenburg, P., & Peter, J. (2008, May). *Getting acquainted through social networking sites: Testing a model of online uncertainty reduction and social attraction.* Paper presented at the annual conference of the International Communication Association, Montreal, Canada.

Baron, N. S. (1998). Letters by phone or speech by other means: The linguistics of email. *Language and Communication, 18,* 133–170.

Berger, C. R., Gardner, R. R., Parks, M. R., Schulman, L., & Miller, G. R. (1976). Interpersonal epistemology and interpersonal communication. In G. R. Miller (Ed.), *Explorations in interpersonal communication* (pp. 149–171). Beverly Hills, CA: Sage.

Bimber, B. (2000). The study of information technology and civic engagement. *Political Communication, 17,* 329–333.

Bradner, E., & Mark, G. (2002, November). Why distance matters: Effects on cooperation, persuasion and deception. In J. Turner & R. Kraut (Eds.), *Proceedings of the 2002 ACM conference on computer-supported cooperative work* (pp. 226–235). New York: ACM Press.

Burgoon, J. K., Bonito, J. A., Ramirez, A., Dunbar, N. E., Kam, K., & Fischer, J. (2002). Testing the interactivity principles: Effects of mediation, propinquity, and verbal and nonverbal modalities in interpersonal interaction. *Journal of Communication, 52,* 657–677.

Byron, K. (2008). Carrying too heavy a load? The communication and miscommunication of emotion by email. *Academy of Management Review, 33,* 309–327.

Caplan, S. E. (2001). Challenging the mass-interpersonal communication dichotomy: Are we witnessing the emergence of an entirely new communication system? *The Electronic Journal of Communication, 11*(1). Retrieved September 15, 2007, from http://www.cios.org/EJCPUBLIC$$463733 1381205$$/011/1/01112.HTML

Caplan, S. E. (2003). Preference for online social interaction: A theory of problematic Internet use and psychosocial well-being. *Communication Research, 30,* 625–648.

Caplan, S. E. (2007). Relations among loneliness, social anxiety, and problematic Internet use. *CyberPsychology & Behavior, 10*, 234–242.

Cramton, C. D. (2001). The mutual knowledge problem and its consequences for dispersed collaboration. *Organization Science, 12*, 346–371.

Culnan, M. J., & Markus, M. L. (1987). Information technologies. In F. M. Jablin, L. L. Putnam, K. H. Roberts, & L. W. Porter (Eds.), *Handbook of organizational communication: An interdisciplinary perspective* (pp. 420–443). Newbury Park, CA: Sage.

Cummings, J., Lee, J., & Kraut, R. (2006). Communication technology and friends during the transition from high school to college. In R. Kraut, M. Brynin, & S. Kiesler (Eds.), *Computers, phones, and the Internet: Domesticating information technology* (pp. 265–278). New York: Oxford University Press.

Daft, R. L., & Lengel, R. H. (1984). Information richness: A new approach to managerial behavior and organization design. In B. M. Staw & L. L. Cummings (Eds.), *Research in organizational behavior* (Vol. 6, pp. 191–233). Greenwich, CT: JAI.

Daft, R. L., Lengel, R. H., & Trevino, L. K. (1987). Message equivocality, media selection, and manager performance: Implications for information systems. *MIS Quarterly, 11*, 355–368.

Dennis, A. R., & Kinney, S. T. (1998). Testing media richness theory in the new media: The effects of cues, feedback, and task equivocality. *Information Systems Research, 9*, 256–274.

Derks, D., Bos, A. E. R., & von Grumbkow, J. (2007). Emoticons and social interaction on the Internet: The importance of social context. *Computer in Human Behavior, 23*, 842–849.

Dibbell, J. (1993, December 23). A rape in cyberspace: How an evil clown, a Haitian trickster spirit, two wizards, and a cast of dozens turned a database into a society. *The Village Voice.* Rpt. retrieved November 12, 2007, from http://www.juliandibbell.com/texts/bungle_vv.html

Douglas, K. M., & McGarty, C. (2001). Identifiability and self-presentation: Computer-mediated communication and intergroup interaction. *British Journal of Social Psychology, 40*, 399–416.

Ellison, N., Heino, R., & Gibbs, J. (2006). Managing impressions online: Self-presentation processes in the online dating environment. *Journal of Computer-Mediated Communication, 11*(2). Retrieved March 12, 2007, from http://jcmc.indiana.edu/v0111/issue2/ellison.html

Epley, N., & Kruger, J. (2005). When what you type isn't what they read: The perseverance of stereotypes and expectancies over e-mail. *Journal of Experimental Social Psychology, 41*, 414–422.

Eveland, W. P. (2003). A "mix of attributes" approach to the study of media effects and new communication technologies. *Journal of Communication, 53*, 395–410.

Fulk, J., & Boyd, B. (1991). Emerging theories of communication in organizations. *Journal of Management, 17*, 407–446.

Fulk, J., Schmitz, J., & Ryu, D. (1995). Cognitive elements in the social construction of communication. *Technology Management Communication Quarterly, 8*, 259–288.

Fulk, J., Schmitz, J., & Steinfeld, C. W. (1990). A social influence model of technology use. In J. Fulk & C. W. Steinfield (Eds.), *Organizations and communication technology* (pp. 117–140). Newbury Park, CA: Sage.

Guadagno, R. E., & Cialdini, R. B. (2002). Online persuasion: An examination of gender differences in computer-mediated interpersonal influence. *Group Dynamics: Theory, Research, and Practice, 6*, 38–51.

Herring, S. C. (2004). Slouching toward the ordinary: Current trends in computer-mediated communication. *New Media & Society, 6*, 26–36.

Hiltz, S. R., Johnson, K., & Agle, G. (1978). *Replicating Bales' problem solving experiments on a computerized conference: A pilot study* (Research report No. 8). Newark: New Jersey Institute of Technology, Computerized Conferencing and Communications Center.

Hiltz, S. R., & Turoff, M. (1978). *The network nation: Human communication via computer.* Reading, MA: Addison-Wesley.

Hiltz, S. R., Turoff, M., & Johnson, K. (1989). Experiments in group decision making, 3:

Disinhibition, deindividuation, and group process in pen name and real name computer conferences. *Decision Support Systems, 5,* 217–232.

Johansen, R., Vallee, J., & Spangler, K. (1979). *Electronic meetings: Technical alternatives and social choices.* Reading, MA: Addison-Wesley.

Joinson, A. N., & Reips, U.-D. (2007). Personalized salutation, power of sender and response rates to Web-based surveys. *Computers in Human Behavior, 23,* 1372–1383.

Kalman, Y. M., & Rafaeli, S. (2008, May). *Chronemic nonverbal expectancy violations in written computer mediated communication.* Paper presented at the annual meeting of the International Communication Association, Montreal, Canada.

Kiesler, S., Siegel, J., & McGuire, T. W. (1984). Social psychological aspects of computer-mediated communication. *American Psychologist, 39,* 1123–1134.

Kock, N. (2004). The psychobiological model: Towards a new theory of computer-mediated communication based on Darwinian evolution. *Organizational Science, 15,* 327–348.

Lea, M., & Spears, R. (1992). Paralanguage and social perception in computer-mediated communication. *Journal of Organizational Computing, 2,* 321–341.

Lee, B. H., Sim, L. C., Trevor, T. M. K., & Detenber, B. H. (2004). Getting to know you: Exploring the development of relational intimacy in computer-mediated communication. *Journal of Computer-Mediated Communication, 9*(3). Retrieved January 1, 2008, from http://jcmc.indiana.edu/vol9/issue3/detenber.html

Lee, E.-J. (2004). Effects of visual representation on social influence in computer-mediated communication: Experimental tests of the social identity model of deindividuation effects. *Human Communication Research, 30,* 234–259.

Lutters, W. G. (2007, November). *Research directions for social computing.* Paper presented at the Group 2007 conference of the ACM, Sanibel Island, FL.

Lutters, W. G., & Ackerman, M. S. (2003). Joining the backstage: Locality and centrality in an online community. *Information: Technology and People, 16,* 157–182.

Markus, M. L. (1994). Electronic mail as the medium of managerial choice. *Organization Science, 5,* 502–527.

McLeod, P. (2000). Anonymity and consensus in computer-supported group decision-making. In T. I. Griffith (Ed.), *Research on groups and organizations* (Vol. III, pp. 175–204). Stamford, CT: JAI.

Mortensen, M., & Hinds, P. J. (2001). Conflict and shared identity in geographically distributed teams. *International Journal of Conflict Management, 12,* 212–238.

Nonnecke, B., & Preece, J. (2001, June). *Why lurkers lurk.* Paper presented at the annual meeting of the Americas Conference on Information Systems, Boston. Retrieved June 30, 2007, from http://www.ifsm.umbc.edu/~preece/Papers/AMCISlurker.01.pdf

Page, S. (2006, October 2). On political track for decades, Foley's career derails in days. *USA Today.* Retrieved January 6, 2008, from http://www.usatoday.com/news/washington/2006-10-02-foley-profile_x.htm

Parks, M. R. (in press). What will we study when the Internet disappears? *Journal of Computer-Mediated Communication.*

Polzer, J. T., Crisp, C. B., Jarvenpaa, S. L., & Kim, J. W. (2006). Extending the faultline model to geographically dispersed teams: How co-located subgroups can impair group functioning. *Academy of Management Journal, 49,* 679–692.

Postmes, T., & Baym, N. (2005). Intergroup dimensions of the Internet. In J. Harwood & H. Giles (Eds.), *Intergroup communication: Multiple perspectives* (pp. 213–238). New York: Peter Lang.

Ramirez, A., Jr. (2007). The effect of anticipated future interaction and initial impression valence on relational communication in computer-mediated interaction. *Communication Studies, 58,* 53–70.

Ramirez, A., Jr., Walther, J. B., Burgoon, J. K., & Sunnafrank, M. (2002). Information seeking strategies, uncertainty, and computer-mediated communication: Toward a conceptual model. *Human Communication Research, 28,* 213–228.

Ramirez, A., Jr., & Wang, Z. (2008). When on-line meets off-line: An expectancy violation theory perspective on modality switching. *Journal of Communication, 58,* 20–39.

Ramirez, A., Jr., & Zhang, S. (2007). When online meets offline: The effect of modality switching on relational communication. *Communication Monographs, 74,* 287–310.

Ramirez, A., Jr., Zhang, S., McGrew, C., & Lin, S. -F. (2007). Relational communication in computer-mediated interaction revisited: A comparison of participant-observer perspectives. *Communication Monographs, 74,* 492–516.

Reicher, S., Spears, R., & Postmes, T. (1995). A social identity model of deindividuation phenomena. *European Review of Social Psychology, 6,* 161–198.

Rheingold, H. (1993). *The virtual community: Homesteading on the electronic frontier.* Reading, MA: Addison-Wesley.

Rice, R. E. (1982). Communication networking in computer-conferencing systems: A longitudinal study of group roles and system structure. In M. Burgoon (Ed.), *Communication yearbook 6* (pp. 925–944). Beverly Hills, CA: Sage.

Rice, R. E., & Associates. (1984). *The new media: Communication, research, and technology.* Beverly Hills, CA: Sage.

Rice, R. E., & Case, D. (1983). Electronic message systems in the university: A description of use and utility. *Journal of Communication, 33,* 131–154.

Sassenberg, K. (2002). Common bond and common identity groups on the Internet: Attachment and normative behavior in on-topic and off-topic chats. *Group Dynamics: Theory, Research, and Practice, 6,* 27–37.

Saunders, C. S., & Ahuja, M. K. (2006). Are all distributed teams the same? Differentiating between temporary and ongoing distributed teams. *Small Group Research, 37,* 662–700.

Scott, C. R., & Bonito, J. A. (2006, November). *Anonymity and participation in online groups: Anonymous, pseudonymous, and named conditions among co-located and remote members.* Paper presented at the annual meeting of the National Communication Association, San Antonio, TX.

Shamp, S. A. (1991). Mechanomorphism in perception of computer communication partners. *Computers in Human Behavior, 7,* 147–161.

Sherry, J. L. (2004). Flow and media enjoyment. *Communication Theory, 14,* 328–347.

Short, J., Williams, E., & Christie, B. (1976). *The social psychology of telecommunications.* London: John Wiley.

Steinfield, C., Pentland, B. T., Ackerman, M., & Contractor, N. (Eds.). (2007). *Communities and technologies 2007: Proceedings of the third communities and technologies conference.* Cambridge, MA: Springer.

Stutzman, F. (2006, April). *The evaluation of identity-sharing behavior in social network communities.* Paper presented at the conference of the International Digital Media and Arts Association, Miami University Center for Interactive Media Studies, Oxford, OH. Retrieved January 7, 2007, from http://www.units.muohio.edu/codeconference/papers/papers/stutzman_track5.pdf

Tanis, M., & Postmes, T. (2008). Cues to identity in online dyads: Effects of interpersonal versus intragroup perceptions on performance. *Group Dynamics: Theory, Research, and Practice, 12,* 96–111.

Tidwell, L. C., & Walther, J. B. (2002). Computer-mediated communication effects on disclosure, impressions, and interpersonal evaluations: Getting to know one another a bit at a time. *Human Communication Research, 28,* 317–348.

Timmerman, C. E. (2002). The moderating effect of mindlessness/mindfulness upon media richness and social influence explanations of organizational media use. *Communication Monographs, 69,* 111–131.

Toma, C. L., Hancock, J. T., & Ellison, N. B. (2008). Separating fact from fiction: An examination of deceptive self-presentation in online dating profiles. *Personality and Social Psychology Bulletin, 34,* 1023–1036.

Turkle, S. (1995). *Life on the screen: Identity in the age of the Internet.* New York: Simon & Schuster.

Turoff, M. (1991). Computer-mediated communication requirements for group support. *Journal of Organizational Computing, 1,* 85–113.

Utne, E. (1995, March–April). Networks are *not* communities. *Utne Reader,* No. 68, p. 3.

Walther, J. B. (1992). Interpersonal effects in computer-mediated interaction: A relational perspective. *Communication Research, 19,* 52–90.

Walther, J. B. (1996). Computer-mediated communication: Impersonal, interpersonal, and hyperpersonal interaction. *Communication Research, 23,* 3–43.

Walther, J. B. (2006). Nonverbal dynamics in computer-mediated communication, or :( :( and the net's with you, :) and you :) alone. In V. Manusov & M. L. Patterson (Eds.), *Handbook of nonverbal communication* (pp. 461–479). Thousand Oaks, CA: Sage.

Walther, J. B. (2007). Selective self-presentation in computer-mediated communication: Hyperpersonal dimensions of technology, language, and cognition. *Computers in Human Behavior, 23,* 2538–2557.

Walther, J. B., & Boyd, S. (2002). Attraction to computer-mediated social support. In C. A. Lin & D. Atkin (Eds.), *Communication technology and society: Audience adoption and uses* (pp. 153–188). Cresskill, NJ: Hampton.

Walther, J. B., Loh, T., & Granka, L. (2005). Let me count the ways: The interchange of verbal and nonverbal cues in computer-mediated and face-to-face affinity. *Journal of Language and Social Psychology, 24,* 36–65.

Walther, J. B., & Parks, M. R. (2002). Cues filtered out, cues filtered in: Computer-mediated communication and relationships. In M. L. Knapp & J. A. Daly (Eds.), *Handbook of interpersonal communication* (3rd ed., pp. 529–563). Thousand Oaks, CA: Sage.

Walther, J. B., Slovacek, C., & Tidwell, L. C. (2001). Is a picture worth a thousand words? Photographic images in long term and short term virtual teams. *Communication Research, 28,* 105–134.

Wang, Z., Walther, J. B., & Hancock, J. T. (2009). Social identification and interpersonal communication in computer-mediated communication: What you do versus who you are in virtual groups. *Human Communication Research, 35,* 59–85.

Wellman, B. (2001). Computer networks as social networks. *Science, 293,* 2031–2034.

# 29

# HUMAN-COMPUTER INTERACTION

◆ Eun-Ju Lee and S. Shyam Sundar

Human-computer interaction (HCI) is an interdisciplinary field that investigates how people perceive and think about computer-based technologies, what human constraints affect human-machine interaction, and what factors improve usability of computer systems (Kiesler & Hinds, 2004). Although HCI research entails both "relatively discursive, qualitative, and conceptual social-behavioral science and relatively formal, quantitative, and device-oriented computer science" (Caroll, 2006, p. 431), it is in the social and behavioral science approach to HCI, or the "soft" science paradigm in Carroll's (2006) words, where we can find the unique contributions of communication scholars. Specifically, unlike management information systems (MIS) research, which treats technology as a tool to accomplish specific task goals and stresses organizational implications of various computer applications (Zhang & Galletta, 2006), HCI researchers consider the interaction between the person and the computer as a sort of conversation (Suchman, 1987) and highlight the importance of communication-related variables. For example, studies pertaining to the effects of human-like attributes of computer systems, such as personality (Moon & Nass, 1996; Nass & Lee, 2001), gender (E.-J. Lee, 2003; Nass, Moon, & Green, 1997), and group membership (Nass, Fogg, & Moon, 1996), closely follow the research tradition on source characteristics. Similarly, studies investigating how structural features of user interfaces, such as modality (Lang, Borse, Wise, & David, 2002;

◆ 507

Sundar, 2000) and interactivity (Kalyanaraman & Sundar, 2006; Sundar & Constantin, 2004), influence individuals' cognitive, affective, and behavioral reactions resemble media effects studies, especially those concerning message and channel characteristics.

In the following sections, we identify two distinct lines of HCI research in the communication field, each representing a slightly different view of the computer: computer as source and computer as interactive medium. Sundar and Nass (2000) posited that the psychology of human-computer interaction is fundamentally premised on the locus of one's orientation to the computer. They suggested that when the computer is viewed as a source (CAS), people respond socially to the technology itself, whereas when the computer is thought of as a medium (CAM), users' social responses are not directed toward the technology but are affected by it. This chapter will summarize research findings and theoretical development within both the CAS and CAM domains and outline future directions in communication-oriented HCI research.

## ◆ Computer as Source

As recent technological advances have augmented computer interfaces with a wide array of social cues, such as natural language use, interactivity, human social roles, speech, and anthropomorphic agents (Steuer, 1995), computers are often treated as a source of information, as opposed to a mere conduit of messages created by another human (Sundar & Nass, 2000). That is, although people are aware that computers simply generate output as programmed, they seem to become oblivious to the asocial nature of interaction and rather automatically apply the same social heuristics toward inanimate machines as they do in human-human interaction (Nass & Moon, 2000; Reeves & Nass, 1996). In this view,

computers are considered to be social actors, if not assigned full humanity, which evoke in users a wide range of social attributions (Nass & Brave, 2005).

## SOCIAL RESPONSES TO COMMUNICATION TECHNOLOGY

Using a research paradigm called "Computers Are Social Actors" (CASA), Nass and colleagues (1997) have tested the applicability of various interpersonal social rules in HCI. For example, several studies have examined users' reactions to computers endowed with human-like *traits*. Specifically, Nass et al. found that individuals rate male-voiced computers as more proficient in technical subjects than female-voiced ones, whereas the opposite is true for topics such as love and relationships. Such gender stereotyping of the computer was replicated in E.-J. Lee's (2003) study, which operationalized computer gender in terms of gender-marked cartoon characters. Another human-like trait bestowed upon the computer is personality. Studies have shown that people not only infer a computer's personality from verbal or paraverbal cues in the interface but also respond more positively to computers whose personalities match their own (Moon & Nass, 1996; Nass & Lee, 2001). Specifically, dominant users preferred a dominant computer that revealed a high level of confidence and used more assertive language, whereas submissive users rated the interaction with a submissive computer more positively (Moon & Nass, 1996). Likewise, users were more willing to buy a book or make a bid for an auction item when the synthesized voice delivering the book reviews or product descriptions expressed a personality (extroverted vs. introverted) that was similar to their own (Nass & Lee, 2001).

Not only do simple cues to uniquely human traits elicit social scripts associated with them, they also seem to trigger spontaneously social behaviors grounded in interpersonal relationships. Following the reciprocity principle, after receiving useful information from the computer to accomplish an experimental task, participants spent more time on the second task to "help" the computer than when the computer had offered them irrelevant information (Fogg & Nass, 1997a). Similarly, Moon (2000) demonstrated that when the computer first provided some information about its technical capacity (self-disclosure), participants' responses were more intimate, in both depth and breadth, than when the computer simply asked the same questions without revealing about itself. Another instantiation of social responses to the computer pertains to flattery effects (Fogg & Nass, 1997b). Despite their awareness that the computer's evaluations were generated randomly and thus were not diagnostic of the actual quality of their performance, participants rated the computer and their own performance more positively when the computer produced praise.

The treatment of computer as a source is more evident in the following studies. Users asked by a computer about its own performance provided more positive evaluations than did those asked by a different computer (Nass, Moon, & Carney, 1999). That is, even though the computer never referred to itself as "I," when a different machine was used for the evaluation session, participants were less subject to the politeness norm and made less positive comments about the computer performance. This seemingly automatic tendency to assign entitativity to a computer was also observed in earlier studies, where praise/criticism about self versus another computer caused significantly different evaluations (Nass & Steuer, 1993; Nass, Steuer, Henriksen, & Dryer, 1994). More recently, K. M. Lee and Nass (2004) found that those who heard multiple synthetic voices reading the reviews of a book at a book-selling Web site were more persuaded than those who heard a single synthetic voice reading all five reviews. Such

findings persisted when participants played with a text-to-speech engine to produce multiple versions of the sentence using different voices, suggesting that "the tendency to use voice characteristics as a mark of individual identity overcomes the fact that one computer generated several voices" (Nass & Brave, 2005, p. 103). These studies underscore the fact that it is not just the box but also the voice of the computer that acts as the psychological source in HCI.

## EMBODIED AGENTS AND HUMAN-ROBOT INTERACTION

According to the CASA paradigm, the tendency to anthropomorphize computers is more or less automatically activated. Sundar (2004a), for instance, showed that the degree to which students anthropomorphized computers predicted their level of loyalty to particular terminals in campus computer laboratories. Other researchers, however, have studied how the extent to which an interface resembles a human, in either its form or functionality, affects user responses. Sproull, Subramani, Kiesler, and Walker (1996) compared how people responded to an ostensible computer-based career counseling system that employed either simple text display or a talking face, one of the clearest human referents. Participants reported greater arousal and displayed a stronger social desirability bias in the talking-face condition, presumably because "the talking-face display reminded subjects of a real human being" (p. 117). In a follow-up study, participants played a social dilemma game with a human confederate via videoconferencing or with one of three interface agents: a person-like agent, a dog-like agent, or a cartoon dog agent. The anthropomorphic agent induced greater cooperation, on a par with a human partner, although the dog-like agent was considered more likeable (Parise, Kiesler, Sproull, & Waters, 1999).

Other studies have employed a more sophisticated rendition of human-like computer agents. Defined as "digital representations of computer programs designed to interact with, or on behalf of, a human" (Bailenson et al., 2005, p. 379), embodied agents can even "understand human communicative behavior and generate integrated spontaneous verbal and nonverbal behavior of their own" (Cassell & Thorisson, 1999, p. 523), simulating human-human interaction more closely. To examine what leads to more satisfactory interaction with a multimodal humanoid, Cassell and Thorisson (1999) compared two different kinds of nonverbal behaviors— envelope feedback (i.e., those related to the process of conversation, such as nods, gaze, manual beat gesture, and head movements) and emotional feedback (i.e., facial displays that reference a particular emotion, such as happiness and puzzlement). The provision of envelope feedback not only elicited more positive evaluations of the interaction but also led people to use fewer utterances to complete the task, indicating greater conversation efficiency. In another study examining the effects of virtual humans' nonverbal behavior (Bailenson, Blascovich, Beall, & Loomis, 2001), when the computer agent in an immersive virtual reality environment displayed realistic gaze, people increased interpersonal distance to maintain an optimal level of immediacy.

Unlike early HCI studies dealing with social actors devoid of actual physical instantiation, researchers have begun to explore how various attributes of a robot affect the way people and robots communicate and work together. In the sense that robots still act according to programmed instructions and an existing knowledge base, they cannot serve as perfect human surrogates (Zhao, 2006). Still, because they are more mobile and designed to make more or less autonomous decisions, people tend to ascribe animacy and intentionality to them (Hinds, Roberts, & Jones, 2004; Kiesler & Hinds, 2004), which prompts social

responses. Analogous to the research on anthropomorphic computer interfaces, Hinds et al. (2004) investigated how the human-like appearance (e.g., facial features, arms and legs, human clothing) of professional service robots, in conjunction with status manipulation (subordinate vs. peer vs. supervisor), affects working relationships. Results showed that "participants retained more responsibility for the successful completion of the task when working with a machine-like as compared with a humanoid robot, especially when the machine-like robot was subordinate" (p. 153), suggesting that anthropomorphic appearance plays a significant role in establishing partnership in human-robot interaction. Similarly, when human likeness was manipulated in the form of the robot's ability to learn new behaviors over time (K. M. Lee, Park, & Song, 2005), it not only evoked more positive perceptions but also facilitated the formation of a stronger bond between human and artificial social actors.

However, the effects of embodied computer agents are not straightforward. In Sproull et al.'s (1996) study, text-only interface was rated higher on social evaluation (e.g., attractive, friendly, cheerful) and sociability, as compared with the talking-face counterpart. Likewise, dog-like agents were rated as more likeable than a person-like agent (Parise et al., 1999). Based on a meta-analysis, Dehn and van Mulken (2000) concluded that "the empirical evidence on the way an animated anthropomorphized agent influences the user's attitudes towards the system (e.g., utility, likeability, and comfortability) appears to be mixed" except that "a system with an agent is perceived as more entertaining than the one without an agent" (p. 15). They also pointed out that when facial display attracts users' attention, it might hinder task performance. On the other hand, Yee, Bailenson, and Rickertsen (2007) reviewed studies that compared interfaces with visually embodied agents with those without agents and found that facial representation yielded more positive social interactions, especially in terms of subjective responses.

Even when animated human-like agents make interactions more engaging and motivating, such systems might create unrealistic expectations about the system's capacity, and the mismatch between appearance and behavior might result in less than optimal user experience (Bailenson et al., 2005). In fact, people more frequently talked over the agent and had greater misunderstanding when the agent provided process-related nonverbal feedback (Cassell & Thorisson, 1999), suggesting that overly anthropomorphic agents might backfire when their behaviors fail to map onto user expectations of human likeness of those agents. Sharing this concern, Heckman and Wobbrock (2000) recommended that agents should inform users of the boundaries of their abilities and that system designers should avoid unnecessary realism. Another potential problem with anthropomorphic interfaces pertains to increased social presence. Given that participants were less willing to perform embarrassing acts (Bailenson et al., 2005) and more likely to engage in impression management in front of more human-looking agents (Sproull et al., 1996), when the task involves socially sensitive topics, users might be better off with more mechanomorphic interfaces. To summarize, while human users have an innate tendency to anthropomorphize computers, they are especially reactive to interface features that invite anthropomorphism, approaching the interaction with heightened expectations of likeness to human-human interactions and letting it influence their perceptions and behaviors.

## WHY SOCIAL RESPONSES?

Researchers have entertained and explored several explanations for the inherent socialness of HCI. First, when individuals interact with a computer, they might actually think of the software programmer (or creator more generally) and respond to that person (Sundar & Nass, 2000). That is, the social responses shown by users are not directed at the computer box per se but at the unseen programmer or imagined other. As Sundar (1994) suggested, users may be carrying on a parasocial interaction with the programmer, just like television viewers form attachments even to fictional characters, especially when the characters seem realistic (Rubin & Perse, 1987) or speak directly to the camera or audience (Auter, 1992). However, when the source was directly manipulated (computer vs. programmer; computer vs. another computer user), individuals' responses varied significantly as a function of presumed source (Sundar & Nass, 2000), thus refuting this "computers-as-a-proxy" or parasocial account. A second explanation is that social treatment of computers might reflect the user's lack of understanding as to how computer systems operate. In direct contrast to the deficiency account, however, Chiasson and Gutwin (2005) reported that praise from a computer improved the evaluations of the computer and feelings about self only among adults, with no corresponding effects among children. Last, on the basis of Langer and colleagues' work on mindlessness (for reviews, see Langer, 1989, 1992), Nass and his associates (Nass & Moon, 2000) argued that when computers emulate human-like attributes, such as interactivity and speech, people tend to focus on those cues and fail to take into account the asocial nature of the interaction. Consistent with this account, the aforementioned flattery effects (Fogg & Nass, 1997b) were more pronounced among high- than low-experience users (D. Johnson, Gardner, & Wiles, 2004), and gender stereotyping of the computer was found only when participants were cognitively busy with a secondary task (E.-J. Lee, 2008). Although these findings seem to comport well with the mindlessness explanation, the presumed mental processes underlying such findings remain to be directly measured and assessed.

## COMPARISONS BETWEEN HCI AND HUMAN-HUMAN INTERACTION

Although a number of studies have demonstrated the operation of social rules in HCI, direct comparisons between HCI and human-human interaction (HHI) have revealed some differences between the two. For example, participants expressed greater excitement, made more sociable comments, and expended more effort to accomplish the task when they believed that they were interacting with another person rather than a computer (Morkes, Kernal, & Nass, 1999; Sundar & Nass, 2000). In a simulated group discussion, the effects of visual representation (stick figures vs. animated cartoon characters) of interactants on source perception were more pronounced when the interactants were thought to be computer agents, as opposed to other participants (E.-J. Lee & Nass, 2002).

Differences between HCI and HHI become more evident when relatively un-restricted communication behaviors are in question. For example, participants talked more and were more likely to use relationship-oriented statements and reciprocate their partners' influence attempts when inter-acting with humans than computer partners (Shechtman & Horowitz, 2003). Likewise, after an online mock job interview, although participants' impressions of the interviewer and self-reported emotional reactions to the interview were not significantly different between human versus computer interviewer conditions, their nonverbal behaviors, such as smiling and silence-filling behavior, were "human biased" (Aharoni & Fridlund, 2007, p. 2186). In addition, people adjusted interpersonal distance from the computer-controlled agent in an immersive virtual environment only when the agent displayed realistic gaze, whereas they maintained the optimal level of distance with a human-controlled avatar regardless of gaze behavior (Bailenson, Blascovich, Beall, & Loomis, 2003). In fact, even when they did not vary the ontological nature of the interactant

(a computer), Nass and Brave (2005) found that claims to humanity (i.e., "I" reference) evoked negative reactions when delivered by a synthetic, as compared with human, voice. Collectively, these findings suggest that people do differentiate between interacting *with* and *via* computer technologies, and yet, in the presence of social cues, they often fail to suppress well-rehearsed social reactions toward the machine, especially when the responses are relatively automatic and require less conscious control (Blascovich, 2001).

## ◆ Computer as Medium

When the computer is conceptualized as a medium rather than as a source, the focus shifts from the computer as an entity with which human users interact to the computer as a conduit of content that human users actively use. The CAM model (Sundar & Nass, 2000) is often equated with computer-mediated communication (CMC), but that would be true only when the computer is considered a medium between *human* inter-actants, that is, interpersonal and group communication mediated by the computer (see Walther, Chapter 28, this volume). It is important to recognize that CAM is not simply about communicating with others via the computer but also about *obtaining content* via the computer. With the arrival and widespread diffusion of the World Wide Web, an ever-increasing portion of interactions via the computer have to do with accessing content on the Internet. This makes all of us users of digitally published content for mass dissemination, an activity much like reading newspapers, watching television, and listening to the radio. In this respect, CAM is akin to mass communication.

### INTERMEDIA COMPARISONS

Under this rubric of computer as a mass communication medium, early research pertained to comparisons between this and older, more traditional media for mass communication, fueled by a McLuhanist conviction that the nature, uses, and effects of content are fundamentally shaped by the medium via which the content is experienced.

*Use.* A random national survey of 1,071 American adults by Perse and Dunn (1998) found that individuals who felt that computers were able to fulfill a media-related need were likely to report greater use of this technology. Guided by uses and gratifications theory, this study also showed a strong ritualistic use of home computers, implying that users focus more on gratifications offered by the medium as a whole than on those obtained from specific content. Flanagin and Metzger (2001) demonstrated that informational use of the Internet was functionally equivalent to the use of traditional mass media. Scholars began to suggest that the Web may be displacing television use, especially for entertainment needs (Ferguson & Perse, 2000), not just because it serves as a functional alternative but because it holds infinite potential for providing pleasure, in keeping with Stephenson's (1988) play theory of communication. Others have become concerned with compulsive use of the Internet and its psychosocial consequences. While social psychologists have noted that Internet use predicted positive outcomes for extroverts and negative ones for introverts and those with low social support (Kraut et al., 2002), communication scholars have theorized about the impact of individual differences on Internet addiction. Caplan (2005), for example, has predicted and found that individuals who lack self-presentational social skills show markedly greater preference for online social interaction (POSI), resulting in problematic Internet use (PIU).

*Credibility.* Researchers have also examined credibility differences between the Web and traditional vehicles of mass communication (e.g., Flanagin & Metzger, 2000), often linking credibility with the degree to which

one uses the medium (e.g., T. J. Johnson & Kaye, 2004; Stavrositu & Sundar, 2008). Aside from the volume of use, researchers have identified several aspects of user interaction that are critical for credibility assessments on the Web, such as paying attention to sources, corroborating obtained information, assessing third-party recommendations, and so on. This has been dubbed the "checklist approach" and found to be quite ineffective because studies overwhelmingly show that users seldom pause to scrutinize and verify information obtained on the Web (Flanagin & Metzger, 2000), relying instead on surface design aspects for assessing credibility (Fogg et al., 2003). Consequently, researchers suggest the use of "credibility markers" (Fogg, 2003) by way of seals and ratings on sites among other means to instantaneously convey the relative expertise and trustworthiness of a given online source. After reviewing research on Web credibility, Metzger (2007) says that there is a pressing need for research on "what users actually do to assess credibility." Working from the perspective of dual-process models in social psychology, communication researchers focus on either user characteristics or system attributes. Metzger argues that user motivation and ability will predict critical evaluation of online information credibility (i.e., use of effortful checklist-style approaches). On the other hand, Sundar (2007a) assumes that most of the time, most users will process most of the information heuristically and proceeds to identify specific cues transmitted by particular technological affordances in the medium. These cues, in turn, will heuristically determine quality and credibility evaluations. His modality-agency-interactivity-navigability (MAIN) model seeks to specify how a given surface or design aspect pertaining to the modality, agency, interactivity, and navigability leads to users' positive or negative credibility evaluations. For example, the interactivity affordance on a political candidate's Web site might transmit the "dialogue" cue by giving users the sense that the content on the site is mutually shaped, thereby triggering a variety of heuristics relating to participation, democracy, consensus, and so on. These heuristics, in turn, will dictate perceptions of the site's and therefore the candidate's credibility, especially in the minds of those who are not heavily involved in content. What started out as a simple intermedia comparison of credibility perceptions has grown into a robust area of research in the field, given the pronounced need for credibility monitoring in a medium characterized by uneven gatekeeping practices and a limitless amount of information.

*Cognitive Effects.* Aside from making credibility comparisons across media, communication researchers have also studied differences in the cognitive impact of computer-based media versus traditional mass media. For example, Sundar, Narayan, Obregon, and Uppal (1998) found that print advertisements were remembered better than Web advertisements. Eveland and Dunwoody (2001) demonstrated greater learning from print than Web versions of identical scientific content. Tewksbury and Althaus (2000) showed that readers of the print version of the *New York Times* were more knowledgeable about public affairs than those reading its online counterpart. With time and increasing diffusion of the Web, scholars began to examine differences between media in terms of information-processing theories borrowed from cognitive psychology and educational technology research. Eveland, Cortese, Park, and Dunwoody (2004) proposed that Web readers may perhaps be engaging in selective scanning, resulting in poorer overall memory compared with their print-reading counterparts. They found that linear site designs (which are similar to print) promoted factual learning, whereas nonlinear designs involving hyperlinks (typical of hypermedia) led to better structuring of acquired information because the nature of their organization triggers the kind of information processing that mimics the associative nature of the human memory system.

Drawing on Bandura's social cognitive theory, Fredin and David (1998) proposed a hypermedia interaction cycle whereby they focused on such user motivations as self-efficacy and shifting goals in explaining user behavior on the Web. LaRose, Mastro, and Eastin (2001) found that social-cognitive variables such as self-efficacy, self-disparagement, and positive as well as negative outcome expectations accounted for 60% of the available variance in Internet usage, a significant improvement over prior uses and gratifications research. In sum, communication research on cognitive aspects of HCI has focused on both user factors and system variables.

## VARIABLE-CENTERED APPROACH

As HCI matures as a field, researchers are moving from considering computer technology as a whole toward investigating the role of specific attributes across technologies. As Nass and Mason (1990) pointed out, studying technologies holistically has serious generalizability limitations in that findings with one technology cannot be applied to other technologies. This is a critical problem in HCI research because computer-based technologies have been evolving rapidly, resulting in a number of new devices and Web-based applications. In advocating a move away from object-centered approaches (i.e., technology as an object or black box), Nass and Mason (1990) proposed a "variable-centered perspective" wherein technologies are studied in terms of their component attributes rather than as a whole package. That is, instead of studying uses and effects of whole technologies such as personal digital assistants (PDAs) or iPods, scholars using the variable-centered approach investigate the role of particular attributes embedded in these technologies, such as screen size, audio fidelity, input type, and output modality.

In a special joint issue of the *Journal of Communication* and the *Journal of Computer-Mediated Communication,* Newhagen and Rafaeli (1996) identified five defining attributes of the Internet— multimedia, hypertextuality, packet switching, synchronicity, and interactivity. While not mutually exclusive, these qualities serve to put the focus on specific attributes of HCI that are worthy of research attention because of their potential for profoundly shaping the interaction between human users and Internet technologies. Nearly 10 years later, however, Walther, Gay, and Hancock (2005) assessed research done in the field about these qualities and found themselves writing mostly about only two of them— multimedia and interactivity. Even though their review was dominated by CMC work, these two variables have also been central to HCI work in communication research.

*Multimedia.* The computer's multimedia capability is perhaps the most obvious distinguishing feature of this relatively new mass communication medium. Most older media, such as newspapers and radio, transmit information exclusively in a single modality (text and audio, respectively), whereas computers communicate in a variety of different modalities, often simultaneously. In addition, newer modalities such as animation, pop-ups, and virtual reality have emerged to vie for user attention. Communication scholars have leaned heavily on cognitive psychology, especially theories relating to sensory perception, to examine the impact of modalities on users. Reeves and Nass demonstrated the greater perceptual importance of audio over video fidelity (1996) and proposed the development of so-called perceptual interfaces (2000) based entirely on human psychology of perception. While some of these perceptions are based on content, many of them are directly related to the modality of presentation.

Invoking psychology theories such as dual coding and separate streams, Sundar (2000) compared the difference between five different modality combinations and found that even though multimedia enhancements to a news Web site were considered highly desirable, they tended to hinder processing and led to more negative evaluations of news content while aiding memory for advertisements. More recently, Rockwell and Singleton (2007) showed that the addition of streaming audio and video had detrimental effects on information acquisition from PowerPoint presentations, with the authors attributing the cause to distraction and cognitive load. Studies employing the limited-capacity model (Lang, 2000) have shown that newer modalities such as animation (Lang et al., 2002) and pop-ups (Diao & Sundar, 2004) command involuntary attention (as indexed by orienting responses) with significant consequences for content memory.

A key outcome variable in the study of multimedia is presence—that is, the degree to which the user feels drawn in by the multiple representation media to the point of believing that the mediated environment is real (Lombard & Ditton, 1997). As Biocca (1997) notes, our senses are the channels to our minds, and since multimedia engages a variety of senses, it has an enhanced ability to immerse us in the mediated world. This immersion arises out of an illusion of "being there" (Steuer, 1992), an illusion made possible by the high level of vividness in multimedia presentations. Conceptualizing vividness of an interface in terms of its sensory breadth (i.e., the number of senses engaged by it) and sensory depth (i.e., the resolution within each perceptual channel), Steuer (1995) arrays various modalities, with text being very low and virtual reality being very high on this dimension. In sum, HCI scholars in the field view multimedia in terms of modalities of interaction with computer-based media and analyze the cognitive impact of various modalities by altering our processing of underlying content and inducing a sense of presence.

*Interactivity.* Interactivity is by far the most controversial concept among technology researchers in the field, with wide disparities in conceptualization and operationalization, but the major point of contention appears to be the locus of interactivity. In a debate titled "Where Interactivity Resides," Bucy (2004a) presented arguments for why interactivity should be a perceptual variable, and Sundar (2004b) argued that interactivity is an attribute of the technology rather than the user. Numerous explications of the concept have been attempted (e.g., Kiousis, 2002; Liu & Shrum, 2002; McMillan & Hwang, 2002; Sundar, Kalyanaraman, & Brown, 2003), with interactivity being equated to dialogue, control, choice, responsiveness, two-way communication, real-time participation, level of user activity, user involvement, speed, mapping, synchronicity, contingency, and content modifiability, among several other definitions. Typologies abound as well. While McMillan (2002) distinguishes between user-to-user, user-to-system, and user-to-documents interactivity, Sundar et al. (2003) make a distinction between functional interactivity (calling up various functions on a site, such as audio downloads) and contingent interactivity (message exchange being threaded, as in a bulletin board). Stromer-Galley (2004) makes a similar distinction between interactivity-as-product (e.g., site features such as click polls) and interactivity-as-process (e.g., interactions between humans via e-mail) but warns of the danger of conflation when process-based definitions are sought to be operationalized as an attribute of the product. This adds yet another locus of interactivity. In addition to the technology and the user, we now have interactivity residing in the process of interaction, either between technology and user (HCI) or between users mediated by technology (CMC).

Recent reviews tend to view interactivity in the HCI context differently than in the CMC context. Of interest to us here is the former, which views interactivity as a technological affordance. In keeping with the functional versus contingency distinction, Sundar (2007b) identifies interactivity as a medium feature (focusing on the number of modalities for user interaction available on the interface) and as a message feature (information organization on the interface leading to contingent exchange of messages between user and system), respectively. He also identifies a third category—namely, interactivity as a source feature (i.e., the degree to which the interface allows the user to choose the source or gatekeeper of information). Under this formulation, the highest level of interactivity is realized when the interface allows users to act as the sources or gatekeepers, as happens in customizable sites and portals on the Web (see also Sundar, 2008). Therefore, there are at least three loci of interactivity, one each corresponding to the three dominant elements of basic communication models (source, message, channel).

Regardless of how interactivity is conceptualized, a steady stream of experimental research has shown that it has significant psychological effects. To begin with, most studies show a strong manipulation check. Whether operationalized in terms of control or contingency, by way of bells and whistles, or in terms of message customizability, user perceptions of interactivity are significantly positively affected by these technological affordances (Kalyanaraman & Sundar, 2006; Liu & Shrum, 2002; Sundar & Kim, 2005). Furthermore, interactivity is shown to induce a sense of telepresence (Coyle & Thorson, 2001) and a need for orientation (Tremayne & Dunwoody, 2001). Interactive devices on a site, such as clicks and drags, tend to trigger conscious processing of stimuli (Sundar & Constantin, 2004). When operationalized in terms of speed of system response, interactivity not only is physiologically significant (Sundar & Wagner, 2002) but also leads to more positive site evaluations (Yun, 2007). However, positive evaluations of the site do not translate directly into positive evaluations of the content on the site. Across several experiments, moderate amounts of interactivity led to the most positive assessments of content, whereas high levels of interactivity had about the same effects on content evaluations as low interactivity (e.g., Sundar et al., 2003)—a phenomenon labeled *interactivity paradox* by Bucy (2004b). When asked, users like increased interactivity, but when considering psychological effects, more is not necessarily better. Different reasons have been cited for this phenomenon, ranging from distraction, disorientation, and cognitive overload to frustration and high expectations (Bucy, 2004b; Bucy & Tao, 2007; Sundar, 2000). Sundar (2007b) argues that high levels of interactivity promote high levels of engagement, thereby forcing central processing and hence close scrutiny of content. Given that content in most of the aforementioned experiments was chosen to be mediocre, it is not surprising that ratings were low when attention was high.

## ◆ Future Trends

Perhaps due to its short intellectual history, as well as the novelty of technological features inviting scientific exploration, HCI research has so far been predominantly driven by a simple stimulus-response formulation. If the initial phase was the study of computer as a holistic technology, the second phase was characterized by a focus on particular technological affordances in computer-based media. These served as independent variables in our attempts to investigate their psychological effects. The third phase is likely to be characterized by efforts to specify the mechanisms by which these affordances have the documented effects (mediating variables) and to uncover important individual differences that are unique to computer use (moderating variables), such as power usage (Marathe, Sundar, Bijvank, van Vugt, & Veldhuis, 2007). Already, work in the area of customization is showing this kind of sophistication. In examining the relationship between degree of personalization and attitudes and behaviors toward Web portals, Kalyanaraman and Sundar (2006) tested

the mediation of five user perceptions—relevance, interactivity, involvement, community, and novelty. Sundar and Marathe (2006) followed up by examining whether it was the tailored content (content put together by the researcher based on individual participants' preference) or a sense of agency (content customized by individual participants) that contributed to positive attitudes toward Web portals. They found that power users rated content more positively in the customization condition, whereas nonpower users gave higher ratings in the personalization condition. Another follow-up experiment investigated why power users and nonpower users differed in their evaluations of customized content and explored such variables as privacy, self-efficacy, sense of control, reported convenience, and perceived utility (Marathe, Sundar, & Reese, 2007). In addition to investigating mediators and moderators, CAM research increasingly has focused on psychological processing of media attributes, with particular reliance on dual-process models in social psychology.

Thus far, the HCI research pertaining to CAS has been dominated by attempts to replicate well-established social psychological theories of interpersonal communication. That is, HCI researchers have applied well-known interaction rules derived from HHI to HCI. However, computer technologies might create a new way in which various interpersonal communication phenomena can be investigated. For example, Bailenson et al. (2003) highlighted the unique value of immersive virtual environment technology (IVET) for proxemics researchers. Unlike past proxemics studies that "employed observational methods with little or no experimental control, confederates who may behave inconsistently, and projective measurement technique," IVET allows near-perfect control over the appearance, behavior, and environment of virtual human representations without sacrificing "ecological validity or mundane realism." Moreover, it offers the advantage of measuring proxemic behavior "accurately, continuously and covertly" (pp. 1–2). Such methodological advantages of using embodied agents as surrogates of human confederates can benefit other domains of interpersonal communication research, such as deception detection and various conversational behaviors.

HCI research offers communication scholars the unique opportunity to participate in the design of tomorrow's media by suggesting psychologically meaningful interface innovations. The influential book *The Media Equation* by Reeves and Nass (1996) led the way in outlining design implications at the end of every chapter. Articles and monographs have started incorporating design suggestions ever since Fredin (1997) proposed a number of hyperstory prototypes for online journalism based on user psychology. A significant number of communication technology scholars participate in the International Society for Presence Research, and many of them also lobbied the International Communication Association (ICA) to establish a separate unit devoted to research on games. Ideas relating to uses and gratifications, self-efficacy, interactivity, and presence have been applied to achieve a social scientific understanding of the culture of games in our field (Vorderer & Bryant, 2006). That said, much of the extant research on the effects of playing games focuses on the psychological impact of game content (e.g., K. M. Lee & Peng, 2006) rather than game technology. Approaching games research as a special case of HCI research (similar to human–Web site interaction) will allow us to better understand the effects of interactivity, modality, and other technological affordances that are an integral part of modern-day computer and video games.

In sum, HCI research in the field of communication is flourishing, especially in terms of finding ready applications in new and emergent forms of interpersonal and mass communication. By treating HCI as a communication situation and drawing upon core concepts such as source and medium, communication scholars have made unique contributions to knowledge that occupy the intersection of basic fields such as psychology and applied disciplines such as information science and technology. As Zhao (2006) observed, with computers increasingly serving as competent communicative agents, "social relationships" are no longer confined to dealings with other human beings (p. 414). Likewise, as the Internet has become one of the most influential sources in people's media repertoire, it prompts numerous research questions that can be effectively addressed by the rich tradition of media effects research. This is why communication scholars, from both interpersonal and mass communication areas, should not limit their inquiries to human-human encounters or traditional mass-oriented media but should take seriously the role of computers and computer-based media in eliciting interactions from human users and facilitating communication that is unprecedented in scale, variety, and quality.

# ◆ References

Aharoni, E., & Fridlund, A. J. (2007). Social reactions toward people vs. computers: How mere labels shape interactions. *Computers in Human Behavior, 23,* 2175–2189.

Auter, P. J. (1992). TV that talks back: An experimental validation of a parasocial interaction scale. *Journal of Broadcasting and Electronic Media, 36,* 173–181.

Bailenson, J. N., Blascovich, J., Beall, A. C., & Loomis, J. M. (2001). Equilibrium revisited: Mutual gaze and personal space in virtual environments. *Presence, 10,* 583–598.

Bailenson, J. N., Blascovich, J., Beall, A. C., & Loomis, J. M. (2003). Interpersonal distance in immersive virtual environments. *Personality and Social Psychology Bulletin, 29,* 1–15.

Bailenson, J. N., Swinth, K., Hoyt, C., Persky, S., Dimov, A., & Blascovich, J. (2005). The independent and interactive effects of embodied-agent appearance and behavior on self-report, cognitive, and behavioral markers of copresence in immersive virtual environments. *Presence, 14,* 379–393.

Biocca, F. (1997). Cyborg's dilemma: Progressive embodiment in virtual environments. *Journal of Computer-Mediated Communication,* 3(2). Retrieved August 29, 2007, from http://jcmc.indiana.edu/vol3/issue2/biocca2. html

Blascovich, J. (2001). Social influences within immersive virtual environments. In R. Schroeder (Ed.), *The social life of avatars* (pp. 127–145). New York: Springer-Verlag.

Bucy, E. P. (2004a). Interactivity in society: Locating an elusive concept. *The Information Society, 20,* 373–383.

Bucy, E. P. (2004b). The interactivity paradox: Closer to the news but confused. In E. P. Bucy & J. E. Newhagen (Eds.), *Media access: Social and psychological dimensions of new technology use* (pp. 47–72). Mahwah, NJ: Lawrence Erlbaum.

Bucy, E. P., & Tao, C. C. (2007). The mediated moderation model of interactivity. *Media Psychology, 9,* 647–672.

Caplan, S. E. (2005). A social skill account of problematic internet use. *Journal of Communication, 55,* 721–736.

Carroll, J. M. (2006). Soft versus hard: The essential tension. In D. Galletta & P. Zhang (Eds.), *Human-computer interaction and management information systems: Applications* (pp. 424–432). Armonk, NY: M. E. Sharpe.

Cassell, J., & Thorisson, K. R. (1999). The power of a nod and a glance: Envelope vs. emotional feedback in animated conversational agents. *Applied Artificial Intelligence, 13,* 519–538.

Chiasson, S., & Gutwin, C. (2005). Testing the media equation with children. In G. C. van der Veer & C. Gale (Eds.), *Proceedings of the Conference on Human Factors in Computing Systems* (*ACM SIGCH,* pp. 829–838). New York: ACM Press.

Coyle, J. R., & Thorson, E. (2001). The effects of progressive levels of interactivity and vividness in Web marketing sites. *Journal of Advertising, 30*(3), 65–77.

Dehn, D. M., & van Mulken, S. (2000). The impact of animated interface agents: A review of empirical research. *International Journal of Human-Computer Studies, 52,* 1–22.

Diao, F., & Sundar, S. S. (2004). Orienting responses and memory for Web advertisements: Exploring effects of pop-up window and animation. *Communication Research, 31,* 537–567.

Eveland, W. P., Jr., Cortese, J., Park, H., & Dunwoody, S. (2004). How Web site organization influences free recall, factual knowledge, and knowledge structure density. *Human Communication Research, 30,* 208–233.

Eveland, W. P., Jr., & Dunwoody, S. (2001). User control and structural isomorphism or disorientation and cognitive load? Learning from the Web versus print. *Communication Research, 28,* 48–78.

Ferguson, D. A., & Perse, E. M. (2000). The World Wide Web as a functional alternative to television. *Journal of Broadcasting & Electronic Media, 44,* 155–174.

Flanagin, A. J., & Metzger, M. J. (2000). Perceptions of Internet information credibility. *Journalism & Mass Communication Quarterly, 77,* 515–540.

Flanagin, A. J., & Metzger, M. J. (2001). Internet use in the contemporary media environment. *Human Communication Research, 27,* 153–181.

Fogg, B. J. (2003). Motivating, influencing, and persuading users. In J. A. Jacko & A. Sears (Eds.), *The human-computer interaction handbook: Fundamentals, evolving technologies and emerging applications* (pp. 358–370). Mahwah, NJ: Lawrence Erlbaum.

Fogg, B. J., & Nass, C. I. (1997a). How users reciprocate to computers: An experiment that demonstrates behavior change. In *CHI Extended Abstract* (pp. 331–332). New York: ACM Press.

Fogg, B. J., & Nass, C. I. (1997b). Silicon sycophants: The effects of computers that flatter. *International Journal of Human-Computer Studies, 46,* 551–561.

Fogg, B. J., Soohoo, C., Danielson, D. R., Marable, L., Stanford, J., & Tauber, E. R. (2003, June). *How do users evaluate the credibility of Web sites? A study with over 2,500 participants.* Paper presented at the ACM conference on Designing for User Experiences, San Francisco.

Fredin, E. S. (1997). Rethinking the news story for the Internet: Hyperstory prototypes and a model of the user. *Journalism & Mass Communication Monographs, 163,* 1–47.

Fredin, E. S., & David, P. (1998). Browsing and the hypermedia interaction cycle. *Journalism & Mass Communication Quarterly, 75,* 35–54.

Heckman, C. E., & Wobbrock, J. O. (2000, June). *Put your best face forward: Anthropomorphic agents, e-commerce consumers, and the law.* Paper presented at the Fourth International Conference on Autonomous Agents, Barcelona, Spain.

Hinds, P. J., Roberts, T. L., & Jones, H. (2004). Whose job is it anyway? A study of human-robot interaction in a collaborative task. *Human-Computer Interaction, 19,* 151–181.

Johnson, D., Gardner, J., & Wiles, J. (2004). Experience as a moderator of the media equation: The impact of flattery and praise. *International Journal of Human-Computer Studies, 61,* 237–258.

Johnson, T. J., & Kaye, B. K. (2004). Wag the blog: How reliance on traditional media and the internet influence credibility perceptions of Weblogs among blog users. *Journalism & Mass Communication Quarterly, 81,* 622–642.

Kalyanaraman, S., & Sundar, S. S. (2006). The psychological appeal of personalized online content in Web portals: Does customization affect attitudes and behavior? *Journal of Communication, 56,* 110–132.

Kiesler, S., & Hinds, P. (2004). Human-robot interaction. *Human-Computer Interaction, 19,* 1–8.

Kiousis, S. (2002). Interactivity: A concept explication. *New Media & Society, 4,* 355–383.

Kraut, R., Kiesler, S., Boneva, B., Cummings, J., Helgeson, V., & Crawford, A. (2002). Internet paradox revisited. *Journal of Social Issues, 58,* 49–74.

Lang, A. (2000). The limited capacity model of mediated message processing. *Journal of Communication, 50,* 46–70.

Lang, A., Borse, J., Wise, K., & David, P. (2002). Captured by the World Wide Web: Orienting to structural and content features of computer-presented information. *Communication Research, 29,* 215–245.

Langer, E. (1989). Minding matters: The consequences of mindlessness-mindfulness. In L. Berkowitz (Ed.), *Advances in experimental psychology* (Vol. 22, pp. 137–173). San Diego: Academic Press.

Langer, E. (1992). Matters of mind: mindfulness/mindlessness in perspective. *Consciousness and Cognition, 1,* 289–305.

LaRose, R., Mastro, D., & Eastin, M. S. (2001). Understanding Internet use: A social-cognitive approach to uses and gratifications. *Social Science Computer Review, 19,* 395–413.

Lee, E.-J. (2003). Effects of "gender" of the computer on informational social influence: The moderating role of task type. *International Journal of Human-Computer Studies, 58,* 347–362.

Lee, E.-J. (2008). Gender stereotyping of computers: Resource depletion or reduced attention? *Journal of Communication, 58,* 301–320.

Lee, E.-J., & Nass, C. (2002). Experimental tests of normative group influence and representation effects in computer-mediated communication: When interacting via computers differs from interacting with computers. *Human Communication Research, 28,* 349–381.

Lee, K. M., & Nass, C. (2004). The multiple source effect and synthesized speech: Doubly disembodied language as a conceptual framework. *Human Communication Research, 30,* 182–207.

Lee, K. M., Park, N., & Song, H. (2005). Can a robot be perceived as a developing creature? Effects of a robot's long-term cognitive developments on its social presence and people's social responses toward it. *Human Communication Research, 31,* 538–563.

Lee, K. M., & Peng, W. (2006). What do we know about social and psychological effects of computer games? A comprehensive review of the current literature. In P. Vorderer & J. Bryant (Eds.), *Playing video games: Motives, responses, and consequences* (pp. 325–346). Mahwah, NJ: Lawrence Erlbaum.

Liu, Y., & Shrum, L. J. (2002). What is interactivity and is it always such a good thing? Implications of definition, person, and situation for the influence of interactivity on advertising effectiveness. *Journal of Advertising, 31,* 53–64.

Lombard, M., & Ditton, T. (1997). At the heart of it all: The concept of presence. *Journal of Computer Mediated Communication, 3*(2). Retrieved August 29, 2007, from http://jcmc.indiana.edu/vol3/issue2/lombard.html

Marathe, S., Sundar, S. S., Bijvank, M. N., van Vugt, H., & Veldhuis, J. (2007, May). *Who are these power users anyway? Building a psychological profile.* Paper presented at the 57th annual conference of the International Communication Association, San Francisco.

Marathe, S., Sundar, S. S., & Reese, C. (2007, August). *Customization vs. personalization: The role of power usage and privacy.* Paper presented at the 90th annual conference of the Association for Education in Journalism and Mass Communication, Washington, DC.

McMillan, S. J. (2002). Exploring models of interactivity from multiple research traditions: Users, documents, and systems. In L. A. Lievrouw & S. Livingstone (Eds.), *The handbook of new media* (pp. 163–182). Thousand Oaks, CA: Sage.

McMillan, S. J., & Hwang, J. S. (2002). Measures of perceived interactivity: An exploration of the role of direction of communication, user control and time in shaping perceptions of interactivity. *Journal of Advertising, 31,* 29–42.

Metzger, M. (2007). Making sense of credibility on the Web: Models for evaluating online information and recommendations for future research. *Journal of the American Society for Information Science and Technology, 58,* 2078–2091.

Moon, Y. (2000). Intimate exchanges: Using computers to elicit self-disclosure from consumers. *Journal of Consumer Research, 26,* 323–339.

Moon, Y., & Nass, C. (1996). How "real" are computer personalities? Psychological responses to personality types in human-computer interaction. *Communication Research, 23,* 651–674.

Morkes, J., Kernal, H. L., & Nass, C. (1999). Effects of humor in task-oriented human-computer interaction and computer-mediated communication: A direct test of SRCT theory. *Human-Computer Interaction, 14,* 395–435.

Nass, C., & Brave, S. (2005). *Wired for speech: How voice activates and advances the human-computer relationship.* Cambridge: MIT Press.

Nass, C., Fogg, B. J., & Moon, Y. (1996). Can computers be teammates? *International Journal of Human-Computer Studies, 45,* 669–678.

Nass, C., & Lee, K. M. (2001). Does computer-synthesized speech manifest personality? Experimental tests of recognition, similarity-attraction, and consistency-attraction. *Journal of Experimental Psychology: Applied, 7,* 171–181.

Nass, C., & Mason, L. (1990). On the study of technology and task: A variable-based approach. In J. Fulk & C. W. Steinfield (Eds.), *Organizations and communication technology* (pp. 46–68). Newbury Park, CA: Sage

Nass, C., & Moon, Y. (2000). Machines and mindlessness: Social responses to computers. *Journal of Social Issues, 56,* 81–103.

Nass, C., Moon, Y., & Carney, P. (1999). Are people polite to computers? Responses to computer-based interviewing systems. *Journal of Applied Social Psychology, 29,* 1093–1110.

Nass, C., Moon, Y., & Green, N. (1997). Are computers gender-neutral? Gender stereo-typic responses to computers. *Journal of Applied Social Psychology, 27,* 864–876.

Nass, C., & Steuer, J. (1993). Voices, boxes and sources of messages: Computers as social actors. *Human Communication Research, 19,* 504–527.

Nass, C., Steuer, J., Henriksen, L., & Dryer, C. D. (1994). Machines, social attributions, and ethopoeia: Performance assessments of computers subsequent to "self-" or "other" evaluations. *International Journal of Human-Computer Studies, 40,* 543–559.

Newhagen, J. E., & Rafaeli, S. (1996). Why communication researchers should study the Internet: A dialogue. *Journal of Communication, 46,* 4–13.

Parise, S., Kiesler, S., Sproull, L., & Waters, K. (1999). Cooperating with life-like interface agents. *Computers in Human Behavior, 15,* 123–142.

Perse, E. M., & Dunn, D. G. (1998). The utility of home computers and media use: Implications of multimedia and connectivity. *Journal of Broadcasting & Electronic Media, 42,* 435–456.

Reeves, B., & Nass, C. (1996). *The media equation: How people treat computers, television, and new media like real people and places.* New York: Cambridge University Press.

Reeves, B., & Nass, C. (2000). Perceptual bandwidth. *Communications of the ACM, 43*(3), 65–70.

Rockwell, S. C., & Singleton, L. A. (2007). The effect of modality of presentation of streaming multimedia on information acquisition. *Media Psychology, 9,* 179–191.

Rubin, A. M., & Perse, E. M. (1987). Audience activity and soap opera involvement: A uses and effects investigation. *Human Communication Research, 14,* 246–268.

Shechtman, N., & Horowitz, L. M. (2003). Media inequality in conversation: How people behave differently when interacting with computers and people. In *Proceedings of the Conference on Human Factors in Computing Systems (ACM SIGCHI,* pp. 281–288). New York: ACM Press.

Sproull, L., Subramani, M., Kiesler, S., & Walker, J. H. (1996). When the interface is a face. *Human-Computer Interaction, 11,* 97–124.

Stavrositu, C., & Sundar, S. S. (2008). If internet credibility is so iffy, why the heavy use? The relationship between medium use and credibility. *Cyberpsychology & Behavior, 11,* 65–68.

Stephenson, W. (1988). *The play theory of mass communication.* New Brunswick, NJ: Transaction.

Steuer, J. (1992). Defining virtual reality: Dimensions determining telepresence. *Journal of Communication, 42,* 73–93.

Steuer, J. (1995). *Vividness and source of evaluation as determinants of social responses toward mediated representations of agency.* Unpublished doctoral dissertation, Stanford University, Stanford, CA.

Stromer-Galley, J. (2004). Interactivity-as-product and interactivity-as-process. *The Information Society, 20,* 391–394.

Suchman, L. A. (1987). *Plans and situated actions: The problem of human-machine communication.* New York: Cambridge University Press.

Sundar, S. S. (1994, August). *Is human-computer interaction social or parasocial?* Paper presented at the 90th annual conference of the Association for Education in Journalism and Mass Communication, Atlanta, GA.

Sundar, S. S. (2000). Multimedia effects on processing and perception of online news: A study of picture, audio, and video downloads. *Journalism & Mass Communication Quarterly, 77,* 480–499.

Sundar, S. S. (2004a). Loyalty to computer terminals: Is it anthropomorphism or consistency? *Behaviour & Information Technology, 23,* 107–118.

Sundar, S. S. (2004b). Theorizing interactivity's effects. *The Information Society, 20,* 387–391.

Sundar, S. S. (2007a). The MAIN model: A heuristic approach to understanding technology effects on credibility. In M. J. Metzger & A. J. Flanagin (Eds.), *Digital media, youth, and credibility* (pp. 73–100). Cambridge: MIT Press.

Sundar, S. S. (2007b). Social psychology of inter-activity in human-Website interaction. In A. N. Joinson, K. Y. A. McKenna, T. Postmes, & U.-D. Reips (Eds.), *The Oxford handbook of Internet psychology* (pp. 89–104). Oxford, UK: Oxford University Press.

Sundar, S. S. (2008). Self as source: Agency and customization in interactive media. In E. Konijn, S. Utz, M. Tanis, & S. Barnes (Eds.), *Mediated interpersonal communication* (pp. 58–74). New York: Routledge.

Sundar, S. S., & Constantin, C. (2004, May). *Does interacting with media enhance news memory? Automatic vs. controlled processing of interactive news features.* Paper presented at the 54th annual conference of the International Communication Association, New Orleans, LA.

Sundar, S. S., Kalyanaraman, S., & Brown, J. (2003). Explicating Website interactivity: Impression-formation effects in political campaign sites. *Communication Research, 30,* 30–59.

Sundar, S. S., & Kim, J. (2005). Interactivity and persuasion: Influencing attitudes with information and involvement. *Journal of Interactive Advertising, 5,* 6–29.

Sundar, S. S., & Marathe, S. (2006, August). *Is it tailoring or is it agency? Unpacking the psychological appeal of customized news.* Paper presented at the 89th annual convention of the Association for Education in Journalism and Mass Communication, San Francisco.

Sundar, S. S., Narayan, S., Obregon, R., & Uppal, C. (1998). Does Web advertising work? Memory for print vs. online media. *Journalism & Mass Communication Quarterly, 75,* 822–835.

Sundar, S. S., & Nass, C. (2000). Source orientation in human-computer interaction: Programmer, networker, or independent social actor? *Communication Research, 27,* 683–703.

Sundar, S. S., & Wagner, C. B. (2002). The world wide wait: Exploring physiological and behavioral effects of download speed. *Media Psychology, 4,* 173–206.

Tewksbury, D., & Althaus, S. L. (2000). Differences in knowledge acquisition among readers of the paper and online versions of a national newspaper. *Journalism & Mass Communication Quarterly, 77,* 457–479.

Tremayne, M., & Dunwoody, S. (2001). Interactivity, information processing, and learning on the World Wide Web. *Science Communication, 23,* 111–134.

Vorderer, P., & Bryant, J. (Eds.). (2006). *Playing video games: Motives, responses, and consequences.* Mahwah, NJ: Lawrence Erlbaum.

Walther, J. B., Gay, G., & Hancock, J. T. (2005). How do communication and technology researchers study the internet? *Journal of Communication, 55,* 632–657.

Yee, N., Bailenson, J. N., & Rickertsen, K. (2007). A meta-analysis of the impact of the inclusion and realism of human-like faces on user experiences in interfaces. In *Proceedings of the Conference on Human Factors in Computing Systems* (*ACM SIGCHI,* pp. 1–10). New York: ACM Press.

Yun, G. W. (2007). Interactivity concepts examined: Response time, hypertext, role taking, and multimodality. *Media Psychology, 9,* 527–548.

Zhang, P., & Galletta, D. (2006). Foundations of human-computer interaction in management information systems: An introduction. In P. Zhang & D. Galletta (Eds.), *Human-computer interaction and management information systems: Foundations* (pp. 1–18). Armonk, NY: M. E. Sharpe.

Zhao, S. (2006). Humanoid social robots as a medium of communication. *New Media and Society, 8,* 401–419.

# AUTHOR INDEX

# SUBJECT INDEX

# ABOUT THE EDITORS

**CHARLES R. BERGER** (PhD, Michigan State University) is Professor in the Department of Communication at the University of California, Davis. His research interests include message production processes and the processing of threat-related messages by intuitive and rational systems. He is a former editor of *Human Communication Research* and coeditor (with Sandra Ball Rokeach) of *Communication Research*. He is currently a member of several editorial boards of communication journals. He is a Fellow and a Past President of the International Communication Association (ICA). Among the books he has published are *Language and Social Knowledge: Uncertainty in Interpersonal Relations* (with James J. Bradac), a volume that received both the National Communication Association (NCA) Golden Anniversary Book Award and the ICA Fellows Book Award. *Social Cognition and Communication* (with Michael E. Roloff) received a book award from the NCA's Social Cognition Division. He also coedited the first edition of the *Handbook of Communication Science* (with Steven H. Chaffee) and *Communication and Social Influence Processes* (with Michael Burgoon). His book, *Planning Strategic Interaction: Attaining Goals Through Communicative Action,* received the NCA Interpersonal Communication Division's Gerald R. Miller Book Award. He is co-recipient (with Judee Burgoon) of the NCA's Mark Knapp Award, and he received the NCA's Distinguished Scholar Award. He is an area editor for the *International Encyclopedia of Communication.*

**MICHAEL E. ROLOFF** (PhD, Michigan State University) is Professor of Communication Studies at Northwestern University. His research and teaching interests are in the general area of interpersonal influence. He has published articles and offers courses focused on persuasion, interpersonal compliance gaining, conflict management, organizational change, and bargaining and negotiation. His current research is focused on conflict avoidance and serial arguing in intimate relationships, the interpretation and construction of persuasive messages, and the effects of planning and alternatives on negotiation processes. He has coedited four research volumes: (1) *Persuasion: New Directions in Theory and Research*, (2) *Social Cognition and Communication*, (3) *Interpersonal Processes*, and (4) *Communication and Negotiation*. He wrote *Interpersonal Communication: The Social Exchange Approach*. He completed a term as the editor of *Communication Yearbook* and is currently coeditor of *Communication Research*. He was co-recipient of the Woolbert Award for Outstanding Contribution to Communication Research from the Speech Communication Association and of a publication award from the Social Cognition and Communication Division of the National Communication Association. He has been the Chair of the Interpersonal Communication Division of the National Communication Association. He is currently Director of the National Communication Association Publications Board. He has received several teaching awards from groups at Northwestern, including the Associated Student Government, the Mortar Board, and the Alumni Association.

**DAVID R. ROSKOS-EWOLDSEN** (PhD, Indiana University) is Professor in the School of Communication at The Ohio State University (OSU). Prior to joining the faculty at OSU in January 2009, he was Professor in the Department of Psychology at the University of Alabama. His research interests focus on media psychology, attitudes, social influence, and health communication. He cofounded the journal *Media Psychology* with Dr. Jennings Bryant in 1999 and founded the journal *Communication Methods and Measures* in 2007. He is the immediate past chair of the Information Systems Division and chair elect of the Mass Communication Division of the International Communication Association and chair elect of the Communication and Social Cognition Division of the National Communication Association. He has published in a variety of journals ranging from the *Journal of Communication, Human Communication Research, Media Psychology, Communication Monographs, Journal of Advertising, Journal of Personality and Social Psychology, Health Psychology,* and *Personality and Social Psychology Bulletin*. In his spare time, he enjoys photography, camping, backpacking, and canoeing.

# ABOUT THE CONTRIBUTORS

**CHARLES ATKIN** (PhD, University of Wisconsin–Madison) chairs the Department of Communication at Michigan State University. He has published six books and 150 journal articles and chapters dealing with media effects on health, political, and social behavior. He is coeditor (with Ron Rice) of two editions of the influential *Public Communication Campaigns* book. He has served as a campaign design consultant or evaluation researcher on numerous national public information and education programs dealing with drunk driving, alcohol and drug abuse, heart disease, and breast and colon cancer. His health campaign work has been recognized with the 2006 Award for Applied Social Science Research from the Decade of Behavior consortium and the 2008 Outstanding Health Communication Scholar Award from the ICA/NCA Health Communication Divisions.

**WILLIAM L. BENOIT** (PhD, Wayne State University) is Professor of Communication at the University of Missouri. He has published in such journals as *Communication Monographs, Human Communication Research, Journal of Communication, Journal of Applied Communication Research, Political Communication, Quarterly Journal of Speech,* and *Journalism and Mass Communication Quarterly.* He has published several books; his most recent is *Communication in Political Campaigns.*

**FRANKLIN J. BOSTER** (PhD, Michigan State University) is Professor in the Department of Communication at Michigan State University. He also is affiliated with the Law School at Michigan State University, where he is a fellow of the Trial Practice Institute, and in the Department of Community and Behavioral Health at the University of Iowa. His substantive interests center on the study of social influence and group dynamics. Presently, he is investigating the attributes of pivotal members of group networks and the manner in which they diffuse health information throughout those networks.

**JENNINGS BRYANT** (PhD, Indiana University) is CIS Distinguished Research Professor, holder of the Reagan Endowed Chair of Broadcasting, and Associate Dean for Graduate Studies and Research at the University of Alabama. He received the university's Blackmon-Moody Outstanding Professor Award for 2000 and was President of the International Communication Association in 2002–2003. In 2006, he received a Distinguished Scholar Award from the Broadcast Education Association and was elected a Fellow of the International Communication Association. He is Advisory Editor of the 11-volume *International Encyclopedia of Communication*. Author or editor of 28 scholarly books or textbooks, he has published more than 120 articles in peer-reviewed journals, has written more than 180 chapters published in edited scholarly books, and has delivered more than 200 papers at conventions of national and international professional associations. His primary research interests are in entertainment theory, mass communication theory, media effects, and media and children.

**JUDEE K. BURGOON** (EdD, West Virginia University) is Site Director for the Center for Identification Technology Research, Eller College of Management, University of Arizona. She holds appointments as Professor of Communication, Family Studies, and Human Development and also a Distinguished Visiting Professor appointment at the University of Oklahoma. She has authored eight books and more than 250 articles, chapters, and reviews on such topics as nonverbal and relational communication, deception, and computer-mediated communication. Her current research—funded by the National Science Foundation, Department of Defense, and Department of Homeland Security—is examining ways to automate analysis of nonverbal and verbal communication to detect deception. She is a Fellow of the International Communication Association, which has also honored her with its Fisher Mentorship and Chaffee Career Achievement Awards. She is

also recipient of the National Communication Association's Distinguished Scholar Award, Golden Anniversary Monographs Award, and Woolbert Award for Research with Lasting Impact.

**BRANT R. BURLESON** (PhD, University of Illinois, Urbana-Champaign) is Professor of Communication and Affiliate Professor of Psychological Sciences at Purdue University. His research examines supportive forms of communication (such as comforting), as well as their effects on varied forms of well-being, and focuses on how people both produce and process supportive messages. Other research interests include communication skill acquisition and development, the effects of communication skills on relationship outcomes, and the role of emotion in communication and relationships. He has authored more than 140 articles, chapters, and reviews and has edited several publications, including *The Handbook of Communication and Social Interaction Skills, Communication of Social Support,* and *Communication Yearbook*. He is a Fellow of the International Communication Association, a Distinguished Scholar of the National Communication Association, and a recipient of the Berscheid-Hatfield Award for Distinguished Mid-career Achievement from the International Association for Relationship Research.

**DONALD J. CEGALA** (PhD, Florida State University) is Emeritus Professor in the School of Communication and the Department of Family Medicine at The Ohio State University. He was on the Ohio State faculty for 35 years. He is the former Chair of the Health Communication Division of the National Communication Association and a member of the OSU Institute for Primary Care Research and the OSU Comprehensive Cancer Center. He has served as a consultant and grant reviewer for the National Cancer Institute and was the recipient of the 2006 NCA/ICA Health Communication Scholar Award. He has published more than 50 book chapters and articles in academic journals and is known nationally and internationally for his research on physician-patient communication, particularly with respect to patient communication skills interventions.

**JAMES PRICE DILLARD's** (PhD, Michigan State University) scholarly interests focus on the communication processes by which individuals attempt to change the opinions and behaviors of others. His work on the impact of interaction goals on message production contributed to our understanding of how and why people create interpersonal influence messages, especially in the context of close relationships. More recently, he has turned his attention to understanding the role of emotion in persuasive health communication. He has received the John E. Hunter Award for Meta-Analysis and the National Communication Association Golden Anniversary Award for article of the year. He was coeditor of *The Persuasion Handbook* and past editor of the journal *Human communication Research*.

**MELISSA A. DOBOSH** (MA, University of Delaware) is a doctoral student in the Department of Communication at the University of Illinois at Urbana-Champaign. Her areas of specialization are organizational and group communication. Specifically, her research focuses on relational communication in organizations, group resiliency, and leadership. Her doctoral dissertation will address the relational capacities that work teams rely upon when faced with organizational stressors. Work from her master's thesis on leadership emergence in small groups was presented in a poster session at the National Communication Association in 2005, and her paper on top management team conflict was presented at the International Association of Conflict Management in 2006.

**DONALD G. ELLIS** (PhD, University of Utah) is Professor of Communication at the University of Hartford. His is interested in communication issues related to ethnopolitical conflicts with particular emphasis on intractable conflicts, intercultural communication, and democracy. He is the past editor of the journal *Communication Theory* and the author of numerous books and articles, including *Transforming Conflict: Communication and Ethnopolitical Conflict*. He has been a Fellow at the Asch Center for the Study of Ethnopolitcal Conflict and a Fulbright Scholar in Israel in 2004–2005. He participates in various national organizations and lectures and writes in the fields of communication, political conflict, conflict resolution, and related topics.

**KORY FLOYD** (PhD, University of Arizona) is Professor of Human Communication and Director of the Communication Sciences Laboratory at Arizona State University. His research focuses on the communication of affection in personal relationships and on the interplay between communication, physiology, and health. He has authored or edited seven books and nearly 75 journal articles and book chapters and recently served as editor of the *Journal of Family Communication*. His work has been supported by the National Institutes of Health and has earned several awards, including the G. R. Miller Early Career Achievement Award from the International Association for Relationship Research.

**HOWARD GILES** (PhD, DSc, University of Bristol) is Professor (and past Chair) of Communication at the University of California, Santa Barbara (with affiliated positions in Linguistics and Psychology). His work is in the general area of intergroup communication, with particular cross-cultural interests in intergenerational encounters as well as police-civilian interactions. Founding editor of the *Journal of Language and Social Psychology* and the *Journal of Asian Pacific Communication* and past editor of *Human Communication Research*, he has been past president of the International Communication Association and the International Association of Language & Social Psychology. Furthering one of his intergroup research interests, he is a Reserve Lieutenant (with many outstanding service awards) in the Santa Barbara Police Department and on-call 24-7 for both their Crisis Negotiation Response and Police Chaplain Teams.

**LAURA K. GUERRERO** (PhD, University of Arizona) is Professor in the Hugh Downs School of Human Communication at Arizona State University. Her research focuses on relational and nonverbal communication, with emphases in attachment, emotion, and the "dark side" of interpersonal communication. She has published numerous articles and chapters on these topics. Her book credits include *Nonverbal Communication in Close Relationships* (with Kory Floyd) and *The Nonverbal Communication Reader* (with Michael Hecht). She received the 2001 Early Career Achievement Award from the International Association for Relationship Research and the 1994 Outstanding Doctoral Dissertation Award (from the Interpersonal Communication Division of the International Communication Association), and she is a two-time recipient of the Western States Communication Association's Dickens Best Article Award.

**R. LANCE HOLBERT** (PhD, University of Wisconsin–Madison) is Associate Professor in the School of Communication at The Ohio State University. His research interests include the study of entertainment media within the context of politics and relations between different types of political communication campaign information outlets. He presently serves on several editorial boards for some of the discipline's top journals, including *Communication Monographs, Journal of Communication,* and the *Journal of Broadcasting & Electronic Media.* He has published more than 40 peer-reviewed journal articles since earning his PhD in 2000, with his most recent research appearing in such journals as *Human Communication Research, Media Psychology,* and *Political Communication.*

**YOUNG YUN KIM** (PhD, Northwestern University) is Professor of Communication at the University of Oklahoma. Her main research aim has been to establish the centrality of communicative competence and engagement in adapting to a new, unfamiliar, or changing cultural environment. Her current research program investigates psychological, situational, and environmental factors that are linked to associative/dissociative communication behaviors of individuals facing ethnically dissimilar others. She has published more than 90 journal articles and book chapters, as well as 12 books, including *Becoming Intercultural* (2001) and *Communicating With Strangers* (4th ed., 2003, with W. Gudykunst). She has served on 11 journal editorial boards, including *Communication Research, Human Communication Research,* and *Journal of Communication.* She is a Fellow of the International Communication Association, a Founding Fellow of the International Academy for Intercultural Research, and a recipient of a Top Scholar Award for Lifetime Achievement in Intercultural Communication.

**CHRISTOPH KLIMMT** (PhD, Hannover University of Music and Drama) is Assistant Professor in the Department of Communication, University of Mainz, Germany. His research is focused on media entertainment, and he has made various theoretical and empirical contributions to the understanding of video game enjoyment. He has published more than 30 articles in international and German peer-reviewed journals and more than 40 book chapters that also reflect his research interest in new media technologies, experimental media effects studies, and methodological issues in communication science.

**ASCAN F. KOERNER** (PhD, University of Wisconsin–Madison) is Associate Professor of Communication Studies and the Donald V. Hawkins Professor for 2008–2009 at the University of Minnesota–Twin Cities. His research focuses mainly on family communication patterns and the cognitive representations of relationships and their influence on interpersonal communication, including message production and message interpretation. His research has appeared in communication journals, such as *Communication Monographs, Communication Theory,* and *Human Communication Research,* and interdisciplinary journals, such as the *Journal of Marriage and Family* and the *Journal of Social and Personal Relationships,* and a number of edited volumes.

**GERALD M. KOSICKI** (PhD, University of Wisconsin–Madison) is Associate Professor in the School of Communication at The Ohio State University. He was Faculty Director of the OSU Center for Survey Research from 2001 to 2004 and principal investigator of the center's largest research project—ongoing studies of economic and political perceptions of Ohioans known as the Buckeye State Poll. Today he is a faculty coordinator of Ohio State's Graduate Interdisciplinary Specialization in Survey Research and a faculty adviser of the undergraduate Survey Research Minor. His research interests are in political communication, public opinion, and media effects, particularly related to framing, media priming, and public construction of public issues. His current teaching areas include public opinion and communication, communication theory, civic journalism, survey research methods, and media and terrorism.

**MICHAEL W. KRAMER** (PhD, University of Texas at Austin) is Professor and Chair of the Department of Communication at the University of Missouri. His research in organizational settings has focused on employee transitions such as newcomers, job promotions, transferees, exit processes, and corporate mergers. In group settings, he has focused on decision making and membership in voluntary groups such as

theater and community choirs. He has made theoretical contributions in the theory of managing uncertainty, in his book *(Managing Uncertainty in Organizational Communication),* group dialectical theory, and a theory of language convergence/meaning divergence. His has used research methods ranging from structural equation modeling to ethnography. His research appears in a wide variety of journals, including *Communication Monographs, Human Communication Research, Journal of Applied Communication, Journal of Communication,* and the *Academy of Management Journal.*

**KATHLEEN J. KRONE** (PhD, University of Texas at Austin) is Professor of Communication Studies at the University of Nebraska–Lincoln. She has published in the areas of upward influence in leader-member relationships, emotion management in organizations, and organizational communication in China. She is a past chair of the Organizational Communication Division of the National Communication Association. She is coeditor with Linda L. Putnam of the multivolume reference *Organizational Communication,* published in 2006. She has served on the editorial boards of the *Journal of Applied Communication Research, Management Communication Quarterly,* and *Communication Monographs* and currently is serving as Forum Editor for *Management Communication Quarterly.*

**EUN-JU LEE** (PhD, Stanford University) is Associate Professor in the Department of Communication at Seoul National University, Seoul, Korea. Her research centers on social cognition and social influence in computer-based communication. Specifically, she has investigated how the restrictions of text-only media affect the ways in which individuals form impressions of anonymous interaction partners, process information, and exhibit group-oriented behaviors, such as group conformity and gender stereotyping. She has also examined what facilitates and inhibits social treatment of computers in human-computer interaction. Her work has won several top paper awards from various divisions of the International Communication Association, the National Communication Association, and the Association for Education in Journalism and Mass Communication and has appeared in journals such as *Human Communication Research, Communication Research, Journal of Communication, Media Psychology,* and the *International Journal of Human-Computer Studies.* She currently serves on the editorial boards of *Human Communication Research, Communication Research,* and *Media Psychology.*

**SHU LI** (PhD, Northwestern University) is Assistant Professor of Communication at the University of Memphis. Her research interests include negotiation strategy, conflict management, and the experience and expression of emotions in organizational and intercultural contexts. She also studies these subjects in health communication projects and is currently working on improving multidisciplinary communication and building an integrated patient/family communication plan at a local hospital.

**DOUGLAS M. McLEOD** (PhD, University of Minnesota) is Professor of Journalism and Mass Communication at the University of Wisconsin. His research develops two lines of inquiry into the antecedents and consequences of mass communication. The former focuses on the role of the media in both domestic and international conflicts, including media coverage of social protest and its impact on the audience. The latter, including research on media framing and priming, examines several factors shaping the information content of mass media and its consequent outcomes on knowledge, attitudes, and perceptions.

**JACK M. McLEOD** (PhD, University of Michigan) is Maier-Bascom Professor Emeritus in Journalism and Mass Communication at the University of Wisconsin–Madison. He recently coauthored the following chapters: "Knowledge as Understanding: The

Information Processing Approach to Political Learning" and "U.S. Election Coverage" (with M. Sotirovic); "Political Communication Effects" and "The Role of Method in Advancing Political Communication Research" (with D. McLeod and G. Kosicki); "Communication and Education: Creating Competence for Socialization Into Public Life" (with D. Shah, D. Hess, and N.-J. Lee); and "Personal Networks and Political Socialization" (with N.-J. Lee). He was coeditor (with D. Shah) of the special issue on communication and political socialization for *Political Communication.*

**SANDRA METTS** (PhD, University of Iowa) is Professor in the School of Communication at Illinois State University, where she teaches graduate and undergraduate courses in interpersonal communication, emotion, language, and communication and aging. Her research interests include relationship transgressions, forgiveness, facework and politeness, sexual communication, and emotions in close relationships. Her work has appeared in a number of edited books on relationship processes and in such journals as *Personal Relationships, Journal of Social Psychology, Journal of Social and Personal Relationships, Family Relations, Western Journal of Communication, Communication Quarterly,* and *Human Communication Research.* She has served as president of the Central States Communication Association, editor of *Communication Reports,* and associate editor of *Personal Relationships,* and currently she is an associate editor for the *Journal of Social and Personal Relationships.*

**RENEE A. MEYERS** (PhD, University of Illinois) is Professor in the Department of Communication at the University of Wisconsin–Milwaukee. She also serves as the Coordinator of the University of Wisconsin System Leadership Site for the Scholarship of Teaching and Learning. Her research interests include the study of small group decision making and argument and investigation of the role of communication in cooperative learning groups. Her articles have appeared in *Human Communication Research, Communication Monographs, Journal of Communication, The Handbook of Group Communication, Communication Studies, Small Group Research,* and *Communication Yearbook,* among other outlets. She has served on the editorial boards of several communication journals, including *Journal of Communication, Communication Studies, Communication Monographs,* and *Communication Theory.* She also served as chair of the Group Communication Division of the National Communication Association.

**ROBIN L. NABI** (PhD, University of Pennsylvania) is Associate Professor of Communication at the University of California, Santa Barbara. Her research focuses on the interplay between emotion and cognition in persuasion and mass media contexts. Her work has appeared in journals such as *Journal of Communication, Communication Theory, Communication Monographs, Communication Research, Human Communication Research, Media Psychology,* and *Cognition & Emotion,* and she serves on the editorial boards of several communication-focused journals. She is currently a coeditor of *Media Psychology,* chair of the Mass Communication Division of the International Communication Association, and vice-chair of the Communication and Social Cognition Division of the National Communication Association. She is coeditor of the forthcoming *SAGE Handbook of Media Processes and Effects.*

**MARY BETH OLIVER** (PhD, University of Wisconsin–Madison) is Professor of Media Studies at the Pennsylvania State University. Her research is in media effects, with an emphasis on media and emotion, as well as media and social cognition. She is former coeditor of *Media Psychology* and associate editor of *Communication Theory* and the *Journal of Communication.* In 1996, she was awarded a Fulbright scholarship to conduct research on media and stereotyping

in New Zealand. She currently serves as a codirector of the Media Effects Research Laboratory at Penn State.

**CHARLES PAVITT** (PhD, University of Wisconsin–Madison) is Professor in the Department of Communication at the University of Delaware. He teaches courses across the entire realm of interpersonal communication but limits his research to content-analytic studies of interpersonal interaction, usually in the small group context. In addition, he has a long-standing interest in the relationship between the philosophy of science and communication theory, with his current thinking in that area reflected in the chapter included here. Finally, he is responsible for the definitions for statistical baseball terminology to be included in the forthcoming third edition of the *Dickson Baseball Dictionary.*

**SALLY PLANALP** (PhD, University of Wisconsin–Madison) is Professor in the Department of Communication at the University of Utah. Her primary area of research is interpersonal communication with emphases in face-to-face interaction, close relationships, emotion, and health communication in interpersonal contexts, especially end-of-life issues. Her work has appeared in journals such as the *Journal of Social and Personal Relationships, Human Communication Research, Cognition and Emotion, Communication Monographs, Health Communication,* and *Communication Theory.* Her 1999 book, *Communicating Emotion: Social, Moral, and Cultural Processes,* addresses wide-ranging communication issues from diverse disciplinary perspectives.

**MARSHALL SCOTT POOLE** (PhD, University of Wisconsin–Madison) is Professor of Communication and Senior Research Scientist at the National Center for Supercomputing Applications at the University of Illinois Urbana-Champaign. His research interests include group and organizational communication, information systems, collaboration technologies, organizational innovation, and theory construction. He is the author of more than 125 articles and book chapters. His articles have appeared in *Communication Monographs, Human Communication Research, Quarterly Journal of Speech, Communication Research, Small Group Research Management Science, Organization Science, Information Systems Research, MIS Quarterly,* and *Academy of Management Review,* among others. He has coauthored or edited 10 books, including *Theories of Small Groups: Interdisciplinary Perspectives, Organizational Change and Innovation Processes: Theory and Methods for Research,* and *The Handbook of Organizational Change and Innovation.* He has been named a Fellow of the International Communication Association and a Distinguished Scholar of the National Communication Association.

**ERIKA J. PRIBANIC-SMITH** (PhD, candidate, University of Alabama) is a graduate student in the mass communication program with a specialization in journalism history. A creative thinker who enjoys finding ways to answer historical questions using new techniques and technology, she has produced a variety of works on 19th- and early 20th-century print media. Drawing on her background as a magazine and newspaper journalist, her teaching focuses include depth reporting and writing for new media. She also moonlights as a Web designer for several College of Communication departments and campus organizations.

**BEVERLY ROSKOS-EWOLDSEN** (PhD, Indiana University) is Associate Dean for the Social Sciences subdivision in the College of Arts and Sciences at The University of Alabama (UA). She also is Associate Professor in the Department of Psychology at UA. Her research focuses on visual-spatial cognition, defined as the comprehension, representation, and use of visual and spatial information. Recent research has investigated comprehension of visual stories, visual working memory, visual creativity/generative thinking, wayfinding, and spatial ability, including individual and group differences in each area (e.g., life span age, intelligence, and gender). Her research has been and is supported by grants from the Office of Naval Research, National Institute on Drug Abuse, and National Science Foundation. She teaches undergraduate and graduate courses on statistics, perception, and visual-spatial cognition.

**CHARLES T. SALMON** (PhD, University of Minnesota) is Dean of the College of Communication Arts and Sciences and Ellis N. Brandt Professor of Public Relations at Michigan State University, as well as Professor in the School of Communication at the Interdisciplinary Center, Herzliya. He has served as a health communication adviser for UNICEF in Kazakhstan, a visiting scientist at the U.S. Centers for Disease Control and Prevention, and codirector of the Center for Health and Risk Communication in the Emory University School of Public Health. He is the editor of *Information Campaigns: Balancing Social Values and Social Change* and, with Theodore Glasser, *Public Opinion and the Communication of Consent.* He is a former recipient of a Fulbright fellowship and the Pathfinder Award for Outstanding Research in Public Relations.

**DAVID R. SEIBOLD** (PhD, Michigan State University) is Professor of Communication (Division of Social Sciences, College of Letters and Science) and Codirector of the Graduate Program in Management Practice (Technology Management Program, College of Engineering) at the University of California, Santa Barbara. He has published two books and more than 100 articles and chapters on persuasion and interpersonal influence, group interaction, organizational communication, and applied communication. A former editor of the *Journal of Applied Communication Research,* he has served as chair of the Interpersonal and Small

Group Interaction Division in the National Communication Association (NCA) and as chair of the Interpersonal Communication Division and the Organizational Communication Division of the International Communication Association. A recipient of numerous awards for scholarship, teaching, and service, he is a Distinguished Scholar of the NCA.

**JOHN L. SHERRY** (PhD, Michigan State University) is Associate Professor in the Department of Communication at Michigan State University (MSU), Principal Investigator in the GEL Laboratory at MSU, and Associate Editor of *Communication Theory*. In addition, he is an Editorial Board member of *Human Communication Research, Journal of Communication*, and *Media Psychology* and is Chair of the International Communication Association Game Studies Special Interest Group. His primary research interest is media effects, focusing on neurophysiological reactivity to media that explains the etiology of the media use and the effects those media have. Recent studies have uncovered a neurophysiological mechanism explaining television and video game use and gender differences in game use.

**MIRIT DEVORAH SHOHAM** (PhD, University of California, Santa Barbara) is Assistant Professor at Ohio University's School of Communication Studies. She is primarily interested in social influence, exploring the spread of attitudes within and across groups. In taking a multilevel and multimethod approach, she incorporates a network-analytic perspective in her investigation of contagion processes, culminating in socially derived attitudes during occasions of sensemaking in organizations. She has published in *Human Communication Research* and frequently presents her research at the International Communication Association and Sunbelt Social Networks conferences. Receiving the Edwin R. Schoell Award for Excellence in Teaching (University of California at Santa Barbara, Department of Communication:

2005–2006) and a top paper award at an International Communication Association meeting (Dresden, Germany, June 2006) reflects her dedication to the field and her enthusiastic optimism for a future of mentorship and scholarship.

**PATRICIA M. SIAS** (PhD, University of Texas at Austin) is Professor of Communication in the Edward R. Murrow College of Communication at Washington State University. Her research centers on workplace relationships. She has published articles in and served on the editorial boards of a variety of academic journals, including *Communication Monographs, Human Communication Research, Management Communication Quarterly, Western Journal of Communication, Communication Quarterly,* and *Journal of Applied Communication Research*. She served as secretary and chair of the Organizational Communication Division of the National Communication Association. She has won numerous awards for her research, including the W. Charles Redding Outstanding Dissertation in Organizational Communication Award from the International Communication Association, several top paper awards from the National Communication Association, and the Distinguished Faculty Achievement Award from the Washington State University College of Liberal Arts.

**ALAN L. SILLARS** (PhD, University of Wisconsin) is Professor of Communication Studies at the University of Montana. His research focuses on conflict and interpersonal perception, particularly in the context of family relationships. He has published numerous articles and chapters on these topics. He received the Franklin H. Knower article award from the National Communication Association on two occasions and recently served as editor-in-chief for *Communication Monographs*.

**JORDAN SOLIZ** (PhD, University of Kansas) is Assistant Professor in the Department of Communication Studies at the University of Nebraska–Lincoln. His research focuses on communication and intergroup processes in family and personal relationships, with an emphasis on grandparent-grandchild relationships, multiethnic families, stepfamilies, and in-law relationships. His research has been published in *Communication Monographs, Journal of Applied Communication Research, Journal of Family Communication,* and *Western Journal of Communication.*

**DENISE HAUNANI SOLOMON** (PhD, Northwestern University) is Professor of Communication Arts and Sciences and Associate Dean for Graduate Studies at Penn State University. Her research focuses generally on the causes and consequences of turbulence in romantic associations, as well as how communication participates in those experiences. Her research has examined how relationship qualities, including interpersonal power, relational uncertainty, and interdependence, shape people's perceptions of and communication about relational irritations, problematic events, uncertainty-provoking events, changes in sexual intimacy, jealousy experiences, hurtful messages, and sexually harassing statements. This work has culminated in the relational turbulence model, which is a theory describing how transitions in romantic relationships promote relationship qualities that polarize cognitive, emotional, and communicative reactions to both ordinary and extraordinary experiences. She also serves on the editorial boards of five journals and is currently an associate editor for *Personal Relationships.*

**RICHARD L. STREET, JR.** (PhD, University of Texas at Austin) is Professor and Head of Communication at Texas A&M University. He is also Director of the Health Communication and Decision-Making Program in the Houston Center for Quality of Care and Utilization Studies, Baylor College of Medicine. He has developed an extensive program of research examining issues related to health care provider–patient communication, medical outcomes, and strategies for increasing patient involvement in

care. He is coauthor (with Ron Epstein at the University of Rochester) of *Patient-Centered Communication in Cancer Care: Promoting Healing and Reducing Suffering* (2007), a monograph for the National Cancer Institute that serves as a roadmap for future cancer communication research. In 2003, he was named Outstanding Health Communication Scholar by both the National Communication Association and the International Communication Association. In 2008, he received the L. Donohew Health Communication Scholar Award from the University of Kentucky.

**S. SHYAM SUNDAR** (PhD, Stanford University) is Professor and Codirector of the Media Effects Research Laboratory at Penn State University's College of Communications. His research investigates social and psychological effects of technological elements unique to Web-based mass communication. He was among the first to publish refereed research on the effects of new media in leading communication journals and has been identified as the most published author of Internet-related research in the field during the medium's first decade. A frequently cited source on technology, he has testified before the U.S. Congress as an expert witness and delivered talks at universities in several countries. He serves on the editorial boards of *Communication Research, Human Communication Research, Journal of Communication, Media Psychology, Journalism & Mass Communication Quarterly, Journal of Broadcasting & Electronic Media,* and *Communication Methods & Measures,* among others. He is Chair of the Communication & Technology division of the International Communication Association.

**SARAH J. TRACY** (PhD, University of Colorado–Boulder) is Associate Professor and Director of the Project for Wellness and Work-Life in The Hugh Downs School of Human Communication at Arizona State University–Tempe. Her critical-interpretive communication scholarship examines emotion and identity within organizations, with a specific focus on emotion labor, workplace bullying, work-life navigation, care work, humor, burnout, and dirty work. She is interested in contextual use-inspired research, qualitative methodologies, public scholarship, and engaging work that can potentially provide space for organizational and societal transformation. She has presented and published her research internationally, and it can be found in *Communication Monographs, Management Communication Quarterly, Communication Theory, Qualitative Inquiry, Human Communication Research, Journal of Applied Communication Research, Journal of Management Studies,* and *Western Journal of Communication.* She is coauthor of the book *Leading Organizations Through Transition: Communication and Cultural Change.*

**ANITA L. VANGELISTI** (PhD, University of Texas at Austin) is the Jesse H. Jones Centennial Professor of Communication at the University of Texas at Austin. Her work focuses on the associations between communication and emotion in the context of close, personal relationships. She has published numerous articles and chapters and has edited or authored several books. Vangelisti has served on the editorial boards of more than a dozen scholarly journals. She has received recognition for her research from the National Communication Association, the International Society for the Study of Personal Relationships, and the International Association for Relationship Research.

**PETER VORDERER** (PhD, Technical University of Berlin) is Scientific Director of the Center for Advanced Media Research Amsterdam (CAMeRA) and head of the Department of Communication Science, VU University Amsterdam, the Netherlands. He specializes in media use and media effects research with a special focus on media entertainment and digital games. Together with Dolf Zillmann and Jennings Bryant, he has edited three volumes on media entertainment and video games.

**JOSEPH B. WALTHER** (PhD, University of Arizona) is Professor in the Department of Communication and the Department of Telecommunication, Information Studies and Media at Michigan State University. His research focuses on the interpersonal dynamics of communication via computer networks, in personal relationships, work groups, social support, and educational settings, areas in which he has published several original theories and numerous empirically based research articles. He has previously held appointments in Cognitive Science, Information Science, or Education and Social Policy at Northwestern University, Cornell University, The University of Manchester, and elsewhere. He was chair of the Organizational Communication and Information Systems division of the Academy of Management and the Communication and Technology division of the International Communication Association.

**STEVEN R. WILSON** (PhD, Purdue University) is Professor in the Department of Communication at Purdue University. He also has been a faculty member at Michigan State, Northern Illinois, and Northwestern Universities. His research and teaching focus on interpersonal communication, social influence, and aggresion/conflict. He is the author of *Seeking and Resisting Compliance: Why Individuals Say What They Do When Trying to Influence Others* (2002) as well as more than 50 articles and book chapters on these topics. His recent research explores patterns of parent-child interaction in families at risk for child maltreatment as well as patterns associated with children's school readiness (funded by the Lilly Endowment). He is a recipient of the National Communication Association's (NCA's) Bernard Brommel Award for Outstanding Scholarship or Distinguished Service in Family Communication and has served as chair of both the International Communication Association's and the NCA's interpersonal communication division as well as associate editor of the interdisciplinary journal *Personal Relationships.*

**Sidney Silverman Library
and Learning Resource Center
Bergen Community College
400 Paramus Road
Paramus, NJ 07652-1595**

**www.bergen.edu**
**Return Postage Guaranteed**